HEALTH PSYCHOLOGY
A BIOPSYCHOSOCIAL APPROACH

HEALTH PSYCHOLOGY
A BIOPSYCHOSOCIAL APPROACH

SECOND EDITION

Richard O. Straub

University of Michigan, Dearborn

Worth Publishers

Publisher: Catherine Woods
Acquisitions Editor: Kevin Feyen
Executive Marketing Manager: Katherine Nurre
Senior Development Editor: Christine Brune
Media Editor: Danielle Pucci
Photo Editor: Ted Szczepanski
Photo Researcher: Donna Ranieri
Art Director: Babs Reingold
Senior Designer: Kevin Kall
Cover and Text Designer: Lissi Sigillo
Associate Managing Editor: Tracey Kuehn
Project Editor: Kate Mannix, Graphic World Publishing Services
Illustrators: Todd Buck and Matthew Holt
Illustration Coordinator: Bill Page
Artist for Cover and Chapter/Part Openers: Nicholas Wilton
Production Manager: Sarah Segal
Composition: Northeastern Graphic, Inc.
Printing and Binding: RR Donnelley

ISBN-13: 978-0-7167-6450-2
ISBN-10: 0-7167-6450-4

Printed in the United States of America

Second printing

Worth Publishers
41 Madison Avenue
New York, NY 10010
www.worthpublishers.com

To my mother, Phyllis,
and my father-in-law, James Hanlon,
whose indomitable Irishy
has sustained us all.

About the Author

Richard O. Straub is professor of psychology, chair of the Behavioral Sciences Department, and founder of the graduate program in Health Psychology at the University of Michigan, Dearborn. After receiving his Ph.D. in experimental psychology from Columbia University and serving as a National Institute of Mental Health fellow at the University of California, Irvine, Straub joined the University of Michigan faculty in 1979. Since then, he has focused on research in health psychology, especially mind–body issues in stress, cardiovascular reactivity, and the effects of exercise on physical and psychological health. Straub's research has been published in such journals as *Health Psychology,* the *Journal of Applied Social Psychology,* and the *Journal of the Experimental Analysis of Behavior.*

A recipient of the University of Michigan's Distinguished Teaching Award and the Alumni Society's Faculty Member of the Year Award, Straub is extensively involved in undergraduate and graduate medical education. In addition to serving on the board of directors of the Southeast Michigan Consortium for Medical Education and lecturing regularly at area teaching hospitals, Straub has created an online learning management system for medical residency programs and authored a series of web-based modules for teaching core competencies in behavioral medicine.

Straub's interest in enhancing student learning is further reflected in the study guides, instructor's manuals, and critical thinking materials he has developed to accompany several leading psychology texts.

Straub's professional devotion to health psychology dovetails with his personal devotion to fitness and good health. He has completed hundreds of road races and marathons (including multiple Boston marathons and the 2006 Ironman-Wisconsin) and is a nationally ranked duathlete and triathlete. With this text Straub combines his teaching vocation with a true passion for health psychology.

Tom Laundroche

Action Sports International

Steelhead Half Ironman Triathlon in Benton Harbor, Michigan, August 2006

Brief Contents

Contents

Part 4
Chronic and Life-Threatening Illnesses 266

Part 6
Future of Health Psychology 463

Preface

"Your cancer is advanced. Inoperable. Try for whatever quality of life you can maintain. You have eleven weeks to live." Irv Kingston refused to believe this prognosis and instead mobilized every psychological, social, and environmental resource he could think of to battle his illness. With his positive, upbeat attitude, he insisted on undergoing a grueling (and useless, according to his doctor) regimen of cancer treatment. And his bravery worked: Twelve months later, he received a clean bill of health and resumed his normal life.

Of course, some diseases take their toll no matter what biological, psychological, or social defenses we offer. However, study after study has shown that attitude and environment matter—that good health is more than a physiological state. Just 30 years ago, health and psychology were separate disciplines, each aware of the other but unable to connect in any meaningful way. Then in 1978, the field of *health psychology* was born, and it has grown explosively since then. From the earliest research linking Type A behavior to increased risk for cardiovascular disease to the most current discoveries regarding psychosocial influences on the inflammatory processes involved in cardiovascular disease, cancer, and other chronic diseases, health psychology has already accomplished much.

More important than individual research findings has been the ongoing refinement of the *biopsychosocial (mind–body) model* as an interdisciplinary template for the study of health issues (the importance of which is reflected in the new subtitle of this text). Increasingly, researchers are able to pinpoint the physiological mechanisms by which anger, loneliness, and other psychosocial factors adversely affect health and by which optimism, social connectedness, and a strong sense of self-empowerment exert their beneficial effects.

Experiencing these exciting and productive early years of health psychology inspired me to write this text—to share with aspiring students this vitally important field. My goals in this text have been to present current, relevant, and well-supported summaries of the main ideas of the field and to model a scientific way of thinking about those ideas in the process. Understanding human behavior and teaching students are my two professional passions, and nowhere have these passions come together more directly for me than in writing this text about how psychology and health are interconnected.

What's New in the Second Edition?

In this thoroughly revised second edition, my aim continues to be to present the science of health psychology clearly, accurately, and in an accessible voice that helps students make meaningful connections with their own lives. Yet I've introduced a number of significant changes.

- Over **200 new research citations** provide a complete and up-to-date picture of the field.

- A **streamlined organization and briefer length** will help you meet the challenge of teaching a one-semester or quarter course.

- The **new text subtitle** reflects an increased, thoroughly integrated emphasis on the interaction of biological, psychological, and social/cultural influences on health.

- New research expands the coverage of **cultural and gender diversity** in health and health care.

- Added coverage of **psychoneuroimmunology** and the associated shift in medical education highlights the growing importance of mind–body issues in health (and best practices in health care).

- **The re-envisioned Chapter 6, "Staying Healthy: Primary Prevention and Positive Psychology,"** focuses on human strengths and building healthy individuals, families, and communities. This chapter adds to the underlying, positive psychology emphasis that flavored the first edition. Table 5 on page xix offers examples of integrated coverage of positive health psychology.

Trademark Features

In an effort to communicate the excitement and value of the field, I have maintained my focus on ensuring that students understand—rather than just memorize—the concepts that make health psychology. I have retained the following key features.

- **Biopsychosocial approach.** The book follows the biopsychosocial model as the basic organizing template. Throughout, I have strived to convey how the components of this model interact dynamically in influencing the well-being of the *whole* person. Each chapter that deals with a specific health problem—AIDS, cardiovascular disease, cancer, and substance abuse, for example—presents a critical analysis of what we know to be the underlying biological, psychological, and social factors in the onset of the health problem, as well as how these factors affect the course of the disease and the outcome. My commitment to this interdisciplinary *systems* perspective on behavior stems from my eclectic graduate training (some would say my inability to make up my mind as to which career path I would follow!) as a student of learning theorist Herbert Terrace, physiological psychologist Richard Thompson, and social psychologist (and health psychology pioneer) Stanley Schachter.

- **Up-to-date coverage.** Few psychological disciplines generate more research each year, and from such a wide variety of related fields, than does health psychology. I have retained the field's classic studies and concepts, but I have also presented the most important recent developments. More than 25 percent of this text's references are from research published since 2005.

- **Fully integrated gender and cultural diversity coverage.** One of my major goals has been to promote understanding of, and respect for, differences among groups of people and how these differences affect health and illness. This effort extends beyond merely cataloging ethnic, cultural, and gender differences in disease, health beliefs, and behaviors. I have made an in-depth effort to stimulate students' critical thinking regarding the origins of these differences. For example, many differences in health-related behaviors are the product of restrictive social stereotypes and norms, economic forces, and other overarching ecological processes. Whenever possible, the text digs deeply into diversity issues by considering the origins of these behaviors and their implications for health-promoting treatments and interventions. Examples of this integrated coverage are provided in Tables 1, 3, and 4 on pages xvii and xviii. The **Diversity and Healthy Living boxes** found throughout the text expand the integrated coverage of gender and multicultural issues by highlighting specific health issues. For example, students will explore differences in how women and men cope with a grave national crisis, why hypertension is so prevalent among African-Americans, and the role of sociocultural factors in AIDS prevention.

■ **The life-course perspective.** In integrated coverage throughout the text, students will learn about the special needs and health challenges of people in every season of life. As with gender and diversity, my approach is to teach students to think critically about aging and health. Increasingly, researchers are realizing that much of what was once considered normal aging is actually disease. Many older people who have made healthy lifestyle choices are rewriting the book on successful aging. The choices people make as children and adolescents may determine their fates in later years. Table 2 on page xviii outlines examples of coverage of life-span issues.

Table 1 Coverage of Culture and Multicultural Experience

Examples of coverage of culture and multicultural experience can be found on the following pages:

Acculturation and immigrant stress, pp. 112–113

African diaspora and health, p. 33

Antismoking campaigns, pp. 256–257

Body mass and hypertension among African-Americans, pp. 32–34

Cancer
 and diet, pp. 308–309
 screening interventions, p. 318

Cardiovascular disease
 racial and ethnic differences in, pp. 275–276

Childbirth pain, pp. 393–394

Community barriers to wellness, p. 171

Eating disorders, pp. 218, 220–221

Environmental stress, pp. 105–107

Health care use, pp. 368–369

Health insurance, p. 170

Health system barriers, pp. 170–171

HIV transmission and AIDS, pp. 335–336

Obesity, pp. 205–207

Pain, pp. 413–414

Racial discrimination and cardiovascular reactivity, pp. 277–278

Smoking cessation programs, p. 261

Sociocultural perspective in health psychology, pp. 18–20

Socioeconomic status
 and cancer, pp. 305–306
 and cardiovascular disease, pp. 275–276
 and health care use, pp. 368–369
 and obesity, pp. 205–207
 and stress, pp. 120–121

Substance abuse, pp. 238–239

Symptom interpretation, pp. 368–369

Tobacco use, pp. 250–251

Table 2 Coverage of Life-Span Issues

Examples of life-span issues are discussed on the following pages:

Adolescence
  and perceived vulnerability to
    risky behaviors, pp. 160–161
  and tobacco use, pp. 250–251
Age differences in sick-role
  behavior, pp. 366–367
Ageism and compliance, p. 367
Age-pain relationship, pp. 410–411
AIDS, p. 334

Asthma and childhood, p. 66
Cancer and age, p. 305
Children coping with pain and
  medical procedures, pp. 389–390
Cigarette advertising and children,
  p. 253
Diabetes and age, p. 294
Eating disorders, treatment of,
  pp. 219–224

Life-course perspective, pp. 16–17
Longevity and lifestyle, pp. 165–166
Obesity–health relationship and
  age, pp. 202–203
Research methods, pp. 37–39
Resilience in children, pp. 126–127
Shaping pain behavior in children,
  p. 415
Smoking and aging, p. 252

Table 3 Coverage of the Psychology of Women and Men

Examples of coverage of the psychology of women and men can be found on the following pages:

AIDS and HIV transmission,
  pp. 334–335
Alcohol
  and dating behavior, pp. 240–242
  gender, and drinking contexts,
    pp. 245–246
Cancer, p. 306
Cardiovascular disease,
  pp. 274–275
Coping styles, pp. 122–123

Gender bias in medicine, pp. 20–21
Gender perspective, pp. 20–21
Gender, stress, and taste,
  pp. 204–205
Hostility and anger, p. 283
Male-pattern and female-pattern
  obesity, pp. 200–201
Pain, pp. 411–412
Reproductive system, pp. 75–76
Retirement and health, p. 147

Role overload and conflict,
  pp. 108–109
Sexism in health care, p. 379
Sick-role behavior, pp. 367–368
Smoking-cessation programs,
  p. 261
Stress response, pp. 113, 119–120
Substance abuse, p. 238
Use of health care services,
  pp. 367–368

Table 4 Coverage of Women's Health

Examples of coverage of women's health can be found on the following pages:

AIDS, pp. 334–335
Alcohol and pregnancy, p. 240
Body image and the media,
  pp. 218–219
Body image dissatisfaction,
  pp. 219–221
Breast cancer
  coping with, p. 321
  and emotional disclosure,
    pp. 323–324

  and heredity, p. 311
  and Nurses Health Study, p. 309
  and social support, pp. 323–324
Caregiving role and stress,
  pp. 112–113
Eating disorders, pp. 213–218
  treatment of, pp. 219–224
Employment and health,
  pp. 108–109

Fertilization, pp. 76–77
Gestational diabetes, p. 295
HIV transmission during pregnancy,
  p. 336
Lung cancer, p. 307
Self-efficacy and high-risk sexual
  behaviors, pp. 348–349

Table 5 Coverage of Positive Health Psychology

Examples of coverage of positive health psychology can be found on the following pages:

Alcohol abuse prevention
  programs, pp. 248–250
Behavioral control, pp. 393–394
Cancer-fighting foods, pp. 308–309
Daily uplifts and stress,
  pp. 103–104
Education programs, pp. 141–144
  197–201
Explanatory style, pp. 127–130
Hardiness, stress, and health,
  pp. 124–127
Health behaviors, pp. 155–157
Health psychology interventions,
  defined, p. 24

Heart and healthy diets,
  pp. 279–280
Hostility and anger, control of,
  pp. 292–293
Hypertension, control of,
  pp. 289–290
Hospitalization, increasing
  perceived control prior to,
  pp. 390–394
Nutrition, pp. 189–192
Optimism and immune system
  health, pp. 128–130
Personal control and self-efficacy,
  pp. 130–131

Self-efficacy beliefs in safer sex
  behaviors, pp. 345–346, 347–349
Reducing cholesterol, pp. 290–291
Relaxation, pp. 144–146
Resilience, pp. 126–127
Self-regulation, pp. 132–134
Smoking inoculation programs,
  p. 258
Social support
  and health and mortality,
  pp. 136–137
  and physiology, pp. 137–138
Work site wellness programs,
  pp. 177–179

- **Coverage of complementary and alternative medicine.** According to a recent *Journal of the American Medical Association* report, 4 out of 10 Americans use acupuncture, massage therapy, naturopathy, or some other form of nontraditional medicine. Chapter 14 carefully explores the validity of these high-interest alternative interventions.

- **Helpful study aids.** This text is designed to bring health psychology alive and to reinforce learning at every step. Its clean, student-friendly visual appeal is enhanced by numerous clear graphs of research findings, useful and interesting photos, and compelling artwork that illustrates anatomical structures as well as important concepts and processes. In addition, each chapter includes the following learning aids:

  a. An engaging **case study** or **vignette** at the beginning of each chapter connects the world of health psychology to some concrete experience and weaves a thread of human interest throughout the chapter. All of these describe real situations. For example, Chapter 10 describes my own family's life-changing battle against the cancer that threatened my young son's life.

  b. All important **terms,** which are boldfaced in the body of the text, are defined concisely and clearly in the margins to enhance students' study efforts. They are also listed, with their page numbers, at the end of each chapter.

  c. **End-of-chapter summaries** distill the important points, concepts, theories, and terms discussed in the chapters.

The Multimedia Supplements Package

As an instructor and supplements author, I know firsthand the importance to a textbook of a good, comprehensive teaching package. Fortunately, Worth Publishers has a well-deserved reputation for producing the best psychology supplements around, for both faculty and students. The supplements package includes several valuable components.

Instructor's Resources and Test Bank

The *Instructor's Resources* feature chapter-by-chapter previews and lectures, learning objectives and chapter teaching guides, suggestions for planning and teaching health psychology, ideas for term projects, and detailed suggestions for integrating audiovisual materials into the classroom—all based on my many years of teaching health psychology. The comprehensive *Test Bank*, also based on my classroom experience and testing, contains almost 1,000 multiple-choice and short-answer essay questions. The questions include a wide variety of applied, conceptual, and factual questions, and each item is keyed to the topic and page in the text on which the answer can be found.

A Full-Featured Web Site (www.worthpublishers.com/straub)

This text's companion Web site offers a variety of simulations, tutorials, and study aids organized by chapter, including:

- **Online Quizzing.** This helpful feature offers multiple-choice quizzes tied to each of the book's chapters (not from the test bank).

- **Check Your Health.** These inherently interesting, automatically tallying self-assessments allow students to examine their own health beliefs and behaviors. For example, students will learn about their stress-management style, their ability to control anger, their potentially high-risk health behaviors, and cognitively restructuring headache pain. Each exercise also gives specific tips that encourage students to more actively manage their own health.

- **Critical Thinking Exercises.** The text has two major goals: to help students acquire a thorough understanding of health psychology's knowledge base and to help students learn to think like health psychologists. The second goal—learning to think like psychologists—involves critical thinking. To directly support this goal, the Web site includes a complete exercise for each chapter designed to stimulate students' critical thinking skills. These skills include asking questions, observing carefully, seeing connections among ideas, and analyzing arguments and the evidence on which they are based. Each exercise emphasizes one of six categories of critical thinking: *scientific problem solving, psychological reasoning, perspective taking, pattern recognition, creative problem solving,* and *practical problem solving.* Sample answers to each exercise and an essay on using critical thinking in everyday reasoning appear in the Instructor's Resources that accompany this text.

- **Interactive Flashcards.** Students can use these flashcards to tutor themselves on all chapter and text terminology and then to quiz themselves on those terms.

- **PsychSim 5.0 and PsychQuest: Interactive Exercises for Psychology.** Key modules from these series (by Thomas Ludwig, Hope College) allow students to explore research topics, participate in experiments and simulations, and apply health psychology to real-world issues.

- **Customized PowerPoint Slides.** This collection was created for use in my health psychology course. These slides focus on key terms and themes from the text and feature tables, graphs, and figures.

- **Chapter Outlines.** These helpful summaries reinforce key points within each chapter.

- **Annotated Web Links.** These links direct students to additional sources related to the study of Health Psychology.

Scientific American Video Collection in Health Psychology

This video series includes selections from the *Scientific American Frontiers* television program hosted by Alan Alda. Created especially for the health psychology course, it includes 16 clips that provide instructors with excellent tools to show current events and classic research in health psychology. Examples of the exciting research topics covered are obesity, pain, the efficacy of complementary and alternative medicine, gene therapy, and jet lag.

Acknowledgments

Although as the author my name is on the cover of this book, I certainly did not write the book alone. Writing a textbook is a complex task involving the collaborative efforts of a large number of very talented people.

Many of my colleagues played a role in helping me develop this text. I am indebted to the dozens of academic reviewers who read part or all of this book, providing constructive criticism, suggestions, or just an encouraging word. Their input made this a much better book, and I hope they forgive me for the few suggestions not followed. I thank the following reviewers for their consultation during the **first edition** process:

David Abwender
State University of New York–Brockport

Christopher Agnew
Purdue University

Jean Ayers
Towson University

Joy Berrenberg
University of Colorado

Marion Cohn
Ohio Dominican College

Karen J. Coleman
University of Texas–El Paso

Eliot Friedman
Williams College

Sharon Gillespie
Andrews University

(continued)

Arthur J. Gonchar
University of La Verne

Bonnie A. Gray
Mesa College

Carol A. Hayes
Delta State University

Robin Kowalski
Western Carolina University

Kristi Lane
Winona State University

Leslie Martin
La Sierra University

Julie Ann McIntyre
Russell Sage College

James P. Motiff
Hope College

Virginia Norris
South Dakota State University

Amy Posey
Benedictine College

Kathleen M. Schiaffino
Fordham University

Elisabeth Sherwin
University of Arkansas–Little Rock

Gabriee B. Sweidel
Kutztown University

Diane C. Tucker
University of Alabama–Birmingham

Rebecca Warner
University of New Hampshire

Eric P. Wiertelak
Macalester College

David M. Young
Indiana University–Purdue University at Fort Wayne

Diane Zelman
California School of Professional Psychology–Alameda

I would also like to thank the following reviewers for their excellent advice and encouraging words in the creation of this thoroughly revised **second edition:**

Mark E. Christians
Dordt College

Dale V. Doty
Monroe Community College

Dennis G. Fisher
California State University– Long Beach

Phyllis R. Freeman
State University of New York– New Paltz

Arthur J. Gonchar
University of La Verne

Linda R. Guthrie
Tennessee State University

Steven Hoekstra
Kansas Weslyan University

Rob Hoff
Mercyhurst College

Marc Kiviniemi
University of Nebraska–Lincoln

Sherri B. Lantinga
Dordt College

Matthias R. Mehl
University of Arizona

Eve Sledjeski
Kent State University

Margaret K. Snooks
University of Houston–Clear Lake

Richard J. Tafalla
University of Wisconsin–Stout

Christy Teranishi
Texas A&M International University

Nancy L. Worsham
Gonzaga Univeristy

At Worth Publishers—a company that lets nothing stand in the way of producing the finest textbooks possible—a number of people played key roles. Chief among these are Publisher Catherine Woods, whose initial interest, vision, and unflagging support gave me the push needed to start the project and sustained me throughout; Acquisitions Editor Kevin Feyen, whose encouragement helped get us through the challenging final stages; Managing Editor Tracey Kuehn, Production Manager Sarah Segal, and Project Editor Kate Mannix, who worked wonders throughout production to keep us on course; Art Director Babs Reingold, Designer Lissi Sigillo, and artists Matthew Holt and Todd Buck, whose creative vision resulted in the distinctive design and beautiful art program that exceeded my expectations; Editor Betty Probert, who edited and produced the *Instructor's Manual* and *Test Bank,* Senior Media Editor Danielle Pucci, who coordinated the production of an unparalleled supplements package and always had an affirming word; and Ted Szczepanski and Donna Ranieri, who supervised the photo research that helped give the book its tremendous visual appeal. Finally, no one deserves more credit than Development Editor Christine Brune. Her vast knowledge of psychology, superb writing and editorial skills, and clear vision for my voice and the book's central messages provided the strong foundation needed to bring this new edition to print.

As ever, my heartfelt thanks go to Pam, for her sage advice and unwavering confidence; to Jeremy, Rebecca, and Melissa, for helping me keep things in perspective; and to the many students who studied health psychology with me and assisted in the class testing of this book. They are a constant reminder of the enormous privilege and responsibilities I have as a teacher; it is for them that I have done my best to bring the field of health psychology alive in this text.

To those of you who are about to teach using this book, I sincerely hope that you will share your experiences with me. Drop me a line and let me know what works, what doesn't, and how you would do it differently. This input will be vital in determining the book's success and in shaping its future.

Richard O. Straub
University of Michigan, Dearborn
Dearborn, Michigan 48128
rostraub@umich.edu

Part 1 | Foundations of Health Psychology

Introducing Health Psychology

*C*aroline Flynn stepped aboard the 32-ton steamer Maure-tania *on what must have been an uncertain morning in the early 1880s. Bound for America, her journey of hope began in Liverpool, England, in a desperate attempt to escape the economic distress and religious persecution she and her family suffered in Ireland. The country's troubles had begun decades earlier with "an Gorta Mór" (the Great Hunger)—a famine caused by the potato fungus that destroyed the primary, and often only, food of most Irish families.*

Caroline's journey was hardly unique. Between 1861 and 1926, four million Irish left the country for similar reasons, and young people like Caroline were brought up for "export" overseas. After a harrowing, five- to six-week voyage across the Atlantic, crowded with other emigrants into a steerage compartment that was rarely cleaned, they endured the humiliating processing of immigrants at Ellis Island. Many of those who were sick or without financial means or sponsors were forced to return to their homeland.

As Caroline doggedly made her way in her adopted country, first north to upstate New York and then west to Chicago, she found that things were better, but life was still hard. Doctors were expensive (and few in number), and she always had to guard against drinking impure water; eating contaminated foods; or becoming infected with typhoid fever, diphtheria, or one of the many other diseases that were prevalent in those days. Despite her vigilance, her survival (and later that of her husband and newborn baby) remained uncertain. Life expectancy was less than 50 years, and one of every six babies died before his or her first birthday. "It would keep you poor, just burying your children," wrote one Irishwoman to her family back home (Miller & Miller, 2001). Equally troubling was the attitude of many native-born Americans, who viewed the Irish as inferior, violent, and drunken. Most of the new immigrants toiled as laborers in the lowest paid and most dangerous occupations, and were banished to ghetto-like "Paddy" towns that sprang up on the outskirts of cities such as New York and Chicago.

More than a century later, I smile as my mother recounts the saga of my great-grandmother's emigration to the United States. Her grandmother lived a long, productive life and left a legacy of optimism and "indomitable Irishy" that fortified her against the hardships in her life—and carried down through the generations. "How different things are now," I think as our phone call ends, "but how much of Caroline's spirit is still alive in my own children!"

Things are very different. Advances in hygiene, public health measures, and microbiology have virtually eradicated the infectious diseases Caroline feared most. Women born in the United States today enjoy a life expectancy of over 80 years, and men often reach the age of 73. This gift of time has helped us realize that health is much more than freedom from illness. More than ever before, we can get beyond survival mode and work to attain lifelong vitality by modifying our diets, exercising regularly, and remaining socially connected and emotionally centered.

My great-grandmother's story makes clear that many factors interact in determining health. This is a fundamental theme of **health psychology,** a subfield of psychology that applies psychological principles and research to the enhancement of health and the treatment and prevention of illness. Its concerns include social conditions (such as the availability of health care and support from family and friends), biological factors (such as family longevity and inherited vulnerabilities to certain diseases), and even personality traits (such as optimism).

The word *health* comes to us from an old German word that is represented, in English, by the words *hale* and *whole,* both of which refer to a state of "soundness of body." Linguists note that these words derive from the medieval battlefield, where loss of *haleness,* or health, was usually the result of grave bodily injury. Today, we are more likely to think of health as the absence of disease rather than as the absence of a debilitating battlefield injury. Because this definition focuses only on the absence of a negative state, however, it is incomplete. Although it is true that healthy people are free of disease, complete health involves much more. A person may be free of disease but still not enjoy a vigorous, satisfying life. **Health** involves physical as well as psychological and social well-being.

We are fortunate to live in a time when most of the world's citizens have the promise of a longer and better life than their great-grandparents, with far less

■ **health psychology** the application of psychological principles and research to the enhancement of health, and the prevention and treatment of illness.

■ **health** a state of complete physical, mental, and social well-being.

disability and disease than ever before. However, these health benefits are not universally enjoyed. Consider:

- The number of healthy years of life that can be expected is at least 70 years in 24 (mostly developed) countries of the world, but is estimated to be less than 40 years in 32 other (mostly developing) countries (World Health Organization, 2002).

- Violence-, drug-, and alcohol-related deaths and injuries, and sexual hazards such as HIV, increasingly mark the transition from adolescence to adulthood, particularly among many ethnic minorities (Yee and others, 1995).

- At every age, death rates vary by ethnic group. For instance, among American men and women aged 20 to 24, death rates are highest among African-Americans (151.3 per 100,000), followed by Native Americans (111.7 per 100,000), European Americans (87.1 per 100,000), and Asian and Pacific Islander Americans (47.6) (National Vital Statistics Reports, 2003).

- Although men are twice as likely as women to die of any cause, beginning in middle age women have higher disease and disability rates (National Vital Statistics Reports, 2003).

- The United States spends a higher portion of its gross domestic product on health care than any other country but ranks only thirty-seventh out of 191 countries in terms of the overall performance of its health care system, as measured by such factors as responsiveness, fairness of funding, and accessibility by all individuals (World Health Organization, 2000).

These statistics reveal some of the challenges in the quest for global wellness. Health professionals are working to reduce the 30-year discrepancy in life expectancy between developed and developing countries; to help adolescents make a safe, healthy transition to adulthood; and to achieve a deeper understanding of the relationships among gender, ethnicity, sociocultural status, and health.

In the United States, the Department of Health and Human Services report *Healthy People 2010* focuses on eliminating health disparities among various sociocultural groups and in general on substantially improving the health of all Americans by 2010. It also notes that nearly one million deaths in this country each year are preventable (see Table 1.1).

This chapter introduces the field of health psychology, which plays an increasingly important role in meeting the world's health challenges. Consider a few of the more specific questions that health psychologists seek to answer: How do your attitudes, beliefs, self-confidence, and personality affect your physiology and your overall health? Why are so many people turning to acupuncture, herbalism, and other forms of alternative medicine? Do these interventions really work? Why do so many people ignore unquestionably sound advice for improving their health, such as quitting smoking, moderating food intake, and exercising more? Why are certain health problems more likely to occur among people of a particular age, gender, or ethnic group? Why is being

The health of women is inextricably linked to their status in society. It benefits from equality and suffers from discrimination.

—World Health Organization, 2000

Table 1.1

Preventable Injury and Death

The *Healthy People 2010* reports that, yearly:

- Control of underage and excess use of alcohol could prevent 100,000 deaths from automobile accidents and other alcohol-related injuries.
- Elimination of public possession of firearms could prevent 35,000 deaths.
- Elimination of all forms of tobacco use could prevent 400,000 deaths from cancer, stroke, and heart disease.
- Better nutrition and exercise programs could prevent 300,000 deaths from heart disease, diabetes, cancer, and stroke.
- A reduction in risky sexual behaviors could prevent 30,000 deaths from sexually transmitted diseases.
- Full access to immunizations for infectious diseases could prevent 100,000 deaths.

Source: U.S. Department of Health and Human Services. (1998). *Healthy People 2010.* Washington, DC: U.S. Government Printing Office.

poor, uneducated, or lonely a potentially serious threat to your health? Conversely, why do those who are relatively affluent, well educated, and socially active enjoy better health?

Health psychology is the science that seeks to answer these and many other questions about how our wellness interacts with how we think, feel, and act. We begin by taking a closer look at the concept of health and how it has changed over the course of history. Next, we'll examine the biopsychosocial perspective on health psychology, including how it draws on and supports other health-related fields. Finally, we'll take a look at the kind of training needed to become a health psychologist and what you can do with that training.

Health and Illness: Lessons from the Past

Although all human civilizations have been affected by disease, each has understood and treated it differently. At one time, people thought that disease was caused by demons. At another, they saw it as a form of punishment for moral weakness. Today, we wrestle with very different questions, such as "Can disease be caused by an unhealthy personality?" We will consider how views regarding health and illness have changed by following a case study—Darrell—through the ages. Darrell presents with a bad headache, shortness of breath, sleeplessness, a racing heart, and a wild, frightened expression. How will he be treated? Current understanding of these symptoms would probably lead most health professionals to suggest Darrell is suffering from anxiety. His treatment today might be a combination of talk therapy, relaxation techniques, and possibly targeted drug therapy. But as we will see, his treatment through the ages would have varied widely. (You may want to refer to Figure 1.1 throughout this section to get a sense of the chronology of changing views toward health and illness.)

Ancient Views

Prehistoric Medicine

Our efforts at healing can be traced back 20,000 years. A cave painting in southern France, for example, which is believed to be 17,000 years old, depicts an Ice Age shaman wearing the animal mask of an ancient witch doctor. In religions based on a belief in good and evil spirits, only a shaman (priest or medicine man) can influence these spirits.

For preindustrial men and women, confronted with the often-hostile forces of their environment, survival was based on constant vigilance against these mysterious forces of evil. When a person became sick, there was no obvious physical reason for it: Rather, the stricken individual's condition was misattributed to weakness in the face of a stronger force, bewitchment, or possession by an evil spirit (Amundsen, 1996).

At this time, Darrell's symptoms might have been treated with rituals of sorcery, exorcism, or even a primitive form of surgery called *trephination.* Archaeologists have unearthed prehistoric human skulls containing irregularly shaped holes that were apparently drilled by early healers to allow disease-causing demons to leave patients' bodies. Historical records indicate that trephination was a widely practiced form of treatment in Europe, Egypt, India, and Central and South America.

About 4,000 years ago, some peoples realized that hygiene also played a role in health and disease and they made attempts at improving public hygiene. The ancient Egyptians, for example, engaged in cleansing rites intended to discourage illness-causing worms from infesting the body. In Mesopotamia (a part of what is now Iraq), soap was manufactured, bathing facilities designed, and public sewage treatment systems constructed (Stone, Cohen, & Adler, 1979).

Greek and Roman Medicine

The most dramatic advances in public health and sanitation were made in Greece and Rome during the sixth and fifth centuries B.C.E. In Rome, a great drainage system, the *Cloaca Maxima,* was built to drain a swamp that later became the site of the Roman Forum. Over time, the *Cloaca* assumed the function of a modern sewage system. Public bathrooms, for which there was a small admission charge, were commonplace in Rome by the first century C.E. (Cartwright, 1972).

The first aqueduct brought pure water into Rome as early as 312 B.C.E., and cleaning of public roads was supervised by a group of appointed officials who also controlled the food supply. This group passed regulations to ensure the freshness of meat and other perishable foods, and they arranged for the storage

Figure 1.1

A Timeline of Historical and Cultural Variations in Illness and Healing From the ancient use of trephination to remove evil spirits to the current use of noninvasive brain scans to diagnose disease, the treatment of health problems has seen major advances over the centuries. A collection of treatments across the ages is shown below (from left to right): trephination (on an ancient Peruvian skull); acupuncture from China; early surgery in seventeenth-century Europe; and vaccination by the district vaccinator in nineteenth-century London.

ANCIENT GREECE Illness caused by an imbalance of bodily humors; good diet and moderation in living would cure it.

PREHISTORIC PERIOD Illness caused by evil spirits and treated by trephination.

MIDDLE AGES (476–1450) Disease was divine punishment for sins, cured by miraculous intervention, invoking of saints, as well as bloodletting.

1800s Disease caused by microscopic organisms. Treatment was surgery and immunization.

TWENTY-FIRST CENTURY Biopsychosocial causes of disease. Modern, flexible methods of treatment.

B.C.E. 10,000 — 5000 — 2000 — 1000 — C.E. — 200 — 500 — 1000 — 1100 — 1400 — 1500 — 1600 — 1700 — 1800 — 1900 — 1960 — 1980 — 2000

ANCIENT EGYPT Demons and punishment by the gods caused illness. Sorcery and primitive forms of surgery and hygiene were treatments.

ANCIENT ROME (200 B.C.E.) "Pathogens" such as bad air and body humors caused illness. Treated by bloodletting, enemas, and baths.

1920s Disease influenced by mind and emotions and treated by psychoanalysis, psychiatry, and other medical methods.

ANCIENT CHINA (1100–200 B.C.E.) Unbalanced forces of nature caused illness. Treated with herbal medicine and acupuncture.

RENAISSANCE Disease was a physical condition of the body, which was separate from the mind. Surgical techniques first used.

Credits (left to right): Trephinated skull engraving by English School (nineteenth century) published 1878 in "Incidents of Travel and Exploration in the Land of the Incas" by E. George Squier: private collection/ Bridgeman Art Library; Illustration showing acupuncture: © Corbis; "The Surgeon," engraving by German School (seventeenth century): private collection/Bridgeman Art Library; "Vaccination" engraving, 1871: Hulton Getty/Liaison Agency.

■ **humoral theory** a concept of health proposed by Hippocrates that considered wellness a state of perfect equilibrium among four basic body fluids, called humors. Sickness was believed to be the result of disturbances in the balance of humors.

of vast quantities of grain, for example, in an effort to forestall famine (Cartwright, 1972).

In Ancient Greece, the philosopher Hippocrates (460–377 B.C.E.) was establishing the roots of Western medicine when he rebelled against the ancient focus on mysticism and superstition. Hippocrates, who is often called the "father of modern medicine," was the first to argue that disease is a natural phenomenon and that the causes of disease (and therefore their treatment and prevention) are knowable and worthy of serious study. In this way, he built the earliest foundation for a scientific approach to healing.

Hippocrates proposed the first rational explanation of why people get sick, and the healers of this period in history may have been influenced by his ideas in addressing Darrell's problems. According to Hippocrates' **humoral theory,** a healthy body and mind resulted from equilibrium among four bodily fluids called humors: blood, yellow bile, black bile, and phlegm. To maintain a proper balance, a person had to follow a healthy lifestyle that included exercise, sufficient rest, a good diet, and the avoidance of excesses. When the humors were out of balance, however, both body and mind were affected in predictable ways, depending on which of the four humors was in excess. Darrell, for example, might have been considered choleric, with an excess of yellow bile and a fiery temperament. He might have been treated with bloodletting (opening a vein to remove blood), liquid diets, enemas, and cooling baths.

Although humoral theory was discarded as advances were made in anatomy, physiology, and microbiology, the notion of personality traits being linked with body fluids still persists in the folk and alternative medicines of many cultures, including those of traditional Oriental and Native American cultures. Moreover, as we'll see in the next chapter, we now know that many diseases involve an imbalance (of sorts) among the brain's neurotransmitters, so Hippocrates was not too far off.

Hippocrates made many other notable contributions to a scientific approach to medicine. For example, to learn what personal habits contributed to gout, a disease caused by disturbances in the body's metabolism of uric acid, he conducted one of the earliest public health surveys of gout sufferers' habits, as well as of their temperatures, heart rates, respiration, and other physical symptoms. Hippocrates was also interested in patients' emotions and thoughts regarding their health and treatment, and thus he called attention to the psychological aspects of health and illness. "It is better to know the patient who has the disease," Hippocrates said, "than it is to know the disease which the patient has" (quoted in Wesley, 2003).

The next great figure in the history of Western medicine was the physician Claudius Galen (129–200 C.E.). Galen was born in Greece but spent many years in Rome conducting dissection studies of animals and treating the severe injuries of Roman gladiators. In this way, he learned much that was previously unknown about health and disease. Galen wrote voluminously on anatomy, hygiene, and diet, building on the Hippocratic foundation of rational explanation and the careful description of each patient's physical symptoms.

Galen also expanded the humoral theory of disease by developing an elaborate system of pharmacology that physicians followed for almost 1,500 years. His system was based on the notion that each of the four bodily humors had its own elementary quality that determined the character of specific diseases. Blood, for example, was hot and moist. Galen believed that drugs, too, had elementary qualities; thus, a disease caused by an excess of a hot and moist humor could be cured only with drugs that were cold and dry. Although such views may seem archaic, Galen's pharmacology was logical, based on careful observation, and similar to the ancient systems of medicine that developed in China, India, and other non-Western cultures. Many forms of alternative medicine still use similar ideas today.

Non-Western Medicine

At the same time that Western medicine was emerging, different traditions of healing were developing in other cultures. For example, more than 2,000 years ago the Chinese developed an integrated system of healing, which we know today as *traditional Oriental medicine (TOM)*. TOM is founded on the principle that internal harmony is essential for good health. Fundamental to this harmony is the concept of *qi* (sometimes spelled *chi*), a vital energy or life force that ebbs and flows with changes in each person's mental, physical, and emotional well-being. Acupuncture, herbal therapy, meditation, and other interventions are said to restore health by correcting blockages and imbalances in *qi*.

Ayurveda is the oldest known medical system in the world, having originated in India around the sixth century B.C.E., coinciding roughly with the lifetime of the Buddha. The word *ayurveda* comes from the Sanskrit roots *ayuh*, which means longevity, and *veda*, meaning knowledge. Widely practiced in India, ayurveda is based on the belief that the human body represents the entire universe in a microcosm and that the key to health is maintaining a balance between the microcosmic body and the macrocosmic world. The key to this relationship is held in the balance of three bodily humors, or *doshas: vata, pitta,* and *kapha,* or, collectively, the *tridosha* (Fugh-Berman, 1997). We'll explore the history, traditions, and effectiveness of these and other non-Western forms of medicine in Chapter 14.

The Middle Ages and the Renaissance

The fall of the Roman Empire in the fifth century C.E. ushered in the Middle Ages (476–1450), an era between ancient and modern times characterized by a return to supernatural explanations of health and disease in Europe. The church exerted a powerful influence over all areas of life at this time. Religious interpretations colored medieval scientists' ideas about health and disease. In the eyes of the medieval Christian Church, humans were regarded as creatures with free will who were not subject to the laws of nature. Because they had souls, both humans and animals were not considered to be appropriate objects of scientific scrutiny, and dissection of both was strictly prohibited. Illness was

The Middle Ages began with an outbreak of plague that originated in Egypt in 540 C.E. and quickly spread throughout the Roman Empire, killing as many as 10,000 people a day. So great in number were the corpses that gravediggers could not keep up. The solution was to load ships with the dead, row them out to sea, and abandon them.

viewed as God's punishment for evildoing, and **epidemic** diseases, such as the two great outbursts of *plague* (a bacterial disease carried by rats and other rodents) that occurred during the Middle Ages were believed to be a sign of God's wrath. Darrell's "treatment" in this era would surely have involved attempts to force evil spirits out of his body. There were few scientific advances in European medicine during these thousand years.

In the late fifteenth century, a new age—the Renaissance—was born. Beginning with the reemergence of scientific inquiry, this period saw the revitalization of anatomical study and medical practice. The taboo on human dissection was lifted sufficiently that the Flemish anatomist and artist Andreas Vesalius (1514–1564) was able to publish an authoritative, seven-volume study of the internal organs, musculature, and skeletal system of the human body. The son of a druggist, Vesalius was fascinated by nature, especially the anatomy of humans and animals. In the pursuit of knowledge, no stray dog, cat, or mouse was safe from his scalpel.

In medical school, Vesalius turned his dissection scalpel on human cadavers. What he found proved some of the medical writings of Galen and earlier physicians to be clearly inaccurate. How, he wondered, could an unquestionable authority such as Galen have made so many errors in describing the body? Then he realized why: Galen had never dissected a human body! Vesalius's volumes became the cornerstones of a new scientific medicine based on anatomy (Sigerist, 1958, 1971).

One of the most influential Renaissance thinkers was the French philosopher and mathematician René Descartes (1596–1650), whose first innovation was the concept of the human body as a machine. He described all the basic reflexes of the body, constructing elaborate mechanical models to demonstrate his principles. He believed that disease occurred when the machine broke down, and the physician's task was to repair the machine.

Descartes is best known for his beliefs that the mind and body are autonomous processes that interact minimally, and that each is subject to different laws of causality. This viewpoint, which is called **mind–body dualism** (or *Cartesian dualism*), is based on the doctrine that humans have two natures, mental and physical.

First Anatomical Drawings
By the sixteenth century, the taboo on human dissection had been lifted long enough that the Flemish anatomist and artist Andreas Vesalius (1514–1565) was able to publish a complete study of the internal organs, musculature, and skeletal system of the human body.

Musculature of a man by Andreas Vesalius, 1543. Fratelli Fabbri, Milan, Italy/Bridgeman Art Library.

Descartes and other great thinkers of the Renaissance, in an effort to break with the mysticism and superstitions of the past, vigorously rejected the notion that the mind influences the body. Darrell's condition and its connection to his emotional well-being was now even less likely to be properly understood. Although this viewpoint ushered in a new age of medical research based on confidence in science and rational thinking, it created a lasting bias in Western medicine against the importance of psychological processes in health. As we'll see, this bias has been rapidly unraveling over the past 25 years.

Post-Renaissance Rationality

Following the Renaissance, physicians were expected to focus exclusively on the biological causes of disease. Hippocrates' ancient humoral theory was finally discarded in favor of this new **anatomical theory** of disease. Physicians at this time would have considered internal causes for Darrell's symptoms, such as heart or brain malfunctions.

Science and medicine changed rapidly during the seventeenth and eighteenth centuries, spurred on by numerous advances in technology. Perhaps the single most important invention in medicine during this period was the microscope. Although a ground lens had been used for magnification in ancient times, it was a Dutch cloth merchant named Anton van Leeuwenhoek (1632–1723) who fashioned the first practical microscope. Using his microscope, Leeuwenhoek was the first to observe blood cells and the structure of skeletal muscles.

Discoveries of the Nineteenth Century

Once individual cells became visible, the stage was set for the **cellular theory** of disease—the idea that disease results when body cells malfunction or die. It was the French scientist Louis Pasteur (1822–1895), however, who truly rocked the medical world with a series of meticulous experiments showing that life can only come from existing life. Until the nineteenth century, scholars believed in *spontaneous generation*—the idea that living organisms can be formed from non-living matter. For example, maggots and flies were believed to emerge spontaneously from rotting meat. To test his hypothesis, Pasteur filled two flasks with a porridge-like liquid, heating both to the boiling point to kill any microorganisms. One of the flasks had a wide mouth into which air could flow easily. The other flask was also open to air, but had a long curved neck that kept any airborne microbes from falling into the liquid. To the amazement of skeptics, no new growth appeared in the curved flask. However, in the flask with the ordinary neck, microorganisms contaminated the liquid and multiplied rapidly. By showing that a genuinely sterile solution remains lifeless, Pasteur set the stage for the later development of *aseptic (germ-free) surgical* procedures. Even more important, Pasteur's successful challenge of a 2,000-year-old belief is a powerful demonstration of the importance of keeping an open mind in scientific inquiry.

Pasteur's discoveries helped shape the **germ theory** of disease—the idea that bacteria, viruses, and other microorganisms that invade body cells cause them to malfunction. The germ theory, which is basically a refinement of the cellular theory, forms the theoretical foundation of modern medicine.

■ **epidemic** literally, *among the people;* an epidemic disease is one that spreads rapidly among many individuals in a community at the same time. A *pandemic* disease affects people over a large geographical area.

■ **mind–body dualism** the philosophical viewpoint that mind and body are separate entities that do not interact.

■ **anatomical theory** the theory that the origins of specific diseases are found in the internal organs, musculature, and skeletal system of the human body.

■ **cellular theory** formulated in the nineteenth century, the theory that disease is the result of abnormalities in body cells.

■ **germ theory** the theory that disease is caused by viruses, bacteria, and other microorganisms that invade body cells.

Louis Pasteur in His Laboratory Pasteur's meticulous work in isolating bacteria in the laboratory, then showing that life can come only from existing life, paved the way for germ-free surgical procedures.

© Bettman/CORBIS

■ **biomedical model** the dominant view of twentieth-century
medicine that maintains that
illness always has a physical
cause.

■ **pathogen** a virus, bacterium,
or some other microorganism
that causes a particular disease.

Following Pasteur, medical knowledge and procedures developed rapidly. In 1846, William Morton (1819–1868), an American dentist, introduced the gas ether as an anesthetic. This great advance made it possible to operate on patients, who experienced no pain and thus remained completely relaxed. Fifty years later, the German physicist Wilhelm Roentgen (1845–1943) discovered x-rays and, for the first time, physicians were able to observe internal organs in a living person directly. Before the end of the century, researchers had identified the microorganisms that caused malaria, pneumonia, diphtheria, leprosy, syphilis, bubonic plague, typhoid, and other diseases that my great-grandmother's generation feared. Armed with this information, medicine began to bring under control diseases that had plagued the world since antiquity.

The Twentieth Century and the Dawn of a New Era

As the field of medicine continued to advance during the early part of the twentieth century, it looked more and more to physiology and anatomy, rather than to the study of thoughts and emotions, in its search for a deeper understanding of health and illness. Thus was born the **biomedical model** of health, which maintains that illness always has a biological cause. Under the impetus of the *germ* and *cellular theories* of disease, this model first became widely accepted during the nineteenth century and continues to represent the dominant view in medicine today.

The biomedical model has three distinguishing features. First, it assumes that disease is the result of a **pathogen**—a virus, bacterium, or some other microorganism that invades the body. The model makes no provision for psychological, social, or behavioral variables in illness. In this sense, the biomedical model embraces *reductionism,* the view that complex phenomena (such as health and disease) derive ultimately from a single primary factor. Second, the biomedical model is based on the Cartesian doctrine of *mind–body dualism* that, as we have seen, considers mind and body as separate and autonomous entities that interact minimally. Finally, according to the biomedical model, health is nothing more than the absence of disease. Accordingly, those who work from this perspective focus on investigating the causes of physical illnesses rather than on those factors that promote physical, psychological, and social vitality. Physicians working strictly from the biomedical perspective would focus on the physiological causes of Darrell's headaches, racing heart, and shortness of breath rather than considering whether a psychological problem could be contributing to these symptoms.

Psychosomatic Medicine

The biomedical model advanced health care significantly through its focus on pathogens. However, it was unable to explain disorders that had no observable physical cause, such as those uncovered by Sigmund Freud (1856–1939), who was initially trained as a physician. Freud's patients exhibited symptoms such as loss of speech, deafness, and even paralysis. Freud believed these maladies were caused by unconscious emotional conflicts that had been "converted" into a physical form. Freud labeled such illnesses *conversion disorders,* and the medical community was forced to accept a new category of disease.

In the 1940s, Franz Alexander advanced the idea that an individual's psychological conflicts could cause specific diseases. When physicians could find no infectious agent or other direct cause for rheumatoid arthritis, Alexander became intrigued by the possibility that psychological factors might be involved. According to his *nuclear conflict* model, each physical disease is the outcome of a fundamental, or nuclear, psychological conflict (Alexander, 1950). For example, individuals with a "rheumatoid personality," who tended to repress anger and were unable to express emotion, were believed to be prone to developing arthritis. Alexander helped establish **psychosomatic medicine,** a reformist movement within medicine named from the root words *psyche,* which means mind, and *soma,* which means body. Psychosomatic medicine is concerned with the diagnosis and treatment of physical diseases thought to be caused by faulty processes within the mind. This new field flourished, and soon the journal *Psychosomatic Medicine* was publishing psychological explanations of a range of health problems that included hypertension, migraine headaches, ulcers, hyperthyroidism, and bronchial asthma. At this time, Darrell might have been treated by Freud's *psychoanalysis*—talk therapy that delves into one's childhood and attempts to uncover unresolved conflicts.

Psychosomatic medicine was intriguing and seemed to explain the unexplainable. However, it had several weaknesses that ultimately caused it to fall out of favor. Most significantly, psychosomatic medicine was grounded in Freudian theory. As Freud's emphasis on unconscious, irrational urges in personality formation lost popularity, the field of psychosomatic medicine faltered. Psychosomatic medicine, like the biomedical model, was also based on reductionism—in this case, the outmoded idea that a single psychological problem or personality flaw is sufficient to trigger disease. We now know that disease, like good health, is based on the combined interaction of multiple factors, including heredity and environment, as well as the individual's psychological makeup.

Although Freud's theories and psychosomatic medicine were flawed, they laid the groundwork for a renewed appreciation of the connections between medicine and psychology. This was the start of the contemporary trend toward viewing illness and health as *multifactorial.* That is, many diseases are caused by the *interaction* of several factors, rather than by a single, invading bacterial or viral agent. Among these are *host factors* (such as genetic vulnerability or resiliency), *environmental factors* (such as exposure to pollutants and hazardous chemicals), *behavioral factors* (such as diet, exercise, and smoking), and *psychological factors* (such as optimism and overall "hardiness").

Behavioral Medicine

During the first half of the twentieth century, the behaviorist movement dominated American psychology. Behaviorists defined *psychology* as the scientific study of observable behavior, and they emphasized the role of learning in the acquisition of most human behavior.

■ **psychosomatic medicine** an outdated branch of medicine that focused on the diagnosis and treatment of physical diseases caused by faulty psychological processes.

■ **behavioral medicine** an inter-disciplinary field that integrates behavioral and biomedical science in promoting health and treating disease.

■ **etiology** the scientific study of the causes or origins of specific diseases.

By the early 1970s, **behavioral medicine** began to explore the role of learned behaviors in health and disease. One of its early successes was the research of Neal Miller (1909–2002), who used operant conditioning techniques to teach laboratory animals (and later humans) to gain control over certain bodily functions. Miller demonstrated, for example, that people could gain some control over their blood pressure and resting heart rate when they were made aware of these physiological states. Miller's technique, called *biofeedback,* is discussed more fully in Chapter 4. By this time in history, our anxiety sufferer, Darrell, would most likely have been correctly diagnosed and treated in a way that brought him some relief from his symptoms—perhaps including a combination of biofeedback and other relaxation techniques.

Although the wellspring for behavioral medicine was the behaviorist movement in psychology, a distinguishing feature of this field is its interdisciplinary nature. It draws its membership from such diverse academic fields as anthropology, sociology, molecular biology, genetics, biochemistry, and psychology, as well as the healing professions of nursing, medicine, and dentistry.

The Emergence of Health Psychology

In 1973, the American Psychological Association (APA) appointed a task force to explore psychology's role in the field of behavioral medicine, and in 1978, the APA created the division of health psychology (Division 38). Four years later, the first volume of its official journal, *Health Psychology,* was published. In this issue, Joseph Matarazzo, the first president of the division, laid down the four goals of the new field:

1. *To study scientifically the causes or origins of specific diseases; that is, their* **etiology.** Health psychologists are primarily interested in the psychological, behavioral, and social origins of disease. They investigate why people engage in *health-compromising behaviors,* such as smoking or unsafe sex.

2. *To promote health.* Health psychologists consider ways to get people to engage in *health-enhancing behaviors* such as exercising regularly and eating nutritious foods.

3. *To prevent and treat illness.* Health psychologists design programs to help people stop smoking, lose weight, manage stress, and minimize other risk factors for poor health. They also assist those who are already ill in their efforts to adjust to their illnesses or comply with difficult treatment regimens.

4. *To promote public health policy and the improvement of the health care system.* Health psychologists are very active in all facets of health education and consult frequently with government leaders who formulate public policy in an effort to improve the delivery of health care to all people.

As noted in Table 1.2, a number of twentieth-century trends helped shape the new field of health psychology, pushing it toward the broader biopsychosocial perspective, which is the focus of this text.

Table 1.2

Twentieth-Century Trends That Shaped Health Psychology

Trend	Result
1. Increased Life Expectancy	Recognize the need to take better care of ourselves to promote vitality through a longer life.
2. Rise of Lifestyle Disorders (for example, cancer, stroke, and heart disease)	Educate people to avoid the behaviors that contribute to these diseases (for example, smoking and a high-fat diet).
3. Rising Health Care Costs	Focus efforts on ways to prevent disease and maintain good health to avoid these costs.
4. Rethinking the Biomedical Model	Develop a more comprehensive model of health and disease—the biopsychosocial approach

■ **biopsychosocial (mind–body) perspective** the viewpoint that health and other behaviors are determined by the interaction of biological mechanisms, psychological processes, and social influences.

Biopsychosocial (Mind–Body) Perspective

As history tells us, looking at just one causative factor paints an incomplete picture of a person's health or illness. Health psychologists therefore work from a **biopsychosocial (mind–body) perspective.** As depicted in Figure 1.2, this perspective recognizes that *bio*logical, *psycho*logical, and *social* forces act together to determine an individual's health and vulnerability to disease; that is, health and disease must be explained in terms of multiple contexts.

• Genetic vulnerability to anxiety

• Reactive nervous system

BIOLOGICAL MECHANISMS

• High stress levels
• Poor coping skills
• Strong feelings of personal responsibility

PSYCHOLOGICAL PROCESSES

• High levels of actual responsibility at work and home and in the community
• Lack of social support

SOCIAL INFLUENCES

Anxiety
• Headaches
• Racing heart
• Feeling breathless
• Lump in the throat
• Insomnia

BEHAVIOR

Figure 1.2

The Biopsychosocial Model of Darrell's Anxiety According to the biopsychosocial perspective, all health behaviors are best explained in terms of three contexts: biological processes, psychological processes, and social influences. This diagram illustrates how these three processes could influence anxiety, as experienced by Darrell.

The Biological Context

All behaviors, including states of health and illness, occur in a biological context. Every thought, mood, and urge is a biological event made possible because of the characteristic anatomical structure and biological function of a person's body. Health psychology draws attention to those aspects of our bodies that influence health and disease: our genetic makeup and our nervous, immune, and endocrine systems (see Chapter 3).

Genes provide a guideline for our biology and predispose our behaviors—healthy and unhealthy, normal and abnormal. For example, the tendency to abuse alcohol has long been known to run in some families (see Chapter 8). One reason is that alcohol dependency is at least partly genetic, although it does not seem to be linked to a single, specific gene. Instead, some people may inherit a greater sensitivity to alcohol's physical effects, experiencing intoxication as pleasurable and the aftermath of a hangover as minor. Such people may be more likely to drink, especially in certain psychological and social contexts.

A key element of the biological context is our species' evolutionary history, and an *evolutionary perspective* guides the work of many health psychologists. Our characteristic human traits and behaviors exist as they do because they helped our distant ancestors survive long enough to reproduce and send their genes into the future. For example, natural selection has favored the tendency of people to become hungry in the presence of a mouth-watering aroma (see Chapter 7). This sensitivity to food-related cues makes evolutionary sense in that eating is necessary for survival—particularly in the distant past when food supplies were unpredictable and it was advantageous to have a healthy appetite when food was available.

At the same time, biology and behavior constantly interact. For example, some individuals are more vulnerable to stress-related illnesses because they angrily react to daily hassles and other environmental "triggers" (see Chapter 4). Among men, increased amounts of the hormone testosterone are positively correlated with this type of aggressive reaction. This relationship, however, is reciprocal: Angry outbursts can also lead to elevated testosterone levels. One of the tasks of health psychology is to explain how (and why) this mutual influence between biology and behavior occurs.

Life-Course Perspective

■ **life-course perspective** theoretical perspective that focuses on age-related aspects of health and illness.

Within the biological context, the **life-course perspective** in health psychology focuses on important age-related aspects of health and illness (Jackson, 1996). This perspective would consider, for example, how a pregnant woman's malnutrition, smoking, or use of psychoactive drugs would affect her child's lifelong development. Her child might be born early and suffer from *low birth weight* (less than 2500 grams [5 pounds]). Low birth weight is one of the most common, and most preventable, problems of prenatal development. Consequences include slowed motor, social, and language development; increased risk of cerebral palsy; long-term learning difficulties; even death (U.S. Bureau of the Census, 2005; Behrman & Rosenzweig, 2004).

The life-course perspective also considers the leading causes of death in terms of the age groups affected. The chronic diseases that are the leading causes of death in the overall population are more likely to affect middle-aged and elderly adults. Young people are much more likely to die from accidents.

The Psychological Context

The central message of health psychology is, of course, that health and illness are subject to psychological influences. For example, a key factor in how well a person copes with a stressful life experience is how the event is appraised or interpreted (see Chapter 5). Events that are appraised as overwhelming, pervasive, and beyond our control take a much greater toll on us physically and psychologically than do events that are appraised as minor challenges that are temporary and surmountable. Indeed, some evidence suggests that, whether a stressful event is actually experienced or merely imagined, the body's stress response is nearly the same. Health psychologists think that some people may be chronically depressed and more susceptible to certain health problems because they replay stressful events over and over again in their minds, which may be functionally equivalent to repeatedly encountering the actual event. Throughout this book, we will examine the health implications of thinking, perception, motivation, emotion, learning, attention, memory, and other topics of central importance to psychology.

Psychological factors also play an important role in the treatment of chronic conditions. The effectiveness of medication and other treatments is powerfully influenced by a patient's attitude. A patient who believes a drug or other treatment will only cause miserable side effects may experience considerable tension, which can actually worsen his or her physical response to the treatment. This reaction can set up a vicious cycle in which escalating anxiety before treatment is followed by progressively worse physical reactions as the treatment regimen proceeds. Psychological interventions can help patients learn to manage their tension, thereby lessening negative reactions to treatment. Patients who are more relaxed are usually better able, and more motivated, to follow their doctors' instructions.

Psychological interventions can also assist patients in managing the everyday stresses of life, which seem to exert a cumulative effect on the immune system. Negative life events such as bereavement, divorce, job loss, or relocation have been linked to decreased immune functioning and increased susceptibility to illness. By teaching patients more effective ways of managing unavoidable stress, health psychologists may help patients' immune systems combat disease.

The Social Context

Turn-of-the-century Irish immigrants like my great-grandmother surmounted poverty and prejudice in the United States by establishing Irish-American associations that strongly reflected an ethic of family and communal support. "Each for himself, but all for one another," wrote Patric O'Callaghan to his sister back home, as he described this system of patronage. In placing health behavior in its

■ **birth cohort** a group of people who, because they were born at about the same time, experience similar historical and social conditions.

■ **sociocultural perspective** theoretical perspective that focuses on how social and cultural factors contribute to health and disease.

social context, health psychologists consider the ways in which we think about, influence, and relate to one another and to our environments. Your gender, for example, entails a particular, socially prescribed role that represents your sense of being a woman or a man. In addition, you are a member of a particular family, community, and nation; you also have a certain racial, cultural, and ethnic identity, and you live within a specific socioeconomic class. You are influenced by the same historical and social factors as others in your **birth cohort**—a group of people born within a few years of each other. For example, those who lived 100 years ago were more likely to die from diseases that we in developed countries today consider preventable, such as tuberculosis and diphtheria (Table 1.3), and infant mortality in the United States has dropped significantly (Figure 1.3). Each of these elements of your unique social context affects your experiences and influences your beliefs and behaviors—including those related to health.

Consider the social context in which a chronic disease such as cancer occurs. A spouse, significant other, or close friend provides an important source of social support for many cancer patients. Women and men who feel socially connected to a network of caring friends are less likely to die of all types of cancer than their socially isolated counterparts (see Chapter 10). Feeling supported by others may serve as a buffer that mitigates the output of stress hormones and keeps the body's immune defenses strong during traumatic situations. It may also promote better health habits, regular checkups, and early screening of worrisome symptoms—all of which may improve a cancer victim's odds of survival.

Sociocultural Perspective

Within the social context, the **sociocultural perspective** considers how social and cultural factors contribute to health and disease. When psychologists use the term *culture*, they refer to the enduring behaviors, values, and customs that

Table 1.3

The 10 Leading Causes of Death in the United States, 1900 and 2001

1900	Rate per 100,000	2001*	Rate per 100,000
Heart disease and stroke	345	Heart disease	245.8
Influenza and pneumonia	202	Cancer	194.4
Tuberculosis	194	Stroke	57.4
Gastritis	143	Chronic lower respiratory diseases	43.2
Accidents	72	Accidents	35.7
Cancer	64	Diabetes mellitus	25.1
Diphtheria	40	Influenza and pneumonia	21.8
Typhoid fever	31	Alzheimer's disease	18.9
Measles	13	Nephritis and nephrosis (kidney disorders)	13.9

Sources: *Historical Statistics of the United States: Colonial Times to 1970, Pt. 1*, by U.S. Bureau of the Census, 1975, Washington, DC: U.S. Government Printing Office; "Deaths: Final Data for 2001," by Arias, E., Anderson, R.N., Kung, H., Murphy, S., & Kochanek, K.D.. 2003, *National Vital Statistics Reports, 52*(3), p. 8.

* Note that the leading causes of death in 2001 were not new diseases; they were present in earlier times, but fewer people died from them or they were called something else.

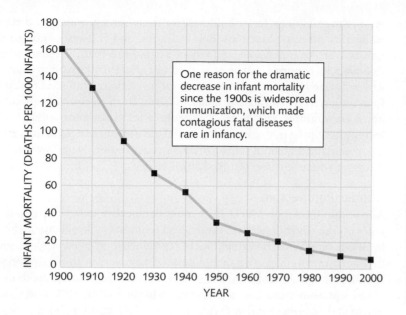

One reason for the dramatic decrease in infant mortality since the 1900s is widespread immunization, which made contagious fatal diseases rare in infancy.

Figure 1.3

Infant Mortality in the United States Less than one hundred years ago, 15 percent of babies born in this country died before their first birthday. For those who survived, life expectancy was only slightly more than 50 years. With improved health care, today more than 90 percent of new-born babies survive to at least 1 year of age.

Sources: *Historical Statistics of the United States: Colonial Times to 1970,* by U.S. Bureau of the Census, 1975, Washington, DC: U.S. Government Printing Office p. 60; "Deaths: Final Data for 2002," by K. Kochanek, S. Murphy, R. Anderson, & C. Scott, 2004, *National Vital Statistcs Reports, 53(5),* Table 30.

a group of people have developed over the years and transmitted from one generation to the next. Within a culture, there may be two or more *ethnic groups*— large groups of people who tend to have similar values and experiences because they share certain characteristics.

In multiethnic cultures such as those of the United States and most large nations, wide disparities still exist between the life expectancy and health status of ethnic minority groups and the majority population. These disparities were even greater among previous cohorts, such as the ethnic groups of my great-grandmother and others who emigrated to America. Some of these differences undoubtedly reflect variation in *socioeconomic status (SES),* which is a measure of several variables, including income, education, and occupation. For example, the highest rates of chronic disease occur among people who are at the lowest SES levels (Cohen, Doyle, & Turner, 2004). Evidence also suggests that bias, prejudice, and stereotyping on the part of health care providers may also be factors. Minorities tend to receive lower-quality health care than whites do, even when insurance status, income, age, and severity of conditions are comparable (Smedley, Stith, & Nelson, 2003).

Sociocultural forces also play an important role in the variation in health-related beliefs and behaviors. For example, traditional Native American health care practices are holistic and do not distinguish separate models for mental and physical illnesses (Johnson and others, 1995). As another example, Christian Scientists traditionally reject the use of medicine in their belief that sick people can be cured only through prayer. And Judaic law prescribes that God gives health, and it is the responsibility of each individual to protect it.

In general, health psychologists working from the sociocultural perspective have found wide discrepancies not only among ethnic groups but also within these groups. Latinos, for example, are far from homogenous. The three major nationality groups—Mexicans, Puerto Ricans, and Cubans—differ in education, income, overall health, and risk of disease and death (Bagley and others, 1995). Socioeconomic, religious, and other cultural patterns may also explain why variations in health are apparent not just among ethnic groups, but also from region to region, state to state, and even from one neighborhood to another. For example, fatal heart attacks are twice as common in West Virginia and Mississippi as in Colorado and Utah (U.S. Bureau of the Census, 2002). As one researcher stated, in terms of your overall health, "The way you age depends on where you live" (Cruikshank, 2003).

Gender Perspective

Also within the social context, the **gender perspective** in health psychology focuses on the study of gender-specific health behaviors, problems, and barriers to health care. With the exceptions of reproductive-system problems and undernourishment, men are more vulnerable than women to nearly every other health problem. In addition, many men consider preventive health care unmanly, but women tend to respond more actively than men to illness symptoms and to seek treatment earlier (Williams, 2003). The effect is cumulative, and by age 80, women outnumber men 2 to 1 (U.S. Bureau of the Census, 2002).

The medical profession has a long history of treating men and women differently. For example, research studies have shown that women treated for heart disease are given more prescriptions, are more likely to be put through unnecessary diagnostic procedures, and receive lower quality medical care overall than men (Ayanian & Epstein, 1991). In one study, 700 physicians were asked to prescribe treatment for eight heart patients with identical symptoms (Schulman and others, 1999). The "patients" were actors who differed only in gender, race, and reported age (55 or 70). Although diagnosis is a judgment call, most cardiac specialists would agree that diagnostic catheterization is the appropriate treatment for the symptoms described by each hypothetical patient. However, the actual recommendations revealed a small, but nevertheless significant, antifemale and antiblack bias. For the younger, white, and male patients, catheterization was recommended 90, 91, and 91 percent of the time, respectively; for the older, female, and black patients, 86, 85, and 85 percent of the time, respectively.

Problems such as these, and the underrepresentation of women as participants in medical research trials, have led to the criticism of gender bias in health research and care. In response, the National Institutes of Health (NIH) issued detailed guidelines on the inclusion of women and minority groups in medical research (Burd, 1994). In addition, in 1991 the NIH launched the Women's Health Initiative, a 15-year study of more than 161,000 postmenopausal women focusing on the determinants, and prevention, of disability and death in older women. Among the targets of investigation in this sweeping study are osteoporosis, breast cancer, and coronary heart disease. The women in this study are now participating in a follow-up phase that will last until 2007 (Anderson and others, 2003).

■ **gender perspective** theoretical perspective that focuses on gender-specific health problems and gender barriers to health care.

Despite the significance of such sociocultural and gender influences, remember that it would be a mistake to focus exclusively on this, or any one context, in isolation. Health behavior is not an automatic consequence of a given social, cultural, or gender context. For example, although, as a group, cancer patients who are married tend to survive longer than unmarried persons, marriages that are unhappy and destructive offer no benefit in this regard and may even be linked to poorer health outcomes.

Biopsychosocial "Systems"

As these examples indicate, the biopsychosocial perspective emphasizes the mutual influences among the biological, psychological, and social contexts of health. It is also based on a **systems theory** of behavior. According to this theory, health—indeed, all of nature—is best understood as a hierarchy of systems in which each system is simultaneously composed of smaller subsystems and part of larger, more encompassing systems. Thus, each of us is a system—a body made up of interacting systems such as the endocrine system, the cardiovascular system, the nervous system, and the immune system. Each of these biological systems is, in turn, composed of smaller subsystems consisting of tissues, nerve fibers, fluids, cells, and genetic material. Moving in the other direction, we are part of many larger systems, including our families, our neighborhoods, our societies, and our culture.

■ **systems theory** the viewpoint that nature is best understood as a hierarchy of systems, in which each system is simultaneously composed of smaller subsystems and larger, interrelated systems.

Sociocultural Bias in Diagnosis Physicians were told that these supposed "heart patients" were identical in occupation, symptoms, and every other respect except age, race, and gender. Although catheterization was the appropriate treatment for the described symptoms, the physicians were much more likely to recommend it for the younger, white, male patients than for the older, female, or black patients.

Source: Schulman, K.A. and others. (1999). The effect of race and sex on physician's recommendations for cardiac catherization. *New England Journal of Medicine, 340,* 618–625.

Applied to health, the systems approach emphasizes a crucial point: A system at any given level is affected by and affects systems at other levels. For example, a weakened immune system affects specific organs in a person's body, which in turn affects the person's overall biological health, which in turn might affect the person's relationships with his or her family and friends. Conceptualizing health and disease according to a systems approach allows us to understand the whole person more fully.

Applying the Biopsychosocial Model

To get a better feeling for the usefulness of biopsychosocial explanations of healthy behaviors, consider the example of *alcohol abuse,* which is a maladaptive drinking pattern in which at least one of the following occurs: recurrent drinking despite its interference with role obligations; continued drinking despite legal, social, or interpersonal problems related to its use; and recurrent drinking in situations in which intoxication is dangerous. Like most disordered behavior, alcohol abuse is best explained in terms of several mechanisms (Figure 1.4). Research studies of families, identical and fraternal twins, and adopted children clearly demonstrate that people (especially men) who have a biological relative who was alcohol dependent are significantly more likely to abuse alcohol themselves. In fact, for males, alcoholism in a first-degree relative is the single best predictor of alcoholism (Plomin and others, 2001). In addition, people who are less sensitive to alcohol's effects may be at a relatively high risk for alcohol dependence because they lack the feedback mechanisms that signal overconsumption (Wolfgan, 1997).

On the psychological side, although researchers no longer attempt to identify a single "alcoholic personality," they do focus on specific personality traits

Figure 1.4

A Biopsychosocial Model of Alcohol Abuse Alcohol abuse is best understood as occurring in three contexts: biological, psychological, and social.

- Genetic predispositions
- Alcohol sensitivity

BIOLOGICAL MECHANISMS

- Negative thinking
- Self-defeating beliefs

PSYCHOLOGICAL PROCESSES

- Stressful events
- Culture/environment that promotes excessive drinking
- Individualistic culture that encourages self-blame for personal failure.

SOCIAL INFLUENCES

Alcohol abuse

BEHAVIOR

that are linked with alcohol dependence and abuse. One such trait is a temperament that includes attraction to excitement and intolerance of frustration (Brook and others, 1992). A second is *behavioral undercontrol,* characterized by aggressiveness, unconventionality, overactivity, and impulsive behavior. A third is *negative emotionality,* which is marked by depression and anxiety (Sayette & Hufford, 1997).

On the social side, alcohol abuse sometimes stems from a history of drinking to cope with life events or overwhelming social demands. Peer pressure, difficult home and work environments, and tension reduction also may contribute to problem drinking. And more generally, as many college students know, certain social contexts promote heavy drinking. Research studies have shown that college students who prefer large social contexts involving both men and women tend to be heavier drinkers than those who prefer smaller, mixed-sex contexts. In addition, men who often drink in same-sex groups (whether large or small) report more frequent drunkenness than men who drink more often in small, mixed-sex groups. This suggests that college men who drink heavily may seek out social contexts in which this behavior will be tolerated (Senchak, Leonard, & Greene 1998). Fortunately, researchers have also found that heavy college drinking does not necessarily predict similar, post-college drinking behavior (Sher, Bartholow, & Nanda, 2001).

Frequently Asked Questions about a Health Psychology Career

We have seen how views regarding the nature of illness and health have changed over the course of history, examined trends that helped shape the new field of health psychology, and discussed the various theoretical perspectives from which health psychologists work. But you may still have questions about the profession of health psychology. Here are answers to some of the most frequently asked questions.

What Do Health Psychologists Do?

Like all psychologists, health psychologists may serve as *teachers, research scientists,* and/or *clinicians.* As teachers, health psychologists train students in health-related fields such as psychology, physical therapy, and medicine. As research scientists, they identify the psychological processes that contribute to health and illness, investigate issues concerning why people do not engage in healthful practices, and evaluate the effectiveness of specific therapeutic interventions.

Health psychologists are on the cutting edge of research testing the biopsychosocial model in numerous areas, including Alzheimer's disease, HIV/AIDS, compliance with medical treatment regimens, and immune functioning and various disease processes. Because the biopsychosocial model was first developed to explain health problems, until recently the majority of this research has focused on diseases and health-compromising behaviors. However, a new movement in psychology, called *positive psychology,* is encouraging psychologists to devote more research attention to optimal, healthy human functioning (Seligman & Csikszentmihalyi, 2000). The scope of this research—covering topics as diverse as optimism and happiness, psychological hardiness, and the traits of people who live to a ripe old age—shows clearly that the biopsychosocial model guides much of it (see Chapter 6).

Applied health psychologists, who generally focus on health-promoting interventions, are licensed for independent practice in areas such as clinical and counseling psychology. As clinicians, they use the full range of diagnostic assessment, education, and therapeutic techniques in psychology to promote health and assist the physically ill. Assessment approaches frequently include measures of cognitive functioning, psychophysiological assessment, demographic surveys, and lifestyle or personality assessment. Interventions may include stress management, relaxation therapies, biofeedback, education about the role of psychological processes in disease, and cognitive-behavioral interventions. Interventions are not limited to those who are already suffering from a health problem. Healthy or at-risk individuals may be taught preventive healthy behaviors.

Where Do Health Psychologists Work?

Traditionally, most psychologists accepted teaching or research positions at universities and four-year colleges. Employment opportunities for health psychologists with applied or research skills have been especially good, particularly in hospital settings (DeAngelis, 1995). This trend continues today, in response to society's increased emphasis on health promotion and meeting the needs of particular groups, such as the elderly (Kaplan, 2000). In addition, medical residency programs in the United States now have a clear mandate to improve physician training in areas such as sensitivity and responsiveness to patients' culture, age, gender, and disabilities. A new model of *collaborative care* involves health psychologists and allied professionals working together in the social and behavioral sciences. As we'll see, this mandate stems from mounting evidence that this type of care results in better health outcomes and helps control health care costs (ACGME, 2001).

In addition to colleges, universities, and hospitals, health psychologists may also be found working in health maintenance organizations (HMOs), medical schools, pain and rehabilitation clinics, and private practice (Figure 1.5). An increasing number of health psychologists may also be found in the corporate world, where they advise employers and workers on a variety of health-related issues. They also help establish on-the-job interventions to help employees lose weight, quit smoking, and learn more adaptive ways of managing stress.

Figure 1.5

Where Do Health Psychologists Work? Besides colleges, universities, and hospitals, health psychologists work in a variety of venues, including health maintenance organizations (HMOs), medical schools, pain and rehabilitation clinics, and independent practices. An increasing number of health psychologists can be found in the workplace, where they advise employers and workers on a variety of health-related issues.

Source: *1993 Doctorate Employment Survey,* by M. Wicherski and J. Kohout, 1995, Washington, DC: American Psychological Association.

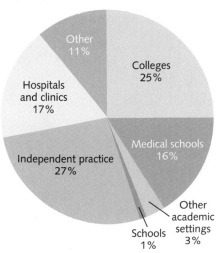

Other 11%
Colleges 25%
Hospitals and clinics 17%
Medical schools 16%
Independent practice 27%
Other academic settings 3%
Schools 1%

How Do I Become a Health Psychologist?

Preparing for a career in health psychology usually requires an advanced degree in any of a number of different educational programs. Some students enroll in medical or nursing school and eventually become nurses or doctors. Others train for one of the allied health professions, such as nutrition, physical therapy, social work, occupational therapy, or public health. An increasing number of interested undergraduates continue on to graduate school in psychology and acquire research, teaching, and intervention skills. Those who ultimately hope to provide direct services to patients typically take their training in clinical or counseling psychology programs.

Many students who wish to pursue a career in health psychology begin with general psychology training at the undergraduate level. Because of health psychology's biopsychosocial orientation, students are also encouraged to take courses in anatomy and physiology, abnormal and social psychology, learning processes and behavior therapies, community psychology, and public health.

Most health psychologists eventually obtain a doctoral degree (Ph.D. or Psy.D.) in psychology. To earn a Ph.D. in psychology, students complete a four- to six-year program, at the end of which they conduct an original research project. Psy.D. programs generally provide slightly more clinical experience and clinical courses but less research training and experience than Ph.D. programs. In 2004, there were 65 identified doctoral training programs in health psychology in the United States.

Graduate training in health psychology is generally based on a curriculum that covers the three basic domains of the biopsychosocial model. Training in the biological domain includes courses in neuropsychology, anatomy, physiology, and psychopharmacology. Training in the psychological domain includes courses in each of the major subfields (biological, developmental, personality, etc.) and theoretical perspectives (social–cultural, cognitive, behavior, neuroscience, etc.). And training in the social domain focuses on the study of group processes and the ways in which the various groups (family, ethnic, etc.) influence their members' health. Our understanding of health has come a long way—from "soundness of body" on the battlefield to today's biopsychosocial approach to overall vitality.

Summing Up

1. Health is a state of complete physical, mental, and social well-being. Health psychology's goals are to promote health, prevent and treat illness, investigate the role of biological, behavioral, and social factors in disease, and evaluate and improve the formulation of health policy and the delivery of health care to all people.

Health and Illness: Lessons from the Past

2. In the earliest known cultures, illness was believed to result from mystical forces and evil spirits that invaded the body. Hippocrates, Galen, and other Greek scholars developed the first rational approach to the study of health and disease. Non-Western forms of healing, including TOM and ayurveda, developed simultaneously.

3. In Europe during the Middle Ages, scientific studies of the body (especially dissection) were forbidden, and ideas about health and disease took on religious overtones. Illness was viewed as punishment for evildoing, and treatment frequently involved what amounted to physical torture.

4. French philosopher René Descartes advanced his theory of mind–body dualism—the belief that the mind and body are autonomous processes, each subject to different laws of causality. Descartes' influence ushered in a Renaissance of medical research based on the scientific study of the body. This research gave rise to the anatomical, cellular, and germ theories of disease.

5. The dominant view in modern medicine is the biomedical model, which assumes that disease is the result of a virus, bacterium, or some other pathogen invading the body. Because it makes no provision for psychological, social, or behavioral factors in illness, the model embraces both reductionism and mind–body dualism.

6. Sigmund Freud and Franz Alexander promoted the idea that specific diseases could be caused by unconscious conflicts. These views were expanded into the field of psychosomatic medicine, which is concerned with the treatment and diagnosis of disorders caused by faulty processes within the mind. Psychosomatic medicine fell out of favor because it was grounded in psychoanalytic theory and predicated on the outmoded idea that a single problem is sufficient to trigger disease.

7. Behavioral medicine was an outgrowth of the behaviorist movement in American psychology. Behavioral medicine explores the role of learned behavior in health and disease.

Biopsychosocial (Mind-Body) Perspective

8. Health psychologists approach the study of health and illness from several overlapping perspectives. The life-course perspective in health psychology focuses attention on how aspects of health and illness vary with age, as well as how birth cohort experiences (such as shifts in public health policy) influence health.

9. The sociocultural perspective calls attention to how social and cultural factors, such as ethnic variations in dietary practice and beliefs about the causes of illness, affect health.

10. The gender perspective calls attention to male–female differences in the risk of specific diseases and conditions, as well as in various health-enhancing and health-compromising behaviors.

11. The biopsychosocial perspective in effect combines these perspectives, recognizing that biological, psychological, and social forces act together to determine an individual's health and vulnerability to disease.

Frequently asked Questions about a Health Psychology Career

12. Health psychologists are engaged in three primary activities: teaching, research, and clinical intervention. Health psychologists work in a variety of settings, including hospitals, universities and medical schools, health maintenance organizations, rehabilitation clinics, private practice, and, increasingly, in the workplace.

13. Preparing for a career in health psychology usually requires a doctoral degree. Some students enter health psychology from the fields of medicine, nursing, or one of the allied health professions. An increasing number enroll in graduate programs in health psychology.

Key Terms and Concepts

health psychology, p. 3
health, p. 3
humoral theory, p. 8
epidemic, p. 11
mind–body dualism, p. 11
anatomical theory, p. 11
cellular theory, p. 11
germ theory, p. 11

biomedical model, p. 12
pathogen, p. 12
psychosomatic medicine, p. 13
behavioral medicine, p. 14
etiology, p. 14
biopsychosocial (mind–body) perspective, p. 15
life-course perspective, p. 16

birth cohort, p. 18
sociocultural perspective, p. 18
gender perspective, p. 20
systems theory, p. 20

Research in Health Psychology

*F*lorence Griffith Joyner, the 38-year-old three-time Olympic gold medalist who revolutionized women's sprinting, died at home on September 21, 1998. "FloJo" not only ran faster than any woman before her, but she also displayed a spectacular flamboyance in the way she ran, dressing in one-legged spandex body suits and sporting 6-inch fingernails. As news of her sudden death spread, the collective reaction was disbelief. How could one of the world's greatest athletes die suddenly at such a young age?

After several weeks of public speculation about drug use or other causes, the coroner concluded that FloJo died in her sleep of suffocation after suffering a seizure caused by a congenital brain abnormality. FloJo had been sleeping on her stomach when the seizure apparently caused her to turn her head into her pillow, restricting the flow of oxygen into her lungs and causing her to become asphyxiated.

Just 14 years earlier, the world had similarly been shocked by the sudden death of another high-profile athlete—running guru Jim Fixx, who helped launch the running boom of the 1970s. Fixx's sudden death while running was, regrettably, taken by many as proof that exercise offered no protection against cardiovascular disease. As with FloJo, however, this quick explanation was simply wrong. For most of his life, Fixx was overweight and consumed a high-fat, high-cholesterol diet. In addition, he had been a chain smoker, smoking three to four packs of cigarettes a day, and a workaholic, working 16 hours or more each day and getting only a few hours of sleep each night. Fixx was also at high risk of heart disease because his father had died from a heart attack at the young age of 43 years.

Fixx ignored early warning symptoms. His fiancée said that he complained of chest tightness during exercise and had planned to travel to Vermont to see whether the fresh air there would alleviate his *symptoms, which he believed to be due to allergies. The change of air did not help, and Fixx died while running on his first day in Vermont.*

Fixx's autopsy showed severe coronary artery disease with near-total blockage of one coronary artery and 80 percent blockage of another. There was also evidence of a recent heart attack. On the day Fixx died, more than 1,000 other Americans succumbed to heart attacks. There is overwhelming evidence that heart attacks occur most commonly in males who have high blood pressure, smoke heavily, have high cholesterol levels, and maintain a sedentary lifestyle. Fixx's midlife change to a healthy lifestyle may very well be what allowed him to outlive his father by 9 years.

Beware of the trap of believing easy, untested explanations for the causes of diseases or seemingly unexpected physiological events. Medical researchers and health psychologists investigate such cases, comparing situations and considering all relevant factors. Researchers must adopt a formal, systematic approach that has a proven ability to find reliable explanations. This approach is called the scientific method. *In this chapter, we will consider how the scientific method is applied to answer questions about health psychology.*

Critical Thinking and the Evidence Base

Health psychology touches on some of the most intriguing, personal, and practical issues of life. Does my family history place me at risk of developing breast cancer? Which of my lifestyle choices are healthy and which are unhealthy? Why can't I quit smoking? Every day we seem to be bombarded with new "definitive" answers to these and countless other vital health questions. For example, in the 1980s, researchers reported that caffeine leads to higher risk of heart disease and pancreatic cancer. In the early 1990s, new research asserted that limited amounts of caffeine were safe, even during pregnancy. In 1996, mothers-to-be were alarmed with reports that pregnant women who drink three or more cups of coffee or tea daily were at increased risk of spontaneous abortion, while caffeine drinkers who were trying to conceive were twice as likely as noncaffeine drinkers to delay conception by a year or more. Less than 2 years later, still more research concluded that women who drink more than half a cup of caffeinated tea every day might actually *increase* their fertility. Researchers also announced that caffeine might offer protection against Parkinson's disease by reducing the destruction of nerve cells in the brain (Hughes and others, 2000). Most recently, a National Institutes of Health study concluded that the caffeine in soft drinks, at least one of which is consumed by 68 percent of boys and 62 percent of girls ages 12 to 17, is "a preventable risk factor for hypertension and cardiovascular disease" (Savoca and others, 2004). So, is caffeine safe? Which conclusion are you to believe?

At the heart of all scientific inquiry is a skeptical attitude that encourages us to evaluate evidence and scrutinize conclusions. This attitude is called *critical thinking,* and it involves a questioning approach to all information. Whether listening to the evening news report, reading a journal article, or pondering a friend's position, critical thinkers ask questions. How did she arrive at that conclusion? What evidence forms the basis for this person's conclusions? Is there an ulterior motive? Can the results of a particular study be explained in another way? Until you know the answers to these and other questions, you should be cautious—indeed, downright skeptical—of all persuasive arguments, including health reports that appear in newspapers and magazines and on television. Learning which questions to ask will make you a much more informed consumer of health information.

The Dangers of "Unscientific" Thinking

In our quest for greater understanding of healthy behavior, we draw on the available information to formulate *cause-and-effect relationships* about our own and other people's behavior. If this information derives solely from our personal experiences, beliefs, and attitudes, then we may be like the quick-reacting reporters who tried to make sense of the deaths of FloJo and Jim Fixx—making snap judgments with little attention to accuracy. It is dangerous to base our explanations on hearsay, conjecture, anecdotal evidence, or unverified sources of information. For example, upon seeing a lean, statuesque female gymnast or dancer, we may admire what we believe to be her healthy eating and exercise habits, wishing we too could possess such willpower and well-being. We may be shocked to learn that she is actually anorexic and suffering from a stress fracture related to poor diet and excessive, exercise-induced skeletal trauma.

Examples of faulty reasoning unfortunately abound in all fields of science. In the early twentieth century, for example, thousands of Americans died from *pellagra,* a disease marked by dermatitis (skin sores), gastrointestinal disorders, and memory loss. Because the homes of many pellagra sufferers had unsanitary means of sewage removal, many health experts believed the disease was carried by a microorganism and transmitted through direct contact with infected human excrement. Although hygienic plumbing was certainly a laudable goal, when it came to pinpointing the cause of pellagra, the "experts" fell into a faulty reasoning trap—failing to consider alternative explanations for their observations. This type of leaping to unwarranted (untested) conclusions is an example of **belief bias,** which explains why two people can look at the same situation (or data) and draw radically different conclusions.

Fortunately, Surgeon General Joseph Goldberger's keener powers of observation allowed him to see that many pellagra victims were also malnourished. To pinpoint the cause of the disease, Goldberger conducted a simple, if distasteful, empirical test: He mixed small amounts of the feces and urine from two pellagra patients with a few pinches of flour and rolled the mixture into little dough

■ **belief bias** a form of faulty reasoning in which our expectations prevent us from seeing alternative explanations for our observations.

All cultures develop incorrect beliefs about human behavior. Some people falsely believe that couples who adopt a child are later more likely to give birth to a child of their own and that more babies are born when the moon is full. Be on guard for examples of unscientific psychology in your own thinking.

balls, which he, his wife, and several assistants ate! When none came down with the disease, Goldberger then fed a group of Mississippi prisoners a diet deficient in niacin and protein (a deficiency that he suspected caused the disease), while another was fed the normal, more balanced prison diet. Confirming his hypothesis, within months the former group developed symptoms of pellagra, while the latter remained disease free (Stanovich & West, 1998). As this example illustrates, seeking information that confirms preexisting beliefs causes researchers to overlook alternative explanations of observed phenomenon.

Health Psychology Methods

Health psychologists use various research methods in their search to learn how psychological factors affect health. The method used depends in large measure on what questions the researcher is seeking to answer. To answer questions regarding how people cope with acquired immune deficiency syndrome (AIDS) or cancer, for example, a psychologist might observe or ask questions of a large sample of victims of these deadly diseases. On the other hand, researchers investigating whether lifestyle factors contribute to the onset of these diseases might conduct laboratory studies under controlled conditions.

There are two major categories of research methods in psychology—descriptive and experimental (Table 2.1). Health psychologists also borrow

Table 2.1

Comparing Research Methods

Research Method	Research Setting	Data Collection Method	Strengths	Weaknesses
Descriptive studies	Field or laboratory	Case studies, surveys and interviews, naturalistic observation	In-depth information about one person; often leads to new hypotheses; detects naturally occurring relationships among variables	No direct control over variables; subject to bias of observer; single cases may be misleading; cannot determine causality; correlation may mask extraneous variables
Experimental studies	Usually laboratory	Statistical comparison of experimental and control groups	High degree of control over independent and dependent variables; random assignment eliminates preexisting differences among groups	Artificiality of laboratory may limit the generalizability of results; certain variables cannot be investigated for practical or ethical reasons
Epidemiological studies	Usually conducted in the field	Statistical comparisons between groups exposed to different risk factors	Useful in determining disease etiology, easy to replicate, good generalizability	Some variables must be controlled by selection rather than by direct manipulation; time consuming; expensive
Meta-analysis	No new data are collected	Statistical combination of the results of many studies	Helps make sense of conflicting reports, replicable	Potential bias due to selection of studies included

methods from the field of **epidemiology,** which seeks to determine the frequency, distribution, and causes of a particular disease or other health outcome in a population. This section describes the research methods employed by psychologists and the tools they use to gather, summarize, and explain their data. The next section will explore the research methods of epidemiologists.

Descriptive Studies

Think about how a health psychologist might set about answering the following three questions: What are the psychological and physiological health outcomes for victims of a grave national crisis, such as the September 11, 2001, attack on the World Trade Center? How can hospital staff reduce the anxiety of family members waiting for a loved one to come out of surgery? Does binge drinking occur more often among certain types of college students? Clearly, the answers to each of these important questions will not be found in a research laboratory. Instead, researchers look for answers about the behavior of an individual or a group of people as it occurs in the home, at work, or wherever people spend their time. In such a study, called a **descriptive study,** the researcher observes and records the participant's behavior in a natural setting, often forming hunches that are later subjected to more systematic study.

Several types of descriptive studies are commonly used: case studies, interviews and surveys, and observational studies.

Case Studies

As we noted in Chapter 1, among the oldest and best-known methods of investigating human behavior is the **case study,** in which psychologists study one or more individuals extensively over a considerable period of time in order to uncover principles that are true of people in general. The major advantage of the case study is that it permits a researcher to gather a much more complete analysis of the individual than ordinarily can be obtained in studies involving larger groups.

Although case studies are useful in suggesting hypotheses for further study, they do have one serious disadvantage: Any given person may be atypical, limiting the "generalizability" of the results. In fact, case studies can be highly misleading. We have to be careful not to leap from especially memorable (although unrepresentative) case studies to broad conclusions. For example, although a mountain of research supports runners' longevity, many people were quick to discount this reality when they heard of jogging guru Jim Fixx's death ("Jim Fixx was a runner, wasn't he? He didn't live as long as my grandfather, who never exercised and was a lifelong cigar smoker."). Personal experience and especially vivid case studies can often overshadow much stronger scientific evidence.

The point to remember: Individual case studies can provide fruitful leads and direct researchers to other research designs to uncover general truths. They can also be highly misleading.

■ **epidemiology** the scientific study of the frequency, distribution, and causes of a particular disease or other health outcome in a population.

■ **descriptive study** research method in which researchers observe and record participants' behaviors, often forming hypotheses that are later tested more systematically; includes case studies, interviews and surveys, and observational studies.

■ **case study** a descriptive study in which one person is studied in depth in the hope of revealing general principles.

■ **survey** a questionnaire used to ascertain the self-reported attitudes or behaviors of a group of people.

■ **observational study** a non-experimental research method in which a researcher observes and records the behavior of a research participant.

■ **correlation coefficient** a statistical measure of the strength and direction of the relationship between two variables, and thus of how well one predicts the other.

Surveys

Surveys examine individual attitudes and beliefs in larger numbers and in much less depth than the case study. In these *self-report measures,* research participants are asked to rate or describe some aspect of their own behavior, attitudes, or beliefs, such as what they think of a new health product or how often they exercise.

Clinical health psychologists use the face-to-face interview as a start for developing a supportive working relationship with a patient. Clinicians also often use surveys for diagnostic assessment as a first step in developing intervention programs. For example, chronic-pain patients may be asked to complete a questionnaire related to their problem that sheds light on the effectiveness of previous treatments and the impact of their condition on their daily functioning. Surveys are among the most widely used research tools in health psychology because they are easy to administer, require only a small investment of time from participants, and quickly generate a great deal of useful data.

Observational Studies

In **observational studies,** the researcher observes participants' behavior and records relevant data. For example, a researcher interested in the physiological effects of everyday hassles might have participants wear a heart rate monitor while commuting to and from school or work in rush hour traffic.

Observational studies may be structured or unstructured. Structured observations often take place in the lab and involve tasks such as role-playing or responding to a very cold stimulus. In unstructured observations, referred to as *naturalistic observation,* the researcher attempts to be as unobtrusive as possible in observing and recording the subjects' behaviors. For example, a health psychologist might observe family members visiting a parent in a nursing home to gain insight into how people cope with watching a parent decline. These observations may be audiotaped or videotaped and then quantified through rating methods or frequency scores.

Correlation

Descriptive studies often reveal information about two variables that may be related, such as caffeine consumption and high blood pressure, or hypertension. To determine the extent of a suspected relationship between two variables, psychologists often calculate the **correlation coefficient,** using a formula that yields a number, or *r value,* ranging from $+1.00$ to -1.00. The sign ($+$ or $-$) of the coefficient indicates the direction of the correlation (positive or negative). A positive correlation is one in which increases in one variable are accompanied by increases in another variable. In contrast, when two variables are negatively correlated, as one goes up, the other tends to go down. Remember that a negative correlation says nothing about the strength or weakness of the relationship between the variables; it simply means the variables are inversely related. The researcher's ability to predict is no less with a negative correlation than it is with a positive correlation.

The absolute value of the correlation coefficient (from 0 to 1.00, regardless of whether the number is positive or negative) indicates the strength of the correlation—the closer to 1.00, the stronger the relationship and the more accurately a researcher can predict one variable from a known value of another.

Suppose, for example, that you are interested in the relationship between body weight and blood pressure. Perhaps you are testing your theory that a lean build lowers a person's risk of cardiovascular disease by reducing hypertension, a documented risk factor. To test your theory with an experiment would require manipulating the body weight variable and then recording blood pressure. Although measuring blood pressure is certainly possible, manipulating body weight would be unethical. So, instead, you calculate a correlation coefficient. Richard Cooper, Charles Rotimi, and Ryk Ward (1999) did just that, measuring body mass index, or BMI (a measure of a person's weight-to-height ratio) and prevalence of hypertension in a large sample of participants of African descent from several countries. Figure 2.1 displays a **scatterplot** of the results of their study. Each point on the graph represents two numbers for a sample of subjects from one country: average BMI and prevalence of hypertension.

The *strength* of a correlation is revealed by how closely together the points in a scatterplot are clustered along an imaginary line. In a *perfect correlation,* the points would align themselves in a perfectly straight line. The *direction*— "positive" or "negative"—is shown by the angle of the line. In a positive correlation, the points in the scatterplot sweep upward, from the lower left to the upper right. In a negative, or inverse, correlation, the points sweep downward, from the upper left to the lower right. Notice in Figure 2.1 that the relationship appears to be both fairly strong (the points fall roughly along a straight line) and positive (the points sweep upward from the lower left to the upper right). So, body mass and hypertension tend to increase together.

■ **scatterplot** a graphed cluster of data points, each of which represents the values of two variables in a descriptive study.

Figure 2.1

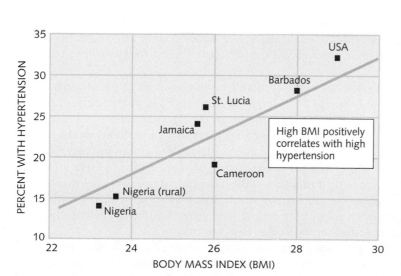

The Relationship between Body Mass Index and Hypertension in People of African Descent Body mass index, or BMI, measures a person's weight-to-height ratio; BMIs over **25** are generally considered a sign of being overweight. In a study comparing key locations in the westward African migration, researchers found that as BMI increased, so did the prevalence of hypertension. The scatterplot reveals a strong positive correlation between BMI and hypertension. The solid line confirms this, showing an upward slope and fairly tight clustering of the data points.

Source: Based on data in Cooper, R. S., Rotimi, C. N., & Ward, R. (1999). The puzzle of hypertension in African-Americans. *Scientific American, 280*(2), 59.

independent variable the factor in an experiment that an experimenter manipulates; the variable whose effect is being studied.

dependent variable the behavior or mental process in an experiment that may change in response to manipulations of the independent variable; the variable that is being measured.

random assignment assigning research participants to groups by chance, thus minimizing pre-existing differences among the groups.

It is tempting to draw cause-and-effect conclusions from the Cooper, Rotini, and Ward study results. However, even when two variables are strongly correlated, one does not necessarily cause the other. Maybe high blood pressure and a high BMI are both caused by a third factor, such as not enough exercise. Correlations do not rule out the possible contributions of other hidden variables. Even if two variables *are* causally related, correlations do not pinpoint directionality, in this case whether a high BMI elevates blood pressure or vice versa. Correlational studies are, however, an important first step. In health psychology, correlations identify relationships, often among several variables, that later may be studied more closely with experiments.

Experimental Studies

Although descriptive studies are useful, they cannot tell us about the *causes* of the behaviors we observe. To pinpoint causal relationships, researchers conduct experiments. Considered the pinnacle of the research methods, experiments are commonly used in health psychology to investigate the effects of health-related behaviors (such as exercise, diet, and so on) on an illness (such as heart disease).

In contrast to descriptive studies, experiments test hypotheses by systematically manipulating (varying) one or more **independent variables** (the "causes") while looking for changes in one or more **dependent variables** (the "effects") and *controlling* (holding constant) all other variables. By controlling all variables except the independent variable, the researcher ensures that any change in the dependent variable is *caused* by the independent variable rather than by another extraneous variable.

Experiments often involve testing the effects of several different *levels* of the independent variable on different groups. For example, in an experiment testing the level at which noise (an independent variable) begins to cause stress (the dependent variable), participants in three different groups might be asked to complete a checklist of behavioral and psychological symptoms of stress (an operational definition of the dependent variable) while listening to 10-, 25-, or 50-decibel noise over headphones (different levels of the independent variable *noise*).

Typically, the researcher randomly assigns a sample of participants to two or more study groups and administers the condition or treatment of interest (the independent variable) to one group, the *experimental group,* and a different or no treatment to the other group, the *control group*. **Random assignment** is crucial, because assigning research participants to groups by chance ensures that the members of all of the research groups are similar in every important aspect except in their exposure to the independent variable. For instance, random assignment would help prevent a large number of participants who were hypersensitive to noise from ending up in one group, thereby potentially masking the true effects of the independent variable.

Health psychology is somewhat unique among the subfields of psychology in that it studies a variety of variables as cause and effect. As possible "causes," health psychologists examine internal states (such as optimism and feelings of self-efficacy), overt behaviors (such as exercise and cigarette smoking), and external stimuli (such as a stressful job or a therapeutic program to promote relaxation). As possible "effects," they investigate overt behaviors (such as coping reactions to stressful employment), physiological measurements (such as blood pressure or cholesterol levels), and psychological states (such as anxiety levels).

To reduce the possibility of **expectancy effects** in experiments, the person who collects data from subjects is often "blind," that is, unaware of either the purpose of the research or of which subjects are in each condition. This is a *single-blind study*. To further ensure that expectancy effects do not contaminate the study, a **double-blind study** may be conducted. In such a case, neither the data collector nor the participants know the true purpose of the study or which participant is in which condition. This way, neither the researchers nor the participants will bias the outcome based on what they expect to happen. See Figure 2.2 for an example of how psychological methods may be used to assess an issue of interest to health psychologists.

Quasi-Experiments

When health psychologists cannot manipulate the variable of interest or randomly assign participants to experimental and control groups, they have other options: quasi-experiments, animal research, or qualitative research. A **quasi-experiment** (*quasi* means "resembling") is similar to an experiment in that it involves two or more *comparison* groups. A quasi-experiment is not a true experiment, however, because it uses groups that differ from the outset on the variable under study (the *subject variable*). Therefore, no cause-and-effect conclusions can be drawn. (Notice that we refer to a comparison group rather than a control group because the group naturally differs from the experimental group and no variable is being controlled.)

For example, suppose researchers wish to investigate the effect of a sedentary lifestyle on the development of cardiovascular disease. For ethical reasons, they cannot use humans in a standard experiment, so they may either use animals or conduct a quasi-experiment. In a quasi-experiment, the subject variable would be a sedentary lifestyle, with the group consisting of people who by their own admission get little or no exercise. The comparison group would be people who exercise regularly. Health psychologists would collect data on the participants' base levels of daily physical activity over a defined period of time, then identify separate "active" and "sedentary" groups. The researchers would follow these comparison groups for a period of years, regularly reassessing the groups' activity levels and cardiovascular health.

Subject variables commonly used in quasi-experiments include age, gender, ethnicity, and socioeconomic status—all variables that are either impossible or unethical to manipulate. Researchers also cannot manipulate variables to produce extreme environmental stress, physical abuse, or natural disasters. In such cases, the researcher finds events that have already occurred and studies the variables of interest.

In a classic study of expectancy effects (Roethlisberger & Dickson, 1939), researchers tried to increase worker productivity at an electric plant by shortening or lengthening coffee breaks, changing lighting conditions, and providing or taking away bonuses. Remarkably, no matter how conditions changed, productivity increased, indicating that the workers were simply responding to the knowledge that they were being studied.

■ **expectancy effects** a form of bias in which the outcome of a study is influenced either by the researcher's expectations or by the study participants' expectations.

■ **double-blind study** a technique designed to prevent observer- and participant-expectancy effects in which neither the researcher nor the subjects know the true purpose of the study or which subject is in each condition.

■ **quasi-experiment** a study comparing two groups that differ naturally on a specific variable of interest.

Figure 2.2

Psychological Research Methods A psychologist interested in studying the relationship between exercise and depression might follow these steps.

1. Using *observation, surveys, interviews*, and *case study* results, determine that there is a *negative correlation* between the amount of exercise and depression levels. Higher exercise levels predict lower levels of depression.

2. Use an *experiment* to test the *hypothesis* that exercising more will lower depression levels in mildly depressed individuals.

   Independent variable: exercise

   Dependent variable: depression levels

McCann & Holmes (1984) Study Results

Administer surveys to volunteer participants that assess depression levels. → Randomly assign the mildly depressed participants to either the experimental or the control conditions for 10 weeks. →

A. Experimental condition: Exercise aerobically for 20 minutes, three times per week.

B. Control condition: No aerobic exercise.

3. Re-administer surveys that assess depression levels. Compare depression levels before and after for each participant, and calculate any differences between the experimental and control conditions.

Lisa McCann and David Holmes (1984) conducted a similar experiment with college women, adding relaxation training as a comparison condition. They found that participants in the exercise condition showed significant decreases in depression.

© Randy M. Ury/Corbis

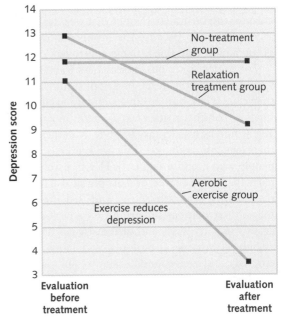

No-treatment group

Relaxation treatment group

Aerobic exercise group

Exercise reduces depression

Depression score

Evaluation before treatment

Evaluation after treatment

Life-Span Studies

Health psychologists working from the life-span perspective are interested in the ways people change or remain the same over time. To answer questions about the process of change, researchers use two basic research techniques, *cross-sectional* and *longitudinal studies.*

In a **cross-sectional study,** the researcher compares groups of people of various ages to determine the possible effects of age on a particular dependent variable. Suppose we are interested in determining whether different age groups are more (or less) likely to eat a well-balanced, low-fat diet. In cross-sectional research, the various age groups need to be similar in other ways, such as ethnicity and socioeconomic status, that might affect the characteristic being investigated. If the groups are similar, then any differences in early patterns among them may be attributed to age-related processes.

Matching different age groups for all subject variables other than age is difficult to do. Despite their best efforts, researchers using a cross-sectional design are well aware that the outcomes of such studies often produce *cohort differences* that reflect the impact of participants having been born and raised at a particular moment in history. A *cohort* is a group of people who share at least one demographic characteristic, such as age or socioeconomic status, in common. A cohort is similar to a generation, but the number of years separating two cohorts often is less than the number of years separating two adjacent generations.

If researchers want to be very sure that age, rather than some other variable, is the reason for differences in the characteristics of different age groups, they may conduct a **longitudinal study,** in which a single group of individuals is observed over a long span of time. This allows information about a person at one age to be compared with information about the same person at another age, revealing how this person changed over time.

Suppose you are interested in studying age-related changes in how people cope with stress. If you choose a cross-sectional approach, you might interview a sample of, say, 25 adults at each of five ages—for example 20, 30, 40, 50, and 60 years—and gather information about the ways in which they handle job stress, family quarrels, financial problems, and so forth. On the other hand, if you choose a longitudinal study to explore the same span of years, you (or, more likely, the researchers who will continue your study 40 years from now) would interview a group of 20-year-olds today and again when they are 30, 40, 50, and 60 years of age. The longitudinal study thus eliminates confounding factors such as differences in the types of stress encountered.

Longitudinal studies may be the "design of choice" from the life-span perspective, but they have several drawbacks. Such studies are very time consuming and expensive to conduct. More important, over the span of years of longitudinal studies, it is common for some participants to drop out because they move away, die, or simply fail to show up for the next scheduled interview or observation. When the number of dropouts is large, the results of the study may become skewed. Another potential problem is that people who remain in

■ **cross-sectional study** a study comparing representative groups of people of various ages on a particular dependent variable.

■ **longitudinal study** a study in which a single group of people is observed over a long span of time.

■ **heritability** the amount of variation in a trait among individuals that can be attributed to genes.

longitudinal studies may change in the characteristic of interest but for reasons that have little to do with their advancing age. For example, our study of age-related coping responses to stress may show that older people cope more adaptively by not allowing everyday hassles to get to them. But suppose a large number of the participants dropped out of the study midway (or perhaps died of stress-related illnesses!), and those who remained tended to be those employed in low-stress occupations. Can the researcher conclude that age has produced the results?

Behavior Genetics Research Techniques

A fundamental question in life-span research is: To what extent is our health—including our health behaviors and attitudes—shaped by our heredity (our nature) and by our life history (our nurture)? In an effort to answer questions about nature–nurture interactions, researchers estimate the **heritability** of a trait; that is, the amount of variation in a trait among a group of individuals that can be attributed to genes. In doing so, they employ two principal methods: twin studies and adoption studies.

Twin studies compare identical twins with fraternal twins. Observed differences between genetically identical twins are generally attributable to environmental factors. In contrast, observed differences between fraternal twins can be attributed to a combination of environmental and genetic factors. For example, a person whose identical twin has Alzheimer's disease has a 60 percent chance of also developing the disease. When a person's fraternal twin has the disease, the risk drops to 30 percent (Plomin and others, 2000). Such a difference suggests that genes play a considerable role in predisposing individuals to Alzheimer's disease.

However, we must be very careful in interpreting twin studies. Identical twins also share a more nearly identical environment than fraternal twins do. They are of the same sex, often are dressed alike, and are frequently confused with each other. Researchers therefore prefer to compare the characteristics of identical twins raised together with those of identical twins raised apart. Unfortunately, because of the time, expense, and the relatively infrequent occurrence of such arrangements, only a small number of such studies have been reported.

Identical Twins Identical twins develop from a single fertilized egg and are genetically identical. Therefore, any observed difference between them must be attributable to environmental factors. Gerald Levey and Mark Newman, shown here being questioned about physical and psychological similarities, were separated at birth and were not reunited until age 31. Although they were raised in different homes, they exhibited many similar characteristics. For example, both had chosen the same vocation, firefighting.

AP/Wide World Photos

Adoption studies provide a way around the problem of similar environments. When a child is placed for adoption, two groups of relatives are created: genetic relatives (biological parents and siblings) and environmental relatives (adoptive parents and siblings). Determining whether an adopted child more closely resembles his or her biological or adoptive parents in specific characteristics or behaviors tells us a lot about the relative effects of genes and environment on those characteristics.

The strongest evidence of a genetic influence comes from the convergence of evidence from family studies, twin studies, and adoption studies. For example, if behavior geneticists discover that hypertension runs in families at a rate that is higher than would be expected by chance, that identical twins are significantly more similar than fraternal twins in their susceptibility to the disorder, and that adopted children resemble their biological parents more than their adopted parents in their levels of hypertension, then a strong argument for genetic influence on hypertension has been made.

Epidemiological Research

When researchers consider the role of psychological and behavioral factors in health, among the first questions to be asked are: Who contracts which diseases, and what factors determine whether a person gets a particular disease? Such questions are addressed by the field of epidemiology.

Although health recordkeeping can be traced back to ancient Greece and Rome (see Chapter 1), epidemiology was not formalized as a modern science until the nineteenth century, when epidemic outbreaks of cholera, smallpox, and other infectious diseases created grave public health threats. In many instances, these diseases were conquered largely as a result of the work of epidemiologists whose painstaking research gradually pinpointed their causes.

The modern era of epidemiology began with the work of John Snow during the 1848 outbreak of cholera in London (Frerichs, 2000). Snow laboriously recorded each death throughout the city. He noticed that death rates were nearly 10 times higher in one part of the city than elsewhere. In some instances, residents on one side of a residential street were stricken with the disease far more often than were their neighbors on the opposite side of the street. Like a good detective solving a mystery, Snow kept looking for clues until he found something different in the backgrounds of the high-risk groups: polluted drinking water. Although two separate water companies supplied most of the residents of south London, their boundaries were laid out in patchwork fashion so that residents living on the same street often received their water from different sources. By comparing the death rates with the distribution of customers getting polluted and nonpolluted water, Snow inferred that the cholera came from an as-yet unidentified "poison" in the polluted water, and thus began the modern era of epidemiology.

One incident during this epidemic became legendary. In the neighborhood at the intersection of Cambridge Street and Broad Street, the incidence of cholera cases was so great that the number of deaths reached more than 500 in 10 days. After investigating the site, Snow concluded that the cause was centered on the Broad Street pump. After the doubtful but panicky town officials ordered the pump handle removed, the number of new cases of cholera dropped

The Pump Handle—Symbol of Effective Epidemiology

Since John Snow's pioneering efforts to eradicate cholera in nineteenth-century London, the pump handle has remained a symbol of effective epidemiology. Today, the John Snow Pub, located near the site of the once troublesome pump, boasts of having the original handle. This cartoon was published in 1866 in the London periodical *Fun* with the caption "Death's Dispensary, Open to the Poor, Gratis, By Permission of the Parish."

The Granger Collection, New York

DEATH'S DISPENSARY.
OPEN TO THE POOR, GRATIS, BY PERMISSION OF THE PARISH.

dramatically. Although the bacterium responsible for transmitting cholera would not be discovered for another 30 years, Snow devised an obvious intervention that broke the citywide epidemic: He simply forced the city to shut down the polluted water main.

Since Snow's time, epidemiologists have described in detail the distribution of many different infectious diseases. In addition, they have identified many of the *risk factors* linked to both favorable and unfavorable health outcomes. In a typical study, epidemiologists measure the occurrence of a particular health outcome in a population, then attempt to discover why it is distributed as it is by relating it to specific characteristics of people and the environments in which they live. For example, some forms of cancer are more prevalent in certain parts of the country than in others. By investigating these geographical areas, epidemiologists have been able to link certain cancers with the toxic chemicals found in these environments.

Epidemiologists record **morbidity,** which is the number of cases of unfavorable health outcomes in a given group of people at a given time. They also track **mortality,** which is the number of deaths due to a specific cause, such as heart disease, in a given group at a given time. Morbidity and mortality are outcome measures that are usually reported in terms of *incidence* or *prevalence.* **Incidence** refers to the number of new cases of a disease, infection, or disability, such as whooping cough, that occur in a specific population within a defined period of time. **Prevalence** is defined as the *total* number of diagnosed cases of a disease or condition that exist at a given time. It includes both previously reported cases and new cases at a given moment in time. Thus, if an epidemiologist wished to know how many people overall have hypertension, she would examine prevalence rates. If, however, she sought to determine the frequency with which hypertension is diagnosed, she would look at incidence rates.

To clarify the distinction between incidence and prevalence, consider Figure 2.3, which compares the incidence and prevalence of heart disease and AIDS between 1982 and 2000. As a result of greater public awareness of this epidemic disease, thanks to epidemiological research, the incidence and prevalence of AIDS have decreased in the United States (although not in other locations, including many African countries).

■ **morbidity** as a measure of health, the number of cases of a specific illness, injury, or disability in a given group of people at a given time.

■ **mortality** as a measure of health, the number of deaths due to a specific cause in a given group of people at a given time.

■ **incidence** the number of new cases of a disease or condition that occur in a specific population within a defined time interval.

■ **prevalence** the total number of diagnosed cases of a disease or condition that exist at a given time.

■ **etiology** the scientific study of the causes or origins of specific diseases.

Objectives

Epidemiologists use several research methods to obtain data on the incidence, prevalence, and **etiology** (origins) of disease. Like research methods in psychology, epidemiological research follows the logical progression from description

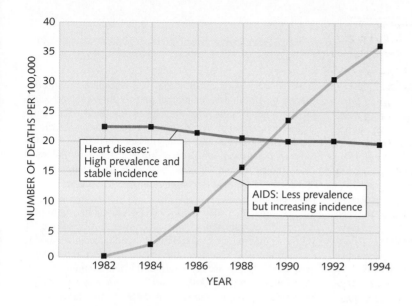

Figure 2.3

U.S. Death Rates for AIDS and Heart Disease in People Aged 25 to 44 Years Between 1982 and 1988, AIDS was less prevalent than heart disease because it claimed fewer lives. However, the rapidly increasing incidence rate of AIDS meant that between 1990 and 1994, in this age group AIDS caused more deaths than heart disease did. Heart disease, on the other hand, has a high prevalence but a stable, or gradually decreasing, incidence.

Sources: *National Vital Statistics Reports,* July 2000, 48(11), 26; *National Vital Statistics Reports,* November 1998, 47(9), 26.

to explanation to prediction and control (Frerichs, 2000). Epidemiologists have three fundamental objectives:

1. Pinpoint the etiology of a particular disease in order to generate hypotheses.
2. Evaluate the hypotheses.
3. Test the effectiveness of specific preventive health interventions.

Epidemiologists start by counting current cases of an illness (prevalence) or measuring the rate at which new cases appear (incidence) to describe the overall health status of a population. Then they analyze this information to generate hypotheses about which subgroup differences are responsible for the disease, just as Snow found water source differences affecting cholera prevalence in different groups. A more recent example comes from epidemiologists' efforts to discern the etiology of hypertension in African-Americans (see Diversity and Healthy Living).

Once epidemiologists have identified the origins of a disease or health condition and generated hypotheses about its causes, they evaluate those hypotheses. For example, some doctors have noted that women who smoke are more likely than men who smoke to develop lung cancer. Could hormonal differences, or some other factor linked to gender, allow the cellular damage that cigarette smoking causes to occur more rapidly in women than in men? Large-scale epidemiological studies have indeed reported this very finding (Prescott and others, 1998).

Epidemiologists test new hypotheses by attempting to predict the incidence and prevalence of diseases. If the predictions are borne out by the epidemiological data, researchers gain confidence that their understanding of the etiology of the disease is increasing. The emerging science of *molecular epidemiology,* which relates genetic, metabolic, and biochemical factors to epidemiological data on disease incidence and prevalence, also promises to improve researchers' ability to pinpoint the causes of human disease.

$\mathcal{D}$iversity and Healthy Living

Hypertension in African-Americans: An Epidemiological "Whodunit"

Although almost 25 percent of all Americans experience rising blood pressure with age, for African-Americans the situation is much more serious: 35 percent suffer from hypertension that contributes to heart disease, stroke, and kidney failure. Hypertension accounts for 20 percent of the deaths among blacks in the United States—twice the number for whites.

In their effort to understand and control disease, epidemiologists have sought to determine whether the disparity between blacks and whites is due to differences in genetic susceptibility, environmental factors, or some combination of the two. As discussed in Chapter 1, evolutionary theory offers one perspective on why a certain ethnic or racial group is at greater risk for a particular health outcome. The argument goes as follows: As a result of natural selection, some members of the group in question (and their genes) survived while others did not. If the survivors primarily mate with members of the same population, their genes are not mixed with those of other groups, and the resulting genetic traits begin to appear with increasing frequency among group members.

Some researchers have suggested that the voyages in slave ships caused exactly the kind of environmental pressure that would select for a predisposition to high blood pressure. During the voyages, many died, often from "salt-wasting conditions" such as diarrhea, dehydration, and infection. Thus, the ability to retain salt might have had a survival value for Africans transported to America against their will. Today, of course, salt retention is *not* adaptive, and it is linked to hypertension.

In 1991, Richard Cooper and his colleagues began a research project that concentrated on the forced migration of West Africans between the sixteenth and nineteenth centuries caused by the slave trade. Knowing that the incidence and prevalence of hypertension in rural West Africa is among the lowest of any place in the world, the researchers compared the prevalence of hypertension in West Africa with that in people of African descent in other parts of the world. The researchers found that people of African descent in other parts of the world, especially in the United States and the United Kingdom, have much higher incidences of hypertension. Perhaps the genes predisposing hypertension have largely disappeared from the West African population, where they are not adaptive. But more likely there is something about the way of life of European and American blacks that is contributing to their susceptibility to high blood pressure.

The researchers then conducted widespread testing of people of African descent in Nigeria, Cameroon, Zimbabwe, St. Lucia, Barbados, Jamaica, and the United States. In addition to monitoring blood pressure, the researchers focused on high-salt diets, obesity, activity levels, and other common risk factors for hypertension. After several years of investigation, the researchers concentrated on Africans in Nigeria, Jamaica, and Chicago as representative of three key points in the westward movement of Africans from their native lands. The findings were startling: Only 7 percent of those in rural Nigeria had high blood pressure, compared with 26 percent of black Jamaicans and 33 percent of black Americans. In addition, several risk factors for high blood pressure became increasingly prevalent as testing moved westward across the Atlantic. As we saw earlier (see Figure 2.2, p. 36), body mass index, a measure of weight relative to height, rose steadily from Africa to Jamaica to the United States, along with hypertension. Being overweight with an associated lack of exercise and poor diet explained nearly 50 percent of the increased risk for hypertension that African-Americans face, as compared with Nigerians.

The researchers' data suggest that rising blood pressure is not an unavoidable hazard of modern life for people of all skin colors. The human cardiovascular system evolved in a rural African setting in which obesity was uncommon, salt intake was moderate, the diet was low in fat, and high levels of physical activity were common. The life of subsistence farmers in Nigeria has

The final goal of epidemiological research is to determine the effectiveness of intervention programs created as a result of this research. For example, AIDS intervention programs, such as needle-exchange and safer-sex initiatives, tested in large groups of high-risk participants have been determined to be effective in reducing the incidence of new cases of AIDS in targeted groups (see Chapter 11).

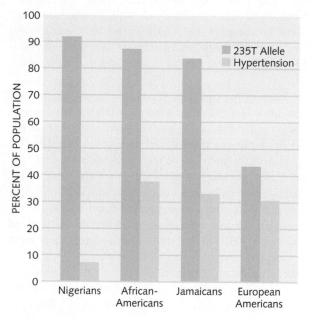

Figure 2.4

Incidence of the *235T* Gene and Hypertension among Different Ethnic Groups Epidemiologists expected that people who carried the *235T* gene would have a higher incidence of hypertension. Surprisingly, *235T* is common in certain groups (such as Nigerians), in whom hypertension is exceedingly rare. These findings suggest that both nature and nurture play a role in the development of high blood pressure.

Source: Redrawn from data in Cooper, R. S., Rotimi, C. N., & Ward, R. (1999). The puzzle of hypertension in African-Americans. *Scientific American, 280*(2), 62.

not changed much, so their blood pressure hardly rises with age, and cardiovascular disease is virtually unknown. This group functions as an epidemiological comparison group against which researchers can test hypotheses about what causes elevated blood pressure in those of African descent.

For instance, blood pressure is higher in the nearby city of Ibadan, Nigeria, than in neighboring rural areas, despite only small differences in the overall level of obesity and salt intake. The researchers suspect that other variables, such as psychological and social stress and lack of physical activity, may help account for the increase. In North America and Europe, those of African descent face a unique kind of stress—racial discrimination. The effect of racism on blood pressure is, of course, difficult to establish, but it is worth noting that the average blood pressure of blacks in certain parts of the Caribbean, including Cuba and rural Puerto Rico, is nearly the same as that of other racial groups. Could it be that the relationships among races in these societies impose fewer insults on the cardiovascular system than those in the continental United States do?

Newer research considering physiological factors seems to lend some support to the genetic, slave-ship theory. Researchers have found that many hypertensive people of African descent have elevated levels of *angiotensinogen II*, a hormone that increases blood pressure by causing blood vessels to constrict excessively, thereby increasing the risk for hypertension. However, they have discovered that the average level of angiotensinogen for each sample studied increased significantly from Nigeria to Jamaica to the United States, paralleling increases in the rate of hypertension. The levels of the hormone, and the gene that produces it, should have been the same in all three populations if it had been selected for on the slave ships.

No single gene or environmental factor can explain why hypertension occurs and why it is so common in African-Americans, although health psychologists continue moving toward a better understanding.

Research Methods

To achieve their purposes, epidemiologists use a variety of research methods, including *retrospective studies, prospective studies,* and *experimental studies.* Like research methods in psychology, each epidemiological method has its strengths and its weaknesses.

■ **retrospective study** a backward-looking study in which a group of people who have a certain disease or condition are compared with a group of people who are free of the disease or condition, for the purpose of identifying background risk factors that may have contributed to the disease or condition.

■ **prospective study** a forward-looking longitudinal study that begins with a healthy group of subjects and follows the development of a particular disease in that sample.

Retrospective and Prospective Studies

Like the cross-sectional studies described earlier, **retrospective studies** (also referred to as *case-control studies*) compare a group of people who have a certain disease or condition with a group of people who do not; those with the condition of interest are considered "cases," and those without are "controls." Whereas cross-sectional studies compare characteristics that are present in the cases and controls at the time of the study, retrospective studies attempt to determine whether the characteristics were present in the cases in the past, usually by a review of records.

Retrospective studies, looking backward in time, attempt to reconstruct the characteristics or conditions that led to the current health status of people who have a particular disease or condition. For example, retrospective research played an important role in identifying the risk factors that led to AIDS. Initially, researchers observed a sharp increase in the incidence of a rare and deadly form of cancer called Kaposi's sarcoma among gay men and intravenous drug users. By taking extensive medical histories of the men who developed this cancer, epidemiologists were able to pinpoint unprotected anal sex as a common background factor among the first men to die from this deadly form of cancer. This was years before the AIDS virus, human immunodeficiency virus (HIV), was isolated (see Chapter 11).

In contrast, **prospective studies** look forward in time to determine how a group of individuals changes or how a relationship between two or more variables changes over time. Does this sound like longitudinal research in life-span studies? The methods are identical. A prospective epidemiological study identifies a group of healthy participants, then tests and retests them over a period of time to determine whether a given condition, such as sedentary living or a high-fat diet, is related to a later health outcome, such as cancer or cardiovascular disease. Health psychologists frequently conduct prospective studies to pinpoint the risk factors that relate to various health conditions.

For example, there is some evidence that smoking may contribute to breast cancer. This is a cause of great concern, considering the recent rise in smoking rates among women (see Chapter 8). In one prospective study that followed healthy women over a 6-year period, researchers found that women who smoked were 1.26 times more likely to die of breast cancer than were women who had never smoked. Among those who smoked two or more packs a day, the relative risk rose to 1.74, whereas those who smoked half a pack or less had a relative risk of only 1.19. In addition, women who started smoking before age 16 were 60 percent more likely to die from breast cancer than those who started after age 20 (Calle and others, 1994).

Prospective studies can yield more specific information than retrospective studies about potential causal relationships between health behaviors (or risk factors) and health outcomes. Suppose we know through retrospective research that men who have suffered recent heart attacks tend to score high on measures of hostility. Although it is tempting to assume that their hostility contributed to heart problems, perhaps suffering a heart attack increases one's feelings of hostility. A prospective study would allow researchers to follow hostile men with healthy hearts over time, to see if they eventually develop cardiovascular disease.

Experimental Studies

Although both retrospective and prospective studies are helpful in identifying various risk factors for illnesses, like the descriptive methods in psychology, neither study can conclusively demonstrate causation in health outcomes. To pinpoint cause and effect, epidemiologists rely on natural experiments, laboratory experiments, and clinical trials. In a natural experiment, a researcher attempts to study an independent variable under natural conditions that approximate a controlled study. Natural experiments are most common in health psychology when researchers compare two similar groups; one group's members are already exposing themselves to a health hazard (such as nicotine, occupational noise, or risky sexual behavior), and the other group's members are not.

In a laboratory experiment, the researcher directly manipulates one independent variable rather than comparing groups of individuals who have self-selected their exposure to a particular independent variable. Like experiments in psychology, epidemiological laboratory experiments use random assignment to ensure that the experimental and control groups are similar in every important way except the level of the independent variable to which they are exposed.

Clinical Trials

The gold standard of biomedical research is the **randomized clinical trial.** This type of study is a true experiment, so researchers can safely draw conclusions about cause-and-effect relationships. Clinical trials test the effects of one or more independent variables on individuals or on groups of individuals.

Although many variations are possible, the most common clinical trial for individuals involves measurement of a *baseline* (starting point) level of a condition followed by a measure of the effectiveness of a treatment. For example, in testing the effectiveness of an analgesic drug on migraine headaches, the researcher first records each participant's pretrial level of headache pain, perhaps using a self-report pain scale. Once the baseline establishes a pretreatment reference value in the dependent variable (the subject's pain), treatment (the drug), which is the independent variable, is administered and the dependent measure (pain) is once again assessed. If the treatment data show improvement over the baseline data, the researcher concludes that the treatment is likely to be effective in the future. To be sure that the treatment itself, rather than some extraneous factor (such as the mere passage of time), produced the improvement, the researcher removes the medication and then observes whether the baseline condition returns and symptoms reappear. If they do, the researcher can be even more confident in accepting the hypothesis that the drug produces a significant (clinical) improvement.

In the most common type of clinical trial involving groups, baseline measures are taken and the participants are then randomly assigned to either an

■ **randomized clinical trial** a true experiment that tests the effects of one independent variable on individuals (single-subject design) or on groups of individuals (community field trials).

experimental group that receives the treatment of interest, such as a new headache medication, or a control group that receives a placebo (see Chapter 1). If outside variables have been properly controlled, then differences in the groups can be attributed to differences in the treatment.

In the final procedure, a *community field trial,* researchers compare people in one community to those in another. For example, children in one school might receive extensive educational information on the benefits of always wearing a helmet when bicycling, skateboarding, or using inline skates. A control group of children from another school would not receive the educational campaign. Researchers would compare pre-trial and post-trial levels of some measure, such as head injuries, in both groups.

Meta-Analysis

Traditionally, when a researcher began investigating a phenomenon, such as the relationship between cigarette smoking and breast cancer, the first step was a thorough review of the relevant research literature. Although the *literature review* has a long and noble history in the annals of science, such reviews are qualitative in nature and therefore subject to bias in how they are interpreted. No matter how skilled the person reviewing the literature may be, the way various results are interpreted essentially remains a subjective process, in which the reviewer's own biases, beliefs, overconfidence, and so forth, may influence the outcome.

To assist researchers in sifting through the sometimes dozens of research studies that pertain to a particular hypothesis, statisticians have developed **meta-analysis,** a quantitative technique that combines the results of studies examining the same effect or phenomenon. Just as an experiment examines the consistency in the responses of individual participants, a meta-analysis determines the overall consistency of individual studies that address the same topics. A meta-analysis does not replace individual studies; rather, it provides a systematic procedure for summarizing existing evidence about focused research hypotheses that already appears in the health psychology literature.

There are several steps to meta-analysis. First, individual research studies are coded according to specific categories such as the size and composition of the sample, presence of a control group, use of randomization, and research methodology. The individual study outcomes are then translated into a common unit, called an *effect size,* to allow results to be compared.

Meta-analysis has a number of advantages. First, by pooling the results of many studies, meta-analysis often reveals significant results simply because combined studies have more participants. Second, demonstrating that a finding holds up across different studies conducted by different researchers at different times and places and with different participants gives researchers much greater confidence in its validity. Finally, like good experiments, meta-analysis is subject to replication. That is, other researchers may repeat the series of statistical steps and should reach the same conclusions.

■ **meta-analysis** a quantitative technique that combines the results of many studies examining the same effect or phenomenon.

Inferring Causality

No matter which research method they use (see Figure 2.5 for a summary), certain basic conditions must be met before epidemiologists can infer a cause-and-effect relationship between a particular risk factor and a particular disease or other adverse health outcome (Beaglehole and others, 1993).

- *The evidence must be consistent.* Studies that report an association between a risk factor and a health outcome must be replicated. When evidence is not entirely consistent (as is often the case in health research), a convincing majority of the evidence must support the alleged association. If not, causality cannot be inferred.

- *The alleged cause must have been in place before the disease actually appeared.* This may seem obvious, but the importance of this criterion cannot be overstated. For example, if a woman starts smoking after her breast cancer is diagnosed, smoking could not have caused the disease. You would be surprised at how often this criterion is overlooked.

- *The relationship must make sense.* This means that the explanation must be consistent with known physiological findings. In the case of the relationship between smoking and breast cancer, for example, a wealth of other evidence suggests several plausible biological links between smoking and other forms of cancer, including that the chemicals in tobacco smoke increase cellular damage caused by free radicals in the body.

- *There must be a dose–response relationship between the risk factor and health outcome. Dose–response relationships* are systematic associations between a

Figure 2.5

Epidemiological Research Methods Epidemiologists working to help resolve the AIDS health crisis have followed these steps.

1. Measure *prevalence* and *incidence* of AIDS in the general population. Determine whether certain subgroups of the population have higher AIDS levels.
2. Use *retrospective* studies to determine which health behaviors or other factors have affected AIDS levels in the subgroups with the highest prevalence rates.
3. Generate hypotheses about what causes AIDS and how it is spread.
4. Test those hypotheses by using *prospective studies, natural experiments,* and *clinical trials.* Use *meta-analysis* to analyze results.
5. Develop intervention programs to stem the spread of AIDS. Continue efforts to understand the etiology of the disease to develop effective treatments.

Retrospective Studies

AIDS rates are highest among intravenous drug users and those having unprotected anal sex.

Clinical Trials:

AIDS is spread through blood and bodily fluids and not through casual contact.

Meta-analysis:

That HIV causes AIDS.

Intervention:

Includes education, needle-exchange programs, and safer sex initiatives.

■ **relative risk** a statistical indicator of the likelihood of a causal relationship between a particular health risk factor and a health outcome; computed as the ratio of the incidence (or prevalence) of a health condition—in a group exposed to the risk factor—to its incidence (or prevalence) in a group not exposed to the risk factor.

particular independent variable, such as cigarette smoking, and a particular dependent variable, such as breast cancer. Such relationships pinpoint the relative risk associated with specific *levels* of an independent variable. Thus, the morbidity rate of breast cancer is highest among women who smoke heavily, somewhat less for women who smoke moderately, less still for light smokers, and lowest among women who do not smoke.

■ *The strength of the association between the alleged cause and the health outcome (relative risk) must suggest causality.* **Relative risk** is statistically defined as the ratio of the incidence or prevalence of a health condition in a group exposed to a particular risk factor to the incidence or prevalence of that condition in a group not exposed to the risk factor. Any relative risk value above 1.0 indicates that the exposed group has a greater relative risk than the unexposed group. For example, a relative risk of 2.0 indicates that the exposed group is twice as likely to develop a health outcome than an unexposed group. Conversely, a relative risk of 0.50 means that the incidence or prevalence rate of the condition in the exposed group is only half that of those in the unexposed group.

■ *The incidence or prevalence of the disease or other adverse health outcome must drop when the alleged causal factor is removed.* Although dose–response and relative risk relationships are necessary to infer causality, they are not sufficient. Before we can infer that smoking causes breast cancer, we must have evidence that women who quit smoking have a reduced risk of this disease. Recent research has, in fact, shown this very thing to be true, thus meeting our fifth criterion (Manjer and others, 2000). When all conditions are met, epidemiologists are able to infer that a causal relationship has been established, even when a true experiment cannot be conducted.

While working to meet these conditions, health psychologists need to evaluate individual research studies very carefully. Quality rating forms, such as the one in Figure 2.6, are very helpful means of achieving this standard. In medicine, too, there is a new emphasis on the importance of basing patient care on the "best available evidence" for a given health condition. Medical residency programs today are required to train new physicians in *evidence-based medicine,* which involves virtually all of the principles we have discussed in this chapter, including learning how to critically appraise research for its validity, reliability, and usefulness in clinical practice (CEBM, 2004).

In this chapter, we have introduced a variety of research methods for studying biological, psychological, and social factors in health. It is natural to ask, Which one is best? Some researchers might quickly answer that the laboratory experiment is most desirable because only in such studies are the variables of interest directly manipulated while all other variables are controlled. But we have also seen that some questions of vital interest to health psychologists do not lend themselves to experimentation for ethical and/or practical reasons. Moreover, experiments are often criticized for being artificial and having little relevance to behavior in the real world.

Figure 2.6

Putting Health Psychology Into Practice: Evaluating Scientific Evidence
Health psychologists use quality rating forms similar to this to evaluate research studies. For each criterion, they rate the study by assigning a number from 0 (no evidence that the criterion was met) to 3 (strong evidence that the criterion was met). Overall scores on the rating system can range from 0 to 21, with higher scores justifying greater confidence in the study's conclusions.

3 = Good, 2 = Fair, 1 = Poor, 0 = No evidence that the criterion has been met

Criterion	Evidence	Score
1. Problem or Question Studied: *(clearly stated hypothesis, significant or relevant issue, operational definitions included)*		
2. Sampling: *(representative of population, random selection and assignment, sample characteristics identified, group differences controlled, low dropout rate)*		
3. Measurement: *(clearly stated methodology)*		
4. Reliability: *(test yields consistent results, even among multiple raters; questions measure single construct, such as anxiety or degree of disability)*		
5. Validity: *(constructs clearly explained, independent and dependent variable levels clear, generalized to appropriate populations)*		
6. Statistical Significance: *(inferred relationships, accurate and appropriate significance supported by data)*		
7. Justification for Conclusions: *(warranted by data and research design)*		
Total		

[1]Adapted from Ramons, K.D., Schafer, S., & Tracz, S.M. (2003). Learning in practice: validation of the Fresno test of competence in evidence based medicine. British Medical Journal, *326*, 319–321; and Bergstrom, N. (1994). Treating pressure ulcers: methodology for guideline development. U.S. Department of Health and Human Services, Publication No. 96-N014.

Increasingly, researchers are combining experimental and nonexperimental methods in order to make their investigations more comprehensive (Murray & Chamberlain, 1999). For example, suppose a researcher is interested in determining whether an educational campaign about safer sex would induce college students to modify their behavior. Conceivably, the researcher might design an experiment in which a randomly assigned group of students who received educational materials related to this issue was compared to a control group that received unrelated materials. The students would be compared on their stated intentions to practice safe sex. However, the researcher would surely want to know whether the educational campaign was equally effective with women, men, members of various ethnic minorities, and so forth. Variables such as these cannot, of course, be manipulated experimentally. Together, however, experimental and nonexperimental methods complement one another, giving health psychologists a larger tool kit with which to study their subject.

This chapter has presented you with the basic tools of the health psychology trade—critical thinking that guards against faulty everyday reasoning and scientific methods that guide researchers in their quest for valid and reliable answers to health-related questions. Armed with this information, you are now ready to begin to address those questions.

Summing Up

Critical Thinking and the Evidence Base

1. Our everyday thinking is prone to bias, including making snap judgments and inferring cause and effect inappropriately. Using scientific research methods to search for evidence will help you become a more careful consumer of health psychology reports.

Health Psychology Methods

2. Descriptive studies, which observe and record the behavior of participants, include case studies, interviews and surveys, and observation.

3. The strength and direction of a relationship between two sets of scores are revealed visually by scatterplots and statistically by the correlation coefficient. Correlation does not imply causality.

4. In an experiment, a researcher manipulates one or more independent variables while looking for changes in one or more dependent variables. Experiments typically compare an experimental group, which receives a treatment of interest, with a control group, which does not. To reduce the possibility of expectancy effects, researchers use double-blind controls.

5. When health psychologists study variables that cannot be manipulated, they may conduct a quasi experiment. In this design, participants are assigned to comparison groups on the basis of age, gender, ethnicity, or some other subject variable.

6. In a cross-sectional study, researchers compare representative groups of people of various ages to determine the possible effects of age on a particular dependent variable.

7. In a longitudinal study, a single group of individuals is followed over a long span of time. To correct the problem of subjects dropping out over the lengthy span of years such studies require, researchers have developed a cross-sectional study, in which different age groups are tested initially and then retested later at various ages.

8. Behavior genetics uses methods such as twin and adoption studies to pinpoint the heritability of specific characteristics and disorders. Identical twins develop from a single fertilized egg that splits in two. Fraternal twins develop from separate eggs. Differences between identical and fraternal twins raised in the same environment suggest a genetic influence.

Epidemiological Research

9. Epidemiological research studies measure the distribution of health outcomes, seek to discover the etiology (causes) of those outcomes, and test the effectiveness of specific preventive health interventions. Among the commonly used epidemiological statistics are morbidity, mortality, incidence, and prevalence.

10. Epidemiologists use several basic research designs. In a retrospective study, comparisons are made between a group of people who have a certain disease or condition and a group that does not. In contrast, prospective studies look forward in time to determine how a group of people changes or how a relationship between two or more variables changes over time. There are also several types of experiments in epidemiology, including laboratory experiments, natural experiments, and randomized clinical trials.

11. Meta-analysis analyzes the data from already published studies, statistically combining the size of the difference between the experimental and control groups to enable researchers to evaluate the consistency of findings.

12. In order to infer causality in epidemiological research, research evidence must be consistent and logically sensible and exhibit a dose–response relationship. In addition, the alleged cause must have been in place before the health outcome in question was observed and must result in a reduced prevalence of the condition when removed.

Key Terms and Concepts

belief bias, p. 29
epidemiology, p. 31
descriptive study, p. 31
case study, p. 31
survey, p. 32
observational study, p. 32
correlation coefficient, p. 32
scatterplot, p. 33
independent variable, p. 34

dependent variable, p. 34
random assignment, p. 34
expectancy effects, p. 35
double-blind study, p. 35
quasi-experiment, p. 35
cross-sectional study, p. 37
longitudinal study, p. 37
heritability, p. 38
morbidity, p. 40

mortality, p. 40
incidence, p. 40
prevalence, p. 40
etiology, p. 40
retrospective study, p. 44
prospective study, p. 44
randomized clinical trial, p. 45
meta-analysis, p. 46
relative risk, p. 48

Biological Foundations of Health and Illness

*L*akeesha's story began in the spring of 1975, with a difficult, slow birth that required the use of excessive anesthetics and forceps to pull her roughly into the world. Together, these medical procedures choked off the supply of oxygen to her young brain. Although she survived, Lakeesha's complicated delivery, coupled with her low birth weight and her mother's heavy use of alcohol during her pregnancy, meant that her problems were just beginning. Lakeesha was born with mild spastic cerebral palsy (CP), a movement disorder that results from damage to the brain's motor centers.

This biological condition cast a lifelong shadow over Lakeesha's health, affecting not only her continuing physical development but her psychological and social development as well. Among the first problems her parents and pediatrician noticed were mild mental retardation, visual and hearing impairment, slight deformities in her teeth and joints, and scoliosis (curvature of the spine). Later, when other children were learning to speak, Lakeesha was having speech difficulties caused by her muscular problems.

Like many children with disabilities, Lakeesha found that everything was harder. From the beginning, she needed extra self-confidence and persistence to master tasks that were routine for other children. During early childhood, when she desperately wanted to be like everyone else, Lakeesha too often found that she couldn't do the same things, look the same way, or keep up with other children. Realizing that her handicap was permanent caused Lakeesha to become depressed and angry.

Lakeesha's condition also challenged the members of her family. Her parents experienced grief, guilt, and disappointment. It took more time and effort to raise Lakeesha than it had taken to raise her older sister, and other people were often hurtful in their comments and behavior toward Lakeesha.

Fortunately, interventions were available for Lakeesha and her family. Dental treatments and orthopedic surgery corrected most of Lakeesha's facial and posture problems. Speech and behavior therapy helped Lakeesha improve her muscular control, balance, and speech.

By age 8, Lakeesha's development had progressed far enough that she was able to attend a "normal" elementary school for the first time. In some areas, her skills were poor. Writing with a pencil, for example, was extremely difficult, and continuing vision problems hampered Lakeesha's efforts to learn to read. In other areas, however, her skills were average, or even advanced. She was one of the first in her class, for example, to understand multiplication and division.

Throughout her childhood, Lakeesha had high emotional and psychological needs, but they were met. Her anger, low self-esteem, and perception of herself as damaged or different were corrected with therapy. Similarly, joining a support group and working with a cognitive behavior therapist helped her parents recognize and cope with their feelings.

Today Lakeesha is living independently, working part-time in an electronics store, and attending classes at the local community college. She maintains a close, warm relationship with her parents, who live nearby, and she has a small but close-knit circle of friends. Most important, she feels good about herself and has confidence in her ability to overcome life's obstacles. Compared with what she's already managed to conquer, the road ahead seems easy.

Lakeesha's story illustrates the importance of the biopsychosocial perspective. Factors in the realms of biology (difficult birth, alcohol exposure), psychology (dealing with being different), and social relations (struggling to connect with others) all contributed to Lakeesha's health problems, and all three areas were addressed through surgery and therapy as part of her triumphant survival. The biopsychosocial perspective is effective because it advocates thinking of the human body as a system made up of many interconnected subsystems (including the abilities to walk and talk for Lakeesha) and externally related to several larger systems, such as society and culture.

Lakeesha's story also makes clear one of health psychology's most fundamental themes: The mind and body are inextricably intertwined. Whether they are focusing on promoting health or treating disease, health psychologists are concerned with the various ways our behaviors, thoughts, and feelings affect and are affected by the functioning of the body.

Although not all of health psychology is directly concerned with biological activity, health and illness are ultimately biological events. An understanding of the body's physical systems is therefore necessary to appreciate how good

■ **central nervous system** the brain and spinal cord.

■ **peripheral nervous system** all the neurons outside the central nervous system; consists of both the somatic nervous system and the autonomic nervous system, which includes the sympathetic and parasympathetic nervous systems.

health habits help prevent disease and promote wellness while poor habits do the opposite.

This chapter lays the groundwork for our investigation into health psychology by reviewing the basic biological processes that affect health. These processes are regulated by the nervous system, the endocrine system, the cardiovascular system, the respiratory system, the digestive system, the immune system, and the reproductive system. For each system, we will consider its basic structure and healthy functioning. In later chapters, you will learn about the major diseases and disorders to which each of these systems are vulnerable.

The chapter ends with a discussion of the mechanisms of heredity and the techniques used by behavior geneticists to evaluate genetic and environmental contributions to health, disease, and various traits.

The material in this chapter is fundamental to an understanding of the specific aspects of health and illness discussed in later chapters. So study this chapter carefully, and be prepared to refer to it frequently throughout the course.

The Nervous System

Major control over the operation of our body's systems belongs to the nervous system, which is made up of the brain, the spinal cord, and all the peripheral nerves that receive and send messages throughout the body. Without the nervous system, our muscles would not expand or contract, our pancreas would not release insulin, and consciousness would not be possible.

Divisions of the Nervous System

The human nervous system contains billions of *neurons* (nerve cells) and trillions of *synapses* (communicating connections between neurons), most of which are in the brain (Figure 3.1). Traditionally, these neurons are grouped into two major divisions: the **central nervous system (CNS),** which consists of the brain and the spinal cord, and the **peripheral nervous system (PNS),** which contains the remaining nerves of the body.

The PNS is further divided into two subdivisions: the *somatic nervous system,* which includes the nerves that carry messages from the eyes, ears, and other sense organs to the CNS, and from the CNS to the muscles and glands; and the *autonomic nervous system,* the nerves that link the CNS with the heart, intestines, and other internal organs. Because the skeletal muscles that the somatic nerves activate are under voluntary control, the somatic nervous system is often referred to as the voluntary nervous system. In contrast, the autonomic, or involuntary, nervous system controls the organs over which we normally have no control.

The autonomic nervous system is also composed of two subdivisions (Figure 3.2 on p. 56). The *sympathetic nervous system* consists of groupings of neuron cell bodies called *ganglia* that run along the spinal cord and connect to the

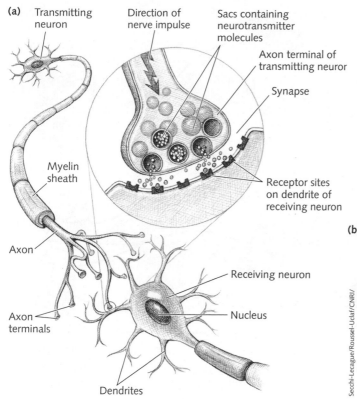

(a) Transmitting neuron

Direction of nerve impulse

Sacs containing neurotransmitter molecules

Axon terminal of transmitting neuron

Synapse

Myelin sheath

Receptor sites on dendrite of receiving neuron

Axon

Axon terminals

Receiving neuron

Nucleus

Dendrites

Figure 3.1

The Neuron (a) A neuron may receive messages from other neurons on any of its dendrites, and then transmits each message down the long axon to other neurons. Nerve impulses travel in one direction only—down the axon of a neuron to the axon terminal. When a nerve impulse reaches the axon terminal, chemical messengers called neuro-transmitters cross the synapse and bind to receptor sites on the receiving neuron's den-drite—rather like a key fits into a lock. (b) This scanning electron micrograph shows three neurons in the human brain.

(b)

Secchi-Lecague/Roussel-Uclaf/CNRI/ Science Photo Library/Photo Researchers

body's internal organs. The sympathetic division prepares the body for "fight or flight," a response generated when a person experiences performance stress (preparing for the big football game or an important job interview) or perceives a significant threat (see Chapter 4). It does so by increasing the heart rate and breathing rate, decreasing digestive activity (this is why eating while under stress can lead to a stomachache), increasing blood flow to the skeletal muscles, and releasing energizing sugars and fats from storage deposits. Because all the sympathetic ganglia are closely linked, they tend to act as a single system, or "in sympathy" with one another.

Unlike the ganglia of the sympathetic division, the ganglia of the *parasympathetic nervous system* are not closely linked and therefore tend to act more independently. This system has opposite effects than those of the sympathetic ganglia; in helping the body to recover after arousal, it decreases heart rate, increases digestive activity, and conserves energy.

The Brain

The human brain weighs about 1,400 grams (3 pounds), is thought to consist of perhaps 40 billion individual neurons, and has the consistency of a soft cheese. Yet this mass is the control center of our nervous system and the storage

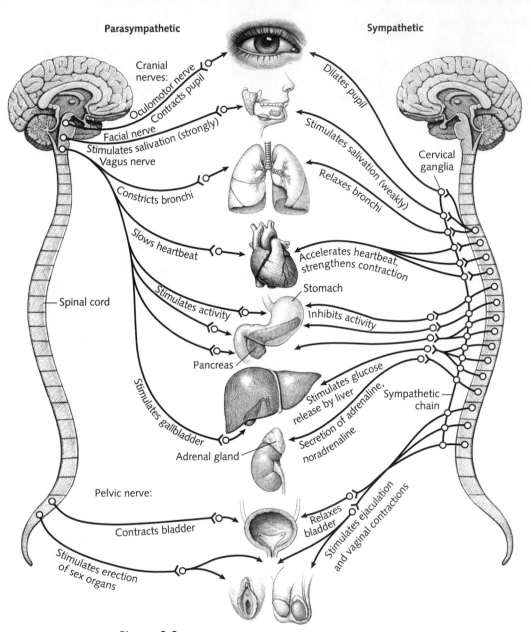

Parasympathetic

Sympathetic

Cranial
nerves:
Oculomotor nerve
Contracts pupil

Dilates pupil

Facial nerve
Stimulates salivation (strongly)

Stimulates salivation (weakly)

Vagus nerve

Cervical
ganglia

Constricts bronchi

Relaxes bronchi

Slows heartbeat

Accelerates heartbeat,
strengthens contraction

Spinal cord

Stimulates activity

Stomach

Inhibits activity

Pancreas

Stimulates glucose
release by liver

Sympathetic
chain

Stimulates gallbladder

Secretion of adrenaline,
noradrenaline

Adrenal gland

Pelvic nerve:

Relaxes
bladder

Contracts bladder

Stimulates ejaculation
and vaginal contractions

Stimulates erection
of sex organs

Figure 3.2

The Autonomic Nervous System The autonomic nervous system is subdivided
into the sympathetic and parasympathetic divisions. The sympathetic division prepares
the body for action, accelerating heartbeat, stimulating the secretion of adrenaline,
and triggering other elements of the "fight-or-flight" response. The parasympathetic
division calms the body by slowing heartbeat, stimulating digestion, and triggering
other restorative activities of the body.

vault for our memories. Without it we couldn't think, move, speak, or breathe. Let's consider the brain's structure and functions so that we can better understand the role of the brain in achieving good health. We'll be considering the three principal regions of the brain: the brainstem, the cerebellum, and the cerebrum (Figure 3.3).

Lower-Level Structures

Located at the point where the spinal cord swells as it enters the skull, the **brainstem** evolved first in the vertebrate brain. Remarkably similar from fish to humans, the brainstem contains the medulla, the pons, and the reticular formation. Together, they control basic and involuntary life-support functions via the autonomic nervous system. (This is why a blow to the head at the base of the skull is so dangerous.) The brainstem is also the point at which most nerves passing between the spinal cord and the brain cross over, so that the left side of the brain sends and receives messages from the *right* side of the body, and the right side of the brain sends and receives messages from the *left* side of the body.

The **medulla** controls several vital reflexes, including breathing, heart rate, salivation, coughing, and sneezing. It also receives sensory information about blood pressure and then, based on this input, varies the constriction or dilation of blood vessels to maintain an optimal state. Damage to the medulla is often fatal. An overdose of an opiate drug such as morphine or heroin may disrupt (or even suppress) breathing because of the drug's effects on the medulla.

As the spinal cord's sensory input travels up through the brain, branch fibers stimulate the **reticular formation,** a brainstem circuit that governs arousal and sleep. The reticular formation is also responsible for alerting the brain during moments of danger and for prioritizing all incoming information. When this region is damaged, a person may lapse into a coma and never awaken.

Above the brainstem is the **thalamus.** Consisting of two egg-shaped groups of nuclei, the thalamus sorts sensory information received from the brainstem and routes it to the higher brain regions that deal with vision, hearing, taste, and touch.

Lying at the back of the brain, the **cerebellum,** or "little brain," is shaped like the larger brain. Its main function is to maintain body balance and coordinate voluntary muscle movement. Damage to the cerebellum produces a loss of muscle tone, tremors, and abnormal posture. In addition, specialized parts of the cerebellum contribute to memory, language, and cognition. Children with learning disabilities, for example, often have damaged cerebellums.

Figure 3.3

The Brain This cross section of the human brain shows its three principal regions: the brainstem, which controls heartbeat and respiration; the cerebellum, which regulates muscular coordination; and the cerebrum, which is the center for information processing. Surrounding the central core of the brain is the limbic system, which includes the amygdala, hippocampus, and hypothalamus. The limbic system plays an important role in emotions, especially those related to sexual arousal, aggression, and pain.

■ **brainstem** the oldest and most central region of the brain; includes the medulla, pons, and reticular formation.

■ **medulla** the brainstem region that controls heartbeat and breathing.

■ **reticular formation** a network of neurons running through the brainstem involved with alertness and arousal.

■ **thalamus** the brain's sensory switchboard. Located on top of the brainstem, it routes messages to the cerebral cortex.

■ **cerebellum** located at the rear of the brain, this brain structure coordinates voluntary movement and balance.

■ **limbic system** a network of neurons surrounding the central core of the brain; associated with emotions such as fear and aggression; includes the hypothalamus, amygdala, and hippocampus.

■ **amygdala** two clusters of neurons in the limbic system that are linked to emotion, especially aggression.

■ **hippocampus** a structure in the brain's limbic system linked to memory.

■ **hypothalamus** lying just below the thalamus, the region of the brain that influences hunger, thirst, body temperature, and sexual behavior; helps govern the endocrine system via the pituitary gland.

■ **cerebral cortex** the thin layer of cells that covers the cerebrum; the seat of conscious sensation and information processing.

The Limbic System

Surrounding the central core of the brain is the **limbic system,** which includes the amygdala, hippocampus, hypothalamus, and the septal area. The limbic system is believed to play an important role in emotions, especially those related to sexual arousal, aggression, and pain.

In 1939, neurosurgeons Heinrich Kluver and Paul Bucy surgically lesioned (destroyed) the **amygdala** in the brain of an especially aggressive rhesus monkey. The operation transformed the violent creature into a docile pussycat. Other researchers have discovered that electrical stimulation of the amygdala will reliably trigger rage or fear responses in a variety of animals.*

Another limbic circuit involves areas within the **hippocampus,** which are thought to be involved in learning and memory. When the hippocampus is injured, people typically develop a form of amnesia in which they are unable to form new memories but retain their memory for previously learned skills. In a famous case, a talented composer and conductor, Clive Wearing, suffered damage to his hippocampus. He now lives from one moment to the next, always feeling as though he has just awakened and not remembering the moment before, yet he has retained his musical skills.

Lying just below (hypo) the thalamus, the **hypothalamus** interconnects with numerous regions of the brain. Neuroscientists have pinpointed hypothalamic nuclei that influence hunger and regulate thirst, body temperature, and sexual behavior. Neuroscientists James Olds and Peter Milner made an intriguing discovery in 1954 about the role of the hypothalamus in the brain's reward system. The researchers were attempting to implant electrodes in the brainstems of laboratory rats when they accidentally stimulated an area in the hypothalamus. Much to the researchers' surprise, the rats kept returning to the precise location in their cages where they had previously been stimulated by the errant electrode. Recognizing that the animals were behaving as if they were seeking more stimulation, Olds and Milner continued to conduct a series of experiments that validated their discovery of the brain's reward circuitry. Indeed, rats have been known to "self-stimulate" their hypothalamic reward centers as many as 7,000 times per hour. As you will see in Chapter 8, some researchers believe that certain addictions—perhaps to food, alcohol, and other drugs— may stem from a genetic *reward deficiency syndrome* in which the brain's reward circuitry malfunctions and leads to powerful cravings.

The Cerebral Cortex

The *cerebrum,* which represents about 80 percent of the brain's total weight, forms two hemispheres (left and right) that are primarily filled with synaptic connections linking the surface of the brain to its other regions. The thin surface layer of the cerebrum, called the **cerebral cortex,** is what really makes us

---

*Given that amygdala lesions transform violent animals into docile ones, might the same procedure work with violent humans? Although this type of psychosurgery has been attempted in a few cases involving patients with severe brain abnormalities, the results have been mixed.

human. This 3-millimeter-thick sheet of some 20 billion nerve cells contains neural centers that give rise to our sensory capacities, skilled motor responses, language abilities, and aptitude for reasoning.

The cortex in each hemisphere can be divided into four principal regions, or lobes; each lobe carries out many functions, and in some cases several lobes work together to perform a function (Figure 3.4). The *occipital lobe,* located at the back of the cortex, receives visual information from the retina of each eye. The *parietal lobe,* in the center of the cortex, receives information from the skin and body. Auditory information from the ears projects to the *temporal lobes.* The *frontal lobes,* lying just behind the forehead, are involved in reasoning, planning, and controlling body movement.

In the parietal lobe, on the edge of the frontal lobe, the **sensory cortex** processes body sensations, such as touch. The **motor cortex,** at the back of the frontal lobes, lies just in front of the sensory cortex. Remember Lakeesha from the chapter introduction? Motor cortex damage caused her cerebral palsy.

In 1870, German physicians Gustav Fritsch and Eduard Hitzig discovered that electrical stimulation of this arch of neurons triggers movement in the limbs of laboratory animals. Little more than half a century later, neurosurgeon Wilder Penfield mapped the motor cortex in conscious patients during surgery to remove brain tumors. In addition to mapping the cortex according to the body parts it controlled, Penfield made the remarkable discovery that the amount of motor cortex devoted to a specific body part is proportional to the degree of control we have over that body part. The muscles of the face and fingers, for example, have much more representation in the motor cortex than does the thigh. Penfield also mapped the sensory cortex and similarly found that the amount of cortical representation was proportional to the sensitivity of that body part.

■ **sensory cortex** lying at the front of the parietal lobes, the region of the cerebral cortex that processes body sensations such as touch.

■ **motor cortex** lying at the rear of the frontal lobes, the region of the cerebral cortex that controls voluntary movements.

Figure 3.4

The Cerebral Cortex (a) Each of the four lobes, or regions, of the cerebral cortex performs various functions, sometimes separately and more often in conjunction with another region. (b) Within these regions are the neural centers that give rise to our sensory capacities, skilled motor responses, language ability, and reasoning ability.

(a)   (b)

The basic functional organization of the primary sensory and motor areas of the cerebral cortex is virtually identical in all mammals, from the rat to the human (Thompson, 2000). However, the sensory and motor areas account for only about one-fourth of the total area of the human cerebral cortex. Researchers are just beginning to understand the functions of the remaining areas, which are called **association cortex.** These areas are responsible for higher mental functions, such as thinking and speaking. Interestingly, humans do not have the largest brains proportionate to size. Porpoises, whales, and elephants have much larger brains. Yet in ascending the evolutionary scale it becomes obvious that more intelligent animals have much greater amounts of "uncommitted" association areas.

The Endocrine System

The second of the body's communication systems, the endocrine system (Figure 3.5), is closely connected with the nervous system in regulating many bodily functions. Whereas the nervous system communicates through neurotransmitters, the endocrine system communicates through chemical messengers called **hormones.** Unlike the much speedier nervous system,

Figure 3.5

The Endocrine Glands and Feedback Control (a) Under the direction of the brain's hypothalamus, the pituitary releases hormones that, in turn, regulate the secretions of the thyroid, the adrenal glands, and the reproductive organs. (b) A complex negative feedback system regulates the production of many hormones. As the levels of hormones produced in target glands rise in the blood, the hypothalamus and pituitary decrease their production of hormones, and the secretion of hormones by the target glands also slows.

(a)

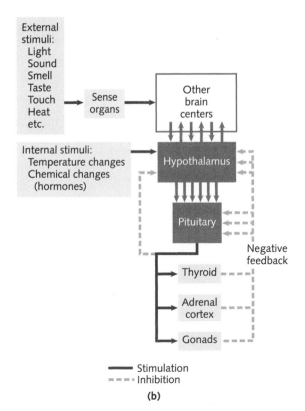

(b)

which is chiefly responsible for fast-acting, short-duration responses, the endocrine system primarily governs slow-acting responses of longer duration.

Endocrine glands secrete hormones directly into the bloodstream, where they travel to various organs and bind to receptor sites. Binding either stimulates or inhibits organs depending on the type of receptor and hormone. In this section, we'll consider the activity of four important endocrine glands—the pituitary, adrenal, and thyroid glands, and the pancreas.

The Pituitary and the Adrenal Glands

The **pituitary gland** secretes a number of hormones that influence other glands. These include hormones that influence growth, sexual development, reproduction, kidney functioning, and aging.

Although the pituitary gland is often referred to as the *master gland* of the endocrine system, the brain's hypothalamus more properly deserves this title because it directly (and rigidly) controls pituitary functioning. Together, the hypothalamus and pituitary act as a master control system. For example, during a stressful moment, the hypothalamus secretes the hormone *corticotrophin-releasing hormone (CRH),* which travels in the bloodstream to the anterior pituitary, where it stimulates the pituitary to secrete *adrenocorticotropic hormone (ACTH).* ACTH binds to receptor cells on the adrenal cortex, causing this gland to release cortisol into the bloodstream. The increased level of cortisol in the blood acts back on the hypothalamus and pituitary gland to inhibit the release of additional CRH and ACTH (see Figure 3.12 on p. 74). This example of *feedback control* is similar to the mechanism by which a household thermostat regulates temperature by turning on or off a furnace or air conditioner as needed.

Located atop the kidneys, the **adrenal glands** secrete several important hormones that play a crucial role in the body's response to stress and emergencies. In a moment of danger, for example, the innermost region of the gland (the adrenal medulla) releases *epinephrine* and *norepinephrine* into the bloodstream, where they travel to receptor sites on the heart. These hormones increase heart rate, blood pressure, and blood sugar, providing the body with a quick surge of energy. The outermost region of the gland (the adrenal cortex) consists of three different regions, each of which produces a different group of steroid hormones. The *gonadocorticoids* include the male androgens and female estrogens. The principal *glucocorticoid* is cortisol, which helps to reduce swelling and inflammation following an injury. The *mineralocorticoids* include aldosterone, which helps maintain normal blood pressure.

The Thyroid Gland and the Pancreas

Located in the front of the neck, the *thyroid gland* is shaped like a butterfly, with the two wings representing the left and right thyroid lobes that wrap around the windpipe. The thyroid gland produces the hormone thyroxin, which helps regulate the body's growth and metabolism (energy use). Located just behind

■ **association cortex** areas of the cerebral cortex not directly involved in sensory or motor functions; rather, they integrate multisensory information and higher mental functions such as thinking and speaking.

■ **hormones** chemical messengers, released into the bloodstream by endocrine glands, that have an effect on distant organs.

■ **pituitary gland** the master endocrine gland controlled by the hypothalamus; releases a variety of hormones that act on other glands throughout the body.

■ **adrenal glands** lying above the kidneys, the pair of endocrine glands that secrete epinephrine, norepinephrine, and cortisol, hormones that arouse the body during moments of stress.

■ **arteries** blood vessels that carry blood away from the heart to other organs and tissues. A small artery is called an arteriole.

■ **veins** blood vessels that carry blood back to the heart from the capillaries.

the thyroid are four parathyroid glands. The hormones secreted by these glands regulate the level of calcium in the body.

Another endocrine gland, the *pancreas,* produces glucagon and insulin, two hormones that act in opposition to regulate the level of the sugar glucose in the blood. Glucagon raises the concentration of glucose in the blood, while insulin controls the conversion of sugar and carbohydrates into energy by promoting the uptake of glucose by the body's cells (see Chapter 7).

The Cardiovascular System

Your heart is about the size of your clenched fist and weighs only about 11 ounces, yet it pumps 5 or more quarts of blood a minute through your circulatory system. Over the course of your life, your heart will beat more than 2.5 *billion* times. The cardiovascular system—the heart, blood vessels, and blood—serves as the body's transportation system. Through the pumping action of the heart, the blood vessels carry blood rich in nutrients and oxygen to our cells and tissues and remove waste products through the lungs, liver, and kidneys.

Blood and Circulation

Human blood is a living tissue; it contains three types of cells that perform different functions. Red blood cells, or *erythrocytes,* carry oxygen from the lungs to the cells of the body. Red blood cells are formed in the bone marrow and contain *hemoglobin,* the iron-rich substance that gives blood its reddish tint. The blood uses hemoglobin to pick up oxygen in the lungs while releasing the carbon dioxide it has carried in from the cells. Blood also carries nutrients from the digestive system to cells and transports cellular waste to the kidneys for excretion in urine.

The white blood cells (*leukocytes*) carried by the blood are part of the immune system, and the *platelets* are small cell fragments that stick together (coagulate) when necessary to form clots along the walls of damaged blood vessels. Without leukocytes, we would have no defenses against infection. Without platelets, we would bleed to death from wounds, even from a small cut.

Blood is transported throughout the body by the *circulatory system,* which consists of several types of blood vessels. **Arteries** carry blood from the heart to the other organs and tissues. The arteries branch into increasingly narrower blood vessels called *arterioles,* which eventually connect with *capillaries.* Capillaries are the smallest of the blood vessels and carry blood directly to the individual cells. **Veins** return blood from the capillaries to the heart.

A blood pressure level of 120/80 ("120 over 80") mmHg (millimeters of mercury) is considered normal. Systolic BP above 140 mmHg and/or diastolic BP above 90 mmHg indicates the presence of hypertension.

The vessels of the circulatory system move blood throughout the body by dilating and contracting as needed. When arteries narrow (constrict), resistance to blood flow increases. Blood pressure is a measure of the force exerted by blood against the blood vessel walls. This force is highest during *systole,* when the heart contracts in order to force the blood out. During *diastole,* the heart relaxes as blood flows into the heart, and blood pressure drops. Thus, diastolic blood pressure is lower than systolic blood pressure.

The Heart

In birds and mammals, the heart is separated into four parts, or chambers: the right and left *atria* in the upper section of the heart and the right and left *ventricles* in the lower section of the heart. These chambers work in coordinated fashion to bring blood into the heart and then to pump it throughout the body (Figure 3.6). Blood returning from the body enters the *right atrium* through two large veins. After expanding to receive the blood, the right atrium contracts,

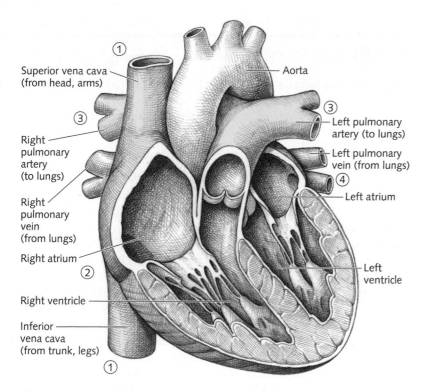

Superior vena cava (from head, arms)

Aorta

Right pulmonary artery (to lungs)

Left pulmonary artery (to lungs)

Left pulmonary vein (from lungs)

Right pulmonary vein (from lungs)

Left atrium

Right atrium

Left ventricle

Right ventricle

Inferior vena cava (from trunk, legs)

① Oxygen-depleted blood returns to the heart from the body through the superior and the inferior vena cava. . . .

② This blood is pumped from the right atrium into the right ventricle. . . .

③ And from there through capillaries of the lungs, where it picks up fresh oxygen and disposes of carbon dioxide. . . .

④ The freshly oxygenated blood is pumped through the pulmonary vein into the left atrium and from there into the left ventricle, from which it flows into the arterial system.

Figure 3.6

The Cardiovascular System The heart is separated into four parts, or chambers: the right and left atria in the upper section of the heart, and the right and left ventricles in the lower section of the heart.

■ **bronchi** the pair of respiratory tubes that branch into progressively smaller passageways, the bronchioles, culminating in the air sacs within the right and left lungs (alveoli).

forcing the "used" blood into the *right ventricle.* Depleted of oxygen, this "used" blood is sent into the pulmonary artery (*pulmonary* refers to lungs), then through the capillaries of the lungs, where it picks up oxygen for later distribution to cells and disposes of waste carbon dioxide (CO_2) (which will be exhaled). The now oxygen-rich blood flows into the pulmonary vein, and pumping action of cardiac muscles forces that blood into the left atrium and then into the left ventricle. The left ventricle propels the oxygen-rich blood into the aorta, from which it flows into the arterial system, carrying nutrients to all parts of the body. If you listen to your heartbeat, the "lubb-dup, lubb-dup" sound represents the closing of the valves between the atria and ventricles ("lubb"), followed by the closing of the valves between the ventricles and the arteries ("dup"). When one of the heart's valves is damaged, as occurs following rheumatic fever, blood leaks back through the valve and produces the "ph—f—f—t" sound of a "heart murmur."

The Respiratory System

Respiration has two meanings. At the level of the individual cell, it refers to energy-producing chemical reactions that require oxygen. At the level of the whole organism, it refers to the process of taking in oxygen from the environment and ridding the body of carbon dioxide.

The Lungs

The most important organs in the respiratory system are, of course, the lungs (Figure 3.7). After air enters the body through the mouth or nose, it passes to the lungs through the *pharynx* and *trachea,* from which it travels through the **bronchi** that branch into smaller tubes, called *bronchioles.* Each bronchiole ends in a cluster of small, bubble-like sacs called *alveoli.* The membranous wall of each alveolus is thin enough to permit the exchange of gases, allowing oxygen to be exchanged for carbon dioxide. Alveoli are surrounded by millions of capillaries so that gases can be transferred efficiently to and from the bloodstream.

How do the muscles that control lung expansion "know" when it's time to breathe? Sensors in capillaries monitor the chemical composition of the blood. As the level of carbon dioxide rises, this information is relayed to the brain's medulla, which signals the muscles of the diaphragm to contract and cause you to inhale. Sensing that the level of carbon dioxide is low, the medulla signals the muscles to slow the rate of breathing until the carbon dioxide level returns to normal.

The respiratory system also has protective mechanisms that eliminate airborne dust particles and other foreign matter from the body. The two reflex mechanisms are sneezing when the nasal passages are irritated, and coughing when the larger airways of the throat are irritated. In addition, the air passages in the nose, mouth, and trachea are lined with tiny hairs called **cilia** that trap germs. Moving in wavelike fashion, the cilia force the mucus that coats

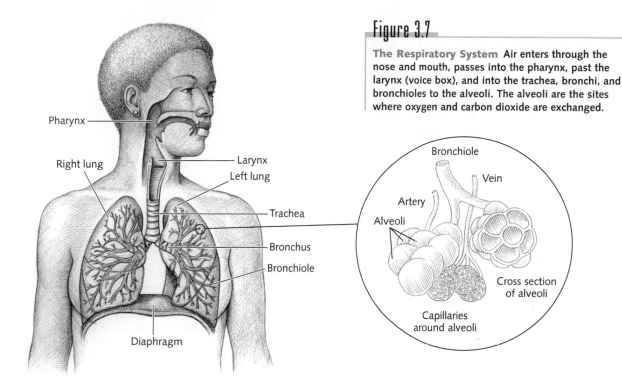

Figure 3.7

The Respiratory System Air enters through the nose and mouth, passes into the pharynx, past the larynx (voice box), and into the trachea, bronchi, and bronchioles to the alveoli. The alveoli are the sites where oxygen and carbon dioxide are exchanged.

them gradually up toward the mouth, where it is either expelled in a cough or swallowed.

The Diversity and Healthy Living box (p. 66) discusses asthma as an example of what can happen when the respiratory system malfunctions, and of how health psychology contributes to the care and well-being of sufferers.

The Digestive System

Digestion is the breaking down of food into molecules that can be absorbed by the blood and distributed to individual cells as nutrients for energy, growth, and tissue repair. The digestive, or **gastrointestinal system,** consists primarily of the *digestive tract*—a long convoluted tube that extends from the mouth to the anus (Figure 3.8 on p. 66). The digestive system also includes the salivary glands, the pancreas, the liver, and the gallbladder.

How Food Is Digested

Digestion begins in the mouth, where chewing and the chemical action of salivary enzymes begin to break food down. Most mammals have teeth that assist in the tearing and grinding of food. As food is chewed, it is moistened by saliva

■ **cilia** the tiny hairs that line the air passageways in the nose, mouth, and trachea; moving in wavelike fashion, the cilia trap germs and force them out of the respiratory system.

■ **gastrointestinal system** the body's system for digesting food; includes the digestive tract, salivary glands, pancreas, liver, and gallbladder.

Diversity and Healthy Living

Asthma

The rapid rise of chronic noncommunicable diseases (NCDs) represents one of the major global challenges to health. Worldwide in 2004, NCDs accounted for 60 percent of all deaths. By 2020, it is estimated that over 70 pecent of the global burden of disease will be caused by NCDs—especially cancer, diabetes, cardiovascular disease, and chronic respiratory diseases such as asthma (WHO, 2004).

Ninety percent of childhood cases of asthma are allergic reactions triggered by animal dander, pollens, dust, indoor mold, or damp conditions in homes and buildings (National Center for Environmental Health, 2006). In the nonallergic form of asthma (which is more likely to affect adults), cold air, viral infections, secondhand smoke, and household chemicals trigger asthma attacks. There are an estimated 6 million chemicals in the environment, and 2,800 of these have allergenic properties. Many people with asthma find that strong emotions, stress, or anxiety can make symptoms of asthma worse, especially during a severe attack.

An asthma attack occurs when the immune system produces an antibody that activates the body's defensive mast cells, causing the muscles surrounding the bronchi in the lungs to constrict and obstruct the flow of air. In addition, the bronchi become inflamed and filled with mucus, further reducing the supply of oxygen. The major symptoms of an asthma attack include wheezing, a whistling sound that may occur throughout the chest or in a local area where the airway has become blocked; coughing as the body attempts to rid itself of any foreign substance (mucus) or irritant (smoke); and shortness of breath caused by fast, shallow breathing as the body attempts to take in sufficient oxygen through narrowed airways.

Although asthma can develop at any age, it usually begins in childhood—it is now the most common chronic childhood disease in the United States—and affects more boys than girls (Dey and others, 2004). Asthma was rare in 1900, but now it has grown into an epidemic: There are more than 20 million people with asthma in the United States (73 per 1,000) and 10 times that many around the world (NCHS, 2004). The prevalence of asthma is highest in Western countries, particularly English-speaking ones; the disease is rare in parts of rural South America and Africa. Each year in the United States, there are nearly 2 million visits to the emergency room for asthma, 10 million outpatient visits to private physician offices, 500,000 hospitalizations, and nearly 5,000 asthma-related deaths, mostly in older adults. Worldwide, there are more than 180,000 asthma deaths each year (WHO, 2000).

Although having one parent with asthma—or, worse still, two parents with asthma—increases a child's risk, geographical variations in the prevalence of asthma are probably due to environmental and lifestyle factors rather than genetic ones. Among the candidates for risk factors is the tendency of children to spend more time indoors than did those in earlier generations, thus increasing their exposure to household allergens, including dust mites, animal dander, and indoor pests such as cockroaches. According to another theory, the immune systems of Western children, unlike those in developing countries, are weaker because they are not conditioned to live with parasites, so the children become more vulnerable to asthma and other allergic diseases such as hay fever.

In the United States, both prevalence and morbidity of asthma are related to ethnicity and socioeconomic status; the disease is particularly prevalent among African Americans, Hispanic Americans, and individuals with lower socioeconomic status (Lehrer and others, 2002). In the largest study of its kind ever conducted, researchers at the National Institute of Allergy and Infectious Diseases studied more than 1,500 children, ages 4 to 11, living in inner cities. In a powerful validation of the biopsychosocial model, the researchers found that a wide variety of factors, rather than a single cause, were responsible for the recent increase in asthma morbidity. Among these factors were environmental toxins, such as indoor allergens and passive smoke; psychological problems of both the children and their caretakers, such as defensiveness and panic disorder; and problems with access to medical care.

Patient education is the most prominent behavioral intervention for asthma, beginning with instruction about basic asthma facts and medications. Most programs instruct patients on avoiding asthma triggers and devising a self-management plan. Some programs also focus on stress management; muscle relaxation techniques that improve breathing; and relating to the health care system, including how to find a doctor, prepare for medical visits, and pay for medical care. Environmental interventions include removing carpeting, draperies, curtains, and upholstered furniture; sealing mattresses and pillows in dust-proof enclosures; finding new homes for pets; and installing high-efficiency particle-arresting (HEPA) filters. The goal of these programs is to eliminate or reduce symptoms, minimize the need for emergency interventions, and improve the overall quality of the asthma sufferer's life. Behavioral interventions often result in significant reductions in symptoms and in the need for medical treatment (Lehrer and others, 2003).

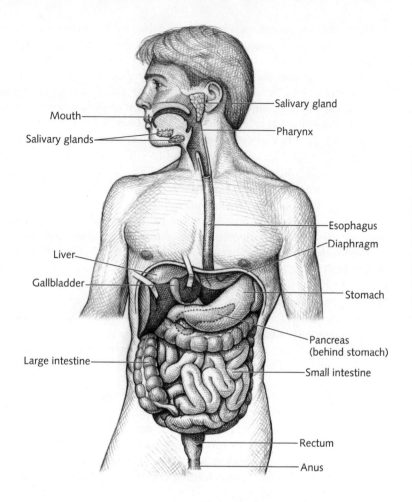

Mouth

Salivary glands

Salivary gland

Pharynx

Esophagus

Diaphragm

Liver

Gallbladder

Stomach

Large intestine

Pancreas
(behind stomach)

Small intestine

Rectum

Anus

Figure 3.8

The Digestive System Digestion is the process of breaking food down into simpler chemical compounds in order to make it absorbable in the digestive tract. The process begins in the mouth, where food is chewed and ground by the teeth. From the mouth, food passes through the esophagus to the stomach, where it is churned and proteins are chemically digested. From there, food passes into the large and small intestines, where chemical digestion of carbohydrates and proteins is completed. Waste products of food are stored as feces in the rectum, and eliminated from the body through the anus.

so that it can be swallowed more easily. Saliva contains a digestive enzyme called *amylase* that causes starches to begin to decompose.

Once food is swallowed, it passes into the *esophagus,* a muscular tube about 9.3 inches (25 centimeters) long in the typical adult. The muscles of the esophagus contract rhythmically, propelling the food downward in an involuntary reflexive motion called *peristalsis.* This reflex is so efficient that you are able to swallow food and water even while standing on your head.

In the stomach, the food is mixed with a variety of gastric juices, including hydrochloric acid and *pepsin,* an enzyme that breaks down proteins. At this point, the food has been converted into a semiliquid mass. The secretion of gastric juices (including saliva) is controlled by the autonomic nervous system. Food in the mouth, or even the sight, smell, or thought of food, is sufficient to trigger the flow of gastric juices. Conversely, fear inhibits digestive activity. When you are in danger or under stress, your mouth becomes very dry, and food remains an uncomfortable, undigested lump in your stomach.

Stomachs vary in capacity. Depending on their success in hunting, carnivores such as hyenas may eat only once every few days. Fortunately, their large-capacity stomachs can hold the equivalent of 30 to 35 percent of their body weight. In contrast, mammals that eat more frequent, smaller meals typically have much smaller stomachs. The capacity of the average college student's stomach is roughly 2 to 4 liters of food—about 2 to 3 percent of the average person's body weight—roughly equal to a burger, fries, and a Coke.

By about 4 hours after eating, the stomach has emptied its contents into the small and large intestines. Digestive fluids from the pancreas, liver, and gallbladder are secreted into the small intestine through a series of ducts. These fluids contain enzymes that break down proteins, fats, and carbohydrates. For example, the liver produces a salty substance called *bile* that emulsifies fats almost as effectively as dishwashing liquid, and the pancreas produces the hormone insulin, which assists in transporting glucose from the intestine into body cells.

The breakdown of food that began in the mouth and stomach is completed in the small intestine. The inner lining of the small intestine is composed of gathered circular folds, which greatly increase its surface area. Fully extended, an average adult's small intestine would be almost 20 feet (approximately 6 meters) in length, with a total surface area of 3,229 square feet (300 square meters)—roughly the size of a basketball court. This vast area is lined with tiny, fingerlike projections of mucus, called *villi,* through which water and nutrient molecules pass into the bloodstream. Once in the bloodstream, nutrients travel to individual cells.

Food particles that have not been absorbed into the bloodstream then pass into the large intestine, or *colon,* where absorption, mainly of water, continues. In the course of digestion, a large volume of water—approximately 7 liters each day—is absorbed. When this process is disrupted, as occurs in diarrhea and other gastric disorders, dehydration becomes a danger. Indeed, dehydration is the reason diarrhea remains the leading cause of infant death in many developing countries.

Completing the process of digestion, food particles that were not absorbed earlier are converted into feces by colon bacteria such as *Escherichia coli.* Fecal matter is primarily composed of water, bacteria, cellulose fibers, and other indigestible substances.

The Immune System

At this moment, countless numbers of microorganisms surround you. Most are not dangerous. Indeed, many, such as those that assist in digestion and the decomposition of waste matter, play an important role in health. However, **antigens**—bacteria, viruses, fungi, parasites, and any foreign microorganism—are dangerous to your health, even deadly. Defending your health against these invaders is the job of the immune system.

You may be exposed to antigens through direct bodily contact (handshaking, kissing, or sexual intercourse) or through food, water, insects, and airborne microbes. Antigens may penetrate body tissue through several routes, including the skin, the digestive tract, the respiratory tract, or the urinary tract. Their impact depends on the number and virulence of the microorganisms, and the strength of the body's defenses.

■ **antigen** a foreign substance that stimulates an immune response.

■ **lymphocytes** antigen-fighting white blood cells produced in the bone marrow.

Structure of the Immune System

Unlike most other systems, the immune system is spread throughout the body in the form of a network of capillaries, lymph nodes (glands), and ducts that comprise the *lymphatic system,* along with the bone marrow, thymus, and tonsils (Figure 3.9). Lymphatic capillaries carry *lymph,* a colorless bodily fluid formed by water, proteins, microbes, and other foreign substances that are drained from the spaces between body cells. Lymph takes its name from the billions of white blood cells it circulates called **lymphocytes.** These cells, which are produced in the bone marrow, patrol the entire body, searching for bacteria, viruses, cancerous cells, and other antigens.

The lymph nodes contain filters that capture infectious substances and debris; as lymph passes through the lymph nodes, the lymphocytes destroy the foreign particles collected there. During an immune response, the lymphocytes expand, which produces swelling and inflammation. You may have noticed how your lymph nodes swell when you are fighting an infection.

Two structures play a role in the activity of lymphocytes: the thymus and the tonsils. The thymus, which also functions as part of the endocrine system, secretes *thymosin,* a hormone that helps control the maturation and development of lymphocytes. Interestingly, the thymus is largest during infancy and childhood and slowly shrinks throughout adulthood, which may partially explain why immune responses are generally more efficient during childhood, and aging is

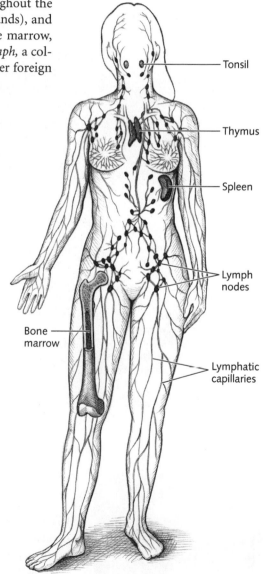

Tonsil

Thymus

Spleen

Lymph nodes

Bone marrow

Lymphatic capillaries

Figure 3.9

The Immune System Positioned throughout the body, the organs of the immune system are home to lymphocytes, white blood cells that are the basis of the body's immune defense against foreign agents or antigens. Other components of the system are the bone marrow, where lymphocytes are produced; lymph nodes, which are glands that help your body fight infection; and the thymus, spleen, and the tonsils. The lymph nodes produce the fluid lymph, which travels throughout the body via the lymphatic capillaries and filters impurities.

associated with reduced immune efficiency. Finally, the tonsils are masses of lymphatic tissue that seem to function as a holding station for lymphocytes as well as a garbage can for worn-out blood cells.

The Immune Response

The body's immune reactions can be divided into two broad categories: *nonspecific immunity* and *specific immunity.* Nonspecific immune defenses fight off any antigen, including those never before encountered. Specific immune defenses occur only when a particular antigen has been encountered before, creating a kind of immunological *memory* for the intruder.

Nonspecific Immune Responses

The body's first line of defense against most antigens consists of the several layers of tightly knit cells that make up the skin. Chemicals found in perspiration, such as the oily *sebum* secreted by glands beneath the skin, prevent most bacteria and fungi from growing on the skin.

The nose, eyes, and respiratory tract—although they lack the tough, protective barrier of the skin—also provide a first line of defense. The mucus membranes of the nose and respiratory tract are armed with hairlike cilia, which, as noted earlier, catch dust, microbes, and other foreign matter. A powerful enzyme in tears and saliva destroys the cell walls of many bacteria. Similarly, gastric acids are able to destroy most antigens that enter the digestive system.

When an antigen penetrates the skin cells, it encounters a second line of defense, called *phagocytosis,* in which two specialized lymphocytes called phagocytes and macrophages attack the foreign particles. *Phagocytes* are large scavenger cells that prowl the blood and tissues of the body for antigens. Phagocytes destroy antigens by engulfing and digesting them. *Macrophages* ("big eaters") are phagocytes found at the site of an infection, as well as in the lymph nodes, spleen, and lungs. These specialized white blood cell "sentries" pass into body tissues, where they hunt antigens and worn-out cells. A single phagocyte can digest 5 to 25 bacteria before dying itself from an accumulation of toxic wastes.

Suppose, for instance, that your skin was punctured by a splinter. Neighboring cells in the area of the wound immediately release several chemicals, particularly *histamine,* which increases blood flow to the area. Circulating phagocytes and macrophages, attracted by these chemicals, rush to the site of the wound, where they begin to engulf the inevitable bacteria and foreign particles that enter the body through the wound. At the same time, blood clots form, sealing off the wound site, and additional histamine is released, creating a hot environment unfavorable to bacteria.

As a consequence of this sequence of nonspecific immune reactions, collectively referred to as the *inflammatory response,* the injured area becomes swollen, red, and tender to the touch. In addition, some lymphocytes release proteins that produce *systemic effects* (effects throughout the entire body), such as fever, in the most serious cases of invasion (for example, food poisoning). In

The Immune System in Action: A Macrophage Attacks Macrophages ("big eaters") are specialized white blood cell "sentries" that pass into body tissues, where they hunt antigens and worn-out cells. A single macrophage can digest 5 to 25 bacteria before dying itself from an accumulation of toxic wastes.

Microworks/Phototake

An Inside Story The clever movie *Osmosis Jones*, which takes place both inside and outside of Frank, humorously showcases the immune system. The star is the white blood cell after whom the movie is named (third from the right), who gallantly fights a fierce, intruding virus to save Frank.

addition to its role in destroying invading microorganisms, inflammation helps restore bodily tissues that have been damaged (Figure 3.10).

In addition to the phagocytes and macrophages, the immune system's non-specific defenses include smaller lymphocytes called *natural killer,* or NK, cells, which patrol the body for diseased cells that have gone awry. Researchers are just now learning how NK cells distinguish normal body cells, or what is *self,* from virus-infected and cancerous cells that are *non-self.* NK cells destroy their

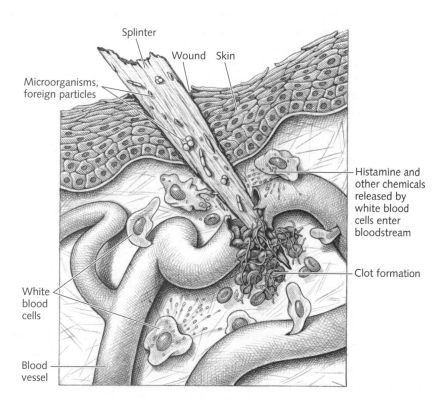

Figure 3.10

The Inflammatory Response When an infection or, as in this case, an injury breaches the body's first line of defense, histamine and other chemicals are released at the site of the wound. These chemicals increase blood flow to the area, attract white blood cells, and cause a clot to form—sealing off the wound site. Some of the white blood cells engulf foreign particles, while others release a protein that produces fever.

targets by injecting them with lethal chemicals. They also secrete various forms of *interferon,* an antimicrobial protein that inhibits the spread of viral infections to healthy cells. Interferons, which differ from species to species, work by preventing viruses from replicating. Interferons are the subject of intensive biomedical research and have the potential for treating influenza, the common cold, and other diseases.

Specific Immune Responses

Some antigens either elude the body's nonspecific defenses or are too powerful to be handled by phagocytes, macrophages, and NK cells alone. In such cases, the immune system calls upon its strongest line of defense: specific immune responses. These reactions occur when a particular antigen has been encountered before. Some specific immunities are acquired when a nursing mother passes a specific immunity to her child through breast milk. Others develop when a person successfully weathers a disease such as measles, or is *immunized.* As a child, you probably were vaccinated against mumps, chickenpox, whooping cough, polio, and other diseases, making your body artificially resistant to these diseases should you ever be exposed to them. Your body's ability to develop "memory" for specific antigens is the basis of acquired immunity. When a child is vaccinated, a dead or nonvirulent form of a specific virus is injected, allowing the body to create a memory for it.

Specific immune responses involve two special lymphocytes, called *B cells* and *T cells,* which recognize and attack specific invading antigens. B cells attack foreign substances by producing specific antibodies, or *immunoglobulins,* proteins that chemically suppress the toxic effects of antigens, primarily viruses and bacteria. A particular antibody molecule fits into receptors on an invading antigen as precisely as a key fits a lock. When a B cell is activated by a particular antigen, it divides into two types: a plasma cell capable of making 3,000 to 30,000 antibody molecules per second and an antibody-producing memory cell (Figure 3.11). The rapid response of memory cells, called the *primary response,* is the basis of immunity to many infectious diseases, including polio, measles, smallpox, and mumps.

Unlike the plasma cell, which lives only a few days, memory cells may last a lifetime, producing a stronger, faster antibody reaction should the particular antigen be encountered a second time. When a memory cell encounters the same antigen during a subsequent infection, the *secondary immune response* is triggered.

For many years, scientists believed that circulating antibodies produced by B cells were the sole basis of immunity. They now know that the immune system has a second line of defense, called *cell-mediated immunity,* in which T cells directly attack and kill antigens without the aid of antibodies.

There are three major varieties of T cells: *cytotoxic cells, helper cells,* and *suppressor cells.* Cytotoxic T cells, known as "killer cells," are equipped with receptors that match one specific antigen. When that antigen is encountered, the killer cell receptor locks onto it and injects it with a lethal toxin. Current esti-

Although 95 percent of kindergarteners in the United States are immunized (a law in most states), only 40 to 60 percent of preschoolers are—a lower rate than in many developing countries. One in five of these is a child without health insurance.

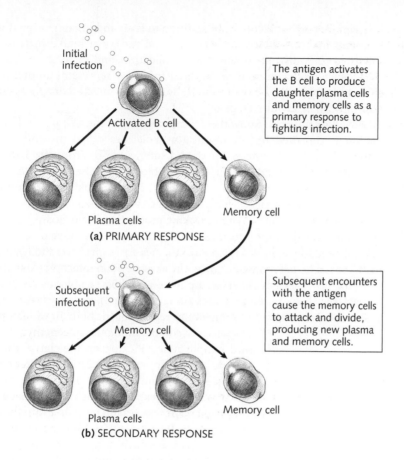

Initial infection

Activated B cell

The antigen activates the B cell to produce daughter plasma cells and memory cells as a primary response to fighting infection.

Plasma cells

Memory cell

(a) PRIMARY RESPONSE

Subsequent infection

Memory cell

Subsequent encounters with the antigen cause the memory cells to attack and divide, producing new plasma and memory cells.

Plasma cells

Memory cell

(b) SECONDARY RESPONSE

Figure 3.11

Primary and Secondary Responses of the Immune System (a) When a B cell is activated by an antigen, it divides into plasma cells, which manufacture antibodies, and memory cells. (b) When memory cells encounter the same antigen during a subsequent infection, the secondary immune response occurs. Memory cells release antibodies that attack the antigen and also divide, producing a new generation of plasma cells and memory cells.

mates suggest that each person is born with enough killer T cells to recognize at least 1 million different kinds of antigens.

Helper T cells and suppressor T cells are the principal mechanisms for regulating the immune system's overall response to infection. They do so by secreting chemical messengers called *lymphokines,* which stimulate or inhibit activity in other immune cells. Helper cells are sentries that travel through the bloodstream hunting antigens. When they find them, they secrete chemical messengers that alert B cells, phagocytes, macrophages, and cytotoxic T cells to attack. Suppressor T cells serve a counterregulatory function. By producing chemicals that suppress immune responding, these cells ensure that an overzealous immune response doesn't damage healthy cells. Suppressor cells also alert T cells and B cells when an invader has been successfully vanquished.

A Bidirectional Immune-to-Brain Circuit

The body's nonspecific immune response, which is triggered by signals originating in the hypothalamus, is called the *acute phase response (APR),* or more simply the "sickness" response, because of the sweeping physiological and

■ **cytokines** protein molecules produced by immune cells that act on other cells to regulate immunity (include the interferons, interleukins, and tumor necrosis factors).

behavioral changes that occur. In addition to fever and inflammation, the APR is accompanied by reduced activity and food and water intake, increased sensitivity to pain, disrupted memory consolidation, and increased anxiety. The APR, which occurs an hour or two after infection, represents an orchestrated effort to mobilize the body's resources for battling infection by preserving energy through behavior changes.

How does the brain know there is an infection in the first place? The information is conveyed by communicator molecules called pro-inflammatory **cytokines,** including interleukin-1 and interleukin-6 (from the Latin *inter,* meaning "between," and "leukin" for white blood cell—thus molecules that signal "between white blood cells") (Sternberg, 2001). Cytokines are produced in the blood by macrophages which, as you'll recall, are the first immune cells on the scene of an infection. When cytokine production is blocked with chemical antagonists for their receptor sites, there is no sign of a sickness response *despite* an infection. Conversely, when cytokines are administered to healthy animals, the sickness response occurs in the absence of an infection (Maier, 2003).

Cytokine molecules, however, are too big to cross the blood–brain barrier. Instead, they bind to receptor sites along the *vagus nerve,* which is one of the 12 cranial nerves. The vagus innervates regions of the body in which immune responses occur, including the spleen, thymus gland, and lymph nodes. Picking up the signal, the vagus signals the brain to make its own interleukin-1, which activates immune cells and triggers the APR. As Steven Maier explains, "Your macrophage chews on a bacteria, it releases interleukin-1 into the neighboring space, the interleukin-1 binds to receptors on the paraganglia, which send neurotransmitters to activate the vagus nerve (quoted in Azar, 2001)." Cutting the vagus nerve (vagotomy) prevents the sickness response from occurring (Maier, 2003).

As shown in Figure 3.12 (from Sternberg, 2001, p. 89) the brain and immune system form a bidirectional communication network in which cytokines produced by immune cells communicate with the brain, and neurotransmitters produced in the brain communicate with immune cells (Sternberg, 2001). Viewed in this way, the immune system functions as a *diffuse sense organ* that alerts the brain to infection and injury. As we'll see in the next chapter, health psychologists working within the subfield of *psychoneuroimmunology* are very interested in this circuit, because stress also taps into it, suggesting that the neural pathways and chemical signals that underly some psychological processes and inflammatory diseases are one and the same.

Figure 3.12

Bidirectional Immune-to-Brain Circuit Once viewed as independent systems, we now know that the brain and immune system communicate with each other through cytokines, which are produced by immune cells, and neurotransmitters, which are produced by nerve cells in the brain.

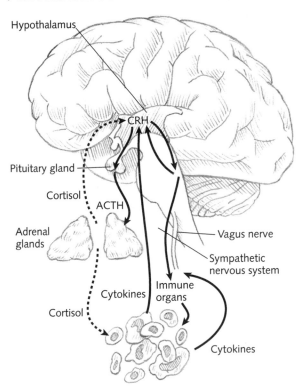

The Reproductive System and Behavior Genetics

The human reproductive system is where life and health begin. The separate development of the female and male reproductive systems begins during prenatal development, when a hormonal signal from the hypothalamus stimulates the pituitary gland to produce the *gonadotropic hormones,* which direct the development of the *gonads,* or sex glands—the ovaries in females and the testes in males. One of these hormones in particular, *GnRH (gonad-releasing hormone),* directs the ovaries and testes to dramatically increase the production of sex hormones, especially *estrogen* in girls and *testosterone* in boys.

The Female Reproductive System

On either side of the female's uterus are two almond-shaped *ovaries,* which produce the hormones estrogen and progesterone. The outer layer of each ovary contains the *oocytes,* from which the *ova* (eggs) develop. The oocytes begin to form during the third month of prenatal development. At birth, an infant girl's two ovaries contain some 2 million oocytes—all that she will ever have. Of these, about 400,000 survive into puberty, and some 300 to 400 reach maturity, generally one at a time, approximately every 28 days from the onset of puberty until menopause, which typically occurs at about age 50. Each ovum is contained in the ovary within a *follicle,* or capsule.

The menstrual cycle is divided into four phases, each of which is timed and controlled by the hypothalamus in a complex feedback system. During the first phase, the *proliferative phase,* which lasts 9 or 10 days, estrogen and progesterone are quite low. Sensing these low levels, the hypothalamus instructs the pituitary to release *follicle-stimulating hormone (FSH)* and *lutenizing hormone (LH).* When FSH reaches the ovaries, it stimulates some follicles to mature and begin producing estrogen, which causes the inner layer of the uterus, called the *endometrium,* to thicken, or "proliferate," in preparation for a possible pregnancy.

During the second phase, the *ovulatory phase,* peak estrogen levels cause one or the other of the ovaries to discharge a mature ovum near the fallopian tubes, or *oviducts,* where it begins its passage to the uterus. When the hypothalamus detects the elevated levels of estrogen, it instructs the pituitary to release additional FSH and LH. Surging levels of LH trigger ovulation within 12 to 24 hours.

The third phase of the cycle, called the *secretory,* or *luteal,* phase, begins just after ovulation and continues to the beginning of the next menstrual phase. Under the continued production of LH, the cells of the emptied follicle enlarge, becoming the *corpus luteum* ("yellow body"). LH also triggers the corpus luteum to begin producing large amounts of estrogen and progesterone.

As the hormone levels increase, estrogen and progesterone inhibit further production of GnRH by the hypothalamus and thus of LH and FSH by the pituitary.

If the released ovum is not fertilized by a sperm, it remains in the uterus for approximately 14 days, after which the corpus luteum is reabsorbed, hormone levels drop, and the corpus luteum is flushed from the body along with the endometrium during the fourth and final phase of the cycle, the *menstrual phase.*

The Male Reproductive System

From puberty until old age, the testes of human males produce an average of several hundred million sperm each day. The testes form during the embryonic phases of prenatal development and are subdivided into some 250 individual compartments, each of which is packed with coiled *seminiferous* ("seed-bearing") *tubules.* Sperm cells form in the tubules. Taken together, the two testes contain a total of approximately 500 meters of tubules.

In contrast to the female's cyclical changes in hormone levels, males maintain fairly constant blood hormone levels. However, the same pituitary hormones that regulate the ovaries—LH and FSH—regulate the testes. FSH stimulates the actual production of sperm, while LH stimulates the testes to secrete testosterone.

As in the female, in the male the hypothalamus monitors blood levels of sex hormones by way of a tight *feedback loop.* Low testosterone levels cause the hypothalamus to secrete a releasing hormone that signals the pituitary to release LH, which in turn causes the testes to secrete testosterone. When testosterone levels rise to an adequate level, the hypothalamus orders the pituitary to cease further production of LH.

Fertilization and the Mechanisms of Heredity

At the moment of conception, a *sperm cell* from the male finds its way upward from the uterus into the fallopian tubes, where it fertilizes an ovum. The resulting single-celled **zygote** travels down the fallopian tube, where the first cellular divisions take place. About 36 hours after fertilization, the zygote divides in half; at 60 hours, the two cells divide again to form four cells. These four cells soon become eight, then sixteen, and so on.

By 5 days after fertilization, the zygote consists of approximately 120 cells and embeds itself in the uterine wall in a process known as *implantation.* Implantation triggers the hormonal changes that halt the woman's usual menstrual cycle, and enables the connective web of the placenta to develop and nourish the organism over the next 9 months.

The zygote contains inherited information from both parents that will determine the child's characteristics. Each ovum and each sperm contain 23 *chromosomes,* the long, threadlike structures that carry our inheritance. At conception, the 23 chromosomes from the egg and the 23 from the sperm unite,

bequeathing to the newly formed zygote a full complement of 46 chromosomes. As the cells of the developing
person divide, this genetic material is replicated over
and over, so that the nucleus of every cell in the person's
body contains the same instructions written at the moment of conception.

The twenty-third pair of chromosomes determines
the zygote's sex. The mother always contributes an **X
chromosome;** the father can contribute either an X or a
Y chromosome. If the father's sperm also contains an X
chromosome, the child will be a girl; a Y chromosome
from Dad will produce a boy. Y chromosomes contain a
single gene that triggers the testes to begin producing
testosterone, which in turn initiates the sexual differentiation in appearance,
and neural differentiation during the fourth and fifth months of prenatal development.

Each chromosome is composed of strings of *genes*—the basic units of
heredity that determine our growth and characteristics. Genes are discrete particles of deoxyribonucleic acid, or *DNA*. Each cell in the body contains 50,000
to 80,000 genes that determine everything from the length of your toenails
to whether you have a tendency toward schizophrenia, a major psychological
disorder.

Before the last decade, scientists knew relatively little about the specific effects of specific genes. Today, with the Human Genome Project, researchers
have been able to locate and determine the role of many of our genes. Even so,
the field of genetics is highly dynamic, and existing knowledge is subject to
change as scientists continue their work.

Genes and Environment

Most human characteristics are not determined by genes alone, but rather are
multifactorial—influenced by many different factors, including environmental
factors. Human traits tend also to be *polygenic*—influenced by many different
genes.

The sum total of genes that a person inherits is that person's **genotype.**
The observable physical and nonphysical traits that are actually expressed
constitute the person's **phenotype.** This distinction is important because
each of us inherits many genes in our genotype that are not expressed in our
phenotype. In genetic terminology, we are *carriers* of these unexpressed bits
of DNA; although we may not manifest them in our own phenotype, they
may be passed on to our offspring, who will then have them in their genotype and may or may not express them in their phenotype. Eye color inheritance is among the most straightforward and is therefore often used to help
us understand this distinction (Figure 3.13 on p. 78). For most traits, a person's phenotype is determined by two patterns of genetic interaction:
gene–gene and gene–environment.

Human Chromosomes At
conception, 23 gene-carrying
chromosomes from each parent
unite to form a zygote with a full
complement of 46 chromosomes
and all the information needed to
create a complex new being nine
months later.

■ **zygote** a fertilized egg cell.

■ **X chromosome** the sex
chromosome found in males
and females. Females have
two X chromosomes; males
have one.

■ **Y chromosome** the sex chromosome found only in males;
contains a gene that triggers
the testes to begin producing
testosterone.

■ **genotype** the sum total of
all the genes present in an
individual.

■ **phenotype** a person's observable characteristics; determined
by the interaction of the individual's genotype with the
environment.

Mother's Eye Color Genes

	BROWN	BLUE
BROWN	BB	Bb
BLUE	Bb	bb

Father's Eye Color Genes

Figure 3.13

Genotype and Phenotype in Eye Color Can brown-eyed parents have blue-eyed children? Yes! As you can see in this simplified illustration, one-fourth of this couple's children may inherit in their genotype a recessive blue eye gene from each of their parents and thus have nothing but blue eyes to express in their phenotype. If, however, the child gets a brown eye gene from even one of the parents, that child will express the dominant brown-eyed trait. Yet these brown-eyed children will still carry a blue eye gene in their genotype that may yet be expressed in future offspring.

Gene–Gene Interactions One common pattern of gene–gene interaction is called *additive* because the resulting phenotype simply reflects the sum of the contributions of individual genes. Genes that determine height and skin color, for example, usually interact additively. For other traits, genes interact in a *non-additive* fashion. With these traits, the resulting phenotype depends on the influence of one gene more than on the other. A familiar example of nonadditive interaction is the *dominant-recessive pattern*. Some traits occur in the presence of a single dominant gene, with its paired recessive gene making little or no contribution. Many physical characteristics, including eye color, follow the dominant-recessive pattern.

Gene–Environment Interaction Worldwide, genes also interact with a person's environment in determining phenotype. When behavior geneticists refer to environment, they are referring to everything that can influence a person's genetic makeup from the beginning of prenatal development until the moment of death. Environmental influences include the direct effects of nutrition, climate, and medical care, as well as indirect effects brought on by the particular economic, cultural, and historical context in which the individual develops.

Health psychologists now recognize that most or all health behaviors are influenced by genetic predispositions and physiological states. As the biopsychosocial perspective reminds us, however, health behaviors are also influenced by personality and thinking style and by social and cultural circumstances. In subsequent chapters, you'll see how physical systems combine and interact with psychological and sociocultural factors to determine health behaviors, as well as overall states of wellness or illness.

Summing Up

The Nervous System

1. The central nervous system consists of the brain and the spinal cord. The remaining neurons comprise the peripheral nervous system, which itself has two main divisions: the somatic nervous system, which controls voluntary movements, and the autonomic nervous system, which controls the involuntary muscles and endocrine glands through the sympathetic and parasympathetic nervous systems.

2. As the oldest and most central region of the brain, the brainstem, including the reticular formation, thalamus, and cerebellum, controls basic life-support functions via

the autonomic nervous system. The limbic system includes the amygdala, which plays an important role in aggression and other emotions; the hippocampus, which is involved in learning and memory; and the hypothalamus, which influences hunger, thirst, body temperature, and sexual behavior.

3. The cerebral cortex is the thin layer of cells that covers the cerebrum. The cortex is the seat of consciousness and includes areas specialized for speaking and decision making (frontal lobe), vision (occipital lobe), hearing (temporal lobe), and touch (parietal lobe). The association cortex includes areas that are not directly involved in sensory or motor functions. These areas integrate information and are involved in higher mental functions such as thinking and speaking.

The Endocrine System

4. Operating under the control of the hypothalamus, the pituitary gland secretes hormones that influence growth, sexual development, reproduction, kidney functioning, and aging. Other glands augment the nervous system in regulating the functioning of heart rate and blood pressure (adrenal medulla), reducing inflammation (adrenal cortex), regulating growth and metabolism (thyroid), and regulating blood glucose levels (pancreas).

The Cardiovascular System

5. The heart is separated into four chambers. Oxygen-depleted blood returning from the body is pumped from the right atrium into the right ventricle, and from there through the capillaries of the lungs, where it picks up fresh oxygen and disposes of carbon dioxide. The freshly oxygenated blood is pumped through the pulmonary vein into the left atrium of the heart, and from there into the left ventricle, from which it flows into the arterial system.

The Respiratory System

6. After air enters the body through the mouth or nose, it travels to the lungs via bronchial tubes that branch into the smaller bronchioles and air sacs of the lungs (alveoli). The thin walls of the alveoli permit the exchange of oxygen and carbon dioxide.

The Digestive System

7. Digestion begins in the mouth, where chewing and salivary enzymes begin to break food down. Once food is swallowed, the rhythmic movements of the esophageal muscles propel food downward to the stomach, where it is mixed with a variety of gastric enzymes under the con-

trol of the autonomic nervous system. Digestive fluids from the pancreas, liver, and gallbladder are secreted into the small and large intestines, where—several hours after eating—the breakdown of food is completed.

The Immune System

8. The body's first line of defense against health-threatening pathogens includes the protective barrier provided by the skin, the mucous membranes of the nose and respiratory tract, and gastric enzymes of the digestive system. A pathogen that penetrates these defenses encounters an army of lymphocytes that filter out infectious substances and debris with the passage of fluids through the lymphatic system. Other nonspecific immune defenses include the action of the antigen-engulfing phagocytes, macrophages, and NK cells. NK cells also secrete antimicrobial proteins called interferon and play a role in the body's inflammatory response.

9. The brain and immune system form a complete, bidirectional communication network in which chemical messengers produced by immune cells (cytokines) communicate to the brain and chemical messengers produced in the nervous system communicate with immune cells.

10. Specific immune reactions occur when B cells and T cells attack specific antigens. B cells accomplish this when memory cells produce specific antibodies that kill previously encountered antigens. In cell-mediated immunity, T cells directly attack and kill antigens by injecting them with lethal toxins. Immune functioning improves throughout childhood and early adolescence and begins to decline as people approach old age.

The Reproductive System and Behavior Genetics

11. The reproductive system, under the control of the hypothalamus and the endocrine system, directs the development of the primary and secondary sex characteristics. Timed and controlled by the hypothalamus, the menstrual cycle has proliferative, ovulatory, secretory (luteal), and menstrual phases. These phases involve three categories of biological changes: changes in blood levels of hormones, follicular changes, and changes in the development of the uterine lining. In contrast to females, males maintain fairly constant blood hormone levels. As in females, the hypothalamus monitors these levels.

12. The sum total of all the genes a person inherits is the person's genotype. How those genes are expressed in the person's traits is the phenotype. Human development begins when a sperm cell fertilizes an ovum, resulting in a single-celled zygote that contains the inherited information from

the 23 chromosomes inherited from each parent. The twenty-third pair of chromosomes determines the zygote's sex. Genes are segments of DNA that provide the genetic blueprint for our physical and behavioral devel-opment. For any given trait, patterns of gene–gene and gene–environment interaction determine the observable phenotype. Two common patterns of gene–gene interaction are additive and dominant-recessive.

Key Terms and Concepts

central nervous system, p. 54
peripheral nervous system, p. 54
brainstem, p. 57
medulla, p. 57
reticular formation, p. 57
thalamus, p. 57
cerebellum, p. 57
limbic system, p. 58
amygdala, p. 58
hippocampus, p. 58
hypothalamus, p. 58

cerebral cortex, p. 58
sensory cortex, p. 59
motor cortex, p. 59
association cortex, p. 61
hormones, p. 61
pituitary gland, p. 61
adrenal glands, p. 61
arteries, p. 62
veins, p. 62
bronchi, p. 64
cilia, p. 65

gastrointestinal system, p. 65
antigen, p. 69
lymphocytes, p. 69
cytokines, p. 74
zygote, p. 77
X chromosome, p. 77
Y chromosome, p. 77
genotype, p. 77
phenotype, p. 77

Part 2 | Stress and Health

Stress

*I*n 1934, Hungarian-born Hans Selye (1907–1982) was a promising young endocrinologist trying to make a name for himself at Montreal's McGill University by identifying a new hormone. Working with an ovary extract, Selye devised a simple plan: Give daily injections of the extract to a sample of laboratory rats and watch for changes in their behavior and health. Easier said than done! Selye quickly learned that rats, like people, are not fond of being injected. Often, as he was about to insert the needle, a rat would squirm, causing Selye to miss the injection site. Squeezing an uncooperative rat more tightly sometimes caused it to nip at the young experimenter, who would then drop the animal on the floor and be forced to chase it around the laboratory before eventually completing the injection.

After several months of these daily sessions, Selye made an extraordinary discovery: most of the rats had developed bleeding ulcers, shrunken thymus glands (which produce disease-fighting lymphocytes), and enlarged adrenal glands. His immediate response was elation, for he believed he had discovered the physiological effects of the as yet unknown ovarian extract. Being a careful scientist, however, Selye realized that without a control group this conclusion was premature. So other groups of laboratory rats were given daily injections of extracts of kidneys, spleen, or a saline solution, instead of the ovarian extract. Otherwise, these control animals were treated the same: they were often squeezed, dropped, and chased around the lab before receiving their injections! Much to Selye's surprise, at the end of the experiment these control rats had the same enlarged adrenal glands, shrunken thymus glands, and bleeding ulcers. Because the same changes occurred in both groups of rats, they could not have been caused by the ovarian extract. What, then, could have caused the changes? What else did the two groups have in common? In a moment of insight (and humility), Selye correctly reasoned that his hapless handling of the animals had triggered some sort of nonspecific response. The rats were stressed out!

W̲e now know that Selye had discovered the *stress response*—a breakthrough that helped to forge an entirely new medical field—*stress physiology*. Although not the first to use the term "stress," Selye is credited with two important new ideas:

- The body has a remarkably similar response to many different stressors.
- Stressors can sometimes make you sick.

That second idea is especially important—that persistent, or chronic stress influences a person's vulnerability to disorders—and it has become a major theme in health psychology. No single topic has generated more research. As we will see in this and later chapters, researchers have established links between stress and many physical and psychological disorders, including cancer, heart disease, diabetes, arthritis, headaches, asthma, digestive disorders, depression, and anxiety.

So, just what is stress? Stress is a part of life. In fact, without some stress our lives would be dull. But when stress overtaxes our coping resources, it can damage our health. Each of us experiences stress in our everyday lives. Stress can come from many directions, including school, family and friends, interactions with strangers, and work. Stress usually happens in real time, as when you are forced to juggle the ever-changing demands of school, work, family, and friends. Sometimes stress persists for a long time, as when a person loses a loved one or is forced to retire.

Despite the pervasiveness of stress, psychologists have not had an easy time coming up with an acceptable definition of the word. *Stress* is sometimes used to describe a threatening situation or *stimulus*, and at other times to describe a *response* to a situation. Health psychologists have determined that **stressors** are demanding events or situations that trigger coping adjustments in a person, and **stress** is the *process* by which a person both perceives and responds to events that are judged to be challenging or threatening. It's important to recognize that we must judge a challenging event or situation to be threatening or even beyond our ability to cope before we will be stressed by it. A significant stressor for one person may be no big deal for another. You will hear much more about this very individual appraisal process later in this chapter. In Chapter 5, we will consider effective ways to cope with stress. In this chapter, we will take a *biopsychosocial* approach to understanding stress and its impact on the body.

- *Biological* processes that occur when we experience stress can differ somewhat according to each individual's unique physiology and levels of physiological reactivity, but the same basic processes affect us all.

- *Psychological* influences affect how we *appraise* challenging situations—either as manageable (not stressful) or unmanageable (stressful)—

■ **stressor** any event or situation that triggers coping adjustments.

■ **stress** the process by which we perceive and respond to events, called stressors, that are perceived as harmful, threatening, or challenging.

Significant stress Catastrophic events, such as the tsunami that struck Southeast Asia in late 2004, provide tragic, real-world examples of stress as both a stimulus and a response. The event that triggers coping behavior is the stressor (the stimulus), and the person attempting to flee the event or trying to compensate for the destruction it causes illustrates the response.

based on our personalities and individual life experiences. Gender, as we will see, also plays a role in whether we fight or flee, or *tend and befriend.*

■ Our own unique *sociocultural* influences affect how we appraise stress from many different sources, including major life events, catastrophes, daily hassles, environmental stress, work, and family.

Let's turn first to the biological perspective with an examination of the body's physiological response to stress.

The Physiology of Stress

A decade before Selye's discovery, physiologist Walter Cannon introduced the term *stress* to medicine (Cannon, 1932). Cannon observed that extremes of temperature, lack of oxygen, and emotion-arousing incidents all had a similar arousing effect on the body. He was the first to call this effect *stress,* and he believed that it was a common cause of medical problems.

In one of Cannon's studies, cats were frightened by the sound of a barking dog. Cannon discovered that large amounts of the hormone epinephrine could later be detected in the cats' blood. Cannon called this response to stressful events the body's *fight-or-flight reaction.* An outpouring of epinephrine, along with cortisol and other hormones, helps prepare an organism to defend itself against a threat, either by attacking or by running away.

Working from an evolutionary perspective, this emergency response system seems highly functional and adaptive. It undoubtedly was essential to our ancestors' survival in a time when human beings faced numerous physical threats and had to either fight or run away. Today, in our modern, highly developed societies, our stressors are apt to be psychological rather than physical, but we still react as though we are facing a standoff with a wild animal (Sapolsky, 1992).

The Role of the Brain and Nervous System

The body's overall reaction to stress is regulated by the central nervous system. Recall from Chapter 3 that the nervous system consists of two parts, the *central nervous system* (the brain and the spinal cord) and the *peripheral nervous system.* The peripheral nervous system is divided into two major branches: the *autonomic nervous system* (ANS) and the *somatic nervous system.* Finally, the ANS is further divided into two branches: the *sympathetic nervous system* (SNS) and the *parasympathetic nervous system* (PNS).

When an external event is first perceived by your sense organs, sensory neurons in the somatic nervous system transmit nerve impulses to lower-level brain regions announcing the impending threat. The *reticular formation,* which runs like a rope through the middle of the brainstem, plays a central role in alerting the brain to an impending threat or challenge.

The reticular formation coordinates two neural pathways of brain–body communication. Through the first, it routes information about the existence of a potential stressor to the *thalamus,* which sorts this sensory information and relays it to the *hypothalamus,* the *limbic system,* and to higher brain regions in the cerebral cortex that interpret the meaning of the potential stressor. Through the second pathway, the reticular formation carries neural instructions back from the higher brain regions to the various target organs, muscles, and glands controlled by the SNS; as a result of these instructions, the body is mobilized for defensive action.

Under instructions from the SNS, the adrenal glands release hormones that cause the fight-or-flight response in which heart rate increases, the pupils dilate, stress hormones are secreted, and digestion slows. In addition, SNS activation increases blood flow to the muscles and causes stored energy to be converted to a form that is directly usable by the muscles. The region of the brain that most directly controls the stress response is the hypothalamus. Nearly every region of the brain interacts in some way with the hypothalamus. For this reason, the hypothalamus reacts to a variety of stimuli, from actual threats to memories of stressful moments to imagined stressors. The hypothalamus coordinates the activity of the endocrine system, and, as we will see, the endocrine system's hormones play a key role in how we respond to stress.

The Role of the Endocrine System: SAM and HPA Systems

As we saw in Chapter 3, the endocrine system is the body's relatively slow-acting communication system consisting of a network of glands that secrete hormones directly into the bloodstream. This communication system is involved in our stress responses in two key ways. First, under stress, the hypothalamus orders the pituitary gland to secrete *adrenocorticotrophic hormone (ACTH),* which is taken up by receptors in the *adrenal glands,* a pair of small endocrine glands lying just above the kidneys. Each of these remarkable structures consists of two nearly independent glands: a central region called the *adrenal medulla* and an outer covering called the *adrenal cortex.* When so ordered by the hypothalamus via the pituitary gland, the adrenal medulla secretes *epinephrine* (also called adrenaline) and *norepinephrine* (also called noradrenaline) into the blood. These endocrine reactions, which help trigger the fight-or-flight response, last much longer than those generated directly by the SNS. Taken together, the interaction of the SNS and adrenal medulla is called the **sympatho-adreno-medullary (SAM) system** (Figure 4.1 on p. 86).

The endocrine system is involved in stress in a second, equally important way. This second way involves the hypothalamus, the pituitary gland, and the adrenal cortex, or what has been called the **hypothalamic-pituitary-adrenocortical (HPA) system.** While the SAM system is the body's initial, rapid-acting response to stress, the HPA system is a delayed response that functions to restore the body to its baseline state, a process known as **homeostasis.** The HPA system is

Research conducted in the mid-1990s demonstrated that the bacterium *Helicobacter pylori*—not stress—is the major cause of most ulcers. Nevertheless, many people continue to believe stress causes ulcers. Even some physicians continue to recommend that their patients with ulcers take antacids rather than the recommended antibiotics.

■ **sympatho-adreno-medullary (SAM) system** the body's initial, rapid-acting response to stress, involving the release of epinephrine and norepinephrine from the adrenal medulla under the direction of the sympathetic nervous system.

■ **hypothalamic-pituitary-adrenocortical (HPA) system** the body's delayed response to stress, involving the secretion of corticosteroid hormones from the adrenal cortex.

■ **homeostasis** the tendency to maintain a balanced or constant internal state; the regulation of any aspect of body chemistry, such as the level of glucose in the blood, around a particular set point.

SAM and HPA: Hypothalamus secretes corticotrophin-releasing hormone (CRH).

SAM and HPA: CRH causes the pituitary gland to secrete adrenocorticotrophic hormone (ACTH).

SAM: ACTH causes the sympathetic ganglia to stimulate the adrenal medulla to release a mixture of epinephrine and norepinephrine that triggers the physiological fight-or-flight responses: increased heart rate, breathing, blood pressure, etc.

HPA: ACTH causes the adrenal cortex to secrete corticosteroids, including cortisol, that combat inflammation, promote healing, and mobilize the body's energy resources.

The Body's Response to Stress During a moment of stress, the hypothalamus secretes releasing factors that coordinate the endocrine responses of the pituitary and adrenal glands. As part of the sympathoadreno-medullary system (SAM), the adrenal medulla releases the stress hormones epinephrine and norepinephrine as the body's initial, rapid-acting response to stress. Epinephrine and norepinephrine increase heart rate, breathing, and blood pressure; slow digestion; and dilate the pupils. A second, delayed response involves the hypothalamic-pituitary-adrenocortical (HPA) system, which triggers secretion of corticosteroids from the adrenal cortex. These steroid hormones fight inflammation, promote healing, and trigger the release of stored reserves of energy.

activated by messages relayed from the central nervous system to the hypothalamus, which in turn secretes *corticotrophin-releasing hormone (CRH)*. CRH stimulates the production of *adrenocorticotrophic hormone (ACTH)* by the pituitary gland, which then activates the adrenal cortex to secrete **corticosteroids,** steroid hormones that reduce inflammation, promote healing, and help mobilize the body's energy resources.

Stressors are normally short-lasting events. Just as the hypothalamus initiates the stress response, it also shuts it down—normally before the body is damaged. The mechanism involves *cortisol,* a corticosteroid hormone that has a potent effect on all the body's tissues, including raising glucose levels in the blood, stimulating the breakdown of proteins into amino acids, and inhibiting the uptake of glucose by the body tissues but not by the brain. In a finely tuned *feedback* mechanism, cortisol acts back on the hippocampus, which has a high density of cortisol receptors and neurons that project to the hypothalamus, signalling the pituitary to suppress the further release of CRH and ACTH. As the amount of ACTH in the blood decreases, the adrenal cortex shuts down its production of cortisol.

The rate of cortisol secretion, which is remarkably sensitive to psychological factors, is so closely linked to stress that the level of this hormone circulating in the blood or saliva is frequently used by health psychologists as a physiological index of stress (Kirschbaum and others, 1998). For some people, even a seemingly ordinary event such as boarding an airplane can trigger a large increase in cortisol, which means, of course, that CRH has already been released from the hypothalamus and ACTH from the pituitary (Thompson, 2000).

All of these endocrine system actions help the organism deal with stress. Faced with a threat, the brain needs energy in the form of glucose, which cortisol helps provide. But too much cortisol can have negative consequences, leading to hypertension, a decrease in the body's ability to fight infection, and perhaps to psychological problems as well. When Robert Sapolsky studied wild-born vervet monkeys that farmers had trapped and caged in groups to protect their crops, he found that a number of the monkeys became sick and died, especially those that were caged with other monkeys that were especially aggressive. Autopsies of the monkeys showed high rates of bleeding ulcers, enlarged adrenal glands, and something else: pronounced damage to the hippocampal regions of their brains, perhaps as the result of prolonged high cortisol levels triggered by the prolonged stress (Sapolsky, 1997). Normally regulated by the hippocampus, cortisol levels can spiral upwards when, in response to unrelenting stress, more and more cortisol is secreted and the hippocampus is damaged, leaving it unable to signal the hypothalamus to shut off the stress response (Morgan and others, 2001). This condition of *hypercortisolism,* which also occurs in individuals with Alzheimer's disease (Greenwald and others, 1986), has been observed in patients suffering from major depressive disorder (Gold and others, 1988) and anorexia nervosa (Newman & Halmi, 1988), and it has been described as evidence of premature biological aging (Sapolsky, 1990). In a less well-understood phenomenon, in some individuals the HPA axis may become underactive in the face of chronic stress, creating a state of adrenal exhaustion and chronically low levels of cortisol (*hypocortisolism)* (Heim and others, 2000). Immune diseases such as fibromyalgia, rheumatoid arthritis, and asthma have all been associated with this state of blunted cortisol production (Kiecolt-Glaser and others, 2002).

■ **corticosteroids** hormones produced by the adrenal cortex that fight inflammation, promote healing, and trigger the release of stored energy.

How Does Stress Make You Sick?

Biomedical researchers who study mind–body connections in disease were once ostracized from the scientific community. Harvard University's Herbert Benson notes that when he began doing his research 30 years ago, he was told he was jeopardizing his medical career (Sternberg, 2000). Things began to change when two remarkable discoveries were made that would forever change the face of medicine. The first was an accident. Working in a laboratory at the University of Rochester, psychologist Robert Ader had been conducting a classic Pavlovian learning experiment, attempting to condition laboratory rats to avoid saccharin-flavored drinking water. The design of the study was simple. After the rats were given a drink of the artificially sweetened water (a neutral stimulus), they received an injection of a drug (unconditioned stimulus), which made them nauseous (unconditioned response)—sick enough so that a single pairing of the two stimuli should have been sufficient to establish a *conditioned aversion* to the water.

But Ader discovered a problem. Over the course of several weeks of training and testing, a number of the rats became very sick and died. Puzzled by this development, Ader found that the number of virus- and infection-fighting

Figure 4.2

Conditioning the Immune Response After Robert Ader and Nicholas Cohen paired saccharin-flavored water with an immune-suppressing drug, the taste of the sweetened water alone elicited a conditioned response (immune suppression) in laboratory rats.

T lymphocytes was significantly reduced in the bodies of the experimental animals. The nausea-inducing drug apparently had a more serious impact on the rats—it suppressed their immune responses (Figure 4.2).

What was most remarkable in Ader's experiment was that when these same rats were given saccharin-flavored water alone, without the drug, their immune systems responded as if the drug was actually circulating in their bloodstream. Classical conditioning had created a learned association between the taste of the water as a conditioned stimulus and the suppression of T cells as a conditioned response. Over time, conditioned responding made the animals increasingly susceptible to disease as their immune reserves were weakened with each drink of sweetened water.

Before Ader's study, most biomedical researchers believed that the mind and body were, for the most part, independent systems that had no influence on one another. So entrenched was this belief that Ader himself had difficulty accepting the results of his own research. Good science demands replication of findings, so Ader teamed up with immunologist Nicholas Cohen to see if his initial findings were a fluke. They were not. In a subsequent series of experiments, Ader and Cohen (1985) demonstrated that the immune system could be conditioned, just as Ivan Pavlov had demonstrated that the salivary response could be conditioned in hungry dogs.

The second key discovery that changed medicine was neuroscientist Candace Pert's demonstration that the brain has receptors for immune molecules that enable the brain to monitor, and therefore influence, the activity of the immune system (Pert, 2003). As an example of this communication network (see Figure 3.12 on page 74), consider that when antigens induce an immune response, cells in the hypothalamus become more active. This may occur when T cells that have been activated by antigens release proinflammatory cytokines. Recall from Chapter 3 that cytokines are protein molecules produced by immune cells that have a multitude of biological effects, including serving as a means of intercellular communication. These chemicals, which attract macrophages and stimulate phagocytosis at wound and infection sites, are similar in structure to neurotransmitters. Cytokines look enough like neurotransmitters to bind to receptor sites on brain cells and trigger nerve impulses. The apparent interchangeability between neurotransmitters and cytokines suggests that the immune system's lymphocytes may, in effect, act as circulating "language translators," converting information from their direct contact with pathogens into the language of the central nervous system so that the brain can monitor and regulate the immune response.

The work of Ader, Cohen, and Pert gave credibility to George Solomon's landmark article, published a decade earlier, in which he coined the term **psychoneuroimmunology (PNI),** referring to a "speculative theoretical integration" of the links among emotions, immunity, and disease (Solomon & Moos, 1964). This word describes a great deal about its focus: *psycho* for psychological processes, *neuro* for the neuroendocrine system (the nervous and hormonal systems), and *immunology* for the immune system. Focusing on three areas of functioning that at one time were believed to be relatively independent, PNI researchers investigate the ways in which behavior and emotions modulate immune function (Kiecolt-Glaser and others, 2002).

Since these watershed studies, the evidence for coordinated interactions among the brain, the neuroendocrine system, and the immune system has quickly mounted. Reduced immune functioning (*immunosuppression)* has been demonstrated following a divorce, bereavement, unemployment, and stressful bouts of exercise or military training; during exam periods; and when one is experiencing occupational stress. Among the changes observed are reduced numbers of natural killer cells, T cells, and total lymphocytes (Kiecolt-Glaser and others, 1994). And there seems to be a "dose–response" relationship between stress and immunosuppression. College students with the highest levels of overall life stress or the tendency to overreact to stressful events, for instance, show the greatest deficit in their immune response during exam weeks (Kiecolt-Glaser and others, 1984; Workman & La Via, 1987).

Stress is also linked to lowered immune resistance to viral infections (Solomon and others, 1997). For example, among a group of 276 students inoculated with common cold viruses, those who reported the most severe chronic stressors (1 month or longer) were most likely to develop colds (Cohen and others, 1998). Other studies demonstrate that both children and adults, when subjected to chronic stress, suffer more bouts of flu, herpes virus infections (cold sores and genital lesions), chicken pox, mononucleosis, and Epstein-Barr virus (Cohen & Herbert, 1996). Psychological stress has also been linked with an accelerated progression of coronary artery disease (Rozanski and others, 1999) and autoimmune disorders, such as arthritis and acquired immune deficiency syndrome (AIDS) (Rabin, 1999).

In addition, stress delays the healing of wounds (Cohen and others, 2001). In one study, dental students who received standardized punch biopsy wounds 3 days before a major test healed an average of 40 percent more slowly than those whose wounds were received during summer vacation (Marucha and others, 1998). In another study, 47 adults were given a standard questionnaire assessing psychological stress before undergoing hernia surgery. Patients who reported

■ **psychoneuroimmunology (PNI)** the field of research that emphasizes the interaction of psychological, neural, and immunological processes in stress and illness.

higher levels of preoperative stress had significantly slower rates of healing and reported a slower, more painful recovery (Broadbent and others, 2003).

Similar wounds in mice subjected to the stress of being held in a restraining harness healed more slowly than wounds placed in unstressed mice (Kiecolt-Glaser and others, 1998). In this study, the researchers also tested the hypothesis that the slower rate of wound healing reflected activation of the HPA system (Kiecolt-Glaser and others, 1998). This was done in two ways: by assessing serum corticosteroid levels, and by blocking the activity of naturally circulating stress hormones in restraint-stressed animals with a chemical that binds to corticosteroid receptor sites. In both cases, the results supported the hypothesis: Corticosteroid levels in the stressed mice were six times higher than in the unstressed mice. When their corticosteroid receptors were blocked, the stressed mice healed as well as control animals.

Pathways from Stress to Disease

How stress influences the immune system is the subject of a great deal of ongoing research. Two hypotheses have been suggested. According to the *direct effect hypothesis,* immunosuppression is part of the body's natural response to stress, for example, through the HPA and SAM systems you've been reading about. Alternatively, the *indirect effect* suggests that immunosuppression is an aftereffect of the stress response (Baum and others, 1987).

The Direct Effect Hypothesis Stress may directly affect immune efficiency through the activation of the HPA and SAM systems. T cells and B cells have receptors for corticosteroid "stress" hormones (which produce immunosuppression), and lymphocytes have catecholamine (epinephrine and norepinephrine) receptors. Stress activates these systems; the hormones released attach to the receptors of T cells, B cells, and lymphocytes, suppressing the immune response.

The Indirect Effect Hypothesis According to the indirect effect hypothesis, stress-induced delays in healing and other adverse health outcomes may occur because stress alters immune processes *indirectly* by encouraging maladaptive behaviors (Kiecolt-Glaser and others, 1998). Among the behavioral risk factors that could delay wound healing through their effects on the immune system are smoking, alcohol and drug abuse, fragmented sleep, less exercise, and poor nutrition, each of which has been associated with increased stress (Steptoe and others, 1996). Smoking, for instance, slows healing by weakening the normal proliferation of macrophages at wound sites and by reducing the flow of blood through vasoconstriction (Silverstein, 1992). In addition to healing more slowly, smokers are more likely to develop infections following surgical procedures, perhaps because nicotine and other toxins in cigarette smoke suppress both primary and secondary immune responses by reducing the activities of white blood cells.

As another example of how stress indirectly alters immune processes, consider that deep sleep is associated with the secretion of growth hormone (GH), which facilitates wound healing by activating macrophages to kill bacteria at the wound site (see Chapter 3). Loss of sleep, or fragmented sleep, results in reduced GH secretion and delayed healing (Leproult and others, 1997).

Duration of Stress

Acute stressors that last half an hour or less (as for example, in laboratory studies of stress) produce transient immune changes, with most immune cell parameters returning to pre-stress levels within an hour or so (Kiecolt-Glaser and others, 1992). Longer-lasting, but nevertheless acute stressors, such as stress associated with upcoming exams, also produce temporary changes in the cellular immune response. For example, a 10-year series of studies of medical students' responses to examinations demonstrated that stressed students' bodies mounted weaker antibody responses to hepatitis B vaccinations than during vacation periods (Glaser and others, 1992). The fact that a stressor as predictable, benign, and transient as an upcoming exam reliably produces immunosuppression suggests that other, everyday stressors probably do so as well.

The ability to recover after a stressful experience strongly influences the total burden that the experience has on an indivdual. The neuroendocrine system plays an important role in the concept of *allostatic load,* which refers to the cumulative long-term effects of the body's physiological response to stress (McEwen, 1998). Stressors that are unpredictable, uncontrollable, of longer duration, and difficult to cope with may continue to be accompanied by hypercortisolism, reduced sensitivity of lymphocytes to regulatory signals (Baum and others, 2000; Baum and others, 1993), and the overproduction of interleukin-6 and other proinflammatory cytokines (Dentino and others, 1999). These adverse neuroendocrine responses have been observed, for example, among prisoners of war (Dekaris and others, 1993), unemployed adults (Arnetz and others, 1991), and earthquake and hurricane survivors (Solomon and others, 1997). We will examine these and other sources of stress later in the chapter.

Stress, Inflammation, and Disease

Investigations of the direct and indirect effect hypotheses have given rise to an immunosuppression model of the relationships among stress, immunity, and disease, which nicely summarizes what we've discussed thus far. According to this model, stress suppresses the immune system, which leaves the individual vulnerable to opportunistic infection and disease (Miller and others, 2002) (Figure 4.3 on p. 92).

The immunosuppression model offers a plausible explanation for how stress influences wound healing, infectious diseases, and some forms of cancer (see Chapter 10). But it does not explain how stress might influence diseases whose central feature is excessive inflammation. These include many allergic, autoimmune, rheumatologic, neurologic, and cardiovascular diseases—all of which are exacerbated by stress (Rozanski and others, 1999). Parkinson's disease, for instance—a neurodegenerative disease that affects more than 1.5 million Americans—involves a loss of brain neurons that produce dopamine and serotonin. Victims of Parkinson's suffer muscular tremors, rigidity of movment, and a

Stress reduces immunity by:

(a) Activating autonomic nervous system fibers that descend from the brain to immune tissue.

(b) Triggering the secretion of hormones that bind to white blood cells and alter their functioning.

(c) Inducing immunosuppressive coping behaviors, such as poor diet and substance abuse.

Figure 4.3

Summary of the Physiology of Stress: Immunosuppression Model These conditions compromise the immune system's capacity to mount an effective response to infection or injury.

slow, 10- to 20-year deterioration in overall health. Inflammation accelerates the development of Parkinson's, which is why ibuprofen and other nonprescription anti-inflammatory drugs may lower the risk of developing the disease.

Following the immunosuppression model, it might be expected that stress would actually *improve* the course of such diseases by suppressing inflammation! This is unfortunately not the case, however, and emotional stress has been implicated as a major risk factor for Parkinson's (Agid and others, 2003). Robert Iacono, a pioneering Parkinson's researcher and neurologist, notes that most of his patients whose bodies become rigid—the worst form of the disease—suffered three or more major emotional crises a few years before the onset of their symptoms (Schwartz, 2004).

To account for the impact of stress on inflammatory diseases, researchers have proposed a *glucocorticoid-resistance model,* the basic premise of which is that chronic stress interferes with the immune system's sensitivity to glucocorticoid hormones such as cortisol, which normally terminate the inflammatory response. In a test of the model, Gregory Miller and his colleagues measured the perceived stress and immune responsiveness of 25 healthy parents of children undergoing active treatment for cancer, in comparison to 25 healthy parents of medically healthy children. Parents of cancer patients reported higher levels of psychological stress than parents of healthy children *and* were found to have diminished sensitivity to a synthetic glucocorticoid hormone, as revealed by higher levels of cytokine production. Remember that glucocorticoid hormones function as *anti-inflammatory* signals by suppressing the production of *proinflammatory cytokines* by immune cells. Parents of cancer patients showed significantly *less suppression* of cytokine production in response to an administered glucocorticoid compared with parents of healthy children (Miller and others, 2002). These findings are signficant because overproduction of cytokines has been linked with a spectrum of chronic inflammatory diseases and adverse conditions, including cardiovascular disease (discussed in Chapter 9), osteoporosis, arthritis, type 2 diabetes, Alzheimer's disease, periodontal disease, and age-related frailty (Kiecolt-Glaser and others, 2003).

To sum up, a growing body of psychoneuroimmunological research evidence demonstrates that the immune system does not work in isolation. Rather, it functions as part of a coordinated system involving the brain and the hormone-secreting endocrine system. The brain regulates the production of stress hormones, which in turn influence the body's immune defenses both directly and indirectly.

■ **general adaptation syndrome (GAS)** Selye's term for the body's reaction to stress, which consists of three stages: alarm, resistance, and exhaustion.

Other Major Models of Stress and Illness

The immune suppression and glucocorticoid resistance models of stress and illness developed from many years of research and from other important models, including Selye's general adaptation syndrome, the transactional model, and the diathesis-stress model. In addition, Shelley Taylor has proposed the influential tend-and-befriend theory. We will consider Selye's work first.

Selye's General Adapation Syndrome

Surely the most significant contribution to our understanding of stress and illness came from the research of Hans Selye, whom you met in the chapter opening story. Selye devised the concept of stress as a "nonspecific response of the body to any demand" (1974, p. 27). The body's reaction to stress was so predictable that Selye called it the **general adaptation syndrome (GAS).**

As Figure 4.4 shows, the GAS consists of three stages. Stage 1, the *alarm reaction,* is essentially the same as Cannon's *fight-or-flight* response, which we

Figure 4.4

The General Adaptation Syndrome Under stress, the body enters an alarm phase during which resistance to stress is temporarily suppressed. From this it rebounds to a phase of increased resistance to stress. The body's resistance can last only so long. In the face of prolonged stress, the stage of exhaustion may be reached. During this final stage, people become more vulnerable to a variety of health problems.

Figure 4.5

Stress-Induced Atrophy of Hippocampal Neurons These neuronal tracings (both oriented with dendrites on top) are from laboratory rats that were either subjected to 21 days of restraint stress (bottom), or not (top). Compared with the neuron from an unstressed control rat (top), the neuron from a chronically stressed rat shows reduced dendritic branching and decreased total dendritic length (bottom).

Source: Magarinos, J. E. and others. (1999). Repeated restrain stress facilitates fear conditioning independently of causing hippocampal CA3 dendritic atrophy. *Behavioral Neuroscience, 13,* 902–913.

considered earlier. The strength of the alarm reaction depends on the degree to which the event is perceived as a threat.

When a stressful situation persists, the body's reaction progresses to Stage 2, the *resistance stage.* In this stage, physiological arousal remains high (but not as high as during the alarm reaction) as the body tries to adapt to the emergency by replenishing adrenal hormones. At this time, there is a decrease in the individual's ability to cope with everyday events and hassles. At this stage, people often become irritable, impatient, and increasingly vulnerable to health problems.

If the stressful situation persists, and resistance is no longer possible, the body enters the final stage of the GAS—the *stage of exhaustion.* At this point, the body's energy reserves are depleted. Hypocortisolism (depletion of cortisol), for instance, is consistent with this final stage of the syndrome. If stress persists, disease and physical deterioration or even death may occur. For example, one result of exhaustion is increased susceptibility to what Selye referred to as *diseases of adaptation.* Among these are allergic reactions, hypertension, and common colds, as well as more serious illnesses caused by immune deficiencies.

Numerous studies have reinforced Selye's basic point: Prolonged stress exacts a toll on the body. People who have endured the prolonged stress of combat, child abuse, or a chronic disease may suffer enlarged adrenal glands, bleeding ulcers, damage to the brain's hippocampus, and abnormalities in several other cerebral areas. The hippocampus, which plays a crucial role in the formation and storage of new memories, is highly activated during the fight-or-flight response. In one study, laboratory rats were chronically stressed by being tightly held in wire mesh restrainers for 6 hours a day for 21 days (Conrad and others, 1999). Compared with unrestrained control rats, the restrained rats suffered significant atrophying of neurons in the hippocampi of their brains. As shown in Figure 4.5, both the number and length of branch points on the dendrites of these neurons were reduced—deficits that could have far-reaching neural and cognitive implications.

Atrophy of the human hippocampus is associated with recurrent clinical depression, post-traumatic stress disorder—which we will discuss shortly—and mild cognitive impairment in normal aging (Lupien and others, 1998). Although some memory loss occurs with age, stress may play an even more important role than simple aging. In one study, older people with low stress hormone levels tested as well as younger people on cognitive tests; those with higher stress levels tested between 20 and 50 percent lower (McEwen & Magarinos, 1997). If stress is chronic or extremely severe, memory loss due to hippocampal damage may become permanent. For instance, in one study, severely stressed Vietnam veterans and women who suffered from sexual abuse displayed up to 8 percent shrinkage in the hippocampus (Sapolsky, 1996). Severe stress may even break down the blood–brain barrier—the physiological mechanism that helps protect the brain from toxins, bacteria, and other potentially harmful substances that may be carried in the blood.

Selye's belief that all stressors produce the same physiological reactions has been revised in the face of more recent evidence. Newer research demonstrates that stress responses are more specific; that is, they are patterned according to the situations encountered and individual coping behaviors. In one of the earliest demonstrations of physiological specificity, John Mason (1975) found different patterns of epinephrine, norepinephrine, and corticosteroid secretion when stressors differed in their predictability. Some stressors led to increases in epinephrine, norepinephrine, and cortisol, whereas others increased only one or two of these stress hormones.

Selye's model has also been revised in the face of evidence that *how* potential stressors are appraised, or perceived, strongly influences their impact on the individual. In one classic study of the role of appraisal, Mason (1975) compared the adrenal responses of two groups of dying patients to a mild physical stressor (heat application). One group consisted of patients who remained in a coma until the moment of death; the other was made up of patients who remained conscious until the moment of death. Postmortem examination revealed that the conscious groups showed symptoms of stress in response to the heat applications, such as enlarged adrenal glands, whereas the coma patients displayed no such symptoms. Results such as these have demonstrated that stress requires the conscious appraisal of potential harm.

Stress as a Transaction

The most influential model describing the importance of conscious appraisal in stress is the **transactional model,** proposed by Richard Lazarus and his colleagues (Lazarus, 1993; Lazarus & Launier, 1978). The fundamental idea behind this model is that we cannot fully understand stress by examining environmental events (stimuli) and people's behaviors (responses) as separate entities; rather, we need to consider them together as a transaction, in which each person must continually adjust to daily challenges.

According to the transactional model, the *process* of stress is triggered whenever stressors exceed the personal and social resources a person is able to mobilize in order to cope. If a person's coping resources are strong enough, there may be no stress, even when—to another person—the situation seems unbearable. On the other hand, if a person's coping resources are weak or ineffective, stress occurs, even when—to another person—the demands of a situation can easily be met.

As shown in Figure 4.6, appraising an event as stressful means seeing it as a potential challenge, a source of harm, or as a threat to one's future well-being. A *challenge* is perceived when a situation is demanding but ultimately can be overcome, and the person can profit from the situation. Appraisals of harm–loss or threat refer to less positive outcomes. *Harm–loss* is the assessment that some form of damage has already occurred as a result of a situation. An event may be appraised as a *threat* when the person anticipates that a situation may bring about loss or harm at some point *in the future.*

When the demands of an event or situation do create stress, our response is not static but instead involves continuous interactions and adjustments—

■ **transactional model** Lazarus's theory that the experience of stress depends as much on the individual's cognitive appraisal of a potential stressor's impact as it does on the event or situation itself.

Potential Stressor (Sound of a car horn)

Primary Appraisal: Am I in Danger?
"Why is someone honking at me?"

Irrelevant: "The driver is honking at someone else."
Benign-Positive: "It's a friend, just saying hello."
Challenging, Harmful, or Threatening: "The driver in the next lane is warning me that my car is drifting out of my lane."

Secondary Appraisal: What Can I Do About It?
"Am I going to be able to steer out of this in time to avoid an accident?"

Behavioral and Cognitive Coping Responses
(Adjust steering to re-center car in lane.)

Reappraisal
"How am I doing? Is this situation under control?"

Figure 4.6

The Transactional Model of Stress The impact of a potential stressor, such as the startling sound of a honking horn, depends on a three-step process of cognitive appraisal. During primary appraisal, events perceived as neutral or benign pose no threat as a source of stress. Events perceived as challenging, harmful, or threatening are subjected to a secondary appraisal, during which the individual determines whether his or her coping resources are sufficient to meet the challenge posed by the stressor. Finally, in the reappraisal process, feedback from new information or ongoing coping efforts is used to check on the accuracy of both primary and secondary appraisals.

called *transactions*—between the environment and our attempts to cope. Each of us is an active agent who can dramatically alter the impact of a potential stressor through our own personal resources.

Lazarus believes that the transactions between people and their environments are driven by our *cognitive appraisal* of potential stressors. Cognitive appraisal involves assessing (1) whether a situation or event threatens our well-being, (2) whether there are sufficient personal resources available for coping with the demand, and (3) whether our strategy for dealing with the situation or event is working.

When we confront a potentially stressful event, such as an unexpected pop quiz, we engage in a **primary appraisal** to determine the event's meaning. In effect, we ask, "Is this situation going to mean trouble for me?" In the primary appraisal, we interpret an event in one of three ways: *irrelevant; benign-positive;* or challenging, harmful, or *threatening* (Figure 4.6).

Once an event has been appraised as a challenge or threat, **secondary appraisal** addresses the question, "What can I do to cope with this situation?" At this point, we assess our coping abilities to determine whether they will be adequate to meet the challenge, or avoid the potential harm, loss, or threat. If these resources are deemed adequate, little or no stress occurs. When a threat or challenge is high and coping resources are low, stress is likely to occur.

Finally, the transactional model emphasizes the ongoing nature of the appraisal process as new information becomes available. Through **cognitive reappraisal,** we constantly update our perception of success or failure in meeting a challenge or threat. New information may allow us to turn a previously stressful appraisal into a benign–positive one, as when we gain confidence in our ability to do well on an unexpected pop quiz after successfully answering the first few questions.

Cognitive reappraisal does not always result in less stress, however; sometimes it increases stress. An event originally appraised as benign or irrelevant can quickly take on a threatening character if a coping response fails or if we begin to see the event differently. For example, a job interview that seems to be going very well may become very stressful when the interviewer casually mentions the large number of well-qualified individuals who have applied for the position.

Lazarus' transactional model has three important implications. First, situations or events are not inherently stressful or unstressful; any given situation or event may be appraised (and experienced) as stressful by one person but not by another. Second, cognitive appraisals are extremely susceptible to changes in mood, health, and motivational state. You may interpret the same event or situation in very different ways on separate occasions. Being forced to wait in traffic may be a minor annoyance on most days; on the day when you are late for an exam, it may seem an insurmountable obstacle. Third, some evidence suggests that the body's stress response is nearly the same whether a situation is actually experienced or merely imagined. This means that even recalled or imagined appraisals of a situation may elicit a stress response.

The Diathesis-Stress Model

Knowing that the stress response varies with how a particular stressor is perceived has led researchers to propose several other models that highlight the interaction of biological and psychosocial factors in health and illness (Fowles, 1992; Levi, 1974). The **diathesis-stress model** proposes that two continuously interacting factors jointly determine an individual's susceptibility to stress and illness: *predisposing factors* that establish a person's genetic vulnerability and *precipitating factors* from the environment. In most cases, the precipitating environmental factors (stress) are not believed to be specific for a given health condition, whereas predisposing genetic factors (diathesis) are.

For instance, some individuals are more vulnerable to illness because their biological systems show greater **reactivity**—they react more strongly to specific environmental triggers. As one example, Jennifer McGrath (2003) recently found stable individual differences (diathesis) in children's blood pressure and heart rate during a stressful mirror-image tracing test. Interestingly, children who displayed the strongest cardiovascular reactivity were more likely to have a family history of hypertension and cardiovascular disease than less reactive children. Other studies have shown that cardiac reactivity to stress is linked to risk of heart attack and stroke. For example, researchers studied the responses of 901 Finnish men on a simple test of memory that was designed to elicit a mild state of mental stress. The men under age 55 who displayed the strongest blood-pressure reaction during the test also had the most severe blockages in their carotid arteries. The researchers speculate that, like cholesterol, over time blood-pressure reactions to stress may injure coronary vessels and promote coronary disease (Kamarck & Lichtenstein, 1998).

Post-Traumatic Stress Disorder (PTSD)

The diathesis-stress model highlights the fact that different people have different vulnerabilities, resulting in many possible health consequences due to stress combined with diathesis. An extreme case in point is **post-traumatic stress disorder (PTSD),** which historically was diagnosed when a person experienced an overwhelming event so fearful as to be considered *outside the range of normal human experience.* More recently, PTSD has been expanded to include "exposure to an extreme traumatic stressor involving direct personal experience of an event that involves actual or threatened death or serious injury" (APA, 1994, p. 424).

■ **primary appraisal** a person's initial determination of an event's meaning, whether irrelevant, benign-positive, or threatening.

■ **secondary appraisal** a person's determination of whether his or her own resources and abilities are sufficient to meet the demands of an event that is appraised as potentially threatening or challenging.

■ **cognitive reappraisal** the process by which potentially stressful events are constantly reevaluated.

■ **diathesis-stress model** the model that proposes that two interacting factors determine an individual's susceptibility to stress and illness: predisposing factors in the person (such as genetic vulnerability) and precipitating factors from the environment (such as traumatic experiences).

■ **reactivity** our physiological reaction to stress, which varies by individual and affects our vulnerability to illness.

■ **post-traumatic stress disorder (PTSD)** a psychological disorder triggered by exposure to an extreme traumatic stressor, such as combat or a natural disaster. Symptoms of PTSD include haunting memories and nightmares of the traumatic event, extreme mental distress, and unwanted flashbacks.

Although the traumatic event most often studied is military combat, researchers now also focus on physical attack; diagnosis of a life-threatening illness; or a catastrophic environmental event such as an earthquake, flood, or act of terrorism. Car accidents are the most frequent cause of trauma in men, and sexual assault is the most frequent source of trauma among women (Blanchard & Hickling, 1997). Children who live in violent neighborhoods or in one of the world's war zones may also show symptoms of PTSD (Garbarino, 1991).

PTSD symptoms include haunting memories and nightmares of the traumatic event, sleep disturbances, excessive guilt, impaired memory, and extreme mental and physical distress. Victims may also suffer flashbacks in which feelings and memories associated with the original event are reexperienced. Other complaints include muscle pains, sensitivity to chemicals and sunlight, and gastrointestinal problems. Those suffering from PTSD also show increased epinephrine, norepinephrine, testosterone, and thyroxin activity that lasts over an extended period of time, and they respond to audiovisual reminders of their trauma with elevated heart rate, blood pressure, and muscle tension (Gottlieb, 1996). In terms of glucocorticoid secretions, however, PTSD is often associated with hypocortisolism (unnaturally low levels of cortisol) (Yehuda, 2000).

Most combat-stress veterans, however, do not suffer from PTSD and are living successful lives. The prevalence of PTSD in the general population is estimated at about 1 percent (Helzer and others, 1987), compared with 20 percent of wounded Vietnam veterans and 35 percent of women who have been the victims of a life-threatening crime (Resnick and others, 1992). The rarity of the disorder has led some skeptics to argue that PTSD is a fad diagnosis (Young & Kane, 1995).

The concept of vulnerability, or diathesis, is important to keep in mind with PTSD (Burstein, 1985). Only a minority of persons exposed to traumatic events develop PTSD, and some people appear to develop clinical symptoms of PTSD following much less traumatic life events, such as marital separation. One of the most striking aspects of PTSD is the frequent simultaneous occurrence (comorbidity) of other psychological disorders, including substance abuse problems, major depressive disorder, panic disorder, generalized anxiety disorder, and personality disorder (Keane & Wolfe, 1990; Kessler and others, 1999). In fact, PTSD patients are twice as likely to meet the diagnostic critera for another major psychological disorder as non-PTSD patients (Helzer and others, 1987).

Biological and familial risk factors have also been implicated in the disorder. For instance, there is a higher prevalence of PTSD among adult children of family members who themselves have PTSD than among children in families without a history of the disorder, even though these adult children, as a group, do not report a greater exposure to traumatic events (Yehuda, 1999). It is difficult to know, of course, to what extent this is due to biological, genetic, or experiential phenomena, because of the large degree of shared environment in families.

Several ongoing studies are expected to shed light on the origins, treatment, and prevention of PTSD. The largest study, which so far has evaluated more than 10,000 veterans of the Gulf War, was started by the U.S. Department of Defense in 1994. Among the findings of this study are these:

- Individuals who develop the symptoms of PTSD are also more vulnerable to other emotional disorders.

- People who feel a lack of social support are more likely to develop symptoms of PTSD, as are soldiers who score lower on *personal hardiness,* a measure of how people cope with stress and adversity (more on this in Chapter 5).

- Soldiers who develop PTSD tend to display more avoidance, wishful thinking, and self-blame than other soldiers. In remembering their childhood, they also believe their families were less cohesive and communicative than others were.

- Female soldiers who reported experiencing harassment or sexual assault report higher-than-average symptoms of PTSD.

- Combat veterans with PTSD symptoms have lower pre- and post-combat scores on standardized intelligence tests, as well as fewer years of total education than other veterans. Researchers do not believe that PTSD lowers intelligence scores, nor do they believe that lower intelligence causes PTSD. Researchers suspect that individuals who have more cognitive resources may be better equipped to cope with combat stress.

Tend-and-Befriend Theory

Although fight-or-flight characterizes the primary physiological response to stress in both females and males, Shelley Taylor and her colleagues have recently proposed that females are more likely than males to respond to the same stressors with *tend-and-befriend* behaviors that: (a) quiet, nurture, and care for offspring in order to protect them from harm (tending), and (b) establish and maintain social networks that facilitate this process (befriending). Physiologically, the tend-and-befriend pattern appears to involve the blunting of SNS responses geared toward aggressing or fleeing by the hormone *oxytocin.* Humans and other animals with high levels of oxytocin exhibit calmer, more social, and more maternal behaviors. Taylor's research suggests that this oxytocin response is more adaptive for females in promoting their own survival, along with that of their offspring (Taylor and others, 2000). Research studies involving both human and nonhuman primates provide support for this hypothesis. In stressful situations, females, compared with males, demonstrate a strong preference to affiliate and mobilize social support, especially from other females (Bell, 1987).

In summary, the six major models of stress and illness that we've discussed have helped us understand several key points.

1. Prolonged stress has harmful effects in the body (*GAS syndrome*).
2. Stress suppresses the immune system, leaving the individual vulnerable to opportunistic infection and disease (*immunosuppression model*).

3. Stress interferes with the immune system's sensitivity to the glucocorticoid hormones that normally help control inflammation, which helps explain the role of stress in disorders such as asthma and arthritis (*glucocorticoid resistance model*).

4. Our cognitive appraisal of challenges determines whether we experience stress. We constantly interact with and adapt to our environment (*transactional model*).

5. Both genetic and environmental factors affect our susceptibility to stress and illness (*diathesis-stress model*).

6. Women and men respond somewhat differently to stressors, with women displaying more behaviors associated with caring for others and relationship building (*tend-and-befriend theory*).

Remember our biopsychosocial approach to this chapter? Well, now you should have a good understanding of the *biology* of stress and also some models that have been used to understand the biological and *psychological* factors involved in the relationship between stress and illness. Next, we'll consider some *psychological* and *social-cultural* sources of stress in our lives.

Psychosocial Sources of Stress

Everyone experiences stress. How and why we experience stress may change as we journey through life, but none of us escapes. Each of us experiences the events of life in a unique way. What you find stressful, your roommate may not. Similarly, some of the leisure activities that you find relaxing may be too stressful for others. Research has focused on several sources of stress: major life events, daily hassles, environmental factors, catastrophes, work, and sociocultural factors. Remember from the transactional model of stress that it is not the event alone but our appraisal of the event that leads us to experience stress.

Major Life Events

Stress may also take a toll on the unborn. Women who reported high levels of stress on a life events scale were more likely to experience a spontaneous abortion (miscarriage) at 11 weeks or later (Boyles and others, 2000).

What impact do major life events, such as changing jobs, having a child, or losing a loved one, have on the quality of our health? In the late 1950s, psychiatrists Thomas Holmes and Richard Rahe of the University of Washington substantially advanced our understanding of how the events of our lives affect our health. They interviewed more than 5,000 people to identify which events forced people to make the most changes in their lives. Then they assigned each event a value in *life change units (LCUs)* to reflect the amount of change that was necessary. For example, a divorce disrupts many more aspects of one's life than does taking a vacation, and thus it would be assigned a larger number of LCUs. The events Holmes and Rahe investigated covered a wide range, even including occasions that called for celebration, such as marriage or a promotion. They then ranked these events and devised the *Social Readjustment Rating Scale*

Table 4.1

The College Undergraduate Stress Scale

Copy the "stress" rating number into the last column for any item that has happened to you in the last year, then add the numbers.

Event	Stress Ratings	Your Items	Event	Stress Ratings	Your Items
Being raped	100		Lack of sleep	69	
Finding out that you are HIV-positive	100		Change in housing situation (hassles, moves)	69	
Being accused of rape	98				
Death of a close friend	97		Competing or performing in public	69	
Death of a close family member	96		Getting in a physical fight	66	
Contracting a sexually transmitted disease (other than AIDS)	94		Difficulties with a roommate	66	
			Job changes (applying, new job, work hassles)	69	
Concerns about being pregnant	91				
Finals week	90		Declaring a major or concerns about future plans	65	
Concerns about your partner being pregnant	90				
			A class you hate	62	
Oversleeping for an exam	89		Drinking or use of drugs	61	
Flunking a class	89		Confrontations with professors	60	
Having a boyfriend or girlfriend cheat on you	85		Starting a new semester	58	
			Going on a first date	57	
Ending a steady dating relationship	85		Registration	55	
Serious illness in a close friend or family member	85		Maintaining a steady dating relationship	55	
			Commuting to campus or work, or both	54	
Financial difficulties	84		Peer pressures	53	
Writing a major term paper	83		Being away from home for the first time	53	
Being caught cheating on a test	83		Getting sick	52	
Drunk driving	82		Concerns about your appearance	52	
Sense of overload in school or work	85		Getting straight A's	51	
Two exams in one day	80		A difficult class that you love	48	
Cheating on your boyfriend or girlfriend	77		Making new friends; getting along with friends	47	
Getting married	76				
Negative consequences of drinking or drug use	75		Fraternity or sorority rush	47	
			Falling asleep in class	40	
Depression or crisis in your best friend	73		Attending an athletic event (e.g., football game)	20	
Difficulties with parents	73				
Talking in front of a class	72		Total		

Note: Of 12,000 U.S. college students who completed this scale, scores ranged from 182 to 2,571, with a mean score of 1,247. Women reported significantly higher scores than men, perhaps because most of the students used in pretesting items were women. This being the case, items that are stressful for women may be overrepresented in the scale.

Source: Renner, M. J., & Mackin, R. S. (1998). A life stress instrument for classroom use. *Teaching of Psychology, 25*, 47.

(SRRS), which was the first systematic attempt to quantify the impact of life changes on health. Table 4.1 is the College Undergraduate Stress Scale, which is a variation of the original SRRS directed specifically at college students.

Holmes and Rahe theorized that the total number of LCUs a person had accumulated during the previous year could predict the likelihood that he or she would become sick over the next several months. In one study (Rahe and others, 1970), researchers obtained SRRS scores on naval crewmen who were about to depart on a 6-month cruise. Over the course of the voyage, the researchers found a positive correlation between life change units and illness rates. Those sailors who reported the highest LCUs were more likely to fall ill than those who reported the lowest LCUs. The message: When life brings many changes at once, the stress that results may make us more vulnerable to health problems.

Although the research of Holmes and Rahe was groundbreaking and influential, the value of the scale for predicting stress and illness has been criticized for several reasons (Monroe & Simons, 1991):

- Many of the items on the SRRS are vague and open to subjective interpretation. "Change in living conditions" or "revision of personal habits," for example, can mean almost anything.

- Assigning specific point values to events fails to take into consideration individual differences in the way events are appraised (and therefore experienced). A divorce, for example, may mean welcome freedom for one person but a crushing loss to another.

- The SRRS lumps all events together—whether positive, negative, chance, or willfully chosen. Many studies have found that unexpected or uncontrollable negative events, such as the premature death of a family member, are much more stressful than are events that are positive, expected, or under one's control, such as changing to a different line of work or taking a vacation (Bandura and others, 1988).

- The SRRS does not differentiate between resolved and unresolved stressful events. There is evidence that stressors that have been successfully resolved have substantially weaker adverse effects on the person's health than events that linger unresolved (Turner & Asvison, 1992).

One measure of a good theory, however, is that it generates research that leads to new understanding, even if it also leads to its own demise. If nothing else, the tremendous number of studies conducted using the SRRS have revealed that there is no simple, direct connection between life stress and illness: Subjected to the same stressors, one person will get sick while another will not. The health consequences of stress depend upon our appraisal of the stressors.

Research has found that college students who were perfectionists were more likely than other students to react to stressful life events with symptoms of depression (Flett and others, 1995).

Catastrophes

On March 28, 1979, the worst commercial nuclear accident in the history of the United States happened at Three Mile Island, a nuclear power plant in Middletown, Pennsylvania. A pump in the reactor cooling system failed, causing an increase in pressure and temperature. For 2 hours, a stuck valve allowed contaminated radioactive water that had cooled the reactor's core to evaporate into the atmosphere. Shortly after the incident, Andrew Baum and his colleagues began one of the first systematic health psychology studies of toxic pollution.

For more than a year after the accident, residents faced a chronically high level of stress, fearing that they had been exposed to radiation (Baum & Fleming, 1993). This fear manifested itself in excessively high blood pressure as well as elevated levels of cortisol, epinephrine, and norepinephrine. Responses to the Three Mile Island incident were not unique. Researchers have uncovered a number of similar responses in situations involving both human error and natural phenomena. For example:

■ The results of a mental health survey conducted after the 9/11/2001 terrorist attacks reported that 40 percent of 4,739 Pentagon staff were at high risk for post-traumatic stress disorder, panic attacks, depression, generalized anxiety, or alcohol abuse (Jordan and others, 2004). Another study reported statistically signficant increases in blood pressure among four large samples of patients hospitalized in Chicago, Washington, DC, Mississippi, and New York at the time of the 9/11 attacks (Chaplin and others, 2003). Elevated blood pressure persisted for 2 months following 9/11. There were no differences in BP in the months preceding and following 9/11/2000—the same period of time, one year earlier.

■ Hypertension, heart disease, and other stress-related ailments tripled in the Republic of Belarus during the stressful aftermath of the world's worst nuclear accident—the Chernobyl nuclear disaster in April 1986 (Nuclear Energy Agency, 1995).

■ Psychologists have observed sharp increases in anxiety, acute stress disorder, post-traumatic stress disorder, depression, and panic attacks among Palestinians living on the Gaza Strip since the al-Aqsa Intifada (uprising) began on September 28, 2000. Among children living on the Gaza Strip, there has been a dramatic surge in bedwetting, nightmares, and behavioral disorders (Crawford, 2002).

Health psychologists continue to learn by monitoring the physiological and psychological effects of such disasters.

Daily Hassles

Major life changes and catastrophes occur infrequently; everyday hassles happen all the time and thus are the most significant sources of stress. These minor annoyances range from missing a commuter train to work, not having the required answer booklet for an exam, or losing a wallet to arguing with a professor or living with an aggravating roommate.

Richard Lazarus (remember his transactional model of stress?) believes that the impact on health of such hassles depends on their frequency, duration, and intensity. In addition, our reactions to minor hassles are influenced by our personality, our individual style of coping, and how the rest of our day has gone.

The counterpart to daily hassles is daily *uplifts:* mood-lifting experiences such as receiving an approving nod from the boss, hearing your favorite song at just the right moment, or even getting a good night's sleep. Just as hassles may cause physical and emotional stress that may result in illness, uplifts may serve as buffers against the effects of stress.

Lazarus and his colleagues devised a scale to measure people's experiences with day-to-day annoyances and uplifts (Kanner and others, 1981). The *Hassles and Uplifts Scale* consists of 117 events that range from small pleasures to major problems. In one study, middle-aged adults completed the scale over a 9-month period while the researchers simultaneously tracked their psychological symptoms, such as anxiety and depression (Kanner and others, 1981). Along with these measures, the participants recorded the occurrence of any potentially stressful major life events, such as those included in the SRRS. Table 4.2 shows the 10 most frequent hassles and uplifts as reported by this sample of adults, together with the percentage of time each event was checked.

How well do our hassles and uplifts predict our overall psychological well-being? Hassles seem to be a better predictor of health problems than either major life events or the frequency of daily uplifts. This finding has been confirmed many times. Everyday hassles or mundane irritants and stressors negatively affect physical and mental health to a degree that exceeds the adverse consequences of major life events (Burks & Martin, 1985; Eckenrode, 1984; Weinberger and others, 1987).

Critics have argued, however, that some of the items listed as hassles may actually be *symptoms of stress* rather than stressors. Items relating to appearance, for example, may tap lowered self-esteem that *results from* rather than contributes to stress (Dohrenwend & Shrout, 1985). In addition, some items refer to alcohol and drug use, sexual difficulties, physical illness, and personal fears—all possible consequences of stress.

Table 4.2

Common Hassles and Uplifts

Hassles	Percentage of Times Checked Over 9 Months	Uplifts	Percentage of Times Checked Over 9 Months
1. Concern about weight	52.4	1. Relating well with your spouse or lover	76.3
2. Health of family member	48.1	2. Relating well with friends	74.4
3. Rising prices of common goods	43.7	3. Completing a task	73.3
4. Home maintenance	42.8	4. Feeling healthy	72.7
5. Too many things to do	38.6	5. Getting enough sleep	69.7
6. Misplacing or losing things	38.1	6. Eating out	68.4
7. Yardwork or outside home maintenance	38.1	7. Meeting responsibilities	68.1
8. Property, investment, or taxes	37.6	8. Visiting, phoning, or writing someone	67.7
9. Crime	37.1	9. Spending time with family	66.7
10. Physical appearance	35.9	10. Home pleasing to you	65.5

Source: Adapted from "Comparison of Two Modes of Stress Management: Daily Hassles and Uplifts versus Major Life Events," by A. D. Kanner, C. Coyne, C. Schaefer, and R. S. Lazarus, 1981, *Journal of Behavioral Medicine, 4*, p. 14.

In addition, other researchers have suggested that individuals who are high in anxiety to begin with will find daily hassles more stressful (Kohn and others, 1991). Paul Kohn and his colleagues found that having an anxious personality triggered stress as often as did daily hassles. This suggests that an overly anxious person may overreact to daily hassles in a way that magnifies their impact. Consistent with the diathesis-stress model, those who are predisposed not to overreact may be less vulnerable to the physical and psychological impact of daily hassles.

Daily hassles also have been demonstrated to interact with *background stressors,* such as job dissatisfaction (Frankenhaeuser & Gardell, 1976), commuting (Singer and others, 1978), and crowded living conditions (Harburg and others, 1973). A dramatic illustration of this interaction is the skyrocketing rates of divorce, murder, suicide, and stress-related diseases that occurred in Russia during the 4 years that immediately followed the breakup of the former Soviet Union (Holden, 1996). It is suspected that persistent social and economic background stress during this difficult period caused many people to overreact to everyday stressors that they would normally have shrugged off. Remarkably, during this same period of time, life expectancy for Russian men fell from about 64 years to 59 years.

Environmental Stress

Crowded subways, noisy street corners, and pollution are daily facts of life for many of us. Unless we are able to escape by moving to a remote part of the world, these largely uncontrollable potential stressors are likely to affect us for many years. Over time, do these environmental stressors take a toll on our health and well-being? Let's see.

Noise

As a student in New York City, I lived with no air conditioning for 2 years in a fifth-floor apartment with an elevated subway train track less than 100 feet from my window. With the window open in the summer, a train rumbling by literally shook the building, and I had to shout to be heard by a friend sitting in the same room. Still, the rent-controlled apartment was all I could afford, and I inadvertently became a case study of the physical and psychological impact of chronic noise.

Using both field studies and laboratory studies, health psychologists have uncovered a number of negative health consequences of long-term living in noisy environments. In one study, children around airports in Munich, Germany, compared with a control group, were found to have higher systolic and diastolic blood pressure levels and elevated levels of cortisol and other stress hormones (Evans and others, 1995).

Animal studies also confirm the damaging effects of chronic noise. The blood pressure of rhesus monkeys exposed to loud noise for 9 months was elevated by one-third, and it persisted more than 1 month after the cessation of noise. Thus, chronic exposure to high intensity noise may increase the risk of cardiovascular problems (Hygge, 1997).

Researchers have also focused on the impact of chronic noise on academic performance. In the Evans study cited earlier, the motivation, long-term memory, and reading and word skills of the children living near noisy airports were impaired. Similarly, Sheldon Cohen, David Glass, and Jerome Singer (1973) found that children who lived in noisy apartments had greater difficulty detecting subtle differences in sounds and had more reading problems than did children who lived in quieter apartments. The longer the children had lived in their present apartment, the greater the discrepancy. Another study found that children attending school in classrooms facing noisy railroad tracks had lower reading scores than did children attending classes in rooms on the quieter side of the building (Bronzaft & McCarthy, 1975).

Just as I did in my noisy apartment, most people attempt to cope with chronic noise by tuning out extraneous sounds and focusing their attention only on relevant cues (such as the voice of a person to whom you are talking). Because they are young, however, children are less likely than adults to be able to differentiate appropriate and inappropriate cues. This may explain why chronic noise is more disruptive to children. Children may have more difficulty with verbal skills because they are more likely to "tune out" verbal elements (along with other noise) in their environment. To test this idea, health psychologists have also investigated the impact of noise on health in the more controlled setting of the laboratory. In such studies, researchers have demonstrated that fairly high levels of noise (80 to 90 decibels in random bursts) disrupt our short-term memory and our ability to attend to even simple cognitive tasks (Hygge, 1997).

Noise alone doesn't necessarily cause stress. The individual's cognitive appraisal plays an important role, as demonstrated by a study of people living on a busy street who were asked about their overall health, sleep, anxiety level, and attitude toward their noisy environment (Nivision & Endresen, 1993). Although noise levels were not significantly correlated with poor health, loss of sleep, or increased anxiety, the residents' subjective attitudes toward noise were strongly linked to the number of their health complaints.

A key factor in how a person appraises noise is the potential he or she has for controlling the noise level. In one study, David Glass and Jerome Singer (1972) demonstrated that college students who were given the possibility of controlling a loud, distracting noise reported less stress than students who had no opportunity to control the noise. This may explain why "self-administered" noise—such as that experienced at rock concerts—is generally appraised as benign, even enjoyable.

Crowding

In a classic study of the effects of crowding on the behavior of animals, John Calhoun (1970) provided ideal living conditions to a group of rats, allowing them to eat, drink, and reproduce freely. When living space was plentiful, the rats behaved normally, forming stable social groups, mating successfully, and rearing their offspring to healthy maturity.

As the population increased, however, the former "good citizenship" of rats began to deteriorate. Frequent fights broke out, as male rats began to stake out and attempt to defend a more crowded territory. In addition, infant mortality increased sharply, the sexual receptivity of females declined, and some rats became cannibalistic.

What about crowding among humans? In yet another example of the importance of cognitive appraisal in the process of stress, some researchers say that we need to make a distinction between crowding and **population density,** which refers to the number of people living in a given area. Crowding is a *psychological* state in which people *believe* they do not have enough space to function as they wish.

Density is necessary to produce crowding, but crowding is not an inevitable consequence of density. Being in a crush of people during a New Year's Eve celebration, for example, may not be perceived as crowding, despite the extreme population density. Conversely, the presence of one other family of campers in a wilderness campground may represent an intolerable crowd to a vacationer seeking solitude.

Crowding has been linked to increased aggression, withdrawal from interpersonal relations, and increased crime rates (Sundstrom, 1978). Crowding also increases unwanted social interactions, a condition that often triggers social withdrawal as a means of coping. In studies of prison inmates, for example, rates of psychiatric commitments and death were higher in years when the prison population was higher. Inmates who live under dense conditions also have higher blood pressure and stress hormone levels (Freedman, 1975).

Other studies have demonstrated that the design of residential space can have far-ranging effects on physical health and subjective well-being. Studies of student housing, for example, reveal that suite-type clusters of dormitory rooms are preferred over the more traditional arrangement of rooms branching off of long corridors. Residents of corridor rooms feel more crowded, report lower feelings of control, are more competitive, and react more negatively to minor annoyances.

Environmental stress is a fact of life. Noise and crowding may cause us to feel anxious and irritable and leave us more vulnerable to physical disorders. For some of us, these reactions, and the stressors that trigger them, come to a point of sharp focus in the workplace.

■ **population density** a measure of crowding based on the total number of people living in an area of limited size.

Work

In recent years, an extensive amount of research has been devoted to examining the causes and consequences of job-related stress. These studies are important for two reasons. First, almost all people at some time experience stress related to their work. Second, work-related stress may be one of the most preventable health hazards and thereby provides a number of possibilities for intervention.

For most of us, job stress is brief in duration and does not pose a serious threat to our health. For some people, however, job stress may be chronic, continuing for years. As the following job-stress findings reveal, more workers today than in the past report high levels of stress (Miller, Smith, Turner, Guijarro, & Hallet, 1997).

■ The Occupational Safety and Health Administration has declared stress a hazard of the workplace. Among federal government workers, for instance, compensation claims for "emotional illness" increased more than 400 percent between 1981 and 1990.

■ Stress costs American industry more than $300 billion annually, or $7500 per worker per year, due to absenteeism, reduced productivity, and workers' compensation benefits.

■ People who handle money on the job, those who work at night, and/or those who work in the inner city are most likely to report stress from fears of being killed on the job.

Let's take a look at some other factors that can make certain jobs more stressful than others.

Overload

One source of occupational stress is *work overload*. People who feel they have to work too long and too hard at too many tasks feel more stressed (Caplan & Jones, 1975). They also have poorer health habits (Sorensen, 1985), experience more accidents (Quick & Quick, 1984), and suffer more health problems than do other workers (Repetti, 1993).

A related form of work stress occurs when people attempt to balance several different jobs at the same time and experience *role overload*.

The problems associated with juggling multiple roles simultaneously have been particularly great for women. Research on the question of whether having a job as well as a home and family enhances or threatens a woman's health is sparse and contradictory, however (Bonebright and others, 2000). Studies have supported two competing hypotheses. One, the *scarcity hypothesis*, maintains that because they have only so much time and energy, women with competing demands suffer from role overload and conflict. The other, the *enhancement hypothesis*, argues that the benefits of meaningful work in enhancing a worker's self-esteem outweigh the costs.

To study this issue further, Ulf Lundberg of the University of Stockholm developed a "total workload scale" to quantify the number of competing demands in women's lives (Lundberg and others, 1994). Using this scale, Lundberg found that age and occupational level don't make much difference in women's total workload. The presence of children, however, makes a huge difference. In families without children, men and women each average 60 hours of work a week. In a family with three or more children, women average 90

Job-Related Stress Japan is notorious for its long work hours and lack of vacation time. Workers begin their stress-filled days with stress-filled subway rides. The number of people crowding into the subway became so dangerous that the system had to hire people to manage the overloads. Work has become such a deeply entrenched ethic in Japanese culture that they have created a term, *karoshi,* to describe death that results from work overload. Under Japanese law, bereaved family members may be entitled to special financial compensation if they are able to prove that the cause of their family member's death was *karoshi.*

Paul Chesley/Stone

hours a week in paid and unpaid work, while men still average only 60. "Women's stress is determined by the interaction of conditions at home and work," notes Lundberg, "whereas men's stress is determined more by situations at work."

In another study of psychological and physiological responses related to work and family, Lundberg and Marianne Frankenhaeuser (1999) investigated female and male managers in high-ranking positions. While both women and men experienced their jobs as challenging and stimulating, women were more stressed by their greater unpaid workload and by a greater responsibility for duties related to home and family. Physiologically, women had higher norepinephrine levels than men did, both during and after work, which reflected their greater workload. Women with children at home had significantly higher norepinephrine levels after work than did the other participants.

Although findings such as Lundberg's seem to support the scarcity hypothesis, other researchers have found that employed women are generally healthier than unemployed women (LaCroix & Haynes, 1987). Moreover, for many working mothers, employment is an important source of self-esteem and life satisfaction. Indeed, researchers have found that those adults—both men and women—who *balance* vocational, marital, and parental roles generally are healthier and happier than adults who function in only one or two of these roles (Hochschild, 1997; Milkie & Peltola, 1999).

From research studies such as these, researchers have concluded that what matters most is not the number of roles a woman occupies, but the quality of her experience in those roles (Baruch & Barnett, 1986). Having control over one's work, a good income, adequate child care, and a supportive family combine to help reduce the likelihood that multiple role demands will be stressful. Similarly, although people often complain that working long hours creates stress, researchers consistently find that stress symptoms, sick days, and overall life satisfaction are more likely to be influenced by other workplace characteristics, such as job autonomy, learning opportunities, supportive supervisors, and scheduling flexibility (Schwartz, 2003).

Burnout

Burnout has been defined as a job-related state of physical and psychological exhaustion that can occur among individuals who work with other people in some capacity. Jobs that involve responsibility for other people, rather than responsibility for products, appear to cause high levels of burnout (Sears and others, 2000). Health care workers, dentists, paramedics, air traffic controllers, and fire fighters are especially susceptible to this type of job stress. One study demonstrated that one-third of nurses report stress-related symptoms that are severe enough to be considered a warning sign of psychiatric problems (Tyler & Cushway, 1992). Although burnout customarily develops over a period of years, its warning signs may appear early on. These signs include feelings of mental and physical exhaustion; hypocortisolism; an increase in stress-related ailments, such as headaches, backaches, and depression; and shortness of temper (Lerman and others, 1999; Pruessner and others, 1999).

Kathleen Finlay/Masterfile

Role Overload The task of managing multiple roles affects both men and women, but the increase in employment of women has triggered more research on role overload and job-related stress in women. Some research findings regarding the stress of role overload have been contradictory; however, the overall conclusion seems to be that what matters most is the quality of a working mother's experiences in her various roles.

■ **burnout** a job-related state of physical and psychological exhaustion.

© Jim Mahoney/The Image Works

Burnout Firefighters have stressful jobs, partly because of their responsibility for others' lives, which makes them highly susceptible to burnout.

Burnout is not, however, an inevitable consequence of employment in certain professions. As the biopsychosocial model reminds us, susceptibility to most health conditions is the product of overlapping factors in every domain of health. For instance, nurses who maintain a hopeful, optimistic view of life are much less likely to experience burnout than their more pessimistic counterparts on chronic care wards, thereby highlighting the protective function of certain personality styles (Sherwin and others, 1992).

Control: Too Little or Too Much

Workers feel more stress when they have little or no control over the procedures, pace, and other aspects of their jobs (Steptoe and others, 1993). The relationship between lack of control and illness was clearly revealed in Marianne Frankenhaeuser's (1975) classic study of Scandinavian sawmill workers. Compared with workers who had more say over aspects of their jobs, those working at dull, repetitive, low-control jobs had significantly higher levels of stress hormones, higher blood pressure, more headaches, and more gastrointestinal disorders, including ulcers.

Other studies have consistently confirmed the relationship between perceived control and work-related stress. A study of British civil servants, for example, found that workers in lower-grade, low-control occupations had poorer health, even after adjustments were made for smoking, diet, and exercise (Hewison & Dowswell, 1994).

Secretaries, waitresses, factory workers, and middle managers are among those with the most stressful occupations marked by repetitive tasks and little control over events. Common to these jobs are complaints of too many demands with too little authority to influence work practices. The sense of powerlessness that results often creates crushing stress (Daniels, 2006). Control issues contribute to the experience of stress among others in our society who have felt powerless, including the impoverished, immigrants, and women. (See Diversity and Healthy Living box on p. 112.)

The Paradox of Choice Psychologist Barry Schwartz (2004) has recently argued that too much choice, in the workplace and elsewhere, may also be detrimental to our well-being. Many workers today face more choices than ever before. The telecommunications revolution, for instance, has dramatically increased flexibility in where and when many people work. E-mail, laptop computers, and cell phones mean that for many of us there are no obstacles to prevent us from working all the time. As another example, people switch jobs today far more often than workers in previous generations. By 30 years of age, the average American has already worked at nine different jobs. And each year an estimated 17 million Americans *voluntarily* switch jobs in hopes of advancement (Clark, 1999). Schwartz believes that as the number of choices people are confronted with in their lives spirals upward, a point is eventually reached at which choice no longer liberates but begins to debilitate.

Other Sources of Job-Related Stress

Several other aspects of jobs increase stress among workers, including these:

- *Role ambiguity or conflict.* Role ambiguity occurs when workers are unsure of their jobs or the standards used to evaluate their performance. Role conflict occurs when a worker receives mixed messages about these issues from different supervisors or coworkers.

- *Shiftwork.* Shiftwork involves continuous staffing of a workplace by groups of employees who work at different times. Shiftworkers face disruption to their family and domestic lives, as well as to their *biological rhythms.* Most human functions have a rhythm with peaks and valleys that occur over a regular 24- to 25-hour cycle. Shiftwork desynchronizes these rhythms and may lead to a number of health complaints, including headaches, loss of appetite, fatigue, sleep disturbances, gastrointestinal problems, and heart disease (Taylor, 1997; Waterhouse, 1993).

- *Job loss.* Downsizing, layoffs, mergers, and bankruptcies cost thousands of workers their jobs each year. The loss of a job can have a serious impact on a worker's well-being, putting unemployed workers at risk for physical illness, anxiety, depression, and even suicide (Vinokur and others, 2000). Job insecurity and the threat of unemployment have been linked to higher levels of several health-compromising risk factors. One study reported higher blood pressure and serum cholesterol levels among Michigan autoworkers who faced the closing of their factory (Kasl, 1997). Other studies have reported increased smoking, alcohol consumption, use of prescription drugs, body weight, and hospital admissions among laid-off workers (Hammarstrom, 1994).

- *Inadequate career advancement.* People who feel that they have been promoted too slowly or that they are not getting the recognition they deserve on the job experience more stress and have higher rates of illness (Catalano and others, 1986).

Although job-related stress is difficult to avoid, there are ways to buffer its negative impact. Better ways of responding include knowing what to expect from certain aspects of work (and coworkers), expressing your feelings to increase your perception of control, keeping things in perspective, and avoiding self-defeating thoughts and overreactions. We'll take up the topic of coping with stress much more fully in Chapter 5.

Social Interactions

Research studies also demonstrate the importance of social relationships to healthy immune functioning (Cohen & Herbert, 1996). Loneliness, for example, appears to affect immune functioning adversely, as does relationship stress (Glaser and others, 1985). Immunosuppression has been linked to interpersonal conflict among married couples (Kiecolt-Glaser and others, 1997), women recently separated from their husbands (Kiecolt-Glaser and others, 1987), and men whose wives have recently died (Schleifer and others, 1983). More recent studies have demonstrated that impaired immunity associated with the loss of a loved one occurs primarily among those people who become depressed in response to their bereavement (Zisook and others, 1994).

The caregiving role, in which one person provides the bulk of care for a relative with a chronic illness, can also be stressful and adversely affect immune functioning. In a series of studies, Janice Kiecolt-Glaser and her colleagues demonstrated that family members who provide care for a relative with Alzheimer's disease report more depression and lower life satisfaction than those in the control group (matched family members with no caregiving responsibili-

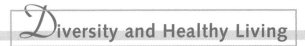

Diversity and Healthy Living

Sociocultural Factors in Stress

Many researchers have argued that sociocultural factors may have a greater impact on health than discrete events of everyday life. Several studies have shown that being African-American, poor, an immigrant, or female can be a source of chronic life stress (Greenwood and others, 1996).

African-Americans, for example, report significantly more stresses in their everyday lives than do nonminority individuals (Young & Zane, 1995). This may stem from the racism and subtle oppression that marginalized people feel because their needs often seem peripheral to the concerns of most Americans.

Poverty People with the lowest *socioeconomic status (SES)* are more likely to suffer ill effects from stress for at least two reasons. First, they invariably experience a greater number of sources of stress, such as overcrowded housing, neighborhood crime, and single parenthood. Second, they are least likely to have the financial resources to help themselves cope with stress (Adler & Matthews, 1994).

Homelessness is one problem faced by many poor people. At least 2.3 million adults and children are homeless each night (Gladwell, 2006). Homeless children have more fears, more fights, fewer friends, more chronic illnesses, and more changes of school than their peers and are about 14 months behind them academically. Homeless families as a unit also lack a supportive social network to assist them in coping with life. Finally, many homeless families are headed by single mothers striving to cope with the after-effects of an abusive relationship.

Immigrant Stress Immigrants are pressured to become **acculturated**—that is, to adopt the cultural values and behaviors of the dominant group in a country. In a diverse, multicultural

country such as the United States, acculturation is an issue of increasing concern to health psychologists. In 2000, 28.4 million foreign-born people lived in the United States, representing 10.4 percent of the total population. Among these, 51.0 percent were born in Latin America, 25.5 percent in Asia, 15.3 percent in Europe, and the remaining 8.1 percent in other regions of the world (U.S. Bureau of the Census, 2000). How do the stresses of acculturation affect health?

There are two major views of acculturation stress (Griffith, 1983). The *melting pot model* maintains that immigrants who quickly strive to become more like the people who make up the dominant culture experience less acculturation stress. According to this theory, immigrants would minimize their adjustment stress by learning and speaking English and by taking up the customs of mainstream American society.

According to the *bicultural theory,* immigrants experience less stress when they maintain their traditional values and customs while also adapting to the mainstream culture. According to this perspective, a flexible combination of ethnic identity and efforts to adapt to the mainstream culture promote well-being.

Although some health problems have been linked with a *failure* to become acculturated, the opposite is more often true. Adapting to a new culture is nearly always stressful, especially when one is a member of a marginalized minority group. Consider:

- Highly acculturated Mexican-Americans who were born in the United States have higher rates of depression and substance abuse than those born in Mexico (Hartung, 1987).
- Highly acculturated Hispanic-American women are more likely to be heavy drinkers than are low-acculturated His-

ties). Caregivers also have lower percentages of T cells and other measures of immunosuppression, and concurrent *overproduction* of proinflamatory cytokines (Kiecolt-Glaser and others, 2003; Kiecolt-Glaser and others, 1996). Overproduction of cytokines have been associated with a broad array of adverse health conditions, including cardiovascular disease, arthritis, type 2 diabetes, and certain cancers. Ethnic minorities, immigrants, those who are poor, and women often experience the most intense social stress (see Diversity and Healthy Living).

In concluding this chapter, it is worth remembering that although stress is inescapable, it does offer mixed blessings. Some stress arouses and motivates us and, in the process, often brings out our best qualities and stimulates personal

■ **acculturation** the process by which a member of one ethnic or racial group adopts the values, customs, and behaviors of another.

panic-American women (Caetano, 1987). Less rigid American gender roles and a loosening of traditional Latin American constraints on drinking among women may explain this finding.

■ Highly acculturated Hispanic-American high school girls are more susceptible than less acculturated girls to eating disorders such as anorexia. Acculturation may make Hispanic-American girls more vulnerable to stereotypes of female attractiveness in mainstream U.S. culture (Pumariega, 1986).

Stress for acculturating persons is usually lower when migration is voluntary rather than forced (that is, for immigrants versus refugees); when there is a functioning social support group (an ethnic community willing to assist during the settlement process); when there is tolerance for diversity within the mainstream culture; and when income, education level, and other background factors help ease the transition from one country to another (Berry, 1997). On this final point, the data are not very encouraging. Consider:

■ In 1999, 16.8 percent of foreign-born U.S. residents were living below the poverty level, compared with 11.2 percent of U.S.-born residents (U.S. Bureau of the Census, 2000).

■ Immigrants are less likely to have graduated from high school than native-born residents (67.0 percent and 86.6 percent, respectively). In 1999, more than one-fifth of the foreign born had less than a ninth grade education (22.2 percent) compared with about one-twentieth of native-born residents (4.7 percent). Interestingly, the proportions with a college bachelor's degree (or higher) were not significantly different for foreign-born and native-born residents (25.8 and 25.6 percent, respectively).

Gender There also seem to be differences in the stress experienced by men and women. In one large-scale study (Silverman and others, 1987), 23 percent of the women and 18 percent of the men reported experiencing significant stress during a 2-week period. Based on these figures, nearly 20 million women and 14 million men regularly feel "a lot" of stress. More recent studies have corroborated this gender difference (Greenglass & Noguchi, 1996).

Marianne Frankenhaeuser (1991) notes that many women today face a particularly heavy daily workload because they have to handle not only an outside job but also most of the chores at home. As people grow older, this gender discrepancy increases even more. Women age 65 and older are twice as likely as men to report a lot of stress in their lives. Furthermore, significantly more women (49 percent) than men (38 percent) believe that stress has had "a lot" or "some" effect on their health.

All of these sociocultural factors cause stress themselves, but they also may increase an individual's vulnerability to the ill effects of discrete stressors. It is important to recognize, however, that the extent to which situations are stressful is largely determined by how the individual understands, interprets, and feels about a situation. The impact of a given stressor also depends on the total number of stressors an individual is experiencing and on the degree to which these affect the overall patterns of everyday life. One classic study reported that children coping with only one major stressor such as poverty were *no more likely* to develop serious psychological problems than children living without this particular stressor. As the number of serious stressors children had to cope with increased, however, the percentage of children diagnosed with serious psychological health problems also increased (Rutter, 1979).

growth. A life with no stress whatsoever would be boring and would leave us unfulfilled. The price we pay, though, is the toll that stress may take on our physical and psychological health. Too much stress can overtax our coping abilities and leave us vulnerable to stress-related health problems. Fortunately, there are many things we can do to keep stress at a manageable level. It is to this topic that we turn our attention in the next chapter.

Summing Up

The Physiology of Stress

1. Stress has been defined as both a stimulus and a response. Researchers distinguish among stimulus events that are stressful (stressors), the physical and emotional responses of a person to a stressor, and the overall process by which a person perceives and responds to threatening or challenging events (stress).

2. Modern research on stress began with Walter Cannon's description of the fight-or-flight reaction. The body's response to stress involves the brain and nervous system, the endocrine glands and hormones, and the immune system. During a moment of stress, the hypothalamus secretes releasing factors that coordinate the endocrine response of the pituitary and adrenal glands. The sympathoadreno-medullary (SAM) system is the primary or first response to stress. Activation of the SAM system leads to increased blood flow to the muscles, increased energy, and higher mental alertness.

3. The hypothalamic-pituitary-adrenocortical (HPA) system is a slower-reacting response to stress that is activated by messages from the central nervous system. HPA activation functions to restore homeostasis to the body. Excessive cortisol production (hypercorticolism) from the adrenal glands, however, may impair immune efficiency.

4. Ader and Cohen's discovery that the immune system can be conditioned, coupled with Candace Pert's demonstration that the brain has receptors for immune molecules, gave rise to the subfield known as psychoneuroimmunology (PNI), which is a biopsychosocial model. PNI focuses on the interactions among behavior, the nervous system, the endocrine system, and the immune system.

5. According to the direct effect hypothesis, immunosuppression is part of the body's natural response to stress. The indirect effect hypothesis maintains that immunosuppression is an aftereffect of the stress response. Animal and human research studies demonstrate that the brain regulates the production of stress hormones, which in turn influence the body's immune defenses.

6. Stress exacerbates many diseases whose central feature is excessive inflammation, including allergic, autoimmune, rheumatologic, neurologic, and cardiovascular diseases. The glucocorticoid-resistance model suggests that this is due to chronic stress interfering with the immune system's sensitivity to glucocorticoid hormones, such as cortisol, which normally terminate the inflammatory response.

Other Major Models of Stress and Illness

7. Hans Selye outlined the general adaptation syndrome (GAS) to describe the effects of chronic stress. This syndrome consists of an alarm reaction, a stage of resistance, and a stage of exhaustion. Persistent stress may increase a person's susceptibility to a disease of adaptation.

8. According to the transactional model, a key factor in stress is cognitive appraisal. In primary appraisal, we assess whether an event is benign-positive, irrelevant, or a potential threat or challenge. In secondary appraisal, we assess the coping resources available for meeting the challenge. Through reappraisal, we constantly update perceptions of success or failure in meeting a challenge or threat.

9. The diathesis-stress model suggests that some people are more vulnerable to stress-related illnesses because of predisposing factors such as genetic weakness. A good example of how this works is seen in post-traumatic stress disorder.

10. Compared with men, women may be more likely to display a tend-and-befriend response pattern during stressful situations.

Psychosocial Sources of Stress

11. Among the sources of stress that have been investigated are major life events, daily hassles, environmental stress, and job-related stress. Major life events and daily hassles

have been studied in relation to the prevalence of illness. Daily hassles may interact with anxiety and background stressors to influence a person's vulnerability to illness. Research exploring environmental stress has focused on the influence of noise, crowding, pollution, and catastrophic events on health.

12. Among the factors that make work stressful are work overload, burnout, role conflict or ambiguity, inadequate career advancement, and lack of control over work.

Key Terms and Concepts

stressor, p. 83

stress, p. 83

sympatho-adreno-medullary (SAM) system, p. 85

hypothalamic-pituitary-adrenocortical (HPA) system, p. 85

homeostasis, p. 85

corticosteroids, p. 87

psychoneuroimmunology (PNI), p. 89

general adaptation syndrome (GAS), p. 93

transactional model, p. 95

primary appraisal, p. 97

secondary appraisal, p. 97

cognitive reappraisal, p. 97

diathesis-stress model, p. 97

reactivity, p. 97

post-traumatic stress disorder (PTSD), p. 97

population density, p. 107

burnout, p. 109

acculturation, p. 113

Coping with Stress

*S*pring break!" shouted Raheema, as she and her two sorority sisters stepped out of the airport into the blessedly warm Florida sunshine. The frozen winter semester at their Michigan college seemed to go on forever, but now they had a whole week to cut loose, soak up some rays, and recharge before midterms. Brittany and Latrice laughed as their roommate, eager to get the adventure under way, snatched the keys of their rental car from the agent's hand before he'd finished giving them directions to the parking lot. For 2 years now, ever since they'd arrived in Ann Arbor as scared freshmen, the three had been inseparable.

"To the beach!" Raheema commanded.

The traffic was light, so Raheema found it easy to drive and still put in her "two cents" as she and her passengers argued about where to go and what to do first. As the conversation grew more animated, she took her eyes off the road for just an instant, glancing back to express her displeasure with Brittany, who had suggested they stop for groceries and sun block before heading to the hotel and beach. Latrice's scream told Raheema that she'd made a terrible mistake.

The light had turned green, but as the women's compact convertible entered the intersection a large sport utility vehicle plowed into their driver's side door, killing Raheema instantly. The driver of the SUV, who was legally drunk, later admitted that his light had turned yellow before he entered the intersection. "It was very close," he stammered. "I thought they saw me coming through."

Miraculously, Brittany and Latrice's injuries were relatively minor, and they were hospitalized for only a few days. Back at school a few weeks later, their bodies were healed but their hearts and minds were not. Brittany seemed unable to overcome her grief, shock, and the feeling that she was at least partly responsible for her friend's death. "If only I hadn't disagreed with Raheema when she wanted to head straight to the beach," she ruminated. "She'd still be alive." As the days *passed, neither Latrice nor anyone else could dissuade Brittany from believing that it was she, and not the drunken SUV driver who ran the stoplight, who was to blame for the tragic accident.*

After taking some time off at home to mend her head and heart, Latrice was ready to get back to her studies. She missed Raheema dearly, and still cried every now and then over her senseless death, but she was putting her life back together. The loving support of her mother and father had helped a lot, and she'd talked things over with a psychologist at the college's counseling center who was helping her work through her grief. And to honor her friend's memory, she'd enrolled in the fitness class the two of them had been pledging to join for more than a year.

Brittany, however, seemed to be in a downward psychological and physical spiral, alternating between states of denial and self-blame. She hadn't gone back to class since the accident, or home for that matter. "My parents wouldn't understand," she said. "Nobody could." To cope with her grief, she tried hard to keep from thinking about the accident. She slept a lot, and when she was awake she was glued to the television, usually with a beer in her hand. When her friends suggested that she talk to a counselor or join a grief support group, Brittany shook her head and said it was hopeless. Asked what she planned to do, she simply said, "My tuition, room, and board are paid up through the end of the school year. I'll worry about it then."

Why was Brittany's response to the tragedy so much more life-disrupting than Latrice's? As you saw in Chapter 4, appraising a situation or event as stressful does not automatically lead to an adverse physiological and psychological response. In fact, how people deal with stressful events is at least as important as the stressors themselves in determining health or illness.

In this chapter, we will take a biopsychosocial approach in considering the factors that affect how people deal with stress. Those factors include biological influences, such as inherited personality traits and our physiological reactivity level, as well as psychological and social influences, such as coping strategies, outlook on life, perception of control, and amount of social support. Through our journey into the biology and psychology of responding to stress, we will see ample evidence supporting the connection between mind and body. At every turn, biological, psychological, and social forces interact in determining our response to stress. We will conclude with a discussion of stress management techniques that can help minimize the ill effects of stress: exercise, relaxation, biofeedback, and cognitive therapy.

■ **coping** the cognitive, behavioral, and emotional ways in which we manage stressful situations.

■ **emotion-focused coping** coping strategy in which we try to control our emotional response to a stressor.

Responding to Stress

When we talk about how people respond to stress, we generally use the word *cope*. **Coping** refers to the cognitive, behavioral, and emotional ways that people deal with stressful situations and includes *any attempt* to preserve mental and physical health—even if it has limited value (Moss-Morris & Petrie, 1997).

Coping is a dynamic process, not a one-time reaction—it is a series of responses involving our interactions with the environment. For example, when you break up with a romantic partner you may experience physical and emotional reactions, such as overall sadness, inability to sleep or eat, and even nausea. It is not just the initial incident but also continuing interactions with the environment that affect your responses. For example, friends' sympathetic comments and revisiting special places may trigger a greater response. Together, these responses form our style of coping with stress.

Emotion-Focused and Problem-Focused Coping Strategies

Coping strategies—the ways we deal with stressful situations—are intended to moderate, or buffer, the effects of stressors on our physical and emotional well-being (Moos, 2002). Not all coping strategies are equally effective, however. Some strategies provide temporary relief but tend to be maladaptive in the long run. For example, although psychological defenses (such as Brittany's choosing not to think about the car accident) may allow us to distance ourselves from a stressful situation temporarily by denying its existence, they do not eliminate the source of stress. Similarly, alcohol or other drugs push the stress into the background but do nothing to get rid of it. As we saw with Brittany, these behaviors are maladaptive because they do not confront the stressor directly and are likely to make the situation worse.

Several researchers have attempted to classify coping strategies. In this chapter, we will consider Richard Lazarus's (1984) approach, which categorizes coping strategies as either emotion-focused or problem-focused.

When we employ **emotion-focused coping** techniques, we attempt to deal with our emotional reactions to stress. We may use behavioral strategies, seeking out others who offer encouragement or keeping ourselves busy to distract attention from the problem. Or we may try cognitive strategies such as changing the way we appraise a stressor or denying unpleasant information. We tend to rely on emotion-focused coping when we believe little or nothing can

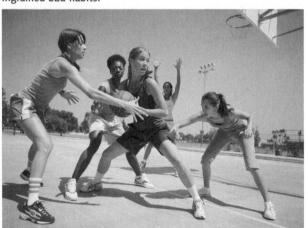

Coping with Stress, the Healthy Way People can choose healthy ways of coping with stress. This is particularly true of teenagers and young adults, who despite their sense of invincibility have yet to develop deeply ingrained bad habits.

be done to alter a stressful situation or when we believe that our coping resources or skills are insufficient to meet the demands of the stressful situation.

We use **problem-focused coping** to deal directly with the stressful situation either by reducing its demands or by increasing our capacity to deal with the stressor. For instance, a student who tackles a seemingly overwhelming course load by breaking her assignments into a series of smaller, manageable tasks is using one of these strategies, as is a recovering alcoholic who joins a support group to share experiences. We use problem-focused coping when we believe our resources and situations are changeable, as Latrice did in working through her grief.

Which is healthier, problem-focused coping or emotion-focused coping? A recent meta-analysis of 34 research studies investigating the association between coping strategies and health found that problem-focused strategies were more often linked with better health outcomes than were distancing, wishful thinking, and other emotion-focused strategies (Penley and others, 2002). However, the relationships varied with the *duration* of the stressor, with problem-focused coping proving more effective with chronic stressors than for acute stressors.

Which coping strategy is likely to work best also depends on whether the stressor is controllable. For example, those caring for terminally ill patients may rely on problem-focused strategies during the period prior to their loved one's death. After the person's death, however, they are likely to see the situation as beyond their control and so lean toward emotion-focused coping (Moskowitz and others, 1996). For these reasons, we often use problem-focused and emotion-focused coping together.

Coping, Gender, and Socioeconomic Status

Our coping strategies vary according to the situation, but also, researchers have found, due to individual differences in gender and socioeconomic status (SES).

Coping begins with our body's response. Men and women exhibit a number of different physiological reactions to stress depending, in part, on the nature of the stressor (Bloor and others, 2004). For example, when experiencing acute laboratory stressors, women exhibit lower blood pressure reactivity than men (Arthur and others, 2004). In addition, although men display greater stress-induced secretions of *catecholamines* (the autonomic nervous system-activating neurotransmitters epinephrine and norepinephrine), women exhibit a stronger *glucocorticoid* response (terminating immune system response) (Gallucci and others, 1993). These neurochemical differences are in keeping with men's tendency to be more aggressive than women, and may help explain gender differences in coronary disease and other chronic illnesses as well.

Several researchers have found that men are more likely to use problem-focused coping strategies in dealing with stress, and women are more likely to rely on emotion-focused strategies (Endler & Parker, 1990; Zuckerman, 1989). However, gender differences in coping styles may have less to do with being

■ **problem-focused coping** coping strategy for dealing directly with a stressor, in which we either reduce the stressor's demands or increase our resources for meeting its demands.

female or male than with the scope of resources available (see Diversity and Healthy Living box on p. 122). When researchers compare women and men of similar SES, gender differences in coping strategies often disappear (Greenglass & Noguchi, 1996). When dealing with interpersonal stress, women may employ more effective coping strategies than men, such as seeking social support (Taylor and others, 2000; Williams, 2003).

Socioeconomic status also affects the way we cope with stress. Stressful experiences are especially common among many ethnic minority families, who tend to be overrepresented in groups of low SES. In 2004, for example, 28.1 percent of African-American families were living below the poverty line (U.S. Census Bureau, 2005). Impoverished families experience more pollution, substandard and overcrowded housing, crime, and dangerous traffic than do more affluent families (Myers and others, 1995). They also suffer poor nutrition, limited education, low-paying work, and a lack of health insurance and access to health care (Johnson and others, 1995). Moreover, children from low-SES homes are more likely to experience divorce, frequent school transfers, and harsh and punitive parenting—events that have been linked with a variety of behavioral and emotional difficulties (Taylor and others, 1997).

Regardless of ethnicity, people of low SES tend to rely less on problem-focused coping than do people with more education and higher incomes (Billings & Moos, 1981). Their demeaning social experiences may cause them to develop a feeling of hopelessness and to believe they have little or no control over events in their lives. So, with repeated exposure to stress and no way to break the cycle, their only recourse is to try to control their emotional responses to stress— because they've learned that they can't control the situation itself.

Judith Stein and Adeline Nyamathi (1999) demonstrated not only that impoverished people have more difficulty coping with stress but also that women in this situation have more problems than men do. The researchers examined a sample of 486 impoverished men and women of African-American, Latino, and European descent who were recruited to participate in a community-based acquired immune deficiency syndrome (AIDS) prevention program. Compared with their male counterparts, the impoverished women reported greater stress and were more likely to resort to *avoidant coping* strategies. These strategies fell into three categories: *passive behaviors,* such as avoiding people and not thinking about their problems; *antisocial behaviors,* such as escapist drug use, risky sexual behaviors, and taking their problems out on others; and *fantasizing,* such as wishing their problems would go away or hoping for a miraculous intervention. The subordinate positions of impoverished women may make them even more vulnerable than men to feelings of hopelessness in the face of chronic stress. This finding points to the need for gender-specific interventions in helping people cope with chronic stress.

Socioeconomic status is also a powerful predictor of health behaviors. The Pitt County, North Carolina, study reported that SES was inversely related, among both African-American women and men, to alcohol consumption and cigarette smoking. The same study found that low-SES African-Americans perceived weaker levels of emotional and instrumental support when under stress than did their higher-SES counterparts (Keenan and others, 1992; Strogatz and others, 1997).

Interestingly, socioeconomic indicators at the level of individual neighborhoods predict the health of residents, including chronic conditions and mortality rates, even after individual differences in SES, lifestyle behaviors, and other risk factors are taken into consideration (Diez Roux and others, 2001). Pamela Feldman and Andrew Steptoe (2004) believe that neighborhood SES is linked to health because it strongly influences the social and psychological experiences of residents living in a particular neighborhood. The researchers compared 19 low SES neighborhoods and 18 high SES neighborhoods in London on four measures: *social cohesion* (trust and solidarity with neighbors); *social control* (confidence that neighbors would take action to maintain the well-being of the neighborhood); *neighborhood problems* (community-wide stressors such as litter and traffic noise); and *neigborhood vigilance* (a measure of feelings of threat and vulnerability in the neighborhood). Londoners living in lower SES neighborhoods perceived greater *neighborhood strain* (weaker social cohesion, more neighborhood problems, and greater vigilance) than people living in more affluent neighborhoods, which in turn was associated with poorer individual health, poorer social relationships, and lower levels of perceived control among residents. Similarly, community violence has been linked to increased stress symptoms, depression, and anxiety among inner-city African-American adolescents *and* to the use of negative coping strategies, such as avoidance and agression (Dempsey, 2002).

Coping and Ethnicity

Although socioeconomic status is a powerful predictor of stress, coping, and health behaviors among women and men in virtually every group that has been studied, the relationship varies with ethnicity. For instance, while SES is inversely related to self-reported stress levels among most groups, including African-American women, the Pitt County study found SES to be positively related to stress in African-American men.

David Williams has identified three factors that help explain the interactions among socioeconomic status, gender, and ethnicity among African-Americans. First, middle-class African-American men report higher levels of racial discrimination than African-American women (Forman, 2002). Racial discrimination is a significant stressor that can adversely affect physical and mental health (Williams, 2000). Significantly, the more years of education an African-American male has completed, the stronger his perception of racial discrimination.

Second, the attainment of middle-class status is often tenuous and marginal for African-Americans (Anderson, 1999). For instance, college-educated African-Americans are more likely than European-Americans to experience unemployment and job insecurity, both of which are associated with higher levels of stress, illness, disability, and mortality (U.S. Bureau of the Census, 2004). African-Americans are also less likely to convert their socioeconomic achievements into more desirable housing and community living conditions

Diversity and Healthy Living

Understanding Gender Differences in Coping Styles

Think back to a moment of significant stress in your family when you were growing up, perhaps a life-threatening illness or job loss, an encounter with a tornado or hurricane, a serious car accident, or some other crisis. Were there differences in how the men and women around you coped with the stressful situation?

Two competing hypotheses have been offered to explain differences in how women and men cope with stress: socialization and role-constraint. The *socialization hypothesis* suggests that because of traditional stereotypes women and men are brought up to cope with stress in very different ways. Traditionally, men are encouraged to take action and remain stoically independent, whereas women are socialized to seek social support from others and to express their emotions freely. As a result, men tend to cope with stress in a *problem-focused* mode, while most women cope in an *emotion-focused* mode.

Although many research studies have reported evidence consistent with the socialization hypothesis (Brems & Johnson, 1989; Carver and others, 1989), others have failed to find gender differences in emotion- or problem-focused coping (Stern and others, 1993). In some studies, the predicted results have actually been reversed, with men reporting greater use of certain emotion-focused strategies (such as denial), and women greater use of problem-focused strategies (Rosario and others, 1988).

Mixed results such as these were the impetus for the *role-constraint hypothesis,* which contends that when stressors are the same for men and women, gender is irrelevant in predicting coping reactions (Ptacek and others, 1992). According to this view, women and men have different social roles, which, in turn, make them more likely to experience different types of stressors. Any differences in coping are therefore due to differences in the types of stressors encountered.

In a fascinating test of the two hypotheses, Hasida Ben-Zur and Moshe Zeidner of the University of Haifa, Israel (1996), compared the coping reactions of Israeli women and men during a stressful national crisis with their reactions during a period of more typical daily stress. During the 10-day Gulf War in

1991, 39 Iraqi missiles were launched at the cities of Haifa and Tel Aviv, causing one death, 290 injuries, and untold damage to homes, buildings, and shops. For Israelis, the Gulf War was a grave national event, which exposed all citizens to a similar environmental stressor.

The researchers surveyed men and women regarding their coping behavior during the Gulf War and again 3 months after the crisis had ended. The participants in both surveys completed the *COPE Inventory*—a personality test consisting of 15 separate subscales that measure various aspects of problem-focused and emotion-focused coping, including denial, disengagement, humor, religion, venting of emotions, and seeking social support. The participants indicated the extent to which they relied on each of the coping strategies, using a scale that ranged from 0 (not at all) to 3 (a great extent).

When the study was concluded, several of the subscales showed an interaction between gender and type of stress (see Figure 5.1). During the war, for example, women scored higher than men on the active and planning subscales (problem-focused coping), whereas during the postwar period they scored lower than men on these subscales. Men scored lower than women on seeking emotional social support during the stress of the war than during the postwar period, but reported more acceptance and types of avoidance behavior, including denial, behavioral disengagement, alcohol/drug use, and humor during the war than they did under everyday stress.

Women also reported using a wider range of coping strategies, scoring higher on 12 out of the 15 subscales during the war period and on 10 out of the 15 subscales during the postwar period. Differences between men and women were small after the war, both in total reported coping and in type of coping strategy, with men reporting slightly more emotion-focused strategies in daily life.

Thus, the data are not entirely consistent with either hypothesis. According to the socialization hypothesis, women should have exhibited more emotion-focused coping and men more problem-focused coping in dealing with everyday events, but

(Alba and others, 2000). And even when they do, the outcome is not necessarily rosy. One study even found that while living in the suburbs predicted lower mortality risk for European-American men, it predicted *higher* mortality risk for African-American men (House and others, 2000).

Third, African-American males may experience a unique source of stress because the educational attainment associated with their higher SES has not been

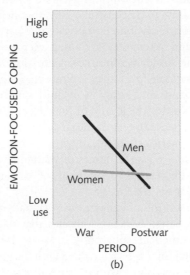

Figure 5.1

Gender Differences in Coping Strategies (a) During a national crisis, women were more likely than men to report problem-focused coping, while men were more likely to report emotion-focused coping. (b) The differences between women and men were smaller after the war, with women reporting slightly more emotion-focused coping strategies in dealing with everyday stressors.

Source: Adapted from Ben-Hur, H. & Zeidner, M. (1996). Gender differences in coping reactions under community crisis and daily routine conditions. *Journal of Personality and Individual Differences, 20*(3), 331–340.

especially during periods of war stress. According to the role-constraint hypothesis, men and women should have exhibited similar reactions during the war because it constituted a similar stressor for both sexes, but not necessarily after the war, when men and women presumably encountered different stressors.

Researchers have suggested possible reasons for the inconsistency between the data and both hypotheses. The socialization hypothesis is not entirely correct because it was based on traditional gender stereotypes that are disappearing in many modern cultures. Women today are expected to have a career of their own, and thus are more likely to be socialized toward greater assertiveness, independence, and active coping.

The role-constraint hypothesis also missed the mark, possibly because although the threat was the same for everyone, men and women may have perceived it differently. For example, many of the coping options that could help protect individuals

were related to creating a safe home environment. Under threat of being bombed by missile warheads with poisonous chemical compounds, families had to stay indoors in a sealed environment, stock up on food, and so forth. Although traditional gender roles are undoubtedly merging, the specific demands of the war situation may have encouraged women to take charge. In contrast, Israeli men, whose defense response more often involves active military service, may have perceived fewer tasks to accomplish. This may explain their relatively higher level of emotion-focused coping.

Think back again to your family crisis. Is either hypothesis consistent with the men and women you saw coping? What about you? Is your coping style more the product of socialization or role-constraint? Do these hypotheses make sense for young women and young men today?

rewarded with equitable increases in income. At every level of education, African-American men have lower incomes than European-American men. Moreover, the pay gap between African-Americans and European-Americans is larger for men than for women (*Changing America*, 1998).

The elevated level of stress among middle-class African-American men may contribute to their increased risk for a variety of chronic diseases, including hypertension. Two decades ago, Sherman James suggested that unrelieved psychosocial stress, generated by the environments in which many African-Americans live and work, triggers *John Henryism* (JH), a pattern of coping behaviors among African-Americans that help explain why they are two to four times more likely than European-Americans to develop hypertension by age 50 (James and others, 1983). Named after the legend of John Henry, an African-American steeldriver in American folklore, African-Americans who score high on the JH Scale for Active Coping engage in high-effort coping with psychosocial demands and stressors, including barriers to upward social mobility. In James's words, "the legend of John Henry is a metaphor of the African-American experience. It tells of the struggle of black Americans to be a part of mainstream America. It is a struggle that has played out against great odds and against very powerful forces of marginalization that continue to create wear and tear on the bodies and minds of African Americans" (Washington University Magazine, 2003, p. 4).

Although John Henryism has generally been viewed as a hazardous coping style, the latest evidence indicates that this hypothesis does not apply to all African-American subgroups, in particular those whose financial and educational attainments provide them with the greatest range of economic and social resources for coping with stress. A recent study demonstrated that the combination of high JH and low SES were associated with increased blood pressure reactivity to, and slower recovery from, a variety of social stressors (Merritt and others, 2004). Conversely, another cross-sectional study of African-American men reported a *positive* association between John Henryism and better overall physical health (Bonham and others, 2004).

Factors Affecting the Ability to Cope

We all know that certain life stresses (such as final exams) tend to give us headaches, queasy stomachs, and other ailments, whereas exhilarating or uplifting experiences (such as a ski weekend or a new intimate relationship) make us feel on top of the world. In this section, we explore several biopsychosocial factors that affect how well we cope with potential stressors and, by extension, how this affects our health. Keep in mind that no one factor by itself determines your well-being. Health is always a result of biopsychosocial factors interacting in various ways.

Hardiness

Do you know people who approach life with enthusiasm, who always seem to be taking on more challenges, who remain healthy in the face of adversity? Salvatore Maddi and Suzanne Kobasa (1991) identified three stress-buffering traits—*commitment, challenges,* and *control*—that appear to influence how people react to potential stressors. Together, these traits form a personality style called **hardiness.**

Hardy people view the everyday demands of life as challenges rather than as threats. They are also committed to their families, jobs, communities, or other groups or activities that give their lives a sense of meaning. And, most important, they have a sense of control over their lives, of having access to needed information, and of being capable of making good decisions regarding the demands of life.

Hardy people may be healthier because they are less likely to become aroused by stressful situations. As a result, they avoid stress-related physical and psychological reactions that lead to illness. One study related personality data from 670 middle- and upper-level managers to self-reported stress and illness experienced during a 2-year period (Kobasa and others, 1982). As Figure 5.2 shows, managers who experienced high levels of stress also reported more illness; however, those in this group who were high in hardiness experienced significantly lower levels of illness than did those low in hardiness.

Researchers have found personal hardiness to be an effective indicator of successful adjustment to numerous health problems, including cancer, chronic obstructive pulmonary disease, cardiovascular disease, diabetes, epilepsy, HIV infection, hypertension, kidney transplant, and stroke (Pollock, 1986). Hardiness has also been linked to lower levels of anxiety, active coping styles, decreased caregiver burden, reduced vulnerability to depression in older people living in a long-term care facility, better adaptation of professional women to the stress of multiple roles, greater spiritual well-being in elderly people, and fewer negative health outcomes during periods of extended stress (Drory and others, 1991; Florian and others, 1995).

Evaluating the Hardiness Hypothesis

Despite the large number of studies in support of the idea that psychologically healthy people are buffered against stress, the concept of hardiness has received its share of criticism. Some researchers have found that the hardiness–health relationship is more applicable to men than women (Klag & Bradley, 2004). Others have questioned whether hardiness consists of certain specific core constructs. On this latter point, Lois Benishek (1996) used *factor analysis*—a statistical procedure that identifies clusters of items on self-report tests that measure a common trait—to show that hardiness actually comprises one to four factors, rather than the three

■ **hardiness** a cluster of stress-buffering traits consisting of commitment, challenges, and control.

Figure 5.2

Stress, Hardiness, and Illness High levels of stress are clearly more likely than low levels to cause illness. However, hardiness can buffer the effects of stress. Hardy managers who reported high levels of stress experienced significantly lower levels of illness than did those low in hardiness. The measure of stress was an adaptation of the familiar *Social Readjustment Rating Scale,* which subjectively quantifies the stressfulness of numerous events (see Chapter 4). The illness index is a composite measure of the frequency and severity of 126 commonly recognized physical and mental symptoms and diseases.

Source: Based on data from Kobasa, S. C., and others. (1982). Hardiness and health: A prospective study. *Journal of Personality and Social Psychology, 42*(1), 168–177. Copyright 1982 by the American Psychological Association. Adapted with permission.

■ **resilience** the quality of some children to bounce back from environmental stressors that might otherwise disrupt their development.

proposed by Kobasa and Maddi. The number of factors seems to depend on the measures used and the population studied.

Skeptics have also suggested that hardy people are healthier because they have greater personal resources, such as income, education, social support, and coping skills, and tend to be younger than the less hardy. To determine whether this is true, Kobasa interviewed executives who remained in good health or became sick during periods of high self-reported stress. Those who remained healthy were not younger, wealthier, or better educated than their sicker counterparts. However, they experienced more commitment in their lives, felt more in control, and had a greater appetite for challenge (Kobasa and others, 1982). In another study, hardiness was shown to have a stronger protective effect against illness than exercise or social support (Kobasa and others, 1985). These and other studies in which hardiness and health-enhancing behaviors were measured separately indicate that hardiness is an independent trait not caused by other variables.

On balance, research studies do seem to demonstrate that some people handle stress more effectively because they view themselves as choosing to live challenging lives. These individuals also appraise potentially stressful events more favorably, seeing them as enriching their lives rather than as intensifying pressure. When confronted with stressful situations, they are more likely than less hardy people to reappraise negative conditions as positive ones (Williams and others, 1992). This reappraisal allows them to feel in control of, rather than controlled by, stressors they encounter. Equally important, hardy people strive to solve their problems with active coping strategies—such as problem-focused coping and seeking social support—rather than trying to avoid them.

Resilience

Closely related to hardiness is the concept of **resilience,** a term that has been applied to children who show a remarkable ability to develop into competent, well-adjusted people despite having been raised in extremely disadvantaged environments (Garmezy, 1993). Resilience allows these remarkable children to shrug off potential stressors.

Psychiatrist Steven Wolin (1993) describes the case of Jacqueline, who at 2 years of age was placed by her birth parents in a foster home. Eighteen months later, Jacqueline's foster father murdered his wife, and Jacqueline was moved to another foster family. After 2 relatively stable years, Jacqueline's birth mother appeared without explanation, taking her daughter to live with her for the next 4 years. During those years, Jacqueline's mother had a string of dysfunctional relationships with men who moved in and out of the house; some of these men physically abused Jacqueline. At age 10, Jacqueline was once again displaced, this time to an orphanage, where she stayed until she was 17. Although many theories of psychosocial development would predict that Jacqueline would develop into an antisocial, problem-ridden woman, this did not happen. Throughout her childhood, she excelled in school, was a leader among her peers, and remained optimistic about her future. Jacqueline is now an adult with a stable marriage. She finds great joy in being "the parent to my children that I never had."

Where does such resilience come from? Research points to two groups of factors. One group relates to individual traits, the other to social support. Resilient children have well-developed social, academic, or creative skills; easy temperaments; high self-esteem; self-discipline; and strong feelings of personal control (Werner, 1997). These elements of *social cognition* foster healthy relationships with others who help such children adjust to adverse conditions. The healthy relationships seem to help these children deflect many of the problems they face at home (Ackerman and others, 1999).

Studies of resilient children point to the importance of at least one consistently supportive person in the life of a child at risk (Garmezy, 1993). This person can be an aunt or uncle, older sister or brother, grandparent, family friend, or teacher. This supportive person, often a caring parent, is a model of resilience who plays a significant role in convincing at-risk children that they can and will beat the odds.

Although early studies of resilience implied that there was something remarkable about these children, recent research suggests that resilience is a more common phenomenon that arises from the ordinary resources of children, their relationships, and their communities (Masten, 2001). Echoing the theme of the positive psychology movement (see Chapter 1), the resilience research now focuses on understanding how these adaptive processes develop, how they operate under adverse conditions, and how they can be protected (or restored).

■ **explanatory style** our general propensity to attribute outcomes always to positive causes or always to negative causes, such as personality, luck, or another person's actions.

Explanatory Style

Your **explanatory style**—whether you tend to attribute outcomes to positive or negative causes—also affects your ability to cope with stress. People who look on the bright side of life—who see a light at the end of the tunnel—have a positive explanatory style and tend to cope well with stress (Peterson & Steen, 2002). Those with a negative explanatory style do not cope as well with stress. They expect failure because they believe that the conditions that lead to failure are all around them or even within them.

Why are some people more prone to one style or the other? Individual attribution styles—whom or what we blame for our failures—are part of the answer. Martin Seligman and his colleagues (1995) believe that negativity and "epidemic hopelessness" are largely responsible for the prevalence of depression among Western people. When failure and rejection are (inevitably) encountered in life, maintains Seligman, the self-focused Westerner is more likely to assume personal responsibility. In non-Western cultures, where individualism is subordinate to cooperation and a sense of community, depression is less common, perhaps because it is less likely to be linked with self-blame for failure.

Pessimism

Those with a negative explanatory style tend to explain failures in terms that are global ("Everything is awful."), stable ("It's always going to be this way."), and internal ("It's my fault, as usual."). Anger, hostility, suppressed emotions,

"A recipe for severe depression is preexisting pessimism encountering failure."

—Martin Seligman (1995)

■ **rumination** repetitive focusing on the causes, meanings, and consequences of stressful experiences.

anxiety, depression, and pessimism are all associated with a negative explanatory style and are believed to lead to harmful health-related behaviors (smoking and alcohol and drug abuse, for example) and disease (Scheier & Bridges, 1995).

Pessimism is also linked with earlier mortality. In a study of personality data obtained from general medical patients at the Mayo Clinic between 1962 and 1965, Toshihiko Maruta and his colleagues (2000) found that patients who were more pessimistic had significantly higher (19 percent) mortality than more optimistic patients. There are at least four mechanisms by which pessimism might shorten life:

1. Pessimists experience more unpleasant events, which have been linked to shorter lives.

2. Pessimists believe that "nothing I do matters," so they are less likely than optimists to comply with medical regimens or take preventive actions (such as exercising).

3. Pessimists are more likely to be diagnosed with major depressive disorder, which is associated with mortality.

4. Pessimists have weaker immune systems than optimists.

Optimism

People with an upbeat, optimistic explanatory style, on the other hand, tend to lead healthier, longer lives than their gloom-and-doom counterparts (Peterson & Bossio, 1991). They also have shorter hospital stays, faster recovery from coronary artery bypass surgery, and greater longevity when battling AIDS (Scheier and others, 1989). Optimists respond to stress with smaller increases in blood pressure and are much less likely to die from heart attacks (Everson and others, 1996). Among college students, optimists—those who agree with statements such as, "In uncertain times, I usually expect the best" and "I always look on the bright side of things"—report less fatigue and fewer aches, pains, and minor illnesses (Scheier & Carver, 1985; Carver & Scheier, 2002).

Why is optimism beneficial to health? According to the *broaden-and-build theory,* positive emotions increase our physical, cognitive, and social resources, which in turn helps us cope more effectively with stressful experiences and live healthier lives (Frederickson, 2001). For example, by shortening the duration of negative emotional arousal, positive emotions may stave off stress-related elevations in blood pressure, immunosuppression, and other disease-promoting processes. Among children, positive emotions experienced during play help build social skills, which in turn may foster lasting social bonds and attachments (Aron and others, 2000). In support of this theory, a recent study found that people who consistently experienced positive emotions with their families as children, and again as adults with their own families, were half as likely to display high levels of cumulative wear and tear on their bodies (Ryff and others, 2001). Another study of older Hispanic-Americans reported that those who generally reported positive emotions were half as likely as those who were more pessimistic and cynical to become disabled or to have died during the 2-year duration of the study (Ostir and others, 2000).

Optimism may also help sustain immune functioning under stress. One study demonstrated that the pressure of first-semester law school took a less negative toll on immune activity in students who were optimistic about their academic success, compared with students who were pessimistic (Segerstrom and others, 1998). As Figure 5.3 shows, the number of CD4 cells in the optimists' bloodstream rose by 13 percent, compared with a 3 percent drop in the number of cells in the pessimists. Similarly, NK cell activity rose by 42 percent in the high-scoring optimists but only by 9 percent in pessimists. (As we saw in Chapter 3, CD4 cells and NK cell activity are immune system factors that help fight infection.)

This is not an isolated finding. For example, other studies have reported that people with AIDS who believe their illness is controllable also display increased T cell (lymphocytes that attack invading antigens) counts over time and they live longer. In contrast, HIV-positive people who are pessimistic about their fate display a decrease in T cell counts and faster onset of AIDS symptoms over the same period of time (Segerstrom and others, 1996).

Back to our law students: Why did optimism enhance their immune function under stress? Segerstrom and Taylor believe that optimists have healthier attitudes and better health habits than pessimists. The optimistic law students may have been more likely to appraise their course work as a challenge (and therefore perceive less stress); to exercise more; and to avoid smoking, alcohol abuse, and other health-compromising behaviors. These health-enhancing behaviors would contribute to stronger immune systems and better functioning under stress.

Optimists and pessimists have different physical reactions to stress but also differ in how they cope with stress. Whereas optimists are more likely to try to alter stressful situations or to take direct problem-focused action against a stressor (Scheier and others, 1986), pessimists are more likely to **ruminate**—to obsess and be overwhelmed by persistent thoughts about stressors (Nolen-Hoeksema and others, 1994). This tendency has been linked to self-criticism, a history of past depression, and excessive dependency on others (Spasojevic & Alloy, 2001). Optimists also perceive more control over stressors, which in turn leads to more effective coping responses, including seeking treatment when illness strikes (Lin & Peterson, 1990; Scheier & Bridges, 1995). In contrast, pessimists are more likely to perceive the world—and their health—as being uncontrollable (Keltner and others, 1993).

Fortunately, pessimism is identifiable early in life and can be changed into *learned optimism* (Seligman & Csikszentmihalyi, 2000). Seligman recommends learning the "ABC's" of optimism (1990). Let's consider how this might work

Figure 5.3

Optimism and Immune Function Two months after beginning law school, optimistic law students showed a 13 percent increase in the blood level (estimated total number) of CD4 cells in the bloodstream, compared with a 3 percent drop in the number of cells in the bloodstream of pessimists. Similarly, natural killer cell cytotoxicity (a measure of cell activity level) rose by 42 percent in the optimists but only by 9 percent in pessimists.

Source: Based on data from Segerstrom, S. C., and others. (1998). Optimism is associated with mood, coping and immune change in response to stress. *Journal of Personality and Social Psychology, 74*(6), 1646–1655. Copyright 1998 by the American Psychological Association. Adapted with permission.

■ **personal control** the belief that we make our own decisions and determine what we do and what others do to us.

to help Brittany overcome her pessimism and develop a more positive explanatory style.

■ Adversity: Brittany should interpret difficulties in terms that are *external* ("It was the SUV driver, not me, who caused the accident."), *temporary* ("This will be a difficult year, but I will get through this."), and *specific* ("I lost one of my best friends, but other things in my life are still going well.").

■ Beliefs: Mindfully practicing such optimistic explanations will lead Brittany to healthier, more upbeat beliefs.

■ Consequences: Healthier, more optimistic beliefs will prompt more positive health consequences for Brittany.

Martin Bolt (2004, p. 176) explains that, "Learning to counterargue, to offer alternative causes for the disappointment, to recognize that you are overreacting, and even to show that the belief is factually incorrect undermine the pessimistic explanation and enable you to cope with setbacks more effectively."

Personal Control and Choice

Consider the following scenario. After a routine physical examination, your doctor tells you that your blood pressure is too high. Because you do not have any other symptoms or a family history of hypertension or coronary heart disease, she suspects that your lifestyle is to blame. She advises gaining control over whatever health-compromising behaviors are elevating your blood pressure.

How do you respond to your doctor's warning? Ideally, you consider how you might alter your diet, activity level, stress level, and other aspects of your daily routine because you believe you can exert a significant degree of control over your blood pressure. Conversely, if you believe that you cannot influence your health or that there is nothing you can do to make your situation better, you do nothing.

Personal control is the belief that we make our own decisions and determine what we do or what others do to us (Rodin, 1986). Healthy children gradually develop a sense of control over their surroundings. Albert Bandura and other researchers have called this *self-efficacy,* which is a belief in our ability to deal with potentially stressful situations (Bandura, 1997; Maddux, 2002).

When faced with repeated, uncontrollable stress, people sometimes learn that they cannot affect what happens to them. In extreme situations, they may even develop the resigned passive behaviors of *learned helplessness* (Seligman & Maier, 1967). In concentration camps and prisons, and even in factories and nursing homes, people who repeatedly fail at a goal often stop trying. Even more important, they may become unresponsive in other environments where success is more likely. For example, college students faced with uncontrollable stress in the form of repeated bursts of noise later make only feeble attempts to turn off a noise that *can* be controlled (Krantz and others, 1974). Elderly people living in long-term care or nursing home facilities, as well as those suffering from chronic illnesses, are particularly vulnerable to learned helplessness. Unwittingly, the well-intentioned staff of many nursing homes (as well as those who provide care in a home setting) encourage passive, helpless behavior in the elderly and chronically ill by denying them the responsibility for even the most fundamental aspects of their care.

Seligman (1975) demonstrated that when people experience outcomes over which they have no control, they lose motivation for responding; display impaired learning; and experience stress, anxiety, and depression. People who feel helpless either do not engage in health-enhancing behaviors or they abandon those behaviors before they have time to exert a positive effect on health. Because of the link between helplessness and depression, and the link between depression and health-compromising behaviors such as substance abuse, there is even reason to believe that feelings of helplessness can be life threatening (Wallston and others, 1997).

Low perceived control may be one reason racial and ethnic minorities are high-risk groups when it comes to health. Among minority men, for instance, the word "crisis" has been used to described the elevated prevalence of disease, disability, and premature death (Williams, 2003). Particularly in Western cultures, where men are socialized under norms emphasizing achievement and competence, an absence of employment opportunities, discrimination, and economic marginalization can have a devastating impact on self-efficacy and on the way men appraise and respond to potentially stressful situations (Myers, 1982).

Racism, for instance, can dramatically affect the cognitive appraisals of African-Americans (Outlaw, 1993). When it does, the stress response can escalate. When African-American college students in a recent study overheard European-American classmates negatively evaluating their performance on a task, those who attributed their poor evaluation to racism and discrimination displayed the strongest stress reactions (King, 2005).

Personal Control and Coping Strategies

In contrast to those with learned helplessness, people with a strong sense of personal control tend to engage in adaptive, problem-focused coping. In one study, health care workers facing layoffs completed questionnaires assessing their levels of stress, personal resources, coping styles, and illness at the beginning of the study and again one year later (Ingledew and others, 1997). The results revealed that increases in perceived level of stress were generally accompanied by increases in emotion-focused coping, but to a lesser degree in those who perceived strong personal control over their lives—for those workers, feelings of control and self-efficacy led to more problem-focused coping. Similarly, African-American adolescents who perceive little or no personal control over racism-related stress have been shown to rely more on avoidance and emotion-focused coping than on problem-focused coping. Conversely, minority teens who perceive high levels of personal control over racial stressors are more likely to use problem-focused strategies (Scott, 2001).

■ **regulatory control** the various ways in which we modulate our thinking, emotions, and behavior over time and across changing circumstances.

Those who feel a strong sense of psychological control are more likely to exercise direct control over health-related behaviors. Niall Pender and colleagues (1990) studied 589 employees enrolled in six employer-sponsored health-promotion programs. Employees who believed that they exerted greater control over their health were far more likely to stick with wellness programs than were employees who felt less responsible for their well-being. Results such as these indicate that feeling in control of aversive events plays a crucial role in determining our response to stressful situations.

Think back to our opening story: Who seemed to feel more personal control—Brittany or Latrice? Who coped more effectively with the stress of the traumatic accident?

Personal Control and Biological Effects

Our sense of control or self-efficacy affects not only our behavioral responses, but also the biological processes activated by stressors, and the way those processes affect our health. People with a strong sense of self-efficacy tend to respond to stressors with minimal physiological arousal and thus little health risk.

For instance, our sense of control over a stressor affects the release of corticosteroids—the endocrine hormones released by the adrenal cortex that mobilize the body's fight-or-flight response. When a stressor is uncontrollable or inescapable—or when we perceive we have no control over it—our body releases more corticosteroids than when we perceive that the stressor can be avoided or terminated (Swenson & Vogel, 1983). A weak sense of control also impairs immune system functioning, increasing a person's susceptibility to bacterial and viral infection and accelerating a disease's progression rate (Schneiderman and others, 1992). In contrast, stress that is aroused while a person is gaining a sense of mastery over a threatening situation can actually enhance immune functioning (Bandura, 1992).

Regulatory Control

Have you ever been so angry with a rude driver that you felt like exploding, yet you didn't? Or perhaps you've been at a religious service when you found something hysterically funny but needed to stifle your laughter? In such situations, we strive to control which emotions are experienced and which are expressed. **Regulatory control,** which refers to our capacity to modulate thoughts, emotions, and behaviors, is a part of everyday life. In fact, nine out of ten college students report making an effort to control their emotions at least once a day (Gross, 1998).

Controlling your responses and emotions has broad implications for your health. Self-regulation is associated with success in dieting (Herman & Polivy, 1980), quitting smoking (Russell, 1971), and maintaining good interpersonal relationships (Kelly & Conley, 1987). In addition, children who have good self-control are calmer, more resistant to frustration, better able to delay gratification (an important factor later in resisting substance abuse), and less aggressive (Muraven and others, 1998). Conversely, undercontrolled people are more likely to become aggressive (Baumeister, 1997), experience depression (Wenzlaff and others, 1988), and dwell obsessively on self-defeating thoughts (Martin & Tesser, 1989).

Individual differences in regulatory control are related to how people cope with stressful events and experiences. People with good self-control are less likely to resort to maladaptive coping responses such as angry venting of emotions or avoidant coping (Aronoff and others, 1994). Similarly, children with good regulatory control are reported by their mothers to be likely to use constructive, problem-focused coping responses and unlikely to use avoidant or aggressive coping responses in stressful situations (Fabes and others, 1994).

Cardiovascular Reactivity Because of the relationship between self-control and physical arousal, researchers are exploring the use of heart rate and other physiological markers to identify individual differences in how people cope with stress (Schneiderman et. al, 2000; Quigley and others, 2002). Physiologically, our reactivity to psychological stress seems to be quite stable. In a recent study, researchers measured participants' blood pressure while they completed stresssful tasks. Years later, follow-up studies demonstrated that those whose blood pressure had increased most during the initial phase of the study were most likely to have chronic hypertension (Matthews and others, 2004).

Several studies have reported that situations that are appraised as threatening are associated with a different pattern of cardiovascular reactivity than situations that are appraised as challenging. Threat appraisals have been linked with enhanced *vascular* responses, as reflected by increases in diastolic blood pressure and *total peripheral resistance* (the cumulative resistance of all the body's blood vessels), whereas challenge appraisals have been linked with increased *myocardial* reactivity, as reflected by increases in heart rate and cardiac output (Tomaka and others, 1993; Maier and others, 2003).

Most changes in heart rate, such as those that occur in response to challenging physical and emotional demands, are controlled by the tenth cranial nerve, which is the longest in the body—extending into each limb all the way from the brain. This is the *vagus* nerve (vagus means "wandering" in Latin). The vagus plays an important role in the parasympathetic nervous system's calming response; its main function is to lower blood pressure and heart rate. When a healthy person inhales, for instance, the vagus becomes less active, increasing heart rate; when he or she exhales, vagal activity increases, and heart rate decreases. In response to stress, the autonomic nervous system speeds heart rate (to meet the metabolic demands of the body's emergency response system) by decreasing vagal action on the heart.

Vagal tone is thus a measure of the relationship between the rhythmic increases and decreases in heart rate associated with breathing in and breathing out. High vagal tone, measured as greater variability in heart rate as a person breathes in and out, reflects greater regulatory control by the vagus nerve. In contrast, low vagal tone (measured as a more stable heart rate pattern) reflects weaker regulatory control. Richard Fabes and Nancy Eisenberg (1997) investigated the relationship among vagal tone, daily stress, and coping responses in

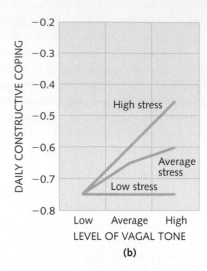

High vagal tone is inversely related to negative emotional arousal and positively related to constructive coping.

Figure 5.4

Vagal Tone and Coping with Stress (a) Students with high vagal tone were less likely than students with lower vagal tone to experience high levels of negative emotional arousal in response to everyday hassles and stress. (b) They were also more likely to rely on constructive coping measures.

Source: Fabes, R. A. & Eisenberg, N. (1997). Regulatory control and adults' stress-related responses to daily life events. *Journal of Personality and Social Psychology, 73*(5), 1107–1117. Copyright 1997 by the American Psychological Association. Adapted with permission.

college students (Figure 5.4). Students with high vagal tone were less likely than students with lower vagal tone to experience high levels of negative emotional arousal in response to everyday hassles and stress. They were also more likely to rely on constructive coping measures (active coping, seeking social support, positive reinterpretation, emotion-focused coping) rather than maladaptive strategies (psychological and physical distancing, venting of emotion, alcohol/drug use).

Cardiovascular reactivity and regulatory control may also partly explain individual and group differences in coronary disease morbidity and mortality rates. Individuals who face repeated threats and challenges in their daily lives and have weaker cardiac autonomic control may be at substantialy greater risk for coronary artery disease than those who have greater regulatory control (Sloan and others, 1999). Researchers at Harvard University's School of Public Health recently reported that Caribbean-Americans and African-Americans, two of the largest black ethnic groups in the United States, display different patterns of cardiovascular reactivity to laboratory stressors than European-Americans do (Arthur and others, 2004). In response to a mental arithmetic task, for instance, African-Americans displayed larger decreases in *heart period variability* (lower vagal tone) than European-Americans, but smaller decreases than their Caribbean-American counterparts.

Choice, Culture, and Control

Psychologists have long argued that choice enhances feelings of personal control (Rotter, 1966). The results from many studies suggest that the positive consequences of choice are apparent even when choice is trivial or illusory. Simply being able to choose the order in which a task is performed appears to reduce anxiety (Glass & Singer, 1972). And in one well-known study, Ellen Langer and Judy Rodin (1976) found that the health of elderly patients in a nursing home was significantly improved when they were permitted to choose their own recreational activities and the placement of the furniture in their rooms.

Conversely, situations in which there is no choice or in which choice has been removed have been linked to detrimental effects on motivation, performance, and health. Interestingly, however, several recent studies have demonstrated that too much choice, in the workplace and elsewhere, may be detrimental to motivation and well-being (Iyengar & Lepper, 2000; Schwartz, 2004) and pointed to cultural differences in the extent to which the perception of choice is associated with well-being. In individualistic cultures, it has been assumed that perceiving oneself as having less choice—as seems to be the case for Asians and Latin Americans—will have negative effects on well-being (Langer & Rodin, 1976). But Sastry and Ross (1998), who examined the impact of people's perceptions of choice and control on psychological distress from participants in 33 different countries, found a much more variable relationship. Among European-Americans, those with a strong sense of freedom of choice and control had lower levels of depression and anxiety than those who perceived less choice and control in their lives. However, this relationship was not observed for Asian-Americans and Asians. Like Asian-Americans, Hispanic-Americans perceived less freedom and control in their lives; however, like European-Americans, Hispanic-Americans also demonstrated the negative association between these perceptions and distress— even after such variables as socioeconomic status were taken into account.

Disclosure

Sometimes we are not aware that we are controlling our emotions. In laboratory studies of stress, some individuals will report feeling relaxed while performing challenging tasks, but physiologically and behaviorally they show signs of significant stress, such as slower reaction times, increased muscle tension, and rapid heart rate. This extreme form of regulatory control—in which there is a discrepancy between verbal and physiological measures of stress—is called **repressive coping** (Weinberger and others, 1979). Using this emotion-focused coping style, *repressors* attempt to inhibit their emotional responses so they can view themselves as emotionally imperturbable. Newton and Contrada (1992) found that repressors displayed the greatest discrepancy between self-report and physiological measures of anxiety when their behavior was being observed. This suggests that repression is most likely to occur in a social context.

Is repression healthy? Accumulating evidence suggests not. Emotional suppression activates the sympathetic division of the autonomic nervous system, functioning much like a stressor in elevating blood pressure and triggering the fight-or-flight response (Butler and others, 2003). In the 1980s, psychologist James Pennebaker began a fascinating series of studies with college students, most of which followed this simple protocol: the students were asked to write about an assigned topic for 15 minutes a day for 4 days. Half of the participants wrote about everyday, ordinary experiences—describing their dorm room, for instance. The other students were told to write about their deepest thoughts and feelings regarding a stressful or traumatic experience. Students in the emotional

■ **repressive coping** an emotion-focused coping style in which we attempt to inhibit our emotional responses, especially in social situations, so we can view ourselves as imperturbable.

disclosure group took immediately to the task and wrote intimate, gripping stories, sometimes crying and displaying other strong emotional reactions. At the end of the study, most reported that the experience had helped them find new meaning in the traumatic experience. The most striking result, however, came 6 months later, at the end of the school year, when Pennebaker discovered that those who had written about stressful experiences had visited the university health center far less often than did the students who had written about everyday things.

Over the past 25 years, Pennebaker's finding has been repeated in dozens of settings with scores of people from different walks of life, ethnicities, and cultural backgrounds. The people writing or, alternatively, confiding verbally to a confidant, have been prison inmates, crime victims, chronic pain suferrers, Holocaust survivors, bereaved widows and widowers, business executives, and laid off workers, among others. In almost every instance, emotional disclosure is related to some sort of positive health benefit.

When people write or talk about traumatic events, for instance, skin conductivity, heart rate, and systolic and diastolic blood pressure all decrease (Pennebaker, Hughes, & O'Heeron, 1997). Over time, keeping a daily journal of thoughts and feelings has been associated with decreased absenteeism, fewer medical visits, and even improved immune functioning (Pennebaker & Francis, 1996; Petrie and others, 1995). In one study, medical students were randomly assigned to write about traumatic events or control topics for four daily sessions. On the fifth day, each received a vaccination for hepatitis B, with boosters 1 and 4 months later. Before each vaccination, and again 6 months later, blood samples revealed that participants in the disclosure group had significantly higher antibody levels against the virus.

There are many reasons that emotional disclosure may help us cope with stress. Confiding in others may allow us to gain helpful advice. It may also provide a source of reinforcement and social support. Finally, writing or talking about a stressful experience may encourage cognitive reappraisal as we gain a new perspective on the event. In support of this latter idea, Pennebaker has found that people who write the most coherent, persuasive, and well-organized stories tend to experience the greatest health benefits (Niederhoffer & Pennebaker, 2002). Similarly, women who had recently lost a close relative to breast cancer, and who were asked to write daily about the death, were most likely to demonstrate a bolstered immune response (increased natural killer cell cytotoxity) when daily written disclosure enabled them to find positive meaning from the loss (Bower and others, 2003).

Social Support

So far, we have focused on a person's *internal* resources for dealing with stress. These resources—hardiness, optimism, personal control, and disclosure—certainly play important roles in our response to stress. Yet external factors are also important, especially the degree of social support we receive. Social ties and relationships with other people powerfully influence us, in both positive and negative ways.

Social support is companionship from others that conveys emotional concern, material assistance, or honest feedback about a situation. In stressful situations, people who perceive a high level of social support may experience less stress and may cope more effectively, as Latrice did in our opening story. Consider the evidence:

1. *Faster recovery and fewer medical complications:* Social support has been associated with better adjustment to and/or faster recovery from coronary artery surgery, rheumatoid arthritis, childhood leukemia, and stroke (Magni and others, 1988). In addition, women with strong social ties have fewer complications during childbirth (Collins and others, 1993), and both women and men with high levels of social support are less likely to suffer heart attacks (Holahan and others, 1997).

2. *Lower mortality rates:* Having a number of close social relationships is associated with a lower risk of dying at any age. The classic example of this association comes from a survey of 7,000 adults in Alameda County, California (Berkman & Syme, 1994). The researchers found that having a large number of social contacts enabled women to live an average of 2.8 years longer and men an average of 2.3 years longer. These benefits to longevity remained even when health habits such as smoking, alcohol use, physical activity, obesity, and differences in SES and health status at the beginning of the study were taken into account. Similarly, a 15-year prospective study of mortality rates among Swedish men, who were 50 years old at the start of the study, revealed that social support was inversely related to mortality. Men with a large circle of friends whom they saw regularly were half as likely to develop heart disease or die compared with men who had little social contact or support. The impact of low levels of social support on mortality was comparable in magnitude to that of cigarette smoking (Rosengren and others, 2004). Another study showed that cancer patients with the fewest contacts each day were 2.2 times more likely to die of cancer over a 17-year period than were those with greater social support (Spiegel, 1996).

3. *Less distress in the face of terminal illness:* AIDS patients who perceive a strong network of social support experience less depression and hopelessness than do patients lacking social support (Varni and others, 1992).

How Social Support Makes a Difference

Clearly, the support of others can benefit our health, but how? According to the **buffering hypothesis,** social support mitigates stress indirectly, by helping us cope more effectively (Cohen &

■ **social support** companionship from others that conveys emotional concern, material assistance, or honest feedback about a situation.

■ **buffering hypothesis** theory that social support produces its stress-busting effects indirectly, by helping the individual cope more effectively.

Friends Can Prevent or Eliminate Stress Throughout our lives, friends can be an important stress-busting resource. If we perceive a high level of social support from our friends, we are better able to cope with stress. Social support is also associated with faster recovery and fewer medical complications after surgery, lower mortality rates, and less distress in the face of a terminal illness.

■ **direct effect hypothesis** the-ory that social support produces its beneficial effects during both stressful and nonstressful times by enhancing the body's physi-cal responses to challenging situations.

McKay, 1984; Cohen & Wills, 1985). For instance, people who perceive strong social support are less likely to ruminate in an effort to cope with stressful experiences. Rumination tends to be counter-productive—leading to more negative interpretations of events, triggering recall of unpleasant memories, in-terfering with problem solving, and reducing the ruminator's interest in par-ticipating in enjoyable activities (Lyubomirsky and others, 1998; Spasojevic & Alloy, 2001).

According to the **direct effect hypothesis,** social support enhances the body's physical responses to challenging situations (Pilisuk and others, 1987). For example, in times of stress, the presence of others who are perceived as sup-portive may dampen sympathetic nervous system arousal, perhaps by reducing the release of *corticotropin-releasing hormone* from the hypothal-amus.

Support for the direct effect hypothesis comes from an investi-gation of the relationships among self-reported stress levels, the availability of social support, and circulating levels of prostate-specific antigen (PSA) in men being screened for prostate cancer (Stone and others, 1999). Men with the highest levels of self-reported stress also had significantly higher levels of PSA—a bio-logical marker of prostate malignancy—than their less-stressed counterparts. Although stress was positively associated with PSA levels, there was an *inverse* correlation between PSA levels and the participants' perceived level of social support, as demonstrated by their scores on the six-item *Satisfaction with Social Contacts (SSC)* scale (see Figure 5.5). The SSC includes items such as, "How has the number of people that you feel close to changed in the past 6 months?" and "How satisfied are you with the amount of social contact you have?" Those low in social support had significantly higher PSA levels than their more socially connected counterparts.

The issue of how social support benefits health continues to be hotly debated. It may be that social support makes potentially stressful events more benign by diffusing or minimizing their initial impact. For example, having a supportive friend may make it less likely that you will in-terpret a low exam grade as evidence of low intelligence. Or perhaps the belief that other people care about you increases your self-esteem and gives you a more positive outlook on life. The result? Greater resistance to disease and a greater chance of adopting health-enhancing habits.

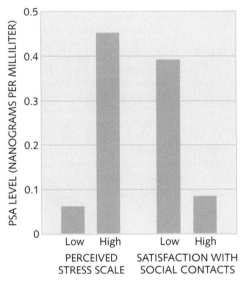

Figure 5.5

Stress, Social Support, and Prostate-Specific Antigen (PSA) Level of PSA was posi-tively associated with stress and inversely related to satisfaction with social contacts. Participants who perceived low levels of stress and high satisfaction with social contacts had significantly lower levels of PSA, a biological marker of prostate malignancy.

Source: Stone, A. A., and others. (1999). Psychosocial stress and social support are associated with prostate-specific antigen levels in men: Results from a community screening program. *Health Psychology, 18*(5) 485.

Who Receives Social Support?

Why are some people more likely than others to receive social support? The an-swer is predictable: People with better social skills—who relate well to others and who are caring and giving—create stronger social networks and thus receive more social support. Some evidence comes from a study of college freshmen (Cohen, Sherrod, & Clark, 1986). Researchers categorized incoming students ac-cording to their social competence, social anxiety, and self-disclosure skills. Over the course of the study, they discovered that students with greater social skills were the most likely to form strong social networks.

Other researchers have found that angry or hostile people receive less social support than agreeable people do. They also report more negative life events and make people around them feel more stress (Hardy & Smith, 1988; Wager and others, 2003). One study found that college hostility predicted low social support, risk for depression, achieving less than expected in career and in relationships, being a current smoker, and excessive alcohol consumption at midlife (Siegler and others, 2003). Results such as these suggest an obvious intervention: To help people increase their social support, help them learn to be friendlier and less hostile.

It would seem, then, that the secret to a long healthy life is to construct a large social network. But can a person be too socially connected? Can some social connections adversely affect our health?

When Social Support Is Not Helpful

Sometimes social support does not reduce stress and benefit health. In fact, it may produce opposite results. There are several reasons for this surprising fact. First, although support may be offered, a person may not *perceive* it as beneficial (Wilcox and others, 1994). This may occur because the person does not want the assistance, thinks the assistance offered is inadequate, or is too distracted to notice that help has been offered. For example, in the first hours of coping with the loss of a loved one, a person may want only to be alone with his or her grief.

Second, the type of support offered may not be what is needed at the moment. For example, a single mother who is struggling to complete her college degree may feel stress during exam weeks. Although what she may need most is *instrumental social support,* such as assistance with child care, all that may be offered is *emotional support,* such as encouragement to study hard. Instrumental social support is especially valuable for controllable stressors, whereas emotional support is more helpful for uncontrollable stressors, such as a cataclysmic event or the loss of a loved one. In one study of young widows, for example, the stress of losing a spouse was best buffered by emotional support (particularly from their parents). Conversely, among working women with young infants the only effective buffer was instrumental support from their spouse (Lieberman, 1982). The role of social support in promoting health, then, is quite specific. It is also subject to social and cultural norms concerning the types of support that are helpful (Abraido-Lanza, 2004).

Third, too much social support may actually increase a person's stress. Perhaps you know someone who is a member of too many organizations or is overwhelmed by intrusive social and family relationships. During periods of stress, this person may feel under siege in the face of all the advice and "support" that is offered (Shumaker & Hill, 1991). The critical factor appears to be having at least one close friend to confide in and share problems with. Having five, six, or even a dozen more may convey no more—perhaps less—benefit than having one or two (Langner & Michael, 1960).

Other Factors

Other factors that affect our ability to cope include practicing gratitude, maintaining a good sense of humor, and interacting with pets.

Gratitude

People who maintain a grateful outlook on life also cope better with stress and therefore experience improved psychological and physical well-being. In one recent study, healthy young adults and persons with neuromuscular disease were asked to keep weekly records of their moods, coping behaviors, health behaviors, physical symptoms, and overall life appraisals. Participants were randomly assigned to groups focused on daily hassles, things to be grateful for, or neutral life events. Those who kept gratitude journals exercised more regularly, reported fewer physical symptoms, and felt better about their lives as a whole, compared with those who recorded hassles or neutral life events (Emmons & McCullough, 2003).

Humor

Laughter and a sense of humor help many people cope with stress. In one of the best-known personal accounts of coping with chronic disease, Norman Cousins (1979) described how a daily dose of viewing comedy films helped relieve his pain. He credited laughter with helping him to regain his health and referred to the healing processes of laughter as "internal jogging."

Although personal accounts such as Cousins' are captivating, they provide only anecdotal evidence of the health-enhancing effects of humor. To date, only a few studies have systematically investigated humor and stress. Nevertheless, evidence is mounting that in addition to boosting mood, laughter bolsters the immune system, as measured by increased natural killer cell activity and reduced secretion of epinephrine and cortisol (Bennett and others, 2003); reduces the risk of coronary disease (Clark and others, 2001); lowers blood pressure (Hassed, 2001); and provides a general sense of well-being. By reducing epinephrine and cortisol secretion, laughing may also allow us to cope more effectively with everyday tension (Martin, 1988; Lefcourt, 2002). Laughter is even aerobic, providing a workout for the heart, diaphragm, and lungs as well as the muscles in the abdomen, shoulders, face, and occasionally the arms, legs, and back. One researcher (Fry, 1977) has estimated that laughing 100 times a day has the same physiological effect as a 10-minute workout on a rowing machine!

Pets

For three decades, Edward Creagan, an oncologist at the Mayo Clinic, has written prescriptions instructing cancer patients to keep pets. Pet ownership can help lower blood pressure responses to stress, decrease physician visits, and increase heart attack survival. "If pet ownership was a medication," Creagan says, "it would be patented tomorrow" (Pets and Aging 2001, pg. 5). In a recent study, hypertensive stockbrokers received the antihypertensive drug lisinopril; half also were given a pet. Those with a pet experienced half the increase in blood pressure to a laboratory stressor as those without a pet (Allen and others, 2001). In other studies, when researchers examined neuroendocrine responses in people before and after 30-minute quiet interaction periods with their pets, they found decreased secretion of cortisol and increased secretion of dopamine, oxytocin, and serotonin—three hormones associated with feelings of well-being (Johnson & Meadows, 2002; Odendaal, 2000). Recognizing that pets can be an important source of social support to the elderly, some assisted living facilities are even beginning to allow residents to keep pets. Even once-a-week exposure to a pet can produce a significant reduction in an elderly person's loneliness (Banks & Banks, 2002).

■ **stress management** the various psychological methods designed to reduce the impact of potentially stressful experiences.

Stress Management

Each of us has coping skills that we have acquired over the years. These include strategies that have worked in the past, techniques we have read about, and behaviors we have observed in other people. In most situations, these skills are probably adequate to keep us from experiencing undue stress. Sometimes, however, the demands of a situation may exceed our coping resources.

Stress management describes a variety of psychological methods designed to reduce the impact of potentially stressful experiences. These techniques were originally introduced in clinical settings to help patients adapt to chronic illnesses and stressful medical procedures, but now they are used widely. For example, occupational groups (especially health care providers, emergency services personnel, students, and teachers) and people in disadvantaged personal circumstances (such as family caregivers, single parents, the unemployed, and victims of assault or abuse) all benefit from stress-management techniques.

There are many techniques available to help people manage stress more effectively. We will consider exercise, relaxation training, biofeedback, and cognitive therapy.

People who take regular vacations are less likely to die prematurely, especially from heart disease. Bring along your pager or cell phone, however, and you won't reap the full stress-busting effects of time off—you'll be on guard for potential stress (Gump & Matthews, 2000).

Exercise

A sedentary lifestyle has been linked to such disorders as cardiovascular disease, obesity, osteoporosis, and back problems. It is also associated with a reduced ability to cope with stress, increased risk of depression, lower work productivity, and greater absenteeism (Long & van Stavel, 1995).

In contrast, many studies demonstrate that regularly taking part in sustained moderate-level exercise can have significant health-protective benefits (Owen & Vita, 1997). In our opening story, Latrice's fitness class may very well have contributed to her healthier adjustment, and Brittany's sedentary approach probably didn't help her cope. How, exactly, does exercise help us cope with stress? Two kinds of explanations have been offered: physiological and psychological.

Physiological Effects of Exercise

A number of researchers consider regular physical activity to be *the most effective* strategy for minimizing the impact of stressful events on physiological health (Thayer and others, 1994). Exercise has a profound affect on physiology. It enhances blood flow to the brain, stimulates the autonomic nervous system, and triggers the release of a variety of hormones. For these reasons, exercise may trigger a neurophysiological "high" that produces an antidepressant effect in some people, an antianxiety effect in others, and, at the very least, an enhanced sense of well-being in most (Sacks, 1990).

Researchers have found that exercise can moderate the effects of stress and help protect against disease (especially stress-linked disorders):

- Physically fit college students report fewer stress-related health problems than less active students (Roth & Holmes, 1985).

- Exercise can dampen the effect of laboratory stress—caused by trying to solve anagrams and math problems, for example—on cardiac reactivity in hypertensive subjects (Perkins and others, 1986). Aerobically fit individuals also display more rapid physiological recovery following stress (Moya-Albiol and others, 2001).

- Adolescents who exercise regularly are less vulnerable to the harmful effects of stressful life events (Brown, 1991; Brown & Siegel, 1988). One team of researchers measured stressful life events, amount of daily exercise, and symptoms of illness in adolescent girls between 12 and 16 years old. The analysis revealed that life stress predicted illness only in those subjects who were physically inactive. Among the physically fit girls, life stress had little relationship to illness.

- Exercise reduces blood pressure, resting heart rate, and cardiovascular reactivity, all of which tend to increase in stressful situations (Dimsdale and others, 1986). Physical activity may also prevent stress-induced suppression of the immune system (Fleshner, 2005).

Psychological Effects of Exercise

According to the psychological view, exercise is like other activities such as going to a movie, reading a book, or relaxing, in that it offers a change of pace. This alone may relieve stress. Exercise may also help people to feel better about their appearance, thus relieving some stressful anxiety. Nancy Norvell and Dale Belles (1993) assigned one-half of a group of law enforcement officers to a weight-training program and one-half to a nonexercising control group. Over the 4 months of the study, participants in the weight-training group reported significantly lower levels of anxiety. The researchers concluded that improved body appearance as well as the time out from stressful work accounted for the results of their study.

Depression, the most common of psychological disorders, is particularly responsive to exercise. A growing body of research suggests that physically active people have lower rates of anxiety and depression than sedentary people (Statistics Canada, 1999). Consider a classic study in which Lisa McCann and David Holmes (1984) randomly assigned one-third of a group of mildly depressed female college students to an aerobic exercise program, another third to a program of relaxation exercises, and the final third to a no-treatment condition (the control group). Ten weeks later, the subjects in the exercise group reported the largest decrease in depression.

Depressed people have low levels of norepinephrine and serotonin, two neurotransmitters that increase arousal and boost mood. Aerobic exercise may counteract depression by increasing the serotonin activity in the brain and thus replacing depression's state of low arousal. In this manner, exercise does naturally what antidepressant drugs such as Prozac, Zoloft, and Paxil are designed to do (Jacobs, 1994).

Aerobic exercise can also be an effective adjunct to counseling or other forms of psychotherapy in decreasing anxiety, improving self-esteem, and reducing depression (Manger & Motta, 2005). In one study, depressed subjects were randomly assigned to a running therapy group, a traditional group psychotherapy program, or a relaxation-training group. Those in the running therapy group received no other form of treatment (they were even forbidden to discuss their depression during the study). During the clinical trial, running therapy patients ran with a group leader in small groups for 1 hour three to four times a week. After 12 weeks, all the subjects reported lower levels of depression. However, 3 months later, only the running and relaxation groups continued to show improvement in their psychological well-being. Patients who had received traditional psychotherapy actually showed some regression toward higher levels of depression.

Interestingly, the type of exercise seems in part to determine its benefits. In one study, researchers induced a depression-like state of reduced activity level and impaired sex drive in rats by administering the drug clomipramine (Dunn and others, 1996). They then allowed one group of the drugged rats 24-hour voluntary access to an activity wheel for 12 weeks. A second group of drugged animals was forced to run on a treadmill for 1 hour each day, 6 days a week, for 12 weeks. A third group was given the antidepressant drug imipramine for the last 6 days of the 12-week experiment. A fourth, control group received no treatment whatsoever—no medication and no exercise—for the duration of the experiment. The rats that received imipramine showed increased brain concentrations of both norepinephrine and serotonin—classic signs that the antidepressant drug was counteracting the drug-induced state of depression. The two exercise groups also showed increases in both neurotransmitters. But only the rats in the voluntary exercise

Exercise Protects against Stress and Illness Regular intense exercise, such as playing soccer, has a profound effect on physiology, enhancing blood flow to the brain, stimulating the autonomic nervous system, and triggering the release of various beneficial hormones. All these physiological effects tend to protect against illness, especially stress-related health problems. Fitness level, more than age, determines what type of exercise we can do. For example, few people of any age can keep up with Ed Whitlock, who is running record-breaking marathon times at age 73.

■ **progressive muscle relaxation**
a form of relaxation training
that reduces muscle tension
through a series of tensing and
relaxing exercises involving the
body's major muscle groups.

group also displayed increased behavioral and sexual activity, the *behavioral* measures the researchers used to rate depression.

Other studies with human subjects have found that significant reductions in tension, anxiety, and stress are more likely to occur following exercise in which the subjects exercised at 60 to 80 percent of their VO_2 *max*—a measure of the maximum rate at which oxygen can be used by a person's body (Farrell and others, 1982). This finding is intriguing because athletes, personal trainers, and exercise physiologists know that this level of intensity is needed to receive aerobic benefit from exercise. Otherwise little, if any, cardiorespiratory benefits are derived.

How do you know if you are exercising at 60 to 80 percent of your VO_2 max? Outside of sophisticated laboratory tests that measure respiratory gases, VO_2 max is often determined from *maximum heart rate* (MHR). You can estimate your MHR from your age: 100 percent of MHR is estimated as 220 minus a person's age. To calculate 60 percent of MHR for a twenty-year-old, for example, you would subtract 20 from 220 and multiply the results times 0.6:

$$220 - 20 = 200$$
$$200 \times 0.60 = 120 \text{ beats per minute}$$

To find out if you are exercising at this level, count your pulse for 10 seconds and then multiply that figure by 6 to determine the number of beats per minute. Interestingly, when they do actually exercise, couch potatoes tend to overestimate how hard they are working (Duncan, 2001).

Research studies such as these imply that simply "prescribing" exercise may not guarantee improved psychological health. Although the forced-exercise treadmill rats in the study described earlier exercised more than the voluntary-exercise activity-wheel rats, the wheel runners displayed the greatest behavioral benefits, suggesting that fitness may only be part of the reason that exercise improves mental health. The ultimate benefits of exercise are probably the result of a combination of biological, psychological, and social factors. And although *any* physical activity is better than none, to derive the greatest benefit—both physically and psychologically—you need to exert yourself, and you need to want to do what you're doing. Start slow and build up to greater exercise intensity. For example, if you want to run, start with brisk daily walks and then begin interspersing walking and jogging. Choose an activity you enjoy and can share with friends, and stick with it!

Relaxation Therapies

Although relaxation techniques have been used since antiquity, modern use is usually traced to Edmond Jacobson (1938), whose **progressive muscle relaxation** technique forms the cornerstone for many modern relaxation procedures. In progressive relaxation, you first tense a particular muscle (such as the forehead) and hold that tension for about 10 seconds. Then you slowly release the tension, focusing on the soothing feeling as the tension drains away. Then you tense, then relax other major muscle groups, including the mouth, eyes, neck, arms, shoulders, thighs, stomach, calves, feet, and toes. After practicing the relaxation technique for several weeks, you will identify the particular spots in your body that tense up during moments of stress, such as the jaw or fists. As you become more aware of these reactions, you can learn to relax these muscles at will.

In another training technique, the **relaxation response,** participants assume the meditative state described below, in which metabolism slows and blood pressure lowers. Cardiologist Herbert Benson became intrigued with the possibility that relaxation might be an antidote to stress when he found that experienced meditators could lower their heart rate, blood lactate level (a by-product of physical exercise that creates the "burn" of muscular exertion), blood pressure, and oxygen consumption (Benson, 1996). Benson identified four requirements for achieving the relaxation response:

- A quiet place in which distractions and external stimulation are minimized
- A comfortable position such as sitting in an easy chair
- A mental device such as focusing your attention on a single thought or word and repeating it over and over
- A passive attitude

There is considerable evidence that relaxation training can help patients cope with a variety of stress-related problems, including hypertension, tension headaches, depression, lower back pain, adjustment to chemotherapy, and anxiety (Smith, 2005). Underlying the effectiveness of these techniques is their ability to reduce heart rate, muscle tension, and blood pressure, as well as self-reported tension and anxiety. Moreover, these techniques have generally been found to be more effective than placebos in reducing pain and alleviating stress.

Deep Breathing and Visualization

When we're stressed, our breathing is often short and hurried. Simply slowing it down by taking long, slow breaths can help induce relaxation. You can try this yourself. Inhale slowly, then exhale slowly. Count slowly to five as you inhale, and then count slowly to five as you exhale. As you exhale, note how your body relaxes. The keys to *deep breathing* are to breathe with your diaphragm, or abdomen, rather than your chest, and to take at least as long to exhale each breath as you did to inhale. Imagine a spot just below your navel. Breathe into that spot, expanding your abdomen as it fills with air. Let the air fill you from the abdomen up, then let it out, like deflating a balloon. Each long, slow exhalation should make you feel more relaxed.

Breathing techniques are often combined with matching *visualization* (guided mental imagery)—a form of focused relaxation used to create peaceful images in your mind—a "mental escape." In *guided imagery* the participant is directed to recall or create a pleasant, relaxing image, focusing attention on sensory details such as sensations of color, sound, and touch. Visualization is powerful enough to reduce, or even to trigger, stress reactions in the laboratory. In one study, participants spent 5 minutes imagining scenes typical of their relationship with a romantic partner. Those who had earlier reported being in an

■ **relaxation response** a meditative state of relaxation in which metabolism slows and blood pressure lowers.

Meditation Many people find meditation to be an effective technique for managing stress. According to research by Herbert Benson, experienced meditators can lower their heart rate, blood lactate level, blood pressure, and oxygen consumption, and so reduce or even eliminate the effects of stress. However, other studies have shown that meditation does not achieve these results more reliably than other forms of relaxation.

■ **biofeedback** a system that provides audible or visible feedback information regarding involuntary physiological states.

unhappy relationship had significantly greater increases in salivary cortisol following the imagery (indicating higher stress) than those in happier relationships (Berry and Worthington, 2001).

To try it for yourself, find a comfortable place where you can close your eyes and begin breathing rhythmically. Breathe deeply, but make sure you do so in a natural rhythm. Now visualize relaxation entering your body as you inhale, and tension leaving your body as you exhale. As you breathe, visualize your breath coming into your nostrils, going into your lungs, and expanding your chest and abdomen. Then visualize your breath going out the same way. Continue breathing, but each time you inhale, imagine that you are breathing in more relaxation. Each time you exhale, imagine that you are getting rid of a little more tension.

Finally, breathing techniques and visualization can be combined with positive *self-affirmations*, or self-talk, as you relax. The goal is to identify negative self-talk and convert it into healthier, positive self-talk. Here are a few positive statements you can practice.

- I am healthy and strong.
- There is nothing that I cannot handle.
- I am safe.

Biofeedback

First described by Neal Miller in the late 1960s, **biofeedback** is a technique for converting certain supposedly involuntary physiological responses—such as skin temperature, muscle activity, heart rate, and blood pressure—into electrical signals and providing visual or auditory feedback about them (Miller, 1969). It is based on the principle that we learn to perform a specific response when we receive information (feedback) about the consequences of that response and then make appropriate adjustments.

Using an electronic monitoring device that detects and amplifies internal responses, biofeedback training begins by helping the person gain awareness of a maladaptive response, such as tense forehead muscles. Next, the person focuses attention on a tone, light, or some other signal that identifies desirable changes in the internal response. By attempting to control this biofeedback signal, the patient learns to control his or her physiological state. Finally, the individual learns to transfer control from the laboratory setting to everyday life. David Shapiro and his colleagues (1969) were the first to show that humans could control their blood pressure via biofeedback. Their participants could lower their systolic blood pressure only a small amount during a single session, however, typically averaging only 5 mmHg.

The most common biofeedback technique in clinical use today is *electromyography (EMG) feedback*. EMG biofeedback detects skeletal muscle activity by measuring muscle tension via the electrical discharge of muscle fibers. Electrodes are attached to the skin over the muscles to be monitored. The biofeedback machine responds with an auditory signal that reflects the electrical activity (tension) of the muscle being measured. EMG biofeedback to decrease muscle tension has been used to treat facial tics, spasmodic movements, and other muscular disorders. It has also been used to treat headaches and lower back pain.

Another common technique, *thermal biofeedback,* is based on the principle that skin temperature tends to vary in relation to a person's perceived level of stress. The rationale for this technique is that high stress, which often causes blood vessels in the skin to constrict, may be linked with cooler surface skin temperatures. Accordingly, by placing a temperature-sensitive instrument on the skin's surface (most often the fingertips), people sometimes are able to raise their skin temperature by monitoring an auditory or visual feedback signal (Sedlacek & Taub, 1996). Thermal biofeedback is often used to help people cope with stress and pain, such as that associated with *Raynaud's disease,* a cardiovascular disorder in which the fingers and toes suffer from a cold, numb aching due to severely reduced circulation. Thermal biofeedback is also frequently used with migraine and tension headache patients (Compas and others, 1998).

Biofeedback Biofeedback is a viable means of treating a variety of anxiety and stress-related disorders in some people. Using computerized imaging, the person affects physiological functions using visual/sound feedback. Although biofeedback does seem to enable control of internal functions, evidence to date suggests that it conveys no advantage over other, less expensive relaxation techniques.

How Effective Is Biofeedback?

Biofeedback has proved to be somewhat beneficial in treating stress-related health problems in some people. For example, research support is relatively strong for alleviation of tension headaches (presumed to involve chronic muscle tension in the neck and head) and migraine headaches (McGrady, 1997). Other disorders for which there is at least some research support to justify the therapeutic use of biofeeback include asthma, chronic pain, irritable bowl syndrome, tinnitus, epileptic seizures, and motion sickness (Moss & Gunkelman, 2002).

Despite some promising results, several important questions remain about biofeedback's medical effectiveness. To date, there have been relatively few well-controlled clinical outcome trials using large numbers of patients who have confirmed medical conditions. Two limitations have emerged in clinical evaluations of biofeedback (Steptoe, 1997). First, people often cannot generalize the training they receive in clinical settings to everyday situations. Second, research has not successfully confirmed that biofeedback itself enables people to control their internal, involuntary responses. Even when biofeedback is effective, it is not clear why, which raises the possibility that relaxation, suggestion, an enhanced sense of control, or even a placebo effect may be operating (Gatchel, 1997).

The few available studies on the use of biofeedback for maladies such as lower back pain and hypertension have produced mixed results. For instance, although biofeedback alone may be no more effective than a drug placebo in treating lower back pain (Bush and others, 1985), when biofeedback is combined with cognitive-behavioral therapy, it may convey some advantages (Flor & Birbaumer, 1993). And although psychologists have reported some success in using biofeedback to treat patients with mild hypertension (Nakao and others, 1997; Paran and others, 1996), the effect apparently is short lived, disappearing after only a few months (McGrady, 1994). However, because stress is often linked to either momentary or long-term increases in systolic and diastolic blood pressure, biofeedback has also been shown to be an effective *complementary* therapy—combined with lifestyle modifications in diet, weight, and exercise—for reducing patients' dependence on medication in managing hypertension (Goebel and others, 1993).

Equally troubling for advocates of biofeedback therapy is the finding that patients with lower back pain or migraine and tension headaches typically report less pain over time, *even without any form of treatment* (Bush and others, 1985). This finding seriously undermines the credibility of biofeedback (and any other treatment) and may help explain why testimonials regarding biofeedback's effectiveness abound. Because people with moderate pain are likely to improve over time anyway, any form of treatment they try in the interim may, as a result of coincidence, seem effective. We'll explore this issue further in Chapter 14, when we take up the topic of alternative medicine.

After reviewing a number of studies, Paul Lehrer and his colleagues (1994) concluded that although biofeedback can help reduce autonomic arousal, anxiety, and stress-related disorders in *some* people, it conveys no advantage over other behavioral techniques (such as simple relaxation training) that are easier and less expensive to use. The positive effects of biofeedback are more general than its pioneers had originally believed and may be the result of enhanced relaxation, a placebo effect, the passage of time, or suggestion, rather than direct control of specific targets or the physical underpinnings of stress (Gilbert & Moss, 2003).

Cognitive Therapies

Cognitive therapy shares commonalities with relaxation therapy and biofeedback. It is based on the view that our way of thinking about the environment, rather than the environment itself, determines our stress level. If thinking can be changed, stress can be reduced. There are a variety of clinical interventions that use cognitive strategies, including distraction, calming self-statements, and cognitive restructuring. In distraction procedures, people learn to direct their attention away from unpleasant or stressful events. Use of pleasant imagery (also called *visualization*), counting aloud, and focusing attention on relaxing stimuli (such as a favorite drawing, photograph, or song) are examples of distraction.

Individuals can also be taught to silently or softly make calming, relaxing, and reassuring self-talk statements that emphasize the temporary nature of a stressor ("Let it go, that rude driver won't get to me."), are aimed at reducing autonomic arousal ("Stay calm now, breathe deeply and count to 10."), or are directed at preserving a sense of personal control ("I can handle this."). In our opening story, Latrice's therapist might have helped her to learn self-calming techniques and to maintain a sense of self-control.

Cognitive restructuring is a generic term that describes a variety of psychological interventions directed at replacing maladaptive, self-defeating thoughts

■ **cognitive therapy** the category of treatments that teach people healthier ways of thinking.

with healthier adaptive thinking. These interventions aim to break the vicious cycle of negative thinking, which pessimistically distorts perceptions of everyday events and prevents adaptive coping behaviors (Belar & Deardorff, 1996) (Figure 5.6). Therapists teach clients to reinterpret their thoughts in a less negative way and to raise awareness of distorted and maladaptive thinking.

This reciprocal relationship between maladaptive thinking and unhealthy behaviors is well documented. For example, focusing on a negative experience at work can affect your mood and lead to a tension headache. Having a tension headache can sour your mood, which can, in turn, make your thoughts more pessimistic.

Rational-Emotive Therapy

One of the first and most effective forms of cognitive restructuring, **rational-emotive therapy (RET),** was developed by Albert Ellis (1962). RET is based on the premise that the stress appraisal processes, which we examined in Chapter 4, becomes dysfunctional when people engage in irrational thinking. There are many examples of irrational thinking, including *catastrophizing,* which occurs when an unpleasant event that might be perceived as a minor inconvenience is psychologically blown out of proportion into a global disaster from which the individual may never recover. Other examples include the tendency to expect negative events at every turn ("I just know something awful is about to happen to me."), to underestimate ability to cope with stressful events ("I can't live if she dumps me."), and to tie a sense of self-worth to performance on a particular task ("I am worthless if I don't get an 'A' in this class.").

Researchers have demonstrated that a tendency to engage in this type of irrational thinking is hazardous to health. For instance, Christopher Peterson and his colleagues analyzed the relationship between explanatory style and mortality among participants in the Terman Life Cycle Study, a longitudinal study of men and women born around 1910 and followed from the 1920s to the present. The participants completed a variety of open-ended questionnaires in 1936 and 1940, including some that tapped their explanatory style. Catastrophizing strongly predicted mortality, especially among men, and especially deaths due to accidental causes and violence (Peterson and others, 1998). Catastrophizing has also been shown to be a particularly harmful cognitive factor among patients with chronic pain (Michael & Burns, 2004).

Once irrational beliefs and thought processes are identified, a cognitive therapist can challenge the person to restructure them into more rational, adaptive thought patterns such as, "If I do poorly on this test, it's not the end of the world. I'll just have to study harder next time," or "My grade in this class doesn't reflect my worth as a person," or "Just because she dumped me, it doesn't mean that I'm unlovable."

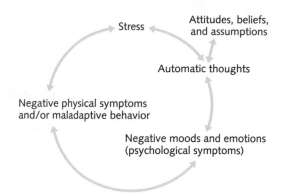

Figure 5.6

The Negative Stress Cycle
Stressful events interpreted through a pessimistic, self-defeating style create a negative mood that leads to stress-related physical symptoms and fuels additional stress. Fortunately, this vicious cycle can be interrupted at any point.

■ **rational-emotive therapy (RET)** a confrontational form of cognitive therapy, developed by Albert Ellis, that challenges people's irrational ideas and attitudes.

Ellis believes people can learn to deal rationally with their problems, use logic to analyze their belief systems, and minimize the impact of unpleasant situations. We cannot always escape stressors, but we can learn to manage our emotional responses to those stressors.

Cognitive Behavioral Stress Management

Cognitive behavioral stress management (CBSM) combines relaxation training, visualization, cognitive restructuring, reinforcement, and other techniques into a multimodal intervention that has helped people suffering from a number of medical conditions (Lau and others, 2003). CBSM often begins by teaching people to confront stressful events with a variety of coping strategies that can be used before the events become overwhelming. In this way, individuals are able to "inoculate" themselves against the potentially harmful effects of stress (Meichenbaum, 1985). Many stress inoculation programs offer an array of techniques, so that a client can choose the strategies that work best for him or her.

Stress inoculation training is a three-stage process, with the therapist using a weakened dose of a stressor in an attempt to build immunity against the full-blown stressor.

■ Stage 1: *Reconceptualization*. Patients reconceptualize the source of their stress. Imagine that you are agonizing over an upcoming dental procedure, such as a root canal. During the first stage of stress inoculation training, you would learn that your discomfort is at least partially the result of psychological factors, such as dwelling on how much the procedure is going to hurt. Once you are convinced that some of your pain is psychological in nature, you will then be more likely to accept that cognitive-behavior therapy can offer some relief.

■ Stage 2: *Skills acquisition*. Next you will be taught relaxation and controlled breathing skills. The logic is inescapable: Being relaxed is incompatible with being tense and physically aroused. Therefore, learning to relax at will is a valuable tool in managing pain. Other techniques you might learn include the use of pleasant mental imagery, dissociation, or humor.

■ Stage 3: *Follow-through*. Now you will learn to use these coping skills in everyday life. You will be encouraged to increase your physical activity and to take pain medication on a timed daily schedule rather than whenever you feel pain. Your family members may be taught ways of reinforcing your new healthier behaviors.

CBSM has proved to be effective in helping people cope with a variety of stress-related problems, including hypertension (Amigo and others, 1991), depression associated with breast cancer (Antoni and others, 2001), prostate cancer (Penedo and others, 2004), and AIDS (Antoni and others, 2001). CBSM has also been shown to reduce HPA axis hormones (see Chapter 4) among symptomatic human immunodeficiency virus (HIV)-infected men (Antoni and others, 2001); and reduce postsurgical pain, rehabilitation, and the number of health service visits among competitive athletes (Perna and others, 2003).

Figure 5.7

A Biopsychosocial View of Coping With and Managing Stress

Biological Influences:
- Greater regulatory control
- Hardy personality

Coping with and managing stress effectively

Social Influences:
- Experiencing helpful social support
- Interacting with pets
- Disclosing emotional experiences articulately to family or friends or in writing

Psychological Influences:
- Using active coping mechanisms
- Developing an optimistic explanatory style
- Being grateful
- Maintaining a sense of humor
- Establishing a feeling of personal control
- Exercising
- Using relaxation techniques
- Utilizing cognitive therapy techniques

We all experience stress, but we don't all cope with it effectively. Our coping resources can best be understood from a biopsychosocial perspective. We cannot control all of the factors. For example, we are affected by our inherited personality type and cardiovascular reactivity level, with the hardiest personalities and the least reactive coping best. However, the many psychological and social factors affecting our ability to cope with and then manage our stress are well within our control, as shown in Figure 5.7. Actively pursue these techniques, and watch your health improve.

Summing Up

Responding to Stress

1. Coping refers to the various ways—sometimes healthy, sometimes unhealthy—in which people attempt to prevent, eliminate, weaken, or simply tolerate stress. Emotion-focused coping refers to efforts to control your emotional response to a stressor, either by distancing yourself from it or by changing how you appraise it. Problem-focused coping refers to efforts to deal directly with a stressor by applying problem-solving skills to anticipate and prevent potential stressors or by directly confronting the source of stress.

2. Compared to women, men react to stress with larger increases in blood pressure, low-density lipoprotein cholesterol, and certain stress hormones. In general, women report more symptoms of stress and are more emotionally responsive to stressful situations. When women and men of similar SES are compared, gender differences in coping styles disappear. People of higher SES are more likely than those of lower SES to use problem-focused coping strategies in dealing with stress. Low SES is often accompanied by a stressful lifestyle that limits a person's options in coping with stress.

Factors Affecting the Ability to Cope

3. Hardy people may be healthier because they are less likely to become overwhelmed by stressful situations. Along with hardiness, resilience in children is positively correlated with physical and mental health.

4. People whose explanatory style is negative tend to explain failures in terms that are global, stable, and internal. This,

in turn, may increase their sensitivity to challenging events and promote self-blame, pessimism, and depression. In contrast, optimists may be healthier and more resistant to stress. Optimism is also related to greater perceived control and self-efficacy, which in turn are related to more effective coping responses.

5. The opportunity to control aversive events plays a crucial role in determining a person's response to a stressful situation. Biologically, exposure to stressors without the perception of control activates the autonomic nervous system. The perception of control buffers stress-related arousal and enhances immune activity.

6. Repeated exposure to uncontrollable stressors may lead to the resigned, passive behavior of learned helplessness. Studies of elderly persons and nursing home residents show that helplessness can lead to depression, a shortened life span, and a variety of health-compromising behaviors.

7. Cardiovascular reactivity is a biological marker of individual differences in regulatory control during moments of stress. People with high vagal tone experience less negative emotional arousal in response to stress. They are also more likely to rely on constructive coping measures than are people who exercise less regulatory control. Repressive coping is an emotion-focused coping style in which the person attempts to inhibit his or her emotional responses.

8. People who perceive a high level of social support may cope with stress more effectively than people who feel alienated. Along with companionship, social ties can provide emotional support, instrumental support, and informational support. Social support produces its beneficial effects indirectly, by helping people cope more effectively (buffering hypothesis), or directly, by enhancing the body's responses to challenging events (direct-effect hypothesis).

9. People with better social skills—who relate well to others and who are caring and giving—create stronger social networks and thus receive more social support. Social support does not always reduce stress and benefit health. Sometimes, support is perceived as intrusive; other times, the type of support offered is not what is needed.

10. Other factors that positively affect our ability to cope include maintaining a grateful outlook on life, enjoying a good sense of humor and frequent laughter, and regularly interacting with pets.

Stress Management

11. Regular physical activity can improve a person's psychological and physiological ability to cope with stress. Exercise produces an antidepressant/antianxiety effect in many people, enhances the efficacy of the immune system, and lowers blood pressure and cardiovascular reactivity.

12. Relaxation techniques such as progressive muscle relaxation and the relaxation response (meditation) can help people cope with a variety of stress-related problems, including hypertension, headaches, chronic pain, and anxiety.

13. Biofeedback is a technique for converting certain supposedly involuntary physiological responses, such as skin temperature, muscle activity, heart rate, and blood pressure, into electrical signals and providing visual or auditory feedback about them. Although results from studies of biofeedback effectiveness are mixed, the method is a viable means of treating some stress-related disorders when combined with other, more conventional treatments.

14. Cognitive therapies are aimed at breaking the cycle of irrational thought patterns that distort people's perception of everyday events and prevent them from adopting appropriate coping behaviors. Rational-emotive therapy is a confrontational—directly challenging people's irrational beliefs. Cognitive behavioral stress management is a multimodal form of therapy that helps people to confront stressful events with coping strategies that can be put in place before stressors become overwhelming.

Key Terms and Concepts

coping, p. 118
emotion-focused coping, p. 118
problem-focused coping, p. 119
hardiness, p. 125
resilience, p. 126
explanatory style, p. 127
rumination, p. 128

personal control, p. 129
regulatory control, p. 132
repressive coping, p. 135
social support, p. 137
buffering hypothesis, p. 137
direct effect hypothesis, p. 138
stress management, p. 141

progressive muscle relaxation, p. 144
relaxation response, p. 145
biofeedback, p. 146
cognitive therapy, p. 148
rational-emotive therapy (RET),
   p. 149

Part 3 | Behavior and Health

Staying Healthy: Primary Prevention and Positive Psychology

*W*hen Sara Snodgrass found the lump in her breast, her first thoughts were of her aunt and mother, both of whom died after battling breast cancer. After her aunt was diagnosed with cancer, she "went home, pulled all the curtains closed, refused to leave the house except for chemotherapy treatments, and allowed very few visitors. She waited for death." (Snodgrass, 1998; p. 3). Sara's biopsy was followed by a lumpectomy (removal of the malignant tumor) and 2 months of radiation treatments. Although she and her doctor were hopeful that she was through with cancer, less than 1 year later metastasized cancer was found in her abdomen. In her words, she has been "submerged in cancer" ever since, having undergone three surgeries, five different courses of chemotherapy, two types of hormone therapy, 3 months of radiation, a bone marrow transplant, and a stem cell transplant. Throughout her treatment, she has also battled unpredictable, debilitating pain 10–14 days per month.

Unlike her aunt, however, Sara continued her work as a university professor throughout her surgery, radiation, and chemotherapy. Determined that cancer would not interfere with her life, she also continued scuba diving, skiing, and other activities that flowed from her natural optimism, sense of self-mastery, and confidence. And she took charge of her health care, learning everything she could about her treatments, making her own decisions, and refusing to work with doctors who did not treat her with respect and honor her desire to maintain a sense of control over her life.

Perhaps most remarkable of all is Sara's conviction that her cancer has led to a reorganization of her self-perception, relationships, and philosophy of life. It has taught her to live more in the present rather than worrying about the future. She stopped worrying about whether

she would find the right man, whether her students would give her good evalua-
tions, and if she would have enough money to live comfortably in retirement. She
also has learned that relationships with friends and family are the most important
part of her life. When thinking about dying, she asserts, "I will not say I wish I had
written more articles. However, I might say I wish I had seen or talked to more
friends or acquaintances with whom I had lost contact." So that is what she is
doing—corresponding, telephoning, and traveling to renew old relationships, and
reveling in new ones that have extended her network of social support throughout
the country.

Statistically, only 15 percent of metastasized breast cancer patients live 5 years.
Yet in 8 years Sara's cancer has not spread and has grown imperceptibly. Equally
important, Sara believes that she is growing as a person and experiencing her life
more positively than before. By her own description, her experience of adversity
has yielded unexpected benefits that have enabled her to thrive psychologically.

The relationship between lifestyle and health has triggered a massive research effort aimed at preventing injury and disease. Sometimes illness cannot be prevented, as in Sara's case. Yet even in such extreme
cases, building our human strengths may allow us the capacity to thrive. In this
chapter, we will start by considering the connection between behavior and
health. Then we will explore how health psychology's biopsychosocial focus on
strength-based approaches to prevention, first, and positive psychology, second, can help build healthy individuals, families, and communities.

Health and Behavior

It is difficult to imagine an activity or behavior that does not influence
health in some way—for better or worse, directly or indirectly, immediately
or over the long term. **Health behaviors** are behaviors that people engage
in to improve or maintain their health. Exercising regularly, using sunscreen,
eating a low-fat diet, practicing safe sex, and wearing seatbelts are all behaviors
that help "immunize" you against disease and injury. Less obvious examples include pleasurable hobbies, meditation, laughter, regular vacations, and even
owning a pet. These activities help many people manage stress and retain an
upbeat outlook on life.

Because health behaviors occur on a continuum, some health behaviors can
have both a positive and a negative impact on health (Schoenborn and others,
2004). For example, exercise and dieting can lead to a beneficial loss of weight;

■ **health behavior** a health-
enhancing behavior or habit; also
called *behavioral immunogen.*

if carried to the extreme, though, they can trigger a "yo-yo" pattern of weight loss and gain that might be hazardous to your health. Similarly, classification of "healthy" use of alcohol is problematic because while studies on the health benefits of light or moderate alcohol use abound, exactly what constitutes "light" or "moderate" drinking seems to depend on a person's gender and other characteristics (Green and others, 2004).

Excessive use of alcohol is an example of a *health-risk behavior* that has a direct negative impact on physical health. Other behaviors influence health indirectly through their association with behaviors that have a direct impact on health. Heavy coffee drinking, for example, may increase the risk of heart disease, because many people who drink coffee excessively also smoke and engage in other risky behaviors that increase the risk of heart disease (Cornelis and others, 2006).

As part of its *Youth Risk Behavior Surveillance* project, the Centers for Disease Control and Prevention (2004) identified six health-risk behaviors—often begun while young—that put people at risk for premature death, disability, and chronic illness:

1. Smoking and other forms of tobacco use

2. Eating high-fat and low-fiber foods

3. Not engaging in enough physical activity

4. Abusing alcohol or other drugs

5. Not using proven medical methods for preventing or diagnosing disease early (e.g., flu shots, Pap smears, colonoscopies, mammograms)

6. Engaging in violent behavior or behavior that may cause unintentional injuries (e.g., driving while intoxicated)

Some behaviors affect health immediately—for example, being involved in an automobile accident while not wearing a seatbelt. Others, such as eating a high-fat diet, have a long-term effect. And some behaviors, such as exercising or cigarette smoking, have both an immediate and a long-term effect on health. Health behaviors also interact and often are interrelated. Someone who smokes, for example, may drink alcohol and excessive amounts of coffee. The combined effect of these behaviors on health is stronger than if the person engaged in only one such behavior. Similarly, exercising regularly, eating healthy foods, and drinking lots of water also tend to come together, but in a positive way. Sometimes a person may engage in both healthy behaviors and unhealthy behaviors—for example, drinking alcohol and exercising. In such cases, one may help offset the effects of the other. Finally, a healthy behavior may replace an unhealthy one. For example, many ex-smokers find that regular aerobic exercise provides a healthy (and effective) substitute for nicotine.

What is the potential impact of adopting a healthier lifestyle? In one classic epidemiological study begun in 1965, Lester Breslow and Norman Breslow began to track the health and lifestyle habits of male residents of Alameda County, California. Over the many years of this landmark study, the salutary effects of seven healthy habits—sleeping 7 to 8 hours daily, never smoking, being

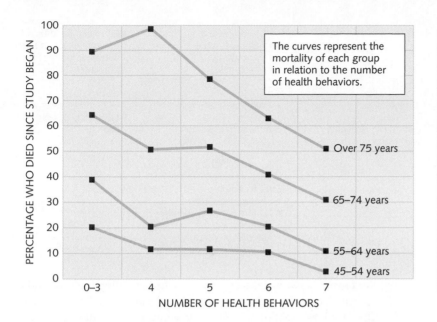

The curves represent the mortality of each group in relation to the number of health behaviors.

PERCENTAGE WHO DIED SINCE STUDY BEGAN

NUMBER OF HEALTH BEHAVIORS

Over 75 years

65–74 years

55–64 years

45–54 years

Figure 6.1

Health Behaviors and Death Rate Nine and a half years into the famous Alameda Health Study, the mortality of men who regularly practiced all seven health habits (sleeping 7 to 8 hours daily, never smoking, being at or near a healthy body weight, moderate use of alcohol, regular physical exercise, eating breakfast, and avoiding between-meal snacking) was 28 percent of the mortality of those who had practiced three or fewer healthy behaviors.

Source: Breslow, L., Breslow, N. (1993). Health practices and disability: Some evidence from Alameda County. *Preventive Medicine, 22,* 86–95.

at or near a healthy body weight, moderate use of alcohol, regular physical exercise, eating breakfast, and avoiding between-meal snacking—have proved striking (Figure 6.1).

Theories of Health Behavior

Health psychologists have developed a number of theories to explain whether or not people engage in healthful or unhealthful behaviors. In this section, we discuss several of the most influential theories.

The Health Belief Model

According to the **health belief model (HBM),** decisions about health behavior are based on four interacting factors that influence our perceptions about health threats (Figure 6.2, p. 158) (Strecher & Rosenstock, 1997):

- *Perceived susceptibility.* Some people worry constantly about their vulnerability to health threats such as HIV; others believe they are not in danger. The greater the perceived susceptibility, the stronger the motivation to engage in health-promoting behaviors. Adolescents especially seem to have a false sense of "invulnerability" that gives them little motivation to change risky behaviors.

- *Perceived severity* of the health threat. Among the factors considered are whether pain, disability, or death may result, as well as whether the condition will have an impact on family, friends, and coworkers. Sara Snodrass recognized the seriousness of her condition and worked hard toward healthful behaviors and ways of thinking.

■ **health belief model (HBM)** non-stage theory that identifies three beliefs that influence decision making regarding health behavior: perceived susceptibility to a health threat, perceived severity of the disease or condition, and perceived benefits of and barriers to the behavior.

Figure 6.2

The Health Belief Model
This non-stage theory emphasizes the interacting factors that influence our decision making about health behaviors. If we believe that an available course of action will reduce our susceptibility to or the severity of the condition, then we will engage in that health behavior.

Source: Strecher, V. J., Rosenstock, I. W. (1997). The health belief model. In A. Baum, S. Newman, J. Weinman, R. West, & C. McManus (Eds.), *Cambridge handbook of psychology, health, and medicine* (p. 115). Cambridge, UK: Cambridge University Press.

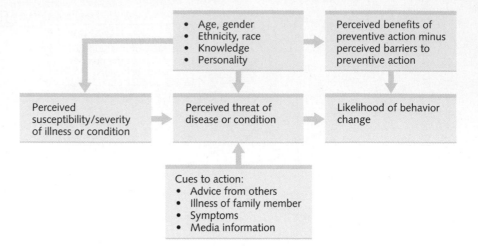

- *Perceived benefits and barriers of treatment.* In evaluating the pros and cons of a particular health behavior, a person decides whether its perceived benefits—such as enabling him or her to avoid a potentially fatal disease—exceed its barriers—such as causing unpleasant side effects or triggering a negative reaction from peers. For example, someone may overlook the huge advantages of quitting smoking due to concerns about becoming obese and unattractive.

- *Cues to action.* Advice from friends, media health campaigns, and factors such as age, socioeconomic status, and gender will also influence the likelihood that the person will act.

In summary, the HBM is a commonsense theory proposing that people will take action to ward off or control illness-inducing conditions: (1) if they regard themselves as susceptible to the condition, (2) if they believe the condition has serious personal consequences, (3) if they believe a course of action available to them will reduce either their susceptibility or the severity of the condition, (4) if they believe that the costs of taking the action are outweighed by the benefits of doing so, and (5) if environmental influences are encouraging change (Strecher & Rosenstock, 1997).

The HBM has been the first health model subjected to extensive research. We have learned that people are more likely to have regular dental checkups, practice safe sex, obtain health screenings for colorectal and other forms of cancer, and engage in other health-protective behaviors if they feel susceptible to the various health problems that might stem from failure to do so (Manne and others, 2002). Studies also show that educational interventions aimed at changing health beliefs do increase health-protective behaviors. For example, women who receive educational messages aimed at enhancing their knowledge of the benefits of mammography are nearly four times more likely to seek mammography than women in a control group (Champion, 1994).

Despite these successes, some studies have found that health beliefs only modestly predict health behaviors, and that other factors, such as perceived barriers to being able to practice a health behavior, are more important determinants (Janz and others, 1997). For instance, in a major prospective study, Ruth Hyman and her colleagues (1994) found that perceived susceptibility to breast cancer did *not* predict their participants' use of mammography services, although both perceived benefits and barriers (such as having an accessible clinic and a physician who recommended a mammogram) did. The same study also found that a woman's ethnicity was the best predictor of all, with African-American women being significantly more likely to obtain regular mammograms than European-Americans. The HBM represents an important perspective, but it is incomplete. Let's expand our thinking with another theory that focuses on the important role that people's intentions and self-efficacy play in their practice of health behaviors.

The Theory of Planned Behavior

Like the health belief model, the **theory of planned behavior (TPB)** specifies relationships among attitudes and behavior (Ajzen, 1985) (Figure 6.3). The theory maintains that the best way to predict whether a health behavior will occur is to measure a person's **behavioral intention**—the decision to engage in a health-related behavior or to refrain from engaging in the behavior. Behavioral intentions are shaped by three factors. The first is our *attitude toward the behavior,* which is determined by our belief that engaging in the behavior will lead to certain outcomes. For example, we may decide that reducing the amount of saturated fat in our diet is a good thing to do because we believe that reducing fat will lead to weight loss and greater personal attractiveness.

The second determinant of intention to act is the **subjective norm,** which reflects our motivation to comply with the views of other people regarding the behavior in question. For example, we may struggle to shift to a low-fat diet if that change is not in line with the behavior of friends and relatives. We have

■ **theory of planned behavior (TPB)** a theory that predicts health behavior on the basis of three factors: personal attitude toward the behavior, the subjective norm regarding the behavior, and perceived degree of control over the behavior.

■ **behavioral intention** in theories of health behavior, the rational decision to engage in a health-related behavior or to refrain from engaging in the behavior.

■ **subjective norm** an individual's interpretation of the views of other people regarding a particular health-related behavior.

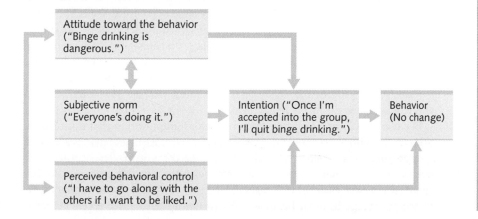

Figure 6.3

Theory of Planned Behavior This theory predicts that a person's decision to engage in a particular health behavior is based on three factors: personal attitude toward the behavior, the subjective norm regarding the behavior, and perceived degree of control over the behavior.

Source: Sutton, S. (1997). The theory of planned behavior. In A. Baum, S. Newman, J. Weinman, R. West, & C. McManus (Eds.), *Cambridge handbook of psychology, health, and medicine* (p. 178). Cambridge: Cambridge University Press.

strong intentions to act when our attitudes toward a behavior are positive and when we believe that others also think the behavior is appropriate.

The third component of behavioral intentions is *perceived behavioral control,* which refers to our expectation of success in performing the contemplated health behavior. The more resources and opportunities to effect a behavior change we believe we have, the greater our belief that we can, in fact, change that behavior. If, in shifting to a low-fat diet, we are confident that we will be able to find healthy recipes, shop for their ingredients, make the time to prepare meals, and still enjoy the flavor despite a more restricted diet, we will have a stronger behavioral intention than someone who is more doubtful.

People's self-reported attitudes and intentions do predict a variety of health-promoting actions, including medication taking (Goldring and others, 2002), weight loss (Schifter & Ajzen, 1985), exercise (Godin and others, 1993), healthy eating (Conner and others, 2002), condom use (Sutton and others, 1999), smoking (Fishbein, 1982), breast and testicular self-examination (Lierman and others, 1991), mammography utilization (Brubaker & Wickersham, 1990), attending childbirth health-information classes (Michie and others, 1992), cancer screening (Conner & Sparks, 1996), and willingness to donate blood (Bagozzi, 1981).

Given its emphasis on planning, it is not surprising that the TPB is most accurate in predicting *intentional* behaviors that are goal oriented and fit within a rational framework (Gibbons and others, 1998). In some cases, such as substance abuse (Morojele & Stephenson, 1994) and drunk driving (Stacy and others, 1994), the model has been less successful. This may be due in part to the fact that for many people, especially adolescents and young adults, these health behaviors are often reactions to social situations. For example, young people may attend a party where others are smoking marijuana or drinking excessively or agree to the demands of an overzealous girlfriend or boyfriend who wants to have sex. As Frederick Gibbons (1998) has noted, in such settings, "What are you willing to do?" probably describes a young person's predicament (and predicts his or her subsequent behavior) more accurately than "What do you plan to do?"

Behavioral willingness refers to our motivation at a given moment to engage in risky behavior. Like *behavioral intention,* behavioral willingness is a function of subjective norms. Greater behavioral willingness is associated with a perception that significant others, especially peers, engage in and approve of the behavior in question. Also, like behavioral intention, greater behavioral willingness is linked to our own positive attitudes toward the behavior. Finally, previously engaging in the behavior is associated with greater intention and willingness to engage in the behavior again.

Behavioral willingness differs from behavioral intention in that it is reactive rather than deliberative (Gibbons and others, 1998). Risky behaviors are often spontaneous social events, in which we follow the group's lead rather than make a personal decision to engage in the behavior. For this reason, risky behaviors often have clear social images that influence a person's momentary willingness to engage in those behaviors. A substantial amount of recent research

■ **behavioral willingness** in theories of health behavior, the reactive, unplanned motivation involved in the decision to engage in risky behavior.

supports the concept of behavioral willingness in health-related behaviors. Surveys conducted with sexually active teens, for example, demonstrate that sexual activity often is reactive rather than planned (Ingham and others, 1991). The same is apparently true of driving while drunk (Gerrard and others, 1996).

The Transtheoretical Model (TTM)

An overweight uncle of mine continued to smoke and eat a high-fat diet despite his doctor's recommendation to modify these health-compromising behaviors. When pressed to explain why he wasn't changing his poor health habits, he replied that he was well aware of the risks and believed that he should improve his lifestyle—but he wasn't "ready." A few months later, after a nearly fatal heart attack, he declared that he was ready to quit smoking. And he did so. Unfortunately, he also "quit" 6 months later. He struggled to reach his goal until the very end of his life. Does my uncle remind you of anyone you know?

The theories of health behavior that we have considered thus far attempt to identify variables that influence health-related attitudes and behaviors and combine them into a formula that predicts the probability that a particular individual will act in a certain way in a given situation. For example, the theory of planned behavior might predict that my uncle continued to smoke because he had a positive attitude about smoking, because it was the accepted thing to do among his friends, and because it gave him a feeling of control over his life. The **transtheoretical model** (also called the *stages of change model*), on the other hand, maintains that behavior often changes systematically through distinct stages (Prochaska, 1994; Prochaska and others, 1992).

The TTM contends that people progress through five stages in altering health-related behaviors. The stages are defined in terms of past behavior and intentions for future action.

> *Stage 1: Precontemplation.* During this stage, people are not seriously thinking about changing their behavior. They may even refuse to acknowledge that their behavior needs changing.
>
> *Stage 2: Contemplation.* During this stage, people acknowledge the existence of a problem (such as smoking) and are seriously considering changing their behavior (quitting smoking) in the near future (typically within 6 months).
>
> *Stage 3: Preparation.* This stage includes both thoughts and actions. In preparing to quit smoking, for example, a person obtains a prescription for a nicotine patch, joins a support group, enlists family support, and makes other specific plans.
>
> *Stage 4: Action.* During this stage, people have actually changed their behavior and are trying to sustain their efforts.
>
> *Stage 5: Maintenance.* People in this stage continue to be successful in their efforts to reach their final goal. Although this stage can last indefinitely, its length is often set arbitrarily at 6 months.

■ **transtheoretical model** a widely used stage theory that contends that people pass through five stages in altering health-related behavior: precontemplation, contemplation, preparation, action, and maintenance.

The stages of change model recognizes that people move back and forth through the stages in a nonlinear fashion. Like my uncle, many recently reformed ex-smokers relapse from *maintenance* to *preparation*, cycling through stages 2 to 5 one or more times until they have completed their behavioral change.

In general, research has confirmed that people at higher stages are more successful at improving health-related behaviors, such as home radon testing (Weinstein & Sandman, 1992), osteoporosis prevention (Blalock and others, 1996), vaccination against hepatitis B (Hammer, 1997), smoking (DiClemente, 1991), colorectal and breast cancer testing (Manne and others, 2002; Lauver and others, 2003), safe sex behaviors (Bowen & Trotter, 1995), HIV prevention (Prochaska and others, 1994), and diet (Glanz and others, 1994).

Other research has shown that stage theories like the TTM have a very practical advantage: They promote the development of more effective health interventions by providing a "recipe" for ideal behavior change (Sutton, 1996). This enables clinical health psychologists and other practitioners to match an intervention to the specific needs of a person who is "stuck" at a particular stage (Perz and others, 1996). The model also acknowledges that different behavioral, cognitive, and social processes may come to the forefront as we struggle to reach our ultimate health goals. These include consciousness raising (for example, seeking more information about a health-compromising behavior), counterconditioning (substituting alternative behaviors for the target behavior), and reinforcement management (rewarding oneself or being rewarded by others for success).

Let's consider an example. Attempting to convince an obese person who is in the precontemplation stage to lose weight is likely to fail because people in this stage do not believe that they have a health problem. The most effective intervention at this time would be to encourage the person to *consider* changing his or her behavior, perhaps by providing information about the health hazards of obesity. On the other hand, a person in the preparation or action stage doesn't need additional persuasion to change his or her behavior. What he or she may need, however, are specific tips about how to enact an effective plan of action.

Addressing the Perceived Benefits of High-Risk Behaviors

Although the health belief model, theory of planned behavior, and transtheoretical model include both perceived benefits and risks, the intention of these models was primarily to explain preventive behaviors motivated by the desire to avoid disease or injury. Consequently, these models tend to focus on the risks of unhealthy behaviors rather than any perceived *benefits* of high-risk behaviors to the individual. Researchers have found, however, that perceived benefits are important predictors of certain behaviors, such as adolescent drinking (Katz and others, 2000), tobacco use (Pollay, 2000), and unprotected sex (Parsons and others, 2000).

In a recent survey of fifth, seventh, and ninth graders, Julie Goldberg and her colleagues (2002) gave the participants the following scenario:

> Now imagine that you are at a party. During the party you have a couple of drinks of alcohol (like two glasses of wine, beer, or hard liquor). Even if this is something you'd never do, please try to imagine it.

After reading the scenario, the students were asked several open-ended questions about the good and bad things that can happen if they drink at a party. The students were also asked about their actual experience with and the consequences of drinking. Six months later, the students were once again asked about their drinking behavior.

The researchers learned a great deal by asking about the perceived benefits of drinking. More than the fifth and seventh graders, the ninth graders perceived the physical and social benefits of alcohol (e.g., "I'll like the buzz I get from drinking"; "I'll have a better time at the party") to be more likely, and the physical and social risks (e.g., "I'll get sick"; "I'll do something that I'll later regret") to be less likely. These results have a profound implication for health education campaigns targeted at teenagers. Although researchers have often concluded that adolescents are irrational in their decision making because they engage in risky behaviors despite knowing the risks, these results suggest that teens are, in fact, weighing the pros and cons of their behaviors. More effective health messages might focus on how adolescents can obtain the perceived benefits of risky health behaviors in safer ways. For example, messages might identify other ways to feel more mature and be more social at parties than by drinking.

For many young adults, health behaviors are often reactions to social situations rather than rationally planned situations. They drink because their friends drink, not because they have made a conscious decision that they enjoy alcohol. Social situations can trigger healthier behaviors, too, such as dancing, exercise, or enjoying another form of recreation.

Prevention

We usually think of prevention solely in terms of efforts to modify one's risk *before* disease strikes. In fact, researchers have differentiated three types of prevention that are undertaken before, during, and after a disease strikes.

Primary prevention refers to health-promoting actions that are taken to prevent a disease or injury from occurring. Examples of primary prevention include wearing seatbelts, practicing good nutrition, exercising, avoiding smoking, and going regularly for health screening tests.

Secondary prevention involves actions taken to identify and treat an illness early in its course. In the case of a person who has high blood pressure, for example, secondary prevention would include regular examinations to monitor symptoms, the use of blood pressure medication, and dietary changes.

Tertiary prevention involves actions taken to contain or retard damage once a disease has progressed beyond its early stages. An example of tertiary prevention is the use of radiation therapy or chemotherapy to destroy a cancerous tumor. Tertiary prevention also strives to rehabilitate people to the fullest extent possible.

■ **primary prevention** health-enhancing efforts to prevent disease or injury from occurring.

■ **secondary prevention** actions taken to identify and treat an illness or disability early in its course.

■ **tertiary prevention** actions taken to contain damage once a disease or disability has progressed beyond its early stages.

Although less cost effective and less beneficial than primary or secondary prevention, tertiary prevention is by far the most common form of health care. Tertiary care is much easier to accomplish because the appropriate target groups (those who are ill or injured) are readily identifiable. In addition, patients under tertiary care typically have the greatest motivation to comply with treatment and to engage in other health-enhancing behaviors.

In this chapter, however, we will focus on health psychologists' primary prevention efforts. Health psychologists encourage doctors and other health care professionals to take the time to give advice to their patients. As effective as this personalized attention would seem to be, many doctors find it hard to follow through with preventive measures. One reason for their difficulty is that medical schools have traditionally placed little emphasis on preventive measures. Another is a lack of time, given the number of people doctors have to see each day.

Health psychologists also promote health by encouraging legislative action and by conducting educational campaigns in the media. These efforts are focused at many levels, from the individual to the community to society as a whole. Table 6.1 illustrates a comprehensive program of primary, secondary, and tertiary disease prevention for AIDS based on the national health goals established by the

Table 6.1

Levels and Timing of Prevention for HIV/AIDS

Level	Primary	Secondary	Tertiary
Individual	Self-instruction guide on HIV prevention for uninfected lower-risk HIV people	Designing an immune-healthy diet	Screening and early intervention for an HIV-positive person
Group	Parents gather to gain skills to communicate better with teens about risky behaviors	Needle exchange program for low SES, high-risk, IV-drug users	Rehabilitation programs for groups of AIDS patients
Worksite	Worksite educational campaign focusing on how HIV is transmitted	Worksite safer sex incentive program (e.g., free condoms, confidential screening)	Extending leave benefits so employees can care for HIV-positive relatives
Community	Focused media campaign to promote safe sex behaviors	Establishing support network for HIV-positive people	Providing better access to recreational facilities for those with AIDS
Society	Enforcing felony laws for knowingly infecting another person with HIV	Enacting antidiscrimination policies for HIV-positive people	Mandating the availability of HIV medications for uninsured AIDS patients

Adapted from: Winett, R. A. (1995). A framework for health promotion and disease prevention programs. *American Psychologist, 50*(5), 341–350.

U.S. Department of Health, Education, and Welfare as part of its *Healthy People Campaign.* As discussed in Chapter 1, these goals are to increase the span of healthy life, to decrease the disparities in health between different segments of the population, and to provide universal access to preventive services.

We are sometimes our own worst enemies in the battle for health. In our teens and twenties, when we are developing health-related habits, we are usually quite healthy. Smoking cigarettes, eating a high-fat diet, and avoiding exercise at this time seem often to have no effect on health. So, young people have little immediate incentive for practicing good health behavior and correcting poor health habits.

Many health-enhancing behaviors such as engaging in vigorous exercise and pursuing a low-fat diet are either less pleasurable or more effortful than their less healthy alternatives. If engaging in a behavior (such as eating when you are depressed) causes immediate relief or gratification, or if failing to engage in this behavior provides immediate discomfort, the behavior is difficult to eliminate.

High-risk sexual behaviors that may result in HIV infection and AIDS are a tragic example of this principle. Within 3 to 6 weeks after first exposure, some HIV-positive persons develop a sore throat, fever, and a rash that often looks like measles. This early form of the HIV illness usually disappears and is often so mild that it is not even remembered. Months or years may pass without any overt symptoms. During this time, of course, HIV is being actively produced and weakening the immune system. The precise length of time before AIDS develops for any individual is not known. Some researchers believe the *incubation period*—the time between exposure to the virus and the first appearance of AIDS symptoms—may be as long as 20 years. Once full-blown AIDS appears, death (if not prevented by new treatments) usually follows within the next 2 years. The far-removed *potential* negative consequences of risky behavior too often are overshadowed by the immediate pleasures of the moment.

Healthy Living

The "fountain of youth" myth is present in the histories of nearly every culture and finds its current expression in the allegedly rejuvenating elixirs, creams, and gadgets that are hawked in infomercials, alternative medicine Web sites, and drugstore displays. Claims that people will soon live to be 200 years old because of megadoses of antioxidants, vitamins, herbs, or some other "magic bullet" have resulted in confusion about *longevity.* For decades, scientists have systematically investigated people's claims of having vastly exceeded the normal life span, and in every instance these claims could not be verified.

Even without a magic bullet, people today can expect to live much longer than previous cohorts. The major diseases of our ancestors, such as polio, smallpox, tetanus, diphtheria, and rheumatic fever, have been almost completely eradicated.

In focusing on healthy life expectancy, health psychologists aim to shorten the amount of time older people spend in *morbidity* (disabled, ill, or in pain).

Many of the world's deadliest diseases are cheap to prevent. For instance (Neergaard, 1999):

- Drugs that treat AIDS may be too expensive for many developing countries, but just $14 for a year's supply of condoms could prevent infection in the first place.

- An insecticide-soaked bednet to protect people from malaria-carrying mosquitoes costs $10.

- One dose of measles vaccine costs 26 cents.

- Five days of antibiotics for pneumonia costs 27 cents.

(a)

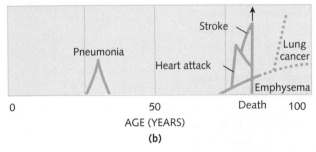

(b)

Figure 6.4

Compression of Morbidity
In focusing on the individual's quality-adjusted life years, health psychologists seek to limit the time a person spends ill or infirm, as illustrated in this diagram of the illnesses and eventual deaths of identical twin brothers. Although the brothers carry the same disease vulnerabilities and life span-limiting genetic clocks, the healthy lifestyle of one (b) keeps disease and disability at bay until primary aging is well advanced. In contrast, the unhealthy lifestyle of his brother (a) takes its toll at a much younger age.

Source: Fries, J. F. (1994). *Living well: Taking care of your health in the middle and later years.* Reading, MA: Addison-Wesley.

To illustrate, consider twin brothers who, although genetically identical and exposed to the same health hazards while growing up, have had very different health experiences since adolescence. The first brother smokes two packs of cigarettes a day, has an obesity-indicating BMI of 30.2, never exercises, has an angry and pessimistic outlook on life, and eats foods containing excessive amounts of animal fat and sugar. The second brother pursues a much healthier lifestyle, avoiding tobacco and excessive stress, exercising regularly, watching his diet, and enjoying the social support of a close-knit circle of family and friends. As Figure 6.4 shows, although the two brothers have the same genetic vulnerabilities to lung, circulatory, and cardiovascular disease, the unhealthy lifestyle of the first brother dooms him to an extended period of adulthood morbidity beginning at about age 45. In contrast, the healthier brother's lifestyle postpones disease until much later in life. If he does contract any of the illnesses, they are likely to be less severe, and recovery will be quicker. In some cases, the illness, such as lung cancer, may be "postponed" right out of his life.

Exercise

Exercise is the closest thing we have to a fountain of youth. It becomes even more important as people age, and it may help slow down or even reverse many of the effects of aging (Fries, 1999). Most important to maintaining physical vitality is *aerobic exercise,* in which the heart speeds up in order to pump larger amounts of blood, breathing is deeper and more frequent, and the cells of the body develop the ability to extract increasing amounts of oxygen from the blood. In addition, weight-bearing aerobic exercises such as walking, jogging, and racquetball help preserve muscular strength and maintain bone density.

Exercise has been demonstrated to protect against *osteoporosis,* a disorder characterized by declining bone density due to calcium loss. Although osteoporosis is most common in postmenopausal women, it also occurs in men, as does the protective effect of exercise. Roughly one woman in four over age 60 has osteoporosis, with white and Asian women being at higher risk than African-American women. Osteoporosis results in more than 1 million bone fractures a year in the United States alone, the most debilitating of which are hip fractures. In one retrospective study, older men and women were asked to describe their level of exercise as adolescents, again at age 30, and again at age 50 (Greendale and others, 1995). Both men and women with the highest reported activity levels had significantly greater bone mineral density than their more sedentary counterparts.

In addition to increasing physical strength and maintaining bone density, regular exercise reduces an older person's risk for two of the most common chronic illnesses of adulthood: cardiovascular disease and cancer. In one study, researchers investigated coronary risk factors in elderly men, aged 65 to 84 (Caspersen and others, 1991). Even moderate exercise, such as gardening and walking, resulted in significant increases in HDL—the so-called "good cholesterol"—and decreased total serum cholesterol. Regular exercise is also linked to lower triglycerides, which have been implicated in the formation of atherosclerotic plaques (Lakka & Salonen, 1992). Focusing on walking, bicycling, running, swimming, tennis, and golf, Goya Wannamethee and his colleagues (1993) found an inverse relationship between the level of physical activity and deaths from all types of cancer.

However, during late adulthood, the intensity of exercise must be adjusted to reflect declines in cardiovascular and respiratory functioning. For some adults, this means that walking replaces jogging; for others, such as former world-class marathoner Bill Rodgers, now 60, this means training at a 6-minute per mile pace rather than a 5-minute pace.

As a guideline, *Healthy People 2000* recommends 150 minutes of total exercise each week, of which at least 60 minutes involve continuous, rhythmic aerobic activity. For many adults, turning off the TV helps promote exercise and better health. The recent *Family Heart Study* found that people who watched TV 1 hour per day exercised more, and had significantly lower body mass indexes (and other coronary risk factors), than people who watched TV 3 hours per day (Kronenberg and others, 2000).

Is It Ever Too Late to Begin Exercising?

No. In one study, frail nursing-home residents aged 72 to 98 participated in a 10-week program of muscle-strengthening resistance training three times a week (Raloff, 1996). After 10 weeks, those in the exercise group more than doubled their muscular strength and increased their stair-climbing power by 28 percent. In another study, Maria Fiatarone and her colleagues (1993) randomly assigned 100 participants, who averaged 87 years of age, to one of four groups. Participants in the first group engaged in regular resistance training exercises. Participants in the second group took a daily multivitamin supplement. Participants in the third group took the supplement and participated in the resistance training. Participants in the fourth group were permitted to engage in three physical activities of their choice (including aerobic exercise) but could not engage in resistance training. Over the course of the study, muscle strength more than doubled in the resistance groups, with an average increase of 113 percent, compared to a miniscule 3 percent increase in subjects in the second group. Interestingly, the group that exercised and took the supplement showed no greater improvement than the groups that exercised but did not take supplements.

Further evidence that it is never too late to start exercising comes from studies demonstrating that exercise even late in life may still help prevent or reduce the rate of loss in bone density. As compared to a control group of sedentary women, 50- to 70-year-old women who had been sedentary but were assigned to an exercise group showed significantly reduced loss in bone mineral content (Nelson and others, 1994). As added benefits, women in the exercise group increased their muscle mass and strength.

Why Don't More Older Adults Exercise?

Despite the well-documented physical and psychological benefits of lifelong exercise, the percentage of people who exercise regularly declines with age (Phillips and others, 2001). Why? For one thing, some older adults are reluctant, even fearful, of exercising too much due to myths associated with exercise. These myths include the idea that exercise can accelerate the loss of bone density, lead to arthritis, and even increase the risk of dying from a heart attack. In fact, the body is far more likely to rust out than it is to wear out. As the saying goes, "Use it or lose it!"

Exercising behavior is also related to an individual's beliefs regarding its health benefits, confidence in his or her ability to correctly perform certain physical skills (*exercise self-efficacy*), and self-motivation. Believing that exercise will help one to live a longer, healthier life is a strong stimulus for initiating exercise. Many older people may lack basic information about the benefits of appropriate exercise and might view exercise as difficult, useless, or unsafe (Lee, 1993). Or they may feel that it is too late to improve their health through exercise because they think declines in health are inevitable and irreversible with increased age (O'Brien & Vertinsky, 1991).

There are several reasons that older adults might lack exercise self-efficacy. For one, they typically have less experience with exercise and have fewer exercising role models than younger people. Older people are also faced with ageist stereotypes about what constitutes appropriate behavior; vigorous exercise, especially for women, is contrary to stereotypes of old age. Finally, many older adults view old age as a time of rest and relaxation and are less likely to initiate and maintain regular exercise.

To further explore why some adults choose to exercise, while others do not, Sara Wilcox and Martha Storandt of Washington University (1996) surveyed a random sample of 121 women aged 20 to 85, focusing on three psychological variables: exercise self-efficacy, self-motivation, and attitudes toward exercise. The sample consisted of two groups: *exercisers* and *nonexercisers.* Women in the exercise group had engaged in aerobic exercise for at least 20 minutes three or more times per week for at least 4 months prior to the study. Nonexercisers reported engaging in little or no aerobic exercise (less than two times per month) over the preceding 4 months.

The findings revealed that desire and willingness to exercise have less to do with age than with attitudes about exercise; the belief that exercise would be enjoyable and beneficial decreased with age, but only among nonexercisers. Those who continued to exercise throughout adulthood were significantly more self-motivated, had greater exercise self-efficacy, and had more positive attitudes toward exercise than did nonexercisers. These results suggest that education stressing the benefits and the required frequency, duration, and intensity of exercise needed to reach these benefits must be a key component in exercise interventions with older adults. In addition, stereotypes of old age as a time of inevitable decline need to be challenged. Finally, older adults will be less likely to begin an exercise regimen if they believe they are unable to do even basic exercises, so intervention efforts should include some basic instruction.

Promoting Healthy Families and Communities

The biopsychosocial model of health is not limited to individuals. Preventive health psychology research is increasingly focused on the various external systems that influence an individual's health. Chief among these systems is the family. In a national survey of over 100,000 adolescents from grades 7 through 12, Resnick and his colleagues (1997) found that the family social context strongly influenced health risk behaviors. In the researchers' words, "parent–family connectedness" strongly predicted the level of emotional distress of teens in the family, their likelihood of using drugs and alcohol, and to some extent how involved in violence they became. Other important factors that affected these teen health behaviors were whether the teen's parents were present during key periods of the day and whether they had high or low expectations of their daughter's or son's academic performance.

More recently, Rena Repetti and her colleagues (2002) have argued that certain family characteristics create a "cascade of risk" that begins early in life by "creating vulnerabilities (and exacerbating preexisting biological vulnerabilities) that lay the groundwork for long-term physical and mental health problems" (p. 336). These risky family characteristics fall into two categories: *overt family conflict,* manifested in frequent episodes of anger and aggression, and *deficient nurturing,* including relationships that are unsupportive, cold, and even neglectful.

In true systems theory fashion, *community health psychology* focuses on the community as the unit of intervention, recognizing that individuals are part of families, as well as cultural, economic, and community contexts. Community health psychologists routinely advocate for public policies that promote social justice, human rights, and equity in access to quality health care and other human services (de La Cancela and others, 2004).

Family Barriers

Health habits are typically acquired from parents and others who model health behaviors. Parents who smoke, for example, are significantly more likely to have children who smoke (Schulenberg and others, 1994). Similarly, obese parents are more likely to have obese children, and the children of problem drinkers are themselves at increased risk of abusing alcohol (Schuckit & Smith, 1996).

Although there may be a genetic basis to these behaviors, children also may acquire expectancies about risky behaviors by observing family members. In one study, Elizabeth D'Amico and Kim Fromme (1997) convincingly demonstrated the impact of older siblings on the behavior and attitudes of their younger adolescent siblings. Their results suggest that vicarious learning from an older sibling is one mechanism through which adolescents may form expectancies about risky health-related behaviors. Other family variables linked with risky health-related behaviors among adolescents include parental conflict and inconsistencies, absence of parental supervision, absence of the father, diffuse family relationships, coercive parent–child relationships, and parental drug and alcohol use (Metzler and others, 1994).

Health System Barriers

Because medicine tends to focus on treating conditions that have already developed (secondary and tertiary care), early warning signs of disease and contributing risk factors often go undetected. People who are not experiencing symptoms of illness see little reason to seek advice regarding potential risk factors, and doctors are oriented toward correcting conditions rather than preventing future problems.

Although health care has begun to change—physicians today are receiving much more training in health promotion—economic forces often undermine the efforts of health care workers to promote preventive measures. Some health insurance plans, for example, still do not cover preventive services such as cholesterol screening. And more than 46 million Americans, including more than 20 percent of working-age adults and 10 percent of children, do not have insurance and therefore are unlikely to undergo preventive screening (United States Census Bureau, 2005). The uninsured receive about one-half of the medical care of people with insurance, which leaves them sicker and likely to die at a younger age. By forgoing regular doctor visits and screening that could catch serious illnesses early, such as cancer and heart disease, many uninsured patients are diagnosed too late to affect the outcome.

It is estimated that the United States loses $65 billion to $130 billion per year because of the poor health and premature deaths of uninsured Americans. More than 8 out of every 10 uninsured are from working families, and only 27 percent come from families with income below the federal poverty level (about $18,244 for a family of four in 2002). Although some ethnic groups are at much higher risk of being uninsured (see Figure 6.5), the uninsured don't fit any stereotype. They come from every race and ethnic group, every community, and every walk of life (Kaiser Foundation, 2004).

As for why people lack health coverage, about 10 percent say they are not covered because they don't feel they need health insurance. More than two-thirds of the uninsured, including many single adults with low incomes, cite the high cost of insurance as the main reason. The costs of health insurance have skyrocketed over the past 2

Figure 6.5

Ethnic Groups That Are More Likely to Be Uninsured
More than one-third of Hispanic-Americans are uninsured, and nearly one-quarter of African-Americans and Native Americans have no health coverage.

Source: Henry J. Kaiser Foundation. (2000). *Uninsured in America: A chart book.* http://www.kff.org/content/archive/1407/

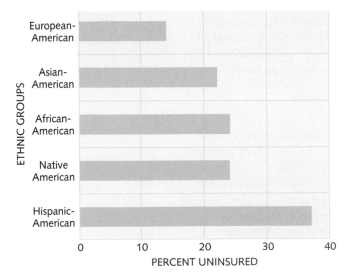

decades, causing employers to pass a greater share of the costs on to their employees. Premiums rose by an average of 13 to 16 percent in 2004—more than six times faster than the growth in the Consumer Price Index and five times faster than overall inflation (Kaiser Foundation, 2004).

Not having insurance can have a devastating impact on a person's health and financial security. Medical bills can quickly wipe out a family's savings, and fear of high bills is a barrier that prevents many of the uninsured from seeking health care. Uninsured adults are four times as likely as those who are insured to report delaying or forgoing needed health services. For example, only 16 percent of uninsured women have recommended mammograms each year, compared with 42 percent of insured women (Kaiser Foundation, 2000). Is it any wonder that uninsured women are 40 percent more likely to be diagnosed with late-stage breast cancer and 40 to 50 percent more likely to die from breast cancer than insured women?

To make matters worse, health insurance companies are using managed care to reduce behavioral health care benefits substantially more than other benefits. Overall, behavioral health care as a percentage of total health care benefits—with its emphasis on primary prevention—has steadily fallen since 1990 (Kaiser Foundation, 2000). Interestingly, a new study sponsored by the Kaiser Foundation (2004) estimates that the United States could provide medical care to every uninsured American for about $48 billion next year—an increase of only 3 percent in national health outlays.

Community Barriers

The community can be a powerful force for promoting or discouraging healthy living. People are more likely to adopt health-enhancing behaviors when these behaviors are promoted by community organizations, such as schools, governmental agencies, and the health care system. In recent years, we have made significant progress in changing attitudes toward exercise and proper nutrition. We are also much better informed about the importance of reducing risk factors for cancer, cardiovascular disease, and other serious chronic conditions. However, there are still powerful social pressures that lead people to engage in health-compromising behaviors.

Consider alcohol use. National surveys indicate that alcohol use is more prevalent among American college students than among their peers who do not attend college (Quigley & Marlatt, 1996). Other surveys reveal that binge drinking among college students is associated with several social risk factors, including living in certain "party" residence halls. For some students, the excitement of being together in a largely unsupervised environment can trigger such risky behaviors (Dreer and others, 2004).

Fortunately, most peer-inspired risk taking is a short-lived experiment that is outgrown before irreversible, long-term consequences are felt. Although drinking rates increase significantly in the transition from high school to the college freshman year (Baer and others, 1994), heavy drinking declines as students grow older, assume increased responsibilities, and display a pattern called *maturing out* (Bartholow and others, 2003).

Community Health Psychology and Injury Control

Each year in the United States, nearly 150,000 people die from injuries, including 41,000 in automobile crashes; 30,500 suicides; 28,000 deaths from fires, drowning, falls, and poisonings; and 25,500 homicides (CDC, 2005). When all people between ages 1 and 44 are considered as a group, injury is the *leading* cause of death, ahead of cardiovascular disease and cancer. Added to this toll in mortality are 3.3 million potential years of life lost prematurely each year as the result of injuries. The terms *injury* and *trauma* are replacing use of the word *accident* to underscore the fact that most injuries are not random, unavoidable events—they are predictable and preventable (Sleet and others, 2004).

Taking a primary prevention approach to injury control is a recent phenomenon. As recently as the 1980s, injury prevention was not even covered in most textbooks on community psychology. Community health psychologists generally focus on three accepted strategies in injury prevention programs: *education and behavior change, legislation and enforcement,* and *engineering and technology.* Education and behavior change strategies typically are aimed at reducing risk behaviors (anything that increases the likelihood that a person will be injured) and increasing protective behaviors (anything that reduces potential harm from a risk behavior).

Community Health Education

There is probably a greater emphasis on health promotion today than at any other time in history. Substantial effort is devoted to shaping the public's views on health issues through educational campaigns in advertisements; on public transportation; in magazines and newspapers; and on television, radio, and Web sites. The importance of these campaigns is revealed in research controversies over how information should be presented. (For example, should HIV-prevention campaigns emphasize safer sex or abstinence?)

Health education refers to any planned intervention involving communication that promotes the learning of healthier behavior. The most widely used model in health education is the *precede/proceed model* (Green & Kreuter, 1990). According to the model, planning for health education begins by identifying specific health problems in a targeted group. Next, lifestyle and environment elements that contribute to the targeted health problem (as well as those that protect against it) are identified. Then, background factors that predispose, enable, and reinforce these lifestyle and environmental factors are analyzed to determine the possible usefulness of health education and other interventions. During the final implementation phase, health education programs are designed, initiated, and evaluated.

Let's examine how the precede/proceed model would apply to a health education campaign for lung cancer. First, health psychologists would identify the target group for the intervention. Next, they would investigate environmental factors that might affect the target group, because the disease might result from unhealthy working or living conditions in which people are exposed to hazardous pollutants. In addition, health psychologists would consider psycholog-

■ **health education** any planned intervention involving communication that promotes the learning of healthier behavior.

ical and social factors. They would begin by determining who smokes. When did they start smoking? Why? Researchers have found that smoking typically begins during adolescence, largely in response to social pressures (Flay, 1985). These pressures include the imitation of family members, peers, and such role models as well-known actors and athletes. Many adolescents find it very difficult to resist social pressure. Being accepted by one's peers is an extremely important source of reinforcement. There are also strong enabling factors: Cigarettes are generally very easy to obtain, and sanctions against smoking are minimal.

Having determined which factors contributed to the health problem, health psychologists would design a health education program to counteract those factors. For example, if social pressure was found to be a major factor, they might design a health education program that focuses on improving the ability of teens to resist social pressure. Such programs might involve role models urging teens not to smoke, adopting antismoking policies in public buildings, imposing stricter sanctions against the sale of cigarettes, and/or levying higher taxes on cigarettes.

How effective are health education campaigns? Researchers have found that education campaigns that merely inform people of the hazards of health-compromising behaviors are typically ineffective in motivating people to change long-held health habits (Green & McAlister, 1984). For example, antismoking messages and other drug education programs by themselves often have little effect—or a negative effect. In one study, teenagers who had participated in a school-sponsored drug education program were actually *more likely* to use alcohol, marijuana, and LSD than a control group of students who had not participated in the course (Stuart, 1974). Simply finding out that one's lifestyle is not as healthy as it could be often is insufficient to provoke change because many people believe they are exempt or invulnerable to the negative consequences of their risky behavior.

Generally speaking, multifaceted community campaigns that present information on several fronts work better than "single-shot" campaigns. For example, 2 decades of antismoking campaigns combining school intervention programs with communitywide mass media messages resulted in a significant decrease in experimental and regular smoking, and a shift in viewing smoking as more addictive and as having more negative social consequences among seventh through eleventh graders in a Midwestern county school system between 1980 and 2001 (Chassin and others, 2003). As another example, a recent skin cancer prevention program focused on the use of sunscreen, wearing hats, sunglasses, and other sun-protection habits by children who were taking swimming lessons at 15 swimming pools in Hawaii and Massachusetts. In addition to targeting the children, the *Pool Cool* program, which combined education, interactive activities, and environmental changes (providing free sunscreen,

Antismoking Campaign in China Although the number of smokers in the United States has decreased recently, the reverse seems to be occurring in other countries, such as China. Everyone, no matter what their native language, can understand billboards such as this one.

portable shade structures, and sun safety posters), was a randomized, controlled trial intervention targeting parents, lifeguards, and swim instructors. Compared with children in a control group at 13 other pools who received a bicycle and rollerblading safety intervention, children in the intervention group showed significant positive changes in use of sunscreen and shade, overall sun-protection habits, and the number of sunburns (Glanz and others, 2002). Similarly, other researchers have found that multicomponent sun-protection behavior interventions are particularly effective with adult beachgoers (Pagoto and others, 2003).

Community programs are on the rise because a large body of research evidence indicates that rates of morbidity and mortality are linked to social conditions such as poverty, unstable living conditions, community disorganization, poor education, social isolation, and unemployment (Adler & Matthews, 1994; Williams & Lund, 1992). The goal of community-based intervention is to create a social infrastructure that supports the efforts of each community member to improve the quality of his or her life (Heller and others, 1997).

Community programs have several advantages. First, they can promote changes that are difficult for individuals to accomplish, such as creating bike paths and other public exercise facilities or banning smoking in public offices. Second, unlike interventions that concentrate on high-risk individuals, community programs reach out to a broader cross section of the public, potentially reaching those in the lower- to moderate-risk categories earlier in the process of disease (Altman, 1995). Third, community programs combine information with the social support of friends, neighbors, and family members.

One of the earliest community campaigns was initiated for residents of a rural county in Finland with a very high incidence of coronary heart disease (Puska, 1999). Launched in 1972 by the government and the World Health Organization, the goal of the *North Karelia Project* was to reduce smoking, cholesterol, and blood pressure levels through informational campaigns. When the program began, the Finns had the highest coronary mortality rates in the world. The initial 5-year follow-up study demonstrated a 17.4 percent reduction in these coronary risk factors among men and an 11.5 percent reduction among women. In addition, coronary disability payments had declined by approximately 10 percent, much more than enough to pay for the entire community program. Most significant of all, over the past 3 decades deaths among the working-age population from heart disease have dropped by 82 percent (Templeton, 2004).

Message Framing

An important factor in the effectiveness of health education is how information is worded, or *framed*. Health messages generally are framed in terms of the benefits associated with a particular preventive action or the costs of failing to take preventive action (Rothman & Salovey, 1997).

Gain-framed messages focus on the positive outcome from adopting a health-promoting behavior ("If you get a mammogram, you are likely to find out that you are healthy") or on avoiding an undesirable outcome ("If you get a mammogram, you decrease the risk of an undetected, potentially life-threatening tumor"). **Loss-framed messages** emphasize the negative outcome from failing to take preventive action ("If you don't utilize mammography, you increase the risk of an undetected, potentially life-threatening tumor"). Loss-framed messages may also emphasize missing a desirable outcome ("If you don't get a mammogram, you will not know whether you are healthy").

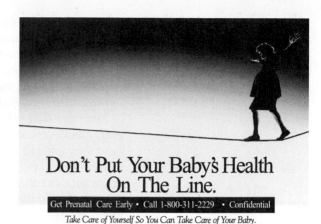

Don't Put Your Baby's Health On The Line.

Get Prenatal Care Early • Call 1-800-311-2229 • Confidential

Take Care of Yourself So You Can Take Care of Your Baby.

Tailored Messaging

A growing body of literature attests to the importance of tailoring health messages and interventions to individual characteristics of participants instead of giving everyone identically framed information. For instance, the effectiveness of gain- or loss-framed messages appears to vary with whether a person tends to be *avoidance oriented* or *approach oriented*. Approach-oriented individuals are highly responsive to rewards and incentives, while avoidance-oriented individuals are highly responsive to punishments or threats. In a recent study, Traci Mann and her UCLA colleagues (2004) found that when college students received loss-framed messages promoting dental flossing, avoidance-oriented students reported taking better care of their teeth, and when given a gain-framed message, approach-oriented students reported flossing more than avoidance-oriented students. These results suggest that tailoring health messages to individuals based on their dispositional motivations is an effective strategy for promoting behavior change.

Message Wording Makes a Difference Educational campaigns may use gain-framed or loss-framed messages, as shown here. A gain-framed message regarding prenatal care might say, "Take care of yourself while you are pregnant, and you'll have a healthy child."

Loss-Framed Fear Appeals

Are fear-arousing messages effective in promoting attitude and behavior change? To find out, Irving Janis and Seymour Feshbach (1953) compared the effectiveness of messages that aroused various levels of fear in promoting changes in dental hygiene. Messages that aroused moderate levels of fear were more effective than more extreme messages in getting junior high school students to change their dental hygiene habits. In accounting for their results, the researchers suggested that individuals and circumstances differ in the optimal level of fear for triggering a change in attitude or behavior. When this level is exceeded, people may resort to denial or avoidance coping measures.

A key factor in determining the effectiveness of threatening health messages is the recipient's perceived behavioral control. Before they can be persuaded, people must believe that they have the ability to follow through on recommendations. In one study, Carol Self and Ronald Rogers (1990) presented highly

■ **gain-framed message** a health message that focuses on attaining positive outcomes, or avoiding undesirable ones, by adopting a health-promoting behavior.

■ **loss-framed message** a health message that focuses on a negative outcome from failing to perform a health-promoting behavior.

threatening messages regarding the dangers of sedentary living with or without information indicating that the subjects could perform the health-enhancing behavior (such as exercise) and succeed in enhancing their health. What did they find? Threat appeals worked only if participants were convinced that they could cope with the health threat; attempts to frighten participants without reassuring them were ineffective.

Recently, Heike Mahler and her colleagues (2003) found college-age beachgoers were particularly responsive to an educational campaign promoting sunscreen use and other sun protection behaviors when it focused on the dangers of sun exposure to each participant's appearance. The intervention began with a 12-minute slide presentation that included graphic photos of extreme cases of wrinkles and age spots. Afterwards, each participant's face was photographed with an ultraviolet (UV) ray filtered camera that accentuated brown spots, freckling, and other existing skin damage from UV exposure. A 1-month follow-up indicated that the intervention resulted in a significant increase in sun protective behaviors and substantially lower reported sunbathing.

However, scare tactics that arouse tremendous fear, such as photographs of grossly decayed or diseased gums, tend to upset people. As a result, such messages may backfire and actually *decrease* a person's likelihood of changing his or her beliefs and hence his or her behavior (Beck & Frankel, 1981). Such messages increase the person's anxiety to such a level that the only coping avenue he perceives open to him is a refusal to face the danger.

Promoting Healthy Workplaces

Occupational health psychologists are leading the way in designing healthy workplaces. Four dimensions of healthy work have been identified: *stress, work–family relations, violence prevention,* and *relationships at work* (Quick and others, 2004). Because job stress is a health epidemic in this country, psychological research and intervention are vital for the health of workers. Increasingly, insurers are recognizing that the causes of disabilities in the workplace are shifting from injuries to job stress.

The workplace has a profound psychological effect on all aspects of our lives and on the lives of our family members. For instance, job stressors may result in family social interactions that are less sensitive and supportive and more negative and conflicted, which can adversely affect children's biological responses to stress, emotional regulation, and social competence (e.g., Perry-Jenkins and others, 2000). Two behavioral *cross-over effects* have been observed between a worker's experiences of job stress and the well-being of other family members. *Negative emotion spillover* occurs when work-related frustrations contribute to greater irritability, impatience, or other negative behaviors at home. *Social withdrawal* occurs when one or more working adult parents or caregivers withdraw behaviorally and emotionally from family life following especially stressful days at work.

Over the past 20 years, there has been a significant shift in how we think about the relationship between work and family life. As more and more families consist of two full-time adult workers, employers and governmental agencies have begun to recognize that all employees face complex challenges in balancing work and family roles. These changing views have triggered an explosion of work–family research. Among the most consistent findings is the fact that in the United States, most employees find little support and have little say in the policies of work that affect them and their families (Quick and others, 2004). Consequently, they are left on their own to arrange child care, balance work schedules, stave off work stress, and so forth. The 1993 *Family and Medical Leave Act* helps some workers by protecting their jobs as they care for new babies and family members who are ill, but many workers are not covered by this legislation.

Workplace violence has received considerable attention in recent years. By some estimates, homicide has become the second leading cause of occupational injury death, exceeded only by motor vehicle deaths (Jenkins, 1996). Most of these deaths occur during robberies, but about 10 percent can be attributed to coworkers or former employees. Another 2 million people or so are assaulted each year at work (Bureau of Labor Statistics, 2006). A number of factors increase a worker's risk of being a victim of violence (Quick and others, 2004):

- Contact with the public
- Exchange of money
- Delivery of passengers, goods, or services
- Having a mobile workplace
- Working with unstable or volatile people (e.g., in health care or social service settings)
- Working alone, late at night, and in high-crime areas

In the area of work relationships, building a healthy work culture requires employees to accept responsibility for their own health and safety and that of their coworkers. More generally, as Dorothy Cantor and her colleagues (2004) have noted, building a healthy work culture requires attention to three factors: the person (individual differences, education, personality), the environment (work conditions, equipment, management systems), and behavior (risk behaviors, procedures, group performance).

In a healthy work culture, *safety triad* policies motivate employees to *behave* in ways that set a healthy example and make the work *environment* safe, while also paying attention to individual *person* factors (Figure 6.6, p. 178).

Worksite Wellness Programs

The workplace is an ideal site for promoting health for several reasons. First, workers find such programs convenient to attend. Some employers even permit their employees to participate in prevention programs during the workday. In addition, the workplace offers the greatest opportunity for continuing contact,

SAFETY CULTURE

| **Person** | **Environment** | **Behavior** |
| Biology, cognition, and experience (knowledge, skills, abilities, training, education, attitude, personality, motivation) | Equipment, tools, machines, management systems, work conditions, workplace design | Individual and group performance (wearing protective equipment, lifting properly, reporting hazards, coaching peers, following procedures) |

Figure 6.6

The Safety Triad A healthy work culture requires attention to three factors: the person, the environment, and behavior.

Source: Cantor, D. W., Boyce, T. E., & Repetti, R. L. (2004). Ensuring healthy working lives. In R. H. Rozensky, N. G. Johnson, C. D. Goodheart, & W. R. Hammond (Eds.), *Psychology builds a healthy world* (p. 277). Washington, D.C.: American Psychological Association.

follow-through, and feedback. Finally, coworkers are available to provide social support and help motivate people during difficult moments.

Worksite programs began to emerge at a rapid pace with the advent of the wellness movement during the 1980s. In the United States today, more than 80 percent of organizations with 50 or more workers offer some sort of health-promoting program (Scott, 1999). Worksite wellness programs offer a variety of activities, including weight management, nutrition counseling, smoking cessation, preventive health screenings, educational seminars, stress management, low back care, fitness centers, immunization programs, and prenatal programs.

At the heart of the wellness movement was the realization that preventing disease is easier, cheaper, and far more desirable than curing disease. Worldwide, health care costs have risen from about 3 percent of world gross domestic product (GDP) in 1948 to about 8 percent today. The United States currently spends over 16 percent of its GDP on health care (Smith and others, 2006). As noted earlier, an ever-increasing proportion of these costs has been passed along to employers who pay their employees' health insurance premiums. According to a 2006 William B. Mercer study, 97 percent of corporate health benefits costs are spent on treating preventable conditions such as cardiovascular disease, lower back problems, hypertension, stroke, bladder cancer, and alcohol abuse. Employers have realized that worksite programs that are even modestly successful in improving employees' health can result in substantial savings.

Are such programs effective? A number of careful studies reveal that they are. The cost of the programs is more than offset by reductions in work-related injuries, absenteeism, and worker turnover. For instance, Union Pacific Railroad employees in a wellness group lowered their risk of high blood pressure (45 percent) and high cholesterol (34 percent), moved out of the at-risk range for obesity (30 percent), and quit smoking (21 percent), yielding a net savings to the company of $1.26 million (Scott, 1999).

Research studies have revealed that, to be successful, work site programs should

- be voluntary.

- include health screenings, which have the greatest impact on a work site's health costs.

- relate to health behaviors of interest to employees.

- ensure confidentiality of health information.

- be convenient and have company support.

- offer additional incentives, such as health insurance rebates, monetary bonuses, or other prizes for success.

Positive Psychology and Thriving

In 2001, the American Psychological Association (APA) modified its 60-year-old mission statement to include the word "health" for the first time. Over 95 percent of the organization's membership endorsed the bylaw change, underscoring their awareness that while within each person there are physical and psychological elements that contribute to illness and disability, there are others that contribute to health, wellness, and thriving. The bylaw change was part of APA's Healthy World Initiative, which aligned with the new **positive psychology** movement described in Chapter 1 to promote a *strength-based, preventive approach* to research and interventions rather than psychology's more traditional approach of attacking problems after they have occurred (Seligman, 2002). As APA President Norine Johnson (2004) stated, "We must bring the building of strength to the forefront in the treatment and prevention of illness, for the promotion of wellness and health."(p. 317)

A central theme of the positive psychology movement is that the experience of adversity, whether physical or psychological in nature, can sometimes yield benefits, as it did for Sara Snodgrass, whom we met at the beginning of the chapter. As Charles Carver (Carver and others, 2005) noted, when we experience physical or psychological adversity, there are at least four possible outcomes:

- A continued downward slide

- Survival with diminished capacity or impairment

- A gradual or rapid return to the pre-adversity level of function

- The emergence of a quality that makes the person somehow better off than beforehand

Thriving refers to this paradoxical fourth outcome, in which adversity somehow leads people to greater psychological and/or physical well-being (O'Leary

■ **positive psychology** the study of optimal human functioning and the healthy interplay between people and their environments.

& Ickovics, 1995). How can this be? According to neuroscientist Bruce McEwen (1994), who introduced the concept of *allostatic load,* "Under conditions of stress, one would expect a physically weakened system, but positive physiological changes can occur—often in the context of psychological thriving. In physiological terms, this translates into greater restorative processes than destructive processes at work" (p. 195). Using the analogy of athletes strengthening their muscles by first breaking them down through exercise, allowing recovery, and then repeating this pattern over time to produce muscles that are stronger and capable of doing more work, positive psychologists point to evidence that adversity can similarly trigger "psychological bodybuilding" (Pearsall, 2004).

Allostasis and Neuroendocrine Health

As we saw in Chapter 4, in response to a stressor, activation of the hypothalamic-pituitary-adrenal (HPA) axis causes a change in the body's overall metabolic state. Most of the time, the cells of the body are occupied with activities that build the body *(anabolism).* When the brain perceives an impending threat or challenge, however, anabolic metabolism is converted into its opposite, *catabolism,* which breaks down tissues to provide energy. Catabolic metabolism is characterized by the release of catecholamines, cortisol, and other "fight-or-flight" hormones that help the body quickly mobilize energy. To counteract these neuroendocrine reactions, the parasympathetic nervous system triggers the release of anabolic hormones, including growth hormone, insulin-like growth factor (IGF-1), and the sex steroids. Anabolic metabolism counters arousal and promotes relaxation, energy storage, and healing processes such as protein synthesis.

Recall from Chapter 4 that allostasis refers to the body's ability to adapt to stress and other elements of rapidly changing environments (McEwen, 1998). One measure of *physical thriving* is a fluid allostatic system that flexibly shifts from high to low levels of SNS arousal, depending on the demands of the environment. Catabolic hormones, for instance, are essential to health over the short term. However, when people are in a constant state of arousal, prolonged elevations of catabolic hormones can damage the body and promote chronic illness. As an example, repeated stress can strongly affect brain function, especially in the hippocampus, which has large concentrations of cortisol receptors (McEwen, 1998). The consequences of long-term elevations of catabolic hormones, when taken together, look very much like aging. Hypertension, wasted muscles, ulcers, fatigue, and increased risk of chronic disease are common signs of both aging and chronic stress. This state, which has been called *allostatic load,* is indicated by a predominance of catabolic activity at rest (McEwen & Stellar, 1993). An elevated resting level of salivary or serum cortisol is one biological indicator of allostatic load and the general functioning of the HPA system. Conversely, a predominance of anabolic hormones at rest reflects enhanced health and a low allostatic load.

A series of classic studies by Jay Weiss and his colleagues (1975) demonstrated that the arousal of stress can lead to enhanced physical health by conditioning the body to be resistant to future stressors. You have learned that when laboratory animals experience chronic stress, they suffer from learned helplessness and catecholamine depletion. Paradoxically, Weiss found that exposing laboratory animals to *intermittent* stressors followed by recovery periods can lead to "physiological toughening," including resistance to catecholamine depletion, suppression of cortisol, and increased resilience to subsequent stressors. This toughening may also be accompanied by better performance on laboratory tasks, greater emotional stability, and even average life spans that were 18 percent longer than normal (Frolkis, 1981).

Psychosocial Factors and Physiological Thriving

Elsewhere in this book, we have seen how the immune system reacts upon encountering pathogens and how its functioning is influenced by cytokines and signals from other bodily systems, including the brain. Much of this discussion has emphasized how psychosocial factors can modify immune functioning in ways that impair health. In this section, we focus on evidence that psychosocial factors can also have beneficial effects on immune functioning and other bodily systems.

A number of psychological variables have been linked to lowered stress hormones or enhanced immunity in response to stress. These include self-esteem and perceptions of personal competence and control over outcomes (Seeman and others, 1995), self-efficacy (Bandura, 1985), and a sense of coherence in one's life (Myrin & Lagerstrom, 2006). In the workplace, a sense of control and autonomy is accompanied by lower baseline levels of catecholamines, even when task demands and stress levels are very high (Karasek and others, 1982).

Self-Enhancement

A growing body of research links positive mental states, even unrealistic ones involving *positive illusions,* to healthier physiological functioning (e.g., Taylor and others, 2003). People who tend toward *self-enhancement* have a disproportionate tendency to recall positive over negative information about their personalities and behaviors, to see themselves more positively than others see them, and to take credit for good outcomes (Taylor & Brown, 1988). Contrary to early views in psychology, which considered this type of inflated self-perception as evidence of narcissism, self-centeredness, and poor mental health, recent studies have suggested that rather than being associated with maladjustment, self-enhancement is indicative of health, wellness, and the ability to feel good about oneself. Self-enhancement has also been linked to the ability to develop and sustain relationships, to be content, and to thrive in environments that are changing or even threatening (Taylor and others, 2003).

Erroneous, but positive, views of our medical condition and of the perception of our control over it appear to promote health and longevity. For instance,

HIV-positive individuals and those diagnosed with AIDS who hold unrealistically positive views of their prognosis show a less rapid deterioration—even a longer time to death (Reed and others, 1999). Although these correlational findings do not prove causality, researchers speculate that *self-enhancing cognitions* might blunt physiological and neuroendocrine responses to stress and thus lessen HPA responses to stress (Taylor and others, 2000).

In a recent study, Shelley Taylor and her colleagues (2003) asked 92 college students to complete the *How I See Myself Questionnaire,* a measure of self-enhancement on which participants rate themselves in comparison with their peers on academic ability, self-respect, and 19 other positive qualities, as well as on selfishness, pretentiousness, and 19 other negative characteristics. They also completed personality scales tapping psychological resources such as optimism, extraversion, and happiness. One week later, the participants reported to a UCLA lab where they first provided a saliva sample for cortisol analysis and then performed several standard mental arithmetic tasks that reliably induce stress. As they did so, their heart rates, and systolic and diastolic blood pressures were monitored. Following completion of the stress-challenge tasks, a second cortisol measure was taken.

The results showed that self-enhancers had lower baseline cortisol levels at the start of the study *and* lower heart rate and blood pressure responses during the stress-challenge tasks. The baseline cortisol results suggest that self-enhancement is associated with lower resting HPA axis levels, indicating a chronically healthier neuroendocrine state. The blunted heart rate and blood pressure responses suggest that positive self-perceptions help people manage acute stressors. Over time, self-enhancers may experience less stress-related wear and tear on their bodies. Equally interesting were the participants' responses to the psychological resources questionnaire, which suggested that the relationship between self-enhancement and neuroendocrine response was mediated by higher self-esteem, optimism, extraversion, stronger social support, and greater work and community involvement than that found in participants who scored low on measures of self-enhancement.

Social Engagement

Sara Snodgrass feels that a key feature of her psychological thriving is the extent to which she has reorganized her life's priorities around her relationships with friends and family. Indeed, the importance of social engagement has been demonstrated by epidemiological studies showing that people who maintain strong social ties are more likely to retain health and live longer (Berkman and others, 2000). Social engagement also appears to be directly linked to neuroendocrine health. Studies have demonstrated, for instance, an increase in lymphocyte count in response to social support. Interventions that include some form of social support have enhancing effects on natural killer (NK) cell cytotoxicity, lymphocyte proliferation, and cell-mediated immunity (Miller & Cohen, 2001). Proponents of alternative medical treatments (see Chapter 14) are also heartened by evidence that massage, which requires physical contact between at least two individuals, promotes immune-enhancing effects such as increased NK cell activity (Ironson and others, 1996).

People often seek the support of others in order to disclose their feelings during moments of adversity. Research conducted over the last 15 years has documented that this type of *emotional disclosure* alters autonomic activity and immune function in ways that promote health. The work of James Pennebacker and his colleagues (1995; 1988) has shown that when individuals communicate events that produce negative emotional states, they exhibit elevations in natural killer cell activity and lymphocyte proliferation.

Relaxation

As we discussed in Chapter 5, wakeful relaxation achieved through meditation, listening to music, simple breathing exercises, and a variety of other simple means is also associated with decreases in negative emotions and alterations of neuroendocrine functions (Daruna, 2004). For instance, research studies have shown that relaxation promotes decreased leukocyte counts, enhanced natural killer cell activity, and, in the case of students who regularly practice relaxation, improved immune functioning during stressful exam periods (Kiecolt-Glaser and others, 1985; 1986). The most consistent finding associated with relaxation is an increase in secretory IgA, one of the anabolic hormones discussed earlier in the chapter. Interestingly, hypnosis, which is also thought to induce relaxation, also produces reliable increases in secretory IgA (Johnson and others, 1996).

Features of Psychological Thriving

A growing body of research reveals that curiosity and a sense of control over one's life contribute strongly to psychological thriving. Let's examine each of these factors.

Curiosity

Curiosity refers to a person's orientation or attraction to novel stimuli. Research suggests that curiosity in older people is associated with maintaining the health of the aging central nervous system. In examining the relationship between curiosity in older men and women and survival rates, researchers have found that, after 5 years, those with the highest levels of curiosity survived longer than those with lower levels (Swan & Carmelli, 1996). It's important to note, however, that this correlational evidence does not indicate that curiosity will automatically increase an older person's chances of survival; it may simply be a sign that his or her central nervous system is operating properly. In some individuals, age-related declines in curiosity reflect declining mental functioning. In partial support of this hypothesis, one study reported decreased curiosity (measured as reduced exploratory eye movements to novel visual stimuli) in individuals with serious central nervous system disease, as compared with age-matched normal controls (Daffner and others, 1994). Because certain brain structures known to be involved in Alzheimer's disease are also involved in directed attention and novelty-seeking behavior, diminished curiosity may be one of the earliest signs of abnormal aging of the central nervous system.

Assuming that the person is a normal, healthy adult, curiosity may enhance healthy aging because it enables older adults to successfully meet daily environmental and physical challenges. Thus, the curious older adult uses active coping strategies (see Chapter 5) to approach potential problems and impediments and in this way manages to reduce the strain on his or her physical and mental resources. It seems that such an individual stands a better chance of being physically and mentally healthy in the later years (Ory & Cox, 1994).

Perceived Control and Self-Efficacy

In one major prospective study of personality traits and health, researchers interviewed 8,723 late-middle-aged and older persons living independently or in adapted housing for elderly people in the Netherlands (Kempen and others, 1997). Three measures of personality were investigated: mastery or personal control, general self-efficacy, and neuroticism (emotional instability). *Mastery* concerns the extent to which one regards one's own life changes as being under one's own control in contrast to being fatalistically ruled. *Self-efficacy* refers to the belief that one can successfully perform specific behaviors. *Neuroticism* is related to a constant preoccupation with things that might go wrong and a strong emotional reaction of anxiety to these thoughts. Research participants with lower levels of neuroticism and higher levels of mastery and self-efficacy perceived significantly higher levels of functioning and well-being.

Why should a sense of control and mastery improve health? Both behavioral and physiological explanations are viable. Those who have a greater sense of control are more likely to take action, to engage in health-promoting behaviors, and to avoid health-damaging behaviors (Rodin, 1986). Because individuals with a high sense of control believe that what they do makes a difference, they behave in healthier ways (Lachman and others, 1994). In contrast, those who feel helpless and fail to see a relationship between actions and outcomes are more prone to illness and disease (Peterson & Stunkard, 1989), perhaps because they fail to engage in health-promoting practices or because they tend toward health-compromising behaviors ("I could get lung cancer no matter what I do, so I might as well smoke").

Having a sense of control also seems to show physiological effects. Research has shown that people with a high sense of control have lower cortisol levels and return more quickly to baseline levels after stress (Seeman & Lewis, 1995). They also have stronger immune systems, as evidenced by their ability to fight off disease (Rodin, 1986).

Additional evidence for the relationship between a strong sense of control and good health comes from research involving people at different socioeconomic levels. Margie Lachman and Suzanne Weaver of Brandeis University (1998) examined three large national samples of 25- to 75-year-old men and women of various social classes and found that for all income groups, higher perceived control was related to better health, greater life satisfaction, and fewer negative emotions. Although the results showed that on average, those with lower income had lower perceived control, as well as poorer health, control beliefs played a moderating role, and participants in the lowest-income group with a high sense of control showed levels of health and well-being comparable with those of the higher-income groups. The results provide some evidence that psychosocial variables such as sense of control may be useful in understanding social-class differences in health.

In this chapter, we have explored the connection between behavior and health. We have seen how health psychology's biopsychosocial focus on strength-based approaches to prevention promotes healthier individuals, families, workplaces, and communities. This focus is a departure from psychology's more traditional approach of attacking problems after they have occurred. As this healthier, more positive model takes hold, we may reach a tipping point in which health care similarly shifts from its traditional emphasis on tertiary prevention to a more balanced delivery system favoring primary prevention.

Summing Up

Health and Behavior

1. Most behaviors affect health in some way: for better (healthy behaviors) or worse (health-risk behaviors), directly or indirectly, immediately or over the long term.

2. The health belief model assumes that decisions regarding health behavior are based on four interacting factors: perceived susceptibility to a health threat, perceived severity of the threat, perceived benefits and barriers of treatment, and cues to action.

3. The theory of planned behavior maintains that the best way to predict whether a health behavior will occur is to measure a person's decision to engage in a health-related behavior (behavioral intention). The decision to engage in a health behavior is shaped by our attitude toward the behavior, our motivation to comply with the views of others regarding the behavior (subjective norm), and our expectation of success in performing the health behavior (perceived behavioral control).

4. The transtheoretical model outlines five stages through which people progress in changing health-related behaviors: precontemplation, contemplation, preparation, action, and maintenance.

Prevention

5. Primary prevention refers to actions to prevent a disease or injury from occurring. Secondary prevention involves actions to treat an illness early in its course. Tertiary prevention involves actions taken to contain damage once a disease has progressed beyond its early stages.

6. In focusing on healthy life expectancy, health psychologists aim to shorten the amount of time older people spend disabled, ill, or in pain (morbidity). Regular exercise, especially aerobic exercise, increases physical strength, helps maintain bone density, and reduces an older person's risk of cardiovascular disease and cancer. Although it is never too late to start exercising, some older adults face several barriers to doing so, including ageist stereotypes, lack of confidence (exercise self-efficacy) and motivation, and myths that exercise can actually undermine their health.

7. Family connectedness, conflict, and nurturance are powerful influences on the individual's health behavior, as are the health habits and attitudes of other family members. Within the health system, prevention remains a relatively minor focus in traditional medicine, and many people cannot afford health coverage. At the community level, people are more likely to adopt health-enhancing behaviors when these behaviors are promoted by community organizations, such as schools, government agencies, and the health care system.

8. Carefully planned health education campaigns that present information on several fronts and are community based often can promote changes that are difficult for individuals to accomplish.

9. Message framing is a critical factor in the effectiveness of health education. Messages can be framed to emphasize either the positive outcomes from adopting a health-promoting behavior (gain-framed messages), or the negative outcomes from failing to do so (loss-framed messages). Tailoring health messages to individuals is an effective strategy for promoting behavior change. Fear-arousing messages may backfire and actually decrease a person's likelihood of adopting a certain health behavior.

10. Most organizations with 50 or more workers offer some form of worksite wellness program. The cost of such programs has proved to be more than offset by reductions in work-related injuries, absenteeism, and worker turnover.

Positive Psychology and Thriving

11. A central theme of the new positive psychology movement—which promotes a strength-based, preventive approach to research and interventions—is that adversity sometimes leads people to greater psychological and/or physical well-being.

12. Although catabolic hormones are essential to our short-term health, when we are in a constant state of arousal (allostatic load), prolonged elevations of catabolic hormones can weaken our immunity and promote illness.

13. A number of psychosocial factors have been linked to enhanced immunity in response to stress. These include self-esteem, perceptions of personal competence and control, self-efficacy, and a tendency to recall positive over negative information about ourselves (self-enhancement).

14. Other key features of psychological thriving include curiosity, wakeful relaxation, social engagement, and emotional disclosure. Relaxation and sharing feelings with family and friends during moments of adversity alter autonomic activity and immune function in ways that promote health. Curiosity may enhance healthy aging because it helps older adults use active coping strategies in meeting daily challenges.

Key Terms and Concepts

health behavior, 155
health belief model (HBM), p. 157
theory of planned behavior (TPB), p. 159
behavioral intention, p. 159
subjective norm, p. 159

behavioral willingness, p. 160
transtheoretical model, p. 161
primary prevention, p. 163
secondary prevention, p. 163
tertiary prevention, p. 163

health education, p. 172
gain-framed message, p. 175
loss-framed message, p. 175
positive psychology, p. 179

Chapter 7

Nutrition, Obesity, and Eating Disorders

*O*ne of my former students (call her Jodi) is 26 years old and weighs 78 pounds. She was once a sleek and muscular 800-meter track champion and an academic All-American. Before that, she was valedictorian of her high school graduating class and voted "most likely to succeed." Today she is hospitalized with serious coronary complications resulting from her 12-year battle with disordered eating. But even now, Jodi sees herself not as emaciated and malnourished but as bloated and obese.

Growing up in an upper-middle-class home, Jodi had two loving parents and a terrific older sister. Yet ever since she was a child, she has felt pressure to live up to her family's high expectations. She found it particularly difficult to follow in the footsteps of her talented and popular sister. By the time she entered college, Jodi felt that she had to be perfect at everything.

Unfortunately, she felt her most significant imperfection was that she did not look like the swimsuit models and actresses she and her friends admired. And her track coaches didn't help. Jodi had a short, powerful build that was well suited for running fast. Even though she was the top runner on her high school and college teams, her coaches and trainers believed that she could run faster if she would only shed a few pounds.

Jodi tried her best to lose weight, but her body simply wouldn't cooperate for very long. She tried several diet plans, including a low-carb diet, but she felt so tired and hungry that she was unable to concentrate on her schoolwork and never stayed on a diet for very long. Her weight bounced up and down like a yo-yo.

Then one day Jodi found a terrible solution for her perceived weight "problem": She would eat whatever and whenever she wanted and then either make herself throw up or take a large dose of laxatives. She also redoubled her training efforts, increasing her daily running mileage and adding cross-training workouts of lap swimming or *spinning on a bicycle trainer. She still felt tired but thought it was worth it to gain some control over her weight.*

Because she maintained a fairly stable weight, Jodi was able to hide her bingeing and purging throughout high school and college. When she was living on her own, however, she started eating less and less, and her weight loss soon became obvious. One holiday, while visiting her family, she fainted while playing basketball with her father. When he picked her up, he realized that she weighed little more than a child.

Jodi's parents insisted that she see a doctor, who quickly placed her into a treatment program in which she was force-fed for a week. Although Jodi's weight has increased, the years of disordered eating have taken a severe toll on her body, and her prospects for regaining her health are not promising.

Not all ancient cultures valued a stout build. Obesity was stigmatized in medieval Japan because it was viewed as the karmic consequence of a moral failing in Buddhism. In some parts of Europe, obesity was frowned upon as a sign of the Christian sin of gluttony.

Throughout most of history and in developing countries today—wherever meals are rarely guaranteed—a full figure has been considered a sign of prosperity and health. Now that super-sized figures are so easy to achieve in our western cultures, we admire the sleek look instead. We are bombarded with media images of movie stars, sports figures, and other celebrities that shape our standards of attractiveness. The current emphasis on thinness strongly influences how we feel about our bodies. Most American women, for example, feel that they weigh somewhat more than men prefer, and much more than their own ideal body weight. Several studies have shown that children as young as 7 years of age have a negative body image and have already engaged in dieting and other weight-loss behaviors (McCabe & Ricciardelli, 2003). As Jodi's heart-wrenching story makes clear, not everyone can have a thin figure. The goal of health psychology is to help people attain and maintain a healthy weight, not necessarily the cultural ideal. Yet the ease with which we fill out has led more of us to suffer serious health risks from being overweight and obese (see Figure 7.1). This epidemic has spread worldwide, including Spain, France, Australia, Brazil, Mexico, Denmark, Italy, and Russia, where more than half the populations are overweight. Is it any wonder that the World Health Organization recognizes **obesity** as one of the top 10 health problems in the world and one of the top 5 in developed nations?

More people are treated for obesity in this country than for all other health conditions combined. Those extra pounds can contribute to diabetes, stroke, hypertension, coronary disease, and other chronic diseases that cost the health care system an estimated $117 billion per year. Add to this the indirect costs for missed days of work, and you begin to understand the scope of the problem—a problem that sends approximately 300,000 North American women and men to early graves each year (DeAngelis, 2004). Each year dozens of new weight "solutions" appear, from liquid diets to appetite-suppressing "aroma sticks," most of which fail (in controlled clinical trials) to reduce the weight of even a handful of obese participants for any length of time.

■ **obesity** excessive accumulation of body fat.

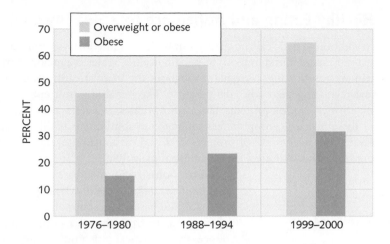

Figure 7.1

Prevalence of Overweight and Obese Americans Data from the National Health and Nutrition Examination Survey (NHANES) reveal that 25 years ago, 47 percent of Americans were classified as overweight or obese (BMI > 25.0); today, 65 percent of U.S. adults between the ages of 20 and 74 years are overweight or obese. Americans are fatter today than their parents and grandparents ever were, and they are getting fatter every year.

Source: Centers for Disease Control and Prevention, National Center for Health Statistics, National Health and Nutrition Examination Surveys http://www.cdc.gov/nchs/products/pubs/pubd/hestats/obese/obse99.htm

Psychologists have joined forces with molecular biologists, genetic engineers, nutritionists, and other health professionals in the search for answers to some of eating behavior's most puzzling questions: Why is obesity becoming more prevalent? Why is it relatively simple to lose a little weight but nearly impossible to keep it off? How is it that some people can eat whatever they want without gaining weight, while others remain overweight despite constant dieting? Why do some of the best and brightest teenagers literally starve themselves to death? Which foods are most healthful to consume, and how can we safely maintain a healthy weight? We will address these and other important questions in our exploration of eating behavior and weight regulation. We begin by examining the components of food and their role in maintaining health.

Nutrition: Eating the Right Foods

In Framingham, Massachusetts in 1948, a "healthy" breakfast consisted of a plate of fried eggs, a slab of bacon, and several pieces of white toast slathered with margarine. Residents spooned sugar and fatty cream from the top of milk bottles into their coffee. In this town, one in four men age 55 or older developed heart disease, yet doctors hadn't yet made the connection to diet and didn't understand what was killing their patients. They often listed "acute indigestion" as the cause of death.

Researchers descended on the town, and after 50 years and over 1,000 scholarly research papers, the Framingham Heart Study has shown that poor nutrition is a leading risk factor in the development of heart disease. We have learned that a healthy diet focused on fruits and vegetables while limiting the consumption of total fat and saturated fat and entirely avoiding trans-fatty acids provides the body with the nutrients it needs to protect and repair itself. We are, indeed, what we eat.

Healthy Eating and Adherence to a Healthy Diet

In addition to daily caloric energy, our bodies require forty-six *nutrients* (essential substances found in food) to remain healthy. Water is a major source of nutrition, transporting nutrients throughout the bloodstream, removing wastes, and regulating the body's temperature. The remaining nutrients are grouped into five categories: proteins, fats, carbohydrates, minerals, and vitamins. Each of these nutrient groups offers unique contributions to bodily function and health, and in the case of proteins, fats, and carbohydrates, the caloric energy our bodies need to meet the demands of daily living.

Nutritionists recommend a balanced daily diet that includes 6–7 ounces of whole grain bread, cereal, rice, and pasta; 2 to 3 cups of vegetables; 2 cups of fruit; 3 cups from the milk group; and about 6 ounces from the meat, fish, poultry, nuts, and beans group (Figure 7.2). The exact amount you should eat from each food group depends on your age, gender, and level of physical activity. (For a quick estimate of your needs, see the online calculator at www.mypyramid.gov.)

The *Glycemic Index (GI)* ranks carbohydrates based on how quickly your body converts them to the sugar glucose. The index ranges from 0 to 100, with higher values given to foods that cause the most rapid rise in blood sugar (Table 7.1). As a reference point, pure glucose has a GI of 100. Paying attention to the GI of the foods you eat is important because your body performs best when its blood sugar is relatively constant. When it drops too low, you feel lethargic and hungry. And when it is too high, your brain signals your pancreas to produce more insulin, which brings your blood sugar back down by converting the excess sugar to stored fat. When you eat foods with a high GI (sweets, processed grains, certain potatoes), you may feel a surge of energy as your blood sugar rises, but this will quickly be followed by increased fat storage, lethargy, and more hunger!

Unfortunately, nutritional advice is frequently ignored, however. In several studies, Jane Wardle and her colleagues (2004; 1995) surveyed the dietary habits of thousands of young adults from 23 countries, including their efforts to avoid animal fat, salt, sugar, and food additives; to emphasize fiber and fruit in their nutrition; and to never skip breakfast. The disappointing results revealed only modest adherence, and only by those who valued health highly, who believed in the importance of diet in determining health, and who felt responsible for determining their health. This was true across all dietary practices, offering convincing support for cognitive models of health behaviors such as the theory of planned behavior (see Chapter 6). Partly because they were more likely than men to be dieting, women tended to consume healthier foods. Equally important, however, was the fact that women professed stronger beliefs than men regarding the importance of healthy food choices.

Whole grains, 7 oz
Vegetables, 3 cups
Fruits, 2 cups
Oils, 6 teaspoons
Milk, 3 cups
Meat and beans, 6 oz

Figure 7.2

A Balanced Diet These amounts are appropriate for a 19-year-old woman who engages in 30 to 60 minutes of moderate or vigorous activity (such as jogging, aerobics, biking, or swimming) most days in addition to her normal daily routine.

Table 7.1

The Glycemic Index of Some Common Foods

Low Glycemic Index Foods (GI = 55 or less)

Skim milk	Plums	Slow cook oatmeal
Soy beverages	Oranges	Lentils, kidney beans, and other legumes
Apples	Sweet potatoes	

Moderate Glycemic Index Foods (GI = 56–69)

Bananas	Brown rice	Whole wheat bread
Pineapple	Basmati rice	Rye bread
Raisins		

High Glycemic Index Foods (GI = 70 or more)

Watermelon	Instant rice	French fries
Dried dates	Sugary breakfast cereals	Table sugar (sucrose)
White potatoes and bread	Bagels	

Not all carbohydrates are created equal! Foods that raise your blood glucose level quickly have a higher GI than foods that raise your blood glucose level more slowly. Choosing low and moderate GI foods—which are usually low in calories and fat, while rich in fiber, nutrients, and antioxidants—may help you keep your energy and cholesterol levels balanced, reduce inflammation, and lower your risk of heart disease and Type 2 diabetes.

In a recent 2-week longitudinal study, Christina Wood Baker and her colleagues (2003) found that social norms and perceived behavioral control also influence the food behaviors of adolescents. Those who professed the most positive attitudes and intentions about healthy eating (a) perceived that their friends and parents felt the same way and were healthy eaters themselves, and (b) felt that their own self-discipline, effort, and other internal resources determined health eating behaviors. These results suggest that to be effective in promoting healthy eating, education and media-based public service campaigns should also focus on social norms and promoting perceived control, self-confidence, and the ability to overcome perceived barriers in healthy eating.

The finding that adherence to healthy eating recommendations is not universal may not surprise students, who often rely on fast foods to satisfy their appetites within the time constraints of a busy lifestyle. Consider breakfast—a meal that can be a mixture of the most and least nutritious foods. One in five people skip this important meal, including one-third of teenagers and those in their 20s (Raloff, 2006). Nutritionists have observed two unhealthy trends in fast-food breakfasts: "dessert for breakfast" and "super-sizing" (Nutrition Action Newsletter, 2001). Health- and **calorie**-conscious students who rarely indulge in ice cream after a meal might be surprised to learn that an almond croissant or cinnamon scone from a popular coffee chain contains 630 calories, five teaspoons of sugar, and 16 to 18 grams of saturated fat—the equivalent of more than two ice cream bars.

Equally dangerous is "super-sizing." Since the 1970s, portion sizes—of restaurant foods, grocery products, and even the servings suggested in cookbooks—

■ **calorie** a measure of food energy equivalent to the amount of energy needed to raise the temperature of 1 gram of water 1 degree Celsius.

have grown dramatically (Brownell, 2003). This is significant because people eat more when given larger portions. In one study in which participants received four different portion sizes of macaroni and cheese on different days, people ate 30 percent more calories when given the biggest compared with the smallest portion (Rolls and others, 2002). In another study of theater-goers, those who were randomly assigned to receive a large size of poporn ate 61 percent more than those who received a smaller size (Wansink & Park, 2001). Interestingly, supersizing is not a universal phenomenon. When Paul Rozin and his colleagues (2003) compared 11 pairs of fast-food chains and ethnic restaurants in Paris and Philadelphia, they found that mean portion sizes in Paris were 25 percent smaller than in Philadelphia.

Diet and Disease

Early dietary habits may set a lifelong pattern. And this pattern may lead to problems in later life. In fact, the foods we eat are implicated in five of the ten leading causes of death: heart disease, cancer, stroke, diabetes, and atherosclerosis (World Health Organization, 2003).

Excess dietary fat has been widely acknowledged as a major health hazard. Once inside the body, dietary fat becomes body fat very efficiently. The body expends only 3 calories to turn 100 calories of fat into body fat. In contrast, the body burns about 25 calories to turn the same amount of carbohydrates into body fat. To make matters worse, we crave fat—a legacy from our prehistoric ancestors, who lived in a time when regular meals and survival were both uncertain. As a result of this craving, an unhealthy 40 to 45 percent of the total calories in the average Western diet come from fat.

There are four main types of fats: *trans fat, saturated fat, monounsaturated fat,* and *polyunsaturated fat.* The toxic *trans fat* or *trans fatty acids* are formed when hydrogen is added to the vegetable oil in a food product to give it a longer shelf-life and a desired taste and texture. *Hydrogenated* and *partially hydrogenated fats* are abundant in margarine, crackers, packaged cookies and snack foods, fried foods, doughnuts, and many other processed foods. Saturated fat is primarily found in foods derived from animal sources, including beef, veal, lamb, pork, butter, cheese, and other whole milk dairy products. Monounsaturated fats are found in oils, such as canola, olive, and peanut, and in avocadoes. There are two kinds of polyunsaturated fats: *omega-6 fatty acids,* which are found in corn, soybean, sesame, and safflower oils; and *omega-3 fatty acids,* found primarily in the oils of coldwater fish such as salmon, and in flax seeds and a few other foods that are often difficult to obtain.

Researchers once thought that all fat was bad, but we now know that they were wrong. Fat is a major source of energy and also helps the body absorb essential vitamins. Trans-fats are indeed unhealthful and should in fact be avoided altogether. Saturated fats should be consumed in extreme moderation, but monounsaturated fats and polyunsaturated fats (especially omega-3 fatty acids) are actually healthful because they reduce cholesterol levels in the blood and have a healthy, anti-inflammatory effect on the body (Brownlee, 2006). As you will see in later chapters, uncontrolled inflammation is implicated in many chronic illnesses. To help consumers sort through the complexities of choosing food products on the basis of their fat contents, beginning in 2006, the U.S. Food and Drug Administration required food companies to list a product's total amount of trans-fat, saturated fat, and cholesterol on its label.

Coronary Heart Disease

Consumption of saturated fat, and especially trans-fat, both of which become dietary cholesterol in the body, is a contributing factor in many adverse health conditions, including coronary heart disease. Cholesterol is a waxy substance essential for strong cell walls, myelination of nerve cells, and the production of hormones. However, the cholesterol we take in from the fats in our foods is nonessential because the liver manufactures all the cholesterol that the body needs. Dietary cholesterol—which comes from animal fats and oils, not from vegetables or plant products—circulates in the blood and so is called *serum cholesterol* (serum is the liquid part of the blood).

Serum cholesterol is found in several forms of proteins called *lipoproteins.* There are three types of lipoproteins, distinguished by their density. *Low-density lipoproteins (LDL,* which carry cholesterol around the body for use by cells), and *triglycerides* (the chemical form in which most fat exists in food), have been linked to the development of heart disease, whereas *high-density lipoproteins (HDL)* may offer some protection against heart disease. Cholesterol carried by LDL is therefore often called "bad cholesterol," while HDL is referred to as "good cholesterol" because it helps clear away cholesterol deposits from cell walls and carries them to the liver, where they are broken down and then removed from the body. Dietary saturated fat and especially trans fat-raise LDL cholesterol levels in the blood, lower HDL levels, and promote inflammation.

Nutritionists recommend keeping overall serum cholesterol below 200 milligrams (mg) of cholesterol per deciliter (dl) of blood, with LDL and triglyceride levels below 100 mg/dl, and HDL levels *above* 40 mg/dl. To help do so, consumption of foods containing saturated fat and cholesterol should be kept as low as possible (while still eating a healthy diet). And, according to a 2002 National Academy of Science panel, the only safe level of trans-fat in a food is "zero." Nutritionists also call for everyone, beginning in their twenties, to obtain a complete serum cholesterol profile (total cholesterol, LDL cholesterol, HDL cholesterol, and triglycerides) every 5 years (NCEP, 2006).

A long-term prospective study of white males found that their serum cholesterol levels at age 22 accurately predicted their cardiovascular health decades later (Klag and others, 1993). At the beginning of the study, the participants were separated into three groups based on their average serum cholesterol level. Those in the high-risk group at age 22 (serum cholesterol between 209 mg and 315 mg) were 70 percent more likely to develop heart disease than were those in the low-risk group (cholesterol levels between 118 mg and 172 mg.)

Although cholesterol levels tend to increase with age, lowering blood cholesterol may not be important for people over the age of 70. Data from the Framingham study demonstrate a positive relationship between serum cholesterol

If approved, a proposal unanimously endorsed by the New York City Board of Health would set a limit of one-half gram of trans fat per serving for every item on the menus of all 20,000 restaurants in the city—from fast food joints to the fanciest bistros. Health psychologists hope that this promising move may encourage other big cities to follow suit.

level and death from coronary disease only up to age 60 (see Chapter 9). In older adults, serum cholesterol may provide some protection from heart disease, particularly among women (Kronmal and others, 1993).

The Framingham study also revealed an important point: The best predictor of heart disease is not total level of serum cholesterol; instead, the culprit is the amount of "bad cholesterol" (LDL and triglycerides) in the body. Even people with lower levels of total serum cholesterol are at increased risk of developing atherosclerosis if their HDL levels are very low. HDL levels below 35 mg/dl are considered unhealthy. Smoking, physical inactivity, and a high dietary intake of cholesterol and saturated fats are linked with increased levels of LDLs and decreased levels of HDLs. Certain types of polyunsaturated and monounsaturated fats, vitamin E, and a low-fat, high-fiber diet may protect against heart disease by elevating HDL levels.

Serum cholesterol level is determined partly by heredity. Some people seem to be able to consume a diet rich in fat without elevating serum cholesterol; others may have high cholesterol levels even though their diet is low in saturated fat. For most people, however, diet and lifestyle play a major role in the amount of serum cholesterol circulating in their bodies.

Cancer

As you will see in Chapter 10, diet is implicated in one-third of all cancer deaths in the United States (Lichtenstein and others, 1998). Saturated fat, especially that found in animal products, is the major dietary culprit. Saturated fat has been linked to several cancers, including breast cancer, prostate cancer, and colorectal cancer (Toribara & Sleisenger, 1995).

Fortunately, there is also evidence that certain foods may protect us against cancer. Vegetables and fruits are rich in *beta-carotene,* which the body processes into vitamin A—a nutrient that helps ensure healthy immune system functioning. Along with beta-carotene, small amounts of the mineral selenium, found in fish, whole grains, and certain vegetables, may help prevent some forms of cancer (Glauert and others, 1990). A diet rich in vitamins C and E may also help prevent cancer by protecting body cells from the damaging effects of *free radicals* (metabolic waste products). Such a diet may also protect against carcinogenic *nitrosamines,* which are produced in the stomach when you eat foods laced with nitrates, nitrites, and other preservatives.

Weight Determination: Eating the Right Amount of Food

Naturally, it's not only what you eat but also how much you eat in relation to your body's caloric needs that determine your weight and your health. Before we discuss obesity—its causes and treatment—you first need to understand the basic mechanisms by which the body determines the type and amount of calories needed.

Basal Metabolic Rate and Caloric Intake

Body weight remains stable when the calories your body absorbs from the food you eat equal the calories it expends for basic metabolic functions plus physical activity. How many calories does your body need to maintain bodily functions while at rest? This figure, called the **basal metabolic rate (BMR)**, is not easily determined because it depends on a number of variables, including your age, gender, current weight, and activity level.

Individual differences in BMR help explain why it is possible for two people of the same age, height, and apparent activity level to weigh the same, even though one of them has a voracious appetite while the other merely picks at food. Several factors determine your BMR, including, first, heredity. Some people have a naturally higher metabolic rate than others, even when they're asleep. Other people need fewer calories for the same amount and level of physical activity. Second, younger people and those who are active generally have a higher BMR than do older adults and those who are sedentary. Third, fat tissue has a lower metabolic rate (burns fewer calories) than muscle does. Once you add fat to your body, you require less food to maintain your weight than you did to gain the weight in the first place. Finally, because men have proportionately more muscle, their bodies burn 10 to 20 percent more calories at rest than women's bodies do.

The Set-Point Hypothesis

Many people believe that their body weights fluctuate erratically, but in fact our bodies balance energy intake and expenditure quite closely. A typical adult consumes roughly 900,000 to 1 million calories a year. Subtract from this figure the energy costs of BMR, and you'll discover that less than 1 percent of the calories you eat are stored as fat, a remarkable degree of precision in energy balance (Gibbs, 1996). Because of this precise regulation, experts have used data from national surveys to estimate that affecting energy balance by only 100 calories per day (as little as 15 minutes of walking or eating a few bites less each meal) could prevent weight gain in most people (Hill and others, 2003).

Evidence of such precision supports the **set-point hypothesis,** the idea that each of us has a body weight "thermostat" that continuously adjusts our metabolism and eating to maintain our weight within a genetically predetermined range, or set point (Keesey & Corbett, 1983). Early evidence for the set-point hypothesis came from experimental studies of voluntary starvation and overeating. During World War II, Ancel Keys studied 36 men who volunteered to participate in a study on semistarvation as an alternative to military service (Keys and others, 1950). For the first 3 months of the study, the participants ate normally. Then, for 6 months, they received half their normal caloric intake, with the goal of reducing their body weight by 25 percent. Initially, the men lost weight rapidly. As time passed, however, the pace of weight loss slowed, forcing the men to consume even fewer calories in order to meet

■ **basal metabolic rate (BMR)** the minimum number of calories the body needs to maintain bodily functions while at rest.

■ **set-point hypothesis** the idea that each person's body weight is genetically set within a given range, or set point, that the body works hard to maintain.

■ **leptin** the weight-signaling hormone monitored by the hypothalamus as an index of body fat.

■ **adipocytes** collapsible body cells that store fat.

their weight-loss goal. An even more dramatic result of this study was its findings regarding the psychological effects of semistarvation. The subjects did nothing but think and talk about food; they even spent time collecting recipes.

The set-point concept (today considered by many researchers to be a *settling-point* range of weight rather than a fixed number of pounds) partly explains why it is difficult to bring weight down. As a study by George Bray (1969) showed, with continued dieting, the body defends its precious fat reserves by decreasing its metabolic rate. When obese dieters reduced their daily intake from 3,500 to 450 calories for 24 days, their bodies quickly started burning fewer calories until their BMRs had dropped by 15 percent. The result: Although their body weight initially dropped 6 percent, with a lower BMR, they found it difficult to lose any more weight. These findings will surely strike a chord with dieters who suffer the frustrating experience of losing a few pounds relatively quickly but then find it harder to lose additional weight as their dieting (and reduced metabolism) continues.

If starvation has this effect on metabolism, what effect does overeating have? To find out, researchers persuaded a group of normal weight volunteers to overeat until their weights increased by 10 percent (Leibel and others, 1995). The results mirrored those of the semistarvation studies. After an initial period of rapid gain, further weight increases came slowly and with great difficulty, even though the participants had access to an abundance of delicious food and kept calorie-burning physical activity to a minimum. Like the men in the semistarvation study, the overfed volunteers found the experiment unpleasant. Food became repulsive, and they had to force themselves to eat. Some even failed to reach their weight gain goal even though they more than doubled the number of calories consumed each day. At the end of the experiment, however, most lost weight quickly.

These studies clearly indicate that over the short term it is normally very difficult to alter our weight substantially, and that even if we are able to do so, the weight differential is difficult to maintain. The body defends its set point by adjusting its basal metabolic rate as necessary. Over the long term, however, even normal weight individuals can override their genetic propensity. For example, over-stuffing ourselves—ignoring our brain's "full" signals—with a corresponding decreasing activity level can lead to modest yearly gains that add up over the years.

Why are our bodies so painfully good at maintaining weight? According to the evolutionary perspective, the capacity to store excess calories as fat was an important survival mechanism for our ancestors. Animals that hibernate and those that must endure periods of nutritional scarcity—as did the human species throughout much of our history—store internal energy reserves when food is plentiful and live off those reserves when food is in short supply. Natural selection favored those human ancestors who developed "thrifty genes," which increased their ability to store fat from each feast in order to sustain them until the next meal. Although those of us who live in well-stocked, developed countries no longer need to store so much fat, many of us continue to do so. For example, obesity is characteristic of Pima Indians living a "Western" lifestyle, whereas Pima Indians living a more traditional lifestyle remain leaner and have low levels of the fat hormone **leptin** (Friedman, 2003).

The Biological Basis of Weight Regulation

Our BMR determines how many calories we need to maintain bodily functioning, but what sets off the initial hunger pangs we all feel? No single question has generated more research in health psychology than this: Precisely what triggers hunger and its opposite—*satiety?* Although it once seemed obvious that hunger and satiety occur in the stomach, this simplistic notion was soon dismissed in the face of evidence that hunger persists in humans and laboratory animals that have had their stomachs removed (Tsang, 1938).

Researchers have tackled this question by focusing on *where* in the brain the signals for hunger and satiety are processed. During the 1960s, researchers located appetite centers in two areas of the hypothalamus: a side region called the *lateral hypothalamus (LH),* which seemed to trigger hunger, and a lower area in the middle called the *ventromedial hypothalamus (VMH),* which seemed to trigger satiety. Animal experiments during the 1960s demonstrated that electrical stimulation of the LH causes an animal that has eaten to the point of fullness to begin eating again; when this area is lesioned, even an animal that has not eaten in days shows no signs of hunger. Conversely, when the VMH is stimulated, animals stop eating; when this area is destroyed, they overeat to the point of extreme obesity (Hoebel & Teitelbaum, 1966). Likewise, hypothalamic brain tumors have been linked to obesity in some human patients (Miller and others, 1995).

Increased feelings of hunger have also been linked to an increase in the number of fat cells, or **adipocytes,** in the body. When adipocytes reach their maximum storage capacity, they divide—a condition called *fat-cell hyperplasia.* Once the number of fat cells increases in a person's body, as a result of genetic predisposition or overeating, they never decrease. People who are not obese have 25 to 30 billion fat cells. Those who are severely obese may have 200 billion or more.

Assuming that the LH and VMH integrate the various internal signals for hunger and satiety, *how* does the brain maintain the body's weight near the set point? One theory proposes that the hypothalamus regulates the number of adipocytes directly. Until recently, fat cells were believed by most researchers to be a passive system of storage. Researchers now consider fat to be a type of endocrine tissue, complete with its own chemical hormones. Researchers have discovered a hormone produced by fat cells that can trigger the formation of new ones, especially in children (Saez and others, 1998).

Researchers have discussed several other specific mechanisms for regulating how often and how much we eat on a given day, and for regulating our body weight over months and years.

Adipocytes Typically, we all have about 30 billion of these fat cells, or adipocytes. They are like little storage tanks. In a thin person, the fat cells are relatively empty; as the person gains weight, the cells begin to fill up. Each of the cells in this electron photomicrograph is filled by a single lipid droplet, mostly formed by triglycerides. Connective tissue fibers, in the upper left, provide support for the fat cells. © Professor P. Motta/ Department of Anatomy/ University "La Sapienza."

Rome/Science Photo Library/Photo Researchers

Short-Term Appetite Regulation

The pancreas produces the hormone insulin and assists the body in converting glucose into fat. When glucose levels fall, insulin production increases and we feel hunger. Conversely, when glucose levels rise, hunger and insulin levels decrease. As time passes since the last meal, the level of glucose in the blood drops. In addition to insulin reduction, low blood glucose triggers a release of stored fat from body cells. As fat is depleted, the hypothalamus also arouses hunger, motivating us to replenish our fat and glucose stores by eating.

Researchers have also identified *cholecystokinin (CCK),* a satiety hormone released into the bloodstream by the intestine that signals when we've had enough to eat. CCK suppresses appetite even when injected into starving animals (Thompson, 2000). Two other short-term appetite-regulating hormones that have been identified are *ghrelin,* an appetite stimulant, and *PYY,* an appetite suppressant. The stomach produces ghrelin, which causes the pituitary gland to release growth hormone and stimulates appetite. This discovery helped clear up a mystery in appetite research: why people want to eat at specific times each day. David Cummings and his colleagues (2004) discovered that ghrelin levels rise an hour or two before mealtimes and decrease afterwards, stimulating appetite by activating neurons in the *arcuate nucleus (ARC)* of the hypothalamus. Ghrelin also stimulates receptors on nerve cells in the hippocampus, a brain area involved in learning and memory (Diano and others, 2006). This finding makes evolutionary sense because hungry animals need to remember where they found a food source. Most obese people have lower levels of ghrelin than those who are thinner, and ghrelin production increases in people who are dieting—explaining in part why dieters may find it increasingly difficult to stick to their regimen.

Long-Term Weight Regulation

Why do some people seem to have more potential to become fat? Molecular biologists speculate that genetic disorders may interfere with the body's ability to regulate the number of fat cells, thereby causing people to gain weight. In 1994, researchers discovered that laboratory mice with a defective gene for regulating the hormone leptin could not control their hunger and became obese. Leptin, produced by fat cells, is found at greater levels in people with higher BMIs and lower levels in those with less body fat. Because they usually have higher body fat content, women generally have higher leptin levels than men do.

As body fat increases, higher levels of leptin signal the normal brain to suppress hunger. Animals with defective leptin genes produce too little leptin and overeat. They become hugely obese and diabetic, and they have a substantially lower BMR than their genetically normal counterparts (Zhang and others, 1994). When given daily injections of leptin, they eat less, they become more active, and their body weights eventually return to normal (Halaas and others, 1995).

The discovery of leptin renewed support for the set-point theory. According to this line of reasoning, if the body's set point is something like a thermostat, leptin acts like the thermometer (Gibbs, 1996). As a person gains weight, more leptin is produced. This shuts off appetite, increases energy expenditure, and triggers other mechanisms to restore body weight to the set point. Conversely, as a person loses weight (as in dieting), levels of leptin decrease, hunger increases, and metabolism falls until the person's weight returns to its targeted level.

Leptin's signaling ability may also explain why most dieters regain lost weight. After dieting, less leptin is available to signal the brain, possibly increasing hunger and slowing metabolism. In normal mice, leptin levels dropped 40 percent after a 3-day fast and 80 percent after a 6-day fast (Nakamura and others, 2000).

Recent studies, however, have pointed to a different function of the hormone in animals and in people. Although some rare cases of human obesity are caused by defects in leptin production, most obese humans have higher than normal blood levels of the hormone (Marx, 2003). Some believe that the leptin receptors of obese people are simply less sensitive to leptin. Following this line of reasoning, leptin's main role may be to protect against weight loss in times of deprivation rather than against weight gain in times of plenty. Obese people simply produce the hormone at a greater rate in order to compensate for a faulty signaling process (Nakamura and others, 2000).

Although injections of leptin are not effective for treating most cases of obesity in humans, the discovery of the hormone helped pinpoint the neural pathways involved in weight regulation. In particular, the ARC, which we have seen to be involved in short-term appetite regulation, contains large numbers of receptors for leptin and other hormones involved in long-term weight control. The ARC also contains two major types of neurons with opposing actions. Activation of one type, which produces a neurotransmitter called *neuropeptide Y (NPY)*, stimulates appetite and reduces metabolism. Activation of the other type causes the release of *-melanocyte-stimulating hormone,* which reduces appetite. For these reasons, the ARC has been called the "master center" for both short-term and long-term weight regulation (Marx, 2003).

Obesity: Some Basic Facts

People are concerned about what and how much they eat because of the negative physiological and psychological effects of obesity. Being overweight carries a social stigma in many parts of the world today, indicating the importance that many societies place on physical appearance. Obese children are frequently teased and, as adults, are often perceived as "ugly" and "sloppy" (Harris and others, 1991) and as lacking in willpower (Friedman & Brownell, 1995).

How our weight affects our psychological well-being depends on our gender. For instance, overweight women are more likely to be depressed, even suicidal, than their thinner counterparts (Carpenter and others, 2000). Interestingly, *underweight* men are more likely to be diagnosed with clinical depression than their heavier counterparts.

How do we define obesity? In recent years, the definition of obesity has been refined to mean the presence of excess body fat. A person with an acceptable

■ **body mass index (BMI)** a measure of obesity calculated by dividing body weight by the square of a person's height.

■ **male pattern obesity** the "apple-shaped" body of men who carry excess weight around their upper body and abdomen.

■ **female pattern obesity** the "pear-shaped" body of women who carry excess weight on their thighs and hips.

Table 7.2

Body Mass Index and Weight

BMI Categories

Underweight = < 18.5
Normal Weight = 18.5–24.9
Overweight = 25–29.9
Obese = 30–39.9
Morbidly Obese = 40+

Source: Department of Health and Human Services. Centers for Disease Control and Prevention. http://www.cdc.gov/nccdphp/dnpa/bmi/index.htm

weight and figure but too much body fat could be considered obese, and his or her health could be at risk. Thus, you can be healthy or not at the same weight—it all depends on your individual fat-to-muscle content.

The most frequently used measure of obesity today is the **body mass index (BMI)**, which is strongly correlated with percentage of body fat. Here's how to determine your BMI: multiply your weight in pounds (without shoes or clothes) by 705. Divide this product by your height in inches. Then divide it again by your height. Alternatively, you could use the BMI calculator at the National Institutes of Health Web Site (www.nhlbisupport.com/bmi/). For example, if you weigh 140 pounds and are 5′6″, your BMI would be 22.66, which is within the normal range (see Table 7.2). A person with a BMI of 40 or greater is considered *morbidly obese*—having reached the point where the excess body fat begins to interfere with day-to-day movement and even breathing. Morbid obesity is equivalent to 294 pounds for a 6-foot man or 247 pounds for a woman 5 feet 6 inches tall.

There is no set ideal amount of body fat for all people, because the amount of body fat changes with age. In healthy adults, acceptable levels of body fat range from 25 to 30 percent in women and from 18 to 23 percent in men.

While the overall amount of body fat is important, the evidence indicates that *where* body fat is distributed may be even more significant. The excess upper body and abdominal fat associated with **male pattern obesity** (also called *abdominal obesity)* has been linked to atherosclerosis, hypertension, and diabetes (Canoy and others, 2004), and—pound for pound—is considered a greater overall health risk than fat that is concentrated on the hips and thighs (**female pattern obesity**). However, the health hazards of a high waist-to-hip ratio apply to both women and men (Sjostrom, 1992) and may even be a more accurate predictor of mortality from all causes than body mass index. To measure your waist-to-hip ratio:

1. Measure your waist at its slimmest point.

2. Measure your hips at the widest point.

3. Divide your waist measurement by your hip measurement: _____ (waist in inches) ÷ (hips in inches) = _____

Two Weight Extremes A Sumo wrestler has a BMI above 30, which puts him well into the obese category. At the other end of the scale, sinewy model Esther Canadas checks in at 5′10″ and 101 pounds, for an unhealthy BMI of 14.4.

Thus, a woman with a waist of 29 inches and a hip measurement of 37 would have a ratio of 0.78, while a man with a 34-inch waist and a 40-inch hip measurement would have a ratio of 0.85. Both ratios fall within the healthy range. As a rule, the desirable waist-to-hip ratio is less than 0.8 for women and less than 0.95 for men.

One study of a large sample of Iowa women reported that the higher the waist-to-hip ratio, the higher the death rate (Folsom and others, 1993). This relationship remained significant even after BMI, smoking, education level, marital status, alcohol consumption, and use of estrogen were factored out. More recently, the Nurses' Health Study showed that women with a waist-to-hip ratio of 0.88 or greater were three times as likely to develop coronary heart disease as were women with a waist-to-hip ratio under 0.72 (Rexrode and others, 1998).

Hazards of Obesity

The National Institutes of Health cite obesity as second only to cigarette smoking in its importance as a behavioral factor in mortality rates. Although being slightly **overweight** appears to pose no health risks (Figure 7.3; Blackburn and others, 2002), obesity presents a major risk: As body fat accumulates, it crowds

■ **overweight** body weight that exceeds the desirable weight for a person of a given height, age, and body shape.

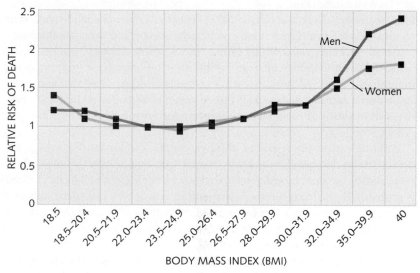

Figure 7.3

Mortality Rates as a Function of Body Mass Index (BMI) Generally speaking, thinner women and men live longer. At a BMI of 40, a woman's risk of dying is approximately 50 percent higher than that of a person with a BMI of 24; for men with a BMI over 40, the risk of death is about 2.5 times higher. However, very thin people do not have the lowest mortality rates, indicating that the relationship between weight and poor health is actually U-shaped, were the graph extended to BMIs below 18.

Source: Calle, E. E., Thun, M. J., Petrelli, J. M., Rodriguez, C., & Heath, C. W. (1999). Body-mass index and mortality in a crospective Cohort of U.S. adults. *New England Journal of Medicine, 341,* 1097–1105.

the space occupied by internal organs and contributes to many chronic health problems. Consider:

- The incidence of hypertension in people who are 50 percent or more overweight is three to five times that of normal-weight people.

- Obesity promotes *hyperinsulinemia,* an endocrine disorder in which insulin progressively loses its effectiveness in sweeping glucose from the blood stream into the 60 trillion or so cells of our bodies. For this reason, obesity is a leading cause of type 2 diabetes.

- The liver manufactures more triglycerides (the most common form of dietary fat in the bloodstream) and cholesterol in those with excess body weight, which increases the risk of arthritis, gout, and gallbladder disease.

- Complications following surgery, including infection, occur more often among the obese.

- There is a strong correlation between obesity and cardiovascular diseases in both men and women, even after statistical adjustments are made for blood pressure, cholesterol, smoking, age, and diabetes.

- Obesity increases the risk of certain cancers.

One in four overweight adults and nearly 30 percent of overweight adolescents have a constellation of risk factors that result in a condition called the *metabolic syndrome* (Cook and others, 2003). These risk factors include abdominal obesity, elevated triglyceride levels and blood pressure, and hyperinsulinemia.

Given the health hazards that obesity poses, it will come as no surprise that being significantly overweight can cut life short. A large-scale study following more than 1 million Americans over a 14-year period reported that white men and women with the highest BMI (40 or higher) had two to six times the relative risk of death of their thinner counterparts with a BMI of 24 (Calle and others, 1999).

Although generally speaking, thinner people live longer, Figure 7.3 also demonstrates that people who are extremely thin do not have the lowest death rates, indicating that the relationship between body weight and health hazards is probably U-shaped (Durazo-Arvizu and others, 1998). Just such a relationship was found in a study that followed a large sample of women over a 26-year period (Lindsted & Singh, 1997). Mortality rates were highest among the very thinnest and the very heaviest individuals.

However, researchers are still debating whether having a BMI between 25 and 30 is truly hazardous. Some experts suggest that people who are short, elderly, African-, Latin-, or Asian-American suffer no ill effects unless they become truly obese (Strawbridge and others, 2000). For instance, while the lowest mortality rates among European-American women and men occur in those with a BMI of 24 to 25, the lowest mortality rates among African-Americans occur in those with a BMI of 27 (Durazo-Arvizu et al., 1998).

Another factor that complicates the obesity–health relationship is age. Being overweight increases the risk of death from all causes among young and middle-aged adults (Oster and others, 1999; Stevens and others, 1998). After about age 65, however, being underweight is actually associated with increased risk of dying from all causes (Diehr and others, 1998) because losing weight in late adulthood generally means less muscle, thinner bones, and greater risk of accidents and chronic disease.

While being excessively under- or overweight is hazardous to health, **weight cycling**—a pattern of repeated weight gain and loss—is also unhealthy. An ongoing study of Harvard alumni has reported that men who maintained a stable weight had significantly lower death rates from all causes (including cardiovascular disease) than did alumni who had either gained or lost a significant amount of weight over the years (Lee and others, 1993). Short-term weight gains and losses, however, are not linked to increased death rates (Maru and others, 2004).

■ **weight cycling** repeated weight gains and losses through repeated dieting.

The Biopsychosocial Model of Obesity

Although it is tempting to take the view that obesity is simply the result of overeating, research shows that this is an oversimplification. Those who are overweight often do *not* eat more than their thin friends do. Rather, obesity is a complex phenomenon involving biological, social, and psychological factors in both its causes and consequences (Pi-Sunyer, 2003).

Biological Factors

Research on the biological factors that contribute to obesity has focused on the roles of heredity, the brain, and hormones in regulating appetite.

Heredity

Twin studies and adoption studies confirm that genes contribute approximately 50 percent to the likelihood of obesity. This heritability is equal to that of body height and greater than the heritability of many disorders for which a genetic basis is generally accepted. (For a review, see Friedman, 2003.) Heredity influences different factors that contribute to obesity. For example, basal metabolic rate (BMR) is determined by genes. People with a naturally lower BMR burn fewer calories than their thinner counterparts.

The role of heredity in obesity is illustrated by a massive study in which researchers analyzed the weights of more than 3,500 adopted Danish children and their biological and adoptive parents (Meyer & Stunkard, 1994). The study found a strong relationship between the body weights of adoptees and their biological parents but little or no relationship between the weights of offspring and their adoptive parents. Additional evidence comes from the strong correlation (0.74) between the body weights and BMIs of identical twins, even when they are raised in separate households (Plomin and others, 1997). The much lower correlation between the body weights and BMIs of fraternal twins (0.32) suggests that genes account for approximately two-thirds of individual differences in BMI (Maes and others, 1997). It is therefore not surprising that the body weights of adopted siblings (who share the same family diet but no genes) are not correlated at all.

Because most studies to date have used primarily European American samples to investigate the genetics of BMI, it is fair to ask whether these estimates of heritability apply equally to all races and ethnic groups. There are, in fact, slight ethnic differences in body composition (Wagner & Heyward, 2000). Nevertheless, a recent examination of BMI among black and white schoolchildren from Philadelphia found no significant differences in estimates of heritability between the two groups (Katzmarzyk and others, 1999).

Destiny? Genetics versus Environmental Factors

Despite the evidence for the role of biological factors in obesity, it is important to recognize that specific genetic defects are involved in only about 4 percent of cases of human obesity (Clement and others, 2002). The role of genetic factors in obestity is complex, determined by the interaction of several genes (polygenic), each of which may have a relatively small effect. Moreover, heredity alone does not destine a person to be fat. Obesity is a product of genetic vulnerability and environmental factors or maladaptive behaviors. What appears to be inherited is a *tendency* to be overweight; the amount a person becomes overweight is affected by diet and activity level. Regular activity and a moderate diet that is low in fat can limit genetic tendencies toward obesity.

Psychosocial Factors

Hunger and eating behavior are not controlled by physiological factors alone. Psychosocial factors also come into play. From an early age, we are conditioned to associate eating with holidays, personal achievements, and most social occasions. And the giving of food is among the first symbols of love between a parent and child. Should we be surprised that people are conditioned to turn to food when they are upset, anxious, or under stress? The idea of stress–eating associations is emobodied in the familiar concept of "*comfort food.*"

Neil Grunberg and I (Grunberg & Straub, 1992) asked groups of men and women seated in a comfortable living room to watch either a stressful film about eye surgery or a pleasant travelogue. Within their reach were bowls of snack foods, including M&M candies. The bowls were weighed before and after each session to determine how much of each snack food the subjects ate. All the men and those women who reported little concern about dieting and body weight ate fewer M&Ms when watching a stressful film than did those who watched the nonstressful film. Women who reported being especially conscious of their weight and who had a history of frequent dieting, however, consumed more sweets when stressed.

A more recent study drew on data from the Health and Behavior in Teenagers Study (HABITS) to determine whether long-term stress is associated with unhealthy eating, particularly fatty foods and snacks (Cartwright and others, 2003). The HABITS sample is a large, socioeconomically and ethnically diverse sample of 4,320 schoolchildren (mean age = 12 years) who completed questionnaire measures of stress and dietary practices. Girls and boys who reported the highest levels of stress ate more fatty food and snacks than their less stressed peers and were less likely to consume the recommended five or more daily fruit and vegetables or to eat breakfast. These data suggest that stress may contribute to long-term disease risk by triggering unhealthy patterns of eating.

Culture, Socioeconomic Status, and Gender

Genes cannot explain why being overweight or obese is more prevalent today than in the past. The average woman's dress size has increased from size 12 in 1951 to size 16 today (Merriman, 1999). Twenty-five years ago, 47 percent of Americans were classified as overweight or obese; today this figure has jumped to 65 percent (Freking, 2006). Americans are fatter today than their parents and grandparents ever were, and they are getting fatter every year.

Genes also cannot explain why the increase in weight in our population is not evenly distributed; there has been a disproportionate increase in the number of massively obese people in recent years, especially in certain ethnic groups (Kumanyika, 2002). Within the United States, obesity is more prevalent among African-Americans, Hispanic-Americans, Native Americans, and other minority groups (NCHS, 2003). It is interesting to note that African-Americans are less concerned about adhering to a thin ideal for women than are European-Americans (Biener & Heaton, 1995), but socioeconomic factors may be more helpful in explaining this relationship. There is an inverse relationship between obesity and socioeconomic status (SES), with people of lower SES more likely to be overweight than those who are more affluent. The fact that members of minority groups are disproportionately represented among lower-SES groups helps explain why they are more likely to be overweight (McMurtrie, 1994).

However, the relationship among income, ethnicity, and weight also varies with gender (Figure 7.4, p. 206). There is a clear income gradient in overweight prevalence among women: Poor women are 1.4 times as likely to be overweight as women with middle incomes and 1.6 times as likely to be overweight as women with high incomes. For men of all races, however, there is little evidence of an income-related gradient in the prevalence of overweight.

Being overweight or obese is also inversely related to education level. Among all young people between 16 and 24 years of age, those who are overweight tend not only to have lower personal incomes, but also to have completed fewer years of education than their normal-weight counterparts (Gortmaker and others, 1993). Men and women of all races with a college degree are less likely to be overweight than men and women with fewer than 12 years of education. Since the mid-1970s, however, the prevalence of being overweight or obese among men and women has increased steadily at all education levels (National Center for Health Statistics, 2000).

Figure 7.4

Prevalence of Overweight Adults by Income, Gender, and Ethnicity Among women of all ethnicities, there is a clear income gradient in overweight prevalence, with overweight prevalence for poor women 1.4 times that of women with middle incomes and 1.6 times that for women with high incomes. In contrast, there is little evidence of an income-related gradient in the prevalence of being overweight among men.

Source: Centers for Disease Control and Prevention, National Center for Health Statistics, National Health and Nutrition Examination Surveys (www.cdc.gov/nchs/nhanes.htm, 2000).

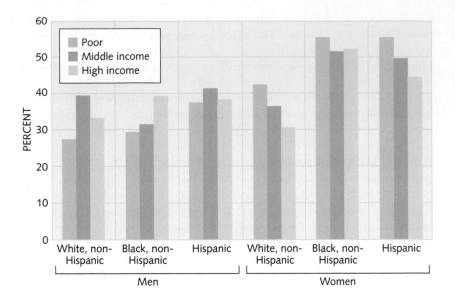

Why are less-educated, lower-SES people at increased risk for obesity? Their risk factors include more limited access to health care services, less knowledge about the importance of a healthy diet and the hazards of obesity, lower perceived self-efficacy in being able to increase their fruit and vegetable intake, and less exercise (Steptoe and others, 2003). It has also been suggested that the greater daily stress associated with poverty—resulting from prejudice, crowding, and crime, for example—may trigger increased eating as a defensive coping mechanism. Thus, it is not surprising that obesity is less prevalent among minority Americans who live in more affluent neighborhoods than among those living in lower-SES neighborhoods (Hazuda and others, 1991). Higher-SES adolescents also display greater awareness of the social ideals of slimness and are more likely to have family and friends who are trying to lose weight (Wardle and others, 2004).

Accessibility to healthy foods can apparently offset the dietary hazards of low income. A recent study compared the dietary composition and food attitudes of a large sample of culturally diverse, low- to middle-income middle school students attending two schools. Students who attended a private school where nutritious lunch and snack food choices were available had significantly lower fat in their overall diets and greater awareness of the benefits of a healthy diet than did students attending a public school where food choices were more limited and less nutritious (Frenn & Malin, 2003). This was true despite the fact that as a group, the private school students came from families with significantly lower incomes than those of students attending the public school.

The issue of access to healthy foods and other barriers to adherence to a healthy-weight lifestyle comes into sharp focus when one considers the plight of residents of a city such as Detroit, where a much higher-than-average percentage of citizens are obese. There are hundreds of fast-food restaurants and convenience stores that stock fatty snack foods within the city limits, but there are only eight major supermarkets that sell fruits, vegetables, and other nutritious foods. To make matters worse, in this sprawling city nearly 22 percent of the population doesn't own a car, and the city has a very weak public transportation system (Freking, 2006).

In the face of results such as these, health psychologists and legislators are calling for wide-scale public health and policy interventions. Among those being considered are bills that would extend nutrition labeling beyond packaged foods to include foods at fast-food restaurants, and the banning of soft drink and snack food machines in schools. Some health psychologists and urban planners are also calling for a shift away from cities built around the automobile toward more "walkable cities" that re-engineer physical activity back into daily routines. In support of this idea, researchers have found that people who live in sprawling cities such as Detroit, and who must therefore rely more on their cars to commute from distant homes to stores and places of employment, weigh more than people who live in more compact cities (Saelens and others, 2003). They also are more likely to suffer from hypertension, another risk factor for obesity.

Food Cues, Restraint, and Hunger

One influential psychological theory proposed that obese and nonobese people respond differently to food cues (Schachter, 1971). According to the *internality-externality hypothesis,* feelings of hunger and satiety in normal-weight people are closely tied to internal stimuli such as stomach fullness, whereas obese people are more responsive to external cues such as the time of day or the taste, smell, or appearance of food. More recent studies, however, have failed to find consistent differences in the responsiveness of obese and normal-weight people to food-related cues. For example, Judith Rodin (1981) discovered that body weight did not predict externality or internality. Some obese people *do* respond to internal cues, such as feeling full, whereas many normal-weight people (especially those who are dieting) do not.

To help explain the apparent contradictions in the varying behaviors of obese and nonobese people, Peter Herman and Janet Polivy (1975) developed the **restraint theory** of eating behavior. This theory contends that heightened sensitivity to body-weight norms results in a pattern of eating that vacillates between strict dieting (restrained eating) and overindulging (unrestrained eating). According to this theory, external sensitivity is a consequence of dietary restraint.

A series of studies by Herman and Polivy (1980) found that externality was tied to restrained eating rather than to body weight. In one study, obese and nonobese college students were divided into high- and low-restraint groups based on their answers to questions such as "How often are you dieting?" and "Do you give too much time and thought to food?" Ostensibly participating in a taste test, half the students in each group were asked to drink a large milkshake "preload" before rating several varieties of ice cream. In fact, the researchers were interested only in how much ice cream each student consumed.

■ **restraint theory** the theory that heightened sensitivity to norms for body weight triggers a pattern of eating that vacillates between strict dieting and binge eating.

disinhibition overeating triggered by an event, emotion, or behavior that causes a restrained eater to abandon his or her restraint.

As expected, unrestrained eaters ate less ice cream following the milkshake preload than their counterparts in the no preload condition. Restrained eaters, who claimed to be dieting frequently and to think a lot about food, however, actually ate more after having just consumed a large milkshake. This paradoxical loss of control over eating when restraint is disrupted has been called **disinhibition.** Restrained eaters who are "forced" off their normally strict diet overeat in the presence of external cues. Some may even engage in *binge eating*—a relatively common behavior pattern observed among people seeking obesity treatment (Spitzer and others, 1993). Risk factors for binge eating—particularly among adolescent girls—include dieting, pressure to be thin, body dissatisfaction, depressive symptoms, emotional eating, low self-esteem, and lack of social support (Stice and others, 2002).

Treatment of Obesity

Obesity is highly stigmatized. Beginning in nursery school, children show a dislike of fatness, rating drawings of fat children as having fewer friends; being less liked by parents; doing less well at school; and being lazier, less happy, and less attractive than thinner children (Latner & Stunkard, 2003; Teachman and others, 2003). And it continues into adulthood, with discrimination against the obese occurring in housing, college admissions, and employment (Puhl & Brownell, 2001). In one clever study, Regina Pingitore and her colleagues (1994) videotaped job interviews in which applicants either appeared to be of normal weight or wore makeup and padding that made them appear 30 pounds heavier. When made up to appear obese, the same applicants, using the same well-rehearsed presentation, received a significantly lower "employability rating" from a group of college students posing as potential employers. The discriminatory bias was especially pronounced when the applicant was a woman.

Because antifat prejudice is so strong and because fat people are generally held responsible for their condition, some psychologists maintain that weight discrimination is even greater than race and gender discrimination and that it affects every aspect of employment, including hiring, promotion, and salary (Roehling & Winters, 2000). Even health professionals who specialize in obesity hold hidden biases toward their obese patients, using words such as "lazy," "stupid" and "worthless" to describe obese people they come into contact with (Schwartz et al., 2003).

This prejudice against obesity has led to a proliferation of different weight-reduction regimens.

Dieting

A stroll through any bookstore will give you a quick idea of the vast array of dieting strategies—everything from preplanned meals with strict calorie limits to single-food plans to hypnosis. It's easy to be cynical about the number of choices. If any of them were truly effective, there would not be a market for such variety. The main beneficiaries of most of these books are their authors.

Successful weight loss in adults is often defined as at least a 10 percent reduction of initial weight that is maintained for 1 year (Rich, 2004). Weight losses of this magnitude generally produce significant improvements in health in most overweight adults. However, many people (especially women who are not overweight) are trying to shed pounds for reasons that have little or nothing to do with health. The increasing popularity of dieting has been attributed to the growing cultural pressure to be slim.

How Effective Are Diets?

Dieting alone usually does not work to take weight off and keep it off (Jeffery and others, 2004). The best way to lose weight and keep it off is to develop sound eating habits *and* to engage in regular physical exercise to raise the BMR. For the overweight and obese, doing so will not only increase the chances of successful weight loss, but it will also improve the individual's perceived quality of life, which is a major reason people seek medical attention for obesity (Rejeski and others, 2002; Kushner & Foster, 2000).

Even though most diets fail, Americans spend billions of dollars each year on them. National surveys suggest that at any given time about 20 percent of the population is on a diet, with more than 72 percent of women and 44 percent of men having dieted at some point in their adult lives (Serdula and others, 1993). In a 1999 Gallup poll, 52 percent of U.S. residents—up from 31 percent in 1951—said they would like to lose weight.

At all ages, women are twice as likely as men to be dieting, even though there is only a small gender difference in the prevalence of obesity (Serdula and others, 1999). Dieting is increasingly prevalent among adolescents, which is cause for concern because of the potential hazards to growth and development. About 65 percent of high school girls and 21 percent of high school boys are dieting at any given time (French and others, 1995).

Why Diets Fail

One reason diets fail is that many people are not very good at calculating the number of calories their bodies need or the size of the food portions they are eating. Underestimating calorie consumption is a common problem in many failed diets. In one study, for example, obese dieters reported eating an average of 1,028 calories per day, but their actual intake was 2,081 calories, more than twice as many calories as reported. To make matters worse, the self-reported daily activity level of the dieters was also substantially in error (Lichtman and others, 1992).

Diets also fail because many people have unrealistic expectations and find it nearly impossible to comply with dietary restrictions for very long (Wadden, 2003). Inconvenience and feelings of deprivation are often cited as factors that undermine adherence (Jeffery and others, 2004). Many dieters practice what has been called "yo-yo" dieting—achieving temporary success, then quitting the diet, regaining weight, and eventually going on a diet again.

The most successful diets are clinical interventions that include some form of post-treatment following weight loss, such as social support, exercise programs, or continued contact with the therapist. One study found that 18 months after finishing a diet program, those who did not participate in a post-treatment phase regained 67 percent of their weight, compared with 17 percent of dieters who participated in a post-treatment program combining exercise and social support (Perri, 1998).

For many people, group treatments produce better results than individual, self-help interventions (Perri and others, 2001). Commercial group programs like *Weight Watchers* typically promote social support, self-monitoring in the form of daily food diaries, and discussion about exercise and nutrition as key components. In one study, two-thirds of the participants who enrolled in a group weight-loss program with friends kept their lost weight off 6 months after the program ended, compared to only one-fourth of those who attended alone (Wing & Jeffery, 1999).

Behavioral and Cognitive Therapy

Behavior modification, particularly in conjunction with cognitive intervention techniques, has become a mainstay of many contemporary weight-loss programs. Behavior modification programs typically include the following components:

- *Stimulus control* procedures to identify and limit the number of cues that trigger eating (for example, confining eating to one particular place)
- *Self-control* techniques to slow the act of eating (for example, chewing each bite a set number of times, putting down silverware between bites)
- *Adding aerobic exercise* to boost metabolism, burn calories, and help curb appetite
- *Contingency contracts* in which therapist-delivered or self-controlled reinforcement is made dependent upon reaching weight-loss goals (for example, the client puts up a sum of money to be earned back as goals are attained)
- *Social support* of family members and friends who are enlisted to provide additional reinforcement for success and compliance
- *Careful self-monitoring* and recordkeeping to increase awareness of what foods are eaten and the circumstances under which eating occurs
- *Relapse Prevention Therapy* to teach people who are trying to maintain changes in their behavior how to anticipate and cope with urges, cravings, and high-risk situations

Self-monitoring is often sufficient, in and of itself, to promote weight loss. In fact, several studies have shown that about 25 percent of weight control success is due to consistent self-monitoring (Boutelle & Kirschenbaum, 1998). Raymond Baker and Daniel Kirschenbaum (1998) examined self-monitoring of eating behaviors during three holiday periods (Thanksgiving, Christmas/ Hanukkah, and New Year's Eve). Compared with the controls who gained weight, those participants who were the most thorough in recordkeeping actually lost weight during the holiday weeks. Other researchers have pointed to the effectiveness of another aspect of self-monitoring in weight loss: memory for recent eating. One study examined the effect of being reminded of a recent eating episode on subsequent food intake (Higgs, 2002). Participants ate less following exposure to a "lunch cue," in which they were simply asked to think about what they had eaten for lunch earlier that day.

Recently, advocates of behavioral treatments have broadened their focus to include a greater concern with the types of foods consumed, the need for exercise and coping skills to aid in overcoming high-risk relapse situations, responses to violating diet and/or binge eating, and primary prevention of obesity during childhood. Consumption of unhealthy food choices can be reduced by increasing the behavioral costs associated with obtaining them—through decreased access, for instance—and by providing healthy alternative foods and enjoyable activities (Goldfield & Epstein, 2002).

Behavioral methods are most successful when they are combined with cognitive techniques that recognize that overweight people often start treatment with unrealistic expectations and self-defeating thoughts. *Cognitive behavior therapies (CBT)* focus on the reciprocal interdependence of feelings, thoughts, behavior, consequences, social context, and physiological processes. The underlying premise of these therapies is that eating habits and attitudes must be modified on a permanent basis for weight loss and the maintenance of that loss to occur.

Rather than attempting to force quick and dramatic weight losses, CBT focuses on the gradual loss of 1 to 2 pounds per week, using a combination of conditioning, self-control, and cognitive restructuring techniques, in which the person learns to control self-defeating thoughts about body weight and dieting. When it comes to weight loss and management in children, CBT generally focuses on prevention, including establishing healthy eating behaviors in the individual and family; reducing television watching, Internet surfing, and video-game playing; and promoting positive attitudes toward food. Positive eating messages are critical because studies have shown that dieting during childhood may actually promote weight gain and unhealthy eating behaviors later in life. Study participants who report that their parents used food to control their behavior are also more likely to struggle with weight cycling, binge eating, and other unhealthy patterns as adults (Schwartz & Puhl, 2003).

Any therapeutic intervention for obesity will be most successful when health psychologists recognize that patients differ in which treatment will be most effective for them. Kelly Brownell and Thomas Wadden (1991) proposed the *stepped-care* process for determining which intervention is most appropriate for a given person (see Figure 7.5, p. 212). A seriously obese person may require more aggressive and intensive treatment than someone who is moderately obese. After considering relevant factors about the client, including degree of

Figure 7.5

Stepped Care in the Treatment of Obesity In general, people at levels 1 or 2 should be able to lose weight through steps 1 and 2. At level 3, treatment should begin with step 2 and extend through 4. Those at level 4 who have medical problems may need surgery to solve their weight-loss problems. However, before a health psychologist sets up a program, he or she considers all factors related to both the client and the program (as listed on the right).

Source: Brownell, K. D. & Wadden, T. A. (1991). The heterogeneity of obesity: Fitting individuals to treatments. *Behavior Therapy, 22,* 153–177.

Weight Classification

Level 1
5–20%
Overweight

Level 2
20–40%
Overweight

Level 3
40–100%
Overweight

Level 4
100% +
Overweight

Stepped-Care Treatment

Step 1
• Self-diet, self-help programs
• Work site programs

Step 2
• Commercial programs
• Behavioral programs

Step 3
• Hospital-based programs
• Very low-calorie diets

Step 4
• Private counseling
• Residential treatment programs

Step 5
• Surgery

Decision must consider:

Client factors
• Weight
• Reasonable weight
• Dietary history
• Metabolic complications
• Body composition
• Eating patterns

Program factors
• Group versus individual treatment
• Dietary counseling
• Structured exercise
• Professional leader
• Meeting frequency
• Prepackaged meals
• Dietary supplements
• Program length
• Severity of diet
• Therapy component
• Behavioral component

obesity, eating patterns, and medical history, a health psychologist structures the safest, least intensive intervention that will meet that person's needs. Only if this treatment is ineffective is a more intensive intervention warranted.

Marlene Schwartz and Kelly Brownell (1995) asked 33 weight-loss experts from several fields (psychology, nutrition, internal medicine, surgery, and neuroendocrinology) to compare 11 popular weight-loss approaches, including self-directed dieting, *Weight Watchers,* behavioral programs, medication, and surgery. Among their findings:

■ Self-directed dieting was recommended for those with mild to moderate obesity, except for people with a history of weight cycling.

■ Commercial programs with group support were recommended for an initial weight-loss attempt or for people who had not been able to diet effectively on their own.

- Very low-calorie diets and surgery were recommended only for those with a medical problem complicated by their obesity.

- Medical supervision was considered necessary for people with diabetes and others with medical conditions that are likely to change with dieting.

- Individual counseling and behavioral weight-loss programs were considered appropriate for those with eating disorders.

Matching individuals to treatment is important because people with different personality styles, levels of obesity, medical histories, and eating practices will respond differently to various treatments (Carels and others, 2005).

■ **anorexia nervosa** an eating disorder characterized by self-starvation, a distorted body image, and, in females, amenorrhea.

■ **bulimia nervosa** an eating disorder characterized by alternating cycles of binge eating and purging through such techniques as vomiting or laxative abuse.

Eating Disorders

For some dieters, especially young, overachieving women like Jodi—the young woman we met at the beginning of the chapter—obsession with weight control may turn into a serious eating disorder.

Anorexia nervosa is an eating disorder characterized by refusal to maintain body weight above a BMI of 18, intense fear of weight gain, disturbance of body image, and amenorrhea (cessation of menstruation) for at least 3 months (APA, 1997). Because a healthy percentage of body fat is necessary for menstruation, postpubescent women develop amenorrhea if they lose enough weight.

Anorexia can lead to many serious medical complications, including:

- slowed thyroid function.
- irregular breathing and heart rhythm.
- low blood pressure.
- dry and yellowed skin.
- brittle bones.
- anemia, light-headedness, and dehydration.
- swollen joints and reduced muscle mass.
- intolerance to cold temperatures.
- starvation.

The other major eating disorder is **bulimia nervosa.** Bulimia involves compulsive bingeing followed by purging through self-induced vomiting or large doses of laxatives. Some sufferers purge regularly, others only after a binge. For example, they may consume as many as 5,000 to 10,000 calories at one time, eating until they are exhausted, in pain, or out of food. People with bulimia also engage in compulsive exercise to try to control their weight. And, unlike those with anorexia, people with bulimia typically maintain a relatively normal weight (Hsu, 1990)—as Jodi initially did until she moved out on her own and began reducing her food intake.

Anorexia Young girls with anorexia look at themselves in the mirror and see not the superthin person we see but someone who is overweight and still needs to shed more pounds. If she continues to lose weight, this girl's systems will become overburdened with the job of trying to maintain a functioning system with minimal caloric intake. At the extreme, the heart may stop pumping.

© Richard T. Nowitz/Corbis

Although as many as half of all college women report having binged and purged at some time (Fairburn & Wilson, 1993), most would not be considered bulimic. The criteria for a clinical diagnosis include at least two bulimic episodes a week for at least 3 months; lack of control over eating; behavior designed to avoid weight gain; and persistent, exaggerated concern about weight (APA, 1997).

Unlike anorexia, which has a mortality rate of 2 to 15 percent, bulimia is rarely fatal. But it puts sufferers at risk for many serious health problems, including:

- laxative dependence.

- hypoglycemia (low blood sugar) and lethargy from eating an unbalanced diet (often one high in sweets but lacking in sufficient fatty acids).

- damaged teeth from purging because hydrochloric acid from the stomach erodes tooth enamel. (Dentists are often the first health care professionals to suspect bulimia.)

- bleeding and tearing of the esophagus from vomiting.

- anemia (a condition involving a lack of hemoglobin in the blood) and electrolyte imbalance caused by loss of sodium, potassium, magnesium, and other body minerals from purging.

Bulimic episodes are reported by 40 to 50 percent of people with anorexia. It is possible for an individual to meet the criteria for both disorders.

History and Demographics

Richard Morton reported the first documented case of anorexia nervosa in 1689. Over the next two centuries, only a handful of additional cases were reported. In London, Sir William Gull studied several cases of self-starvation during the 1860s, concluding that the disorder was psychological in origin and later giving the disorder its name, which means "nervous loss of appetite." Bulimia nervosa has only been recognized as a distinct disorder in the past 30 years or so (Russell, 1979).

Anorexia and bulimia are unique among psychological disorders in having a strong gender bias (a 10 to 1 ratio of women to men) and in the substantial increase in these disorders during the past century. Before the 1970s, eating disorders also were generally found only among upper-middle-class women in Western cultures (Garfinkel & Garner, 1984). Since then, disordered eating has been increasing among other populations, leading researchers to conclude that SES and ethnocultural identity are no longer reliable predictors (Dolan & Ford, 1991; Whitaker, 1989).

Today, approximately 0.5 to 1 percent of young adult and adolescent females have anorexia, and between 1 and 3 percent have bulimia (APA, 1997). College women are at particular risk, as are young women between 15 and 19 who attend ballet or modeling academies. Athletes also are at increased risk of eating disorders, even those who participate in sports that do not emphasize appearance or an overly thin body. Men make up about 5 to 10 percent of all anorexia victims. Male athletes—especially swimmers, rowers, and wrestlers—are especially vulnerable (Weinberg & Gould, 1995).

Applying the Biopsychosocial Model

Until the late 1930s, many doctors linked anorexia exclusively with a pituitary gland disorder, but this view was soon determined to be too narrow. During the 1940s and 1950s, psychiatrists hypothesized that anorexia involved a denial of femininity and a fear of motherhood, but this view too was discarded in the face of mounting evidence that anorexia is a learned syndrome. Current research focuses on the multiple components of these complex disorders, reflecting biological, psychological, and sociocultural influences.

Biological Factors

A young person's body image at the onset of puberty may foretell healthy or disordered eating behaviors (Graber and others, 1994). Girls who perceive the timing of their development to be early tend to feel the least positive about their bodies, whereas girls who perceive their development to be on time feel the most attractive and have the most positive body images (McLaren and others, 2003; Striegel-Moore and others, 2001). Early maturing girls may feel less comfortable with their bodies because at a time when peer acceptance is crucial to self-esteem, their bodies are different from those of the majority of their peers. On-time development may present the fewest psychological challenges to adolescent girls.

Biochemical abnormalities at all levels of the hypothalamic-pituitary-adrenal axis are associated with both anorexia and bulimia. These include abnormal levels of norepinephrine and other neurotransmitters that may promote clinical depression (Fava and others, 1989). There is also evidence that bulimia may be caused in part by disturbances in the brain's supply of *endorphins,* the opiatelike neurotransmitters linked to pain control and pleasure (Jonas & Gold, 1988). Researchers have found that *opiate antagonists,* which block the action of the endorphins, may be an effective treatment in reducing the frequency of binge-purge episodes. Researchers have also discovered that serum levels of leptin are significantly reduced in people with anorexia (Calandra and others, 2003).

Biochemical theories are inconclusive, however. While it is possible that abnormal brain biochemistry caused by an unrelated factor could alter mood and lead to abnormal eating, researchers have found that neurotransmitter levels often return to normal when disordered eating stops. Thus, biological abnormalities may be consequences rather than causes of eating disorders (Wardle, 1997).

Might people inherit a predisposition to eating disorders? Studies of eating disorders within families and among twins reveal a possible genetic influence on anorexia and bulimia. Consider:

- When one twin has bulimia, the chances of the other twin's sharing the disorder are substantially greater if they are identical twins (a 75 percent concordance rate) rather than fraternal twins (a 27 percent rate) (Walters & Kendler, 1995).

- The chances that a young adult woman will be diagnosed with a clinical eating disorder are much greater if she has a female relative who has anorexia (Strober and others, 1985).

Psychological Factors

Other theorists argue that the roots of eating disorders can be found in certain psychological situations, such as the competitive, semiclosed social environments of some families, athletic teams, and college sororities (Lester & Petrie, 1998).

The families of people with anorexia tend to be high achieving, competitive, overprotective, and characterized by intense interactions and poor conflict resolution (Pate and others, 1992). The families of people with bulimia have a higher-than-average incidence of alcoholism, drug addiction, obesity, and depression (Miller and others, 1993). Researchers caution, however, against assuming that all children from such homes are alike. Eating disorders are *not,* for example, a telltale sign of an alcohol abuser's home environment (Mintz and others, 1995). Young women with anorexia and bulimia rate their relationships with their parents as disengaged, unfriendly, and even hostile (Wonderlich and others, 1996). They also feel less accepted by their parents, who are perceived as overly critical, neglectful, and poor communicators (Calam and others, 1990).

Until recently, researchers focused almost exclusively on the role of the mother in her daughter's disordered eating, tracing its roots to the relationship between infant and primary caregiver (Bruch, 1982). Following this model, the mother of the girl with anorexia was described as overnurturing, overprotective, and demanding, whereas the mother of the girl with bulimia was seen as undernurturing, rejecting, and unaffectionate. Although research studies of this model are sorely limited, there *is* evidence that the mothers of daughters with an eating disorder tend to be more controlling and demanding (Humphrey, 1987), as well as critical of the weight and appearance of their daughters (Pike & Rodin, 1991).

More recent research encourages a shift away from the once popular "blame mother" view of adolescent eating disorders. Apparently *both* parents play important roles in influencing the development of healthy eating behaviors in their children. For example, Amy Swarr and Maryse Richards of Loyola University (1996), who investigated family relationships and disordered eating in adolescent females, found that positive relationships with *both* parents predicted healthier eating scores both concurrently and in the future. Girls who felt close to both Mom and Dad reported the fewest weight and eating concerns during the seventh, eighth, and ninth grades. Those who spent more time with both parents reported fewer eating problems two years later.

Despite living in a society that stigmatizes obesity and idealizes thinness, there are many more Americans who are overweight or obese (65 percent) than suffering from eating disorders (0.5–3 percent). As a result of this disparity between ideal and reality, body image dissatisfaction is so pervasive in the

United States that it represents a "normative discontent" among women of all shapes and sizes (Striegel-Moore and others, 1993). Judy Rodin has argued that women too often are brought up to believe that their appearance is not solely their own business. How daughters look, for instance, is an open topic of conversation in many families, making them feel their bodies are fair game for public scrutiny. Sadly, given the common gap between their *actual selves* and *ideal selves,* many come away feeling exposed and shamed. The increased prevalence of eating disorders during the last half-century has coincided with this epidemic of body image dissatisfaction (Feingold & Mazzella, 1996). Figure 7.6 illustrates one test of the *self-ideal discrepancy* that has been widely used in body image dissatisfaction research.

How much blame for girls' plump body image should be placed on the unrealistic body dimensions of Barbie and other popular dolls? By one estimate, to achieve "Barbie doll proportions" a female of average height would have to gain 12 inches in height, lose 5 inches in her waistline, and gain 4 inches in her bustline!

Figure 7.6

Self-Ideal Body Image Discrepancy Working first with the top part (head to waist) of the drawings for your gender, choose the number below the figure that best illustrates (A) how you think you currently look (that is, the figure that best represents your actual size). Then choose the figure that illustrates (B) how you would like to look (your ideal figure). Each figure has a number associated with it, so you can calculate your body discrepancy score. The numerical difference between your views of how you think you look and how you would like to look (A–B) represents your self-ideal discrepancy. Repeat the same procedure for the figures from waist to feet. Finally, rate how ashamed you are of any body image discrepancy from 0 (not at all) to 5 (extremely). If you have a shame score of 3 or more, you should consider talking to a close friend, family member, or counselor about these feelings.

Source: Rodin, J. (1992). *Body traps* (pp. 76–77). New York: William Morrow. Reprinted by permission of HarperCollins Publishers, Inc.

Sociocultural Factors

Sociocultural factors may explain why anorexia and bulimia occur more often in women than in men and more often in weight-conscious Western cultures, and why the prevalence of eating disorders has increased in recent years (see Diversity and Healthy Living box on p. 220). According to the sociocultural view, dieting and disordered eating are understandable responses to social roles and to cultural ideals of beauty (Seid, 1994). Binge eating, self-starvation, and thin standards of female beauty have characterized female cohorts who reached adolescence in periods when educational opportunities for women increased but have not characterized cohorts who reached adolescence when educational opportunities remained stable or decreased (Perlick & Silverstein, 1994).

Interestingly, the "thin is beautiful" standard is absent in many developing countries. In Niger, West Africa, for instance, fat is the beauty ideal for women, who often compete to be crowned the heaviest (Onishi, 2001). Among the Calabari of southeastern Nigeria, brides are sent to "fattening farms" before their weddings, where they gorge themselves on food and take steroid drugs to gain bulk and other pills to increase their appetites. At the end of their stay, they are paraded in the village square where their fullness can be admired.

The Thin Ideal Over the years, judges have selected increasingly thin women as Miss Universe, showing the current idealization of the "slim" Western-style woman around the world.

In recent years, Western cultures have increasingly emphasized the positive attributes of slender bodies, in particular for women. As Roberta Seid has noted, "Our culture has elevated the pursuit of a lean, fat-free body into a new religion. It has a creed: 'I eat right, watch my weight, and exercise.' Indeed, anorexia nervosa could be called the paradigm of our age, for our creed encourages us all to adopt the behavior and attitudes of the anorexic" (Seid, 1994, p. 4). Nowhere is this "religion" more apparent than in how women's bodies are represented in the media.

Body Image and the Media

The ideal female weight—represented by actresses, supermodels, and Miss Americas—has progressively decreased to that of the thinnest 5 to 10 percent of American women. Consequently, over three-fourths of normal-weight women think they weigh too much, and more than half are dieting at any given time (Mintz & Kashubeck, 1999).

A survey of 15,000 American women between the ages of 17 and 60 revealed an average weight-loss goal of 30 pounds, which, if attained, would have made most of them underweight (Williamson and others, 1992). Another survey of American dieters found that those who were most likely to diet were young, well-educated, employed, and least likely to need to diet. In fact, half these dieters had a BMI under 25 (Biener & Heaton, 1995). Most disturbing of all is that even very young girls are now preoccupied with body weight. One study reported that 80 percent of fourth-grade girls in the San Francisco Bay area were watching their weight (Kilbourne, 1994).

Society's current emphasis on thinness may be the clearest example of the power of advertising to influence cultural norms and individual behavior. Like clothing styles, body types go in and out of fashion and are promoted by advertising. Media images constantly reinforce the latest ideal, and the impact of the media in establishing role models is undeniable. In the United States, women of European ancestry are particularly vulnerable to these role models (Cash & Henry, 1995). With increasing Americanization and globalization, body image dissatisfaction is becoming more common among young women in Egypt, Russia, Japan, Brazil, and many other nations (Nasser, 1997).

On a more encouraging note, long-term exposure to ultrathin celebrities and magazine models does not automatically lead to excessive dieting and other unhealthy behaviors. Eric Stice and his colleagues (1998) randomly assigned 13- to 17-year-old girls either to a group that received a 15-month subscription to *Seventeen* magazine or to a control group that did not receive the magazine. Over the next 20 months, only those who initially expressed body dissatisfaction experienced significant increases in dieting, depression, and symptoms of bulimia. The researchers suggested that previous studies probably found that brief exposure to ads showing lean, sinewy models resulted in sharply decreased satisfaction with personal appearance because the studies were nearly always conducted in a laboratory environment. Over a longer period of time in the more natural home environments of their participants, the feedback of supportive parents, peers, and dating partners might overshadow the media's influence. The researchers caution, however, that their findings don't mean that media influences should be discounted, since teenagers with poor body images might be more likely to read fashion magazines to learn more about weight-loss techniques.

Treatment of Eating Disorders

A range of therapies has been used to treat anorexia and bulimia, from force-feeding to family therapy. Experts agree that treatment must address both the behavior and the attitudes that perpetuate disordered eating.

Restoring body weight is, of course, the first priority in treating anorexia. In extreme cases, inpatient treatment includes force-fed diets that gradually increase from about 1,500 to 3,500 calories per day. In many cases, a number of secondary biological and psychological disturbances are reduced once body weight is restored.

Many different drugs have been used in the treatment of binge eating. These include antidepressants, appetite suppressants, and opiate antagonists. Pharmacological treatments remain controversial, however, and have an especially high relapse rate. For this reason, most clinicians view such treatment as supplementary and consider psychotherapy as the treatment of choice for most patients. Antidepressants and other drugs are generally prescribed only when there is clear evidence of a coexisting affective- or impulse-control disorder, especially one that preceded the onset of the eating disorder (Fairburn & Wilson, 1993).

$\mathcal{D}$iversity and Healthy Living

Eating Disorders and Ethnocultural Identity

Traditional American standards of attractiveness are oppressive for many women, but especially for those whose own body ideals do not stem from European American culture.

Cultures differ in the flexibility of the ideal body image. Colleen Rand and John Kuldau (1990) compared body image satisfaction in African-Americans and European-Americans, finding a greater tolerance for diversity of body type and shape in the former group. Similar differences among college students have been reported. One study found that African-American college women had a less restricted definition of ideal body weight and were less likely to become depressed after binge eating (Gray and others, 1987).

Most eating disorder research has focused on white women, to the exclusion of other racial or ethnic groups. Maria Root (1990) identified stereotypes, racism, and ethnocentrism as reasons underlying this lack of attention. She suggested that many have adopted the stereotype of the individual with an eating disorder as a white, upper-class woman despite evidence that African-American women do suffer from eating disorders (Abood & Chandler, 1997; Wilfley and others, 1996).

It has also been suggested that many experts believe that certain factors within minority cultures, such as an appreciation of a healthier (larger) body size and less emphasis on physical appearance, make minority women invulnerable to eating disorders. Although research has demonstrated that African-American women generally do have more positive attitudes toward their bodies, food, and weight than white women (Abood & Chandler, 1997), they certainly are *not* immune to developing hazardous patterns of eating.

Newer studies reveal that for women of color, eating disorders may be "a means of suppressing one's ethnocultural concept of beauty by replacing it with a Eurocentric one of thinness" (Harris & Kuba, 1997). According to this view, eating disorders among members of minority groups are a symptom of identity confusion. Although the *Diagnostic and Statistical Manual of Mental Disorders* (DSM-IV=TR) includes ethnicity and culture in its review of anorexia nervosa and bulimia nervosa, it does not refer to compulsive eating. This is problematic, given that many women of color suffer from this eating disorder. In a recent study of women assessed for eating disorders, 84 percent of African-American women were diagnosed as compulsive eaters (Harris & Kuba, 1997).

For the adolescent who is attempting to assimilate into a different culture, learned ways of behavior may conflict with the messages from the majority community and result in a crisis. Thus, if the Latin-American culture accepts a robust figure but the European-American culture values thinness, young Latina

---

Cognitive Behavioral Treatments

Behavioral treatments for eating disorders are based on the assumption that they are learned habits maintained by some source of reinforcement. Following this reasoning, one form of treatment for bulimia, called **exposure-response prevention,** attempts to prevent purging after bingeing (Rosen & Leitenberg, 1982). This treatment is based on an anxiety model of bulimia, in which binge eating is believed to increase anxiety (over weight gain), which in turn is relieved by purging. When purging is prevented, a powerful source of negative reinforcement for bingeing (relief from anxiety) is removed. Over time, and in conjunction with interventions that promote more realistic thinking about food and body image, binge eating may disappear (extinction).

Other aspects of behavioral programs include relapse prevention training, in which the patient learns to identify circumstances that trigger disordered eating and to develop strategies to avoid those situations or to cope with them more effectively. Relaxation training and stress-management skills are also taught.

■ **exposure-response prevention** a behavioral treatment of bulimia nervosa that attempts to prevent purging (and therefore, reinforcement) following binge eating.

women may find themselves in conflict over the appropriate body image and eating behaviors. Similarly, Toshiaki Furukawa (1994) reported that Japanese exchange students developed maladaptive eating patterns (and experienced weight changes) during their time in the United States.

Ethnocultural identity develops as children learn about themselves in relation to the norms and expectations of others within their group. Most models of identity formation among people of color identify four or five distinct psychological states (Helms, 1995).

Precultural awakening Those in this stage often experience low self-esteem as they struggle to identify with a majority frame of reference. The roots of disordered eating can often be found in this struggle. For example, a young African-American woman may decide to stop eating certain foods because she is preoccupied with the size of her hips or thighs as she compares herself with European-American actresses.

Dissonance stage In the next stage, the individual becomes aware of her internal conflict and vacillates between the desire to be thin and to accept her body as it is. She may develop bulimic symptoms that represent the push and pull of two different cultures.

Immersion-emersion The third stage is characterized by greater self-appreciation as the young person immerses herself in her culture of origin. Although it may appear that she has formed a healthy identity, she may exaggerate her ethnocultural stereotype, even rejecting any attempt to appear physically attractive. Anger and mood swings are a predominant emotional theme of this stage. Compulsive eating may reflect this stage of thinking.

Internalization stage The final stage is marked by improved self-esteem and an integration of positive attitudes toward self and culture, with less anger and a greater appreciation for differences in attractiveness across cultures.

One implication of these models is the need for preventive interventions that are sensitive to each individual's stage of identity development. When the patient is in the precultural awakening stage, an appropriate strategy is to increase the young person's awareness of her ethnocultural legacy as well as the prejudice inherent in majority cultures. Intervention during the dissonance stage should focus on the grief caused by the client's sense of loss of culture. Development beyond this stage might be hastened by encouraging contact with others of similar ethnocultural identity.

Since the 1970s, cognitive behavior therapy (CBT) has become the most widely used method of treating both anorexia and bulimia (Agras, 1993). First, therapists monitor food intake, binge-eating episodes, and stimulus triggers of those episodes. They then use this information to gradually mold the patient's eating into a pattern of three or more meals per day; introduce feared foods into the diet; and change faulty thinking and distorted attitudes about food intake, weight, and body image.

How Effective Are Treatments for Eating Disorders?

Anorexia remains one of the most difficult behavior disorders to treat, because many victims see nothing wrong with their eating behavior and resist any attempt to change. Consequently, from 5 to 18 percent will eventually die from starvation, cardiac arrest, or suicide (Wardle, 1997).

Christopher Fairburn, a leading bulimia researcher, has suggested that the long-term success rate of all eating disorder interventions is a function of two participant variables: self-esteem and body image. Regardless of the type of treatment used, patients with lower self-esteem and persistent body-image distortions tend to be less successful in terms of their long-term recovery (Fairburn & Wilson, 1993).

Although there are relatively few controlled studies comparing the results of treatments for anorexia, most therapies result in some weight restoration in the short term but a high relapse rate (often in excess of 50 percent) and poor long-term outcome (Wardle, 1997). Longer-term follow-up studies show that the majority of people with anorexia persist in their preoccupation with food and weight and that many continue to show psychological signs of the disorder, have low weight, and exhibit social or mood disturbances (Sullivan and others, 1998).

There have been more controlled clinical trials of the treatment of bulimia, which is more prevalent than anorexia. As with anorexia, longer-term evaluations have not produced entirely favorable results (Wardle, 1997). One study compared the effectiveness of behavior therapies with CBT. The behavior therapy group received eight sessions of individualized treatment that focused on restructuring the patient's environment to gain greater control over environmental triggers for disordered eating. The group was also taught self-monitoring and relapse prevention strategies through the use of contingency contracts. The CBT group received the behavioral training as well as treatment sessions designed to challenge irrational food attitudes, promote coping skills, and prevent relapse. A third, control group received training in self-monitoring only. At the end of the treatment phase, all three groups experienced a significant decrease in binge-purge episodes. Six months later, however, only 15 percent of the control subjects and 38 percent of the behavior therapy group remained free of binge-purge episodes. In contrast, 69 percent of the CBT group remained free of such episodes (Thackwray and others, 1993).

CBT has also proved to be fairly effective as a primary prevention for binge eating in high-risk women (Kaminski & McNamara, 1996). The researchers recruited college women with warning signs for eating disorders: low self-esteem, poor body image, perfectionism, and a history of repeated dieting. The students were randomly assigned to either a treatment group or a control group. The treatment group received training in cognitive strategies for increasing self-esteem, challenging self-defeating thinking, improving body image, and combating social pressures for thinness. After 7 weeks, students in the treatment group showed greater improvement in self-esteem and body image than did students in the control group. They also reported significantly fewer disordered eating episodes.

Controlled studies of treatments for disordered eating show dropout rates ranging from 0 to 34 percent and long-term abstinence from disordered eating ranging from 20 to 76 percent. As Stewart Agras (1993) has noted, out of a treatment group of 100 binge eaters treated with cognitive behavior therapy (generally the most effective treatment), 16 will probably drop out of treatment, and 40 will be abstinent by the end of treatment. A failure rate of 60 percent suggests that researchers have not yet found the ideal treatment for eating disorders.

Some programs fail because they try to do too many things at once. Traci Mann and colleagues (1997) evaluated eating disorder interventions aimed at both primary and secondary prevention. Because of their very different aims, the ideal primary and secondary prevention strategies often oppose each other. As Mann suggests, to prevent disordered eating in healthy young women (primary prevention), the ideal strategy might be to stress the abnormal and hazardous nature of anorexic and bulimic behaviors. In contrast, to encourage those who already have problems to come forward for help (secondary prevention), it might be advisable to suggest the opposite—that eating disorders are common and easy to treat. Interventions for eating disorders may be more effective if they do not try to simultaneously achieve both primary and secondary prevention.

Despite the relatively poor success rate of formal treatment programs and preventive interventions for eating disorders, there is evidence that some people with eating disorders respond to simple interventions, such as instruction in self-help techniques. Jacqueline Carter and colleagues (1998) found that pure self-help and guided self-help had a substantial and sustained impact on eating behavior, with almost half the participants ceasing to binge eat at the end of treatment and at treatment follow-ups 3 and 6 months later.

There is also good news in the finding that some victims of eating disorders may recover on their own with the passage of time. One longitudinal study followed a cohort of 509 women and 206 men who were teenagers in the late 1970s and early 1980s. The researchers surveyed the participants' eating attitudes and behaviors while in college and again 10 years later (Heatherton and others, 1997). The results showed that body dissatisfaction, chronic dieting, and eating disorder symptoms generally diminished among many of the women in the 10 years following college, with rates of apparent eating disorder dropping by more than half. However, a substantial number of the women, particularly those who were dissatisfied with their body weight or shape in college, continued to have eating problems 10 years after college. More than 1 in 5 of the women who met clinical criteria for an eating disorder in college also did so 10 years later.

These results suggest that some degree of disordered eating may be normative for college women and that diminuation of these problems after graduation is also normative. However, body dissatisfaction and chronic dieting remain problems for a substantial number of women. Changes in maturation and gender role status may partly explain why eating problems diminish after college.

It is also possible that these findings reflect a more general societal trend. Todd Heatherton and his colleagues (1995) compared the eating behavior of college students in 1982 and 1992. They found that eating disorder symptoms, dieting, and body dissatisfaction declined during that decade. Heatherton attributes the decline in eating disorders to greater public awareness. The increased media focus may have increased awareness of the potential consequences of fasting or bingeing and purging.

Along with greater awareness of disordered eating, today there is an increased emphasis on healthful eating and nutritious low-fat rather than low-calorie diets. Sociocultural messages about thinness have changed somewhat as well, again with greater emphasis on health and fitness and less on actual weight.

Health psychologists hope to continue this increased focus on overall good health rather than on attempting to achieve unattainably perfect physiques. This would help many of us avoid the dangers of obesity or eating disorders, as well as the anxiety and dissatisfaction caused by the dispairity between our real and longed-for body images.

Summing Up

Nutrition: Eating the Right Foods

1. Besides water and daily caloric energy, the body requires 46 nutrients, which are grouped into five categories: proteins, fats, carbohydrates, vitamins, and minerals.

2. Poor nutrition has been implicated in five of the ten leading causes of death: heart disease, cancer, stroke, diabetes, and atherosclerosis. There are three types of lipoproteins: Low-density lipoprotein (LDL) has been linked to heart disease, whereas high-density lipoprotein (HDL) may protect against atherosclerotic plaques. Dietary saturated fat and especially trans fat raise LDL cholesterol levels in the blood. Saturated fat has been implicated as a dietary factor in some forms of cancer. Nutritionists recommend a healthful balance of unprocessed foods, especially those with a low glycemic index.

Weight Determination: Eating the Right Amount of Food

3. Basal metabolic rate (BMR) depends on a number of variables, including your age, gender, current weight, and activity level. Many people believe that their body weights fluctuate erratically, but in fact their bodies actually balance energy intake and expenditure quite closely. This supports the concept of a body weight set point. Once the number of fat cells in a person's body increases, it never decreases.

4. Researchers have located appetite centers in two areas of the hypothalamus: a side region called the lateral hypothalamus (LH), which may trigger hunger, and a lower area in the middle called the ventromedial hypothalamus (VMH), which may trigger satiety. One region of the hypothalamus, the arcuate nucleus, appears to be the master center for short-term regulation of appetite and long-term regulation of body weight.

5. Two hormones produced by the digestive tract, known as *ghrelin* and *PYY*, have been linked to short-term feeding behaviors, whereas *leptin*, and to a lesser extent, insulin, are key to weight maintenance over months and years.

Obesity: Some Basic Facts

6. Obesity is a risk factor for many diseases. In addition, the obese also have social problems because they are the objects of discrimination. The most frequently used measure of obesity today is the body mass index (BMI), which is strongly correlated with percentage of body fat. Distribution of fat is also important, with abdominal (male pattern) fat being less healthy than lower-body (female pattern) fat. Furthermore, weight cycling may be more hazardous to health than a somewhat high but stable weight.

The Biopsychosocial Model of Obesity

7. Obesity is partly hereditary. Researchers have discovered that laboratory mice with a defective gene cannot control their hunger and tend to become obese. The gene appears to regulate the production of leptin, a hormone produced by fat, which the hypothalamus monitors as an index of obesity. The amount of leptin is generally correlated with how much fat is stored in the body.

8. Hunger and eating behavior are not controlled by physiological factors alone. Psychosocial factors, such as stress, socioeconomic status, and culture also come into play.

9. According to the internality-externality hypothesis, feelings of hunger and satiety in normal-weight people are closely tied to internal stimuli such as stomach fullness, whereas obese people are more responsive to external cues such as the time of day or the taste, smell, or appearance of food. In contrast, the restraint theory of eat-

ing proposes that external sensitivity is the result of dietary restraint. Restrained eaters vacillate between strict dieting and overeating triggered by disinhibition.

Treatment of Obesity

10. At all ages, women are twice as likely as men to be dieting, even though there is only a small gender difference in the prevalence of obesity. Dieting is increasingly prevalent among adolescents, which is cause for concern because of the potential hazards to growth and development.

11. Today, health psychologists recognize that patients differ in which treatment will be most effective for them. The stepped-care process can be used for determining which intervention is most appropriate for a given person.

Eating Disorders

12. Eating disorders are multifactorial—determined by the interaction of biological, psychological, social, and cultural factors. The changes in fat distribution in adolescent girls, particularly those who mature early, may provide the foundations for body image dissatisfaction. A social and family environment in which there is an emphasis on slimness may foster additional frustration with body weight. At the individual level, competitiveness and perfectionism, combined with the stresses of adolescent peer pressure, may promote disordered eating.

13. Anorexia nervosa is an eating disorder characterized by refusal to maintain body weight above a BMI of 18, intense fear of weight gain, disturbance of body image, and amenorrhea for at least 3 months. Bulimia nervosa involves compulsive bingeing followed by purging through self-induced vomiting or large doses of laxatives. Women with low self-esteem are particularly likely to have a negative body image and to be vulnerable to eating disorders. The families of people with bulimia have a higher-than-usual incidence of alcoholism, obesity, and depression. People with anorexia often come from families that are competitive, overachieving, and protective. Eating disorders may also be partly genetic and linked to abnormal levels of certain neurotransmitters.

14. Cultural factors may explain why anorexia and bulimia occur more often in women than in men and more often in weight-conscious Western cultures, and why the prevalence of eating disorders has increased in recent years. Eating disorders are more common among women in occupations that emphasize appearance (for example, dance).

15. A range of therapies has been used to treat anorexia and bulimia, from force-feeding to family therapy. Experts agree that treatment must address both the behavior and the attitudes that perpetuate disordered eating. One behavioral treatment for bulimia, called exposure-response prevention, is based on an anxiety model of bulimia nervosa, in which binge eating is believed to increase anxiety (over weight gain), which in turn is relieved by purging. The most widely used therapy for anorexia and bulimia, cognitive behavior therapy, attacks faulty thinking about food intake, weight, and body image and gradually molds the patient's eating into a healthier pattern.

Key Terms and Concepts

obesity, p. 188
calorie, p. 191
basal metabolic rate (BMR), p. 195
set-point hypothesis, p. 195
leptin, p. 196
adipocytes, p. 196

body mass index (BMI), p. 200
male pattern obesity, p. 200
female pattern obesity, p. 200
overweight, p. 201
weight cycling, p. 203
restraint theory, p. 207

disinhibition, p. 208
anorexia nervosa, p. 213
bulimia nervosa, p. 213
exposure-response prevention, p. 220

Substance Abuse

*J*ack was one of the first students I met when I entered Columbia University's graduate program in the fall of 1975. Like the rest of us, Jack was a highly motivated overachiever, eager to get on with the business of becoming a research psychologist.

But Jack was different, too. He seemed older and surer of himself and what it took to be successful. And he was smart. I admired his ability to "think on his feet" during a particularly stressful seminar taught in the Socratic style. Confident in his preparation for each class and a gifted speaker, Jack would not be intimidated when questioned by cranky full professors eager to reduce a young student to a quivering mass of jelly.

We all looked up to Jack, but we also worried about him. While the rest of us spent our nights studying in the library, Jack had a part-time job as a New York City cab driver. Although each of us received a teaching or research fellowship that covered tuition and provided a modest monthly stipend for living expenses, Jack apparently couldn't make it on this amount alone. Some of us suspected that he was sending money to some less fortunate relative who was unable to work. Or maybe he didn't want to admit, like the rest of us mere mortals, that the first year of graduate school required his full, undivided attention.

For a few months, Jack seemed unfazed by the double workload. I don't know when he slept or studied, but he seemed fully functional in class, and except for an occasional yawn during a particularly boring lecture, he performed about as well academically as any of us.

But the loss of sleep and mounting academic pressure eventually took its toll on Jack. Something had to give, and we first noticed it when our classmate stopped attending postexam parties and other social functions. Soon Jack began coming late to class, then missing an occasional seminar, then—worst of all—showing up unprepared to discuss the day's reading assignment.

When Jack did make it to class, his appearance belied his lifestyle. He appeared haggard and worn out, with huge circles under his eyes.

He looked to be 50 or 60 years of age rather than 22. Rumor had it that he was drinking heavily and using an assortment of pills—"uppers" and "downers" mostly—to medicate himself into a "functional state." When a group of us confronted Jack's roommate, he shrugged off our concern about Jack's drug use, saying, "Don't worry about Jack. He knows what he's doing. Those pills are all prescription drugs, and Jack never takes more than the prescribed dosage."

Well, you can guess what happened. A few weeks later, the department chair interrupted our seminar in physiological psychology to inform us that Jack's body had been found early that morning. Jack had died of an apparent overdose of alcohol and barbiturate tranquilizers.

Since antiquity, human beings like Jack have sought ways to alter mood, thought processes, and behavior—often with significantly negative health effects. This chapter examines the different facets of substance, or drug, abuse—its causes, effects, and prevention, including research pointing to a biopsychosocial common ground in the origins of addiction to many habit-forming substances. We will focus primarily on the two most commonly abused drugs: tobacco and alcohol.

Substance Use and Abuse: Some Basic Facts

Drug use is simply the ingestion of any drug, regardless of the amount taken or its effect. **Drug abuse,** however, is the use of a chemical substance to the extent that it impairs the user's well-being *in any domain of health:* biological, psychological, or social. By this definition, legal drugs—such as prescription medicines—can also be abused. The spread of drug abuse is often described as a global pandemic, with similarities to epidemic diseases. The most widely used drug is tobacco. Although tobacco use is decreasing in affluent countries, its use is climbing in low- and middle-income countries. Next to tobacco, alcohol is the most widely used and abused drug and is available in all but the most isolated areas of the world and a few countries with strict religious prohibitions (WHO, 2004). Although alcohol consumption has recently declined in many developed countries, its use has also been increasing in developing countries. Moreover, alcohol problems are now occurring in many Asian and Western Pacific countries where they did not exist before.

The health hazards and costs of drug abuse are incalculable. The abuse of illegal drugs, alcohol, and tobacco causes more deaths, illnesses, and disabilities than any other preventable health condition (Robert Wood Johnson Foundation, 2001). Alcohol, for instance, is implicated in 44 percent of the more than

■ **drug abuse** the use of a drug to the extent that it impairs the user's biological, psychological, or social well-being.

■ **blood–brain barrier** the network of tightly packed capillary cells that separates the blood and the brain.

■ **teratogens** drugs, chemicals, and environmental agents that can damage the developing person during fetal development.

Figure 8.1

The Blood–Brain Barrier
Unlike the porous blood capillaries in most other parts of the body, those in the brain are tightly packed, forming a fatty glial sheath that provides a protective environment for the brain. The glial sheath develops from the nearby astrocyte cells. In order to reach the brain, a drug must first be absorbed through the capillary wall and then through the fatty sheath.

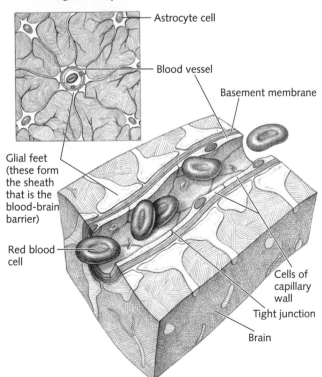

Astrocyte cell

Blood vessel

Basement membrane

Glial feet (these form the sheath that is the blood-brain barrier)

Red blood cell

Cells of capillary wall

Tight junction

Brain

40,000 annual traffic fatalities (NIAAA, 2001). Half of all murders in the United States involve alcohol or some other drug, and 80 percent of all suicide attempts follow the use of alcohol. And each year tobacco use, the number one preventable cause of death in the United States, globally claims more than 5 million deaths and results in a net loss of $200 billion dollars due to medical expenses and lost work time (WHO, 2004).

Why, despite these enormous financial, health, and social costs, do people continue to abuse drugs? To answer this question, you first need to know how drugs move through and affect the body.

Mechanisms of Drug Action

As a first step, the drug must be ingested, or administered. Drugs are administered in one of five ways: orally, rectally, by injection, by inhalation, and by absorption through the skin or the mucous membranes. The manner in which a drug is administered can alter its physiological effects. Because they enter the bloodstream faster, drugs that are injected or inhaled, for example, usually have stronger and more immediate effects than those that are swallowed.

Within minutes after a drug is absorbed from its point of entry, it is distributed by the bloodstream to its site of action (receptors). How quickly a drug reaches its target receptors depends on the rate of blood flow to the target and how easily the drug passes through cell membranes and other protective barriers in the body. Blood flow to the brain is greater than to any other part of the body. Therefore, drugs that are able to pass through the network of cells that separate the blood and the brain—the **blood–brain barrier** (Figure 8.1)—move quickly into the central nervous system. The ease with which a drug passes through this barrier depends on its lipid (fat) solubility. Most recreational drugs as well as those that are widely abused are lipid soluble, which means they easily pass through the barrier to their target receptor sites in the brain.

Fat-soluble drugs that cross the blood–brain barrier are usually also able to permeate the *placental barrier* that separates the blood of a pregnant woman from that of her developing child. For this reason, alcohol, nicotine, or other drugs as well as chemicals in cosmetics, foods, and elsewhere in the environment absorbed by the mother can affect her unborn child. Scientists now understand a great deal about **teratogens**—drugs, pollutants, and other substances that cross the placental barrier and damage the developing person. Alcohol, tobacco, heroin, and marijuana, for example, can stunt fetal growth and permanently damage the developing brain. The extent of their damaging effects, however, depends on when exposure occurs; the greatest damage occurs during critical periods of development when specific organs and systems are developing most rapidly.

Drugs and Synapses

Once in the brain, drugs affect behavior by influencing the activity of neurons at their synapses. Drugs can achieve their effects in one of three ways: by mimicking or enhancing the action of a naturally occurring neurotransmitter, by blocking its action, or by affecting its reuptake.

Drugs that produce neural actions that mimic or enhance those of a naturally occurring neurotransmitter are **agonists** (see Figure 8.2). Recall that synaptic

■ **agonist** a drug that attaches to a receptor and produces neural actions that mimic or enhance those of a naturally occurring neurotransmitter.

Figure 8.2

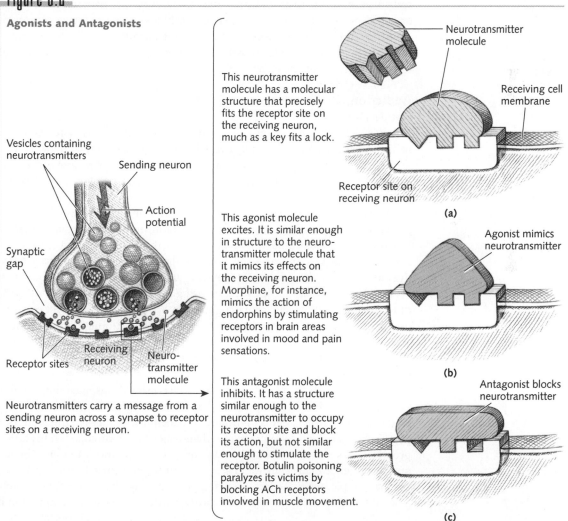

Agonists and Antagonists

Vesicles containing neurotransmitters

Sending neuron

Action potential

Synaptic gap

Receptor sites

Receiving neuron

Neuro-transmitter molecule

Neurotransmitters carry a message from a sending neuron across a synapse to receptor sites on a receiving neuron.

This neurotransmitter molecule has a molecular structure that precisely fits the receptor site on the receiving neuron, much as a key fits a lock.

Neurotransmitter molecule

Receiving cell membrane

Receptor site on receiving neuron

(a)

This agonist molecule excites. It is similar enough in structure to the neurotransmitter molecule that it mimics its effects on the receiving neuron. Morphine, for instance, mimics the action of endorphins by stimulating receptors in brain areas involved in mood and pain sensations.

Agonist mimics neurotransmitter

(b)

This antagonist molecule inhibits. It has a structure similar enough to the neurotransmitter to occupy its receptor site and block its action, but not similar enough to stimulate the receptor. Botulin poisoning paralyzes its victims by blocking ACh receptors involved in muscle movement.

Antagonist blocks neurotransmitter

(c)

■ **antagonist** a drug that blocks the action of a naturally occurring neurotransmitter or agonist.

■ **drug addiction** a pattern of behavior characterized by physical as well as possible psychological dependence on a drug as well as the development of tolerance.

■ **dependence** a state in which the use of a drug is required for a person to function normally.

■ **withdrawal** the unpleasant physical and psychological symptoms that occur when a person abruptly ceases using certain drugs.

■ **drug use** the ingestion of a drug, regardless of the amount or effect of ingestion.

receptors are cellular locks that wait for neurotransmitters with a particular shape to act like a key and trigger activity within the cell. For example, nicotine is an acetylcholine agonist, which means that it fits the lock meant for acetylcholine and binds to postsynaptic receptors on the same neuron, thus enhancing activation of the receiving neuron and causing the tobacco user to feel more alert.

Drugs that produce their effects by blocking the action of neurotransmitters or agonist drugs are **antagonists.** Caffeine, for example, is an antagonist that blocks the effects of *adenosine,* a neurotransmitter that normally inhibits the release of other transmitters that excite (cause to fire) postsynaptic cells. Thus, the excitatory cells continue firing, resulting in the stimulation felt when caffeine is ingested.

Finally, drugs can alter neural transmission by enhancing or inhibiting the reuptake of neurotransmitters in the synapse; that is, the natural breakdown or reabsorption of the neurotransmitter by the presynaptic neuron. Cocaine, for example, produces its stimulating effects by blocking the reuptake of norepinephrine and dopamine. Because these neurotransmitters are not reabsorbed by the sending neuron, they remain in the synapse and continue to excite (or inhibit) the receiving neuron.

Addiction, Dependence, and Tolerance

Not everyone who starts using a drug becomes addicted. How can you tell whether a person is addicted? Health experts today define **drug addiction** as a behavior pattern characterized by overwhelming involvement with the use of a drug, a preoccupation with its supply, a high probability of relapse if the drug is discontinued, and the development of physical and psychological dependence on the substance.

Dependence is a state in which the body and mind have adjusted to the repeated use of a drug and require its presence in order to maintain "normal" functioning. In this context, *normal* refers to the absence of the withdrawal symptoms that will appear when use of a drug is discontinued. Drug **withdrawal** refers to the unpleasant physical and psychological symptoms that occur when a person abruptly ceases using a drug. The symptoms of withdrawal, which vary widely from drug to drug, are generally the direct opposite of a drug's primary effects. Amphetamines and other stimulants, for example, create a rush of euphoria. Amphetamine withdrawal triggers the opposing state of depression. Other symptoms include nausea and vomiting, sleep disturbances, anxiety, and even death.

Consistent with the biopsychosocial model, most drugs, including alcohol and nicotine, give rise to both physical and psychological dependence. For example, alcohol, which seems to produce biochemical changes in the brain (see page 239), also seems to improve mood and allow a person to forget his or her problems. For many former stimulant drug users, memories of the "highs" once experienced fade slowly and are constant triggers for relapse.

The complementary effects of **drug use** and drug abstinence have led to a general theory—the *hypersensitivity theory*—which proposes that addiction is the result of efforts by the body and brain to counteract the effects of a drug in order to maintain an optimal internal state. For example, among its many physical effects, nicotine accelerates heart rate. To compensate and maintain a constant internal state, the brain and nervous system respond to nicotine by stimulating the vagus nerve, which slows the heart rate. Over time, regular use of nicotine and the associated vagus nerve stimulation seem to create a new, higher "set point" for vagus nerve activity. If the person quits smoking, vagal tone remains high, (meaning heart rate stays slow), higher than normal in fact, because there is no nicotine in the system to increase the heart rate.

One sign of dependence is the development of *tolerance,* a state of progressively decreasing behavioral and/or physiological responsiveness to a frequently used drug. As a person's body adjusts to a drug, increased dosages are necessary to produce the effect formerly achieved by a smaller dose. There are at least two reasons that tolerance develops. With repeated use, some drugs are metabolized at a faster rate by the liver, so that more of the drug must be administered simply to maintain a constant level in the body. Second, brain receptors adapt to the continued presence of a particular drug either by increasing the number of receptor sites or by reducing their sensitivity to the drug. In either case, more of the drug is required to produce the same biochemical effect.

Psychoactive Drugs

Chemical substances that act on the brain to alter mood, behavior, and thought processes are known as **psychoactive drugs.** Psychoactive drugs are grouped into three major categories: hallucinogens, stimulants, and depressants.

Also called psychedelic drugs, *hallucinogens* such as marijuana and LSD alter sensory perception, induce visual and auditory hallucinations as they separate the user from reality, and disrupt thought processes. *Stimulants,* including nicotine, caffeine, cocaine, and the amphetamines, make people feel more alert and energetic by boosting activity in the central nervous system. At low doses, the moderate stimulants (nicotine and caffeine) reduce fatigue, elevate mood, and decrease appetite. In higher doses, and with the more extreme drugs, however, the stimulants may cause irritability, insomnia, and anxiety. Like all psychoactive drugs, stimulants produce their effects by altering the action of neurotransmitters at synapses. The stimulants have a dramatic impact on acetylcholine, the catecholamines, dopamine, and, to a lesser extent, norepinephrine. For example, amphetamines like nicotine are agonists, stimulating the release of dopamine from presynaptic storage sites in nerve terminals. Cocaine blocks the reuptake of dopamine and norepinephrine. The alertness that follows derives from the resulting overstimulation of dopamine and/or norepinephrine receptors in postsynaptic neurons.

Because of their powerful reward effects, stimulants are widely abused. Dependence develops rapidly along with tolerance that forces the addict to take progressively higher doses. Withdrawal symptoms associated with amphetamines

■ **psychoactive drugs** drugs that affect mood, behavior, and thought processes by altering the functioning of neurons in the brain; they include stimulants, depressants, and hallucinogens.

■ **drug potentiation** the effect of one drug to increase the effects of another.

include increased appetite, weight gain, fatigue, sleepiness, and, in some people, symptoms of paranoia.

Depressants dampen activity in the central nervous system. These drugs include the barbiturates, opiates, alcohol, general anesthetics, and antiepileptic drugs. Low doses reduce responsiveness to sensory stimulation, slow thought processes, and lower physical activity. Higher doses result in drowsiness, lethargy, and amnesia; they can also lead to death by shutting down vital physiological functions such as breathing.

One group of depressants, *barbiturates,* is used to block pain during surgery and to regulate high blood pressure. They are also popular street drugs because they produce a mild sense of euphoria that can last for hours. Up until about 1960, the barbiturates were also the most commonly prescribed drugs for treating anxiety and insomnia. However, because they are highly addictive and were implicated in thousands of suicides, accidental overdose deaths, and dependency, barbiturates are no longer prescribed for these complaints. To take their place, researchers developed synthetic tranquilizers, the benzodiazepines, such as *Librium* and *Valium*

Barbiturates are considered particularly dangerous because, taken in combination with another drug, their effects will increase the effects of that drug, a reaction known as **drug potentiation.** In combination with alcohol, for example, a barbiturate may suppress the brain's respiratory centers and cause death. Another example of this type of drug interaction involves the concurrent use of alcohol and marijuana. The driving ability of a person under the influence of both alcohol and marijuana will be profoundly impaired because of the interaction of the two drugs. Drug potentiation may have caused the death of Jack, whom we met at the opening of the chapter.

Another group of depressants, the *opiates,* such as morphine, heroin, and codeine, derive from the opium poppy. Morphine has been used for more than a century as a potent painkiller (analgesic). In one of medicine's greatest historical ironies, heroin was developed following the Civil War to be a *nonaddictive* alternative to morphine. So many war veterans returned from the battlefield addicted to morphine (the "soldiers' disease") that physicians sought to synthesize a nonaddictive analgesic. The truth, of course, is that heroin induces physical dependence even more rapidly than morphine. Globally, it is estimated that 13.2 million people take opiates, including 9.2 million heroin users (WHO, 2004).

Opiates produce their effects by mimicking the body's natural opiates, the *endorphins.* Endorphins are neurotransmitters that help regulate our normal experience of pain and pleasure. When the brain is flooded with artificial opiates such as heroin, molecules of these synthetic drugs bind to the receptor sites for the endorphins, and the brain stops producing its own naturally occurring opiates. If the drug is discontinued, withdrawal symptoms soon occur, including rapid breathing, elevated blood pressure, severe muscle cramps, nausea and vomiting, panic, and intense cravings for the drug.

Models of Addiction

Theories about how people become addicted to drugs can be grouped into three general categories: biomedical models, reward models, and social learning models.

Biomedical Models: Addiction as Disease

Biomedical models of addiction view physical dependence as a chronic brain disease caused by the biological effects of psychoactive drugs (Leshner, 2001). The simplest model maintains that addicts inherit a biological vulnerability to physical dependence. Researchers point to evidence from studies that compare the **concordance rate,** or rate of agreement, of physical dependence among identical and fraternal twins. A pair of twins is concordant for the trait—in this case, addiction—if both of them have it or if neither has it.

Although concordance studies suggest that genes play a role in physical dependence on many psychoactive drugs, researchers are cautious in interpreting the results from such studies. Even in rare studies in which identical twins who have been raised in different environments are compared and found to have a high concordance rate, it is impossible to completely rule out possible confounding effects due to other variables. Moreover, twin studies do not pinpoint the specific gene or genes that might promote physical dependence.

Another biomedical model points to altered neurochemistry as the basis for both physical and psychological dependence. According to the *withdrawal-relief hypothesis,* drug use serves to restore abnormally low levels of dopamine, serotonin, and other key neurotransmitters (Giannini & Miller, 1989). Depression, anxiety, low self-esteem, and other unpleasant emotional states are indeed associated with neurotransmitter deficiencies and with substance use (Kim and others, 2003). By elevating the release of presynaptic dopamine, drugs such as cocaine and the amphetamines restore neural functioning *and* produce a sense of psychological well-being.

For most of the twentieth century, the withdrawal-relief model was based primarily on evidence from opiate addiction. By suppressing the brain's natural production of endorphins, heroin and other opiates trigger dependence. As the first receptor-based theory of addiction, the opiate model was quickly adopted as the basic biomedical model for addiction to all drugs that induce physical dependence. Nicotine acts on acetylcholine receptors, amphetamine and cocaine act on catecholamine receptors, and barbiturates presumably act on receptors for gamma-aminobutyric acid. In each case, addiction might involve the same sequence of receptor adaptation to an artificial source as occurs with opiate addiction. One glaring exception to the opiate receptor theory as a general model, however, is alcohol, which does not appear to act on specific receptors.

■ **gateway drug** a drug that serves as a stepping-stone to the use of other, usually more dangerous, drugs.

The withdrawal-relief model was appealing because the idea that addicts need more of their drug to relieve physical distress made their intense determination to obtain drugs seem understandable—a rational response to their withdrawal sickness. However, the model does not explain why addicts begin taking a drug in sufficient dosages and with enough frequency to develop physical dependence in the first place. A second problem with this model is its inability to explain why many users suffer a relapse, even long after withdrawal symptoms have subsided.

Reward Models: Addiction as Pleasure Seeking

Researchers trying to explain the initial motivation for repeated use have focused on the pleasurable effects of psychoactive drugs. The impetus for this shift in thinking stems from several bodies of research, including animal studies of brain reward circuits and the 1990s epidemic of cocaine abuse (Lyvers, 1998).

The Brain's Reward System

While attempting to locate the sleep-control system in the brainstems of laboratory rats, James Olds and Peter Milner (1954) accidentally stimulated the septal area of the hypothalamus. To their surprise, the rats refused to leave the area of their cages in which they had been stimulated.

All major drugs of abuse, including nicotine and other stimulants, overstimulate the brain's reward system, which also becomes active when a person engages in pleasurable behaviors that promote survival, such as eating or having sex. Given the choice between psychoactive drugs that put this reward circuit into overdrive—repeatedly activating the neurons until the drug leaves the body—and other, more mundane pleasures, physically dependent animals and human addicts will often choose the former. Rats allowed to press a lever to electrically stimulate their reward systems have been observed to do so up to 7,000 times per hour (Figure 8.3).

Evidence for Reward Models

According to the reward models, addiction may best be understood as being motivated by pleasure seeking. Cocaine, alcohol, nicotine, and other psychoactive drugs may induce physical dependence because they increase the availability of dopamine in the brain, overstimulating the brain's reward system (Thompson, 2000).

Evidence for the reward system link in addiction comes from the fact that people who develop dependence for one drug are more likely to be addicted to others as well. Smokers, for example, consume twice as much alcohol as nonsmokers, are 10 to 14 times more likely to abuse alcohol, and are 4 times as likely to use illicit drugs (Leutwyler, 1995).

Use of tobacco, alcohol, and marijuana plays a pivotal role in the development of other drug dependencies and high-risk behaviors. So, these drugs are often referred to as **gateway drugs**

Figure 8.3

Intracranial Self-Stimulation Whenever the small lamp on the panel is lit, pressing the lever will cause an electrical stimulus to be delivered to the reward system of the rat's brain. Using this experimental arrangement, rats have been observed to lever-press at rates faster than one response per second.

Lamp

Electrode for dispensing electrical stimulus

Lever

because they "open the door" to experimentation with other drugs (Gerstein & Green, 1993). In a nationwide survey of high school seniors, Richard Clayton and Christian Ritter (1985) found that cigarette smoking and alcohol use were the most powerful predictors of marijuana use.

Shortcomings of the Reward Model

Despite its seeming logic, the reward model does not provide the final answer. Although it is true that cocaine, heroin, and other drugs with the greatest potential for addiction evoke the most powerful euphoria, marijuana and several other psychoactive drugs that are not considered physically addictive also produce feelings of well-being (Jones, 1992). In contrast, tobacco, which is highly addictive and as difficult to abstain from as cocaine or heroin (Kozlowski and others, 1982), induces a euphoria that is hardly on the same scale as that elicited by cocaine (Jarvis, 1994).

Reward models by themselves are also unable to explain why drug use continues even when unpleasant side effects occur. Why don't alcohol abusers abstain given the nausea and vomiting they often experience? And changes in drinking behavior over time are not strongly related to changes in smoking behavior over time (Murray and others, 2002). Terry Robinson and Kent Berridge's (2000) two-stage theory, known as the *incentive-sensitization theory* of addiction, provides a rationale for this behavior. In the first stage, the original good feelings from drug use prevail; in the second stage, drug use becomes an automated behavior. Repeated drug use sensitizes the brain's dopamine-serotonin reward systems to drug-related cues (Lyvers, 1998). Thus, even though pleasure may not increase, the systems continue to respond to the cues because they have become conditioned stimuli that evoke dopamine release and craving. In support of their theory, Robinson and Berridge note that sensitization of the dopamine-serotonin systems, which mediate responses to other incentives such as money, may explain the tendency of former addicts to engage in substitute compulsive behaviors such as gambling.

Social Learning Models: Addiction as Behavior

Although psychoactive drugs trigger neurochemical changes, and research points to hereditary risk factors in dependence, there is good reason to also view addiction as a *behavior* that is shaped by learning as well as by social and cognitive factors. For instance, smokers "learn" to smoke in a variety of situations, such as socializing with friends or after eating a meal. Through conditioning, the pleasurable physiological effects of nicotine, together with other rewarding aspects of social situations, transform these situations into powerful triggers for smoking. Furthermore, treatment outcomes for drug abuse are strongly influenced by the presence of social support, the user's employment, and the presence of effective skills for coping with the stress of withdrawal (Westmaas and others, 2002).

A person's identification with a particular drug also plays a role in both the initiation and the maintenance of addiction. Adolescents are preoccupied with their public images and are thus very sensitive to the social implications of their behaviors. Risky health behaviors are often neither intended nor planned; rather, they are reactions to circumstances that are conducive to risk behavior. Seeing oneself as a heavy drinker or smoker, for example, may lead to the adoption of a certain lifestyle that makes abstinence a monumental task involving a new sense of self. Drinkers whose social networks revolve entirely around the neighborhood bar may find it especially hard to stop drinking, especially if they avoid thinking about the consequences of their behavior. Conversely, Meg Gerrard and her colleagues (2002) have found that adolescents who are encouraged to think about the positive social consequences of abstaining from alcohol use subsequently have lower levels of willingness to drink when opportunities arise.

As another example of social influence on drug use, people, especially young people, may be protected by family, school, religion, and other social institutions. According to the *social control theory,* the stronger a young person's attachment to such instititions, the less likely he or she will be to begin using drugs (or to break *any* social norm). Data from the *Monitoring the Future Study,* a survey of more than 53,000 tenth-grade students, found that those who said that religion was a very important part of their lives were much more likely never to have used alcohol, tobacco, or marijuana than students who said religion was not important (Wallace and others, 2003).

The closely related *peer cluster theory* maintains that peer groups are strong enough to overcome the controlling influence of family, school, or religious values. Research studies have consistently demonstrated similarity in substance use among adolescent and young adult peers (Andrews and others, 2002). This may partly be due to the fact that some group settings, such as college campuses, develop false beliefs about social norms regarding drug use. In two large survey studies, Jerry Suls and Peter Green (2003) found that students at a large Midwestern university mistakenly believed that their personal misgivings about alcohol practices were not shared by large segments of the campus population.

Now that you understand more about addiction, let's turn to two of the most common addictions: alcohol and nicotine.

Alcohol Use and Abuse

Alcohol is a depressant that slows the functioning of the central nervous system in a manner similar to tranquilizers such as Valium. When you drink an alcoholic beverage, approximately 20 percent of the alcohol is rapidly absorbed from the stomach directly into the bloodstream. The remaining 80 percent empties into the upper intestine, where it is absorbed at a pace that depends on whether the stomach is full or empty. Drinking on a full stomach delays absorption up to about 90 minutes.

Once alcohol is absorbed, it is evenly distributed throughout body tissues and fluids. It takes a 175-pound man about 1 hour to metabolize the amount of alcohol contained in a 1-ounce glass of 80 proof liquor, a 4-ounce glass of wine, or a 12-ounce bottle of beer (Julien, 2005). Drinking at a faster pace results in intoxication, because a larger amount of alcohol remains in the bloodstream. Women metabolize alcohol more slowly because they produce less of the enzyme *alcohol dehydrogenase,* which breaks down alcohol in the stomach. Women also tend to weigh less than men. As a result of both of these factors, women have a higher blood alcohol content than men after consuming the same amount of alcohol.

The amount of alcohol in the bloodstream is your **blood alcohol level (BAL)**. In most states, a BAL of 0.08 grams per 100 milliliters of blood (g%) constitutes legal intoxication. It is illegal to attempt to drive an automobile with a BAL at this level or higher. A typical male college student would reach an illegal BAL after consuming one standard drink an hour for every 30 to 35 pounds of body weight. Women would reach an illegal BAL sooner. Some people develop a higher tolerance and are able to drink larger amounts of alcohol before becoming visibly impaired. For others, however, obvious intoxication may occur with BALs as low as 0.03 or 0.04 g%. Regardless of the visible effects, the damaging, internal, physiological effects are comparable for all drinkers.

The short-term effects of alcohol are dose dependent. At BALs ranging from about 0.01 to 0.05 g%, a drinker usually feels relaxed and mildly euphoric. As the level increases to 0.10 g%, memory and concentration are dulled, and reaction time and motor functioning are significantly impaired. At 0.10 to 0.15 g%, walking and fine motor skills become extremely difficult. By 0.20 to 0.25 g%, vision becomes blurry, speech is slurred, walking without staggering is virtually impossible, and the drinker may lose consciousness. Death may occur at a BAL of 0.35 or more.

A Profile of Alcohol Abusers

As Figure 8.4 shows, 51.8 percent of Americans aged 12 or older (126 million people) reported being current drinkers in 2005 (defined as having at least one drink during the preceding month). Of these, 22.7 percent (55 million people)

■ **blood alcohol level (BAL)** the amount of alcohol in the blood, measured in grams per 100 milliliters.

Figure 8.4

Alcohol Use in the U.S. among Those 12 Years and Older 51.8 percent of those 12 years or older in the United States are classified as current drinkers and 48.2 percent are abstainers. Among those who drink, 22.7 percent are classified as binge drinkers, and 6.6 percent are heavy drinkers.

Source: Substance Abuse and Mental Health Services Administration. (2006). *Results from the 2005 national survey on drug use and health: National findings.* Office of Applied Studies, NSDUH Series H-30, DHHS Publication No. SMA 06-4194. Rockville, MD.

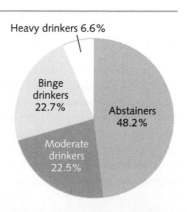

Heavy drinkers 6.6%

Binge drinkers 22.7%

Abstainers 48.2%

Moderate drinkers 22.5%

reported binge drinking during the past month. Binge drinking is defined as having 5 or more drinks for males, and 4 or more drinks for females, on one occasion or within a short period of time (Naimi, 2003; NIAAA, 2006). In 2005, 6.6 percent (16 million people) reported heavy drinking in the past month, defined as daily consumption of greater than 1 drink per day for women and greater than 2 drinks per day for men (SAMHSA, 2006). The Institute of Medicine considers "at-risk drinking" as two or more episodes of binge drinking in the past month, or consuming an average of two or more alcoholic drinks per day in the past month. At-risk drinking is a major public health concern because it is linked with poor health, premature death, and a variety of social consequences such as injury, unplanned and unprotected sex, and hostile encounters with police. A recent, 4-year longitudinal study estimated the prevalence of at-risk drinking among employed adults residing in the Southeastern United States to be 11 percent (Mazas and others, 2006).

The prevalence of the various categories of drinking behavior varies by age, gender, education level, ethnicity, and culture. Adults between 25 and 44 years of age have the highest overall rates of drinking, but the 18 to 24 cohort has the highest rates of binge and heavy drinking (Schoenborn and others, 2004). Alcohol use among adolescents age 12 to 17 dropped substantially after the legal age for purchasing alcohol was increased to 21 in most states. In 1979, before these laws were put in place, fully 50 percent of those in this age group used alcohol; by 1992, however, only 1 out of 5 reported using alcohol (USDHHS, 1998).

Compared with women, significantly more men are current drinkers, binge drinkers, and heavy drinkers (Schoenborn et al., 2004). Approximately 30 to 50 percent of drinkers meet the criteria for major depressive disorder (compared with 17.1 percent in the general population); 33 percent have a coexisting anxiety disorder (compared with 5.1 percent in the general population); 14 percent have antisocial personalities (compared with 1 to 3 percent in the general population), and 36 percent are addicted to other drugs (Julien, 2005).

Despite the fact that college campuses began to be inundated with alcohol education programs in the 1980s, studies indicate that most U.S. college students use alcohol and that nearly one-quarter of college students can be classified as heavy, or problem, drinkers (Kim and others, 1997). When heavy, episodic, or binge drinking is considered, "problem drinker" rates rise to nearly one-half of all students. In 2000, a survey by the Harvard School of Public Health found that 44 percent of college students are binge drinkers, and 74 percent say they binged in high school.

The prevalence of drinking also varies by ethnic and cultural background. In the United States, alcohol addiction rates are extremely low among the Amish, Mennonites, Mormons, and Orthodox Jews (Trimble, 1996). Furthermore, European-Americans have higher rates of drinking than African-Americans, Asian-Americans, or Hispanic-Americans. African-Americans are less likely to be heavy drinkers than European-Americans and Hispanic-Americans. Contrary to popular stereotypes, African-American high school students have the lowest reported use rates for virtually *all* psychoactive drugs (Wallace and others, 2003).

Several recent studies suggest that teen drinking is especially damaging to the brain. Although researchers once thought that the brain is fully developed by age 16 or 17, significant neurological development continues at least until age 21. Heavy drinking at a young age may impair that development.

Although the specific causes of ethnic and cultural group differences in risk are not known, researchers have pointed to several possibilities. Religion is a powerful protective factor against drug use for ethnic and cultural groups (Wallace and others, 2003). People in certain groups may also be at higher or lower risk because of the way they metabolize alcohol. One study of Native Americans, for instance, found that they are less sensitive to the intoxicating effects of alcohol (Wall and others, 1997). People who "hold their liquor" in this way may therefore lack (or can more easily ignore) warning signals that ordinarily make people stop drinking. Asian-Americans, on the other hand, may be less prone to alcohol abuse because they have genetically lower levels of *aldehyde dehydrogenase,* an enzyme used by the body to metabolize alcohol (Suddendorf, 1989; Thomasson & Li, 1993). Without this enzyme, toxic substances build up more quickly after a person drinks alcohol and they cause flushing, dizziness, and nausea.

The Physical Effects of Alcohol Consumption

Alcohol affects all parts of the body. At the most basic level, because cell membranes are permeable to alcohol, alcohol enters the cell and disrupts intracellular communication. Alcohol also affects genes that regulate cell functions such as the synthesis of dopamine, norepinephrine, and other important neurotransmitters.

Alcohol and the Brain

The craving that some people develop for alcohol, the adverse reactions that occur during withdrawal, and the high rate of relapse are all due to biochemical changes in the brain brought on by heavy, long-term use of alcohol. Alcohol has major effects on the hippocampus, a brain area associated with learning, memory, emotional regulation, sensory processing, appetite, and stress (see Chapter 3). It does so by inhibiting neurotransmitters that are strongly associated with emotional behavior and cravings. Dopamine transmission, in particular, is strongly associated with the rewarding properties of alcohol, nicotine, opiates, and cocaine.

Alcohol abuse also indirectly affects other parts of the brain. For example, it may interfere with the body's absorption of thiamin, one of the B vitamins. The absence of thiamin may contribute to **Korsakoff's syndrome,** a neurological disorder characterized by extreme memory difficulty, including the inability to store new memories.

Alcohol and the Immune and Endocrine Systems

Chronic alcohol abuse weakens the immune system, damages cellular DNA, interferes with normal endocrine system development, and disrupts the secretion of growth hormone, which may cause a problematic variety of other endocrine changes.

■ **Korsakoff's syndrome** an alcohol-induced neurological disorder characterized by the inability to store new memories.

Korsakoff's Syndrome These PET scans show brain activity in a normal patient (left) and a patient suffering from Korsakoff's syndrome (right inset). The frontal lobes are seen at the bottom center of each scan; the darker areas represent low metabolic activity. In a PET scan, low metabolic activity in response to thought-provoking questions indicates problems with memory and other cognitive functioning.

Courtesy Dr. Peter R. Martin from Alcohol Health & Research World, Spring 1985, 9, cover.

■ **fetal alcohol syndrome (FAS)**
a cluster of birth defects that
include facial abnormalities, low
intelligence, and retarded body
growth caused by the mother's
use of alcohol during pregnancy.

Alcohol abuse has been linked to decreased testosterone levels in men, leading
to impotence and decreased fertility. In women, menstrual disturbances, spontaneous abortions, and miscarriages increase with the level of alcohol consumption. Alcohol may also decrease estrogen levels in women, which may
partly explain the association between alcohol use and increased risk of breast
cancer (Wolfgan, 1997).

Alcohol and the Cardiovascular System

Alcohol promotes the formation of fat deposits on heart muscle, which lowers
the efficiency of the heart and contributes to cardiovascular disease. It also increases heart rate and causes blood vessels in the skin to dilate, resulting in a loss
of body heat. Chronic abuse may increase blood pressure and serum cholesterol
levels and accelerate the development of atherosclerotic lesions in coronary arteries. Although women experience alcohol-related heart damage at lower levels
of consumption than men, both men and women who abuse alcohol are equally
likely to suffer a fatal heart attack before age 55 (Hanna and others, 1992).

Alcohol and the Gastrointestinal System

Excessive use of alcohol contributes to stomach inflammation and the formation
of gastrointestinal ulcers. Severe inflammation of the liver (*hepatitis*) and the replacement of normal liver cells by fibrous tissue (*cirrhosis*) are two common
chronic diseases caused by alcohol abuse. Cirrhosis of the liver is an irreversible
disease that causes approximately 26,000 deaths each year in the United States.

Fetal Alcohol Syndrome If a
woman drinks heavily during critical periods of fetal development,
she puts her unborn child at risk
of having fetal alcohol syndrome.
Besides the malformed facial
structures seen here, the child is
also likely to be mentally retarded.
These foster parents took on the
task of raising this FAS child,
despite known problems.

© David H. Wells/Corbis

Alcohol and Pregnancy

Alcohol freely crosses the placenta of pregnant women,
making alcohol a potent teratogen. Alcohol levels in a
developing fetus quickly match those of the drinking
mother. Pregnant women who drink during critical stages
of fetal development place their infants at risk of developing **fetal alcohol syndrome (FAS)**. FAS causes severe birth
defects, including low intelligence; microcephaly (small
brain); mental retardation; retarded body growth; facial
abnormalities such as malformed eyes, ears, nose, and
cheekbones; and congenital heart defects.

The behavioral, psychological, and social effects of alcohol abuse are just as dangerous as its physical effects, as
the next section will explain.

Psychosocial Consequences of Alcohol Use

As blood alcohol level initially rises, many drinkers feel cheerful, self-confident,
and more sexually responsive. As levels continue to rise, however, higher-order
cognitive functions are disrupted, including planning, problem solving, and
self-awareness. Furthermore, by focusing the drinker's attention on the imme-

diate situation and away from any possible future consequences, alcohol impairs judgment and facilitates urges that might otherwise be resisted (see Chapter 6). This alcohol-induced sense of confidence and freedom from social constraints is known as **behavioral disinhibition.** Too often, the result of this condition is increased aggressiveness, risk taking, or other behaviors the individual would normally avoid.

Alcohol also makes it difficult for the drinker to interpret complex or ambiguous stimuli, partly because drinkers have a narrower perceptual field; that is, they find it harder to attend to multiple cues and easier to focus on only the most salient ones (Chermack & Giancola, 1997). This *alcohol myopia* (nearsightedness) was demonstrated by Antonia Abbey, Tina Zawacki, and Pam McAuslan (2000), who invited unacquainted college students (88 male–female pairs) to converse for 15 minutes after consuming either alcoholic or nonalcoholic drinks.

Both men and women who drank alcohol perceived their partners and themselves as behaving more sexually and in a more disinhibited way than did those who did not drink. The effects were stronger in males, perhaps confirming social stereotypes about intoxicated behaviors being more acceptable in men. However, the effects also depended on the type of cue being evaluated. Intoxicated participants exaggerated the meaning of dating availability cues and *ignored* the meaning of ambiguous attention cues (more ambiguous signals possibly indicating friendliness or sociability, rather than sexual interest). Thus, alcohol seems to make it even easier for people to concentrate on salient cues that fit their current beliefs (or hopes) and disregard more ambiguous cues that do not.

These results have implications for college prevention programs. Most students realize that intoxication is dangerous, although this does not necessarily keep them from drinking heavily (Norris and others, 1996). As the researchers note, "two drinks are enough to affect perceptions of disinhibition and sexuality. Students who feel sexy and uninhibited are at risk for having sex with someone they do not know well, having unprotected sex, feeling comfortable forcing sex on someone, or being the victim of forced sex" (p. 137). Health psychology's challenge is to make students take these risks seriously, rather than feeling that they are invulnerable. One suggestion offered by the researchers is that students could watch videotapes simulating risky situations and discuss them in mixed-sex groups. "Hearing the other gender's perceptions of the actors might help them realize they may not always understand their opposite sex companion's motives and intentions"(p. 137).

Alcohol-induced cognitive impairments are especially destructive during adolescence, perhaps because even low doses can impair the judgment of teens who are already distracted by the ongoing psychological, physiological, and social challenges of puberty. Indeed, students who use alcohol, compared with their nondrinking counterparts, tend to have more sexual partners, to be less likely to use condoms (MacDonald and others, 1996), and to have more unwanted pregnancies (Perez and others, 2002). Frequent drinkers are also absent from school nearly four times more often, more likely to ride in a car

■ **behavioral disinhibition** the false sense of confidence and freedom from social restraints that results from alcohol consumption.

with a driver who has been drinking, and nearly three times as likely to engage in antisocial behaviors such as stealing and vandalizing property (Lammers and others, 2000).

Alcohol abuse has been associated with a variety of other social problems, including difficulties in interpersonal relationships and various types of violence, including homicides, assault, robbery, suicides, and spousal abuse (Wolfgan, 1997). Half of all people convicted of rape or sexual assault were drinking before the commission of their crimes (Crowell & Burgess, 1996; Seto & Barbaree, 1995). Drinking also increases the chances of being a victim of crime. Approximately 72 percent of rapes committed on college campuses occur when victims are so intoxicated they are unable to consent or refuse (Wechsler, 2004).

Alcohol contributes to violence not only by loosening restraints due to behavioral disinhibition but also by increasing a person's sensitivity to pain and frustration. Under the influence of alcohol, people are more sensitive to electric shocks and react with more aggression to frustration than when they are sober. In addition, brain imaging studies show that repeated heavy use of alcohol, stimulants, and other drugs disrupts frontal lobe activity, which impairs decision making and planning and lowers a person's normal threshold for violence. In one study, Antoine Bechara and his colleagues (2001) had alcohol abusers participate in a laboratory gambling task. One-fourth of the participants performed almost exactly as patients with frontal lobe damage do on the same task (Grant and others, 2000), invariably opting for a small, immediate payoff in the game, even when that strategy proved unprofitable in the long run.

Factors Contributing to Alcohol Dependence

In the late 1950s, the American Medical Association first described the symptoms of *alcoholism*. Although the term is still widely used, experts prefer the more descriptive *alcohol dependence* and *alcohol abuse*. Like any form of drug dependence, **alcohol dependence** involves the use of the drug in order for the person to function normally. About 4 percent of Americans are dependent on alcohol (SAMSHA, 2006), defined as reporting three or more of the following symptoms in the past year (DSM-IV-TR, 2000):

- Tolerance.
- Withdrawal. The *alcohol withdrawal syndrome* consists of a cluster of symptoms that include nausea, sweating, shaking ("the shakes"), hypertension, and anxiety. In severe cases, these symptoms coalesce into a neurological state called **delirium tremens**—or the DTs.
- Use for longer periods than intended.
- Unsuccessful efforts to cut down or control use.
- Considerable time spent obtaining, using, or recovering from alcohol.
- Important social, work, or recreational activities given up because of use.
- Continued use despite knowledge of problems.

■ **alcohol dependence** a state in which the use of alcohol is required for a person to function normally.

■ **delirium tremens (DTs)** a neurological state induced by excessive and prolonged use of alcohol and characterized by sweating, trembling, anxiety, and hallucinations; a symptom of alcohol withdrawal.

Alcohol dependence is often closely related to **alcohol abuse,** defined as a maladaptive drinking pattern in which at least one of the following occurs: recurrent drinking despite its interference with role obligations; continued drinking despite legal, social, or interpersonal problems related to its use; and recurrent drinking in situations in which intoxication is dangerous (DSM-IV, 1994).

Various factors have been implicated in explaining why certain people are more likely than others to abuse alcohol. No single factor or influence, however, completely explains the origins of alcohol dependence or abuse.

■ **alcohol abuse** a maladaptive drinking pattern in which drinking interferes with role obligations.

Genes and Alcohol Dependence

Alcohol dependence is at least partly genetic, although it does not seem that a single, specific gene causes this disorder. Instead, some people inherit a greater tolerance for the aversive effects of alcohol as well as a genetically greater sensitivity to the pleasurable effects (Devor, 1994). Both tendencies may be factors in early excessive drinking, leading to dependence. Consider the evidence:

■ Researchers have located a gene in some alcohol abusers that alters the function of the dopamine receptor *DRD2*. Genetic variation in *DRD2* may influence concentrations of and responses to synaptic dopamine. This gene is also found in people with attention deficit disorder, who have an increased risk for alcohol dependence (Cook and others, 1995). Investigators have focused on the *DRD4* gene, which expresses differences in dopamine receptors that moderate alcohol craving (Hutchison and others, 2002).

■ When either the mother or father of a male child is alcohol-dependent, that child is significantly more likely to later abuse alcohol himself (Cloninger and others, 1985). In fact, for males, alcoholism in a first-degree relative is the single best predictor of alcoholism (Plomin and others, 2001).

■ Adopted children are more susceptible to alcohol dependence if one or both of their biological parents was alcohol dependent (Wood and others, 2001).

■ Identical twins have twice the concordance rate (76 percent) of fraternal twins for alcohol abuse or dependence. This is true whether the twins were raised together or apart and whether they grew up in the homes of their biological parents or with adoptive parents (Kendler and others, 1997).

■ Alcohol's anxiety-relieving effects may also be enhanced among children of alcohol abusers (Sayette, 1993). People who are at increased risk for alcohol dependence also appear to lack the feedback mechanisms that signal overconsumption (Wolfgan, 1997).

■ The personalities of those most likely to abuse alcohol have several common traits, each of which is, at least in part, genetically determined: a quick temper, impulsiveness, intolerance of frustration, vulnerability to depression, and a general attraction to excitement (Brook and others, 2001).

As we saw in Chapter 2, heritability refers to the variation in a trait, in a particular population, in a particular environment, that can be attributed to genetic differences among the members of that group. Heritability refers to *group* rather than *individual* differences in a trait. It does not indicate the degree to which genes determine the likelihood of a trait in a particular person.

Based on such evidence, researchers have estimated the *heritability* of alcohol dependence to be about 0.357 for males and 0.262 for females.

Even if additional genetic factors in alcohol dependence are identified, however, it is unlikely that heredity can explain all cases of alcohol dependence. In fact, another view is that the *lack* of genetic protection may play a role. Like fat and sugar, alcohol is not readily found in nature, and so genetic mechanisms to protect against alcohol dependence may not have evolved in humans as they frequently have for protection against naturally occurring threats such as bacteria, viruses, and other pathogens (Potter, 1997).

Gene–Environment Interactions

Current models of the origins of alcohol dependence emphasize the interaction of environmental and genetic factors (for example, Milby and others, 2004; Cloninger, 1987). Certain person–environment combinations may mutually reinforce each other and lead to substance abuse or interact in a way that constrains use (Hawkins and others, 1992). In one study, students between 12 and 15 years old were tested over a 3-year period, as were their parents and siblings (Bates & Labouvie, 1995). The participants were presented with a list of 53 alcohol-related problems (for example, getting into fights, neglecting responsibilities, experiencing memory loss, or being unable to complete homework due to being under the influence) and asked to indicate how many times each had happened to them. Each participant also completed a variety of scales assessing sensation seeking, impulsiveness, need for achievement, and the quality of interpersonal relationships. Person–environment combinations that included impulsiveness, disinhibition, deviant peer group associations, and low parental control acted as catalysts for alcohol use. Conversely, high educational goals and parental control were protective factors in preventing alcohol and other drug experimentation.

Other studies have found that the parents of alcohol-dependent children are more likely to be of lower socioeconomic status than are the parents of offspring who are not problem drinkers. These parents, according to their children, also tended to be less supportive and to be involved in less-than-ideal marriages (Hunt, 1997). Lynne Cooper, Robert Pierce, and Marie Tidwell (1995) also found that although neither paternal nor maternal drinking problems consistently predicted substance use among adolescent offspring, chaotic and unsupportive family situations were strongly predictive of early alcohol consumption.

Alcohol, Temperament, and Personality

Research studies that link temperament and personality to alcohol dependence provide another clear indication of the interaction of nature and nurture. Our personality is determined in part by heredity and in part by upbringing. Age also plays a role, with adolescents and young adults being more vulnerable to the alcohol-abusing temperament predictors than those in other seasons of life.

Researchers no longer attempt to identify a single "alcoholic personality," focusing instead on specific personality traits that appear to be linked to alcohol dependence. One such trait is a temperament that includes attraction to excitement and intolerance of frustration (Brook and others, 1992; Kaplan & Johnson, 1992).

A second is **behavioral undercontrol** (also called *deviance proneness*), character-ized by aggressiveness, unconventionality, overactivity, and impulsive behavior. A third is **negative emotionality,** which is characterized by depression and anxiety (Sayette & Hufford, 1997). Marked by such traits, high-delinquent teens show consistently elevated levels of alcohol-related problems (Stice and others, 1998).

Alcohol and Tension Reduction

One of the most popular behavioral explanations of alcohol abuse is the **tension-reduction hypothesis.** According to this hypothesis, alcohol and other addictive drugs are reinforcing because they relieve tension, in part by stimulating the re-lease of neurotransmitters that calm anxiety and reduce sensitivity to pain (Par-rott, 1999). Many people, including those who treat alcohol abuse and those who are dependent upon alcohol, believe that some people may cope with stress by drinking, but evidence for the tension-reduction hypothesis is actually mixed. One difficulty with this hypothesis is that although anxiety level may decrease early in a drinking bout, both anxiety and depression levels often *increase* there-after (Nathan & O'Brien, 1971). (Remember: alcohol is a depressant.) Thus, the model may explain why a bout of drinking *begins,* but it does not explain why it continues.

Social-Cognitive Factors

For some, alcohol abuse may stem from a history of drinking to cope with a va-riety of life events or overwhelming situational demands. Alcohol may help some people cope defensively with difficult environments by altering their thought processes. Jay Hull's *self-awareness model* (1987) proposed that alcohol distorts information processing, making the drinker's thinking more superfi-cial and less self-critical. By focusing attention away from thoughts such as "I'm no good at anything," alcohol may allow some people to feel better about them-selves. In other words, people may drink to avoid self-awareness. A similar, *self-handicapping model* proposes that some drinkers use alcohol as an excuse for personal failures and other negative outcomes in their lives ("I was drunk"). A third model proposes that behavior under the effects of alcohol represents a welcomed *time out* from the everyday rules of life. Each of these models under-scores the importance of the social context in which drinking occurs, as well as the drinker's expectations about the drug's effects.

Alcohol and Context Marilyn Senchak, Kenneth Leonard, and Brian Greene (1998) questioned college students to determine the frequency of drinking in different social contexts. Participants were asked, "With whom do you usually or most frequently drink?" Typical social drinking context was strongly related to the students' level of alcohol consumption and their individual personalities. The riskiest drinking context, particularly for men, was either large, mixed-sex groups or small, same-sex groups, but perhaps for very different reasons. Drink-ing in a large, mixed-sex group was associated with low depression and a socially outgoing personality. The second style, drinking in small, same-sex groups,

■ **behavioral undercontrol** a general personality syndrome linked to alcohol dependence and characterized by aggressive-ness, unconventionality, and impulsiveness; also called deviance proneness.

■ **negative emotionality** a state of alcohol abuse characterized by depression and anxiety.

■ **tension-reduction hypothesis** an explanation of drinking behavior that proposes that alcohol is reinforcing because it reduces stress and tension.

■ **alcohol expectancies** individuals' beliefs about the effects of alcohol consumption on behavior—their own as well as that of other people.

seemed to indicate more introverted individuals (especially men) drinking in response to negative internal states. Other researchers have made a similar distinction between two types of heavy drinkers—one influenced by sensation seeking and another influenced by personal problems (Brennan and others, 1986; Fondacaro & Heller, 1983). The interaction of individual characteristics and social drinking contexts may be important in predicting heavy drinking.

A recent study shows that members of fraternities and sororities drink more heavily than other students, dubbed the *Greek effect* by the researchers (Sher and others, 2001). Researchers surveying students 3 years after graduation found that postcollege drinking was more moderate—perhaps due to being removed from a social environment that supported heavy drinking.

Alcohol and Expectations As is true of all psychoactive drugs, alcohol's impact depends not only on the dose but also on the circumstances under which the drug is taken—the user's personality, mood, and **alcohol expectancies** regarding the drug's effects. People who believe they have received alcohol behave just like those who have imbibed, whether or not they have (Leigh, 1989). In one study, people drove more recklessly in a driving simulator when led to believe they had just consumed alcohol (McMillen and others, 1989).

Personal beliefs and expectations about alcohol use influence drinking behavior in another way as well. In a 5-year study conducted at 56 public schools in upstate New York, Lawrence Scheier and Gilbert Botvin (1997) found that adolescents' beliefs about their peers' alcohol use and attitudes predicted their own alcohol use. Those who were certain that many of their friends drank regularly—and enjoyed doing so—were more likely to begin using alcohol themselves. As another example, people who believe that alcohol promotes sexual arousal become more responsive to sexual stimuli if they believe they have been drinking (Abrams & Wilson, 1983).

The impact of alcohol expectancies on drinking behavior is explored more fully in the Your Health feature on this text's companion web site, http://www.worthpublishers.com/straub

Treatment and Prevention of Alcohol Dependence

Most problem drinkers are able to quit drinking without formal intervention. Those who seek treatment generally receive outpatient rather than inpatient care (McMurran, 1994). The treatments generally involve the use of drugs or therapy, or some combination of the two.

Factors that appear to influence the willingness of a person to enter treatment for alcohol dependence include gender, age, marital status, and ethnicity. Among women, factors that predict entry into treatment include being older and unmarried and having a lower level of education, employment, and income. For men, factors that predict entry include having experienced alcohol-related social consequences, being older, and belonging to an ethnic minority (Wolfgan, 1997). Although evaluations of the effectiveness of self-help groups are limited (Sayette & Hufford, 1997), drinking-related beliefs, readiness and motivation to change, and social support for abstinence are important predictors of the success or failure of treatment.

Drug Treatment

Researchers working to understand the physiological mechanisms by which alcohol affects the brain have uncovered a number of pharmacological treatments for alcohol dependence. Medications include *detoxification* agents to manage alcohol withdrawal, alcohol-sensitizing agents to deter future drinking, and anticraving agents to reduce the risk of relapse.

As noted, many people who are dependent on or abuse alcohol also suffer from clinical depression. Antidepressants that increase levels of serotonin by inhibiting its reuptake at synapses are sometimes used to treat those in the early stages of abstinence from alcohol. The best known of these is *fluoxetine* (Prozac). Some researchers believe that deficiencies of serotonin may cause alcohol craving (Anton & Kranzler, 1994). Other researchers have taken a different approach, focusing instead on the role of dopamine in alcohol dependence. By treating alcohol dependence with drugs that block the release of dopamine, they decrease the reward properties of alcohol (Thompson, 2000).

Aversion Therapy

Researchers generally agree that treatment of alcohol dependence is more successful when drugs are combined with behavioral and psychological therapy. One technique, **aversion therapy,** associates a nauseating drug such as *Antabuse* with alcohol, with the goal of getting the patient to avoid alcohol. Although the drug does not reduce cravings for alcohol, if the patient takes a single drink within several days of ingesting Antabuse, a variety of unpleasant effects occur, including nausea, sweating, racing heart rate, severe headaches, and dizziness.

The logic behind the use of Antabuse stems from learning theory. Drugs like this, which produce sickness when a person drinks, are designed to produce a *conditioned aversion* to alcohol. When taken daily, Antabuse can result in total abstinence. A major problem, however, is patient adherence. Many people simply stop taking the drug on a regular basis, which dramatically reduces its effectiveness (Gessner & Gessner, 1992).

Because of adherence problems with Antabuse, some therapists prefer to conduct aversion therapy in a controlled, clinical setting. The client drinks alcohol then takes an *emetic drug,* which induces vomiting. By carefully timing the interval between the drink and the emetic drug, the latter functions as an unconditioned stimulus and becomes associated with the taste, smell, and act of taking a drink of alcohol. These stimuli thus become conditioned stimuli and trigger the unpleasant reaction of nausea.

Relapse Prevention Programs

Because of the unusually high rate of relapse in alcohol dependence (roughly 60 percent a year following treatment), many treatments, while helping the person to remain alcohol free, focus on enabling the person to deal with situations that tempt relapse. When faced with a situation such as a party at which other people are happily imbibing, many former drinkers may become physically aroused and

■ **aversion therapy** a behavioral therapy that pairs an unpleasant stimulus (such as a nauseating drug) with an undesirable behavior (such as drinking or smoking), causing the patient to avoid the behavior.

begin to crave alcohol. Many relapse prevention programs therefore emphasize gaining control over situations that may precipitate a return to drinking (Marlatt & Gordon, 1985).

One form of relapse prevention is based on the gradual *extinction* of drinking triggers. Treatments have been developed in which drinkers are repeatedly exposed to alcohol-related stimuli, such as the aroma of their favorite drink, but they are not allowed to drink. The patients' initially powerful, conditioned physical and psychological responses diminish with repeated exposure over a number of sessions (Monti and others, 1993).

Many relapse prevention programs also incorporate *coping* and *social-skills* training, which helps "inoculate" drinkers by teaching specific strategies for coping with high-risk situations without the help of alcohol. Such situations typically involve social pressure, negative emotions such as anger and frustration, and communication difficulties. Inoculation focuses on improving the person's assertiveness, listening skills, ability to give and receive compliments and criticism, and on enhancing close relationships (Foxhall, 2001). In addition, the recovered drinker is taught skills that permit him or her to abstain in drinking situations. *Drink refusal training* entails the modeling and rehearsal of skills needed to turn down offers to drink.

Self-Help Groups

One of the most widely accepted nonmedical efforts to deal with alcohol dependence is Alcoholics Anonymous (AA). Founded in 1935, AA's 12-step approach recognizes the biochemical model of alcohol abuse and suggests calling on a higher power to help battle what is viewed as an incurable disease. Its theory is that "once an alcoholic, always an alcoholic," and it disagrees entirely with the belief that alcoholics can be reformed into moderate, responsible drinkers. AA counts more than two million members worldwide.

Self-help groups such as AA generally involve group discussions of members' experiences in recovering from alcohol abuse. Members benefit by connecting with a new, nondrinking network and sharing their fears and concerns about relapse. Another self-help group, Rational Recovery, offers a nonspiritual alternative to treating alcohol dependence.

Preventing Alcohol Problems

Alcohol prevention researchers target individual drinkers as well as the social environments in which drinking occurs. Preventive treatments therefore aim to change attitudes about drinking, strengthen coping skills, and restructure environments to reduce the risk of alcohol-related problems.

Most prevention programs stem from one of two theoretical perspectives: *wellness theory* and *problem behavior theory.* Wellness theory proposes that healthy behavior is a "conscious and deliberate approach to an advanced state of physical and psychological/spiritual health" (Ardell, 1985, p. 2). Young people who have a sense that their worlds are coherent and understandable, who feel confident that they have the skills necessary to meet life's demands, and who feel a commitment to themselves and to their lives are generally also the ones who choose a health-enhancing lifestyle (Antonovsky, 1990). In contrast, problem behavior theory suggests that drug use, early sexual activity, truancy, and other risky behaviors often occur together as a syndrome and trigger other problems later in life (Jessor, 1987).

Eleanor Kim and her colleagues (1997) questioned a random sample of college freshmen to determine whether drinking was part of an isolated group of unconventional social behaviors (as problem behavior theory suggests) or more accurately understood as part of a more general health or wellness orientation. The results supported the problem behavior theory. The very different health behavior choices made by abstainers, light to moderate drinkers, binge drinkers, and heavy drinkers showed clear trends.

Prevention programs are most effective when they target children and adolescents before they have succumbed to the habit. The efforts that have proved at least partly effective include strict enforcement of drunk-driving laws, higher prices of alcohol and cigarettes, and harsher punishments for those who sell (or make available) alcohol and cigarettes to minors, as well as classes that inform parents of the hazards of various drugs, improve parent–child communication, and/or realistically delineate the potential hazards of drug use.

As noted earlier, peer culture is a major social influence on drug use. Several primary prevention programs, including the Alcohol Misuse Prevention Study (AMPS), are based on correcting faulty reasoning about peers' drug use and improving social skills in targeted groups. The AMPS was designed to help preadolescent students resist social pressures leading toward alcohol consumption. For instance, role-playing exercises allow students to practice declining alcohol, marijuana, and other drug offers in various social situations. Should students actually encounter such situations, they will have behavioral and cognitive *scripts* for declining the drug offer. The program's beneficial effects have been shown to persist through grade 12 (Wolfgan, 1997).

Since the Drug Free Schools and Communities Act of 1986, most elementary and secondary schools have included some classroom programming aimed at preventing drug use. Does it work? So far, the results have been mixed (Smith, 2001). One longitudinal study evaluated the effectiveness of middle school social influence programs that teach children to resist peer pressure and try to change their perceptions that teen use of drugs is widespread. Sadly, the researchers found no difference in drug use in these schools compared with control schools (Peterson and others, 2000). Results such as these suggest that psychologists' understanding of substance abuse prevention is far from complete and that much more research is needed. The most promising new research takes a systems approach (see Chapter 2), recognizing that a person's choice to use drugs is the result of many interrelated environmental factors and contexts.

Realistically, however, health psychologists recognize that as long as drugs are available and are not perceived as serious threats to health, many young people will try them, and many will eventually abuse them. Following this line of reasoning, one strategy is to delay the young person's experimentation as long as possible. Doing so will increase the odds that he or she is realistically informed about the hazards of the drug and has the cognitive maturity to avoid the faulty reasoning that often leads to drug abuse. The younger a person is when he or she starts drinking, for example, the more likely he or she will be to abuse or become dependent on alcohol. One study sponsored by the National Institutes of Health found that people who began drinking before they turned 15 were four times more likely to become alcohol abusers than were those who started drinking at the legal age of 21. For every year drinking alcohol is delayed, the risk of becoming alcohol dependent decreases by 14 percent.

Figure 8.5

Who Smokes? Smoking is most prevalent among men and people with less than a high school education. Overall, 50 million adults in the United States, about one in every four, currently smoke. Clearly, the nation failed to meet the national health goal set by the Healthy People 2000 project of limiting smoking to 15 percent of the population by the year 2000.

Sources: Satcher, D. (2000). *Reducing tobacco use: A report of the surgeon general—2000.* Washington, DC: U.S. Department of Health and Human Services; Grunberg, N. E., Brown, J. J., & Klein, L. C. (1997). Tobacco Smoking. In A. Baum, S. Newman, J. Weinman, R. West, and C. McManus (Eds.), *Cambridge handbook of psychology, health, and medicine* (pp. 606–610). Cambridge: Cambridge University Press.

Tobacco Abuse

Along with caffeine and alcohol, nicotine is one of the three most widely used psychoactive drugs. Native to the New World, the tobacco plant is first represented in history on a Mayan stone carving dated from around C.E. 600 to 900, and tobacco smoking is first mentioned in Christopher Columbus' log books for his legendary voyage of 1492.

Prevalence of Smoking

Cigarette smoking in the United States peaked in the early 1960s, when half of all adult men and one-third of adult women smoked. From the late 1960s until the mid-1990s, the number of U.S. smokers declined steadily—to about 25 percent of all adults (Grunberg and others, 1997). However, the decline was not evenly distributed, with most of the decrease occurring among upper socioeconomic status (SES) groups and men. Lower-SES individuals continued to smoke, and the prevalence of smoking among women increased sharply. Today, smoking is most prevalent among men (25.2 percent), young adults 18 to 24 years of age (28.5 percent), people with a General Education Development (GED) diploma (42.3 percent), and adults who live below the poverty level (32.9 percent) (CDC, 2004) (Figure 8.5).

Smoking has also become increasingly prevalent in Asian countries such as China, where 70 percent of men (but only 10 percent of women) smoke, and Japan, where 40 percent of men and 11 percent of women smoke (Global Tobacco Control, 2006). In developed countries as a whole, tobacco is responsible for an estimated 24 percent of all male deaths and 7 percent of all female deaths (Peto and others, 1996). Equally troubling is the fact that smoking rates are

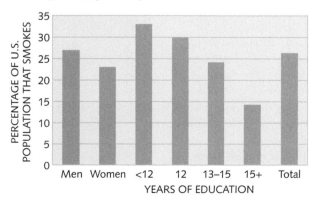

skyrocketing in developing countries such as Kenya and Zimbabwe, causing the World Health Organization to predict that by the year 2025, 7 out of every 10 tobacco-related deaths will occur in developing countries, where many people are still uninformed about the dangers of smoking (WHO, 2000).

Still, the news is not all bad. The most recent "Surgeon General's Report on Tobacco Use Among High School Students" (CDC, 2005) found that although smoking increased among twelfth graders between 1991 and 1999 (39.6 percent to 42.8 percent), smoking rates among eighth, tenth, and twelfth graders have declined each year since, perhaps indicating that teen smoking rates have peaked (see Figure 8.6).

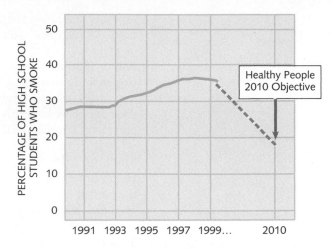

Physical Effects of Smoking

Cigarette smoking is the single most preventable cause of illness, disability, and premature death in this country and in much of the world. In the United States alone, more than 440,000 people a year die from smoking-related illness—more than the combined number of deaths from murders, suicides, AIDS, automobile accidents, alcohol and other drug abuse, and fires (CDC, 2004). Because each cigarette smoked reduces a person's life expectancy by an estimated 14 minutes, an adult who has smoked two packs of cigarettes a day (40 cigarettes) for 20 years can expect to lose about 8 years of life.

Each time a person lights up, 4,000 different chemical compounds are released. It is these chemicals that provide pleasure and energy, and disease and death. For example, the nicotine in cigarette smoke activates specific neural receptors, which in turn causes an increase in heart rate and blood pressure and the constriction of arteries, all of which contribute to the development of cardiovascular disease. The presence of nicotine also causes serum cholesterol levels to rise, hastening the formation of artery-blocking lesions.

Cigarette smoke leads to bronchial congestion by increasing the production of mucus in the throat and lungs while simultaneously damaging the hairlike *cilia* that line the respiratory tract. This leads to higher-than-normal incidence rates of bronchitis, emphysema, and respiratory infections.

The link between smoking and cancer is no longer a matter of debate. Benzo[a]pyrene (BPDE), a chemical in cigarette smoke, has been identified as a causative agent in lung cancer (Denissen and others, 1996). BPDE damages a cancer suppressor gene, causing a mutation of lung tissue. Smoking is also a significant factor in cancers of the mouth, larynx, stomach, pancreas, esophagus, kidney, bladder, and cervix (CDC, 2004).

Given the same lifetime exposure to tobacco smoke, the risk for developing lung cancer is 20 to 70 percent higher in women than men at every level of

Figure 8.6

Smoking among U.S. High School Students Although adult smoking decreased sharply over the past 25 years, especially among people with more years of education, it made a partial comeback among U.S. teens during the 1990s. Still, researchers are hopeful that this trend has peaked and that the Healthy People 2010 objective of fewer than 1 in 5 high school students as smokers will be met.

Sources: National Alternative Youth Risk Behavior Survey. Centers for Disease Control and Prevention, October 28, 2000, www.cdc.gov/nccdphp/dash/yrbs/; Johnston, L. D., O'Malley, P. M. & Bachman, J. G. (2001). *Monitoring the future: National results on adolescent drug use.* Bethesda, MD: National Institute on Drug Abuse.

By one estimate, tobacco companies need to recruit 2 million new smokers every year to replace those who have died or finally quit smoking (Lynch and others, 1995).

exposure, indicating that women are more susceptible to the carcinogens in tobacco. Women who smoke during pregnancy are also more likely to miscarry or to have low-birth-weight infants and infants who die from sudden infant death syndrome (CDC, 2004). Because cigarette smoke reduces the delivery of oxygen to the developing child's brain, the resulting *fetal hypoxia* can cause irreversible intellectual damage. Schoolchildren whose mothers smoked during pregnancy have lower IQs and an increased prevalence of attention-deficit hyperactivity disorder (ADHD) (Milberger and others, 1996).

Smoking Effects Disguised as Aging

Health experts are discovering that a number of disorders once believed to be the normal consequences of aging are, in fact, caused by long-term smoking and other behavioral pathogens. For example, some of the mental decline observed among elderly persons may be caused by tobacco-related bleeding in the brain ("silent strokes") that goes unnoticed. A meta-analysis of four European studies of 9,223 people aged 65 and older compared smokers, nonsmokers, and former smokers once and then again 2 years later on short-term memory, attention, and simple mathematical calculations. All three groups showed a decline in cognitive performance over the 2-year period, but the decline was by far the greatest among smokers (Launer & Kalmijn, 1998).

Second-hand Smoke

The hazards of smoking extend beyond the direct risks to the smoker. Second-hand smoke contains an even higher concentration of many carcinogens than smoke inhaled directly from a cigarette. According to the Centers for Disease Control, nearly 9 out of 10 nonsmoking Americans are exposed to environmental tobacco smoke (ETS). The study reported measurable levels of *cotinine* (a chemical the body metabolizes from nicotine) in the blood of 88 percent of the nonsmokers. The presence of cotinine is proof that a person has been exposed to, and absorbed, tobacco smoke (Domino, 1996).

It is estimated that 4,000 Americans die each year from lung cancer caused by ETS. Female nonsmokers whose husbands smoke, for instance, stand a 1.32 greater chance of developing lung cancer than do nonsmoking wives of nonsmoking husbands. Exposure to ETS is also recognized as an independent risk factor for cardiovascular disease (Torpy and others, 2005). Children who live with smokers have a significantly higher prevalence of pneumonia, ear and nasal infections, asthma, and the skin disorder eczema. As adults, they also have an increased risk of chronic illness and sickness-related work absences (Eriksen, 2004).

Why Do People Smoke?

To understand why people smoke, we need to consider each of the major stages of smoking behavior: initiation, maintenance, cessation, and relapse (Grunberg and others, 1997).

Initiation

Initiation of drug use often occurs through social contacts. Initial use of many psychoactive drugs, with the exception of cocaine and amphetamines, is often unpleasant. As a result, a period of experimentation typically precedes the development of regular drug use, thus suggesting that factors other than physical effects are important in the initiation and maintenance of drug use until dependence develops.

Advertising is a powerful influence. The tobacco industry spends more than $11.2 billion per year marketing its products in the United States alone, where *Joe Camel,* for instance, once ranked second only to Mickey Mouse in face recognition among American schoolchildren (Tobacco Free Kids, 2006).

In a clever twist of this once highly effective advertising campaign, Sonia Duffy and Dee Burton showed kindergarten through twelfth-grade Chicago students two currently used antismoking messages: "Smoking kills" and "Smoking causes lung cancer, heart disease, emphysema and may complicate pregnancy." The messages were either plain, printed messages or featured a Joe Camel-like cartoon character leaning nonchalantly against a sign bearing the message. All of the cartoon messages received higher ratings of importance and believability than the plain ones (cited in Azar, 1999).

Role modeling and peer influence also lead many teenagers to start smoking. Celebrities who smoke create the image that smoking is linked with success, beauty, and even sexual arousal. Image, smoking among friends, relaxation, and pleasure are most often cited as reasons teens begin smoking (Soldz & Cui, 2002; Stanton and others, 1993). Having parents, older siblings, and friends who smoke is also predictive of teen smoking (Chassin and others, 1998). Among adolescents whose parents and close friends do not smoke, smoking is rare (Moss and others, 1992).

The college years are a time of transition in smoking behavior—when many young adults begin to smoke regularly. A 4-year national study that followed nearly 1,500 students from high school into college identified several personal and environmental factors as important predictors of smoking in college (Choi and others, 2003). Students who were more likely to begin smoking were those who did not like school as much and were more rebellious. High school students who had tried smoking were more likely to become regular smokers if they thought their college peers approved of smoking, and if they believed that experimentation with smoking was not dangerous. Finally, the longer a student avoided smoking, the less likely he or she was to experiment in college. Not surprisingly, therefore, students who lived in smoke-free dormitories were less likely to smoke than those who lived where smoking was permitted. The results of this study suggest that interventions that reinforce the message that nonsmoking is the norm among students and that increased access to smoke-free environments

Between 1987 (when Joe Camel was first introduced by R. J. Reynolds) and 1997, Camel's share of the teenage cigarette market increased from less than 3 percent to over 13 percent. Is it any wonder that in 1997 the Federal Trade Commission accused Reynolds of targeted appeals to teenagers?

AP/Wide World Photos

The Long-Term Effects of Smoking These photos of identical twins make the effects of smoking—and tanning—obvious and tangible—perhaps even to those fighting social influences to take up smoking. Sixty-year-old Gay Black (left) was a smoker and a sunbather. Her twin, Gwen Sirota (right) did neither.

would discourage initiation of smoking among college students and prevent occasional smokers from progressing to established smokers.

In light of the evidence linking social influences with the initiation of smoking, the U.S. Surgeon General has concluded that situational factors are more important than personality factors in explaining why people start smoking. Nevertheless, a number of *vulnerability factors* differentiate teens who are more likely to become dependent on nicotine and other psychoactive drugs. Smoking is especially prevalent among those who feel less competent and less in control of their future and who perceive a lack of social support (Camp and others, 1993). This is particularly true among people of lower socioeconomic status, whom recent studies have shown continue smoking because they believe that their personal life and health can only be slightly controlled by their own behavior (Droomers and others, 2002). In addition, rebelliousness, a strong need for independence, and perceptions of benefits such as weight control, increased alertness, and stress management are also linked to smoking initiation. Teenagers who smoke are also more likely to feel alienated from school, to engage in antisocial behavior, to have poor physical health, and to feel depressed (Kandel & Davies, 1996). They also tend to spend more time in passive activities such as watching television, and are more likely to be living with a single parent (Soldz & Cui, 2002).

Maintenance

Once a person has begun to smoke, a variety of biological, psychological, and social variables contribute to making it difficult for him or her to abstain.

Heavy smokers are physically dependent on nicotine. Support comes from evidence that laboratory animals will learn difficult new behaviors in order to self-administer nicotine, suggesting that the drug has powerful properties as a reinforcer. Nicotine stimulates the sympathetic nervous system and causes the release of catecholamines, serotonin, corticosteroids, and pituitary hormones (Grunberg and others, 2001). In addition, nicotine induces relaxation in the skeletal muscles and stimulates dopamine release in the brain's reward system (Nowak, 1994).

Stanley Schachter and his colleagues (1977) first advanced the idea of the **nicotine-titration model,** suggesting that long-term smokers attempt to maintain a constant level of nicotine in their bloodstream. Schachter discovered that smokers smoke roughly the same amount day after day. When they are unknowingly forced to switch to lower-nicotine brands, they compensate by smoking more cigarettes, inhaling more deeply, and taking more puffs (Schachter, 1978).

Evidence of a genetic component in explaining why people continue to smoke comes from a large meta-analysis of twin studies, which estimated a 60 percent heritability for smoking (Heath & Madden, 1995). Smokers and nonsmokers also appear to differ in a gene for a *dopamine transporter*—a protein that "vacuums up" dopamine after it has been released by a neuron. Caryn Lerman and her colleagues (1999) found that people with one form of the gene (the

■ **nicotine-titration model** the theory that smokers who are physically dependent on nicotine regulate their smoking to maintain a steady level of the drug in their bodies.

"9-repeat allele") were less likely to be smokers than people with other forms of the dopamine transporter gene. Other studies have linked the 9-repeat allele to increased levels of dopamine, indicating reduced efficiency at removing excess dopamine compared with those who inherit other forms of the gene. In addition, former smokers are more likely than current smokers to have the 9-repeat allele and the same DRD2 dopamine receptor gene implicated in alcohol dependence, indicating that these genes may boost people's ability to quit smoking (Lerman, 2003).

Psychosocial factors also contribute to maintenance. Adolescents who smoke often believe that their behavior is only temporary. When asked, they often report they will no longer be smoking in 5 years and that the long-term consequences of tobacco will not affect them. Adolescents are also oriented toward the present, so warnings of the long-term health hazards of cigarette smoking generally are not sufficient to deter smoking, especially in the face of immediate social pressures to smoke.

For many smokers, coping with stress is a key psychological factor in their habit. Schachter (1978) discovered that nicotine metabolism varies with the smoker's level of stress, providing a physiological explanation for why smokers tend to smoke more when anxious. When a smoker feels stressed, more nicotine is cleared from the body *unmetabolized,* forcing the smoker to smoke more to get his or her usual amount of nicotine.

Closely related to the idea of the nicotine-titration model, the *affect management model* proposes that smokers strive to regulate their emotional states (Tomkins, 1966). Accordingly, *positive affect smokers* are trying to increase stimulation, feel relaxed, or create some other positive emotional state. In contrast, *negative affect smokers* are trying to reduce anxiety, guilt, fear, or other negative emotional states.

In support of the affect management model, researchers have uncovered a link between nicotine use and depression, naturally leading to questions of whether one causes the other or whether some third factor contributes to both. A recent longitudinal study of high school students suggests that smoking and depression have a reciprocal effect, triggering a vicious cycle of smoking and negative mood (Windle & Windle, 2001). Every 6 months, students completed questionnaires assessing their emotional state, cigarette smoking, family dynamics, and friends' drug use. Teens who were heavy smokers at the beginning of the 18-month study were more likely than those who smoked less to report symptoms of depression. In addition, students who had persistent symptoms of depression at the start of the study were more likely than other students to increase smoking, even when other factors were taken into consideration.

Prevention Programs

Because it is so difficult for ex-smokers to remain nicotine free, health psychologists have focused a great deal of energy on primary prevention. Their efforts have included educational programs in schools, public health messages,

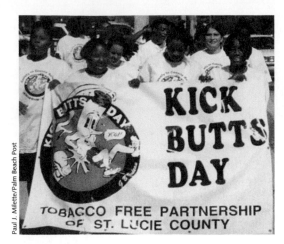

Paul J. Milette/Palm Beach Post

Effective Prevention The state of Florida directed a huge, youth-oriented anti-smoking campaign in 1998, which reduced rates of smoking within 1 year.

tobacco advertising bans, increasing tobacco taxes, and campaigns to ban smoking in public places. Over the past 3 decades, these campaigns have changed in ways that reflect the broader social changes in how smoking is viewed. In the 1970s, for instance, school-based prevention programs focused on providing information regarding the hazards of smoking. In the 1980s, programs were increasingly based on social influence models that portrayed smoking as undesirable and taught skills to resist social pressures to smoke. Most recently, smoking has been portrayed as an addictive disorder as well as a problem behavior. As a result, smoking interventions have increasingly incorporated some form of nicotine replacement therapy (see Chassin et al., 2003 for a review).

Information Campaigns

The most successful antismoking campaigns provide nonsmoking peer role models that change our idea of what behaviors are acceptable and valued (Azar, 1999). Kim Worden and Brian Flynn (1999) followed more than 5,000 children in Vermont, New York, and Montana. Half the children participated in a school-based antismoking intervention program and were also exposed to a variety of radio and television commercials featuring nonsmoking role models. The other half only participated in the school program. Instead of focusing on the health hazards of smoking, the commercials featured teens who were enjoying life without smoking, who demonstrated how to refuse a cigarette, and who emphasized that most kids today don't smoke and don't approve of smoking. Four years later, children from the commercial intervention group were less likely to smoke than children who participated only in the school program.

In another study, Cornelia Pechmann and Chuan-Fong Shih (1999) tested the effectiveness of 196 antismoking ads on seventh- and tenth-grade California students. Out of seven different types of antismoking ads, only three were effective in reducing the teenagers' desire to smoke. Two of the successful ads showed peers who think smokers are misguided and young people choosing not to smoke; the third ad showed how smokers endanger family members through secondhand smoke.

Antismoking Campaigns and Ethnic Minorities

Cultural stereotypes help explain why smoking is more prevalent among some groups than others (Johnsen and others, 2002). Antismoking campaigns have been less effective among ethnic minorities, perhaps partly because tobacco companies have targeted a disproportionate amount of advertising toward minority communities, especially the African-American and Hispanic-American communities. African-American men have the highest smoking rates among the major racial/ethnic groups in the United States (Schoenborn and others,

2004). They also have the highest rates of death due to lung cancer—six times that of European-American men (see Chapter 10).

Overall, Hispanic men smoke at about the same rate as non-Hispanic men, while Hispanic women smoke somewhat less than non-Hispanic women and Hispanic men (Schoenborn and others, 2004). Acculturation partly explains these smoking patterns. Traditional Hispanic culture frowns upon smoking in women but not in men. In an unhealthy twist, the generally less rigid American gender roles have meant that smoking rates among more acculturated Hispanic-American women in the United States are higher than those among less acculturated women. Asian-American women and men are less likely to be current smokers than any other single-race group studied (Schoenborn and others, 2004).

Increasing Aversive Consequences

Successful primary prevention programs also strive to increase the aversive consequences of smoking. For example, increasing the tax paid on cigarettes is quite effective. Consider the experience of Canadian smokers, whose cigarette tax has increased more than 700 percent since 1980. When a pack of cigarettes costs more than $5, many teenagers think twice about smoking. The tax impact is the sharpest among teenagers, who have less disposable income and are in the age group most vulnerable to smoking behavior. According to a Health Canada survey, the smoking rate among 15- to 19-year-olds dropped to 18 percent in 2003 from 28 percent in 1999 after the tobacco tax was increased by $2.50 per carton (CTUMS, 2004).

The price of a pack of cigarettes in the United States increased 90 percent between 1997 and 2003, which may be part of the reason the Centers of Disease Control and Prevention (CDC) reports that the percent of high school students who smoke decreased from 36 percent to 22 percent during the same time period. This is the lowest reported teen smoking rate since the CDC began tracking it in 1975 (CDC, 2004). To counter the arguments of those who object to increasing taxation, it is worth noting that tobacco-caused health care costs increase the average American household's federal tax bill by about $320 each year (Campaign for Tobacco-Free Kids, 2006).

As another example, teens caught smoking, possessing, or buying tobacco products in Broward County, Florida, must appear in court with their parent or guardian and watch a video on the dangers of smoking. The judge also orders either a $25 fine or a day of community service picking up cigarette butts around public buildings. Underage offenders who fail to comply with the sentence may also lose their driver's licenses. So far, the tactic seems to be working. A survey of 402 offenders and their parents or guardians showed that nearly one-third of the teens reported using less tobacco than they did before their citation, and 15 percent had not used tobacco at all (Chamberlin, 2001).

Another way to increase smoking's immediate aversive consequences is to legislate change in the workplace, such as by imposing smoking bans. A growing number of American universities prohibit smoking in public areas and in residence halls. The success of such programs is mixed. Banning smoking from the work environment appears to be most helpful for those who have low habit strength, a desire to quit, and other social supports for their efforts (Borland and others, 1991).

Inoculation

Most effective for deterring smoking in adolescents have been "inoculation" programs that teach practical skills in resisting social pressures to smoke. Because smoking generally begins during the junior high and high school years, prevention programs are typically conducted in schools before children reach their teens.

The most successful programs are based on a *social learning model* that focuses on three variables: social pressure to begin smoking, media information, and anxiety. A program, designed by Richard Evans (2003), used films, role-playing, and rehearsal to help young teens improve their social skills and refusal skills. In the films, same-age models were depicted encountering and resisting social pressure to smoke. The students also role-played situations, such as when someone is called "chicken" for not trying a cigarette. The students were instructed to give responses such as "I'd be a real chicken if I smoked just to impress you." After several sessions of "smoking inoculation" during the seventh and eighth grades, these students were only half as likely to start smoking as were those in a control group at another school, even though the parents of both groups had the same rate of smoking.

As noted in Chapter 6, multifaceted community campaigns that intervene on several fronts work better than "single-shot" campaigns. In one midwestern county school system, 2 decades of antismoking campaigns have combined school intervention programs with community-wide mass media messages. The results have been gratifying. Between 1980 and 2001 among seventh through eleventh grade students, there has been a significant decrease in experimental and regular smoking, and a shift in viewing smoking as more addictive and as having more negative social consequences (Chassin and others, 2003).

Cessation Programs

Since 1977, the American Cancer Society has sponsored the annual Great American Smokeout, in which smokers pledge to abstain from smoking for 24 hours. For many smokers, the Smokeout has been a first step in successfully quitting tobacco for good. The percentage of smokers who said they participated increased from 18 percent in 1995 to 26 percent in 1996. Now in its ninth year, "Kick Butts" is a similar program, sponsored by the Campaign for Tobacco-Free Kids, that encourages children and teenagers to avoid tobacco and attacks the image of smoking as being cool (http://kickbuttsday.org/).

Campaigns such as these, along with print and broadcast ads, no-smoking pledge drives, smoking bans and other programs—many of which have been funded from the 1998 $226 billion tobacco settlement—appear to be working

(Pierce, 2004). It is estimated that over 3 million deaths have been prevented as a result of people either quitting smoking or not beginning in the first place. Yet we need to continue these efforts. Each day, more than 4,000 kids in the United States try their first cigarette, and 2,000 other kids under 18 years of age become new, daily smokers (SAMHSA, 2002).

Smoking cessation programs generally fall into two categories: those based on an addiction model and those with cognitive-behavioral approaches. Programs based on an addiction model of smoking emphasize the physiological effects and habitual behavior engendered by nicotine (Henningfield and others, 1993). Cognitive-behavioral models focus on helping smokers better understand the motivation, conditioning, and other psychological processes that trigger smoking (Lando, 1986). Intervention is aimed at helping the smoker develop coping skills to gain control over smoking triggers and to deal with anxiety, stress, and other emotions without smoking.

Addiction Model Treatments

A variety of pharmacological replacement therapy programs have been developed for smokers, including transdermal nicotine patches, nicotine gum, and inhalers. These *nicotine replacement programs* have helped millions of smokers in their efforts to quit smoking. Once available only as expensive prescription drugs, most are now available over the counter.

People who smoke continuously day in and day out are good candidates for *transdermal nicotine patches,* which have become the most common pharmacological treatment for smoking. Worn during the day, the bandage-like patches release nicotine through the skin into the bloodstream. Users are able to gradually reduce the daily dose in a series of steps that minimize withdrawal symptoms and help ensure success in remaining smoke-free (Fiore and others, 1994; Wetter and others, 1995).

However, nicotine patches are only moderately successful as a stand-alone treatment for smoking. After 10 years of research, abstinence rates in patients using the nicotine patch are generally about 1.9 times higher than those observed in patients using a placebo (Corelli, 2002). The effectiveness of the patch varies with the user's genotype with respect to the now-familiar dopamine *D2* receptor gene. Oxford University researchers genotyped more than 750 people in 1999 and 2000. All had tried to quit smoking during an earlier clinical trial. At the 8-year mark, 12 percent of women with a particular allele of the dopamine *D2* receptor gene who had received the patch had remained abstinent. Only 5 percent of women without that *D2* receptor gene had maintained their nonsmoking status. Although the same gene variants are found in men, no differences in abstinece based on genotypes was noted (Yudkin and others, 2003).

Like all pharmacological treatments, the effectiveness of nicotine gum varies with the strength of the smoker's dependency on nicotine and his or her particular smoking habits. Nicotine gum appears to be most helpful for smokers who tend to smoke many cigarettes in a short period of time—after work, for example. Nicotine gum may be most effective when used as part of a comprehensive behavioral treatment program (Hall and others, 1984). Some researchers believe that the relief of withdrawal symptoms and cravings is largely a placebo effect rather than a pharmacological effect of the actual nicotine in the gum (Gottlieb and others, 1987). Although less effective than the nicotine patch, nicotine gum improves cessation rates by about 50 percent compared with control interventions (Davies and others, 2004).

The most recent intervention is the oral inhaler, a plastic tube filled with 4 mg of nicotine that smokers can "puff" on 2 to 10 times a day. Patients who use the nicotine inhaler are 1.7 to 3.6 times more likely to remain abstinent than patients using a placebo inhaler. Smokers often find inhalers appealing because the hand-to-mouth ritual associated with their use is similar to that with smoking (Fiore and others, 2000).

Recognizing the possible biochemical common ground of nicotine and alcohol addiction, researchers are experimenting with new medications for treating addiction. *Bupropion* (Zyban), a powerful antidepressant, may curb nicotine cravings by mimicking tobacco's ability to increase brain levels of dopamine (Lerman and others, 2003). Like many other pharmacological discoveries, Zyban's efficacy in treating nicotine addiction was discovered by accident. Researchers knew that depression was a common symptom of nicotine withdrawal and so began experimenting with antidepressants to alleviate addiction rather than depression. Cessation rates in patients who use sustained-release bupropion are generally 2.1 times higher than those observed in patients receiving a placebo (Fiore, 2000). Most effective is *combination therapy,* in which one intervention (such as the nicotine patch) provides steady levels of nicotine in the body and a second form (such as Bupropion) is used as needed to control cravings and suppress nicotine withdrawal symptoms (Corelli, 2002).

Cognitive-Behavioral Treatments for Smoking

Given the importance of modeling, reinforcement, and principles of learning in the development of drug abuse, it makes sense that health experts rely on a number of cognitive and behavioral techniques to help people quit smoking. As with its use in treating alcohol dependence, *aversion therapy* involves pairing unpleasant consequences with smoking in order to condition an aversion to smoking. In one of the most frequently used techniques, smokers increase their usual smoking rate until the point of **satiation,** an unpleasant state of "fullness." One variation involves *rapid smoking,* in which a smoker periodically is asked to smoke a cigarette as fast as he or she can. Rapid smoking and satiation are both designed to associate nausea with smoking. Aversion strategies have also used electric shock and nausea-inducing drugs. For many smokers, aversion therapy is an effective way to begin to quit (Kamarck & Lichtenstein, 1985).

Cognitive restructuring of health beliefs and smoking attitudes is also important in successful quitting and avoiding relapse. Research studies demonstrate that those who sucessfully quit smoking typically change their beliefs to

■ **satiation** a form of aversion therapy in which a smoker is forced to increase his or her smoking until an unpleasant state of "fullness" is reached.

see less psychological benefit and more health threat from smoking, while those who relapse may come to view smoking as having *more* psychological benefits and being less of a personal threat over time (Chassin and others, 2003).

Smoking Cessation Programs for Ethnic Minorities and by Gender

Health organizations are beginning to realize that no single approach to smoking cessation is likely to work with all smokers. Interventions need to be targeted to specific groups, especially in order to take into account cultural traditions, values, and gender. For instance, women have more difficulty quitting smoking than men, and nicotine replacement therapy is less effective in women than in men, possibly because women may be more responsive to non-nicotine stimuli associated with smoking. That's not to say that nicotine isn't important for women. Rather, the external pleasures of smoking, such as holding and smelling a cigarette and the social context in which smoking occurs, may be more important to women than they are to men. More generally, in laboratory studies women are less able than men to perceive physiological changes such as increased blood pressure, heart rate, or blood glucose levels (Roberts & Pennebaker, 1995).

There is also evidence that Hispanic-American smokers appear to be more perceptive of social cues than are smokers from other groups (Nevid, 1996). This includes the positive connection between smoking and socializing with friends as well as the negative connection between their smoking and setting a bad example for their children. It makes sense, then, that appropriate interventions in helping Hispanic-Americans quit smoking would be to teach them how to refuse a cigarette politely, and to provide antismoking messages that incorporate concerns about modeling, secondhand smoke, and other negative social consequences of smoking.

In one example of the development of a culturally sensitive smoking cessation program, Jeffrey Nevid and his colleagues (1996) organized an 8-week "Si, PUEDO" ("Yes, I Can") intervention in a predominantly Hispanic community in New York City. This successful intervention incorporated videotaped vignettes of Hispanic actors remaining smoke free in a variety of social situations. In addition, deep-seated cultural values such as *machismo* (masculinity), *familiarismo* (responsibility to family), and *respeto* (respect for self and others) were used to convey antismoking messages.

Which Smoking Cessation Programs are Effective?

There have been relatively few randomly controlled studies examining the effectiveness of smoking cessation programs for adolescents. The conventional wisdom seems to have been that teens are not going to quit smoking until they're older, so why bother? A review of 17 adolescent smoking cessation studies indicated that, on average, about 21 percent of teenagers in such programs quit smoking (Sussman and others, 1999). Six months later, however, this figure dropped to 13 percent. For comparison purposes, about 11 percent of all

Figure 8.7

Factors in Smoking Cessation According to this model, readiness motivation is the primary, proximal causal factor in determining whether a person makes a serious attempt to quit. Social and environmental supports or prompts, such as a workplace no-smoking policy, increases in the price of tobacco, persistent reminders from one's child to stop smoking, or a physician's advice can also affect readiness motivation.

Source: Lichtenstein, E. & Glasgow, R. E. (1997). A pragmatic framework for smoking cessation. *Psychology of Addictive Behaviors*, 1997, *11*(2), 142–151 (Figure 1).

INFLUENCES   TEMPORAL STAGES

Motivation
Readiness ───────────────→ Quit Attempt
Persistence
Physical Dependence ──────→ Short-Term Quitting or Failure
Barriers/Support ─────────→ Maintenance or Relapse

───────→ Solid arrow = primary influence
- - - -→ Broken arrow = secondary influence

people who attempt to quit smoking on their own, without an intervention, are able to do so (Carpenter, 2001). The programs that were most effective for adolescents were those that:

- enhanced intrinsic and extrinsic motivation to quit with rewards and education designed to reduce ambivalence about quitting.
- were tailored to adolescents' developmental needs (rather than adult programs with only superficial changes) and made intervention programs fun.
- provided social support to help teens persevere and avoid relapse.
- showed teens how to make use of community resources for remaining nicotine free.

In contrast, there is an abundance of research on adult smoking cessation efforts. Research studies involving adult smokers have found that smoking treatment programs are most effective when two or more methods are used together. For example, treatment programs that combine behavioral methods with nicotine replacement are more effective than either approach used alone (Cinciripini and others, 1996; Levesque and others, 1999).

Whichever combination of techniques is used, Edward Lichtenstein and Russell Glasgow (1997) of the Oregon Research Institute argue that quitting smoking is determined by three interacting factors: motivation to quit (including persistence despite withdrawal symptoms and stress), level of physical dependence on nicotine, and barriers to or supports in remaining smoke-free (Figure 8.7). The extent of a smoker's physical dependence, for example, will certainly influence both readiness to quit and persistence. The presence of a smoking spouse, workplace smoking bans, a child pressuring a parent to quit, and other barriers and supports may also influence motivation (Hammond and others, 2004).

James Prochaska (1996b) suggests that many smoking cessation programs dilute their effectiveness by targeting multiple behaviors and failing to recognize that different smokers have different needs. Prochaska proposes, instead, that planned interventions be organized according to each smoker's stage of quitting. His transtheoretical model outlines six stages of behavior change: 1) precontemplation, 2) contemplation, 3) preparation, 4) action, 5) maintenance, and 6) termination. Smokers in the precontemplation stage, for example, are often defensive and resistant to action-oriented programs. They often are demoralized by previous failures to quit smoking and consequently are put off by information campaigns condemning their unhealthy behavior. Historically, health experts considered such people as unmotivated or not ready for therapy. Prochaska, however, would suggest that treatment for people at this stage include reassurance that becoming a nonsmoker—like becoming a smoker in the first place—is not something that happens overnight. Rather, there are stages in its development, and many smokers who attempt to quit are not successful the first time.

The stage approach has several advantages over traditional, nonstage interventions. First, it generates a much higher rate of participation. When free smoking clinics are provided by health maintenance organizations (HMOs), only about 1 percent of subscribers participate. In two home-based interventions involving 5,000 smokers each, Prochaska and his colleagues recruited smokers to stage-matched interventions. Using this approach, the researchers generated remarkably high participation rates of 82 to 85 percent (Prochaska and others, 1995).

A second strength of stage-based interventions is a dramatic improvement in the number of participants who complete the treatment (retention rate). A meta-analysis of 125 nonstage smoking cessation programs revealed an average retention rate of only about 50 percent (Wierzbicki & Pekarik, 1993). Remarkably, Prochaska and his colleagues have reported nearly 100 percent retention rates when treatment is individualized according to a stage approach.

The third advantage of stage-based approaches is the most important: Progress in remaining smoke free is directly related to the stage participants were in at the start of the interventions. This *stage effect* is illustrated in Figure 8.8, which shows that smokers in the precontemplation phase displayed the smallest amount of abstinence from smoking over 18 months, whereas those in the preparation stage showed the most progress in 6-, 12-, and 18-month follow-ups. As discussed in Chapter 2, stage-based interventions proceed in a gradual series of steps, with the reasonable goal of helping smokers advance one stage at a time.

Relapse: Back to the Habit

Unfortunately, only a small percentage of people who quit remain smoke free for very long. Although 70 percent of adult smokers claim they want to quit, fewer than 1 in 10 is able to do so, and as many as 80 percent of smokers who quit smoking relapse within 1 year (Shiffman, 2006).

Many factors are involved in relapse, the most fundamental being the severity of withdrawal symptoms and craving. In one recent study of 72 long-term smokers (38 men and 34 women), 48 percent relapsed within the first week of quitting. Participants who relapsed experienced greater distress and withdrawal symptoms during the first 24 hours of nicotine abstinence (al'Absi and others, 2004). Interestingly, the researchers found that stressful experiences affect men and women who are trying to quit smoking differently. For instance, cortisol responses

Figure 8.8

Percentage of Abstinent Former Smokers by Stage of Quitting The amount of progress former smokers make in remaining abstinent is directly related to the stage they were in at the start of the intervention. Smokers in the precontemplation phase display the smallest amount of abstinence from smoking over 18 months, whereas those in the preparation stage show the most progress in 6-, 12-, and 18-month follow-ups.

Source: Prochaska, J. O. (1996). Revolution in health promotion: Smoking cessation as a case study. In R. J. Resnick and R. H. Rozensky (Eds.), *Health psychology through the life span: Practice and research opportunities* (pp. 361–375). Washington, DC: American Psychological Association.

before and after performing a public-speaking test were stronger in the men than in the women. Ex-smokers also may experience other side effects, which are immediately eliminated by a return to smoking. For example, some ex-smokers gain weight (perhaps because of slower metabolism, increased preference for sweet-tasting foods, or substituting eating for smoking), have trouble sleeping, are more irritable, and find it difficult to concentrate (Grunberg, 1986).

Another factor in relapse is the strength of previously conditioned associations to smoking (Killen and others, 1992). Smoking behaviors, as well as nicotine's physiological effects, become conditioned to a variety of environmental stimuli. Many ex-smokers relapse in the face of an irresistible urge (conditioned response) to smoke in certain situations or environments—for example, with that first cup of coffee in the morning or after a meal.

Because of this dismal prognosis for ex-smokers, smoking relapse has received considerable research attention in recent years. A working conference sponsored by the National Institutes of Health (NIH) took a first step in addressing the relapse problem by encouraging health experts to adopt a "stages of change" model in developing programs to prevent relapse. For example, rather than encouraging ex-smokers to attend an occasional follow-up session reminding them of the hazards of smoking, the NIH group encouraged training in relapse-prevention strategies much earlier in the stages of quitting.

Researchers will continue to study all aspects of substance abuse in an effort to help many more of us become "former users" or, better yet, to avoid altogether the life disruption that substance abuse brings.

Summing Up

Substance Use and Abuse: Some Basic Facts

1. The combined health hazards and costs of drug abuse are incalculable. During pregnancy, many drugs will cross the placenta and act as teratogens to adversely affect fetal development.

2. Drugs affect behavior by influencing the activity of neurons at their synapses. Some (agonists) do so by mimicking natural neurotransmitters, others (antagonists) by blocking their action, and still others do so by enhancing or inhibiting the reuptake of neurotransmitters in the synapse.

3. Drug addiction is a pattern of behavior characterized by dependence, the development of tolerance, and the presence of a withdrawal syndrome when the drug is not available.

4. Psychoactive drugs act on the central nervous system to alter emotional and cognitive functioning. Stimulants, such as caffeine and cocaine, increase activity in the central nervous system and produce feelings of euphoria.

Depressants, such as alcohol and the opiates, reduce activity in the central nervous system and produce feelings of relaxation. Hallucinogenic drugs, such as marijuana and LSD, alter perception and distort reality.

Models of Addiction

5. Biomedical models propose that dependence is a chronic disease that produces abnormal physical functioning. One aspect of these models is based on evidence that some people inherit a biological vulnerability toward dependence. The withdrawal-relief hypothesis suggests that drugs deplete dopamine and other key neurotransmitters. Another model proposes that psychoactive drugs are habit-forming because they overstimulate the brain's dopamine reward system.

6. Reward models suggest that the pleasurable effects of psychoactive drugs provide the initial motivation for repeated use. All major drugs of abuse, including nicotine and the other stimulants, overstimulate the brain's reward system.

7. Shortcomings in the biomedical and reward models of addiction were the impetus for social learning models, which view addiction as shaped by learning and by other social and cognitive factors.

Alcohol Use and Abuse

8. Alcohol depresses activity in the nervous system, clouds judgment, and is linked to a variety of diseases. Alcohol is also involved in half of all traffic accidents. Genes play a role in alcohol dependence, especially in men. Psychosocial factors such as peer pressure, a difficult home environment, and tension reduction may contribute to problem drinking.

9. Individuals marked by behavioral undercontrol and negative emotionality are especially prone to alcohol dependence. As is true of all psychoactive drugs, alcohol's impact depends in part on the user's personality, mood, past experiences with the drug, and expectations regarding its effects. Alcohol abuse is continued drinking that becomes linked with health problems and impaired functioning. Alcohol dependence is an abnormal state of physical dependence characterized by loss of control over drinking behavior. Alcohol dependence is generally accompanied by tolerance.

10. Alcohol treatment usually begins with detoxification from alcohol under medical supervision. Counseling, psychotherapy, and support groups such as AA also may help. Pharmacological treatments for alcohol dependence include aversion therapy, which triggers nausea if alcohol is consumed. Antidepressants such as Prozac may help reduce alcohol cravings.

Tobacco Abuse

11. Cigarette smoking is the single most preventable cause of death in the Western world today. A stimulant that affects virtually every physical system in the body, nicotine induces powerful physical dependence and a withdrawal syndrome. Social pressures most often influence the initiation of smoking.

12. Most people start smoking in their teenage years. Once a person begins smoking, a variety of psychological, behavioral, social, and biological variables contribute to make it difficult to abstain from nicotine. Researchers have reported a connection between smoking and the gene for a dopamine transporter—a protein that "vacuums up" dopamine after it has been released by a neuron.

13. According to the nicotine-titration model, long-term smokers may smoke in order to maintain a constant level of nicotine in their bodies. Smoking prevention programs that focus on refusal skills and other inoculation techniques prior to the eighth grade may be the best solution to the public health problems associated with smoking.

14. The most successful antismoking advertisements provide culturally sensitive nonsmoking peer role models that shift people's overall image of what behaviors are "normal" and valuable within one's peer group.

15. No single treatment has proved most effective in helping smokers quit smoking. Most programs have an extremely high relapse rate. Modern treatments for smoking deal with psychological factors through relapse prevention and physiological factors through nicotine replacement.

Key Terms and Concepts

drug abuse, p. 227
blood–brain barrier, p. 228
teratogens, p. 228
agonist, p. 229
antagonist, p. 230
drug addiction, p. 230
dependence, p. 230
withdrawal, p. 230
drug use, p. 230

psychoactive drugs, p. 231
drug potentiation, p. 232
concordance rate, p. 233
gateway drug, p. 234
blood alcohol level (BAL), p. 237
Korsakoff's syndrome, p. 239
fetal alcohol syndrome (FAS), p. 240
behavioral disinhibition, p. 241
alcohol dependence, p. 242

delirium tremens, p. 242
alcohol abuse, p. 243
behavioral undercontrol, p. 245
negative emotionality, p. 245
tension-reduction hypothesis, p. 245
alcohol expectancies, p. 246
aversion therapy, p. 247
nicotine-titration model, p. 254
satiation, p. 260

Part 4 | Chronic and Life-Threatening Illnesses

Cardiovascular Disease and Diabetes

*B*ryan McIver, M.D.—a dedicated young endocrinologist at the Mayo Clinic—was driving to his laboratory to check on an experiment. He thought nothing of the mild case of indigestion he'd been feeling since having a curry dinner with some friends. Mild stomach acidity was something he often experienced, so it seemed like a normal night.

When he arrived at the hospital, he again felt some discomfort in his chest, but he ignored it. When he walked past the emergency room 3 minutes later, however, things changed dramatically. In his words, "the world went blank . . . and I died."

What happened was a sudden and complete blockage of one of his heart's main coronary blood vessels. Within seconds, McIver's heart floundered into a chaotic rhythm, his blood pressure dropped to zero, the oxygen supply to his brain was cut off, and he passed into unconsciousness.

When the brain doesn't have oxygen, it begins to die within about 3 minutes. After 6 minutes, brain death occurs, and there is almost no chance for recovery. This would almost certainly have happened to McIver had his heart attack happened a minute earlier as he strolled through the darkened parking lot or a minute later once he'd reached the seclusion of his laboratory. Miraculously, he collapsed in the hospital corridor, just a few feet from the emergency room.

As a 37-year-old nonsmoker with no history of high blood pressure, vascular disease, or diabetes, McIver hardly fit the typical profile of a cardiac patient. Although one grandmother had died of a stroke (in her 80s), his family is generally long lived. McIver did have some risk factors. Although he was not overweight (6-foot-1 inch, 197 pounds), he rarely exercised, had a high-stress job, and had unhealthy cholesterol levels. Even so, less than a month before his heart attack, McIver had been given a clean bill of health during a thorough *physical exam. He was told only to try to exercise a bit more and lose a pound or two. Yet here he was, being resuscitated from the near-death experience of a massive heart attack.*

Although he continues his high-pressure work as a medical researcher, McIver has taken steps to improve his coronary risk factor profile to ensure that he lives a long, healthy life. Many others, however, are far less fortunate, and cardiovascular disease remains the number one cause of death in the United States and many other developed countries.

In this chapter, we will consider the biological, psychological, and social risk factors in two major chronic illnesses: cardiovascular disease (including high blood pressure, stroke, and heart disease) and diabetes. Although some of the risk factors in these diseases are beyond our control, many reflect lifestyle choices that are modifiable. Because each of these disorders involves the circulatory system, let's first review how the heart and circulatory system should work, then take a look at what goes wrong when each of these diseases strikes.

The Healthy Heart

As you'll recall from Chapter 3, the cardiovascular system comprises the blood, the blood vessels of the circulatory system, and the heart. About the size of your clenched fist and weighing on average only about 11 ounces, the heart consists of three layers of tissue: a thin outer layer, called the *epicardium;* a thin inner layer, called the *endocardium;* and a thicker middle layer, the heart muscle itself, or *myocardium* (derived from the Greek roots *myo* [muscle] and *kardia* [heart]). The myocardium is separated into four chambers that work in coordinated fashion to bring blood into the heart and then to pump it throughout the body. Like all muscles in the body, the myocardium needs a steady supply of oxygen and nutrients to remain healthy. And the harder the heart is forced to work to meet the demands of other muscles in the body, the more nutrients and oxygen it needs.

In one of Mother Nature's greatest ironies, the heart's blood supply comes not from the 5 or more quarts of blood pumped each minute through the internal chambers of the heart but rather from two branches of the aorta (the major artery from the heart) lying on the surface of the epicardium. These left and right *coronary arteries* branch into smaller and smaller blood vessels called arterioles until they become the capillaries that supply the myocardium with the blood it needs to function. (See page 63 for a diagram of the heart and the flow of blood through it.)

■ **cardiovascular disease (CVD)** disorders of the heart and blood vessel system, including stroke and coronary heart disease (CHD).

■ **coronary heart disease (CHD)** a chronic disease in which the arteries that supply the heart become narrowed or clogged; results from either atherosclerosis or arteriosclerosis.

■ **atherosclerosis** a chronic disease in which cholesterol and other fats are deposited on the inner walls of the coronary arteries, reducing circulation to heart tissue.

Cardiovascular Disease

When the blood supply from the coronary arteries is impeded beyond a critical point, the risk of developing cardiovascular disease increases substantially. About 60 million Americans suffer from some kind of disorder of the heart and blood vessel system, collectively referred to as **cardiovascular disease (CVD).** Leading all diseases in killing about 1,408,000 people (38.5 percent of all deaths) each year in the United States, CVD appears in many guises, including stroke and **coronary heart disease (CHD),** a chronic illness in which the arteries that supply the heart become narrowed or clogged and cannot supply enough blood to the heart. Before discussing the biological, social, and psychological factors that contribute to the onset of these diseases, we need to describe their underlying physical causes: atherosclerosis and arteriosclerosis.

The Causes: Atherosclerosis and Arteriosclerosis

Most cases of CVD result from **atherosclerosis,** a condition in which the linings of the arteries thicken with an accumulation of cholesterol and other fats. As these *atherosclerotic plaques* develop, the arterial passageways become narrowed, impeding the flow of blood through the coronary arteries (Figure 9.1). Although plaques tend to develop in most people in their thirties and forties, these plaques will not threaten their health—at least not until age 70 or older. Those not so fortunate, like Bryan McIver, may develop damaging plaques as early as their twenties or thirties—or even younger.

Inflammation in the circulating blood (*systemic inflammation*) can contribute to the development of atherosclerosis and help trigger heart attacks and strokes. As we saw in Chapter 3, inflammation is the body's response to injury, and blood clotting is often part of that response. Although researchers are not certain what causes the low-grade inflammation that seems to put otherwise healthy people at increased risk for atherosclerosis, many believe

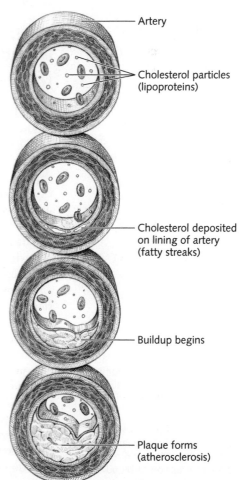

Artery

Cholesterol particles (lipoproteins)

Cholesterol deposited on lining of artery (fatty streaks)

Buildup begins

Plaque forms (atherosclerosis)

Figure 9.1

Atherosclerosis Atherosclerosis is a common disease in which cholesterol and other fats are deposited on the walls of coronary arteries. As the vessel walls become thick and hardened, they narrow, reducing the circulation to areas normally supplied by the artery. Atherosclerotic plaques cause many disorders of the circulatory system. How atherosclerosis begins is not clear; possibly, injury to the artery causes scavenger macrophages to attack cholesterol deposits.

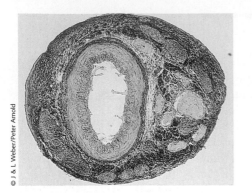

© J & L Weber/Peter Arnold

Figure 9.2

Arteriosclerosis In arteriosclerosis, the coronary arteries lose their elasticity and are unable to expand and contract as blood flows through them.

■ **arteriosclerosis** also called "hardening of the arteries," a disease in which blood vessels lose their elasticity.

■ **angina pectoris** a condition of extreme chest pain caused by a restriction of the blood supply to the heart.

■ **myocardial infarction (MI)** a heart attack; the permanent death of heart tissue in response to an interruption of blood supply to the myocardium.

that a chronic bacterial or viral infection might be the underlying cause (Desvarieux and others, 2003). One of the proteins that increases during the inflammatory response, *C-reactive protein (CRP)*, is increasingly being used to assess a person's risk of CVD. The risk for heart attack in people with the highest CRP levels is twice that of people whose CRP levels are at the lowest levels (Genest, 2004; Mazer & Rabbani, 2004).

Closely related to atherosclerosis is **arteriosclerosis,** or "hardening of the arteries" (Figure 9.2). In this condition, the coronary arteries lose their elasticity, making it difficult for them to expand and contract. (Imagine trying to stretch a dried-out rubber band.) This makes it difficult for them to handle the large volumes of blood needed during physical exertion. In addition, a blood clot is much more likely to form in, and block, a coronary artery that has lost its elasticity due to arteriosclerosis.

The Diseases: Angina Pectoris, Myocardial Infarction, and Stroke

Left unchecked, atherosclerosis and arteriosclerosis may advance for years before a person experiences any symptoms. This was the case with Dr. McIver. Once the process gets underway, however, the risk of developing one of three diseases increases with time.

The first begins with a gradual narrowing of the blood vessels. Any part of the body that depends on blood flow from an obstructed artery is subject to damage. For example, if the narrowing affects arteries in the legs, a person may experience leg pain while walking. When the arteries that supply the heart are narrowed with plaques, restricting blood flow to the heart—a condition called *ischemia*—the person may experience a sharp, crushing pain in the chest, called **angina pectoris.** Although most angina attacks usually pass within a few minutes without causing permanent damage, ischemia is a significant predictor of future coronary incidents.

Although angina attacks can occur anytime—including while a person is sleeping—they typically occur during moments of unusual exertion, because the body demands that the heart pump more oxygenated blood than it is accustomed to handling—for example, when a casual runner tries to complete a 26-mile marathon. Angina may also occur during strong emotional arousal or exposure to extreme cold or heat. Mental stress during daily life, including feelings of tension, frustration, and sadness, increases the risk of ischemia (Rosenfeldt and others, 2004).

The second, much more serious cardiac disorder occurs when a plaque ruptures within a blood vessel, releasing a sticky mass that can further reduce blood flow or even obstruct it completely. Within seconds of the complete obstruction of a coronary artery, a heart attack, or **myocardial infarction (MI),** occurs, and a portion of the myocardium begins to die (an *infarct* is an area of dead tissue). Unlike angina, which lasts only a brief time, MI involves a chronic deficiency in the blood supply and thus causes permanent damage to the heart.

The third possible manifestation of cardiovascular malfunction is cerebrovascular disease, or **stroke.** Strokes affect 500,000 Americans annually, claiming more than 150,000 lives each year. They are the third leading cause of death, after myocardial infarctions and cancer (Arias and others, 2003). The most common type of stroke—*ischemic stroke*—occurs when plaques or a clot obstruct an artery, blocking the flow of blood to an area of the brain (Figure 9.3). *Hemorrhagic stroke* occurs when a blood vessel bursts inside the brain, increasing pressure on the cerebrum and damaging it by pressing it against the skull. Hemorrhagic stroke is associated with high blood pressure, which stresses the artery walls until they break, or exposes a weak spot in an artery wall (*aneurysm*) that balloons out because of the pressure of the blood circulating inside.

The effects of stroke may include loss of speech or difficulty understanding speech, numbness, weakness or paralysis of a limb or in the face, headaches, blurred vision, and dizziness. Strokes usually damage neural tissue on one side of the brain, with a resulting loss of sensation on the opposite side of the body. An estimated 11 million American adults each year (4 percent of the population) have "silent strokes," which damage tiny clusters of cells inside the brain but cause no immediately obvious symptoms. These strokes tend not to be detected until, over time, memory loss, dizziness, slurred speech, and other classic stroke symptoms begin to appear.

Diagnosis and Treatment

Medicine has made great strides in diagnosing and treating cardiovascular disease in recent years. Although CVD was once a quiet killer with seemingly no warning signals, there now is an array of techniques for detecting its precursors—atherosclerosis and arteriosclerosis—early in their development. And while a heart attack was once an almost certain death sentence, in many cases today patients can be successfully treated with medication or with such techniques as angioplasty, bypass surgery, or even a heart transplant.

Diagnostic Tests

The most commonly used test of cardiac health is an **electrocardiogram (ECG or EKG),** in which electrodes attached to key points on the body measure the electrical discharges given off by the heart as it beats. A graphic representation of the discharges can reveal patterns of abnormal heart rhythms (*arrhythmia*), although in many cases abnormalities are not apparent unless the heart is stressed. When this is suspected, doctors administer an *exercise electrocardiogram,* or stress test, which is essentially an EKG done while a person walks or runs on a treadmill.

Another scanning technique, the *echocardiogram,* uses the echo of sound waves bounced against the chest to create an image of the heart. This image can

© Mehau Kulyk/Science Photo Library/Photo Researchers

Figure 9.3

Stroke Damages the Brain
This CT scan of the brain of a 70-year-old stroke victim shows that when blood flow to the brain is blocked, cells in the brain may be destroyed. The darkened area on the right shows where brain tissue has died because of an inadequate blood supply. The lack of blood may be due to an obstruction in a cerebral artery or to the hemorrhaging of a weakened artery wall. The result is paralysis or weakness on the left side of the body (since the tissue destroyed is on the right side of the brain).

■ **stroke** a cerebrovascular accident that results in damage to the brain due to lack of oxygen; usually caused by atherosclerosis or arteriosclerosis.

■ **electrocardiogram (ECG or EKG)** a measure of the electrical discharges that emanate from the heart.

Remember:

CVD = cardio**vascular** disease (includes heart disease and stroke)

CHD = coronary **heart** disease

© Greenlar/The Image Works

Coronary Angiography In this method of diagnosis, a small cardiac catheter is threaded through an artery into the aorta, then to the coronary artery suspected of blockage. The dye injected through the catheter enables the surgeon to x-ray the artery (see video monitor) and locate the blockage.

■ **coronary angiography** a diagnostic test for coronary heart disease in which dye is injected so that x-rays can reveal any obstructions in the coronary arteries.

■ **coronary artery bypass graft** cardiac surgery in which a small piece of a healthy vein from elsewhere in the body is grafted around a blocked coronary artery, allowing blood to flow more freely to a portion of the heart.

■ **coronary angioplasty** cardiac surgery in which an inflatable catheter is used to open a blocked coronary artery.

reveal damage to the myocardium, the presence of tumors or blood clots, valve disorders, and even weakened regions of arteries where aneurysms have formed.

Coronary angiography is the most accurate means of diagnosing CHD. A small cardiac catheter (a thin, flexible tube) is threaded through an artery (typically in the groin) into the aorta, and from there into a coronary artery that is suspected to be blocked with plaque. Dye is injected through the catheter so that the artery becomes visible when x-rays are taken, revealing the extent of the blockage. Patients remain awake and only partially sedated during the procedure.

Treatments

Depending on the severity of the problem, coronary disease patients may be given medication to treat or prevent cardiac malfunction, or they may need surgery.

Cardiac Medications Several types of drugs may be used to treat CHD. These include *nitroglycerine,* which increases the blood supply to the heart and stabilizes the heart electrically; *beta-blockers* and *calcium-channel blockers,* which lower blood pressure and reduce the pumping demands placed on the heart; *vasodilators,* which expand narrowed blood vessels; and *anticoagulants,* which help prevent the formation of blood clots. If a heart attack is diagnosed within the first few hours, doctors commonly give an intravenous infusion of a *thrombolytic agent* to quickly dissolve any blood clots.

Cardiac Surgery If angiography reveals substantial blockage in one or more coronary arteries, several surgical treatments may be recommended. In **coronary artery bypass graft** surgery, an incision is made in the patient's breastbone, and a small piece of a vein is removed from elsewhere in the body (typically from a leg but sometimes from an arm or the chest) and grafted around the region of a blocked or narrowed artery. The bypass allows blood to circumvent the blockage and flow more freely to the undernourished section of myocardium. Bypass surgery is typically recommended when blockages are severe and when the patient has not responded to other forms of treatment.

Another surgical intervention is **coronary angioplasty.** In this procedure, a catheter is threaded into a leg artery up into a blocked coronary artery, and a balloon at the tip is then inflated to press the plaque against the wall of the blood vessel. The balloon is then deflated and the catheter removed. In most cases, a fine metallic mesh tube called a *stent* is inserted into the artery to reduce the likelihood that it will become narrowed again. In other cases, an *atherectomy* is performed, and blockages are surgically removed or destroyed by laser, a rotating blade, or a diamond-studded drill.

Although medication and surgical procedures have been fairly successful in prolonging life in heart patients, some medical researchers are taking an entirely different approach that attempts to get around the fact that the heart, unlike other muscles, does not regenerate after it is damaged. Among the promising new techniques is transplanating embryonic muscle cells into diseased portions of the myocardium. Still in the earliest stages of development, this experimental treatment may someday restore function to human hearts damaged by myocardial infarctions.

Framingham's Risk Factors for Cardiovascular Disease

What causes plaque to form in the coronary arteries? Why do the coronary arteries of some people escape the buildup of scar tissue while those of others become obstructed at a young age? Research has identified a number of risk factors that are linked to CVD. Much of this knowledge comes from the Framingham Heart Study, one of the most celebrated epidemiological studies in the history of medicine. When the study began in 1948, the mortality rate due to CVD in the United States was nearly 500 cases per 100,000 people. This rate increased to a peak of 586.8 cases per 100,000 in 1950 and has dropped steadily ever since (Figure 9.4). Much of the credit for this dramatic improvement in mortality rates is due to "healthy heart" initiatives that stem from the Framingham study. The results of this remarkable study have undoubtedly extended the lives of millions.

Before Framingham, epidemiologists studied disease by examining medical records and death certificates. Framingham set a new standard for epidemiological research by inaugurating the concept of studying the health of living persons over time. This landmark study used a *prospective design* that included 5,209 healthy people in the small town of Framingham, Massachusetts.

The plan of the original researchers was to follow the subjects for 20 years to see what factors—demographic, biological, and/or psychological—predicted the development of CVD. Although more than half of the original study group has died, the study has continued with researchers now also collecting data from the children of the original participants.

Every 2 years, the original participants received a complete physical exam that included an electrocardiogram, blood pressure test, and more than 80 separate medical tests. (Their children have exams every 4 years.) In addition, each participant completed a battery of psychological tests and health questionnaires. The researchers asked questions about the participants' level of anxiety, sleeping habits, nervousness, alcohol and tobacco use, level of education, and their typical response to anger.

The Framingham study has identified two basic categories of *risk factors* for CVD: those that are largely

Figure 9.4

Annual U.S. Cardiovascular Disease Mortality Although the mortality rate from CVD has decreased in the United States and other affluent countries, it has increased in Eastern Europe and the developing world. In Europe, for instance, the CVD mortality rates range between 981 and 1,841 per 100,000 people. In the Western Pacific and Southeast Asia, CVD mortality rates are as high as 3,527 and 3,752 per 100,000 people, respectively (WHO, 2000).

Sources: National Center for Health Stastics. (2005). *Health, United States.* Washington, D.C.: U.S. Government Printing Office. Table 36, pp. 193–195; World Health Organization. (2000). *The World Health Report, 2000.* Geneva: World Health Organization, Annex Table 3, pp. 164–169.

uncontrollable, such as family history, age, and gender; and those that are more controllable, such as obesity, hypertension, cholesterol level, and tobacco use. Of course, there is some overlap in these dimensions, because there are controllable and uncontrollable elements to almost any risk factor. Still, for organizational purposes, we will follow the Framingham study's break-down.

Uncontrollable Risk Factors

A number of risk factors for CVD stem from genetic or biological conditions that are largely beyond our control.

Family History and Age

Family history strongly predicts CVD. This is especially true for those who have a close male relative who suffered a heart attack before age 55 or a close female relative who had a heart attack before age 65. Advancing age is also a risk factor for CVD. Indeed, approximately one-half of all CVD victims are over the age of 65.

Gender

The risk of CVD also rises sharply in men after age 40. Except in women who smoke cigarettes, the risk of CVD remains low until menopause, when, as we will explain, it begins to accelerate. However, the risk is still much higher among men until about age 65. In fact, men have roughly the same rate of CVD as women who are 10 years older (American Heart Association, 2004). Although the gap narrows with advancing age, this gender difference explains in part why women live longer than men do. In all developed countries and most developing countries, women outlive men by as many as 10 years. U.S. life expectancy at birth is currently about 80 years for women and 74 years for men.

Some experts believe that the gender difference in CVD mortality may be caused by differences in the sex hormones testosterone and estrogen. Testosterone has been linked with aggression, competitiveness, and other behaviors that are thought to contribute to heart disease (Sapolsky, 1998). Coincidentally, testosterone levels increase during early adulthood, just when the difference in mortality between men and women is at its peak. Some researchers therefore attribute the spike in mortality to "testosterone toxicity" (Perls & Fretts, 1998).

Although women may be at lower risk for CVD than men, heart disease takes the lives of more American women than any other cause, affecting one of about every three women (as opposed to one in eight for breast cancer). Still, many women and their doctors believe that breast cancer is the biggest threat to their health, despite the fact that CVD takes the lives of five times as many women as breast cancer (Figure 9.5). This may explain why men who complain of chest pain are more likely to be referred for heart diagnostic tests than women and why women are less likely to receive cholesterol-lowering drugs than men, despite having similar blood levels of cholesterol (Fischman, 2000).

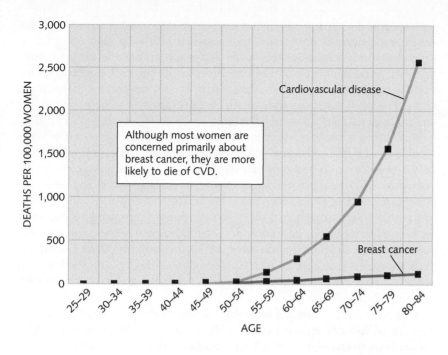

Figure 9.5

Mortality Rates for Cardio-vascular Disease and Breast Cancer in Women by Age Although women may be at lower risk for CVD than men, heart disease takes the lives of more American women than any other cause, affecting one of about every three women.

Source: National Center for Health Statistics. (1999). *Health, United States, 1997.* Washington, DC: U.S. Government Printing Office.

Men and women also differ in their prognosis for recovery following a heart attack. Compared to men, women are twice as likely to die following a heart attack. Among survivors, women are more likely to suffer a second heart attack and more likely to die after bypass surgery than men are.

Several factors may explain these differences. For one, women with CVD tend to be older than their male counterparts. In addition, CVD tends to be recognized sooner in men than in women, perhaps reflecting the medical bias that CVD is more of a male problem. And until recently, women have been underrepresented in clinical studies of CVD. As a result, the gold standard in diagnosing and treating CVD is based on male physiology.

Studies have also shown that men receive more aggressive diagnostic and treatment procedures than do women (Ayanian & Epstein, 1997; Mehilli and others, 2002). Men, for example, are twice as likely to be referred for coronary angiography and bypass surgery. This gender bias is particularly strong for patients presenting CHD symptoms in the context of stressful life events (Chiaramonte & Friend, 2006).

Race and Ethnicity

The prevalence of CVD also varies across racial and ethnic groups. Compared to Americans of European ancestry, for example, African-Americans are at increased risk, and Asian-Americans and Hispanic-Americans are at lower risk (American Heart Association, 2004). Economic factors may contribute to these differences. People of low socioeconomic status (SES) tend to have more total risk factors for CVD, including high-fat diets, smoking, and stressful life experiences such as racial discrimination (Gillum and others, 1998), and African-Americans are disproportionately represented among groups with lower SES.

Lack of exercise may also be a factor. As a group, affluent people tend to exercise more, perhaps because they have more free time, can more easily afford exercise equipment, or may be better informed about the hazards of sedentary living. European-American women, for example, are two to three times as active as African-American women during leisure time (Nevid and others, 1998).

It is natural to wonder whether ethnic and racial differences in risk of CVD would persist if disparities in education, family income, and disease risk factors for CVD did not. To find out, Marilyn Winkleby and her colleagues (1998) compared CVD risk factors among groups of African-American, Hispanic-American, and European-American women. Regardless of their ethnic background, low-SES women had elevated risk factors compared to high-SES women. However, after education and family income were controlled for, African-American and Hispanic-American women still had more risk factors than European-American women. These findings strongly indicate that both ethnicity and socioeconomic factors are involved in determining our risk of developing CVD.

Differences in psychosocial stress such as single parenting, may also help explain racial and ethnic disparities in CVD (Macera and others, 2001). Many African-American neighborhoods are segregated from the general population and include primarily low SES, female-headed families (Jargowsky, 1997). For example, a 1990 study of urban neighborhoods in which at least 40 percent of the households fell below the poverty line found that nearly 75 percent of African-American families were female headed. These women are more likely to die of coronary disease, perhaps as a result of the high levels of stress associated with raising a family without a partner (Leclere and others, 1998).

Another factor in racial and ethnic differences in CVD mortality rates involves limited access to and use of health care, as well as preferential medical treatment. As noted in Chapter 6, there are vast differences among ethnic groups in the availability of affordable health care. Furthermore, African-Americans—male or female—are less likely than white males to receive aggressive treatments such as bypass surgery and angioplasty. This double standard of care may be due to many factors, including, of course, discrimination, which causes some minority patients to mistrust the health care system in general (Peterson, 1997).

Controllable Risk Factors

Uncontrollable risk factors do not necessarily doom a person to death by heart attack. Knowing one's inherent risk profile is an important step in reducing the risk of CVD, however, because it allows high-risk individuals to minimize their total risk profile by changing those things they *can* control. Even with a family history of heart disease, for example, a person can reduce overall risk by working toward lowering blood pressure, eating a healthy diet, exercising regularly, and maintaining a normal body weight. These efforts can reap huge benefits. For instance, the Chicago Heart Association Detection Project evaluated the health outcomes for men between ages 18 and 39, men between 40 and 59, and women between ages 40 and 59 years. Younger men with the healthiest lifestyles had a life expectancy 9.5 years longer than other men in their age group. For healthy men aged 40 to 59 years, life expectancy was extended by 6 years. For women with the healthiest lifestyles, life was extended by 5.8 years (Stamler and others, 1999).

Hypertension

Blood pressure is the force exerted by blood as it pushes out against the walls of the arteries. When pressure is too high, it can damage the vessels and lead to atherosclerosis. Before the Framingham study, physicians believed that blood pressure increased as a natural consequence of aging. A rule of thumb had been that normal systolic blood pressure was equal to one's age plus 100. Thus, a 65-year-old was considered normal if his or her systolic pressure was as high as 165. We now know that the risk of CVD, beginning at 115/75 mmHg, doubles with each increment of 20/10 mmHg (Chobanian and others, 2003).

Under new guidelines issued in 2003, blood pressure is considered normal if it is below 120/80 mmHg (Chobanian and others, 2003). Although the condition is not called **hypertension** until it consistently exceeds 140/90, with the increased incidence of hypertension-related mortality, the Centers for Disease Control and Prevention recently introduced a *prehypertension* category (blood pressure of 120–139/80–89 mmHg) associated with an increased risk of progression to full-blown hypertension (Chobanian and others, 2003).

Most cases of high blood pressure are classified as *primary,* or *essential, hypertension,* meaning that the exact cause is unknown. Hypertension is the result of the interaction of biological, psychological, and social factors. Obesity, lack of exercise, dietary salt, and excessive stress can produce hypertension in biologically predisposed people. Hypertension is also related to anxiety and anger, especially in middle-aged men. In a major longitudinal study, researchers measured anxiety, anger, and blood pressure in middle-aged and older men. An 18- to 20-year follow-up revealed that men 45 to 59 who scored high on a standardized measure of anxiety were twice as likely to develop hypertension (Markovitz and others, 1993).

Stress is also linked with hypertension, particularly among people who have poor coping mechanisms, or limited coping resources. Exposure to environmental stressors at a young age can be particularly harmful. Adolescents who report experiencing large numbers of chronic, uncontrollable negative family stressors exhibit greater systolic blood pressure throughout the day, regardless of their gender, ethnicity, body mass index, and activity level (Brady & Matthews, 2006). These early experiences may increase their risk of developing hypertension later in life.

Heredity plays a role in hypertension as well, as evidenced by the fact that the prevalence of hypertension varies widely among racial and ethnic groups. For

■ **hypertension** a sustained elevation of diastolic and systolic blood pressure (exceeding 140/90).

Deadly Stress Kenneth Lay, 65, died of a heart attack unexpectedly just seven weeks after his 2006 conviction of conspiracy and fraud in his role as founder and former chairman of Enron. The experience of a severely stressful event can indeed trigger a myocardial infarction, and the stress of conviction and impending jail time appears to have been a contributor to Lay's death.

■ **cardiovascular reactivity** an individual's characteristic reaction to stress, including changes in heart rate, blood pressure, and hormones.

instance, the prevalence of hypertension among African-American women and men in the United States is among the highest in the world. Compared with European-Americans, African-Americans develop hypertension at a younger age, and their average blood pressures are much higher (American Heart Association, 2004).

Although genes may create a biological predisposition to hypertension, heredity alone cannot explain the widespread variation in the prevalence of hypertension among different ethnic and cultural groups. Within the African-American community, for instance, rates of hypertension vary substantially. Those with the highest rates are more likely to be middle-aged or older, overweight or obese, physically inactive, less educated, and to have diabetes (NHANES III, 2002). A number of researchers have proposed that the greater exposure to social and environmental stressors among lower-SES African-Americans, rather than genetic differences, may promote sodium retention by the kidneys, causing vasoconstriction and a corresponding increase in blood pressure (Anderson and others, 1992). Others have suggested that the prevalence of hypertension among African-Americans might reflect greater **cardiovascular reactivity (CVR)** to social stress—especially the stress of racial discrimination—in the form of larger increases in heart rate and blood pressure and a greater outpouring of epinephrine, cortisol, and other stress hormones. Researchers have found that acute exposure to stressors such as mental arithmetic tasks (Arthur and others, 2004), racially provocative speeches (Merritt and others, 2006), and role-playing scenarios such as being accused of shoplifting (Lepore and others, 2006) are associated with increases in cardiovascular activation (see Brondolo and others, 2003 for a review). Interestingly, low-SES African-American men tend to display greater CVR to racial stressors than high-SES African-American men *or women*. They also report significantly greater firsthand experience with racial prejudice (Krieger and others, 1998). As noted in Chapter 5, however, the impact of a stressor such as racism may depend on the individual's past experience and coping resources. The presence of other factors, including anger, defensiveness, interpersonal skills, and coping style all are potential mediators and moderators of CVR (Rutledge & Linden, 2003).

Obesity

Recall from Chapter 3 that high-density lipoprotein, or HDL, is the so-called good cholesterol, and low-density lipoprotein, or LDL, is the so-called bad cholesterol. Triglycerides, also called very-low-density lipoproteins (VLDL), are especially bad.

Excess body weight increases a person's risk of hypertension and all CVD, in part because of its association with high cholesterol. The risk of excess fat depends somewhat on how the fat is distributed. *Abdominal obesity* associated with excess fat in the midsection (the "beer belly") promotes the greatest risk of CVD, perhaps because it is often associated with lower levels of HDL cholesterol and higher triglyceride levels. People who carry excess weight in their midsections also have thicker artery walls, increasing blood pressure and the risk of stroke (De Michele and others, 2002). Indeed, waist circumference may be a more accurate predictor of hypertension than body mass index (Gus and others, 2004). Differences in where body fat is distributed may help to explain why men have higher rates of CVD than women, at least until menopause. Abdominal obesity is more common in men than women.

Cholesterol Level

Doctors have known for years that people with a genetically high level of cholesterol also have a high rate of CVD, beginning at a young age. Before the Framingham Heart Study, however, there was no prospective evidence that excess dietary cholesterol was a coronary risk factor. The Framingham study found that people with low serum cholesterol rarely developed CVD, whereas those with high levels had a high risk.

How High Is Too High? A blood cholesterol level lower than 200 milligrams per deciliter (mg/dl) is generally associated with a low risk of CVD. A level of 240 or greater doubles the risk.

Total cholesterol is only part of the story, however. As noted in Chapter 3, a more complete picture comes from comparing the relative amounts of *high-density lipoprotein (HDL)*, *low-density lipoprotein (LDL)*, and *triglycerides*. Men and women who have high total cholesterol levels and low HDL levels have the highest risk of CVD. However, even people with low levels of total cholesterol are at increased risk if these proportions are faulty. The higher a person's HDL cholesterol level is, the better, but a level below 40 mg/dL in adults is considered a risk factor for CVD (AHA, 2004).

Some studies have suggested that regular consumption of antioxidant nutrients (agents believed to promote health by reducing the buildup of cell-damaging waste products of normal metabolism), such as vitamin E, beta-carotene, selenium, and riboflavin (which are plentiful in fruits and vegetables), may help prevent CVD. Antioxidants neutralize oxygen free radicals and prevent them from causing the oxidation of LDL cholesterol (Stampfer and others, 1993). Oxidation would otherwise lead to injury, scarring, and the buildup of fatty plaque in the blood vessel walls. In one longitudinal study, researchers found that men with the highest levels of antioxidants had a two-thirds lower risk of CVD than those with the lowest levels (Morris and others, 1994).

Research also suggests that moderate alcohol consumption may lower total cholesterol and raise HDL levels. Consider the *French paradox:* Mortality rates from CVD are markedly lower in France than in other industrialized countries, despite the fact that the French people eat more rich, fatty foods; exercise less; and smoke more (Hackman, 1998). Studies suggest that the French may suffer less CVD because of their regular consumption of red wine, which contains natural chemical compounds called *flavonoids.* Scientists think biologically active flavonoids lower the risk of CVD in three ways: reducing LDL cholesterol, boosting HDL cholesterol, and slowing platelet aggregation, thereby lessening the chances of a blood clot forming (Hackman, 1998). Despite this interesting possible relationship between moderate wine consumption and a healthy heart, the issue remains controversial. We *do* know that excessive alcohol consumption increases the risk of suffering a myocardial infarction.

■ **metabolic syndrome** a cluster of conditions that occur together—including elevated blood pressure and insulin levels, excess body fat, and unhealthy cholesterol ratios—that increase a person's risk for heart disease, stroke, and diabetes.

Metabolic Syndrome

For an estimated 47 million Americans, obesity, hypertension, and a poor cholesterol profile combine into the **metabolic syndrome,** defined as three or more of the following:

■ Waist circumferance greater than 40 inches in men and 35 inches in women
■ Elevated serum triglyceride level
■ HDL cholesterol level less than 40 mg/dL in men and 50 mg/dL in women
■ Blood pressure of 130/85 mmHg or higher
■ Glucose intolerance (commonly found in those suffering from diabetes, as we will see)

People with the metabolic syndrome have a significantly higher risk of developing CVD and diabetes (NHANES III, 2002). The age-adjusted prevalence of metabolic syndrome varies substantially among racial and ethnic groups in the United States; it is highest among Mexican Americans (31.9 percent), followed by European-Americans (24.3 percent) and African-Americans (21.6 percent) (American Heart Association, 2004).

Tobacco Use

Smoking more than doubles the chances of having a heart attack and is linked to one of every five deaths due to CHD. Smokers have twice the risk of having a stroke and are less likely to survive an MI than are nonsmokers.

On the positive side, 1 year after quitting smoking, the risk of CVD decreases by 50 percent. Fifteen years after quitting, the relative risk of dying from CVD is about the same as that of a lifetime nonsmoker (American Heart Association, 2004). Since 1965, smoking in the United States has declined by more than 40 percent among people age 18 and older (*Health, United States,* 2005). Even so, 25.2 percent of men and 20.7 percent of women continue to smoke, with rates highest among those with only 9–11 years of education (35.4 percent), and people living below the poverty level (33.3 percent).

Psychosocial Factors in Cardiovascular Disease: The Type A Personality

Puzzled by the fact that many coronary patients were *not* obese, middle-aged men with elevated cholesterol, researchers decided that they must be overlooking something. So they broadened their search for risk factors that might offer an explanation. In the late 1950s, cardiologists Meyer Friedman and Ray Rosenman (1959) began to study personality traits that might predict coronary events. They found a coronary-prone behavior pattern that included competitiveness, a strong sense of time urgency, and hostility, which they labeled **Type A.** In contrast, people who are more relaxed and who are not overly pressured by time considerations tend to be coronary disease resistant. This they called **Type B** behavior.

In the 1960s and 1970s, hundreds of studies supported the association between Type A behavior and risk of future CVD in both men and women. In an effort to explain this relationship, researchers have focused on physiological differences between Type A and Type B people. Among their findings: Type A people have more rapid blood clotting and higher cholesterol and triglyceride levels under stress than their Type B counterparts (Lovallo & Pishkin, 1980). Type A people also often display greater autonomic arousal (see Chapter 3), elevated heart rate, and higher blood pressure in response to challenging events (Jorgensen and others, 1996). In relaxed situations, both types are equally aroused. When challenged or threatened, however, Type A people are less able to remain calm. This pattern of "combat ready" hyperreactivity is most likely to occur in situations in which Type A persons are subjected to some form of feedback evaluation of their performance (Lyness, 1993).

A secondary cluster of traits combining depression with high levels of anxiety—both of which are independently linked to hypertension and CVD (Rutledge & Hogan, 2002)—has also been observed in Type A individuals (Frasure-Smith and others, 1995). Depression appears to be particularly lethal, as shown by a 12-year Centers for Disease Control study (Anda and others, 1993). Depressed people were more vulnerable to CVD, even after the researchers controlled for differences in age, gender, smoking, and other CVD risk factors. Moreover, depressed people have four times the risk of recurrence of a heart attack compared to MI survivors with no depressive symptoms (Frasure-Smith and others, 1999).

Believing that the Type A syndrome was too global, researchers began to analyze component behaviors, including competitiveness, hostility, time urgency, and anger, to determine whether one or more of these components might more accurately predict CVD.

Competitiveness, Hostility, and Time Urgency

In a classic study, Charles Carver and David Glass (1978) attempted to learn whether Type As and Type Bs responded differently to anger-provoking situations or interruptions in their efforts to reach a goal. A Type A or a Type B student was placed in a room with an actor hired by the experimenters. In the first part of the experiment, the actor and the student were asked to solve a difficult wooden puzzle in a short period of time. In the *instigation condition,* the actor disrupted the student's attempts at the puzzle and made insulting comments about his or her performance (for example, "I don't know what's taking you so long; it's not that difficult!"). In the *no instigation* condition, the actor did not interact at all with the student.

In the second phase of the study, the student was required to "teach" the actor a concept by delivering an electric shock whenever the actor made an incorrect response (no actual shocks were delivered). The student was free to

■ **Type A** Friedman and Rosenman's term for competitive, hurried, hostile people who may be at increased risk for developing cardiovascular disease.

■ **Type B** Friedman and Rosenman's term for more relaxed people who are not pressured by time considerations and thus tend to be coronary-disease resistant.

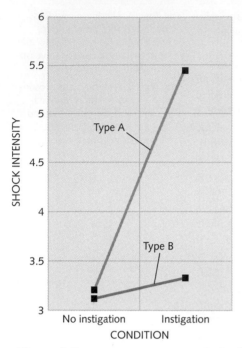

Figure 9.6

Type A Behavior and Hostility When provoked, Type A students retaliated against their instigators by choosing higher shock intensities. Type B students were less likely to show this tendency to retaliate. Note that the numbers representing shock intensity are arbitrary numbers; the students read their own meaning into each level of intensity.

Source: Carver, C. S., & Glass, D. C. (1978). Coronary-prone behavior pattern and interpersonal aggression. *Journal of Personality and Social Psychology, 36,* 361–366.

choose which of 10 shock intensities would be delivered each time the actor made an error.

In the instigation condition, Type A students chose significantly higher shock intensities than did Type B students. However, in the no instigation condition, both types administered about the same level of shock. These results suggest that when provoked or prevented from reaching a goal, Type As have a more hostile reaction than do Type Bs (Figure 9.6).

In another probe of the key variables in the Type A–CVD relationship, researchers used data from the 20-year Coronary Artery Risk Development in Young Adults (CARDIA) study of over 5,000 women and men between the ages of 18 and 30 years to investigate the relationships among three components of Type A behavior (time urgency, hostility, and competitiveness) and risk of developing hypertension. Regardless of participants' age, sex, race, education, body mass index, alcohol consumption, and fitness levels, those characterized by the highest levels of two variables—time urgency and hostility (but not competitiveness)—had an 80 percent greater risk of developing hypertension (Lijing and others, 2003).

Lately, researchers have focused most closely on hostility as the possible "toxic core" of Type A behavior. Hostility has been characterized as a chronic negative outlook that encompasses feelings (anger), thoughts (cynicism and mistrust of others), and overt actions (aggression). As such, it is considered an attitude that is generally longer in duration than specific emotions that trigger short-lived strong physical arousal. With hostility, as with other attitudes, it's not so much *what* is said as *how* it is said (Kop & Krantz, 1997). Erika Rosenberg and her colleagues (1998), for example, showed that facial expressions of contempt were significantly related to hostility and defensiveness (defined as the tendency to deny the existence of undesirable traits in oneself).

Redford Williams and his colleagues administered a questionnaire called the Cook-Medley Hostility Scale (Ho Scale) to a large group of coronary patients. They found a striking correlation between patients' scores on the questionnaire and the severity of blockage in their coronary arteries. Hostile patients had significantly more severe coronary artery blockages than did less hostile patients (Williams, 1996).

In another study, Richard Shekelle and his colleagues (1983) reviewed the hostility scores of middle-aged men who had earlier participated in a study of Type A behavior. High hostility—but not designation as Type A—accurately predicted a patient's risk of suffering a fatal heart attack as well as his risk of dying at an early age from other stress-related diseases. The hostility–CVD relationship remained significant even when other risk factors (such as smoking, high serum cholesterol, and family history) were controlled for.

Compared with high blood pressure or smoking, how strong an effect does hostility have on coronary risk? Hostility is nearly as poisonous (Figure 9.7).

Figure 9.7

Hostility and Heart Attacks Even after other risk factors (such as hypertension and smoking) are controlled for, the highest scorers on a hostility scale are more than 1.5 times as likely to suffer an acute MI as are the lowest scorers. Similarly, people with untreated hypertension are 3.1 times as likely to suffer an acute MI as are people without hypertension. For treated hypertension, the relative risk drops to 2.0. Compared with nonsmokers, those who smoke 30 g of tobacco per day (about one and a half packs of cigarettes) have a relative risk of 2.8. Angry people are 2.66 times as likely to have an acute MI as are nonangry people.

Sources: Barefoot, J. C., Larsen, S., von der Lieth, L., & Schroll, M. (1995). Hostility, incidence of acute myocardial infarction, and mortality in a sample of older Danish men and women. *American Journal of Epidemiology, 142,* 477–484; Whiteman, M. C., Fowkes, F. G. R., Deary, I. J., & Lee, A. J. (1997). Hostility, cigarette smoking and alcohol consumption in the general population. *Social Science and Medicine, 44,* 1080–1096.

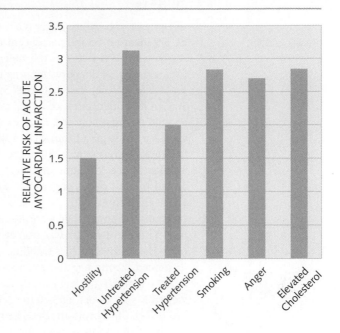

People with the highest scores on the Ho Scale are more than 1.5 times as likely to suffer an acute MI as are people with the lowest scores (Barefoot and others, 1995).

Some researchers have speculated that hostility may underlie the relationship between CVD and several seemingly uncontrollable risk factors, including gender, age, and possibly ethnicity. For example, men have a higher incidence of CVD than do women; they also tend to be more hostile. Interestingly, Karen Matthews has provided evidence that male children also have higher hostility scores than their female peers (Matthews and others, 1992). Both hostility scores and incidence of CVD increase after people reach age 40 (Colligan & Offord, 1988). Furthermore, African-American men, who have an extremely high incidence of CVD, score higher on standard hostility tests than do African-American women and white men (Scherwitz and others, 1991).

Although hostility is related to CVD mortality, its status as an independent risk factor for cardiovascular disease continues to be debated (Smith & Gallo, 2001). Hostility is also related to other behaviors that promote CVD, including obesity, hypertension, alcohol and tobacco use, negative life events, and little social support (Siegler and others, 1992). Children and adolescents who exhibit high hostility scores are also more likely to develop the metabolic syndrome than those who score low on measures of hostility (Raikkonen and others, 2003). These relationships have caused researchers to narrow their investigations to a specific component of hostility—anger.

In a controversial study, researchers noted a correlation between the estimated hostility scores of U.S. cities and the incidence of CVD. Philadelphia had the highest hostility score and the highest incidence of cardiovascular diseases (Huston, 1997). What other factors might explain this result?

Anger

In contrast to hostility, anger is a transient emotional response that is triggered by provocation or the perception of mistreatment (Hogan & Linden, 2004). *Anger expression* refers to the specific behaviors a person uses in response to feeling angry, with people tending toward either *expressive* (*anger-out*) or *suppressive* (*anger-in*) styles (Laux & Spielberger, 1983).

Can a sudden burst of anger lead to a heart attack? It does happen often enough to cause concern. By one estimate, 20 percent of fatal MIs occur in response to an angry outburst (Ferroli, 1996). In the massive Atherosclerosis Risk in Communities study, 256 of the 13,000 middle-aged participants had heart attacks. Janice Williams and her colleagues (2000) found that people who scored highest on an anger scale were three times more likely to have a heart attack than those with the lowest scores. People who scored in the moderate range on the anger scale were about 35 percent more likely to have a heart attack. This elevated risk was true even after taking into account the presence of other risk factors such as smoking, diabetes, elevated cholesterol, and obesity.

Indeed, strong negative emotions such as anger may be as dangerous to the heart as smoking, a high fat diet, or obesity. In one study, researchers interviewed MI survivors, ages 20 to 92, for information about their emotional state just before their heart attacks. The researchers devised a seven-level anger scale ranging from calm to very angry to enraged. Heart attacks were more than twice as likely to occur in the 2 hours that followed an episode of anger than at any other time. The largest jump in risk occurred at level 5 anger (enraged), in which the person is very angry and tense, with clenching fists or gritting teeth. Arguments with family members were the most frequent cause of anger, followed by conflicts at work and legal problems (Hilbert, 1994).

However, the anger that generates a heart attack may have been preceded by countless such episodes, reflecting a maladaptive pattern of coping with stress that has developed over a lifetime. In a massive longitudinal study, researchers studied the long-term effects of anger responses among lawyers divided according to their anger and hostility levels. Over the course of the 25-year study, there was a roughly equivalent rate of death due to coronary disease in Type A and Type B personalities. But when the researchers adjusted for hostility and anger, they found that the hostile and angry lawyers were dying at seven times the rate of the nonhostile and nonangry lawyers—in both Type A and Type B personalities (Williams, 1989).

Suppressed anger may be as hazardous to health as expressed anger. James Pennebaker (1992) has developed a general theory of inhibition that is based on the idea that to hold back one's thoughts or feelings requires work that, over time, results in levels of stress that can create or exacerbate illness. In support of this theory, cardiac patients who deny their anger or frustration are 4.5 times more likely to die within 5 years than are other cardiac patients (Bondi, 1997). Suppressed anger was an even stronger predictor of mortality than elevated cholesterol level or cigarette smoking.

Taken together, research studies of anger expression and suppression suggest that too much, or too little, can be hazardous to health. In a recent 2-year longitudinal study of over 23,000 male health professionals, researchers found that men with *moderate* levels of anger expression had a reduced risk of nonfatal MI and stroke compared with those with lower levels of anger expression, even after adjusting for other health behaviors and coronary risk factors (Eng and others, 2003).

More generally, there is evidence that a number of the main psychosocial factors implicated in CVD, including social isolation, clinical anxiety, depression, socioeconomic status, and job stress, may act at least partly through their effects on an individual's mood (Eng and others, 2003). Over an 18-month period, Tessa Pollard and Joseph Schwartz (2003) found women and men who reported the highest and most frequent levels of *tense arousal* (feeling anxious, jittery, and nervous) and negative emotions (feeling dissatisfied, sad, and sorry) had elevated blood pressure, compared with their more relaxed and happier counterparts. In addition, in the Normative Aging Study of older men, negative emotions strongly predicted the development of CHD even after adjusting for health behaviors, stress hormones, and sociodemographic differences among the participants (Kubzansky and others, 2006; Todaro and others, 2003).

Why Do Hostility and Anger Promote Cardiovascular Disease?

An angry, hostile personality predicts an increased risk of CVD, but how do these traits work their damage? The key theoretical models differ in their relative emphasis on biological, psychological, and social factors.

Psychosocial Vulnerability

Some theorists maintain that hostile adults lead more stressful lives and have low levels of social support, which, over time, exerts a toxic effect on cardiovascular health. In support of this *psychosocial vulnerability hypothesis,* researchers have found that chronic family conflict, unemployment, social isolation, and job-related stress are all linked to increased risk of CVD (Kop and others, 2001).

The Work Environment The work environment can be an important source of satisfaction or stress (Mills and others, 2004). As we saw in Chapter 5, jobs associated with high productivity demands, excessive overtime work, and conflicting requirements accompanied by little personal control tend to be especially stressful. Data from the 20-year CARDIA study reveal that *job strain,* defined as high job demands and low decision latitude, predicts the incidence of hypertension, even after adjusting for baseline blood pressure, education, body mass index, and age (Markovitz and others, 2004). Over time, it is not surprising then that assembly-line workers as well as those who wait tables and perform similarly stressful jobs are, in fact, more susceptible to coronary disease (Bosma and others, 1998). In addition, workers who feel they have been promoted too quickly or too slowly, those who feel insecure about their jobs, and those who feel that their ambitions are thwarted are more likely to report stress and to show higher rates of illness, especially coronary disease (Taylor and others, 1997).

Researchers have also found that especially complex jobs that make mental demands requiring skill and training may promote coronary disease, especially among hostile, hurried workers. Complex jobs may cause susceptible individuals to manifest Type A behavior because they elicit the impatience and hurriedness that is characteristic of the Type A person (Schaubroeck and others, 1994). In general, however, "white collar" workers evidence lower baseline blood pressure levels when compared with "blue collar" workers, even afer controlling for body mass index, smoking status, and other risk factors for hypertension (Gallo and others, 2004).

Social Support As we saw in Chapter 5, coping with stressful events is especially difficult when an individual feels cut off from others. William Ruberman and his colleagues (1984) found that 3 years after surviving an acute MI, those with a combination of high stress and social isolation had four times the death rate of people with low stress and strong social support.

Living alone after suffering a heart attack is also associated with a higher risk of a recurrence of CHD. Redford Williams (1996) found that coronary disease patients who were unmarried and/or had no one with whom they could share their innermost concerns were three times more likely to die in the next 5 years than patients who had a confidante—a spouse or a close friend. More recently, among a sample of 180 older adults, greater loneliness, low levels of emotional support, and lack of companionship were all strongly associated with an increased probability of CHD (Sorkin and others, 2002).

Other researchers have reported an elevated rate of coronary death among women who perceive little support either in the workplace or at home (Kawachi and others, 1994). They suggest that stress accompanied by social isolation and feelings of subordination are independent risk factors for CHD. This relationship held true even after the researchers controlled for other traditional risk factors such as hypertension, total serum cholesterol, obesity, and smoking. On a positive note, the perception of social support from supervisors and coworkers has a powerful moderating effect on workers' blood pressure during high-stress conditions (Karlin and others, 2003).

Interestingly, Julianne Holt-Lunstad and her colleagues (2003) have found that the quality of people's relationships with others actually predicts their blood pressure during everyday social interactions with these people. Interactions with family members and friends for whom the participants reported generally positive, supportive ties were accompanied by lower systolic blood pressure (measuring the force of the heart's contraction), while interactions with people for whom participants reported ambivalent feelings (both positive and negative emotions) were associated with elevations in systolic blood pressure.

The Health Behavior Explanation

We have seen that hostility, anger, job strain, and social isolation may affect health directly. Some researchers believe that they may also have an indirect effect on health. For example, people with poor support may not take care of themselves as well as those who have someone to remind them to exercise, eat in moderation, or take their medicine. Similarly, a person with a cynical attitude may perceive health-enhancing behaviors, such as adhering to a healthy diet and active lifestyle, as unimportant and may ignore warnings about smoking and other health-compromising behaviors. Hostility and anger have indeed been linked with excessive alcohol and caffeine consumption, greater fat and caloric intake, elevated LDL cholesterol, lower physical activity, greater body mass, hypertension, sleep problems, and nonadherence to medical regimens (Miller and others, 1996).

Psychophysiological Reactivity Model

Stress, hostility, and anger may act slowly over a period of years to damage the arteries and the heart. When we vent our anger, our pulse quickens, the heart pounds more forcefully, and blood clots more quickly. In addition, blood vessels constrict, blood pressure surges, and blood levels of free fatty acids increase. Our immunity also decreases as adrenaline, cortisol, and other stress hormones suppress the activity of disease-fighting lymphocytes.

To pinpoint the physiological bases of hostility, researchers have studied hostile men and women who were harassed while trying to perform a difficult mental task. The stress caused an unusually strong activation of the fight-or-flight response in these people. When challenged, they displayed significantly greater cardiovascular reactivity (CVR) in the form of larger increases in blood pressure and greater outpourings of epinephrine, cortisol, and other stress hormones (Kop & Krantz, 1997). Recent data from the Healthy Women Study also show that women who express Type A anger and symptoms of anxiety and depression also have impaired functioning in the endothelial cells lining the internal surface of the coronary arteries. Normally, these cells promote vascular health by releasing substances that cause the blood vessels to relax or contract as needed to promote homeostasis. When these cells do not work properly, this delicate balance is disrupted. Consequently, the coronary arteries may become constricted and inflamed, thus promoting the development of CHD (Harris and others, 2003).

Interestingly, nighttime cardiac response is normal in hostile people, suggesting the reaction is not innate but rather a direct response to daytime stressors. Hostile people apparently have a lower threshold for triggering their fight-or-flight response than do nonhostile people (Williams, 2001).

However, the association between anger expression and psychophysiological reactivity is far from perfect and varies with such factors as the tendency to dwell on anger-provoking events and a person's tendency to forgive others. Hypertensive women and men who ruminate—that is, agree with such statements as, "I think repeatedly about what I really would have liked to have done but did not"—tend to have higher resting blood pressure levels (Hogan & Linden, 2004). Conversely, college students who have a generally forgiving personality and are therefore less likely to ruminate have lower blood pressure levels and CVR during interviews about times when they felt betrayed by a parent or friend (Lawler and others, 2003).

The Biopsychosocial Model

Health psychologists have combined the insights of these findings to provide a biopsychosocial explanation for how hurriedness, hostility, and anger contribute to cardiovascular disease. This model suggests that in order for a chronic disease such as CVD to develop, a person must first have a physiological predisposition. This is determined by family history of CVD and previous health history (other diseases, poor diet, tobacco use, and so on). Whether or not CVD develops then depends on a variety of psychosocial factors in the person's life, including the level of stress from the work and home environments, and the availability of social support. Hostile individuals with a strong sense of time urgency tend to elicit aggressive behaviors from others, producing interpersonal conflict and more hostility. This in turn leads to a reduction in social support, more negative effect, and artery-damaging cardiac reactivity. Thus, hostile attitudes create a self-fulfilling prophecy for the mistrusting, hostile person by producing a hostile environment.

Fortunately, most people can minimize the health-compromising effects of hostility. Although changing one's personality is not easy, hostility can be countered with efforts to control hostile reactions and treat others as you would have them treat you.

Reducing the Risk of Cardiovascular Disease

Although epidemiological research has provided a wealth of information that should help us prevent cardiovascular disease—limit fat intake, quit smoking, lose excess weight, and get regular exercise—we persist in making heart-unhealthy choices. Working from an evolutionary perspective, some researchers believe that our poor decisions are made by brains that were shaped to cope with an environment substantially different from the one our species now inhabits (Nesse & Williams, 1998). On the African savanna, where our species originated, those who had a tendency to consume large amounts of usually scarce fat were more likely to survive famines that killed their thinner companions. Those with a rapid-fire fight-or-flight reaction had a clear advantage in hunting and reacting to hostile threats and were more likely to survive and pass on these traits to their offspring. And we, their descendants, still carry these evolved urges and hostile tendencies.

Health psychology aims to help us overcome these evolved tendencies by establishing heart-healthy habits and modifying behaviors that increase the risk of CVD. Lifelong behaviors such as a poor diet, tobacco use, and a sedentary lifestyle are particularly difficult to modify. Studies of high-risk children (those with elevated cholesterol, obesity, and hypertension) typically reveal that such children remained at increased risk of developing CVD throughout adulthood (Myers and others, 1995). Yet perception of control is also a factor. Patients who have experienced an MI or angina who report the highest levels of *perceived behavioral control* (see Chapter 6) over being able to exercise regularly, give up smoking, and modify other CVD risk behaviors are more likely to report doing so 1 year later (Johnston et al., 2004).

Next, we focus on interventions aimed at controlling hypertension, reducing elevated serum cholesterol, and reversing atherosclerosis. The most serious behavioral risk factor in CVD, cigarette smoking, was discussed in Chapter 8.

Controlling Hypertension

For every 1-point drop in diastolic blood pressure, which measures the pressure between heartbeats, there is an estimated 2 to 3 percent reduction in the risk of an MI (Massey and others, 2000). Interventions aimed at lowering high blood pressure typically begin with pharmacological treatment. However, because hypertension is often symptom free, many patients fail to adhere to prescribed treatment regimens.

Changing behavior can also go a long way toward lowering blood pressure. For example, lowering sodium intake can bring about significant improvement in blood pressure readings. Many people with hypertension are sodium sensitive, meaning that excess sodium raises their blood pressure. Because there is no test for sodium sensitivity, almost everyone with hypertension should restrict dietary sodium to 2,000 mg per day.

Numerous studies have shown that even moderate amounts of physical activity can help lower the resting blood pressure of people with hypertension (Ishikawa-Takata and others, 2003). It can also improve a person's cholesterol profile by increasing HDL cholesterol and reducing body mass index (Nordstrom and others, 2003). Even when exercise fails to reduce hypertension or improve a person's lipid profile, it conveys a heart-protecting benefit: Physically fit hypertensives with elevated cholesterol actually have a lower overall risk of CVD than unfit individuals who have normal blood pressure and cholesterol (Blair and others, 1989). Most impressively, data from the CARDIA study reveal that even after adjustment for age, race, sex, smoking, family history of hypertension, diabetes, and CHD, participants with low fitness levels (below the 20th percentile in performance on a treadmill test) were three to six times more likely to develop hypertension, diabetes, and the metabolic syndrome than participants with high fitness levels (above the 60th percentile) (Carnethon and others, 2003). Regular exercise is also associated with significant reductions in the risk of ischemic and hemorrhagic strokes (Lee and others, 2003).

To be most beneficial, physical exertion should occur in the context of leisure and not work. In a recent case-control study of 312 patients with stable

Risk Reduction—and Preventing Recurrence Regular exercise and good nutrition are significant factors in preventing CVD, and in preventing *recurrence* of CVD. At top, a former heart-attack victim (center) saw his illness as a wake-up call and changed his life. He now has the highest karate level in his area. The person above is improving his cholesterol ratios with a vegetarian diet and a glass of wine.

CHD, researchers found that participants who engaged in regular leisure time physical activity also had lower levels of C-reactive protein—a protein that we have seen to be linked to the inflammatory response—and interleukin 6, a proinflammatory cytokine linked with immunosuppression (see Chapter 4) (Rothenbacher and others, 2003). By contrast, *work-related* physical exertion was strongly associated with *increased* risk of CHD. These results suggest that one mechanism of the heart-protective effects of regular exercise is a beneficial effect on the body's inflammatory response.

Even if a person has had a heart attack, preventive behaviors can play an important role in controlling the negative effects of CVD. For example, exercise improves the heart's ability to pump blood to working muscles as well as the muscles' ability to extract and make use of oxygen from the blood. Neil Oldridge (1988) conducted a meta-analysis of studies involving over 4,000 heart attack patients. The results showed that patients who participated in cardiac rehabilitation exercise programs were 25 percent less likely to die from CVD.

Reducing Cholesterol

Reducing serum cholesterol levels requires consuming less saturated fat (no more than 10 percent of your total daily calories). Saturated fats raise serum cholesterol by signaling the body to manufacture fewer LDL receptors, which help the liver to remove cholesterol from the body. The major sources of saturated fats are animal fats, butter fat, tropical oils, and heavy hydrogenated oils. Even more important is never consuming trans-fatty acids (found in any foods with partially-hydrogenated oils) due to the dangerous way they increase LDL and triglyceride levels.

Monounsaturated and polyunsaturated fats such as those contained in olive and canola oil are a much healthier choice. Although they have just as many calories as saturated fats, they help lower serum cholesterol and improve the HDL/LDL cholesterol ratio. When saturated fat is replaced by carbohydrates, the reduction in LDL cholesterol is often accompanied by an unhealthful increase in triglycerides and reduction in HDL cholesterol. However, when monounsaturated fats are substituted for saturated fats, the same beneficial degree of LDL cholesterol lowering often occurs, with less or no change in triglyceride or HDL levels. A Mediterranean-type diet, rich in fruits and vegetables, whole grains, olive oil and other monounsaturated fats, fish, and moderate consumption of red wine, has been associated with lower heart rates and a reduction in the risk of CVD that is independent of its effect on LDL-cholesterol (Massey and others, 2000). This is true even after adjustment for differences in physical activity, smoking status, alcohol consumption, and body mass index (Dallongeville and others, 2003). Eating more fiber, fruits, vegetables, and grains also has a cholesterol-lowering effect, perhaps by binding with acids that cause cholesterol to be pulled from the bloodstream.

Regular exercise, too, can improve an individual's lipid profile. How much exercise is needed? In a recent prospective study, William Kraus and his colleagues

(2002) randomly assigned 111 sedentary, overweight men and women with mild-to-moderately high HDL and triglyceride levels to participate for 8 months in either a control group or one of three exercise groups: *high amount-high intensity exercise* (the caloric equivalent of jogging 20 miles per week at 65 to 80 percent of peak oxygen consumption), *low amount-high intensity exercise* (the caloric equivalent of jogging 12 miles per week at 65 to 80 percent of peak oxygen consumption), or *low amount-moderate intensity exercise* (the caloric equivalent of walking 12 miles per week at 40 to 55 percent of peak oxygen consumption). Although the greatest benefit on lipid profiles occurred in the high amount-high intensity group, both lower amount exercise groups had significantly better lipid profiles than did sedentary participants in the control group. Other researchers have found that the combination of a low-fat, high-fiber diet and daily exercise for 45 to 60 minutes for 3 weeks can produce a significant decrease in total cholesterol and improved cholesterol ratios (Roberts and others, 2002).

After CVD: Preventing Recurrence

It is estimated that over 355,000 people undergo coronary artery bypass graft (CABG) surgery in the United States each year (American Heart Association, 2004). Most people who survive an MI recover well enough to resume near-normal lives within a few weeks or months. However, they remain high-risk individuals and need to make lifestyle adjustments in order to improve their chances of living a long life and avoiding a recurrence of CHD. Longitudinal research reveals that even 5 years after CABG surgery, damage is still evident in measures of recognition memory, word recall, verbal learning, and other cognitive tasks (Stygall and others, 2003). Following discharge from the hospital for a cardiac event, both women and men tend to resume traditional gender-typed activities, with women assuming greater responsibility for domestic tasks such as laundry, cleaning, and cooking (Lemos and others, 2003). This imbalance in responsibility may help explain the poorer prognosis of female cardiac patients, who may not heed signs of overexertion.

A number of social and psychological factors contribute to how well patients adapt to CABG. Perceived social support (Kulik & Mahler, 1993), dispositional optimism (Scheier and others, 1989), low hostility (Jenkins and others, 1996), and religious involvement (Contrada and others, 2004) have all been shown to have beneficial effects in the recovery of heart surgery patients.

Many stroke victims are not so lucky. Extensive paralysis of one side of the body prevents them from resuming anything like a normal life. However, with a lot of work and social support from their family and friends, some do return to a near-normal existence. Like those with CHD, they can make lifestyle adjustments that will increase their longevity.

In addition to enlisting physical assistance with household tasks, those with CVD may avoid recurrence by quitting smoking, improving cholesterol ratios, losing excess weight, exercising regularly, and keeping blood pressure within a healthy range. CVD survivors may need assistance in managing their levels of stress and controlling anger and hostility.

Managing Stress Following a Cardiovascular Episode

A heart attack or stroke can cause substantial distress to both the patient and his or her family members. Although many patients make a complete recovery and are able to resume most of their previous activities, some remain psychologically impaired for a long time. A major goal of many intervention programs is to deal with the approximately one-third of the patients who experience significant stress, anxiety, or depression lasting more than 1 year after their hospitalization (Bennett & Carroll, 1997).

In one program, Nancy Frasure-Smith and Raymond Prince (1989) assigned nurses to contact post-MI patients regularly during the year following their heart attacks to evaluate whether they were experiencing stress. When a patient indicated that stress was indeed a problem, the nurses instigated what they considered the appropriate stress-reduction procedure. In some cases, this simply entailed talking through the source of stress with the patient; in more serious instances, patients were referred to other health professionals such as a psychologist, social worker, or cardiologist. Over the course of the 7-year study, patients in the stress-management group had significantly lower rates of cardiac mortality and morbidity compared with control patients, who received standard posthospitalization contact.

Controlling Hostility and Anger

A number of studies have reported positive effects of CVD interventions directed at reducing Type A behavior and hostility. These interventions are based on two premises:

1. Hostile people are more likely to encounter stress, which increases the prevalence of atherosclerosis-promoting experiences involving anger.

2. Hostile people are less likely to have stress-busting resources such as social support, partly as a result of their antagonistic behavior.

Intervention studies focus on helping hostile people gain control over their angry emotions. In the typical program, the psychologist first attempts to gain insight into the triggers of anger-inducing incidents by having participants self-monitor their behavior. Next, the participants develop strategies for coping with aggravation—for example, by avoiding especially stressful situations such as rush hour traffic, and controlling their reactions, perhaps by counting to 10 before reacting to a provoking incident. As the participants become increasingly able to cope with problem situations, the psychologist turns to a more cognitive intervention, helping participants learn to challenge cynical attitudes and modify unrealistic beliefs and expectations about life. Dozens of studies have supported the efficacy of these interventions.

Clinical health psychologists have used a variety of other strategies to help individuals cope with anger. One effective strategy is relaxation training, which was discussed in Chapter 5 as an effective means of coping with stress. Another method involves teaching angry persons new social and communication skills in which they learn to be more civilly assertive and to become aware of other people's cues that would normally provoke anger in them. Teaching participants to avoid provocative situations and to take themselves less seriously are also common goals of anger-intervention programs.

Jerry Deffenbacher and Robert Stark (1992) have demonstrated the efficacy of anger-control interventions. Using a combination of progressive relaxation, deep breathing, imagery, and cognitive restructuring, people who learned these skills experienced significant reductions in anger compared with those in a no-treatment control group. Promoting regular laughter, too, has been shown to decrease blood pressure, reduce stress hormones, and help reduce anger and improve mood (Hayashi and others, 2003; Hassed, 2001).

■ **diabetes mellitus** a disorder of the endocrine system in which the body is unable to produce insulin (Type 1) or is unable to properly utilize this pancreatic hormone (Type 2).

Diabetes

One of the most important risk factors for the development of CVD is **diabetes mellitus,** which involves the body's inability to produce or properly use insulin, a hormone that helps convert sugar and starches from food into energy. There is no cure for diabetes, and its cause remains a mystery, although both heredity and lifestyle factors appear to play roles. Diabetes mellitus affects more than 18 million Americans, is the sixth leading cause of death in this country, and has an annual cost of more than $132 billion. It is estimated that 41 million more Americans have *prediabetes,* characterized by blood glucose levels that are higher than normal but have not yet risen to the level that indicates a diagnosis of diabetes (CDC National Diabetes Fact Sheet, 2004).

Prevalence rates for diabetes vary markedly around the world: The disease is absent or rare in some indigenous communities in developing countries in Africa, the Eastern Mediterranean, and the Western Pacific, with prevalence rates of 14 to 20 percent in some Arab, Asian Indian, Chinese, and Hispanic-American populations (World Health Organization, 2000). In the United States, African-Americans, Hispanic-Americans, and Native Americans are at higher risk for adult-onset diabetes than European-Americans, Asian-Americans, and Cuban-Americans (Figure 9.8).

Figure 9.8

Estimated Age-Adjusted Prevalence of Diabetes in the United States by Ethnicity, 2005 Diabetes takes a greater toll on some ethnic groups than others, especially American Indians, Alaska Natives, Non-Hispanic blacks, and Hispanic-Americans.

Source: Centers for Disease Control and Prevention. (2005). National Diabetes Fact Sheet, United States, 2005. Washington, D.C.: U.S. Government Printing Office.

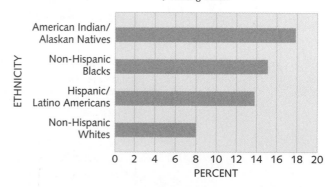

Types of Diabetes

There are two basic types of diabetes: juvenile-onset diabetes (called insulin-dependent diabetes mellitus or *Type 1 diabetes*), and adult-onset diabetes (called non-insulin-dependent diabetes mellitus or *Type 2 diabetes*) (Table 9.1). Type 1 diabetes, which first appears in childhood (usually between 5 and 6 years of age) or sometimes later during adolescence, is an autoimmune disease in which the person's immune system attacks the insulin- and glucagon-producing *islet cells* of the pancreas (Roberts, 1998). In a healthy person, the opposing actions of these hormones help regulate the blood level of the sugar glucose. Glucagon stimulates the release of glucose, causing blood sugar levels to rise, and insulin decreases blood sugar levels by causing cells to take up glucose more freely from the bloodstream. Without functioning islet cells, the body is unable to regulate blood sugar levels, and the individual becomes dependent on insulin injections. The symptoms of Type 1 diabetes, which include excessive thirst and urination, craving for sweets, weight loss, fatigue, and irritability, are largely the result of

Table 9.1

Characteristics and Risk Factors of Type 1 and Type 2 Diabetes

Type 1	Type 2
Autoimmune disorder in which insulin-producing cells of the pancreas are destroyed	Chronic illness in which the body fails to produce enough or to properly use insulin
Peak incidence occurs during puberty, around 10 to 12 years of age in girls and 12 to 14 in boys	Onset occurs after age 30
Accounts for 5–10 percent of all cases of diabetes	Accounts for 90–95 percent of all cases of diabetes
Symptoms may mimic flu, including excessive thirst, frequent urination, unusual weight loss, extreme fatigue, and irritability	Symptoms include any of the Type 1 symptoms and blurred vision, frequent infections, cuts that are slow to heal, tingling or numbness in hands or feet
Requires insulin injections	Requires strict diet and exercise
Who Is at Greater Risk?	**Who Is at Greater Risk?**
Children of parents with Type 1 diabetes	People over age 45 with a family history of diabetes
Siblings of people with Type 1 diabetes	Affects more women than men
Affects women and men equally	People who are overweight
Higher prevalence among European-Americans than other ethnic groups	Women who had gestational diabetes or who had a baby weighing 9 pounds or more at birth
	People who don't exercise regularly
	People with low HDL cholesterol or high triglycerides
	African-Americans, Native Americans, Hispanic-Americans, Asians, and Pacific Islanders
	People of low socioeconomic status

the body's inability to metabolize glucose for energy, which forces it to begin feeding off its own fats and proteins.

Type 2 diabetes—a milder form of the disease that usually appears after age 30—is found in more than 90 percent of all people with diabetes. It results from *insulin resistance* (also called *glucose intolerance*—a condition in which the islet cells of the pancreas fail to make enough insulin) and/or an insensitivity to insulin caused by a decrease in the number of insulin receptors in target cells. The symptoms of Type 2 diabetes include frequent urination, irregular menstruation in women, fatigue, slow healing of cuts and bruises, dryness of the mouth, and pain or cramps in the legs, feet, and fingers. Type 2 diabetes is more common among women, overweight people, members of certain ethnic groups, and those of low socioeconomic status. *Gestational diabetes* is a temporary form of glucose intolerance that usually occurs about halfway through a pregnancy as a result of the mother's inability to produce sufficient insulin. Gestational diabetes usually goes away after the baby's birth, but women who have had gestational diabetes have a greater risk of later developing Type 2 diabetes, as do women who gave birth to babies weighing 9 pounds or more at birth.

In both types of diabetes, two types of blood sugar problems can develop: *hypoglycemia* (blood sugar level that is too low) and *hyperglycemia* (blood sugar level that is too high). An estimated 50 to 75 percent of individuals with diabetes develop one or more long-term health complications as a result of their body's inability to regulate blood sugar (Talbot and others, 1999). Elevated levels of glucose, for instance, cause the walls of arteries to thicken, accelerating the development of atherosclerosis and CVD. Men and women with diabetes have CHD mortality rates that are two to four times higher than adults without diabetes. Because unregulated glucose levels in the blood can damage the retinas of the eyes, diabetes is also the leading cause of blindness among adults. People with diabetes are 17 times more likely to go blind than those without the disease. Diabetes is also the leading cause of end-stage renal (kidney) disease, and is associated with cancer of the pancreas, damage to the nervous system that may cause memory impairments (especially among older adults), and loss of sensation or pain in the extremities. In severe cases of poor circulation and loss of sensation in the extremities, amputation of the toes or feet may be required. Overall, the risk of death for people with diabetes is twice that of people without diabetes (CDC National Diabetes Fact Sheet, 2004).

Causes of Diabetes

As with other chronic illnesses, diabetes seems to be caused by multiple factors, including viral or bacterial infections that damage the islet cells of the pancreas, an overactive immune system, and genetic vulnerability. Nutritional "Westernization," which includes a diet high in fat and processed foods as well as total calories, may also be a contributing factor in diabetes. Ethnic groups that follow those diets, such as African-American females, experience higher rates of diabetes (Christoffel & Ariza, 1998). Increased television watching associated with reduced physical activity and poor nutrition may also contribute to Type 2 diabetes (Rosenbloom and others, 1999).

Stress has also been suggested as a precipitating factor in both Type 1 and Type 2 diabetes, especially among individuals with a strong family history of the disease (Dougall & Baum, 2001). People who have already been diagnosed with diabetes, as well as those at high risk for the disease, react to laboratory and environmental stressors with abnormally greater changes in their blood glucose levels than do people not at risk for diabetes (Surwit & Williams, 1996). Following the *diathesis-stress* model of disease (see Chapter 4), some investigators have suggested that abnormal blood sugar responses to challenging events (a symptom of an overreactive sympathetic nervous system), in conjunction with long-term exposure to high levels of stress, may be a *direct* path in the development of diabetes (Esposito-Del Puente and others, 1994). Indirectly, stress may also promote the development of diabetes by adversely affecting the individual's diet, level of compliance with treatment regimens, and tendency to exercise (Balfour and others, 1998).

Treatment of Diabetes

Fortunately, most people with diabetes can control their disease through lifestyle modifications—by changing their diet, regulating their weight, and exercising regularly, for example—and, in some cases, with daily injections of insulin. The goal of treatment, of course, is to keep blood sugar at a stable, healthy level. The medical community is currently debating whether both types of diabetes should be treated in the same way, including medication for precise glucose control, or differently (Tucker, 2002). Type 1 diabetes treatment requires insulin management, but Type 2 diabetes treatment could focus on weight control, exercise, and diet—reducing sugar and carbohydrate intake and keeping the total number of calories consumed each day within a narrow range In practice, a combination of treatments is used with Type 1 diabetes, depending on the severity of the individual case and the effectiveness of dietary and exercise modifications. For preventing diabetes, moderate exercise, improved diet, and other lifestyle interventions win hands down over medications (Zepf, 2002).

Health Psychology and Diabetes

The knowledge, beliefs, and behavior of patients strongly affect their ability to manage their diabetes and its impact on every domain of their health (Feifer & Tansman, 1999). This makes the health psychologist's role in the care and treatment of people with diabetes particularly important, as underscored by the standards of treatment recommended by the American Diabetes Association (ADA). Educational interventions are vitally important. People with diabetes often have deficits in their knowledge about diabetes and their increased risk for heart disease and other chronic conditions (Wagner and others, 2006). The ADA standards focus on lifestyle, cultural, psychological, educational, and economic factors in addition to medication (ADA, 1997). The ADA also emphasizes that *self-management* is the cornerstone of treatment for all people with diabetes. As a result, psychologists are increasingly becoming involved in the primary care of people with diabetes (Feifer & Tansman, 1999).

◾ **illness intrusiveness** the extent to which a chronic illness disrupts an individual's life by interfering with valued activities and interests and reducing perceptions of personal control, self-efficacy, and self-esteem.

Promoting Adjustment to Diabetes

A patient who receives a diagnosis of diabetes may experience a range of emotions, including shock, denial, anger, and depression (Jacobson, 1996). Helping patients accept their diagnosis is the first step in promoting self-management. Consider the case of Beatrice, a 64-year-old woman with a 20-year history of hypertension and a 4-year history of Type 2 diabetes. Beatrice reported feeling anger at her initial diagnosis. Over the next few months, she began exhibiting symptoms of depression and anxiety, and her already poor glucose control got even worse (Feifer & Tansman, 1999). Using *rational-emotive therapy,* psychologists challenged Beatrice's negative perceptions about her disease and helped her to feel better about herself, manage her moods, and deal with her self-care tasks on a day-to-day basis. As her acceptance of the disease and the once seemingly overwhelming tasks of self-management improved, Beatrice ultimately gained much stronger control over her blood sugar levels.

Illness Intrusiveness Even after accepting their diagnosis, many patients with diabetes continue to struggle with **illness intrusiveness,** which refers to the disruptive effect of diabetes on their lives. Illness intrusiveness can adversely affect an individual's well-being in at least two ways: directly, when the condition interferes with valued activities and interests, and indirectly, as a result of reduced perceptions of personal control, self-efficacy, and self-esteem (Devins and others, 1997). One study found that illness intrusiveness was strongly correlated with symptoms of depression among a large sample of Canadian Type 2 diabetes patients (Talbot and others, 1999). However, research has shown that having strong social support and good personal coping resources—including high self-esteem, a sense of mastery, and feelings of self-efficacy in the face of adversity—are associated with fewer depressive symptoms in people with diabetes (and, for that matter, those with lung cancer or CVD) (Penninx and others, 1998).

Self-Management of Diabetes The goal of diabetes treatment is to keep blood sugar at a stable, healthy level. Here a health care professional instructs a group of young people with diabetes on how to safely draw their own blood in order to monitor their blood sugar levels.

Psychologists have designed interventions to help those without the support or resources needed to cope with diabetes. They reduce diabetes intrusiveness on daily living by teaching people to redefine personal priorities, increase participation in enjoyable activities, and restructure irrational expectations regarding the intrusiveness of the disease. They also help patients mobilize social support and improve personal coping skills.

Blood Glucose Awareness Diabetes patients often lack proper understanding of their disease and its symptoms. One study found that more than 50 percent of patients with diabetes had inaccurate beliefs about blood glucose levels, including the symptoms of hypoglycemia and hyperglycemia (Gonder-Frederick and others, 1989). As a result, the patients often overlooked or missed some potentially serious symptoms and overreacted to other, irrelevant ones. Health psychologists have reported impressive results from *blood glucose awareness training*, in which patients learn to gauge their blood sugar levels from environmental cues (such as time of day or ongoing activity), physical symptoms (such as nausea and mouth dryness), and mood (such as fatigue and irritability). Through such training, which is similar in many ways to biofeedback training, most people with diabetes can learn to reliably recognize various cognitive and behavioral indicators of different blood glucose levels (Cox and others, 1994). Compared with untrained control patients, those patients trained in blood glucose awareness have achieved these additional health benefits:

- Improved glucose control and fewer long-term health complications
- Fewer automobile and other accidents resulting from states of hypoglycemia
- Fewer hospitalizations for blood sugar level abnormalities

Treating Diabetes-Related Psychological Disorders

People with diabetes tend toward feelings of depression, especially during the early stages of adjusting to the disease. Psychologists have also found that diagnosable clinical disorders such as major depression, anxiety, and eating disorders are more prevalent among adults with diabetes than they are in the general population (Katon & Sullivan, 1990). Prevalence rates for major depressive disorder, for example, which range from 5 to 25 percent in the general population, have been found to range from 22 to 60 percent among those with diabetes (Gavard and others, 1993; Talbot and others, 1999).

The physical and emotional demands placed on the individual with diabetes, including strict compliance to a complex treatment regimen of daily self-monitoring of blood glucose levels, preparing special meals, and taking medication, can be difficult and frustrating. This task is made all the more challenging when the individual suffers from unusual psychosocial distress or a psychological disorder. Many research studies have found an association between the presence of psychological disorders and poor adherence (Littlefield and others, 1992). With depression, for instance, self-care tasks such as daily monitoring of glucose levels or preparation of special foods may seem futile or too difficult to accomplish. Many health professionals have suggested that individuals with diabetes should have psychosocial evaluations at some point during their medical treatment, preferably soon after the time of diagnosis (King and others, 1998). Health psychologists who are involved in the primary care of people diagnosed with diabetes are in a good position to refer them to appropriate clinical psychologists, if needed (Feifer & Tansman, 1999).

Managing Weight and Stress

Effective weight management is particularly important for patients with diabetes because it improves the body's ability to regulate glucose, and thereby reduces the need for medication. Weight-loss programs often produce substantial success among people with diabetes by using a multimodal approach that combines nutrition, education, low-calorie diets, and regular exercise. As with all weight-loss programs, however, the main problem has been in maintaining the loss (Bradley, 1997; Wing, 1993).

Regular exercise can also help prevent Type 2 diabetes. One prospective study of male alumni of the University of Pennsylvania found that physically active men had the lowest incidence of Type 2 diabetes over a 15-year period (Helmrich and others, 1991). This protective effect remained even after the researchers controlled for other major diabetes risk factors, including obesity, hypertension, and family history of the disease. Interestingly, people with Type 2 diabetes have the greatest difficulty maintaining healthy concentrations of blood sugar in March and April, perhaps because the preceding months of cold weather have promoted inactivity (Doro and others, 2006).

Equally important is stress management. In people with diabetes, reactions to stress strongly influence whether and how well they follow a particular regimen. For example, stress may begin the vicious cycle of overeating, poor control over diabetes, more stress, more overeating, and so on. Relaxation training and other stress management techniques appear to be beneficial for many individuals with diabetes.

Increasing Adherence to Diabetes Treatment Regimens

Health psychologists have approached the issue of adherence in two ways: by seeking to identify factors that predict compliance or noncompliance and by developing interventions to improve adherence to different aspects of a treatment regimen. Sociodemographic factors such as age, gender, ethnicity, and personality do not predict adherence to diabetes treatment regimens (Goodall & Halford, 1991). Several factors contribute to noncompliance, including the sheer complexity of a lifelong regimen of self-care (Landis and others, 1985). Patients with diabetes may also perceive prescribed treatment as recommended and discretionary rather than mandatory, and they fail to comply. Those newly diagnosed with diabetes often feel no ill effects—severe medical complications of diabetes may not arise for a decade or more—and may find their current lifestyle too enjoyable to change. Social and environmental circumstances are also factors in poor adherence. During periods of unusual stress or social pressure to behave in unhealthy ways, for instance, dietary and exercise compliance often decreases among those with diabetes (Goodall & Halford, 1991).

Working from the transtheoretical model discussed in Chapter 6, health psychologists might try to get diabetes patients to adhere to treatment regimens by helping them cycle through the stages of precontemplation, contemplation, preparation, action, and maintenance. For example, the psychologist would al-

The general topic of why certain people are more likely to delay making healthy lifestyle changes and seeking health care is discussed in Chapter 12.

most certainly tell an obese woman newly diagnosed with Type 2 diabetes to lose weight. However, since she probably does not feel sick, she sees no reason to change from her delicious high-calorie, high-carbohydrate diet (precontemplation). To move her to the stage of contemplation, the psychologist would try to explain the connection between diet and diabetes. (She perceives a link, but she still isn't ready to give up her favorite foods.) Further education and support for change (family members are enlisted to help her modify her diet, for instance) may nudge the patient into the stage of preparation (she knows she will diet), and then to action (the patient works hard at dieting). Finally, during the maintenance stage (working to avoiding relapse to unhealthy eating habits), she is likely to benefit from interventions that focus on how to maintain the treatment regimen in the face of circumstances that undermine it (such as unusual stress or social pressure to eat unhealthy foods). For example, maintenance interventions for Beatrice, who abandoned her medical regimen each time she encountered a stressful life event, involved exercises to promote stress management and improve her communication coping skills.

Enhancing Communication and Increasing Social Support

Empowering individuals with diabetes (or any chronic illness) to actively participate in decision making in their treatment regimen has a variety of benefits. Among these are an increased perception of control, enhanced doctor–patient communication, greater confidence in prescribed treatment regimens, and improved compliance. In one study, diabetes patients who were taught to be more assertive in acquiring knowledge about the disease and in using that information to negotiate treatment decisions with their physicians showed significant increases in their perceived self-efficacy, regulation of blood glucose, and satisfaction with their treatment regimen (Greenfield and others, 1988). Beatrice had received from her physician basic information about living with diabetes. She was too intimidated, however, to discuss her fears, self-care needs, and difficulty complying with her treatment regimen. She did, however, discuss these issues with her psychologist, who used assertiveness training to prepare Beatrice to approach her doctor to resolve these issues, which she later did.

The problems of managing diabetes extend beyond the individual to members of the family, who may react in ways that adversely (or favorably) affect the patient. The quality of marital relationships, for example, is an accurate predictor of diabetes regimen adherence (Trief and others, 2004). Family therapy is often helpful. Therapy often begins with education about diabetes, what must be done to achieve control, and how the behaviors of family members affect the individual's control. This can be particularly important in the management of Type 1 diabetes in children and adolescents. Parents, for example, may become overly protective of a teenager newly diagnosed with diabetes, unnecessarily restricting activities and promoting a sense of helplessness. Family therapy directed at improving communication and conflict resolution among family members has been demonstrated to improve diabetes control among children who perceive deficiencies in these areas in their families (Minuchin and others, 1978). When parents are actively involved in their child's diabetes management (such as helping with blood glucose monitoring), greater control is achieved (Andersen and others, 1997).

From our biopsychosocial perspective, we have seen that many factors play a role in the development of chronic conditions such as cardiovascular disease and diabetes. Healthy living helps many people avoid or significantly delay the development of chronic conditions. Even those who are already suffering chronic disease may still improve their health by following better health practices, including eating well, exercising, maintaining normal weight, and avoiding tobacco. And physical and psychological coping strategies help many limit the life disruption of chronic conditions.

Summing Up

The Healthy Heart

1. The cardiovascular system consists of the blood, the blood vessels of the circulatory system, and the heart. The heart consists of three layers of tissue: a thin outer layer, called the *epicardium;* a thin inner layer, called the *endocardium;* and a thicker middle layer, the heart muscle itself, or *myocardium.* The myocardium is separated into four chambers that work in coordinated fashion to bring blood into the heart and then to pump it throughout the body.

Cardiovascular Disease

2. Cardiovascular disease (CVD), which includes coronary heart disease (CHD) and stroke, is the leading cause of death in the United States and most developed countries.

3. CVD results from *atherosclerosis,* a chronic condition in which coronary arteries are narrowed by fatty deposits and plaques that form over microscopic lesions in the walls of blood vessels, and *arteriosclerosis,* or hardening of the arteries.

4. When the arteries that supply the heart are narrowed with plaques, restricting blood flow to the heart (*ischemia*), the person may experience heart pain, called *angina pectoris.* When severe atherosclerosis or a clot causes a coronary artery to become completely obstructed, a heart attack, or *myocardial infarction (MI),* occurs, and a portion of the myocardium begins to die. A third possible manifestation of cardiovascular malfunction is a *stroke,* which occurs when a blood clot obstructs an artery in the brain.

5. Medicine has made great strides in diagnosing and treating heart disease. Diagnostic techniques include *electro-*

cardiogram (EKG) monitoring, and *coronary angiography.* Treatment interventions include medications for controlling blood pressure, cholesterol level, and preventing blood clots, and also cardiac surgery in the form of *coronary artery bypass grafts* and *balloon angioplasty.*

Framingham's Risk Factors for Cardiovascular Disease

6. The Framingham Heart Study, a prospective study of CVD that has collected data for over half a century, has identified a number of coronary risk factors.

7. The "uncontrollable risk factors" for CVD include family history of heart disease, age, gender, and ethnicity. The risk of CVD increases with age, is much higher among men than women, and varies across racial and ethnic groups. Economic and social factors may be the actual causes of racial and ethnic variation in CVD.

8. The major "controllable risk factors" for CVD are hypertension, obesity, elevated serum cholesterol, and smoking. Most cases of high blood pressure are classified as essential hypertension, meaning that the exact cause is unknown.

9. Cholesterol levels that are too high promote the development of atherosclerosis. Those with metabolic syndrome are at particularly high risk of developing CVD and diabetes.

Psychosocial Factors in Cardiovascular Disease

10. Characterized by a competitive, hurried, hostile nature, the Type A behavior pattern has been linked to increased risk of CVD. Researchers now point to hostility and anger as the toxic core of Type A behavior.

11. Several theoretical explanations have been proposed to explain the relationship between a hostile, angry personality and cardiovascular disease. The psychosocial vulnerability model maintains that hostile people have more stressful life events and low levels of social support, which, over time, have a toxic effect.

12. The health behavior model proposes that hostile people are more likely to develop cardiovascular disease because they tend to have poorer health habits than less hostile people.

13. The psychophysiological reactivity model maintains that frequent episodes of anger produce elevated cardiovascular and stress hormone responses that damage arteries and contribute to coronary disease.

14. The biopsychosocial model suggests that in order for CVD to develop, a hostile person must first have a biological predisposition toward it. CVD may then be more likely to develop because the hostile person's attitude has chased away social support and continues to elicit negative responses from others, which leads to more hostility and damaging cardiac reactivity.

Reducing the Risk of Cardiovascular Disease

15. Lifestyle modifications can significantly reduce a person's risk of cardiovascular disease. Interventions for hypertension include reducing weight, limiting salt and alcohol intake, increasing exercise, and improving cholesterol ratios. Eating more fiber, fruits, vegetables, grains, and mono- and polyunsaturated fats and less saturated fat can reduce serum cholesterol levels and improve the ratio of HDL cholesterol to LDL cholesterol.

After CVD: Preventing Recurrence

16. Comprehensive interventions that combine stress management, aerobic exercise, relaxation training, and low-fat diets may prevent CVD recurrence.

17. Interventions for hostility help people gain control of environmental triggers for their anger and learn to modify their negative emotions and cynical thought processes. Reducing hostility can substantially reduce the risk of future ischemia in cardiac patients.

Diabetes

18. *Diabetes mellitus* is a chronic disease in which the body is unable to produce or properly use the hormone insulin. Diabetes can develop in either childhood (Type 1) or adulthood (Type 2), with Type 1 diabetes generally involving more serious health complications and the need for daily insulin injections. Many individuals with diabetes also benefit from lifestyle modifications that include a strict diet and exercise.

19. Many individuals with diabetes also suffer from psychological disorders, including major depression, anxiety, and eating disorders. Health psychology's role has included studying factors in adjusting to the disease, such as psychological distress, personal coping skills, and social support, as well as factors that affect compliance with treatment regimens.

20. Health psychologists are increasingly becoming involved in the primary care of diabetes by reducing illness intrusiveness, increasing weight control and stress management, enhancing communication, and increasing compliance with complex treatment regimens.

Key Terms and Concepts

cardiovascular disease (CVD), p. 268
coronary heart disease (CHD), p. 268
atherosclerosis, p. 268
arteriosclerosis, p. 270
angina pectoris, p. 270
myocardial infarction (MI), p. 270
stroke, p. 271

electrocardiogram (ECG or EKG), p. 271
coronary angiography, p. 272
coronary artery bypass graft, p. 272
coronary angioplasty, p. 272
hypertension, p. 277
cardiovascular reactivity, p. 278

metabolic syndrome, p. 280
Type A, p. 281
Type B, p. 281
diabetes mellitus, p. 293
illness intrusiveness, p. 297

Cancer

"Dad, can we go home now? I don't feel sick, and I don't want to be poked any more." So said my 6-year-old son, Jeremy, at the end of a very long day in which he was diagnosed with cancer. It was the day my family's world seemed to turn upside down.

It began in a relatively uneventful manner, as childhood health problems often do: soreness and swelling on the left side of Jeremy's neck that seemed to appear overnight and wouldn't go away. An almost-casual visit to the family pediatrician revealed that the discomfort was due to swollen lymph glands yet did not seem to be a cause for alarm. Just to be safe, Jeremy was referred to the university's pediatric hospital for a few more tests to rule out any (unlikely) serious health problems. After a morning of blood tests; physical examinations by a stream of nurses, doctors, and interns; and finally magnetic resonance imaging (MRI) of Jeremy's neck, we grew increasingly worried. We were ushered into a small waiting room in the pediatric oncology wing of the hospital, where we were stunned by the diagnosis: non-Hodgkin's lymphoma.

Our immediate reaction was disbelief. How? Why? As a health psychologist, I knew that there were probably no simple answers to those questions. There were no warning signs or symptoms. Jeremy had always been a healthy, active kid. He wasn't overweight, ate a nutritious diet, and to my mind had no known risk factors for cancer (other than several relatives who'd battled skin cancer). Just as our son's life was beginning, it seemed, inexplicably, to be in danger of ending.

Fortunately, we were not defenseless against this disease, which only a few decades earlier would almost certainly have been fatal. We immediately enacted a full biopsychosocial assault, including state-of-the-art biomedical interventions that arrested the cancer, a healthy diet and exercise program, and relaxation training to ease the discomfort of chemotherapy and promote a positive outlook. Jeremy's family,

■ **cancer** a set of diseases in which abnormal body cells multiply and spread in uncontrolled fashion forming a tissue mass called a tumor.

■ **metastasis** the process by which malignant body cells proliferate in number and spread to surrounding body tissues.

friends, classmates, primary care physician, and especially nurses provided extensive social support, and Jeremy himself showed incredible strength of character— especially for a young child. He was stoic throughout his treatment, which was sometimes painful (as in the needle pokes), and included many nausea-inducing bouts of chemotherapy. But his stoicism was not accompanied by withdrawal. He shared his feelings, fears, and determination to beat the disease with us, and we grew stronger because of his strength. At times he could even laugh at himself and turn adversity into an apparent asset. When chemotherapy caused his hair to fall out, Jeremy—who remains an ardent Star Trek: The Next Generation *fan—joked that he looked like a young Captain Picard!*

Today, more than 15 years later, Jeremy is a healthy computer science graduate who has gone on to earn an MBA and start a successful company that generates popular mapping software for handheld computers. He travels extensively, pilots his own plane (so that his wonderful mutt "Red" can sit beside him), and credits his survival to the powers of mind–body medicine.

While I wouldn't wish this painful chapter of our lives on anyone, our family survived and thrived after bringing Jeremy back to health. We all became more health-conscious . . . and more aware of the interconnections among our physical, psychological, and social well-being.

© Moredun Animal Health Ltd/Science Photo Library/Photo Researchers, Inc.

A Malignant Tumor This scanning electron micrograph shows a tiny lung tumor (center) filling an alveolus (one of the air sacs that make up the lungs). The individual cancer cells are coated with microscopic, hair-like structures known as microvilli.

What Is Cancer?

Few of us have avoided the life-changing effects of cancer—either in ourselves or a loved one. Indeed, **cancer** is the second leading cause of death in the United States, and many more suffer through nonfatal varieties, as Jeremy did. It is not one disease but a set of more than 100 related diseases in which abnormal body cells multiply and spread in uncontrolled fashion forming a tissue mass called a *tumor.*

Not all tumors are cancerous. *Benign* (noncancerous) tumors tend to remain localized and usually do not pose a serious threat to health. In contrast, *malignant* (cancerous) tumors consist of renegade cells that do not respond to the body's genetic controls on growth and division. To make matters worse, malignant cells often have the ability to migrate from their site of origin and the ability to attack, invade, and destroy surrounding body tissues. If this process of **metastasis** is not stopped, body organs and systems will be damaged, and death may result. Although some malignant cells remain as localized tumors and do not automatically spread, they still pose a threat to health and need to be surgically removed.

Types of Cancer

Most cancers can be classified as one of four types:

- **Carcinomas** attack the *epithelial cells* that line the outer and inner surfaces of the body. Carcinomas are the most common type of cancer, accounting for approximately 85 percent of all adult cancers. They include cancer of the breast, prostate, colon, lungs, pancreas, and skin. Affecting one out of every six people in the United States, skin cancer is the most common (and most rapidly increasing) type of cancer in America (American Cancer Society, 2004).

- **Sarcomas** are malignancies of cells in muscles, bones, and cartilage. Much rarer than carcinoma, sarcomas account for only about 2 percent of all cancers in adults.

- **Lymphomas** are cancers that form in the lymphatic system. Included in this group are *Hodgkin's disease,* a rare form of lymphoma that spreads from a single lymph node, and Jeremy's *non-Hodgkin's lymphoma,* in which malignant cells are found at several sites. Over 60,000 new cases of lymphoma are diagnosed each year, of which 90 percent are non-Hodgkin's lymphoma.

- **Leukemias** are cancers that attack the blood and blood-forming tissues, such as the bone marrow. Leukemia leads to a proliferation of white blood cells in the bloodstream and bone marrow, which impair the immune system. Although often considered a childhood disease, leukemia strikes far more adults (an estimated 25,000 cases per year) than children (about 3,000 cases per year).

Cancer Susceptibility

Many individual factors, such as gender, age, and ethnic background, affect susceptibility to cancer. For example, although over the course of a lifetime more men (just under 1 in 2) develop cancer than women (just over 1 in 3), women are more likely to develop any cancer before age 60. Although women are more commonly diagnosed with breast cancer and men with prostate cancer, lung cancer is the top killer of both genders (Figure 10.1, p. 306) (American Cancer Society, 2004). Whether and where cancer strikes also vary with age. As is true for many other chronic diseases, the older people become, the greater their chances of developing and dying of cancer. But in the United States cancer is also the second leading cause of death (after accidents) among children between 1 and 14 years of age.

Variations in the distribution of cancers by race and ethnicity add to the complexity of cancer's epidemiology. For instance, African-Americans have the highest incidence rates for cancer overall—60 percent greater risk than Hispanic-Americans and Asian-Americans—primarily because of high rates of lung and prostate cancer among men. Not only are African-Americans more

■ **carcinoma** cancer of the epithelial cells that line the outer and inner surfaces of the body; includes breast, prostate, lung, and skin cancer.

■ **sarcoma** cancer that strikes muscles, bones, and cartilage.

■ **lymphoma** cancer of the body's lymph system; includes Hodgkin's disease and non-Hodgkin's lymphoma.

■ **leukemia** cancer of the blood and blood-producing system.

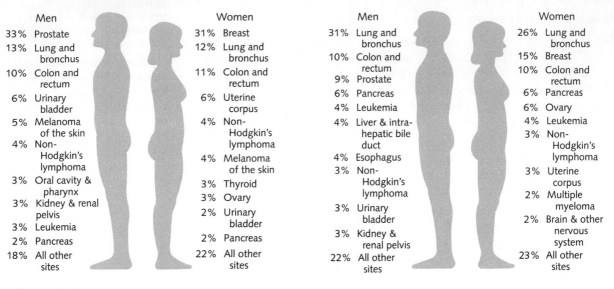

CANCER INCIDENCE RATES

Men		Women	
33%	Prostate	31%	Breast
13%	Lung and bronchus	12%	Lung and bronchus
10%	Colon and rectum	11%	Colon and rectum
6%	Urinary bladder	6%	Uterine corpus
5%	Melanoma of the skin	4%	Non-Hodgkin's lymphoma
4%	Non-Hodgkin's lymphoma	4%	Melanoma of the skin
3%	Oral cavity & pharynx	3%	Thyroid
3%	Kidney & renal pelvis	3%	Ovary
3%	Leukemia	2%	Urinary bladder
2%	Pancreas	2%	Pancreas
18%	All other sites	22%	All other sites

CANCER MORTALITY RATES

Men		Women	
31%	Lung and bronchus	26%	Lung and bronchus
10%	Colon and rectum	15%	Breast
9%	Prostate	10%	Colon and rectum
6%	Pancreas	6%	Pancreas
4%	Leukemia	6%	Ovary
4%	Liver & intra-hepatic bile duct	4%	Leukemia
4%	Esophagus	3%	Non-Hodgkin's lymphoma
3%	Non-Hodgkin's lymphoma	3%	Uterine corpus
3%	Urinary bladder	2%	Multiple myeloma
3%	Kidney & renal pelvis	2%	Brain & other nervous system
22%	All other sites	23%	All other sites

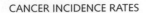

Figure 10.1

Estimated New Cancer Cases and Deaths by Type and Gender, 2006 Although the breasts in women and the prostate in men are the leading sites of new cases of cancer (left), lung cancer continues to be the leading cause of cancer deaths in both men and women (right).

Source: American Cancer Society, Inc., Surveillance Research.

likely to develop cancer, but they are also about 33 percent more likely to die of the disease than are European-Americans, and more than twice as likely to die of cancer as Asian/Pacific Islanders, Native Americans, and Hispanic-Americans.

As noted in Chapter 1, several variables contribute to ethnic differences in chronic disease incidence and mortality, and cancer is no exception. Among these variables are socioeconomic status, knowledge about cancer and its treatment, and attitudes toward the disease, which may affect access to health care and adherence to medical advice (Meyerowitz and others, 1998). For example, consider breast cancer. Although white women are more likely to develop breast cancer than African-American women, African-American women are more likely to die of the disease. African-American women historically have been less likely to perform regular breast self-examination and to obtain mammograms, the two most effective means of early detection (Murray, 1999). African-Americans and other minorities also tend to have less access to health insurance and health care facilities and greater distrust of the medical establishment, which may be perceived as insensitive and even racist. This explains why cancer of all types is generally diagnosed in later (usually more serious) stages in African-Americans than it is in white Americans. African-Americans have lower 5-year relative survival rates than European-Americans when all cancers are considered together (American Cancer Society, 2004). Finally, ethnic differences in diet, tobacco use, and other risk factors for cancer also play a role. For example, African-Americans more than other Americans tend to smoke more and consume fattier diets—two behaviors implicated in many forms of cancer.

Risk Factors for Cancer

■ **carcinogen** a cancer-causing agent such as tobacco, ultraviolet radiation, or an environmental toxin.

It is interesting to speculate about the number of cancer cases that would arise naturally in a population of otherwise healthy people who completely avoided all environmental carcinogens. By one estimate, epidemiologists suggest that less than 25 percent of all cancers would develop anyway as a result of uncontrollable genetic and biological processes (Trichopoulos and others, 1996). In most cases of cancer, controllable factors such as smoking and diet play the most important role.

This section examines a number of risk factors for cancer. Although risk factors increase a person's chance of developing cancer, not every person with those risk factors will develop the disease. Many people with one or more risk factors never develop cancer, whereas others who develop the disease have no known risk factors.

Tobacco Use

As we saw in Chapter 8, smoking is the most preventable cause of death in our society. The American Cancer Society estimates that about one in every five deaths in the United States is caused by tobacco, and most of those tobacco-related deaths were the result of cancer. Tobacco is the single most lethal **carcinogen** (agent that causes cancer) in this country (American Cancer Society, 2004).

Smoking is linked to cancers of the lungs, mouth, pharynx, larynx, esophagus, pancreas, uterus, cervix, kidney, bladder, and breast. In one prospective study that followed healthy women over a 6-year period, researchers found that women who smoked were 1.26 times more likely to die of breast cancer than were women who had never smoked. Among those who smoked two packs or more each day, the relative risk rose to 1.74, whereas those who smoked half a pack or less had a relative risk of only 1.19. In addition, women who started smoking before age 16 were 60 percent more likely to die from breast cancer than those who started after age 20 (Calle and others, 1994).

Up to 20 percent of lung cancer patients who smoked prior to diagnosis continue to do so (see Schnoll and others, 2003 for a review). Continued use of tobacco after a cancer diagnosis increases the risk of recurrence and the development of additional tumors, reduces the effectiveness of chemotherapy and other cancer treatments, and exacerbates unpleasant side effects of treatment.

Diet and Alcohol Use

Only diet rivals tobacco as a cause of cancer, accounting for nearly the same number of deaths each year (Trichopoulous and others, 1996). Diet is a primary factor in as many as one-third of all cancer deaths (Brody, 1998c). A number of dietary factors can affect cancer risk, including the types of foods you eat, how the food is prepared, the size of your portions, whether you eat a balanced diet, and your overall caloric balance.

Although little is known about the mechanisms by which specific foods convey their health-related effects, we generally know which foods people should avoid and which they should eat in abundance if they want to minimize their risk of getting cancer.

Cancer-Causing Foods

Foods to avoid are animal (saturated) fat in general and red meat in particular, which are linked to a number of specific cancers, including cancer of the colon, rectum, and prostate. The cancers that have been most directly linked to foods are those that affect the cells that line bodily tissues, including those in the lungs, colon, bladder, stomach, and rectum, and, to a lesser degree, the uterus, prostate, breasts, and kidneys. It should come as no surprise that these cancers are most prevalent in cultures noted for high-fat diets, such as the United States.

Cross-cultural studies have found that Japanese-American women are more likely to develop breast cancer when they live in the United States and consume a high-fat American diet (Wynder and others, 1991). The traditional soy-rich Asian diet may partially explain the normally low risk of breast, uterine, and other hormone-related cancers in Asian women. Soy products contain plant-derived *phyto-estrogens* that may be slightly protective against breast cancer when used in place of meats—especially if initiated before puberty (Adlercreutz, 2002). On the other hand, data from the Nurses' Health Study, as well as a meta-analysis of research studies of more than 300,000 women, found *no* conclusive link between dietary fat and breast cancer (White, 1999). More research is needed before we can draw any definitive conclusions about the relationship between dietary fat and breast cancer.

Cancer-Fighting Foods

Healthy foods include vegetables, fruits, legumes (such as beans and peas), whole grain carbohydrates (such as brown rice and whole-wheat bread, as opposed to processed or refined "white" flours and grains), good fats (unhydrogenated fats that come primarily from plant sources), and organic coffee (caffeinated or decaf) in moderation.

Foods that may play a protective role against some cancers do so by blocking carcinogenic processes in body cells. For example, *antioxidants* such as vitamins A and C may buffer against the cell-damaging activities of free radicals (Ames & Wakimoto, 2002).

Especially beneficial are dark green, yellow, and orange vegetables that are rich in **carotenoids,** light-absorbing pigments found in certain plants. Carotenoids are responsible for the color of carrots, tomatoes, pumpkins, broccoli, cauliflower, brussels sprouts, citrus fruits, and strawberries. One carotenoid, *beta-carotene,* is broken down by the body as a rich source of vitamin A. Vitamin A is essential in maintaining the health of the cells that line the lungs and stomach. Diets that include five to nine servings daily of foods that are rich in beta-carotene are linked to reduced risk of cancer of the lung, stomach, colon

■ **carotenoids** light-absorbing pigments that give carrots, tomatoes, and other foods their color and are rich sources of antioxidant vitamins.

and rectum, and, to a smaller degree, the breasts, bladder, and pancreas. Cooked tomato products, which are rich in the carotenoid *lycopene,* may reduce the risk of prostate cancer (Brody, 1998c).

Other studies have found that diets rich in fruits, vegetables, and fiber may offer some protection against colon and rectal cancers, most likely because they promote rapid removal of cancer-causing wastes from the body (Steinmetz and others, 1994). In a massive study of Seventh-Day Adventists, George Fraser (1991) found that people who ate fruit at least twice a day had one-fourth the risk of developing lung cancer as those who ate fruit less than three times a week. Participants who ate fruit three to seven times each week had about one-third the risk of developing lung cancer.

Data from the Nurses' Health Study reveal that premenopausal women who consumed five or more servings per day of fruits and vegetables were 23 percent less likely to develop breast cancer than those who ate fewer than two servings per day (Zhang and others, 1999). Although this level of protection appears to be modest, we should remember that the link between obesity and breast cancer is very strong (see Chapter 7), and eating a lot of fruits and vegetables also helps to maintain a healthy weight level.

Researchers are studying many other foods as possible weapons against cancer. Protective foods include garlic, onions, and leeks (which contain a compound called *allium* that may protect against breast cancer), and *selenium*-rich foods such as fish, liver, garlic (which has both allium and selenium), eggs, and whole grains (which may reduce the risk of prostate cancer). The newest anticancer candidates are green tea, olive oil (which may reduce the risk of breast cancer when used to replace other fats), and foods rich in Vitamin D and calcium (which may reduce both breast and colon cancer). Table 10.1 summarizes the sources of several cancer-fighting foods and their possible benefits.

Table 10.1

Foods That May Prevent Cancer

Substance	Source	Possible Health Benefit
Garlic	Garlic powder, cloves, supplements	May have antioxidant properties that protect against breast and stomach cancer
Flavonoids	Red wine, grapes, apples, cranberries	May reduce the risk of lung and colorectal cancer
Lycopene	Tomatoes, red peppers, watermelon	May have stronger antioxidant properties than beta-carotene that protect against several cancers, including prostate cancer
Beta-carotene	Dark yellow and orange fruits, leafy dark green vegetables, apricots, pumpkins, carrots, spinach, and squash	Associated with reduced risk of cancer of the lung, stomach, colon and rectum, and, to a smaller degree, the breasts, bladder, and pancreas
Selenium	Liver, mushrooms, garlic, fish	Believed to increase the antioxidant effects of vitamin E and protect against prostate cancer
Isoflavones	Beans, grains, soy products	May reduce the risk of breast and prostate cancer
Indoles	Cruciferous vegetables such as broccoli, brussels sprouts, and cabbage	May reduce the risk of several forms of cancer

Alcohol

Although moderate consumption of alcoholic beverages may reduce the risk of cardiovascular disease (see Chapter 9), excessive drinking, especially among tobacco users, has been shown to be a major risk factor for cancer of the upper respiratory and digestive tracts. Alcohol may also contribute to breast, colorectal, and liver cancer. Women who consume two or more alcohol-containing drinks a day have at least a 25 percent greater risk of developing breast cancer than women who do not use alcohol (Diez-Ruiz and others, 1995). Alcohol-related cirrhosis is a frequent cause of liver cancer and may place the immune system in "overdrive," even when no threat (other than excessive alcohol) is present. Recent animal research shows that drinking the equivalent of two to four alcoholic drinks per day also dramatically increases the growth of an existing tumor (Tan and others, 2006).

However, we must be cautious in drawing conclusions about alcohol and immunocompetence. People who abuse alcohol may also suffer from poor nutrition and sleep deprivation and may be exposed to other pathogens that compromise their health.

Physical Activity

Lack of physical activity may be a risk factor for certain cancers. One prospective study of men with colon cancer, men with rectal cancer, and healthy men found that the more sedentary a man's job, and the longer he had worked at that job, the greater his risk of colon cancer (Vena and others, 1985). More recently, researchers have similarly reported an inverse relationship between overall physical activity levels and the risk of colon cancer in both women and men (White and others, 1996). These results suggest that a sedentary lifestyle is indeed a risk factor for colon cancer, one of the leading causes of cancer mortality.

Regular physical activity—either work-related or recreational—may also protect against breast cancer. For example, Suzanne Shoff and her colleagues (2000) found that physically active women who had lost weight since they were 18, or had gained only minimal amounts of weight, were only half as likely as their inactive counterparts to develop breast cancer after menopause. The most compelling evidence comes from the Nurses' Health Study, which reported that women who exercised 7 hours or more per week were 20 percent less likely to develop breast cancer than women who exercised less than 1 hour per week (Rockhill and others, 1999). Walking, the most frequently reported exercise, was as effective in protecting against cancer as more strenuous forms of exercise. Similarly, data from the massive Women's Health Initiative Cohort Study indicate that women who engaged in the equivalent of as little as an hour and a half of brisk walking each week had an 18 percent decreased risk of breast cancer compared with inactive women (McTiernan and others, 2003).

Family History

Only a small percentage of all breast cancer cases are inherited. The vast majority (nearly 95 percent) are linked to a combination of genetic and nongenetic risk factors. Nongenetic risk factors include obesity, younger age at menarche, lack of exercise, smoking, poor diet, use of oral contraceptives, the presence of other diseases of the breast, radiation exposure, and use of alcohol.

Genetic vulnerability can, however, interact with other risk factors to increase an individual's risk (Ellenhorst-Ryan, 1997). For example, approximately one-third of the 175,000 women diagnosed with breast cancer each year in the United States have a family history of the disease (Esplen and others, 1998). Evidence again comes from the Nurses' Health Study, which found that the daughters of women diagnosed with breast cancer before age 40 were more than twice as likely to develop breast cancer, as compared with women whose mothers had no history of the disease. The daughters of women with breast cancer after age 70 were one and a half times more likely to develop breast cancer. Participants who had a sister with breast cancer were more than twice as likely to develop this cancer themselves; when both mother *and* sister were diagnosed with breast cancer, the risk increased to two and a half times (Colditz and others, 1993).

Both men and women can inherit and pass on defective genes. Families in which breast cancer is inherited typically demonstrate the following characteristics:

- Breast cancer in two or more close relatives, such as a mother and two sisters
- Early onset—often before age 50—of breast cancer in family members
- History of breast cancer in more than one generation
- Cancer in both breasts in one or more family members
- Frequent occurrence of ovarian cancer
- Ashkenazi (Eastern and Central European) Jewish ancestry, with a family history of breast and/or ovarian cancer.

Other forms of cancer are also linked to mutant genes. One example is *basal cell carcinoma*—the most common (and usually localized) form of skin cancer (Gailani and others, 1996). Other examples include cancer of the ovaries, prostate, pancreas, and larynx (Smith, 1998). Men who carry this mutant gene are nearly twice as likely as noncarriers to develop prostate cancer by age 80.

Environmental and Occupational Hazards

The degree of cancer hazard posed by environmental toxins depends on the concentration of the carcinogen and the amount of exposure to the toxin. However, even low-dose exposure can represent a significant public health hazard when a large segment of the population is involved (Willett and others, 1996).

Toxic Chemicals

Various chemicals are clearly carcinogenic, including asbestos, vinyl chloride, and arsenic. In addition, some researchers believe that exposure to chlorine-containing compounds found in some household cleaning and pest-control products may increase the risk of breast cancer and, possibly, other hormone-related cancers. Although the popular media have focused on the dangers of pesticides, the very low concentrations found in some foods are generally well within established safety levels and pose minimal risks.

Environmental toxins in the air, soil, and water are estimated to contribute to about 2 percent of fatal cancers, mainly of the bladder and the lungs. Although long-term exposure to high levels of air pollution—especially by smokers—may increase the risk of lung cancer by as much as 50 percent, this pales in comparison to the 2,000 percent increased risk caused by heavy smoking itself.

Although a few studies have linked water chlorinating and fluoridation with bladder cancer, most experts believe that the potential health risk is small and is outweighed by the greater danger of the spread of diseases such as cholera and typhoid fever by germs in unchlorinated water (Trichopoulous and others, 1996). Moreover, fluoride in drinking water is an effective agent in preventing tooth decay.

Radiation

Beginning in the 1960s, a well-tanned complexion became fashionable. However, many people burn rather than tan, and we now know that a serious long-term effect of sunburn is skin cancer. In those days, when skin-protective sunscreens were generally unknown, sunbathing was especially risky. Is it any wonder that 40 to 50 percent of all Americans who reach 65 develop skin cancer (American Cancer Society, 2004)? Even today skin cancer is the most common and most rapidly increasing type of cancer in the United States.

High-frequency radiation, ionizing radiation (IR), and ultraviolet (UV) radiation are proven carcinogens. Ultraviolet B rays, which can damage DNA, cause more than 90 percent of all skin cancers, including **melanoma,** a potentially deadly form of cancer that forms in skin cells. A number of researchers believe that the overall frequency of sunburns during childhood is a key factor in melanoma. This explains why people who take longer to develop a sunburn have a lower incidence of melanoma than those who burn quickly (Leffell & Brash, 1996). Another factor in the rising trend in skin cancer is the thinning of the earth's ozone layer, which filters skin-damaging ultraviolet (UV) radiation.

Given the evidence that the sun's ultraviolet rays can cause cancer, why do so many people continue to bask in the sun? In one study, researchers interviewed sunbathers at California beaches to determine the factors that influenced their decision to lie in the sun (Keesling & Friedman, 1987). Those with the deepest tans (who also reported spending the largest amounts of time in the sun) were least knowledgeable about skin cancer. They also were more relaxed, more sensitive to the influence of peers who valued a good tan, more likely to take other risks, and more focused on their appearance.

■ **melanoma** a potentially deadly form of cancer that strikes the melatonin-containing cells of the skin.

Non-ionizing, or low-frequency, radiation (such as that arising from microwaves, radar screens, electricity, and radios) has not been shown to cause cancer. Another common fear—living near a nuclear plant—is largely unfounded. In a 35-year study of over 40 million people, researchers compared cancer death rates of Americans who lived near nuclear plants with cancer death rates of people who lived in counties that had no nuclear sites. No differences were found in the two groups (Jablon and others, 1991). Similarly, although toxic wastes in dump sites can threaten health through air, water, and soil pollution, most community exposures involve very low dose levels and do not pose serious health threats.

Occupational Carcinogens and Pollution

People whose work involves exposure to certain chemicals have long been known to be at greater risk of developing cancer than others. Work-related cancers mostly affect the lung, skin, bladder, and blood-forming systems of the body (Trichopoulous and others, 1996). For example, those who work with asbestos, chromium, and chromium compounds are much more likely than other workers to develop lung cancer. Workers exposed to benzene, a solvent used in making varnishes and dyes, are at high risk for developing leukemia.

Other substances now known to be carcinogenic include diesel exhaust and radon. In recent years, however, strict control measures in the workplace, at least in the developed world, have reduced the proportion of cancer deaths caused by job-related carcinogens to less than 5 percent. Unfortunately, such control measures generally lag behind the pace of industrialization in developing countries, where job-related cancers are still likely to increase.

Stress and Immunocompetence

With advances in *psychoneuroimmunology* (PNI), researchers are paying more attention to psychological risk factors—in particular, the role of stress—in the development of cancer. In Chapter 4 we saw how PNI researchers study the relationships among the mind, the body, and immunity. **Immunocompetence**—our immune system's ability to mount an effective defense against disease and harmful foreign agents—depends on many factors, including our overall health, the nature of the health-threatening disease or foreign agent, and perceived stress.

How might perceived stress promote the development of cancer? According to the **immune surveillance theory,** cancer cells, which develop spontaneously in the body, are prevented from spreading and developing into tumors by NK (natural killer) cells and other agents of the immune system. However, when the immune system is overwhelmed by the number of cancer cells or weakened by stress or some other factor, the immune system's surveillance is suppressed, and cancer may develop.

Perceived stress from exams, work, divorce, bereavement, caring for a terminally ill relative, environmental catastrophes, and unemployment, for example, adversely affects our immune functioning (see Cohen and others, 2001 for a review). Based on such findings, one early PNI model, the *global immunosuppres-*

■ **immunocompetence** the overall ability of the immune system, at any given time, to defend the body against the harmful effects of foreign agents.

■ **immune surveillance theory** the theory that cells of the immune system play a monitoring function in searching for and destroying abnormal cells such as those that form tumors.

sion model, proposed that stress always suppresses immune responses. This type of blunted immunity was assumed to be responsible for the increased incidence of infectious diseases and some cancers found in chronically stressed people.

Although the global immunosuppression model dominated the thinking of PNI researchers for years, and continues to be influential, to some researchers the concept of broad decreases in immunity does not make sense as a species' response to all stressors. They reason that if the stress-immune response did indeed evolve, a healthy person should not be adversely affected when it is triggered because this would be maladaptive; natural selection would have selected against this over the course of evolution. Indeed, after more than 30 years of research, there is little evidence that specifically links stress-related changes in the immune system of healthy individuals to disease vulnerability (Segerstrom & Miller, 2004). For instance, although many studies have demonstrated that stress can adversely impact neuroendocrine and immune function, the *clinical significance* of these changes for cancer patients is not clear (Luecken & Compas, 2002). Nor does stress in the years preceding a diagnosis appear to influence a person's cancer risk or mortality (Maunsell and others, 2001).

To address this problem, a more recent *biphasic model* proposes that only the most chronic stressors cause global immunosuppression. Short-term stressors that trigger our fight-or-flight response either have no effect on immunity, or might actually *enhance* immunity to help prepare us to defend against possible infection or injury (Dhabhar & McEwen, 2001; Segerstrom & Miller, 2004). Examples of acute stressors that enhance natural immunity include challenging computer tasks, mental arithmetic, and loud noises. In contrast, chronic stressors such as bereavement, long-term caregiving, and suffering a traumatic injury produce global suppression of most measures of immune function.

Personality

Personality is another psychological factor researchers have studied to determine its relationship to cancer (Smith & Gallo, 2001). It is difficult to determine whether personality attributes such as explanatory style or mood are *causes* or *consequences* of chronic diseases such as cancer. Specific personality dispositions *have* been linked with cancer development, psychological adjustment, survival, and recurrence. However, being diagnosed with a serious illness could itself trigger anger and other mood alterations rather than vice versa. And, of course, chemotherapy and other biomedical interventions may induce physiological changes that directly alter mood as well. Before we can conclude that the mind can cause cancer, however, we need evidence from prospective research studies that investigate psychosocial factors in a large sample of healthy people over a period of years.

In a massive prospective study, Patrick Dattore and his colleagues (1980) compared scores from the Minnesota Multiphasic Personality Inventory (MMPI) that had been obtained from a group of patients several years *before* cancer was detected with the personality profiles of a healthy control group. Those who subsequently developed cancer differed from the disease-free control subjects in two ways: They were more likely to suppress their emotional reactions to events, and they *reported* less depression.

To test the relationship between personality type and cancer, Hans Eysenck and other researchers conducted two major prospective studies (Eysenck and others, 1991; Grossarth-Maticek and others, 1997). At the beginning of the studies, the participants were designated as one of four personality types on the basis of their responses to personality questionnaires. Over the next decade, the researchers compared the causes of death among the four personality types. In both studies, cancer was the top killer among people who had difficulty expressing emotion and tended toward hopelessness in response to stress. Cardiovascular disease was the leading cause of death for people who were easily frustrated, had short tempers, tended to blame others for their stress, and tended toward hostile, angry responses. The third type was a mixture of the first two personalities, and the fourth type had a positive, trusting outlook. Neither the third nor fourth type was especially vulnerable to either cancer or heart disease.

The Type C Personality

These and other studies led researchers to describe the **Type C (cancer-prone) personality.** Cancer-prone individuals were hypothesized to be passive, uncomplaining, and compliant and to have difficulty expressing their emotions. As nurses, oncologists, and other health care professionals have long noted, cancer patients tend to be "nice people" (Holland & Lewis, 1996).

A number of researchers have begun focusing on suppression and denial of emotions as the toxic core of the Type C personality. Brian Esterling and his colleagues (1994) found that subjects who scored high on a personality test that measured repression showed reduced immunocompetence, as indicated by higher levels of herpes virus antibody. This relationship was significant, even after controlling for medication use and a range of other health practices.

Depression has also received considerable attention as a personality disposition that may contribute to cancer (Cohen & Herbert, 1996). In a 20-year study of men who completed the MMPI in 1957, those with higher depression scores had twice the risk of their nondepressed counterparts of dying of cancer 2 decades later (Perskey and others, 1987). A prospective study by researchers at the National Institute on Aging analyzed the case histories of women and men over age 70. Ten years into the study, the cancer rate among those who had been diagnosed as chronically depressed—*after* accounting for age, sex, smoking, and other habits—was 88 percent higher than for nondepressed participants (Penninx and others, 1998). Depression has also been linked with more rapid progression of tumors (possibly due to lower NK cell activity) and shorter survival time among patients diagnosed with breast cancer (Cohen & Herbert, 1996).

Despite these compelling findings, critics have questioned the validity of the link between an emotionally unexpressive, depressed personality style and cancer because these studies have not always been successfully replicated. In fact, some studies have not been able to establish *any* link between cancer and personality type—depressed or otherwise (Zonderman and others, 1989). Furthermore, several studies have reported that depression *does not* place people at increased

■ **Type C (cancer-prone) personality** a passive, uncomplaining person who tends to repress emotions and may be prone to developing cancer.

risk for either cancer incidence or cancer mortality (Kaplan & Reynolds, 1988; Zonderman and others, 1989).

Why the inconsistency in results? One possibility is that research on the role of depression in cancer has generally focused on cancer as a generic disease. It is possible that a greater focus on particular disease sites may clarify the relationship between specific personality dispositions and specific cancers (Cohen & Herbert, 1996).

One meta-analysis examined the relationship between personality and other psychosocial factors and breast cancer (McKenna and others, 1999). The researchers found only a moderate association between the development of breast cancer and psychosocial factors including the tendency to use denial or repression in coping with life stressors, recent experiences of separation and loss, a history of stressful life experiences, or a personality style characterized by conflict avoidance. The remaining hypothesized psychosocial contributors to breast cancer received little statistical support. These findings, therefore, fail to support many of the popular assumptions regarding the influence of personality or psychological factors on the development of breast cancer.

Any link between emotional depression/suppression and other personality characteristics and cancer is also subject to the influence of other factors, such as occupation and health attitudes and behaviors. It is important to show, for example, that the relationship is not due to the fact that people who gravitate toward occupations involving possible exposure to toxic chemicals and other carcinogens are also more likely to be depressed—or that depressed people tend to "let themselves go" by smoking more, eating a fatty diet, and in other ways increasing their health risk.

The safest conclusion we can draw at this point is that the link between specific personality traits and cancer is *suggestive* but inconclusive. Additional research is needed, but to be convincing, future prospective studies must do more than merely establish (or fail to establish) correlations between certain traits and the development of cancer. As several researchers have argued, they should attempt to pinpoint the *mechanisms* by which such factors lead to the development of malignancies (Linkins & Comstock, 1988).

Cancer Treatment

When cancer does develop, early detection and treatment can prevent death and perhaps reduce overall treatment time.

Early Diagnosis

A cancer diagnosis may result in months or years of painful or uncomfortable treatment. This is because cancer develops over time, as neoplastic cells grow into tumors that may metastasize to surrounding tissues. Detecting this process

Figure 10.2

Five-Year Relative Survival Rates by Race and Stage at Diagnosis Five-year relative survival rates are commonly used to monitor progress in the early detection and treatment of cancer. This includes all survivors, whether in remission, disease-free, or under treatment. *Localized* refers to a malignant tumor confined entirely to the organ of origin. *Regional* refers to a malignant tumor that has extended beyond the limits of the organ of origin into the surrounding organs or tissues, and/or involves regional lymph nodes by way of the lymphatic system. *Distant* refers to a malignant cancer that has spread to parts of the body remote from the primary tumor either by direct extension or by metastasis, or via the lymphatic system to distant lymph nodes. The earlier the detection, the greater the likelihood that the tumor will be localized; thus, survival increases markedly the earlier the cancer is diagnosed.

Source: Surveillance, Epidemiology, and End Results (SEER) Program, by National Cancer Institute (search.nci.nih.gov/).

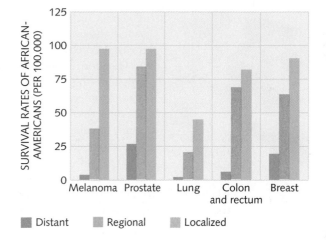

early on, before malignant cells have gained a strong foothold, can dramatically improve a person's chances of survival (Figure 10.2). Unfortunately, many people refuse to perform self-examinations and do not follow recommended screening schedules for cancer of the prostate, breasts, colon, rectum, and cervix (Table 10.2, p. 318). Also, as many as 30 to 50 percent of people with noticeable cancer symptoms delay 3 or 4 months before seeking medical attention (Singer, 1988). (See Table 10.3, p. 318.)

For those with family histories of cancer, genetic screening has become a useful method of early detection. A simple blood test can now detect genetic mutations linked to an increased risk of many types of cancer. Such tests, however, have raised a host of ethical and practical questions. On the practical side, many laboratories administering these tests do not follow the admittedly vague and inadequate regulatory controls that help ensure the validity

Table 10.2

Prevalence of Cancer Screening among Five Racial and Ethnic Groups

Cancer Screening	European-American	African-American	Hispanic-American	Native American	Asian/Pacific Islander
Prostate test (protoscopy) within the past 5 years	30.4%	28.2%	22.4%	27.6%	California*: 24.3%; Hawaii*: 40.7%
Colorectal test	18.2	20.3	14.2	12.3	California*: 2.6; Hawaii*: 23.8
Mammogram within the past 2 years	73.7	76.1	63.5	Alaska*: 93.5	Hawaii*: 80.7
Cervical/uterine test within the past 3 years	84.7	91.1	80.9	90.5	Hawaii*: 84.2

*Indicates state-specific prevalence estimates available for the corresponding race/ethnic group.

Source: Behavioral Risk Factor Surveillance System, Surveillance Summary Report, 2000. National Center for Chronic Disease Prevention and Health Promotion, Centers for Disease Control and Prevention.

Detecting Lung Cancer Most important in the treatment of cancer is early detection. A basic x-ray can provide useful preliminary information regarding a patient's condition. Here a Polish doctor displays an x-ray of a cancerous lung. Although about 40 percent of adults in Poland smoke every day, more than 3 million Poles have quit smoking since the first nationwide antismoking campaigns were launched in the early 1990s.

of genetic tests. And some labs market tests to physicians, obstetricians, and primary care providers who lack expertise in medical genetics.

The more significant problem has to do with the ethics of genetic testing and the knowledge it provides. The ability to predict someone's genetic future also raises a host of psychosocial concerns, both for the individual being tested and for other family members who might be at risk (Cella and others, 2002). If you were fated to develop cancer, would you want to know? What would you do in response? Providing people with a diagnosis of an untreatable disease raises concerns, especially when dealing with children who may not fully understand the implications of the tests. Others fear that children identified as carriers of serious diseases will

Table 10.3

Warning Signs of Cancer

Remembering the word *Caution* will help you identify the most common warning signs of cancer. Although some of these symptoms can be caused by less serious conditions, you should definitely see a doctor to rule out cancer as the cause. Most important, don't wait until you feel discomfort or pain. In their early stages of development, most cancers do not cause pain.

C   Change in bowel or bladder habits.

A   A sore that does not heal.

U   Unusual bleeding or discharge.

T   Thickening or lump in the breast or elsewhere.

I   Indigestion or difficulty swallowing.

O   Recent change in a wart or mole.

N   Nagging cough or hoarseness.

Source: American Cancer Society, 2006.

be discriminated against. A related concern is the real possibility that insurance companies will deny coverage to individuals who have a predisposition toward developing a particular disease.

Treatment Options

Until recently, the treatment options for most forms of cancer were severely limited, and cancer was often a death sentence. Today, there are many effective treatment options that have reduced death rates from most types of cancer. These options include surgery, chemotherapy, radiation therapy, and combination regimes such as those involving both bone marrow transplantation and radiation therapy (Varmus, 2006).

Surgery

Surgery is the oldest form of cancer treatment, and it generally offers the greatest chance for cure for most types of cancer. Approximately 60 percent of cancer patients have some form of surgery, which is usually recommended to achieve one or more of the following goals.

- *Diagnostic* surgery is used to obtain a tissue sample for laboratory testing in order to confirm a diagnosis and identify the specific cancer. A procedure to remove all or part of a tumor for diagnostic tests is called a *biopsy*.

- *Preventive* surgery is performed to remove a growth that is not presently malignant but is likely to become so if left untreated. Sometimes preventive surgery is used to remove an organ when people have an inherited condition that makes development of a cancer likely.

- *Staging* surgery is used to determine the extent of disease. In *laparoscopy*, for example, a tube is passed through a tiny incision in the abdomen to examine its contents and remove tissue samples.

- *Curative* surgery involves the removal of a tumor when the tumor appears to be localized and there is hope of taking out all of the cancerous tissue.

- *Restorative* (or reconstructive) surgery is used to restore a person's appearance or the function of an organ or body part. Examples include breast reconstruction after mastectomy, or use of bone grafts or *prosthetic* (metal or plastic) bone or joint replacements after surgical treatment of bone cancer.

Chemotherapy

Chemotherapy is the use of medicines to treat cancer. While surgery and radiation therapy destroy or damage cancer cells in a specific area, chemotherapy can destroy cancer cells that have spread, or metastasized, to parts of the body far from the original, or primary, tumor. These *systemic drugs* travel through the bloodstream to reach all areas of the body.

Depending on the type of cancer and its stage of development, chemotherapy can be used to cure cancer, to keep the cancer from spreading, to slow the cancer's growth, to kill cancer cells that may have spread to other parts of the

When child psychologist Elizabeth King was diagnosed with cancer, her son created a story and illustration about a character named "Kemo Shark," who swam around in his mother's body eating cancer cells and sometimes healthy ones by mistake, causing her to get sick. When King completed her treatment, she developed her son's story into a children's comic book and funded the nonprofit organization KIDSCOPE to raise money to distribute the book at no cost.

(See http://www.kidscope.org.—Courtesy of KIDSCOPE; Concept by Mitchell McGraugh.)

■ **immunotherapy** chemotherapy in which medications are used to support or enhance the immune system's ability to selectively target cancer cells.

body from the original tumor, or to relieve symptoms caused by the cancer. In one of the newest forms of chemotherapy, **immunotherapy,** medications are used to enhance the immune system's ability to selectively target cancer cells (Disis, 2006).

Anticancer drugs are made to kill fast-growing cells; however, because these drugs travel throughout the body, they can affect normal, healthy cells as well. The normal cells most likely to be affected are blood cells that form in the bone marrow and cells in the digestive tract, reproductive system, and hair follicles (which is why Jeremy temporarily lost his hair). Some anticancer drugs can also damage cells of the heart, kidneys, bladder, lungs, and nervous system.

The most common side effects of chemotherapy are nausea and vomiting, hair loss, and fatigue. Less common side effects include bleeding, infections, and anemia. Although side effects are not always as bad as expected, their reputation makes chemotherapy an anxiety-provoking treatment.

Radiation Therapy

All cells, cancerous and healthy, grow and divide. But cancer cells grow and divide more rapidly than many of the normal cells around them. Radiation therapy delivers high doses of x-rays, gamma rays, or alpha and beta particles to cancerous tumors, killing or damaging them so that they cannot grow, multiply, or spread. Although some normal cells may be affected by radiation, most appear to repair themselves and recover fully from the effects of the treatment. Unlike chemotherapy, which exposes the entire body to cancer-fighting chemicals, radiation therapy affects only the tumor and the surrounding area.

An estimated 350,000 cancer patients receive radiation therapy each year, more than half of all cancer cases. It is the primary treatment for cancer in almost any part of the body, including head and neck tumors, early-stage Hodgkin's disease, non-Hodgkin's lymphomas, and cancers of the lung, breasts, cervix, prostate, testes, bladder, thyroid, and brain. Radiation therapy also can be used to shrink a tumor prior to surgery (so that it can be removed more easily) or after surgery to stop the growth of any cancer cells that remain.

Like chemotherapy, radiation is often associated with side effects, including temporary or permanent loss of hair in the area being treated, fatigue, loss of appetite, skin rashes, and loss of white blood cells. On the positive side, thousands of people have become cancer free after receiving radiation treatments alone or in combination with surgery or chemotherapy.

Alternative Treatments

Alternative treatments for cancer will be discussed more fully in Chapter 14.

Many cancer patients have tried one or more alternative treatments. Among these are aromatherapy, biofeedback, meditation, music therapy, prayer and spiritual practices, yoga, t'ai chi (an exercise-based form of "moving meditation"), art therapy, massage therapy, and herbal treatment. Although alternative therapies are generally unproven and have not been scientifically tested, many *can* be used safely along with standard biomedical treatment to relieve symptoms or side effects, to ease pain, and to improve a patient's overall quality of life.

Coping with Cancer

Life-threatening chronic diseases such as cancer create unique stresses for both victims and their families. Cancer is a dreaded disease, which most people realize can be intensely painful and lead to disability, disfigurement, or death. As patients' expectations of survival have increased, so has the need for psychosocial supports aimed at restoring or maintaining quality of life. Health psychologists are helping focus attention and resources on enabling patients and their families to cope with the adverse effects of cancer treatment. They also are helping health care professionals recognize that the course of adjustment to cancer is not the same for all patients (Helgeson and others, 2004).

Research on the emotional and behavioral responses of cancer patients to surgery consistently shows high levels of anxiety both before and after an operation. Compared with patients who are undergoing surgery for benign conditions, cancer surgery patients have higher overall levels of distress and slower rates of emotional recovery. In one study, breast cancer patients' presurgery expectations were significant predictors of their *postsurgery* pain, fatigue, and nausea (Montgomery & Bovbjerg, 2004).

Even when cancer treatment is successful and the disease is in remission, the fear, stress, and uncertainty do not go away. The threat of recurrence looms, for some patients for the rest of their lives. In fact, the distress associated with cancer recurrence is often greater than that following the initial diagnosis (Vickberg, 2003). The words of one breast cancer survivor poignantly illustrate this anxiety:

> "This is what cancer is about to me, living with possible recurrence. Cancer is not about two months of treatment and a couple of minor surgeries . . . I think the hardest thing for women like me who have found their cancers early and kept their breasts is to believe we are going to get away with all this. Am I really going to be OK?" (as quoted in Vicksberg, 2003).

Feelings such as these argue for educating cancer patients about what's normal following treatment, and for improving the quality of life of cancer patients. Unfortunately, many health insurance providers do not distinguish between mental illness and psychosocial interventions for cancer patients. As a result, many patients find that psychological healing is not covered by their health care insurance.

Personality, Ethnicity, and Coping

Although the link between personality traits and the development of cancer is tenuous, personality does predict how well a person copes with cancer. For instance, cancer victims who psychologically "give in"—who are unwilling to fight the disease—seem to have a poorer prognosis than those who maintain the kind of "fighting spirit" that my son, Jeremy, found within himself. In one 15-year study of women with breast cancer, this spirit was associated with a significantly lower mortality rate than denial, helplessness, or even stoic acceptance (Greer,

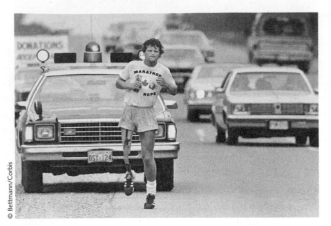

© Bettmann/Corbis

True "Fighting Spirit" Canadian Terry Fox's refusal to be defeated by cancer has inspired several generations. In this photo, Terry, who lost his right leg to cancer, runs along a highway just before reaching the halfway mark in his cross-Canada run. Terry ran coast to coast on an artificial limb—often as far as a marathon each day—to raise money to fight the killer disease.

1991). In a sense, then, *poor* adjustment and nonacceptance of the diagnosis are *positive* traits for cancer victims.

Other researchers have found that an optimistic disposition at the time the cancer is diagnosed is associated with an active, engaged coping style and less psychological distress over time (Carver and others, 1993). Breast cancer patients who scored very low on a measure of dispositional optimism at the time of diagnosis reported greater symptoms of anxiety and depression and relied more often on avoidant, emotion-focused coping than did their more optimistic counterparts (Epping-Jordan and others, 1999). At 3 and 6 months after diagnosis, symptoms of anxiety and depression tended to occur only in those who continued to be troubled by persistent, intrusive thoughts about their illness.

Health psychologists are paying increasing attention to the experiences of ethnically diverse samples of people following the diagnosis of cancer. As an example, among breast cancer survivors, African-Americans report more difficulties with physical functioning and activities of daily living than do European-Americans; European-Americans report more sexual difficulties than do African-Americans; Latinas score higher than the other groups on measures of distress; and Filipina patients report the most difficulties with emotional functioning (see Giedzinska and others, 2004 for a review).

Other researchers have found that women of lower socioeconomic status, and African-American and Hispanic women, are more likely than European-Americans to perceive *benefits* from a diagnosis of breast cancer, such as a renewed focus on relationships in their lives (Tomich & Helgeson, 2004). The researchers suggest that impoverished and minority women are more likely to face discrimination in their daily lives that has prepared them to derive benefits from traumatic events. Low-SES and minority persons also are more likely to turn to religion to cope with trauma, which has been characterized as a way of cognitively restructuring events to search for their significance (Harrison and others, 2001).

Because ethnicity often serves as a proxy for other sociodemographic variables, such as income, education, and the nature of the medical treatment received, interpreting differences in coping such as these is difficult. At the very least, however, these findings demonstrate that psychologists and health care providers should not assume that the experiences provided by one ethnic group can be generalized to all others.

A number of studies have found that the ability to find positive meaning from stressful life events, including a diagnosis of cancer, is associated with improved immune responses. In one study, Julienne Bower and her colleagues (2003) asked women who had lost a close relative to breast cancer to write about the death (cognitive processing/disclosure group) or about nonemotional topics weekly for 4 weeks. Women in the cognitive processing/disclosure group who, following the intervention, placed greater importance on goals such as cultivating relationships and striving for meaning in their lives had stronger measures of immune functioning.

Knowledge, Control, and Social Support

Considering the stress associated with being treated for cancer, most patients display remarkable physical and psychological resilience. Important factors in adjusting to cancer treatment include having access to information, perceiving some degree of control over treatment, and being able to express emotions while feeling supported by others.

Knowledge and Control

Health psychologists have made considerable progress in understanding the psychological reactions of patients to cancer treatment and the types of interventions that are effective in assisting their adjustment. They have found, for example, that procedural information (such as how the surgery, radiation, or chemotherapy regimen will be administered, as well as what the patient can expect before and after treatment) has wide-ranging benefits. Among these are fewer negative emotions, reduced pain, and briefer hospitalization (Johnston & Vogele, 1993).

The Internet is an increasingly important source of information for many cancer survivors. A 2001 survey revealed that over 100 million individuals in the United States spent some time looking for health information on the Internet, with cancer being one of the top two diseases researched (Satterlund, 2003). One study found that using the Internet for as little as 1 hour per week to search for breast health information was associated with greater feelings of social support and less loneliness in women with breast cancer (Fogel and others, 2002).

Also beneficial are interventions that focus on preventing patients from feeling helpless during their treatment. Even something as simple as encouraging patients to make choices about the hospital environment can improve a patient's well-being (Patenaude and others, 1990). For this reason, patients often are encouraged to decorate their room with pictures, photographs, and other personal items from home. Although the sense of doom and the stigma that once were attached to a diagnosis of cancer have largely disappeared, interventions aimed at *self-presentation* can help patients overcome difficulties in managing social relationships with family, friends, and coworkers that result from changes in their physical appearance (Leary and others, 1994; Leary & Kowalski, 1990). Such interventions can range from the use of wigs by patients who have lost their hair as a result of chemotherapy to cognitive-behavioral therapy to improve self-esteem.

Emotional Disclosure

Key to any effective intervention is providing cancer patients with emotional support and an opportunity to discuss their fears about the disease and its treatment. For example, women with metastatic breast cancer who were allowed to

For many cancer patients, there is a wide gap between optimal care and the care they actually receive. A report from the Institute of Medicine's National Cancer Policy Board, for instance, found that physicians often fail to recognize signs of depression and other long-term psychological effects of cancer and its treatment (Rabasca, 1999).

discuss their fears showed an 18-month increase in survival (Spiegel and others, 1989). Similarly, men and women with melanoma who met regularly with a support group showed increased survival rates and reduced recurrence after 5 to 6 years, as compared to control patients who received standard biomedical treatment (Fawzy and others, 1993).

A more recent study examined the importance to patients of being able to actively process and express the emotions involved in coping with breast cancer. The participants were recruited within 20 weeks of completing surgery, chemotherapy, or radiation. Over the next 3 months, women who expressed their emotions about cancer had fewer medical appointments for cancer-related health problems and reported significantly lower stress levels compared with their less expressive and less socially receptive counterparts (Stanton and others, 2000). The researchers suggest that by openly expressing one's fears—for instance, a loss of perceived control—"one may begin to distinguish what one can and cannot control [in order] to channel energy toward attainable goals, and to generate alternate pathways for bolstering control" (p. 880). They also suggest that repeated expression of emotions may decrease negative emotions and the physiological arousal that comes with them, leading cancer patients to believe that their situation is not as dire as originally thought and to derive some benefit from their adversity. Other studies have reported that experimentally inducing individuals to write or talk about stressful experiences can enhance physical and psychological health (for example, Smyth & Pennebaker, 2001).

A spouse or significant other provides an important source of social support for many cancer patients. When this relationship is perceived as solid and supportive, the patient's physical and emotional well-being benefits greatly. For example, cancer patients who are married tend to survive the disease better than unmarried persons (Pistrang & Barker, 1995). This is due in part to the fact that married patients—often because of input from their spouse—generally detect cancer and other diseases at an earlier stage of development, and they are more likely to seek early treatment.

The benefits of social support extend beyond marriage. Women and men who feel "socially connected" to a network of caring friends are less likely to die of all types of cancer than their socially isolated counterparts (Reynolds & Kaplan, 1990).

Emotional Intelligence

A growing body of research indicates that cognitive and emotional processing is critical in coping with traumatic events such as a diagnosis of cancer (Green and others, 2000; Lepore, 2001). People who possess good skills at identifying and articulating emotions might therefore be expected to fare better at coping with traumatic events than people who lack these skills. One dispositional characteristic that psychologists have focused on is *emotional intelligence (EI)*, defined as the ability to accurately perceive, understand, express, and regulate emotions (Mayer and others, 2001).

In a recent study, John Schmidt and Michael Andrykowski (2004) investigated the relationships among several social and dispositional variables and adjustment to breast cancer among 302 members of five Internet-based breast cancer support groups. In all cases, women who scored higher on a 30-item dispositional measure of EI reported less anxiety, depression, and overall distress than women with lower levels of EI. The beneficial effects of EI were especially pronounced among participants who perceived weaker social support and more social constraints from others that discouraged them from sharing their thoughts and feelings regarding their cancer. The researchers suggest that the presence of social contraints and absence of social support may have caused the women to actively avoid thinking about their cancer experience, thus inhibiting active processing and coping. To make matters worse, women who score low in EI may be less able to effectively identify, communicate, and control their emotions and "thus may be seen as irrational, demanding, or aversive" by others around them, who then respond in a manner that further discourages discussion (Schmidt & Andrykowski, 2004; p. 264). Those who are low in EI might also be less effective in eliciting social support from others and less capable of recognizing and responding to supportive responses that they may make.

Social Support and Other Systematic Interventions

Other, more systematic interventions focus on improving the ability of patients to cope with their anxiety and stress during and immediately following cancer treatments. For example, Nancy Fawzy and her colleagues (1993) evaluated survival rates in patients suffering from malignant melanoma. For 6 weeks following surgery, half the patients attended weekly group meetings that centered on health education, stress-management skills, and social support. The others (the control group) did not attend any such meetings. A 6-year follow-up revealed that the intervention group had significantly better survival rates than the control group did. However, several large-scale, well-controlled studies have failed to find a significant effect of psychosocial interventions on cancer progression or survival (for example, Edelman and others, 1999; Cunningham and others, 1998).

Other studies have demonstrated that specific interventions are most effective at certain times. For example, one group of researchers divided breast, colon, lung, and uterine cancer patients into two groups: one that began a group intervention soon after entering the study and the other after 4 months (Edgar and others, 1992). At the start of the study, both groups were measured on depression, anxiety, illness worry, and perceived personal control; follow-up measures were taken at 4-, 8-, and 12-month intervals. The intervention consisted of five 1-hour sessions that focused on developing coping skills, using such techniques as goal setting, problem solving, cognitive reappraisal, and relaxation training, and providing workshops on health care resources. Coping improved for all patients, but the greatest reduction in stress levels occurred in the group whose intervention began 4 months after being diagnosed with cancer. According to the researchers, patients' needs shortly after being diagnosed with cancer are probably quite different from their needs a few months later, after the emotional shock of the situation has been overcome.

A limited number of studies have also suggested that behavioral and psychoshocial interventions may lower stress hormone levels and improve immune function in cancer patients and people coping with cancer in a loved one. For instance, among breast cancer patients, biofeedback training, cognitive therapy, relaxation training, guided imagery, and stress management have all been associated with significant decreases in cortisol levels and increases in the number of circulating lymphocytes (for example, Cruess and others, 2002). Although a few studies have even shown lower recurrence rates among cancer patients who participate in psychosocial interventions relative to waiting-list control participants, as noted earlier, the potential effects of such interventions on clinical outcomes remain speculative (see Luecken & Compas, 2002 for a review).

Holistic Medicine

Health psychologists have made considerable progress in developing cognitive-behavioral interventions in comprehensive cancer care. For adults, they have focused on pain relief, control of aversive reactions to treatment (such as nausea during chemotherapy), and enhancement of emotional well-being. For children, they have focused on increasing adherence and reducing suffering (Redd & Jacobsen, 2001). Among the most widely used interventions are hypnosis, progressive muscle relaxation with guided imagery, systematic desensitization, biofeedback, and cognitive distraction. For instance, before Jeremy's attending physician performed a *lumbar puncture* (spinal tap) to sample my son's spinal fluid, the nurse engaged Jeremy in a detailed (and distracting) discussion of the most recent *Star Trek* program. In this section, we describe two of the more common techniques: guided imagery and systematic desensitization.

Many of these interventions stem from the field of psychoneuroimmunology (PNI). PNI researchers believe that the risk for many diseases, including cancer; the course that a particular disease follows; and the remission and recurrence of symptoms are all influenced by the interaction of behavioral, neuroendocrine, and immune responses.

Guided Imagery

Guided imagery draws on patients' psychophysiological reactions to the environment to help them optimize physiological activity in various body systems and thus relieve pain or discomfort. For example, a patient who views an impending surgery as a life-threatening trauma may exhibit hypertension, cardiac arrhythmia, and other health-compromising responses prior to surgery. Conversely, a patient who looks forward to the same operation as a life-saving event is more likely to remain relaxed before, during, and following treatment.

In guided imagery, the therapist uses one or more external devices to help the patient relax and then form clear, strong, positive images to replace the symptoms. Effective images draw on several sensory modalities, including vi-

■ **guided imagery** the use of one or more external devices to assist in relaxation and the formation of clear, strong, positive images.

sion, hearing, touch, and even smell or taste and may be stimulated by taped music, sounds of nature, verbal suggestions, pictures of objects or places, aromas from scented candles, or a variety of other devices (Naparstek, 1994).

Guided imagery begins with the patient assuming a comfortable position, either lying down or sitting, with eyes closed or open. After taking several slow, deep breaths, the person begins a process of systematically attending to any areas of bodily tension, which are then relaxed. A variety of techniques may be used to assist relaxation, including progressive muscle relaxation, biofeedback training, or autogenic training (see Chapter 5).

Once a relaxed state is reached, the person visualizes a safe, peaceful place and strives to make the image as clear and intense as possible by focusing on sights, sounds, smells, and other sensory aspects of the moment. At this point, the patient follows taped suggestions (or a nurse or therapist's verbal suggestions) and forms a mental image of a symptom, such as pain or nausea. The patient then imagines the symptom changing. For example, the "red" fiery pain changes to a cool shade of blue; queasiness is expelled from the body with each exhalation.

After a few minutes of focusing on the altered symptom (sometimes describing its changed appearance to the nurse or therapist), the patient is instructed to relax, breathe deeply, and return to the peaceful place. After several sessions, which may last only 5 or 10 minutes, most patients are able to perform imagery without assistance.

Imagery may be beneficial for several reasons (Naparstek, 1994):

- Imagery triggers a state of relaxed concentration that enhances the person's sensitivity to health-promoting images.

- Imagery gives the patient an increased sense of control and a decreased sense of helplessness over stressful aspects of disease or treatment.

- Imagery may also work through the *placebo effect*. People who believe that imagery and relaxation have the potential to improve their health may, in fact, experience physiological changes that enhance the ability to fight disease.

Systematic Desensitization

After several sessions of chemotherapy, nearly one-third of all patients begin to feel nauseated in anticipation of an upcoming treatment session. Many health psychologists consider this *anticipatory nausea* to be a form of classical conditioning, in which events leading up to treatment (such as driving to the hospital and sitting in the waiting room) function as *conditioned stimuli,* becoming linked to the powerful physiological reactions elicited as *unconditioned responses* by the cancer drug.

Health psychologists have learned that incorporating guided imagery into **systematic desensitization** effectively counters this classically conditioned side effect of chemotherapy. In this form of behavior therapy, commonly used to help people overcome phobias, the person is gradually exposed to increasingly fearful stimuli or situations, while remaining deeply relaxed. In one study, Gary

■ **systematic desensitization** a form of behavior therapy, commonly used for overcoming phobias, in which the person is exposed to a series of increasingly fearful situations while remaining deeply relaxed.

Morrow and his colleagues (1992) trained a group of oncologists and nurses to use desensitization with cancer patients. The patients were then randomly assigned to one of two treatment groups (one conducted by a psychologist and one conducted by a nurse) or to a control group that received no intervention.

In the first stage, cancer patients established a hierarchy of difficult moments related to an approaching chemotherapy session, such as awakening on the morning of treatment, driving to the hospital, and sitting in the treatment room. After instruction in several relaxation-inducing techniques, the patients used guided imagery to visualize each moment in the hierarchy while remaining in a relaxed state. As they gradually worked their way up from the least threatening image to the most threatening image, the patients were *reconditioned* to feel relaxation rather than anxiety and nausea.

Both treatment groups experienced a substantial decline in the duration of their nausea following treatment. In contrast, the control group's nausea actually lasted 15 hours *longer* than ever, perhaps as a result of additional classical conditioning. In follow-up studies, Morrow and his colleagues have found that the benefits of desensitization often increase over time. Like athletes who gradually improve their visual imagery skills, many patients report much less nausea and vomiting over time as they improve their control over their anxiety in anticipating treatment.

The intervention studies we have discussed provide substantial evidence that psychosocial factors can influence a cancer patient's response to treatment and, quite possibly, the course of recovery (or the likelihood of recurrence). Those studies that have reported longer survival for cancer patients are especially vivid demonstrations of the value of such interventions.

Summing Up

What Is Cancer?

1. Cancer is the second leading cause of death in the United States. It is actually more than 100 different but related diseases. They result from the uncontrolled multiplication and spread of body cells that form tumors.

2. There are four general types of cancer: Carcinomas are cancers of the epithelial cells, which line the outer and inner surfaces of the body. Lymphomas are cancers of the lymph system. Sarcomas are cancers that develop from muscle, bone, fat, and other connective tissue. Leukemias are cancers of the blood and blood-forming system.

3. Cancer defies a simple description because its occurrence varies with gender, age, ethnicity, and race.

Risk Factors for Cancer

4. The leading risk factor for cancer is smoking. Cancers of the lungs, mouth, pharynx, larynx, esophagus, pancreas, uterus, cervix, kidney, bladder, and breast are linked to all forms of tobacco use, including smokeless tobacco and cigars.

5. Diet is a factor in as many as one-third of all cancer deaths. Fatty diets promote cancer of the colon, prostate, testes, uterus, and ovary. Excessive intake of salt, sugar, and alcohol may increase the risk of certain types of cancer. Diets that include plenty of fruits, vegetables, and whole grains may play a protective role against some cancers. Regular exercise may also be a protective factor for certain cancers. Alcohol use, espe-

cially among tobacco users, is a major risk factor for cancer.

6. Some forms of cancer are inherited. Most cases of breast cancer, however, are caused by nongenetic factors.

7. Research has linked a variety of environmental factors to cancer, including ultraviolet light, toxic chemicals, and occupational carcinogens.

8. According to the immune surveillance theory, cancer cells are prevented from spreading by agents of the immune system that constantly patrol the body for abnormal cells. Prolonged stress may compromise the immune system and allow malignant cells to spread. Reduced immunocompetence has been demonstrated following exams, divorce, bereavement, unemployment, and occupational stress.

9. Personality factors have also been linked to cancer. A pattern of traits, including a hopeless attitude, depression, and the suppression of emotion may be related to the development of cancer. Nonacceptance of cancer as a death sentence and a "fighting spirit" appear to be positive traits that tend to prolong survival among cancer patients.

Cancer Treatment

10. When cancer does develop, its impact on health can nearly always be minimized through early detection and treatment. Advances in genetic screening, mammography, CT scans, and other detection technologies have dramatically improved the survival rates for many types of cancer. Many people fail to heed early warning signs of cancer, however.

11. Biomedical treatments for cancer include surgery, chemotherapy, and radiation therapy. Surgery generally offers the greatest chance for cure for most types of cancer. Chemotherapy is used to destroy fast-growing cancer cells that have spread to parts of the body far from the primary tumor. Unlike chemotherapy, radiation therapy affects only the tumor and the surrounding area.

12. Many cancer patients try one or more alternative treatments (such as meditation, biofeedback, or herbal treatments) to relieve side effects and to improve their overall quality of life.

Coping with Cancer

13. Cancer and cancer treatment create unique stresses for both patients and their families. Even when treatment is successful, the threat of the disease's recurrence looms.

14. A variety of psychosocial interventions have been used to assist patients in coping with cancer. Effective interventions enhance patients' knowledge about what to expect from treatment, increase the perception of control over their lives, and offer a supportive social environment in which to share fears and concerns.

15. Interventions that provide health education and teach specific skills for solving problems and managing stress are also beneficial to patients' well-being. Guided imagery and systematic desensitization effectively help patients control the side effects of chemotherapy and other cancer treatments.

Key Terms and Concepts

cancer, p. 304
metastasis, p. 304
carcinoma, p. 305
sarcoma, p. 305
lymphoma, p. 305

leukemia, p. 305
carcinogen, p. 307
carotenoids, p. 308
melanoma, p. 312
immunocompetence, p. 313

immune surveillance theory, p. 313
Type C (cancer-prone) personality, p. 315
immunotherapy, p. 320
guided imagery, p. 326
systematic desensitization, p. 327

HIV and AIDS

*M*ercy Makhalemele—a 23-year-old woman from Durban, South Africa—discovered that she was HIV-positive when she became pregnant with her second child. She had always been faithful to her husband of 5 years, but fearing what might happen if her husband and employer found out, Mercy kept her secret for almost a year. When she finally realized that her husband's infidelity must have been the source of the virus and confronted him with the news, he became violent, beating her and pushing her against a hot stove that badly burned her wrist. Then he threw her out of the house, refusing to admit that he had given her the virus. Later, he stormed into the shoe store Mercy managed, shouting in front of coworkers and customers that he wanted nothing to do with someone with AIDS. Mercy was fired later that day.[1]

Mercy's experience is not an isolated story. Already, AIDS has killed more than 20 million people and become the world's leading cause of death and lost years of productive life among adults aged 15 to 59 years (World Health Organization, 2004). In most African towns, however, asking whether AIDS is common will lead to a quick denial. The social stigma attached to AIDS is so strong that few will admit to being HIV-positive. Those who do come forward are shunned.

AIDS arouses such passion because it is associated with two highly taboo subjects: sex and death. The shame that AIDS victims feel and the treatment they receive from their neighbors, coworkers, and even family members is the greatest barrier in the battle to stop the spread of the disease. Even when AIDS testing is available, many Africans don't want to know if they have the virus. Those who know they have the disease are ashamed and afraid to admit it, so they act as if nothing is wrong, which often contributes to the spread

[1]Mercy Makhalemele's story is adapted from Daley, S. (1998). *Dead Zones: The Burden of Shame.* The New York Times. http://www.nytimes.com

of the disease. Similarly, many AIDS victims do not go to the clinics because they are too ashamed to be seen there, even though early treatment can prolong survival and dramatically improve the quality of life among those who are infected.

This tendency to "blame the victim" for his or her plight is not confined to developing countries. Many Americans also believe that AIDS patients are being punished for their immorality (Herek and others, 2003). Because of fears about AIDS and because many people link drug abuse and homosexuality to AIDS, patients and their families typically feel stigmatized. Afraid that disclosing their illness will lead to rejection by friends, neighbors, and coworkers, some may withdraw and become secretive. In so doing, they cut off the social support that can play a vital role in their survival.

A lthough AIDS is a newly discovered disease, some health experts believe that it actually may be thousands of years old. AIDS has become a global problem only recently because of the dramatic increase in mobility of most of the world's population, which has allowed the disease to spread from continent to continent. Although the initial panic created by the outbreak of the HIV virus has subsided somewhat in developed countries, where early screening and aggressive new drug treatments have given cause for hope, in developing countries the picture is bleaker than ever.

This chapter takes a thorough look at the AIDS epidemic. We begin by examining the origins of the virus that causes AIDS, its impact on the body, and how the virus is spread. Next, we will take up the issue of medical and psychosocial interventions for HIV/AIDS. The chapter concludes with a discussion of health psychology's role in the design and implementation of programs to help AIDS patients, partners, and family members cope with their crisis.

The AIDS Epidemic

A cquired immunodeficiency syndrome (AIDS) is a life-threatening disease caused by the **human immunodeficiency virus (HIV)**. The virus attacks the body's immune system and leaves it vulnerable to infection. As HIV sickness develops into full-blown AIDS, its victims usually struggle with infections that would otherwise be handled with relative ease if their immune systems were not compromised. In this way, AIDS increases its victims' vulnerability to *opportunistic infections,* such as pneumonia and certain cancers, which prey on their weakened immune systems.

■ **AIDS (acquired immunodeficiency syndrome)** a life-threatening disease caused by the human immunodeficiency virus in which the body's CD4 lymphocytes are destroyed, leaving the victim vulnerable to opportunistic diseases.

■ **HIV (human immunodeficiency virus)** the retrovirus that causes AIDS; it injects its genome into lymphocytes so that it reproduces when the cells are activated.

■ **Kaposi's sarcoma** a rare cancer of blood vessels serving the skin, mucous membranes, and other glands in the body.

A Brief History of AIDS

In the late 1970s, unrecognized cases of what we now know to be AIDS began to appear. Although no one knows exactly how the AIDS virus affected the first human, it appears to have originated in west central Africa, spreading quickly through neighboring countries. HIV is one of a family of primate viruses similar to a harmless virus found in certain subspecies of chimpanzees and green monkeys.

Patient Zero

Whatever the origins of HIV, the role of international travel in its spread through the population is underscored by the case of "Patient Zero," a Canadian flight attendant named Gaetan Dugas, whose job and sexual habits made him a potent carrier for spreading HIV.

The disease was first noticed in humans in 1980, when 55 young men (including Dugas) were diagnosed with a cluster of similar symptoms with an unknown cause. The symptoms were indicative of **Kaposi's sarcoma,** a rare cancer usually found only among the elderly. Epidemiologists suspected that the cause of the unexpected illness was a weakened immune system. Since most of the first reported victims were gay men and intravenous (IV) drug users, it appeared that the disease was being transmitted sexually or through the exchange of infected blood.

The Centers for Disease Control (CDC) finally tracked down Dugas in 1982, a year after they published the first report on the disease. Dugas freely disclosed his sexual habits. Unaware that he had infected scores of homosexual men, Dugas estimated that he had as many as 250 sexual contacts in a typical year, even boasting that over 10 years, he'd easily had 2,500 sexual partners (Shilts, 1987). Although he refused to believe that he may have been an original carrier, Dugas cooperated by providing the names and telephone numbers of as many of his previous sexual partners as he could remember. By April 1982, epidemiologists were certain that 40 of the first gay men diagnosed with AIDS could be linked to Dugas: 9 in Los Angeles, 22 in New York City, and 9 in several other American cities.

In 1983, the National Institutes of Health (NIH) in the United States and the Pasteur Institute in France simultaneously concluded that a new virus was the probable cause of the disease. In March 1984, Dugas died. One month later, the U.S. Department of Health announced that it had isolated the new virus—HIV.

The Spread of AIDS

During the last half of the 1980s, AIDS began to threaten the general population. Once limited mostly to white gay men, AIDS began surfacing among other ethnic groups. In January 1991, AIDS claimed its 100,000th victim. Public fear escalated when in November of that year basketball legend Magic Johnson announced

AP/Wide World Photos

AIDS Awareness On November 7, 1991, NBA superstar Earvin "Magic" Johnson stunned the world by announcing that he was HIV-positive. Because of Johnson's fame and the esteem and affection his fans felt for him, this statement was a major factor in increased AIDS awareness, both in the United States and around the world.

that he was HIV-positive. This furor increased even more in February 1993, when tennis player Arthur Ashe died of AIDS contracted through a blood transfusion during heart surgery. But no cure was yet in sight; prevention was still the only weapon against AIDS as it claimed its 200,000th victim in 1993. The disease continued to grow exponentially, reaching 400,000 cases worldwide by 1994, with increased incidence among women and still no effective drug treatments.

As the millennium approached, new anti-HIV drugs were finally proving to be effective, but they weren't available to everyone who needed them, and, worldwide, the AIDS **pandemic** was spiraling out of control (see Table 11.1). Twenty-five years into the still-emerging pandemic, HIV has reached every corner of the globe, infecting more than 65 million people (of whom 25 million have died), and with a death toll that has risen every year since the first reported cases (Fauci, 2006). Worldwide, 11 people are infected every minute. Ten percent of these are under age 15. We can only guess how many people have been exposed to HIV and are therefore carriers who can spread the virus without being aware of doing so. Sadly, the battle against AIDS has not yet been won anywhere. Two-thirds of all HIV-infected people live in Africa, where about 1 in 12 adults is infected, and one-fifth live in Asia. Worldwide, unprotected heterosexual intercourse is the predominant mode by which the virus is transmitted (World Health Organization, 2004).

■ **pandemic** a worldwide epidemic such as AIDS.

Of the 42,514 newly diagnosed cases of AIDS in the United States during 2004, nearly 9,000 involved adults age 50 and older (CDC, 2004).

Table 11.1

Regional HIV/AIDS Statistics, May 2006

Region	Adults & children living with HIV/AIDS	Percentage who are women	Main mode(s) of transmission
Sub-Saharan Africa	24.5 million	54%	Hetero
North Africa & Middle East	440,000	43%	IDU, Hetero
East Asia	680,000	28%	IDU, Hetero, MSM
South & Southeast Asia	7.6 million	29%	IDU, Hetero, MSM
Latin America	1.6 million	30%	MSM, IDU, Hetero
Caribbean	330,000	48%	Hetero, MSM
Eastern Europe & Central Asia	1.5 million	28%	IDU, MSM
Western Europe & Central Europe	720,000	28%	MSM, IDU
North America	1.3 million	24%	MSM, IDU, Hetero
Oceania	78,000	45%	MSM, IDU
Total	38.6 million	45%	

MSM (sexual transmission among men who have sex with men), IDU (transmission through intravenous drug use), Hetero (heterosexual transmission)

Source: UNAIDS. May 2006. Report on the global AIDS epidemic. http://www.unaids.org/en/HIV_data/2006GlobalReport/default.asp

AIDS Is Out of Control in Africa In Africa, more than 50 percent of women aged 15 to 25 are HIV-positive. This native of Kitwe, Zambia, is 27 years old. Her husband has already died of AIDS, and she has been diagnosed as HIV-positive.

The Epidemiology of AIDS

As you learned in Chapter 2, the first step in fighting and preventing a chronic disease like AIDS is taken by epidemiologists, who investigate the factors that contribute to its prevalence and incidence in a particular population. Keeping track of the distribution of AIDS by demographic traits is a difficult job because of the fluidity of the disease. However, it is most prevalent among certain populations. In the United States, the AIDS epidemic has taken the greatest toll on young men, particularly African-Americans and Hispanic-Americans. At the beginning of 2003, 82 percent of the persons living with AIDS in the United States were men, and 73 percent were between the ages of 25 and 44. Very few young people have been diagnosed with AIDS—1 percent of those between the ages of 0 and 14—even though they make up over 25 percent of the total U.S. population (Centers for Disease Control and Prevention, 2004). This figure may be misleading, however, due to the long incubation period associated with the HIV virus. Many AIDS victims who are now in their twenties undoubtedly were infected while still in their teens.

Gender

Since 1985, the *proportion* of all AIDS cases in the United States reported among women has more than tripled, with the largest rate of growth occurring among women of color. African-American and Hispanic women together account for more than three-fourths (78 percent) of AIDS cases in women in the United States, even though they together represent less than one-fourth of all women in this country. AIDS is the third leading cause of death of African-American women aged 25 to 44 (CDC, 2003).

These statistics are sobering, but the situation elsewhere in the world is much worse. Throughout Africa, 12 to 13 women are infected for every 10 men (WHO, 2004). What accounts for this gender difference? One reason is that women are often less able to protect themselves from HIV because they often are subordinate to men in intimate relationships (Ickovics and others, 2001). Women who use illegal drugs are likely to use a needle only after their male counterparts have used it. They also have less control over whether a condom will be used during sexual intercourse.

Another reason is that more of the virus is found in ejaculate than in vaginal and cervical secretions. After intercourse, the infected lymphocytes in semen may remain in the vagina and cervix for many days, thus giving the virus more time to infect the woman. In contrast, secretions from an HIV-positive (HIV1) vagina and cervix are easily washed from the penis. Male-to-female transmission of HIV through vaginal intercourse is far more common than is female-to-male transmission (Allen & Setlow, 1991; WHO, 2004) (see Figure 11.1).

Another difference between women and men is that on average, HIV levels in women are about half that of men with similar lymphocyte counts. Women progress to AIDS at a lower overall viral load than men (Farzadegan and others, 1998). These findings suggest the need for gender-based specificity in HIV/AIDS

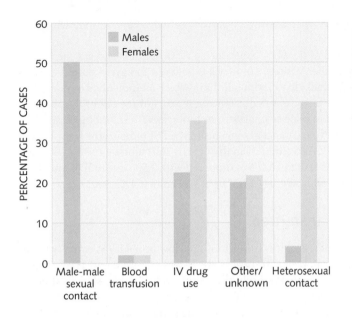

Figure 11.1

AIDS Cases by Exposure Category The rate of AIDS among women is increasing at a faster rate than that among men. One reason is that male-to-female transmission of AIDS is far more common than female-to-male transmission. Another is that women are less in control of the decision to use a condom. A third is that women generally use IV needles after their male partners.

Sources: *Health, United States,* by National Center for Health Statistics, 1998, Hyattsville, MD: United States Government Printing Office; *HIV/AIDS Surveillance Report, 9,* by Centers for Disease Control and Prevention (CDC), 1998, http://www.cdc.gov/hiv.

treatment, such as the need for lower HIV level cut-off points for women in determining their drug treatment regimens. Indeed, when drug treatment cut-off points are adjusted, women have the same rate of disease progression as men (Greiger-Zanlungo, 2001).

Sadly, among many impoverished young women, the risk of HIV infection is linked to sex that is used to obtain food and shelter or to support a drug habit. These women are much less likely to practice safe sex (Allen & Setlow, 1991).

Demographic Patterns

Worldwide, at least three large-scale patterns of HIV transmission have been identified. The first pattern is found in North America and Western Europe, where the most commonly affected groups are gay men and IV drug users. The second pattern includes sub-Saharan Africa and the Caribbean, where HIV and AIDS are commonly found in heterosexuals and equally distributed among men and women (Cohen, 2006). The third pattern involves areas where HIV-infection rates are still relatively low and there are no specific lines of transmission. This pattern is found in Asia, Eastern Europe, North Africa, and some Pacific countries.

Figure 11.2 shows the devastating effect AIDS has had on certain minority populations in the United States. Ethnic and racial differences in rates of HIV transmission are thought to reflect sociocultural differences in drug use and the acceptance of homosexual and bisexual practices. For example, in impoverished minority communities, drug users commonly share needles; of course, when they share with HIV-positive drug users, they become infected themselves and expose their sexual partners. Injection drug use (IDU) is therefore considered a cause of roughly 45 percent of AIDS cases among both African-Americans and

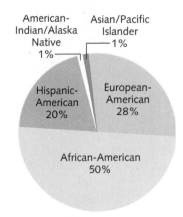

Figure 11.2

AIDS and Ethnicity in the United States In 2004, the estimated number of diagnosed AIDS cases was 42,514. Although AIDS ocurs in every racial and ethnic group, it has taken a disproportionately greater toll on African-Americans.

Source: Centers for Disease Control and Prevention. *HIV/AIDS Surveillance Report: HIV infection and AIDs in the United States, 2004.* http://www.cdc.gov/hiv/topics/surveillance/resources/reports/index.htm

■ **hemophilia** a genetic disease in which the blood fails to clot quickly enough, causing uncontrollable bleeding from even the smallest cut.

Hispanic-Americans, whereas only 17 percent of AIDS cases among whites are linked to shared needles.

The initial spread of the HIV virus among IV drug users and gay men in the United States and other Western countries is believed to have occurred because these are relatively small, closed populations in which an individual is more likely to be exposed to the virus repeatedly. For many years, three out of four cases of AIDS were the result of male-to-male sexual contact (MTM). Although rates due to IDU and heterosexual contact are increasing, MTM remains the largest exposure category among AIDS sufferers in the U.S. In 2002 alone, 11,515 AIDS cases were diagnosed as the result of MTM, compared with 7,596 due to IDU and 9,056 in men and women who acquired HIV heterosexually (CDC, 2003).

How HIV Is Transmitted

As with all serious illnesses, it is important to know how HIV is actually transmitted. Present in high concentration in the blood and semen of HIV-positive individuals, HIV can enter the body through any tear in the skin or mucous membranes, including those not visible to the human eye. Certain sexual behaviors and drug-related activities are by far the primary means by which AIDS is spread, but HIV may be transmitted through the sharing of any virus-infected lymphocytes in bodily fluids—blood, semen, vaginal and cervical secretions, and breast milk. Fortunately, HIV is less easily transmitted than most other less deadly viruses (such as malaria). Without a supportive environment of blood, semen, or the cytoplasm of a host cell, the virus quickly dies.

A less common route of infection involves a transfusion of infected blood. In the early years of the AIDS epidemic, HIV spread rapidly through transfusions of infected blood to victims of **hemophilia,** a genetic disease in which the blood does not clot quickly enough and the person suffers uncontrollable bleeding. Since 1985, however, blood banks have been screening all donor blood for HIV antibodies, and the risk of contracting HIV through transfusion has all but disappeared, accounting for only about 2 percent of all AIDS cases in the United States (Schreiber and others, 1996).

Children are usually infected through exposure to white blood cells from the mother's blood that pass through the placenta during labor and birth. Worldwide, it is estimated that one in four offspring of HIV1 women are so infected. Another 10 percent become infected after birth via breast feeding.

AIDS is NOT transmitted by

• donating blood.

• exposure to airborne particles, contaminated food, or insect bites.

• shaking hands, drinking from the same cup, closed-mouth kissing, hugging, sharing drinking fountains, public telephones, or toilets.

• sharing a work or home environment.

Symptoms and Stages: From HIV to AIDS

HIV infects mostly lymph tissues, where *lymphocytes* develop and are stored. Recall from Chapter 3 that lymphocytes are immune cells that help prevent cancer and other chronic illnesses by controlling cell growth. They also guard against infection by producing antibodies. HIV invades and destroys a type of lymphocyte called the T cell, which is a crucial player in the immune response because it recognizes harmful microbes and triggers production of antibodies. It also coordinates the release of natural killer (NK) cells.

How HIV Progresses

HIV is classified as a **retrovirus** because it works by injecting a copy of its own genetic material, or **genome,** into the DNA of the T cell (the host cell). Like all viruses, HIV can replicate only inside cells, taking over their machinery to reproduce. However, only HIV and other retroviruses incorporate their own genetic instructions into the host cell's genes.

The infected DNA may remain dormant in the chromosome of the host lymphocyte for a period of time. Eventually, however, the infected lymphocyte is certain to become activated against another virus or some other foreign substance. At that point, it divides, replicating HIV along with itself. As infected cells continue to divide, vast numbers of HIV particles emerge from the infected host and invade other lymphocytes.

Healthy human blood normally contains approximately 1,000 T cells per cubic milliliter. Despite the fact that HIV is reproducing in an infected person's body, this level may remain unchanged for years following HIV infection. Then, for reasons that biomedical researchers are still struggling to understand, T cell levels begin to decline, and the immune system grows steadily weaker. Eventually, the victim is left with few functional immune cells and is unable to mount an effective defense against cells harboring HIV, HIV itself, and other invading microorganisms.

The Four Stages of HIV

HIV progresses through four stages of infection that vary in length from person to person (see Figure 11.3, p. 338). During the first stage, which lasts from 1 to 8 weeks, the immune system destroys most HIV, and so people experience only mild symptoms that are similar to those of many other illnesses, such as swollen lymph glands, sore throat, fever, chronic diarrhea, skeletal pain, gynecological infection in women, neurological problems (for example, forgetfulness, decreased alertness, etc.), and, in some cases, a skin rash. These symptoms are often so mild they go unnoticed or unremembered.

The second stage, which may last for months or years, appears to be a period of latency. The person has no obvious symptoms except perhaps for swollen lymph nodes, which may go unnoticed. HIV is far from inactive during this period. In fact, during stage 2, as T cell concentration falls, HIV is constantly being replicated. Within 5 years, 30 percent of infected people move to stage 3, when T cells are further reduced, immune function is impaired, and opportunistic infections occur. Among the most common opportunistic infections are Kaposi's sarcoma (a cancer of blood vessels that causes purplish spots in the skin, mouth, and lungs), lymphoma, parasitic gastrointestinal infections,

■ **retrovirus** a virus that copies its genetic information onto the DNA of a host cell.

■ **genome** all of the DNA information for an organism; the human genome consists of approximately 3 billion DNA sequences.

The AIDS Virus Close-up view of the AIDS virus. HIV is classified as a retrovirus because it destroys lymphocytes by injecting a copy of its own genetic material into the host cell's DNA.

Figure 11.3

The Course of HIV/AIDS
HIV infection may be carried for many years in the unsuspecting victim before symptoms appear. Unfortunately, this long "dormant" period often means that carriers who are unaware of their infection spread HIV unwittingly.

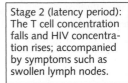

Stage 1: Soon after the initial HIV infection, the immune system destroys most virus; symptoms are mild or nonexistent.

Stage 2 (latency period): The T cell concentration falls and HIV concentration rises; accompanied by symptoms such as swollen lymph nodes.

Stage 3: As T cells are further reduced, immune function is impaired, and opportunistic infections occur.

Stage 4: Finally, almost all natural immunity is lost and full-blown AIDS occurs.

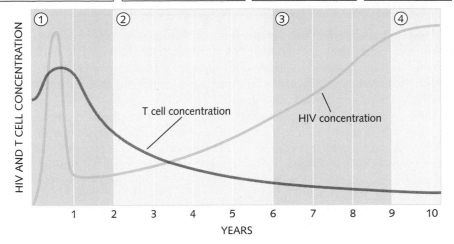

and *pneumocystis carinii pneumonia (PCP)*. This type of pneumonia is caused by a parasite that infects the lungs and is the cause of death in 60 percent of AIDS victims.

During stage 4, the number of T cells drops from a healthy count of 1,000 to 200 or less per cubic milliliter of blood, and almost all natural immunity is lost. At this point, HIV has developed into full-blown AIDS. As T cell levels drop below 100, the balance of power in the immune system shifts to favor the invading virus. HIV levels soar, and microorganisms that the immune system normally would destroy easily begin to proliferate. Without treatment, death generally occurs within a year or two.

The Neurological Impact of AIDS

HIV affects many body systems, including the central nervous system. When HIV migrates to the brain and attacks brain cells, it triggers a variety of emotional and cognitive problems in half of all HIV-positive patients. In most cases, these disturbances involve forgetfulness, inability to concentrate, general confusion, and language impairment. In the later stages of AIDS, patients may display signs of depression, paranoia, and hallucinations that signal the **AIDS dementia complex,** a progressive cognitive deterioration that involves more substantial memory loss and confusion as well as shifts in personality. This complex may be caused by the dramatic loss of brain cells that accompanies the HIV infection. Researchers comparing samples of tissue from the brains of people who died from AIDS with those who died from other causes found a 40 percent lower density of neurons in the HIV group (Everall and others, 1991).

"What HIV has done is tap into the most fundamental aspect of the immune system, and that is its immunological memory. It's the perfect mechanism for the virus to ensure its survival. Perfect because the virus lies silent inside cells that are programmed to do nothing but sit and wait. Their only job is to store a record of the germs they encounter, keeping the body prepared for the next time it sees them."

(Haney, 2001; p. 11-A)

Physiological Factors in the Progression of AIDS

Biomedical researchers have long been puzzled by the unpredictability of AIDS. The period from diagnosis of full-blown AIDS until death may be as short as several months or as long as 5 years. Although the average time from HIV infection to AIDS is about 10 years, a lucky 5 percent of HIV-positive people live more than 15 years. Several factors are thought to play a role in the prognosis of AIDS.

One factor in a patient's prognosis is the strength of the initial immune response. HIV progresses much more slowly among patients whose immune systems mount strong lymphocyte activity in the acute stage of HIV sickness (stage 2). This strong defense apparently helps preserve the body's later ability to produce the T cells that target HIV (Bartlett & Moore, 1998).

As with many chronic diseases, genetic vulnerability may also affect the rate at which AIDS develops. For viruses to attain their full impact on cells, they require collaboration from the body, which in the case of AIDS is the existence of the protein receptor to which HIV particles bind. AIDS researchers suspect that some people have genes that protect against the development of this receptor. Indeed, it appears that 1 percent of people of Western European descent inherit a gene from both parents that blocks the development of the receptor, giving them apparent immunity to HIV infection. Another 20 percent inherit the protective gene from only one parent and, while not immune to HIV, display a much slower progression of symptoms. Researchers have also found racial and ethnic differences in responsiveness to anti-HIV drugs, suggesting the importance of considering a person's genetic profile prior to treatment (Mays and others, 2001).

Psychosocial Factors in the Progression of AIDS

After HIV exposure, the pace at which clinical symptoms of AIDS begin to appear and the severity of illness at all stages of the disease vary tremendously. Poor nutrition, drug use, repeated HIV exposure, and other viral infections can all accelerate the progression of the disease. As with other diseases, however, epidemiologists have discovered that even after these physical risk factors are accounted for, there is still a tremendous amount of unexplained variability in the course of AIDS.

Stress and Negative Emotions

Stress, negative emotions, and social isolation may influence the pace at which AIDS progresses, perhaps by altering hormonal and immune environments that affect the resistance of host cells to the invading virus (Cohen & Herbert, 1996). Several researchers have reported that low self-esteem, a pessimistic outlook, and chronic depression are all linked with a decline in T cells and a more rapid onset of AIDS among HIV-infected individuals (Burack and others, 1993; Byrnes and others, 1998; Segerstrom and others, 1996). HIV-infected individuals who maintain hope and are able to find meaning in their struggle

■ **AIDS dementia complex** an AIDS-related syndrome involving memory loss, confusion, and personality changes.

tend to show slower declines in T cell levels and are even less likely to die (Bower and others, 1997).

As is true of cancer victims, AIDS patients who deny their diagnosis may experience a more rapid development of AIDS-related symptoms. George Ironson and colleagues (1994) studied the progression of AIDS symptoms in a group of HIV-positive men who participated in a behavioral intervention program. At the start of the study, all the men were asymptomatic. Two years later, those who refused to accept their HIV-positive status showed a greater decline in T cells, a decreased lymphocyte response, and other symptoms not seen in patients who accepted their status.

The relationship between denial and AIDS may be part of a larger syndrome of emotional inhibition, which has been linked to more rapid development of cancer and other chronic illnesses. For example, gay men who hide their sexual orientation deteriorate more rapidly following HIV infection than do men who more openly express their sexual identity (Cole and others, 1996).

Not all studies have found a positive relationship between negative emotions and changes in T cell counts, AIDS onset, or mortality rates, however (Kessler and others, 1991). In fact, some evidence indicates the opposite—that HIV-positive men who refuse to accept their diagnosis actually survive *longer* than those who accept their fate more readily (Reed and others, 1994).

Why are the results of AIDS research studies inconsistent? One problem is that many of the studies measured stress, depression, or self-reported feelings of social support only at the *start of the study.* However, feelings of stress and depression are not static emotions; they may differ from one day or month to the next, depending on events in a person's life. Comparing the results of studies of different people with different statuses and at different times in their lives could be misleading.

Stress and Social Support

Social support is also a factor in the progression of HIV sickness and AIDS. In one study, patients who tested positive for HIV were followed for 5 years. Those who reported greater isolation and less emotional support at the start of the study showed a significantly greater decline in T cells over the course of the study than those who reported feeling more socially connected (Theorell and others, 1995). In another study, Margaret Kemeny and her colleagues (1994) reported that HIV-positive men who recently lost an intimate partner to AIDS showed more rapid disease progression.

Lack of social support may cause AIDS to develop more quickly partly because it leaves those who are HIV-positive less able to cope effectively with stressful life events. In a prospective study of stressful life events, social support, coping, and AIDS that began in 1990, Jane Leserman and her colleagues (2000) studied 82 HIV-infected gay men every 6 months. The participants reported the number of stressful events in their lives, their styles of coping with stressful events, and their satisfaction with the social support available to them. The researchers also measured blood levels of T cells, as well as serum levels of cortisol and other stress hormones.

Although none of the HIV-positive men had any AIDS symptoms at the start of the study, one-third of them have thus far exhibited some symptoms. For every increase in the number of stressful life events—equivalent to one severely stressful event (a death in the family or the loss of a job, for instance) or two moderately stressful events (illness in the family or strained relations with the boss, for example)—the risk of developing AIDS symptoms doubled. The risk of AIDS has also doubled for every significant *decrease* in the average score on the satisfaction with social support scale, every *increase* in the use of denial as a coping strategy, and every 5 mg/dl increase in the level of serum cortisol.

Given the health benefits of having a strong social network, it is particularly tragic that AIDS is often a stigmatizing condition and that many of its victims lose friends and companions. Interestingly, at least one study suggests that pet ownership can provide a buffer against the isolation-induced depression that can accompany AIDS. Judith Siegel and her colleagues (1999) surveyed more than 1,800 gay and bisexual men, 40 percent of whom were HIV-positive and 10 percent of whom had already developed AIDS. As other studies have found, men with AIDS, particularly those with the lowest levels of satisfaction with their social networks, showed markedly higher levels of depression than did HIV-positive men without AIDS and HIV-negative men in a control group. But whereas men with AIDS without pets were 300 percent more likely to report symptoms of depression than men without AIDS, men with AIDS who owned a pet were only 50 percent more likely to report symptoms of depression. The benefits of owning a dog or cat were strongest for men who felt the closest attachment to their pets, sleeping in the same room as their pets, for instance, and petting them frequently.

Understanding how psychosocial factors affect the course of AIDS may improve a person's chances of surviving HIV infection. The results of these studies will also help us gain a perspective on the interaction of biological, psychological, and social factors in health and disease and thus to refine our understanding of the connections between mind and body.

Medical Interventions

Until very recently, HIV infection was almost always a progressive, fatal disease. Medical interventions focused almost exclusively on treating the pneumonia and other opportunistic diseases that resulted from immune failure, not on eliminating (or even controlling) the rapidly replicating HIV virus. Today, however, scientists have a much better understanding of how the virus behaves in the body; they also have a number of potent weapons at their disposal. Several tests directly monitor levels of the virus in the body, thus giving doctors a more accurate means of determining how well a treatment regimen is working. In addition, several new classes of drugs have made it possible to treat HIV aggressively, improving overall health and dramatically increasing chances of survival.

Once they have determined that HIV has infected a person, doctors continue to monitor levels of the virus in the patient's blood because these levels

HIV infection is a highly stigmatizing disease because it is difficult to conceal as the disease progresses, it is disruptive to the person's life and relationships, and it can cause physical disfigurement as part of its degenerative course. AIDS-related stigmas result in discrimination, prejudice, and isolation and are a major factor in limiting social support and assistance for coping with HIV.

(American Psychological Association. Public Interest Directorate. Major HIV/AIDS topics and issues [www.apa.org/pi/aids]).

■ **zidovudine (AZT)** the first anti-AIDS drug; a reverse transcriptase inhibitor.

strongly predict the pace at which AIDS develops. By doing so, they are able to modify ineffective treatments before immune failure results and the invading virus gets the upper hand.

The HAART Regimen

Today's optimum treatment regimen is *highly active antiretroviral therapy,* or *HAART* for short. HAART involves multiple anti-HIV drugs that prevent the virus from replicating within host cells. Multiple drugs are used so that if one proves ineffective, the second (or third) may provide the needed insurance. In addition, HIV tends quickly to become resistant to drugs that do not completely suppress its replication. Because no single drug has been able to completely suppress the virus, any one drug may quickly lose its effectiveness if used in isolation—often within a matter of weeks.

One of the most commonly used drugs in the HAART regimen is **zidovudine (AZT)**. Introduced in 1983, AZT is one of a class of drugs called *reverse transcriptase inhibitors* because they block replication of the HIV virus by inhibiting production of reverse transcriptase—the enzyme HIV needs to reproduce itself. AZT reduces AIDS symptoms, increases T cell levels, and may prolong the patient's life. However, many patients on AZT unfortunately experience a variety of side effects, including anemia, which requires frequent blood transfusions; reduced white blood cell formation, which increases the risk of other infections; headaches; itching; and mental confusion. In addition, AZT's effectiveness wears off as the virus becomes resistant to it (Kinloch-de Loes and others, 1995). For this reason, AZT is often combined with a promising new group of anti-HIV drugs called *protease inhibitors,* which attack HIV at a different phase of its life cycle (Deeks and others, 1997). This combination of drugs has reduced HIV to undetectable levels in some patients (Balter, 1996).

Clinical trials of HAART have been quite promising. Recent studies of HIV1 patients at San Francisco General Hospital and Johns Hopkins University Hospital reported that 50 percent of patients given HAART therapy reached the treatment goal of only 500 HIV per milliliter—some within 6 weeks of beginning treatment. Although a 50 percent success rate would be considered disappointing in the treatment of many serious diseases, for HIV it represents a huge improvement from just a few years ago. In some patients, HAART appears to stop HIV replication completely, giving health experts hope that treatment will work indefinitely.

One drawback of HAART, however, is that the regimen is difficult to follow, making adherence a challenge. Patients often must take 16 or more anti-HIV pills a day, some with food and some on an empty stomach, according to a precise schedule that can challenge even the most motivated and highly organized patient. Patients who are homeless, confused, or lacking in social support find such a regimen almost impossible. Another drawback is that many AIDS patients simply can't afford it. The average cost of a year's treatment on the HAART regimen is $10,000 to $15,000. Even in the affluent developed countries where such care is available, many people lack the income or health insurance

AIDS Intervention Over the last few years, AIDS patients have been required to take a large variety of pills each day on a very strict timetable. However, with research advances, more streamlined pharmacological regimens have been used and have been equally effective.

coverage necessary to handle such costs. Of course, the countless impoverished people in undeveloped countries have little hope of getting these drug treatments. Worldwide, fewer than one in five people who need anti-HIV drugs are receiving them (Fauci, 2006).

Slowing the development of AIDS in developing nations (where 90 percent of those infected with HIV live) is a top priority for researchers. By one estimate, making the aggressive HAART treatment protocol available worldwide would cost $36.5 billion. The inequities in HIV treatment and prevention hit children the hardest. In some parts of Africa, for example, four out of every ten children lose at least one parent to AIDS before age 15—and every day 1,600 babies are born with HIV. To help stop the transmission of HIV to infants, the United Nations AIDS agency began a program of prenatal care, AZT, and delivery assistance to women in 11 of the world's poorest nations. In the face of mounting evidence that HIV also passes to a child through breast milk, the program helps infected mothers find safe alternatives to breast feeding.

A Preventive Vaccine

Given the capacity of HIV to become integrated in a host cell's DNA, prospects are bleak for a true cure that would detect and destroy every HIV-infected cell in the body. Despite 25 years of research, there hasn't been a single well-documented case of an infected person whose immune system has been completely cleared of the virus (Fauci, 2006). Is there an alternative? A number of biomedical researchers are searching for a vaccine to minimize and control the impact of HIV on the body. One of the major stumbling blocks is the enormous variability of HIV. Some researchers estimate that in an infected person with replicating HIV, more than 10 billion new viruses are made every day. New strains are constantly appearing; even if a vaccine is developed that proves effective against one strain, it may provide no protection against other strains. A second difficulty is the unusual life cycle of HIV. The rapid speed with which the virus infects T cells and the long life of infected cells make the prospects for an effective protective vaccine quite unlikely.

Still, researchers are hopeful of developing a treatment that will completely block one of the many steps in the HIV life cycle (Figure 11.4). If this is accomplished, the virus may be stopped dead in its tracks. Scientists at the University of Montana are following a promising line of research that may lead to an AIDS control vaccine. They have developed antibodies in mice that attack HIV just as the virus

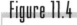

Figure 11.4

Strategies to Combat HIV Reproduction Doctors have a number of potent anti-HIV drugs at their disposal. These widely used drugs block specific steps in the HIV life cycle.

1. Virus binds to host cell

Vaccines may prevent HIV from binding to CD4(T) cell

CD4 receptor protein

2. HIV copies its RNA onto host's DNA (reverse transcription)

Reverse transcriptase inhibitors restrain the reverse transcription process

3. HIV is integrated into host DNA

4. Infected CD4 cell produces HIV proteins

5. The CD4 cell, after producing HIV proteins, sprouts a new HIV "bud"

Protease inhibitors block the production of mature functional viral proteins begins to fuse to host cells. When the antibodies were injected into samples of HIV, the antibodies destroyed 23 of 24 strains of the virus (Gainetdinov & Caron, 1999).

Although biomedical researchers are quick to point out that there still is no "cure" for AIDS, advances in treatment that have been achieved since 1995 are unparalleled in the history of medicine. Before 1995, "treatment" for HIV patients consisted almost entirely of making patients as comfortable as possible as they prepared to die. Today, the use of reverse transcriptase inhibitors, protease inhibitors, and the "AIDS cocktail" approach of HAART has increased hope that AIDS will someday become a manageable chronic disease—much like diabetes—rather than a terminal illness and that AIDS patients may look forward to long, productive lives (Chartrand & Seidman, 1996).

Psychosocial Interventions

As researchers press on in their search for effective medical interventions, psychosocial interventions remain the primary means of battling AIDS. Health psychologists play a number of roles in the battle against AIDS, including counseling people about being tested for HIV, helping individuals modify high-risk behaviors, helping AIDS patients cope with emotional and cognitive disturbances, and conducting bereavement therapy for those in the last stages of the illness and their loved ones.

Since the beginning of the AIDS epidemic, many different interventions have been implemented. The earliest programs targeted high-risk groups such as gay males or IV drug users, using behavior modification and educational interventions to try to change attitudes and behaviors. Programs at the high school and college level have typically focused on increasing knowledge of AIDS and promoting safe sex. Mass media campaigns have emphasized awareness of how AIDS is transmitted—and they have been quite successful: By 1987, nearly all U.S. adults were aware of AIDS and more than 90 percent could correctly state the primary modes by which HIV is transmitted (Coates and others, 1990). Despite a slow beginning, AIDS education and other intervention programs skyrocketed during the late 1980s and 1990s, paced initially by the efforts of the gay community in the United States. As a result, public awareness of AIDS increased, and a corresponding reduction in risk-related behaviors occurred, accompanied by a sharp decline in the number of new cases of HIV infection. Worldwide, a number of innovative prevention programs have appeared in the past 5 years, including programs in Belize and other Caribbean countries that attempt to link violence reduction with HIV/AIDS education in gang members, who are particularly vulnerable to HIV (Cohen, 2006). Let's take a look at the theories on which the intervention programs are based and then at some of the interventions that are effective in reducing HIV/AIDS risk-related behavior.

The Basis for Psychosocial Interventions

Many of the theoretical models described in Chapter 6 have been used to predict whether and when people will change a risky health-related behavior, so they often form the basis for HIV/AIDS intervention programs.

Social cognitive theory, which focues on the interaction of environmental events, our internal processes, and our behaviors (Bandura, 1997), has served as the framework for a number of interventions (Kalichman and others, 1996; Kalichman & Hospers, 1997). Three factors addressed by this model appear to be particularly important in successful intervention programs: *perceived social norms* regarding peer acceptance of HIV risk-reducing behaviors; *self-efficacy beliefs* controlling one's own thoughts, emotions, and behaviors in order to avoid unsafe behaviors; and *social skills,* the ability to respond assertively in negotiating risky behaviors. This was demonstrated by Seth Kalichman and his colleagues (1998), who found that gay men who practice high-risk behaviors also score lower on measures of perceived safer sex norms, safer sex self-efficacy, and social skills.

The health belief model, which is based on the idea that beliefs predict behavior, has achieved modest success with a variety of high-risk groups in predicting condom use, the number of sexual partners, and knowledge of partners' past sexual history (Abraham and others, 1992; Aspinwall and others, 1991). The theory of reasoned action, which also considers the person's attitude toward complying with other people's views, has achieved greater success, probably due to the influence of social norms on sexual activity of many at-risk populations, including teenagers (Schaalma and others, 1993; Winslow and others, 1992). Researchers have consistently found that people with more favorable attitudes toward condoms, as well as those who believe their friends are supportive of condom use, are more likely to engage in protected sex (Jemmott and others, 1992).

Support for stage models comes from evidence that certain individuals may profit more than others from a specific intervention. For example, younger, less knowledgeable individuals tend to benefit from educational interventions that close gaps in knowledge about how AIDS is transmitted, while older individuals in certain high-risk groups may be more likely to profit from interventions that stir them into preventive action.

In an investigation of the structure of beliefs about condom use, Dolores Albarracin and her colleagues (2000) interviewed a large, multiethnic sample of HIV-negative heterosexual males and females. Four psychosocial themes were analyzed for their ability to predict consistent condom use among heterosexual adults during vaginal sex. The themes investigated were the participants' beliefs that condom

Education Should Begin at a Young Age In the absence of a vaccine, preventing HIV infection remains our best weapon against AIDS. Throughout the world, educational campaigns are the major means of primary prevention.

use: 1) does or does not provide effective *protection* from AIDS and other *sexually transmitted infections (STIs),* including herpes, hepatitis B, chlamydia, and HPV (human papilloma viruses); 2) is or is not compatible with their *self-concept* concerning responsible sexual behavior; 3) either contributes to or takes away from their sexual *pleasure;* and 4) would or would not have a negative impact on their *interaction* with their sexual partner. The results showed that the more closely condom use conformed to a person's self-concept and the less condoms were perceived as decreasing sexual pleasure, the more positive were the attitudes toward condom use. There was an association between intentions and behavior in all four areas examined: protection, self-concept, pleasure, and social interaction; but the association was much stronger with self-concept and pleasure.

Educational Programs

Educational programs and media campaigns are most likely to be effective when messages are adapted to the target group. One study, for example, compared the impact on African-Americans of an AIDS risk-reduction message delivered by white broadcasters with the same message delivered by African-American women that focused on culturally relevant themes, such as cultural pride and family responsibility (Kalichman and others, 1993). Two weeks after watching the taped message, the African-American participants who had viewed the culturally relevant tape reported more concern and fear about AIDS than participants who had viewed the standard tape. They also reported either engaging or intending to engage in more preventive behaviors, such as being tested for HIV.

Another successful program targeted people 50 years of age and older who were living with HIV/AIDS (Heckman and others, 2006). The 12-session intervention, which was delivered via teleconference, provided age-appropriate counseling focused on reducing loneliness, depressive symptoms, and avoidant coping. The success of this intervention is especially important because it is predicted that by 2015 one-half of all cases of HIV/AIDS in the United States will be in persons 50 years of age or older (CDC, 2006).

However they are delivered, all educational messages have one thing in common—to make people aware of AIDS and how to prevent it. There are a number of simple precautions that will protect against AIDS and other STIs. Obviously, abstaining from both drugs and sex or maintaining a monogamous sexual relationship with an uninfected partner are still the safest ways to prevent AIDS and other STIs. For those who are sexually active, it is important to limit the number of partners in the *sexual network,* the range of sexual activities, and the extent of *sexual mixing* with people from other sexual networks (Catania and others, 2001). If a person has sex or shares a drug needle with someone who is HIV-positive, he or she may become a carrier of the virus. If the person then has sex or shares a drug needle with two other people, each of whom has sex or shares needles with two other people, and so forth, the initial infection has the potential to spread to hundreds of other victims.

Health experts also offer the following specific precautions:

- Stay sober. (Alcohol and many other drugs lower inhibitions and increase the likelihood of high-risk behaviors.)

- Avoid anal intercourse. (The thin lining of the rectum makes this the most hazardous form of sex for transmitting HIV.)

- Be selective in choosing partners. Avoid sexual contacts with people who are known to engage in high-risk sexual or drug-use behaviors.

- Use latex condoms during vaginal, anal, and oral sex. These barriers block nearly all sexually transmitted microorganisms, including HIV. Doctor-prescribed and fitted vaginal diaphragms or cervical caps that block semen and spermicides that paralyze sperm (and lymphocytes) are also advisable.

- Build caring, meaningful relationships with those with whom you are intimate.

- Never share hypodermic needles, razors, cuticle scissors, or other implements that may be contaminated with another person's blood or bodily fluids.

- Do not be lulled into a sense of complacency about AIDS and STIs by media reports about treatment breakthroughs. There is still no cure for AIDS.

Mass Screening and HIV Counseling

While education is important, it is often not enough. HIV screening and basic counseling are also primary preventive interventions in most state and federal programs. In the most ambitious screening program to date, 110 million Japanese citizens were tested, resulting in the detection of 1,700 HIV-positive cases and 400 cases of full-blown AIDS (Gilada, 1991).

People being screened for HIV benefit from interventions that help reduce their anxiety over testing positive. In a series of studies by Michael Antoni and his colleagues (2000), gay men were randomly assigned to intervention and control groups several weeks *before* HIV screening. Those in the intervention group participated in a multifaceted program that included aerobic exercise, relaxation training, and cognitive therapy aimed at modifying self-defeating attitudes. Each participant's psychological status and immunocompetence were assessed several times before and after receiving the results of screening. Among men who tested positive for HIV, those in the intervention group reported significantly lower anxiety and depression than those in the control group. They also displayed significantly stronger immune functioning, including increases in the levels and activity of T cells and NK cells.

Health psychologists have also developed interventions to counteract the reality that many sexual encounters, especially with new partners, are emotionally intense, rushed, and not conducive to clear thinking and negotiating about safe sex (Miller and others, 1993). The goal of such interventions is therefore to teach young men and women how to exercise self-control in sexual relationships and how to resist coercive sexual pressure. For example, intervention participants have been asked to use mental imagery to visualize risky sexual encounters that result in HIV infection. When coupled with role-playing exercises, modeling, and feedback, this type of intervention can be highly effective in giving young people the skills needed to avoid high-risk behaviors (van der Velde & Van der Pligt, 1991).

One study of African-American inner-city teenagers randomly assigned some subjects to an AIDS risk-reduction group and the rest to a control group (Jemmott and others, 1992). Those in the intervention group received educational materials and participated in workshops on high-risk behaviors conducted by African-American adults. Compared to control subjects, the teens in the intervention group reported greater condom use, fewer instances of intercourse, fewer sexual partners, and fewer instances of anal intercourse.

Unfortunately, successful counseling interventions are more often the exception than the rule. Over an 18-month period, researchers compared HIV-risky behaviors in women who voluntarily sought HIV testing and counseling at four urban clinics and women who used other clinic services, such as physical examinations or vision tests. Although women in the counseling group were more concerned about AIDS than women in the comparison group, the two groups did not differ in the prevalence of HIV-risky behaviors. Both groups engaged in high-risk sexual behaviors, including having unprotected intercourse with partners of uncertain or high risk (Ickovics and others, 1998). Why is HIV counseling not automatically effective in changing high-risk sexual behaviors? One reason is that a person—even one who knows all about AIDS—must feel capable of controlling his or her risk-related behaviors in specific situations. Increasingly, health psychologists recognize that modifying sexual behaviors is a complex process involving two people with different agendas and different attitudes toward safe sex practices. For example, they have found that they cannot assume that both partners are equally empowered to consent to sex and to make decisions about risk. Many women report that in their first sexual experience (and too often, in subsequent experiences) their male partner coerced them to have intercourse (Bor, 1997). And although the female partner often is held responsible for ensuring the use of a contraceptive, she may not be empowered to insist that her male partner use a condom.

Research to date has shown a strong association between perceived *self-efficacy* and the prevalence of high-risk behaviors. For example, self-efficacy is linked to greater condom use among college students (Wulfert & Wan, 1993), gay men (Emmons and others, 1986), African-American teenagers (Jemmott and others, 1992), and Hispanic-American women (Nyamathi and others, 1995). Gay men who have strong feelings of self-efficacy also tend to have fewer sexual partners and to be better informed about the sexual history of those with whom they are intimate (Wulfert and others, 1996).

Researchers have also found a relationship among outlook on life, self-efficacy, and the tendency to engage in high-risk sexual behaviors. A recent study showed that among sexually active inner-city minority adolescents (aged 15 to 18 years), those who were more optimistic were also more confident of their ability to practice safe sex (such as using a condom). Optimists also were more aware of and concerned about the dangers of unsafe sex (Carvajal and others, 1998). Pessimists, on the other hand, were less concerned about the potential danger of unsafe sex, perhaps because they felt they had less to lose than their more optimistic counterparts. Furthermore, the pessimists' lack of feelings of self-efficacy led them to believe that there was nothing they could do to avoid those dangers, or the behaviors.

And finally, in a longitudinal study of heterosexual women, those who avoided unprotected intercourse had more favorable attitudes toward condoms and had a greater internal locus of control regarding their health. That is, they felt more personally responsible for protecting their bodies against HIV infection (as well as other health threats) than did women who more often had unprotected intercourse (Morrill and others, 1996).

All these results suggest that the frequency of unprotected sex can be dramatically reduced with a few steps: Help people to improve their outlook on life, their feelings of self-efficacy, and their sense of personal control; and encourage them to talk more openly about safe sex.

Promoting Disclosure of HIV-Positive Status

Because of fears about AIDS, and because the disease is commonly associated with homosexuality and IV drug use, HIV-positive people often feel ashamed and conceal their status. Many don't even tell their immediate family (Mansergh and others, 1995). Recent survey data indicate that concerns about AIDS stigma still discourage many concerned individuals from even being tested for HIV infection (Herek, Capitanio, & Widaman, 2003).

Withholding one's HIV-positive status or misrepresenting one's sexual history obviously prevents a partner from making an informed decision about sexual behavior and may result in the transmission of the virus to that person and others. The results of one survey revealed that many college students would lie about their sexual history in order to obtain sex (Cochran & Mays, 1990).

Does preventive counseling at the time of HIV diagnosis lead to greater self-disclosure of HIV status to sexual partners? Among a sample of HIV-positive men, researchers found that men who were counseled to disclose their status were indeed more likely to do so than men who were not counseled. HIV-positive partners who disclose their HIV status are also more likely to engage in safer sexual practices (DeRosa & Marks, 1998).

Although most HIV/AIDS interventions have focused on preventing infection in at-risk uninfected persons, a growing number are aimed at preventing risky behaviors in people who have tested positive for HIV. One in three HIV-positive people continues to practice HIV transmission risk behaviors *after* they test positive for the virus (Kalichman, 2000). In one recent intervention, Thomas Patterson and his colleagues (2003) found that a brief (90-minute), targeted behavioral intervention among HIV-positive individuals that focused only on changing those risky behaviors that had been identified as problematic for the individual (for example, unprotected sex, disclosure) resulted in a significant reduction in HIV transmission risk behaviors over the next year. In another study, Seth Kalichman and his colleagues (2002) designed targeted interventions that successfully assisted HIV-positive men in developing adaptive coping behaviors to replace alcohol use (a risk behavior) as a means of coping or ecaping from the stress of living with HIV/AIDS.

Cognitive-Behavioral Stress Management

One of health psychology's roles in the AIDS pandemic is helping people who are HIV-positive to live with the infection. Several comprehensive intervention programs have proven effective in improving the emotional and physiological well-being of HIV-positive individuals.

One study evaluated the effectiveness of a 10-week cognitive-behavioral stress management (CBSM) intervention in reducing stress among HIV-positive men (Antoni and others, 2000). Men who were randomly assigned to the experimental (intervention) condition participated in 10 weekly, 2½ hour meetings, which included both stress management and relaxation training components. The stress management portion focused on helping the men to identify cognitive distortions in their thinking and to use cognitive restructuring to generate more rational appraisals of everyday stressors. The meetings also taught the men techniques to improve their coping skills, be more assertive, manage their anger, and make greater use of social support. Through group discussions and role-playing exercises, the men also learned to share experiences, disclose their fears, and apply various stress management concepts. The relaxation portion included progressive muscle relaxation training, meditation, abdominal breathing exercises, and guided imagery.

The results showed that the men who participated in the CBSM intervention reported significantly lower post-treatment levels of anxiety, anger, total mood disturbance, and perceived stress compared to the men who were assigned to an untreated control group (Figure 11.5). Moreover, those in the intervention group also displayed less norepinephrine output and significantly greater numbers of T cells 6 to 12 months later.

Figure 11.5

Pre- and Post-CBSM Treatment Anxiety and Anger in HIV-Positive Men Prior to the intervention, men assigned to CBSM showed mood and anxiety scores similar to those men assigned to the control condition, as measured by scores on the *Profile of Mood States*. Following the intervention, CBSM participants reported significantly lower post-treatment anxiety and anger than their control group counterparts.

Source: Antoni, M. H., and others. (2000). Cognitive-behavioral stress management intervention effects on anxiety, 24-hour urinary norepinephrine output, and T-cytotoxic/suppressor cells over time among symptomatic HIV-infected gay men. *Journal of Consulting & Clinical Psychology, 68,* 31–45.

Interestingly, men participating in CBSM also experienced significant increases in testosterone levels. Diminished levels of testosterone, which seems to cause decreased muscle mass, have been documented in HIV-infected men and seem to become more pronounced as the disease progresses to AIDS (Christeff and others, 1996).

Because of the biopsychosocial, interactive nature of cognitive, affective, behavioral, and social elements of stress responses, it appears that the most effective way to "package" stress management interventions for HIV-infected persons may be a multimodal CBSM program (Antoni & Schneiderman, 2001). Those who test positive may also need counseling and other interventions to help them cope with a wide array of problems over the course of the illness, including pain management, adherence to complicated medical regimens, and facing the possibility of death.

Communitywide Interventions

Intensive, coordinated, communitywide interventions have proved to be the best way not only to educate people about HIV and its modes of transmission but also to change social norms that influence sexual behavior. The most massive communitywide AIDS prevention program to date was implemented in San Francisco in 1982. The *San Francisco Model* involved seven different organizations chosen to reach people at different levels of risk (Coates, 1990): the mass media, schools, family planning centers, drug abuse clinics, health care organizations, churches, and clubs.

Each organization developed an educational program on how HIV is transmitted that was appropriate for its clientele. At each site, classes, videos, and models were used to teach safer sex practices. In addition, mass-media motivational messages and social action groups focused on increasing awareness of high-risk behaviors and reducing the social stigma attached to HIV-positive persons.

The comprehensive program proved immediately successful. At the start of the program, 60 percent of the sample reported engaging in high-risk behavior. By 1987, this figure had dropped to 30 percent. The continuing success of the program indicates that HIV/AIDS interventions need to strike on several fronts. Effective interventions are those that

■ target high-risk behaviors among at-risk individuals.

■ teach specific skills to reduce risk (such as proper condom use and needle cleaning).

■ promote interpersonal assertiveness and other communication skills necessary to initiate and maintain lower-risk sexual relationships.

■ address social and cultural norms that surround sexual activity.

■ focus on improving self-esteem and feelings of self-efficacy regarding how to practice safer sex.

- address faulty, even "magical" thinking regarding HIV transmission and personal vulnerability.
- involve coordinated, community-level education.

Psychosocial Barriers to AIDS Interventions

Despite massive efforts to educate the public and discourage high-risk behaviors, condom use remains startlingly low. Results from the National College Risk Behavior Survey indicate that 84 percent of college men and 88 percent of college women report having engaged in sexual intercourse. Only one-third, however, reported consistent condom use (Douglas and others, 1997; Pluhar and others, 2003). Media depictions of sexual encounters, which almost never include the awkward search for and fumbling with a condom, do little to promote AIDS interventions aimed at promoting safe sex. This is particularly damaging for teenagers, who acquire a *script* of how things are supposed to progress and attempt to follow that script during their first intimate experiences. If a condom is not in the script, is it any wonder they would feel awkward introducing one?

A surprisingly common example of faulty reasoning about HIV/AIDS is the belief that the danger of HIV infection depends on the depth of the relationship with the HIV-positive person. This line of thinking causes many people to worry needlessly about casual contact with HIV-positive coworkers and strangers but to behave recklessly in their behaviors with people they know more intimately. Among college students, for instance, condom use appears to drop off abruptly over the time of a college relationship (Pluhar and others, 2003). In one study, 43 percent of college women who reported using a condom at the start of their relationships no longer did so 6 months later (Kusseling and others, 1995). Our faulty AIDS/HIV thinking is often the result of believing that we are somehow less vulnerable to infection than others are. This *optimistic bias* and *perceived invincibility* contribute to our tendency to underestimate the risk that results from casual, unprotected sex; needle sharing; and other high-risk behaviors.

Ironically, a significant impediment to AIDS prevention programs is the success of recent advances in medical treatment, which has brought new hope and optimism for HIV-infected people but at the cost of greater public complacency regarding the dangers of the disease. Widespread news of AIDS treatment breakthroughs has led to premature claims that HIV is more of a chronic than a life-threatening illness and that a complete cure is on the horizon. As we've seen, anti-HIV drugs have become increasingly successful in reducing the concentrations of HIV in the infected person's body, suggesting to some that people under treatment may be less infectious. Those who perceive a reduced threat of HIV/AIDS are more likely to engage in high-risk sexual behaviors, as are people who suppress HIV-related thoughts during intimate encounters (Hoyt and others, 2006).

Researchers have also found that some individuals engage in risky sexual behavior because the risk makes the behavior more exciting and pleasurable. A particularly important variable is the *sensation-seeking personality,* defined as the tendency to seek optimal arousal and sensory stimulation. In a survey of

HIV-negative gay and bisexual men, Jeffrey Kelley and Seth Kalichman (1998) found that the subjective reinforcement value (pleasure) of unprotected anal intercourse more strongly predicted condom use than perceived vulnerability to infection. The emotional meaning of having unprotected sex, including trust of one's partner, may also be a factor in the failure of some individuals to practice safe sex. In another study, Kalichman and his colleagues (2002) found that HIV-positive men who score high in measures of sensation seeking tend to have cognitive expectancies that alcohol use enhances sexual performance and pleasure, which may promote their engaging in unprotected sex. Current condom use messages are neutral in tone, cognitively focused in their appeal, and oriented to disease prevention rather than to the positive or affective benefits of safe sex. In the future, HIV interventions may need to seek more explicitly to lessen the reinforcement value of high-risk sexual practices and to increase the perceived value of safe sex, particularly among those who score high in sensation seeking.

Coping with HIV and AIDS

Chronic illnesses such as AIDS can have a dramatic impact on the individual as well as on family, friends, and caregivers. Those who have AIDS often find themselves isolated from social support networks as coworkers, neighbors, and even family and friends withdraw from them. Early studies suggested that psychological and emotional difficulties were common, with as many as half of AIDS patients having diagnosable psychological and emotional disorders (Selwyn, 1986). However, most of the studies involved only gay men, making it difficult to rule out the impact of other variables (such as social stigma) on the individual's adjustment to the disease. More recent studies have indicated that the rates of persistent psychological disorders among AIDS patients are no different from those associated with other life-threatening diseases (Bor, 1997).

Impact on the Individual

People who test positive for HIV face the challenges of coping with the stigma of AIDS, acknowledging the possibility of dying young, and developing strategies for minimizing the impact of the disease on their physical and emotional health (Swendeman and others, 2006; Siegel & Krauss, 1991). Ironically, with advances in biomedical technology, the fear of developing symptoms may actually be magnified. New tests are now able to forecast when symptoms will probably appear.

When the challenges and fears associated with AIDS become overwhelming, victims may suffer depression and suicidal thinking. This is especially true for those who feel a withdrawal of family and social support, lose their jobs, or become disfigured as a result of the disease's progression or treatment. In a large national sample of HIV-infected women and men, John Fleishman and

The National AIDS Quilt HIV-positive individuals who remain socially connected fare better than those who feel shunned or isolate themselves. The National AIDS quilt, shown here in Washington, D.C., is being transported around the country to increase AIDS awareness and to prompt people to provide social support to sufferers.

Barry Fogel (1994) found that more than 40 percent of those with AIDS were diagnosed with depression. HIV-positive people who tend to rely on avoidant-oriented coping strategies, such as denial and behavioral and mental disengagement, rather than approach-oriented coping strategies, such as active problem solving and support seeking, are especially likely to experience psychological distress (Penedo and others, 2003). HIV-infected people are also more likely to think about and actually commit suicide than their HIV-negative counterparts (Heckman and others, 2002; McKegney & O'Dowd, 1992).

Not all patients who test HIV-positive develop psychological problems. As with other chronic illnesses, AIDS patients who use active coping strategies to solve their problems and maintain an upbeat outlook tend to fare much better than those who distance themselves physically or emotionally from their plight (Fleishman & Fogel, 1994). Active coping measures that have proved effective in reducing AIDS-related stress reactions include seeking information and social support (Siegel and others, 1997), and taking an active role in one's medical treatment regimen (Baum & Posluszny, 1999).

A number of researchers have studied long-term AIDS survivors in an effort to identify behavioral factors that might promote longevity (LaPerriere and others, 1990; Patterson and others, 1996; Solomon, 1991). Three factors, in particular, seem to distinguish long-term survivors from those who succumb more quickly.

- *Maintaining physical fitness by engaging in regular exercise.* A number of researchers have reported that aerobic exercise interventions bolster immunocompetence in AIDS patients by preventing declines in level and activity of NK cells (LaPerriere and others, 1990). These interventions also help prevent the dramatic weight loss and other telltale signs of disease that often accompany the later stages of AIDS (Lox and others, 1996).

- *Keeping an upbeat, positive outlook.* AIDS progresses more rapidly among patients who are chronically depressed, leading to significantly shorter survival times (Patterson and others, 1996).

- *Avoiding social isolation.* In fact, having a large social network is strongly correlated with longevity among AIDS patients (Patterson and others, 1996).

Impact on Family Members, Partners, and Caregivers

The effects of AIDS extend beyond the individual to family members, partners, and other caregivers. Research into the effects on families is lacking because AIDS poses several unique problems. First, in most cases, AIDS changes the family structure and roles, often reversing standard developmental patterns. For example, children may die before their parents. When parents die, many young children and grandparents are forced to become caregivers at a time when they would normally expect to be in a more dependent role themselves (Bor & Elford, 1994). Second, AIDS places the additional burden of the disease's social stigma on its victims and their families. Uninfected family members may find their friends shying away from or even harassing them. And the social rejection may persist even after the AIDS victim has died.

AIDS can have a profound impact on a surviving partner. Most common is the fear of loneliness and, for those who are HIV-positive themselves, a fear of dying with no one to care for them. Anger at their partner's "abandonment" by dying first is also common. Even for partners who are not infected, the fear of being "tarnished" by having shared a relationship with an infected partner may cast a long shadow, making it difficult for the survivor to establish new relationships (Bor, 1997).

AIDS also has a powerful impact on health care providers and caregivers, many of whom have concerns about being infected themselves. Despite the relatively low risk, anxiety about working with AIDS patients persists and may lead to unusual occupational stress and burnout.

It is estimated that about 3 percent of the entire adult population in the United States has provided informal care to a person living with HIV or AIDS (Turner and others, 1994). Although women predominate in most caregiving situations, many AIDS caregivers are men caring for other men (Turner and others, 1994). On average, caregivers devote over 20 hours per week solely to providing care. Almost two-thirds experience at least one chronic physical symptom; the most common are severe backaches and headaches.

The biggest factor in the impact of caregiving on a person's health is the length of the patient's illness. Those who act as caregivers for a long time and who rate their patient's health as very poor are less likely to report good health than those who have been providing care for a short time to a person living with AIDS or HIV in comparatively good health. This is true regardless of the nature of care-related activities or the amount of time devoted to caregiving each day (Wight and others, 1998).

At present, no cure for AIDS exists, and the disease continues to infect people throughout the world. Health psychologists play an important role in battling the HIV pandemic. In the early years, psychologists were key players in designing and implementing primary and secondary prevention efforts to reduce the spread of HIV and to help those who were HIV-positive cope with their illness. These efforts included interventions to reduce risky behaviors for AIDS and to help those who were HIV-positive adhere to complex treatment regimens. More recently, health psychologists have teamed up with immunologists and other scientists to study how psychosocial factors such as beliefs about AIDS and disclosing HIV status, perceived social support, coping style, and possible symptoms of anxiety and depression influence the course of HIV infection and its progression to AIDS. Based on the growing evidence from these investigations, we have seen that psychologists are designing interventions that not only improve the quality of life of HIV-positive persons but also increase the odds of their long-term survival.

Summing Up

1. The first human cases of acquired immunodeficiency syndrome (AIDS), which is caused by the human immunodeficiency virus (HIV), appeared in 1980, when 55 young men (most of whom were gay or intravenous drug users) were diagnosed with a rare form of cancer. During the last half of the 1980s, AIDS began to threaten the general population.

2. In the United States, the AIDS epidemic has taken the greatest toll on young men, particularly African-Americans and Hispanic-Americans. For a variety of biological, economic, and sociocultural reasons, women are more vulnerable than men to HIV infection and tend to contract the virus at a younger age and lower HIV viral load level.

3. In other parts of the world, AIDS affects men and women equally, and heterosexual sex is the most common mode of transmission. Ethnic and racial differences in rates of HIV transmission are thought to reflect sociocultural differences in drug use and the acceptance of homosexual and bisexual practices.

Symptoms and Stages: From HIV to AIDS

4. HIV is transmitted primarily through the sharing of virus-infected lymphocytes in bodily fluids—blood, semen, vaginal and cervical secretions, and breast milk.

5. High-risk behaviors that promote HIV infection include having unprotected sex with multiple partners, using IV drugs, and sharing needles. HIV may also be transmitted from an infected mother to her unborn child during pregnancy, as well as from mother to child during breast feeding.

6. The chances of casual transmission of AIDS without sexual contact or IV drug use are very low. The best ways to guard against HIV infection are limiting sexual partners, choosing partners carefully, and avoiding sexual contacts with those who are known to engage in high-risk behaviors.

7. HIV is a retrovirus that causes host cells to reproduce the virus's genetic code. In doing so, HIV destroys T cells, progressively reduces immunocompetence, and leaves its victims vulnerable to a host of opportunistic infections.

8. HIV sickness progresses through four stages, which vary in length from person to person. The average time from HIV infection to AIDS is about 10 years, although 5 per-

cent of HIV-positive people live more than 15 years. HIV progresses much more slowly among patients whose immune systems mount strong lymphocyte activity in the acute stage of HIV sickness.

9. Stress, negative emotions, and social isolation may influence the pace at which the disease progresses, perhaps by altering hormonal and immune environments that affect the resistance of host cells to the invading virus.

Medical Interventions

10. Until recently, HIV infection was almost always a progressive, fatal disease. Today, however, doctors in developed nations have a number of potent drug treatment regimens to offer HIV-positive patients to improve quality of life and longevity. These drugs include antiretroviral drugs, reverse transcriptase inhibitors, protease inhibitors, and "cocktail" combinations of these drugs.

11. Researchers continue to work toward developing a vaccine that will minimize and control the impact of HIV on the body. However, the capacity of HIV to become integrated in a host cell's DNA and HIV's enormous variability make this a challenging proposition.

Psychosocial Interventions

12. Health psychologists play a number of roles in the battle against AIDS, including counseling people about being tested for HIV, helping individuals modify high-risk behaviors, helping AIDS patients cope with emotional and cognitive disturbances, and conducting bereavement therapy for those waiting to die and for their loved ones.

13. Although AIDS prevention programs have had some success, many barriers to prevention remain. Misinformation, feelings of personal invulnerability, cultural norms, and personal resources are all factors in the success (or failure) of AIDS prevention measures.

14. HIV screening is readily available in most developed countries, but complacency or fear of knowing prevent some people from seeking out their HIV status. Many people who know their HIV status avoid telling their partners and relatives.

15. A particularly effective way to package stress management interventions for HIV-positive patients seems to be a multimodal, cognitive behavioral stress management (CBSM) approach.

Coping with HIV and AIDS

16. Chronic illnesses such as AIDS can have a dramatic physical and psychological impact on the individual as well as on family members, partners, friends, coworkers, and caregivers. The main problems faced by AIDS victims are adjusting to the possibility of dying young and coping with heightened anxiety and depression.

17. Health psychologists have designed a variety of psychosocial interventions to help people cope with AIDS. These include aerobic exercise, active coping strategies, relaxation training, and avoiding social isolation.

Key Terms and Concepts

AIDS (acquired immunodeficiency syndrome), p. 331
HIV (human immunodeficiency virus), p. 331
Kaposi's sarcoma, p. 332

pandemic, p. 333
hemophilia, p. 336
retrovirus, p. 337

genome, p. 337
AIDS dementia complex, p. 339
zidovudine (AZT), p. 342

Part 5 | Seeking Treatment

The Role of Health Psychology in Health Care Settings

*E*ven *though the event happened 30 years ago, it is as vivid in my mind today as it was on that unusually warm afternoon in April when one of my fraternity brothers was nearly blinded. A bunch of us were watching the Detroit Tigers battle the St. Louis Cardinals in a spring training baseball exhibition game. "Anybody want to play handball?" asked Bruce, bounding through the lobby. I declined, as did everyone but Chris. "I'll play," he said, "but only for about half an hour. I've got a chemistry final tomorrow."*

The rest of us turned our attention back to the game and thought nothing more about handball until about 45 minutes later, when a worried-looking Chris came through the door with a woozy Bruce leaning heavily on him for support. It was easy to see that Bruce had been hurt—his left eye was discolored and growing puffy.

"Bruce took a handball right in the eye," Chris explained. "I wanted to take him right over to the health center, but he refused."

"It's nothing," Bruce said shakily. "I'll probably have a black eye tomorrow, but I'll be fine. Just get me some ice and a couple of aspirin."

As Bruce stretched out on a couch, somebody ran for the ice and aspirin. The rest of us looked at one another doubtfully. As the minutes passed, Bruce's eye was looking angry and red, and the swelling was starting to force his eyelid closed. He was clearly in pain, wincing with every word he spoke. Vision was not something to mess around with, even if you were trying to keep up a stoic front for a bunch of college buddies, and especially if, like Bruce, you were hoping one day to become an airline pilot.

For all of these reasons, I knew what we had to do. In less than five minutes Glenn, Jack, and I had phoned Campus Safety, the Health Center, and Bruce's parents. Following their instructions, we drove

■ **collaborative care** a cooperative form of health care in which
physicians, psychologists, and
other health care providers join
forces to improve patient care.

*Bruce to the emergency room at County Medical Hospital, paced by a police
cruiser with siren blaring and lights flashing. Half an hour after being hit by the
handball, Bruce was rushed into the operating room, where a board-certified surgeon sutured his ruptured eyeball and saved his vision.*

Why was Bruce reluctant to seek medical care? Why wasn't the severe
pain in his eye sufficient to sound the alarm that his health was in
jeopardy? In considering why people do or do not seek treatment
and how they interact with the health care system, we shift our focus from *primary* prevention to *secondary* prevention, that is, from actions designed to prevent a disease or injury to actions intended to identify and treat an illness early
in its course.

Sooner or later, each of us comes into contact with a health care provider and
the health care system. In most cases, these encounters are brief, perhaps involving a visit to the doctor because of the flu. In other cases, they involve more extended contact, such as a hospital stay following surgery, recuperating in a
rehabilitation center following an accident, or living in an extended-care facility.

This chapter explores health psychology's role in the relationships between
patients and the health care system. Social and psychological factors have both
a direct and an indirect impact on those relationships. First, such factors
strongly influence when and how people initially decide they are sick. Second,
people's confidence in their health care providers influences their satisfaction
with treatment as well as how they respond to it. Third, the extent and quality
of communication between patients and health care providers indirectly influence almost every aspect of health care, including how patients decide when
they need medical attention, why people sometimes choose to ignore health-
related symptoms, and why people sometimes carefully follow their provider's
instructions but sometimes they do not.

As a result of our improved understanding of these psychosocial influences,
a significantly increasing number of psychologists now work in general health
care settings, and medical school curricula include a greater focus
on the behavioral and social sciences (IOM, 2006). Working from
the other direction, many graduate programs in psychology are
now placing more emphasis on training students to work in primary care settings such as psychopharmacology, which is part of
an interdisciplinary movement to permit specially trained psychologists to prescribe medication (Dittman, 2002). A growing
number of hospitals are also encouraging greater use of **collaborative care,** in which physicians, psychologists, and other health
care providers join forces to improve patient care (Daw, 2001).
Optimum health care is not achieved by defining the separate responsibilities of patients and health care providers, but through
their harmonious interaction.

Collaborative Care Today, the
health care system is increasingly
focused on collaborative care, the
combined efforts of physicians,
psychologists, and other health
care people, such as this social
worker talking with a nurse and
her patient.

© Mitch Wojnarowicz/The Image Works

Recognizing and Interpreting Symptoms

How and when do we decide that we are sick? At what point does a nagging headache, upset stomach, or other symptom become serious enough for us to recognize a problem? The criteria that people use to recognize and interpret symptoms vary enormously. However, certain broad psychosocial factors play an important role in the process.

Attentional Focus and Coping Strategies

Attentional focus influences our awareness of physical symptoms. If we have a strong *internal focus* on our bodies, emotions, and overall well-being, we are more likely to detect symptoms—and to report them more quickly—than if we are more *externally focused* (Pennebaker & Epstein, 1983). People who are socially isolated, bored with their jobs, and living alone are more likely to be internally focused, whereas people with more active lives are subject to more distractions that keep their minds off their own problems.

Momentary situational factors have a substantial impact on whether a symptom is registered. People tend to become more aware of physical sensations when they are bored than when they are deeply involved in a task. For example, they are far less likely to cough in response to a tickle in their throats during exciting parts of a movie than during boring parts (Pennebaker, 1980). Similarly, injured athletes often play through the pain, focusing only on the game. In situations such as these, the distractions of external events may temporarily overshadow internal symptoms.

Attentional focus also determines how we cope with health problems and other stressful events. When threatened with an aversive event, **sensitizers** actively monitor the event and their reaction to it; repressors avoid and psychologically blunt their reactions to such events (Miller & Nuessle, 1978). Sensitizers cope with health problems by closely scanning their bodies and environments for information. As we'll explain later, sensitizers also prefer high levels of information about their health in medical contexts and seem to fare better when it is provided.

The distinctive characteristics of sensitizers become most apparent when the sensitizer is confronted with potentially high levels of stress (Wardle and others, 1994). For example, in the face of a potentially major or life-threatening illness, sensitizers report significantly greater physiological and behavioral distress and dysfunction, are slower to recover, and exhibit greater treatment side effects (Lerman and others, 1996; Schwartz and others, 1995).

In contrast, **repressors** tend to ignore or deny health-related information. They seem to look at life through rose-colored glasses, coping with negative events without bother or irritation and often by defending themselves from unwanted thoughts or unpleasant mood states. As we discussed in Chapter 5, research with different stressors suggests that avoidant-type strategies are often maladaptive over time and may be associated with a variety of long-term health

Cancer patients at Delaware County Memorial Hospital in Drexel Hill, Pennsylvania, are offered an integrative approach to care. It includes an 8-week class that teaches mindfulness meditation and cognitive-behavioral strategies to reduce stress. Patients can also take advantage of a massage therapist and a free weekly yoga class. The psychologists may employ hypnosis to help people harness the strengths of the mind over the body's pain.

—(O'Connor, 2001)

■ **attentional focus** a person's characteristic style of monitoring bodily symptoms, emotions, and overall well-being.

■ **sensitizers** people who cope with health problems and other aversive events by closely scanning their bodies and environments for information.

■ **repressors** people who cope with health problems and other aversive events by ignoring or distancing themselves from stressful information.

■ **illness representation** how a person views a particular illness, including its label and symptoms, perceived causes, timeline, consequences, and controllability.

effects, including more rapid cancer progression (Epping-Jordan and others, 1994). These adverse effects are most evident when efforts to ignore the stressor fail and the individual resorts to more extreme defensive attempts, such as denial (Foa and others, 1995).

Repressing may create an especially powerful reluctance to seek medical screening procedures, which are typically oriented toward detecting serious illnesses. The distress of thinking about the possibility of disease may create a barrier to noticing symptoms (Millar & Millar, 1995).

Illness Representations

Our personal views of health and illness, called **illness representations,** also affect our health in at least two ways: by influencing our preventive health behaviors, and by affecting how we react when symptoms appear.

Researchers have studied several components of how we represent illnesses. Each component by itself can substantially affect our motivation to seek medical care.

1. *Identity* of the illness—its label and symptoms. There appears to be a symmetrical bond between a disease's label and its symptoms. Thus, a person who has symptoms will seek a diagnostic label for those symptoms; a person who has been diagnosed (labeled) will seek symptoms that are consistent with that label. In a vivid example of this symmetry, Linda Baumann and her colleagues (1989) found that research participants who were told that they had high blood pressure were more likely than others to report symptoms commonly associated with this illness, such as tightness in the chest, jittery feelings, and so forth. This was true regardless of whether or not they really were hypertensive. Another example of the impact of labels on symptom recognition is *medical student's disease.* As many as two-thirds of aspiring physicians imagine that they themselves have symptoms of diseases they have studied (Mechanic, 1978).

   All medical conditions are at least partly *social constructions,* meaning that their identity and diagnosis are shaped by culture, advertising, and other nonbiological forces. As an example, consider that German medicine and culture pay special attention to the heart and its workings. German physicians are far more likely than their counterparts in France, England, or the United States to diagnose and treat low blood pressure. Any patient of 60 years or so in age who reports feeling tired, excessive urination at night, and fluid retention is likely to be diagnosed with "Herzinsuffzienz" (cardiac insufficiency) and be given prescription medication (Moerman, 2002). Another example is the epidemic of *attention deficit hyperactivity disorder (ADHD)* in the United States. The diagnostic criteria for ADHD include failing to give close attention to details, careless mistakes in schoolwork, losing things necessary for tasks, fidgeting with the hands, and squirming in one's seat. Nowhere in the world are these behaviors treated with the same intensity as in the United States. The point to remember:

people in different places can experience the same biological phenomena in very different ways.

2. *Causes*—attributing syptoms to external factors such as infection or injury, or internal factors such as genetic predisposition. A student who interprets her tension headache as a by-product of cramming for an exam will react quite differently from the student who attributes the same symptoms as signs of a brain tumor.

3. *Timeline*—the duration and rate of the disease's development. For example, four out of ten patients being treated for hypertension believe that their condition is *acute;* that is, short in duration, caused by temporary agents, and not a serious threat to long-term health. In contrast, *chronic illnesses* are long in duration, caused by multiple factors, and represent potentially serious threats to long-term health. Patients who believe their illness is acute often drop out of treatment earlier than those who believe it to be chronic (Meyer and others, 1985).

4. *Consequences*—the physical, social, and economic impact of illness and disease. We are far more likely to ignore symptoms that minimally disrupt our daily lives (such as minor muscle soreness following a strenuous workout) than we are to ignore symptoms that have a serious disruptive effect (such as a severe muscular strain that prevents a laborer from earning a paycheck).

5. *Controllability*—beliefs regarding whether the illness can be prevented, controlled, and/or cured (Leventhal and others, 1997). If we view our disease or condition as incurable, we may skip appointments, neglect treatment, or even behave in self-destructive ways because we feel helpless and lack hope.

Note that the key to these components is our *perception* of the symptoms rather than the actual facts about the disease. How we initially react to a stomachache, for example, depends not on its actual cause, about which we are unaware, but on what we *believe* is causing the pain.

Explanatory Style and Psychological Disturbances

Explanatory style (optimistic or pessimistic) and psychological health also influence the reporting of symptoms. People who have a more positive outlook on life generally report fewer symptoms than do people who are more negative (Scheier & Bridges, 1995). Those in a good mood also consider themselves healthier and less vulnerable to future illness than do people in bad moods (Leventhal and others, 1996; Salovey, and others, 1991). This may be a cognitive rather than a physiological phenomenon, however. Research on *state-dependent memory* reveals that people who are in a bad mood tend to think of illness-related memories more easily than people in a good mood (Croyle & Uretsky, 1987).

People who are anxious and those who score low on tests of emotional stability tend to report more physical symptoms, perhaps because they tend to

■ **comorbidity** the simultaneous occurrence of two or more physical and/or psychological disorders or symptoms.

exaggerate the seriousness of minor complaints that others are more likely to ignore (Larsen, 1992). In addition, symptoms of psychological or emotional disorders are sometimes misattributed to physical problems (Simon and others, 1996). Actually, there is substantial **comorbidity** of psychological and physical disorders—physical and psychological symptoms and disorders occurring simultaneously. Psychological disorders such as anxiety or depression can predispose physical disorders through biological, behavioral, cognitive, and social pathways (Figure 12.1). For example, depression might trigger poor health practices, such as alcohol abuse, and a general apathy regarding treatment regimens. Anxiety and depression can also lead to an excessive focus on bodily symptoms.

Prior Experience

How we interpret symptoms is further influenced by our prior experiences and our expectations. If we have a personal or family history of a particular medical condition, we tend to be less concerned about familiar symptoms than others with no history of the condition, at least for minor medical conditions (Jemmott and others, 1988). However, for more serious conditions—such as cancer—we are likely to react strongly to symptoms we've seen in stricken family members.

Prior experience can be good, leading to increased accuracy, as when experienced parents calmly seek medical care for their second child, who exhibits a symptom familiar from their first child's younger days (Turk and others, 1985).

Figure 12.1

Psychological Disorders, Physical Disorders, and Illness Behavior Psychological disorders can predispose physical disorders and illness behavior via a number of biological, behavioral, cognitive, and social pathways. Among these are stress-induced physiological arousal, abuse of alcohol, an excessive focus on bodily symptoms, and social isolation. For example, depression might lead to alcohol abuse, which could result in a variety of physical disorders such as cirrhosis of the liver.

Source: Adapted from: Cohen, S. & Rodriguez, M. S. (1995). Pathways linking affective disturbances and physical disorders. *Health Psychology, 14,* 374–380.

Psychological disorders
- Negative emotional states and traits
- Mood and anxiety disorders

Biological pathways
- Sympatho-adreno-medullary arousal
- Hypothalamic-pituitary-adrenal arousal

Behavioral pathways
- Poor health practices
- Misuse of health services
- Poor medical adherence

Cognitive pathways
- Faulty interpretation of physical stimuli
- Inaccurate illness representations
- Focus on health decision processes

Social pathways
- Interference with daily life and social roles
- Isolation from others

Physical disorders
- Onset
- Progression
- Increased severity

Illness behaviors
- Symptom reporting
- Care seeking
- Pain and disability

Or prior experience can be bad, causing us to overlook or misinterpret symptoms, as when older adults mistakenly assume that unusual fatigue, muscle weakness, or memory loss are merely symptoms of aging rather than signs of disease (Leventhal & Prohaska, 1986). Another example of experience gone awry occurs when busy workers mistakenly attribute physical symptoms of disease to the temporary effects of stress (Cameron and others, 1995). This tendency to attribute symptoms to nondisease sources is particularly noticeable in the early stages of many diseases, when symptoms are most likely to be mild, slow to develop, and ambiguous (Benyamini and others, 1997).

People also often exaggerate expected symptoms while ignoring or not detecting unexpected symptoms. In a classic study, Diane Ruble (1972) told one group of women that they were within 1 or 2 days of beginning menstruation and told another group that their periods were not due for 7 to 10 days. In fact, they were all about 1 week from beginning their periods. The first group reported significantly more psychological and physical symptoms of premenstruation than did the latter group, who did not expect their periods for another week or so. Although Ruble's findings indicate that *premenstrual syndrome (PMS)* may result not only from physical changes but also from a woman's beliefs, the results do not mean the women did not experience actual symptoms. Rather, they suggest that women who believe themselves to be premenstrual may overstate naturally fluctuating bodily states. Similarly, women who believe that most women experience unpleasant premenstrual changes are more likely to recall and amplify their own premenstrual changes than women who perceive PMS as an unusual complaint (Marvan & Cortes-Iniestra, 2001).

Seeking Treatment

At any given moment, perhaps one out of every four people in the population has a health condition that is potentially treatable. However, the presence of symptoms is not always enough to get us into the health care system (Cameron and others, 1993). Why do some of us keep up our normal activities even in the face of undeniable evidence that something is wrong, while others take time off in response to the slightest symptoms?

We fail to respond to potentially serious medical symptoms for many reasons. We may avoid seeing a doctor because we believe that our symptoms are not serious, and that all we need is a day or two of rest, an over-the-counter medication, or some other form of self-care. We may avoid the use of health services because we lack health insurance or are afraid we can't afford it. We may be fearful that our symptoms *are* a sign of a serious condition, and our inaction is a result of denial. Finally, we may avoid medical care because we are suspicious of the health care system and doubt its ability to treat our condition effectively.

Several demographic and sociocultural factors play important roles in determining whether a person will take the next step and seek medical treatment.

Age and Gender

In general, the very young and the elderly use health services more often than do adolescents and young adults. As any parent knows, children develop many different infectious diseases as their immune systems are developing. They need check-ups, vaccinations, and regular health services. In general, however, our younger years are among the healthiest of the entire life span. The frequency of illness and the need to visit physicians declines steadily throughout late childhood, adolescence, and young adulthood. Health services begin to increase again in middle age and late adulthood as a result of the increasing prevalence of chronic, age-related diseases (Figure 12.2).

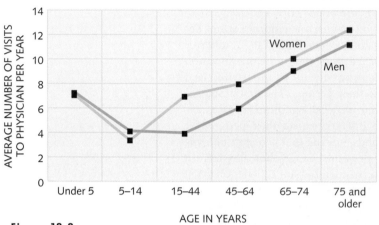

Psychologists have long recognized that every age has its own special way of viewing the world. Childhood concepts of disease often include magical notions about causality. Only at a later age do children begin to understand the concept of contagion and the mechanisms by which infectious diseases are transmitted. Still later, as their concept of self-efficacy continues to mature, they begin to realize that they can take steps to control their health (Burbach & Peterson, 1986).

During adolescence, thinking is typically distorted by a self-view in which teenagers regard themselves as more significant than they actually are. This *adolescent egocentrism* manifests itself in many ways, including an optimistic bias, in which some young people believe that they will never be seriously harmed by dangerous actions (Weinstein, 1982). As a result of this false sense of invulnerability, they are more likely to engage in risky behaviors such as cigarette smoking, substance abuse, unsafe sexual behavior, and dangerous driving.

As adults grow older, they increasingly tend to blame their age for mild symptoms that gradually appear, while sudden severe symptoms are more likely to be attributed to illness (Leventhal & Diefenbach, 1991). When symptoms are attributed to age, many people—especially the middle aged—tend to delay the seeking of health care. Older people, however, are more likely to seek prompt care for ambiguous symptoms, perhaps due to intolerance of uncertainty.

During late adulthood, *ageist* stereotypes, which are widely held among health care professionals and even by some older adults, can be significant barriers to achieving and maintaining good health. Chief among these are the views that old age is a period of inevitable decline, that elderly people are generally unable or unwilling to change their lifestyles and behaviors, that their adherence to treatment regimens and preventive interventions is poor, and that the bene-

Figure 12.2

Age, Gender, and Physician's Contacts In general, young children and older adults are more likely than adolescents and young adults to use health services. Starting in adolescence, women contact their physicians more than men do.

Source: United States Department of Health and Human Services (USDHHS). (1995). *Healthy People 2000 Review, 1994.* Washington, DC: U.S. Government Printing Office.

fits gained from lifestyle and behavioral interventions at this stage of life are minimal. This is unfortunate because most people aged 65 years or older suffer from at least one chronic health condition and many suffer from two or more—and in many cases these conditions may be cured or at least controlled.

Ageist stereotypes may also prevent older adults from seeking (or receiving) optimal preventive health care. For instance, cancer screening programs often are not directed at people over age 65, despite the increased prevalence in this age group (Black and others, 1990). Ageist stereotypes can also be a barrier to older adults' motivation to adopt healthier lifestyles aimed at increasing their overall health expectancy. Fortunately, research studies indicate that many elderly people remain optimistic about their health status—a good thing, because self-assessed health is the strongest predictor of life satisfaction during old age (Hart, 1997).

Gender is another factor in using health services. Beginning in adolescence and continuing throughout adulthood, women are more likely than men to report symptoms and to use health services (Baum & Grunberg, 1991; Fuller and others, 1993). This difference is due in large part to pregnancy and childbirth. New mothers are staying in the hospital about half a day longer than they did in the mid-1990s, when insurance companies cut childbirth stays to 24 hours and sparked outcries about "drive-by deliveries" (Meara and others, 2004). However, even when medical visits for pregnancy and childbirth are not counted, women still visit their physicians more often than do men.

Men, especially young men, more often dodge the doctor, even when faced with potentially serious problems. Large-scale surveys conducted by CNN and the National Center for Health Statistics revealed the following (NCHS, 2006; Papas, 1999):

- More than one-third of the sample of men wouldn't go to a doctor immediately, even if experiencing severe chest pains (34 percent) or shortness of breath (37 percent)—two possible signs of a myocardial infarction.

- Fifty-five percent of the women had undergone a cancer screening in the past year, mostly for cervical or breast cancer. Only 32 percent of the men sampled had been checked for cancer, mostly of the prostate gland.

- The women were more conscious than the men of taking care of their health and more likely to perceive that they had a medical need. Men were less likely than women to report having unmet medical needs (18.7 percent compared to 22.9 percent).

- Gender differences in visits to physician offices vary by age, with the largest difference occurring among adults 18–44 years of age. The gender difference narrows among middle-aged adults and disappears among the oldest age group.

Why are women more likely than men to seek health care? One possible reason is that women are exposed to more illness. They are more likely to be involved in direct care of the elderly and children, who have the highest incidence

Charles Gupton/Stone/Getty

Women, the Elderly, and Sick Role Behavior In general, women are more likely than men to seek health care, and women over 65 are more likely than younger women to seek health care.

of illness. Women also are more likely to be nurses, elementary school teachers, and day-care providers. As a consequence, women have an increased risk of becoming ill themselves.

Research has also found that women are more sensitive to their internal bodily symptoms than are men, causing them to report more symptoms (Pennebaker, 1982). Many younger men delay visiting the doctor because they perceive themselves as healthy, even invincible. At age 25, the average male doesn't worry about injury or chronic disease. However, many women of the same age have already experienced a pregnancy and so may be more aware of the fragility of perfect health. This explanation does not imply that women get sick more often than men do, merely that they are more likely to notice and report any symptoms they experience.

The gender difference in the seeking of health care may also be partly due to social factors. For instance, women visit doctors more than men do because their health care tends to be more fragmented. For a routine physical exam, most men are "one-stop shoppers." That is, they visit a general practitioner or nurse practitioner who is able to perform most, if not all, of the needed tests. In contrast, a woman may need to visit three or more specialists or clinics for a thorough check-up: an internist for her physical, a gynecologist for a Pap smear, a mammography specialist to screen for breast tumors, and so forth. Some researchers see this fragmentation as an indication that Western medicine is male biased and not well structured to meet women's basic needs (Rosenthal, 1993).

Socioeconomic Status and Cultural Factors

Socioeconomic status (SES) predicts both symptom reporting and the seeking of health care. High-income people generally report fewer symptoms and better health than do low-income people (Kaplan & Keil, 1993). However, when high-SES people do get sick, they are more likely to seek health care. This may explain why low-SES people are overrepresented among those who are hospitalized. People in lower-SES groups tend to wait longer before seeking treatment for their symptoms, making it more likely that they will become seriously ill and require hospitalization. In addition, people with lower family incomes are more likely to use outpatient clinics and hospital emergency rooms for medical care, because they are less likely to have health insurance and regular physicians than their financially advantaged counterparts (Flack and others, 1995). This helps explain why morbidity and mortality are highest among people at the lowest-SES levels.

Cultural factors also influence the way in which people respond to physical symptoms. Some cultures encourage a strong reaction to symptoms, while others socialize group members to deny pain and keep their symptoms to themselves (Sue & Zane, 1995). In one study, researchers compared the overall functioning of chronic back pain sufferers in six different countries (Sanders and others, 1992). American patients reported the greatest overall suffering and disruption of daily activities, followed in order by Italian, New Zealand, Japanese, Colombian, and Mexican patients. As another example, there are marked cultural differences in the experience of menopause. As many as 75 percent of American women report experiencing hot flashes and sweating. In Japan, however, fewer than 10 percent of women report experiencing these same symptoms (Moerman, 2002).

Cultural factors also influence a person's tendency to seek treatment. People who hold illness beliefs that conflict with Western medicine are less likely to seek traditional biomedical care and more likely to rely upon a **lay referral system**—an informal *social network* of family members, friends, and other nonprofessionals who offer their own impressions and experiences regarding a set of symptoms (Burnam and others, 1984). A member of the referral system might help interpret a symptom ("My niece had a growth like that, and it turned out to be nothing at all") or give advice about seeking treatment ("Jack waited until his cancer had metastasized and it was too late to treat. You'd better call your doctor right away").

Several researchers have studied ethnic and cultural variations in the lay referral system. They have found, for example, that ethnic groups differ widely in the degree to which they believe that human intervention in health outcomes is possible, or desirable. Some groups, for instance, attribute disease to nonphysical factors, such as God's will (Landrine & Klonoff, 1994). In such cases, people may be more inclined to employ non-Western practices for treatment (see Chapter 14). This poses an interesting problem for Western health care providers because the closer a patient's cultural background or ethnicity is to that of Western physicians, the more the patient's *reported* symptoms will approximate those that are recognizable as signs of disease.

Upbringing is a related cultural factor in determining the likelihood of a person's seeking treatment for a particular symptom. People whose parents paid close attention to physical symptoms and sought regular health care may be more likely to do the same. Conversely, those whose parents were suspicious of doctors and more likely to rely on self-care or some form of alternative treatment may be more likely to carry that suspicion with them.

Delay Behavior

Do you, or does someone you know sometimes avoid thinking about health care until a *serious* need arises? Do you tend to ignore symptoms for as long as possible in the hope that they will disappear? Clearly, for medical emergencies such as heart attacks, getting help as quickly as possible is of the utmost importance. Although other chronic diseases and conditions may not present this kind of minute-by-minute urgency in survival, seeking timely care when symptoms first appear can make the difference between dying from the disease or condition and catching it when it may still be treatable. For example, beginning treatment for certain types of cancer while it is still localized and before it has

■ **lay referral system** an informal network of family members, friends, and other nonprofessionals who offer their own impressions, experiences, and recommendations regarding a set of bodily symptoms.

■ **delay behavior** the tendency to avoid seeking medical care because symptoms go unnoticed *(appraisal delay)*, sickness seems unlikely *(illness delay)*, professional help is deemed unnecessary *(behavioral delay)*, the individual procrastinates in making an appointment *(scheduling delay)*, or the perceived benefits of treatment do not outweigh the perceived costs *(treatment delay)*.

metastasized to other areas of the body often makes the difference between a long, full life and one that is shortened prematurely.

Despite the benefits of seeking care when symptoms first appear, many people, like my friend Bruce, whom you met at the beginning of the chapter, ignore their symptoms and do not seek medical help. This is called **delay behavior.** Despite seemingly overwhelming evidence of the need for immediate medical attention for myocardial infarction, sufferers frequently wait hours before admitting their chest pain is serious. Patients who feel lumps in their breasts or testicles sometimes postpone a visit to a doctor for months. Why do people delay seeking medical attention for such serious conditions?

In one analysis of factors in delay behavior, Martin Safer and his colleagues (1979) described five stages in the decision-making process for seeking medical care; at each stage, a person can exhibit delay behavior (see Figure 12.3). The model predicts that people will avoid seeking medical care because symptoms go unnoticed *(appraisal delay)*, sickness seems unlikely *(illness delay)*, professional help is deemed unnecessary *(behavioral delay)*, the individual procrastinates in making an appointment *(scheduling delay)*, or the perceived benefits of treatment do not outweigh the perceived costs *(treatment delay)*.

What determines the amount of delay during each stage? During the appraisal delay stage, the sensory prominence of the symptoms is the most important factor. Interviews with patients seeking care at hospital clinics indicated that patients delayed less when they were in pain or bleeding. Myocardial infarction patients who stopped to research their symptoms by consulting books and other sources delayed more than five times as long as patients who did not research their symptoms. Initial pain led to a short delay, whereas talking with others about one's symptoms resulted in a significantly longer delay (Matthews and others, 1983).

In the illness delay stage, other factors, such as previous experience with the symptoms, also came into play. Patients who had previously experienced similar symptoms were more likely than those who experienced symptoms for the first time to delay seeking medical attention. For example, with *carpal tunnel syndrome,* a nerve disorder caused by repeti-

Figure 12.3

Stages of Delay in Seeking Medical Attention The delay model proposed by Martin Safer and colleagues shows that noticing symptoms does not automatically lead to treatment. People have to make a concerted effort to take each step, so it's possible for intervening factors to interrupt the process.

Source: Anderson, B. L., Cacioppo, J. T., & Roberts, D. C. (1995). Delay in seeking a cancer diagnosis. Delay stages and psychophysiological comparison processes. *British Journal of Social Psychology, 34,* 33–52.

tive motion, the symptoms may come and go over a long period of time, and so people tend to ignore them. Only when the symptoms (numbness in the fingers and shooting pain up the arm) become persistent will the person start moving through the stages toward seeking treatment. In addition, patients who spent more time thinking about their symptoms and imagining the consequences of being sick were more likely to delay seeking medical attention.

In the last three stages, delay was longest for patients who were more concerned about the cost of treatment, had little pain, and were doubtful that their symptoms could be cured. The association between not feeling pain and delaying medical care is unfortunate because pain is not a major symptom in the early stages of a number of chronic diseases, including cancer, hypertension, and diabetes.

Overusing Health Services

At the opposite extreme are people who misuse health services by seeking care when they do not have a diagnosable health condition. The magnitude of this problem for the health care system is revealed in a startling statistic: Physicians estimate that as much as two-thirds of their time is taken up by people with problems that are either medically insignificant or the result of emotional disturbances (Miranda and others, 1991).

Hypochondriasis

Why do some people visit their physicians when there is no real need? A commonsense explanation is that such people suffer from **hypochondriasis,** or the false belief that they have a disease when they do not. Most people with hypochondriasis experience vague or ambiguous symptoms that they exaggerate and misattribute to disease. They also may have an exaggerated fear of contracting a disease, even in the face of information that nothing is, in fact, wrong and that there is no real danger. An underlying factor in many cases of hypochondriasis appears to be *neuroticism* (emotional instability), a state of emotional maladjustment that encompasses a number of specific traits, including self-consciousness, the inability to inhibit cravings, vulnerability to stress, and the tendency to experience anxiety, depression, and other negative emotions (Costa & McCrae, 1985).

Is this commonsense view of hypochondriasis correct? Or are people who report imaginary symptoms feigning illness, or **malingering,** in order to derive **secondary gains;** that is, whatever benefits they can from sick role behavior (for instance, sympathy from others and time off from work)? Generally speaking, people suffering from hypochondriasis amplify vague or ambiguous symptoms that are, in fact, benign into excessive worry about their health. To find out whether hypochondriasis is linked with emotional maladjustment, Paul Costa and Robert McCrae (1985) administered to average adults the Emotional Stability Scale and the Cornell Medical Index, which assesses a broad range

■ **hypochondriasis** the condition of experiencing abnormal anxiety over one's health, often including imaginary symptoms.

■ **malingering** making believe one is ill in order to benefit from sick role behavior.

■ **secondary gains** the "rewards" associated with sick role behavior, including increased attention, the ability to rest, freedom from responsibility, and so forth.

*D*iversity and Healthy Living

Chronic Fatigue Syndrome

Katie Lucas was so exhausted that she could barely get out of bed or perform even the simplest physical or mental task. "I remember one occasion having to take out a calculator to subtract 12 from 32," she said. "That's pretty bad." In Atlanta, Wilhelmina Jenkins was unable to complete her doctoral training in physics due to chronic fatigue that made thinking and writing all but impossible. "All they could recommend to me was changing my lifestyle—getting more rest," she said. "I tried every kind of change I could think of, and nothing helped; I just continued to go downhill."

Lucas and Jenkins suffer from chronic fatigue syndrome (CFS), a puzzling disorder suffered by an estimated 1 million patients in the United States, 80 percent of whom are women. In addition to persistent fatigue that lasts for months or longer, other symptoms of CFS include headaches, infections of unknown origins, and difficulties with concentration and memory (Ray, 1997). People afflicted with CFS are often so debilitated they are unable to carry out their normal, everyday activities. Making matters worse is the widespread view that they are not really sick but are merely malingerers whose symptoms are self-induced to gain attention, sympathy, or release from overwhelming responsibilities.

The cause of CFS has been much debated; the majority of patients report that it began with an apparent infection, and a significant number state that they were under considerable stress at the time (Komaroff & Buchwald, 1991). Because there is no diagnostic test for CFS and no known treatment, some doctors believe the condition is actually a form of hypochondri-asis, or even a *hysterical epidemic* caused by modern culture. Throughout history, *hysteria* has served as a physical manifestation of distress—a form of expression for people who otherwise are unable to verbalize their problems. First described in women during the late nineteenth century, hysteria involved puzzling physical disabilities—blindness or paralysis, for example—that Sigmund Freud believed to be the result of emotional conflicts. Many historians and sociologists believe that hysteria was really a "Victorian disorder," a female reaction to sexual repression and limited career opportunities, which all but disappeared with the advent of feminism. Along with those who have *recovered memories* of childhood trauma and abuse or suffer from *Gulf War syndrome* or *dissociative identity disorder* (formerly called multiple personality disorder), CFS "victims," say the critics, are merely manifesting contemporary signs of hysteria (Showalter, 1999).

There is evidence, however, that those who consider CFS to be a form of hysteria or hypochondriasis are probably wrong. For example, researchers at Johns Hopkins University have established a link between chronic fatigue and low blood pressure. Strapping CFS patients on a tilt table and then gradually moving them upright to a 70-degree angle, researchers found that at one point the patients' blood pressure drops suddenly from about 125 to 45, immediately triggering CFS symptoms. By boosting the patient's water and salt intake and providing pressure-elevating medication, researchers have been able to help about 75 percent of the CFS patients. Other researchers have found that administering low doses of the stress hor-

---

■ **chronic fatigue syndrome (CFS)** a puzzling disorder of uncertain causes in which a person experiences headaches, infections of unknown origins, extreme tiredness, and difficulties with concentration and memory.

of medical symptoms. The results showed that adults who scored high on emotional instability averaged two to three times as many physical complaints as those who scored low on emotional instability. But does this prove that neuroticism causes hypochondriasis? As we have seen, correlational evidence such as this cannot pinpoint causality. Even if it could, we would be unable to discern the *direction* of causality. It could be that having many aches, pains, and illnesses causes an excessive preoccupation with one's health. Those suffering from **chronic fatigue syndrome,** for example, have struggled with false assumptions about the causality of their condition (see Diversity and Healthy Living above).

It is particularly unfair—and inaccurate—to denounce everyone who calls a health provider in the absence of indisputable physical symptoms, because stress and anxiety often create a number of physical symptoms that may resemble the symptoms of a biologically based disorder (Miranda and others, 1991).

mone hydrocortisone, known to be in short supply in many people with CFS, boosts energy, mood, and activity level (Rutz, 1998). The research also indicates that a high percentage of CFS patients suffer from a persistent viral infection and immune system dysfunction and that treatment of these problems can alleviate some of the symptoms (Ablashi and others, 2000; Pall, 2000). Evidence such as this is helpful to frustrated patients, who have frequently been told by doctors who can find nothing wrong with them that they are imagining their symptoms.

The role of psychological factors in CFS, however, continues to be debated. Some experts suggest that CFS and depression have a common cause because of similar symptoms such as fatigue. Others have pointed to differences between the two disorders. For example, weight loss, suicidal thinking, guilt, and low self-esteem are all less common in CFS than in depression, while flu-like symptoms, muscle weakness and pain, and fatigue are more common.

The time course of CFS varies from patient to patient, with some experiencing rapid improvement and full recovery, while others worsen over time and/or experience repeated cycles of relapse and remission (Hinds & McCluskey, 1993). Because there is no generally accepted drug treatment for CFS, treatment usually involves managing the symptoms and engaging in moderate activity. Cognitive-behavioral interventions designed to increase tolerance of symptoms and to modify maladaptive illness beliefs have also been effective in some patients (Sharpe and others, 1996). The disorder can be so debilitating, unresponsive to traditional medical regimens, and frustrating that some CFS sufferers turn to various forms of alternative and fringe medicine. One nurse suffering from CFS actually took her own life with the help of Dr. Jack Kevorkian (Showalter, 1999).

Because the debate appears to be shifting from whether the symptoms of disorders such as CFS are real—those affected are definitely sick, according to an increasing number of experts—some health experts question whether there is any point in continuing the search for specific, organic causes. Simon Wessely, professor of psychological medicine and director of the Chronic Fatigue Syndrome unit at King's College in London, believes that doing so is a disservice to patients: "Doctors have been searching for the Holy Grail to explain these syndromes for the last 150 years without success. . . . If a patient is told the problem is due to a permanent deficit in the immune system or a persistent virus or chronic disability of the nerves or brain, this just generates helplessness and the patient becomes a victim," he said. "And if you say the problem is psychological, this generates anger on the part of patients who don't regard psychological ills as legitimate. Looking for any single cause misses the point. Regardless of how or why they may have started, these syndromes are multifactorial, like heart disease" (as quoted in Brody, 1999a, p. B11). This understanding suggests that a multifactorial approach to treating CFS would therefore be most effective, and certainly better than being turned away from the medical system entirely, or told that "it's all in your head."

For example, anxiety (perhaps about upcoming exams) may disrupt sleeping and concentration, trigger diarrhea and nausea, suppress appetite, and/or result in a state of general agitation (Pennebaker and others, 1977).

Patient Adherence

Surprisingly, even when people seek health care, many simply ignore (or fail to closely follow) the treatment that is prescribed for them. Every health care professional can tell stories about this phenomenon: the patient who cheats on a special diet; the coronary case who, without consulting her doctor, stops taking her hypertension medication; or the accident victim who misuses a prescribed painkiller.

■ **adherence** a patient both agreeing to and then closely following a treatment regimen as advised by his or her health care provider.

Adherence is broadly defined as closely following the advice of a health care provider. This includes advice pertaining to medications and lifestyle changes (for example, losing weight or quitting smoking) as well as recommendations about preventive measures (such as avoiding fatty foods or starting an exercise program). Adherence is both an attitude and a behavior. As an attitude, it entails a willingness to follow health advice; as a behavior, it is related to the actual carrying out of specific recommendations. Nonadherence would include refusal to adhere to instructions or the lack of sustained effort in following a treatment regimen.

The potential costs associated with nonadherence are enormous (Dunbar-Jacob & Schlenk, 2000). In patients with organ transplants, for example, failure to adhere to immunosupressant drug regimens can lead to organ rejection. In addition, nonadherence causes 10 to 20 percent of patients to require an otherwise unnecessary refill of prescription medications, 5 to 10 percent to require further visits to their doctor, and another 5 to 10 percent to need additional days off from work. It is estimated that nonadherence has an annual economic impact of over $100 billion in additional treatment and hospitalization costs and lost productivity (HRSA Care Action, 2005).

How Widespread Is Nonadherence?

Philip Ley (1988) reviewed nine studies comparing patients' self-reports of adherence with more direct methods such as pill counts and urine or blood screening. Although 75 percent of patients stated that they had followed their treatment regimens, direct measures indicated the actual percentage to be closer to 46 percent.

Estimating the prevalence of nonadherence is difficult because the problem takes so many different forms. For example, a patient may not show up for a scheduled appointment or may fail to complete the course of an antibiotic. A person may "cheat a little" on a special diet, rehabilitative exercise program, or in following some other treatment regimen. In other words, there are many degrees of nonadherence.

In broad terms, the average rate of adherence is estimated to be only about 60 percent—only three out of every five patients follow their treatment regimens closely (DiMatteo, 1994). Here are some specifics:

■ Only 20 to 40 percent of participants in treatment programs for smoking, alcohol, and drug abuse continue to comply with treatment after one year.

■ In the treatment of obesity, between 10 and 13 percent of participants stop attending program meetings after 2 to 3 months, and from 42 to 48 percent after 3 to 4 months.

■ Only 50 percent of patients comply fully with physician-directed dietary restrictions. Up to 80 percent of patients drop out of programs that prescribe other lifestyle changes (such as fitness programs).

What Factors Predict Adherence?

Are some people more likely than others to comply with treatment? Is adherence more likely for certain kinds of treatment than for others? In their search for answers to these questions, biomedical researchers have examined three broad categories of variables: *patient variables, treatment regimen variables, and patient-provider communication.*

Patient and Provider Variables

Although a substantial amount of adherence research has focused on age, gender, ethnicity, education, and income, it is now generally understood that sociodemographic factors are not very accurate predictors of adherence (Dunbar-Jacob & Schlenk, 2001). In general, this is because people are inconsistent in their adherence behaviors. A patient who follows a medication regimen, for example, may not necessarily adhere to a dietary regimen (Eitel and others, 1995). Among certain groups of patients, however, problematic alcohol or drug use (Turner and others, 2001) and a history of depression, anxiety, and other mental health problems have been associated with nonadherence (Tucker and others, 2004).

At the consumer level, what does affect adherence? Being in a good mood, having optimistic expectations, and having trust in one's care provider are important factors (Leedham, 1995; Thom and others, 2004). Having the support of family and friends is also important. For instance, studies have shown that marital support improves adherence to diabetes care regimens that include food purchase and preparation, medication administration, glucose testing, and exercise involvement (Trief and others, 2004).

Perceived control and preference for control of treatments also help to explain adherence. Patients who express greater preference for control and involvement in their health care demonstrate better adherence with medical treatments that are largely self-directed and that take place in the home (Christensen and others, 1990). However, greater preference for control predicts *poorer* adherence when treatments take place in a clinic or hospital (Cvengros and others, 2004).

Provider variables, too, have a predictable influence on patient adherence. Robin DiMatteo (1993) conducted a 2-year study of patient adherence with medication, exercise, and dietary restrictions prescribed by 186 doctors who were treating patients for heart disease, diabetes, and high blood pressure. Among the factors that correlated with patient adherence were the doctor's level of job satisfaction, the number of patients seen per week, and communication style (for example, his or her willingness to answer a patient's questions).

Treatment Regimen Variables

Patients are more likely to follow recommendations that they believe in and that they are capable of carrying out (DiMatteo, 1994). Even when a treatment is deemed useful, whether the patient is actually able to carry out the regimen depends on how difficult the regimen is to follow and the support available to the patient. Researchers have generally found that the more complex a treatment regimen, the lower the likelihood of complete adherence.

Health care providers can take several steps to improve adherence in their patients, including the following (Jeffery and others, 1993; Christensen and others, 2002):

- Tailor the treatment to fit the patient's lifestyle. Adherence will increase in response to anything that makes a treatment regimen easier to follow, such as daily reminders about taking medicine, individually packaged meals for those on a restricted diet, or breaking down a complicated or long-term regimen into smaller segments.

- Simplify instructions with clear language to ensure that the patient understands the amount, timing, and duration of treatment.

- Make sure that the patient understands enough of the treatment rationale to gain confidence in the treatment schedule.

- Involve family members, friends, and other patient supporters in the treatment and the explanation of its rationale.

- Provide feedback about progress.

Patient–Provider Communication

Interpersonal communication between health care consumers and providers is used to gather information for making an accurate diagnosis, to elicit informed consent from patients when selecting treatment strategies, and to encourage patients to follow prescribed treatment regimens. The quality of these interactions directly influences a number of health care outcomes (Arora, 2000; Kreps 2002).

At the heart of the consumer–provider relationship are the nature and quality of communication. Patients too often emerge from consultations with insufficient information or even a misunderstanding of their problems. Particularly during difficult consultations, patients often are under considerable stress and find it difficult to take in everything the doctor says. To improve the situation, communication-skills training is now an integral component of the medical school curriculum (ACGME, 2004).

Health care providers who are good communicators, who are less businesslike, and who meet their patients' expectations regarding the information they are entitled to receive tend to have patients who are more likely to adhere to treatment recommendations (Thompson and others, 1995). Physicians' nonverbal skills are also linked with patient satisfaction and adherence. We will explore the patient–provider relationship more fully next.

The Patient–Provider Relationship

"I really don't have time to explain all this," Dennis Moore's physician said as he hurried away, and for the second time that day Moore saw red. Earlier that day

Moore, a former army officer who had commanded a river gun boat in Vietnam, had also seen the red of his own blood as he urinated. He desperately needed answers to questions—"Why am I bleeding? Do I have cancer? Will I be alive in a year?"—but he was too frightened and angry to stick around, and he stormed out of his doctor's office. A week later, he learned from a more responsive doctor that the bleeding came from ulcers in his colon and a noncancerous tumor.

The relationship between health care provider and patient is the backbone of all medical treatment. A full 60 to 80 percent of medical diagnoses and treatment decisions are made on the basis of information that arises from the medical consultation process alone. Yet patients and providers do not always share the same view of the effectiveness of the process. Too often, providers overestimate how well a consultation went and how likely it is that the patient will follow through on their advice. The quality of the patient–provider relationship plays an important role in promoting patient adherence to treatment instructions.

Factors Affecting the Patient–Provider Relationship

Research has demonstrated that the central elements of the patient–provider relationship are *continuity of care, communication,* and the overall *quality of consultations* (Sihvonen and others, 1989). The same principles apply to this relationship, regardless of the provider (physician, nurse, physician's assistant, or medical technician) or the health care system. Under the fee-for-service model, 78 percent of patients reported being "very satisfied with their doctors." Today, under **managed care,** only 54 percent of patients report this same level of satisfaction (Brink, 1998). One reason for this decrease in satisfaction is that half of all patients are convinced that treatment decisions—including which providers they can see and whether they can develop long-term relationships with those providers—are based strictly on what their health plan will cover. General communication problems may result from a lack of continuity in care, but other factors—from both provider and patient perspectives—also play a role.

Provider Communication Problems
The information exchanged between doctor and patient during a consultation is often crucial to formulating diagnoses and in deciding on the course of treatment. Effective communication ensures that a patient's symptoms and concerns are understood by the health care providers and that information and treatment instructions are accurately received and carried out by the patient.

Patients often leave a consultation dissatisfied due to a lack of information, poor understanding of medical advice, and the perception that they are unable to follow recommended treatment or advice (Weinman, 1997). And, as Dennis Moore's story illustrates, faulty communication about their condition and treatment is also a major source of anxiety for many patients. Ideally, health

■ **managed care** health care that seeks to control costs by eliminating waste and unnecessary procedures and by providing economically sound treatment guidelines to hospitals and physicians.

care providers listen carefully to patients, ask questions to ensure that patients understand their condition and treatment, and fully inform patients about every aspect of their care.

Lack of information is a direct by-product of "too little time, too much to do." Many health care providers simply do not spend enough time with their patients. Research consistently shows that the more time physicians spend with their patients, the more satisfied the patients are, particularly when their doctors take some time just to chat. People are also more likely to follow their treatment plans to a successful conclusion when they understand their care and have a voice in it. Faster doctors who see more patients each day have less-satisfied patients who are also less likely to be up to date on immunizations, mammograms, and other health-enhancing procedures and tests (Zuger, 1998).

Some health care providers also *miscommunicate* with patients by failing to listen carefully or by treating them either like medical school faculty or children. In one study of 74 physician consultations, researchers reported that in nearly two-thirds of the cases the physician interrupted the patient's description of symptoms after only 18 seconds (Beckman & Frankel, 1984). Another early series of studies by Phillip Ley (1988) analyzed the content of physicians' comments during their consultations in terms of complexity, clarity, and organization. The findings of these studies showed that far too often the medical information provided was too detailed or complex for patients to understand or retain and that patients and doctors frequently interpreted the same information in different ways. To make matters worse, doctors and other providers often mix the complicated lingo with a patronizing tone that can leave patients feeling like helpless children.

Why such poor communication skills in such highly intelligent and skilled professionals? People are typically chosen for medical training based on their technical expertise, not their social skills. Until relatively recently, medical schools placed little emphasis on communication. Few providers, for instance, were trained to deliver bad news, and many—out of sheer ignorance or in response to time pressures—say things to patients and families that cause unnecessary emotional pain and may even reduce the effectiveness of treatment.

The harm that stems from poorly delivered bad news can be long lasting, even permanent. One study reported that, even after months had passed, cancer survivors and their loved ones were able to recall what made getting the news more or less difficult. Many expressed persistent negative feelings about how the news was conveyed (Ptacek & Eberhardt, 1996). In the worst instances, providers seemed to adopt coping strategies to minimize *their* discomfort with delivering bad news and failed to realize what was needed to minimize their patients' and the patients' loved ones' trauma. What the patients wanted

Seeking Social Skills Medical school students now regularly participate in communication skills training along with all the technical learning. This will help them establish better patient–provider and other relationships as they move along in their careers.

© Royalty-Free/Corbis

was to hear all available information about their condition; to have ample opportunity to vent their feelings and ask questions; to be informed about available support services, including support groups for family members; and to be given as much time with their providers as needed to fully understand the medical condition, its treatment, and the likelihood that treatment would be successful.

Another problem is that like people everywhere, some health care providers hold prejudicial patient stereotypes. Several studies have reported that physicians provide less information to and are less supportive of African-American and Hispanic patients and patients of lower socioeconomic status (SES) than other patients in the same health care setting (van Ryn & Fu, 2003). Patients who present themselves for treatment for certain disorders also seem to evoke more negative reactions from physicians. For example, psychological disorders such as anxiety or depression may provoke especially brief visits. There is also evidence that many physicians have negative perceptions of the elderly, which are made even worse when older patients have difficulty communicating. Is it any wonder that among patients aged 65 and older, only 54 percent state high confidence in their physicians (Haug & Ory, 1987)?

Sexism is also present in health care, making communication between male physicians and female patients, for example, sometimes less than perfect. A number of research studies demonstrate that female physicians demonstrate more proficient clinical performance than do their male counterparts, conducting longer office visits, asking more questions, and showing significantly more verbal and nonverbal support (Hall and others, 1994). As with many things, patients often are most comfortable communicating and interacting with health care providers who are of the same gender and similar in other ways to themselves.

Patient Communication Problems

Health care providers should not receive all the blame for miscommunications. Patients themselves often are uninformed and unprepared to communicate about sensitive health matters. Moreover, a surprising number of patients give faulty information or mention the symptom of greatest concern in an almost off-hand manner, fearing either that doctors will not be fully forthcoming in telling the truth about serious conditions or that their fears may be confirmed.

The differing educational and social backgrounds of patient and provider also can adversely affect communication. Traditionally, physicians have been upper-middle-class and white. Their patients, however, reflect a much more heterogeneous group, often of lower SES and from different ethnic and cultural backgrounds. While the provider may think he or she is clearly explaining a problem, the patient may be reading a whole different meaning into the explanation. Research has shown that such misunderstandings are widespread and that patients with the most extensive and complicated health care problems are at greatest risk for misunderstanding their diagnoses, medications, and treatment instructions (Parker, 2000). Contributing to this problem of medical misinformation is the reality that health promotion and patient education information has traditionally been written at reading levels at or above the tenth grade. Such material is clearly not accessible to the millions of patients with lower-level reading skills. The health care system needs reshaping, including providing nonwritten materials for health education, and surrogate readers, so that patients with low literacy levels have access to information.

Patient–provider cultural misunderstandings were demonstrated in a study of Israeli doctors and Ethiopian immigrant patients that compared patient evaluations of health consultations with evaluations made by their doctors (Reiff and others, 1999). Physicians rated the health status of these patients and the effectiveness of their consultation significantly higher than did the patients. Although immigrant patients who had been in their new countries longer had somewhat greater agreement with their providers than did more recent immigrants, many continued to report symptoms and concerns that were culturally specific—and completely lost on their new doctors.

Models of the Patient–Provider Relationship

Over half a century ago, Thomas Szasz and M. Hollender (1956) proposed three models of the doctor–patient relationship that parallel the prototypical styles of parent–infant, parent–adolescent, and adult–adult models of communication: *activity-passivity, guidance-cooperation,* and *mutual participation.* The traditional model of this relationship is a paternalistic one in which providers take the active, upper hand—treating patients either as passive infants (activity-passivity) or as adolescents who, although older and more mature, still require a steady, mature hand to direct their health care (guidance-cooperation).

These traditional relationships were challenged by the consumer movement of the 1960s and 1970s, which promoted a more active role for patients and the mutual participation of providers and patients. Patients have continued to become more assertive, insisting that they be heard and fully informed. They are "well-informed consumers" who insist on playing a more active role in the patient–provider interaction (Haug, 1994). This growing sense of shared responsibility is not universal, however, and is much more typical of health care systems in Western, developed countries. A recent study of Lebanese women's experiences with maternity care found that the vast majority accorded total trust to their physicians and rarely questioned their decisions regarding various procedures. When questioned, the women reported that many aspects of their care were intimidating and unsatisfactory. However, the extent of passivity and feelings of dissatisfaction varied with the participants' SES and the amount of psychosocial support they received throughout the process of childbirth. Higher SES levels and more extensive support were strongly associated with less passivity and greater satisfaction with treatment (Kabakian-Khasholian and others, 2000).

The quality of the patient–provider relationship often reflects directly on patient health. Patients who are satisfied with their consultation, their provider's communicative style, and the overall patient–provider relationship are more likely to comply with treatment instructions once they return home. This was dramatically revealed in a study of patients with diabetes. Paul Ciechanowski and his colleagues (2001) attempted to correlate treatment adherence among patients with three categories of attachment. Patients who showed *secure attachment* reported the highest levels of confidence and trust in their physicians. Patients who demonstrated *insecure attachment* reported less confidence and trust in their providers, either because they seemed too busy or simply unresponsive to their patients' needs and concerns. Patients in the insecure subgroups had less control of glucose levels than did patients in the secure group, especially if they also rated patient–provider communications as poor. A follow-up study found that patients in the insecurely attached subgroups were also less likely to see their primary care provider than those in the securely attached group.

Although many patients welcome a new, more active role in their health care, people differ in their abilities and willingness to assume this type of role. Patient lifestyle and adherence to treatment regimens are indeed determining factors in the outcome of health care treatment, and patients and providers today continue to debate where the responsibility for optimum care lies. However, overemphasis on patient responsibility can have the negative effect of making some patients feel responsible for conditions over which they have little or no control. Even when patients assume a relatively passive role in their relationships with providers, there are many things that providers and patients can do to ensure that their communication is smooth and clear, as we will see next.

Improving Patient–Provider Communication

Health care providers increasingly realize that patients are more likely to follow instructions and respond well to treatment when their knowledge is recognized and incorporated into the treatment regimen. And doctors and patients alike increasingly recognize that approximately half of all causes of morbidity and mortality in the United States are linked to behavioral and social factors (IOM, 2004; NCHS, 2006). In order to practice good medicine, doctors must treat these risk factors as well as physical symptoms, which requires the patients' active cooperation and good patient–provider communication.

Communication training for health care providers includes a focus on *active listening* skills in which providers echo, restate, and seek to clarify patients' statements to achieve a shared understanding of symptoms, concerns, and treatment expectations. It also includes training in developing good rapport with patients through appropriate eye contact and other responses designed to acknowledge patients' feelings and to help them talk. In addition, providers receive instruction in how to communicate with patients about sensitive or difficult health topics, as well as in how to give bad news (Bellack and others, 1999).

A number of communication-enhancing interventions have also been targeted at patients, especially those about to receive an important consultation. These interventions generally have focused on increasing patients' level of participation, specifically in order to ensure that their concerns will be clearly heard and that they leave the consultation with a clear understanding of the information that has been provided (Weinman, 2001).

To help patients who are overly passive, Sheldon Greenfield and Sherrie Kaplan (1985) developed a program of *assertiveness coaching* for patients waiting to see their physicians. The 20-minute intervention begins with a careful review of the patient's medical record. From this review, a psychologist helps the patient formulate a set of clear questions for the doctor. The psychologist also offers a brief pep talk in which the patient is reminded that being assertive doesn't mean being aggressive. It means taking an active role and entering the doctor's office with a clear sense of one's goals. It means telling the doctor about feelings, fears, and symptoms without being hindered by embarrassment or anxiety.

Assertiveness coaching can pay huge dividends. By establishing a greater degree of control in their office visits, patients who have been coached obtain more information. Follow-up interviews reveal that 4 months later, they had missed less work, rated their overall health as better, and reported fewer symptoms than control patients who did not receive the assertiveness coaching.

The Internet and the Patient–Provider Relationship

When Julie Remery had a bout with the flu, she was coughing so badly one night that her husband Kevin nearly took her to the emergency room at 3 A.M. Instead, he logged onto their HMO's Web site and learned that the over-the-counter antihistamine Julie was taking could actually worsen phlegm and that switching to an expectorant might help. After picking up the recommended medication at a 24-hour pharmacy, he e-mailed his wife's doctor for an appointment the next day.

As this story illustrates, the Internet has become a major vehicle for health care. Surveys of users indicate that most believe the Internet has made them better consumers of health information. In one survey, nearly half had urged a family member or friend to visit a doctor, changed their exercise or eating habits, or made a treatment decision for themselves as a result of their cyber search (Miller & Reents, cited in Kassirer, 2000). Patients who access authoritative medical information also visit emergency rooms and doctors' offices less frequently, cutting health care costs (Landro, 2001).

Telemedicine (telehealth) is becoming part of every health care provider's training (Saab and others, 2004). Physicians are beginning to treat minor health problems such as common low back pain, upper respiratory infections, and urinary infections by e-mail, just as they have previously done by telephone. Using patients' test results from reliable home monitoring equipment, uploaded to Internet sites that provide two-way video and audio communication, physicians prescribe and adjust doses of drugs, send laboratory reports, and refer patients to other providers. Increasingly, health care professionals are expected to offer these services, and health care insurers will cover them just as they cover medications, surgery, and other medical procedures.

Telemedicine: Making New Connections Advances in technology are providing greater access to health care, especially for people in remote areas. This American cardiologist is using video technology to help a patient and his doctor in Manila, Phillipines, where comparable equipment and expertise is not typically available.

Paul Morris/TimeLife Pictures/Getty Images

Some experts caution that the patient–provider relationship may change for the worse in the wake of enhanced electronic communication, greater access to health and medical information online, and other changes in technology. For instance, e-mail exchanges can be impersonal and mechanical, and e-mail lacks context. The multiple nonverbal cues available during a face-to-face consultation such as a patient's appearance, body language, and tone of voice, may be lost with online care. However, some more positive changes from advancing technologies, especially for people in remote areas, are already being seen in the area of telemedicine.

The Health Care System

The World Health Organization defines a health care system as *all activities whose primary purpose is to promote, restore, or maintain health* (World Health Report, 2006). Formal health services, including the professional delivery of personal medical services by physicians, physicians' assistants, midwives, nurses, and technicians, are clearly within these boundaries, as is the use of all medication, whether or not prescribed by a provider. By this definition, health care is one of the largest sectors in the economy, with the United States spending yearly an estimated $1.9 trillion, which amounts to 16 percent of our gross domestic product, or $6,280 per person (Smith and others, 2006).

The resources devoted to health care systems are very unequally distributed throughout the world, and not in proportion to the distribution of health problems. For instance, 84 percent of the world's population lives in low- and middle-income countries, which account for only 11 percent of global health spending (4 percent of gross domestic product in those countries), despite the fact that these countries bear 93 percent of the world's disease burden.

In both rich and poor nations, health needs today are very different from those of 100 or even 50 years ago. Expectations of access to some form of health care continue to increase, as do demands for measures to protect individuals against the financial cost of poor health. People today also turn to health systems for a much more diverse array of problems than before—not just for pain relief or the treatment of debilitating diseases and conditions, but also for information on nutrition, substance abuse, childrearing, and countless other issues. The hospital remains at the heart of the modern health system.

Home Care The cost of health care accounts for 8 percent of the world gross domestic product. Home care services across the world account for the majority of this cost, except in the United States, where hospitalization accounts for the majority of health care costs. Here, a nurse practitioner cares for an elderly woman at home.

The Administrative Structure of the Modern Hospital

There are 5,759 registered hospitals in the United States, admitting over 34 million people as patients each year (AHA, 2006). Many hospitals now specialize, for example treating only acute diseases or trauma that results from injury. This

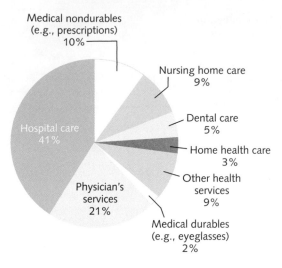

Medical nondurables
(e.g., prescriptions)
10%

Nursing home care
9%

Dental care
5%

Hospital care
41%

Home health care
3%

Other health
services
9%

Physician's
services
21%

Medical durables
(e.g., eyeglasses)
2%

Figure 12.4

The Health Care "Pie" Out
of every dollar spent on health
services in the United States, 41
cents go to pay for hospitalization. Small wonder that
economic pressures have dramatically reduced the average
length of a hospital stay from
about 8.3 days in 1965 to
around 4.8 days in 2003. Health
psychologists believe that if
more efforts were placed on
promoting health and preventive
care, the need for expensive
hospitalization would be dramatically reduced (NCHS, 2006).

shift in focus is due in large part to economic pressure to reduce the high cost of hospitalization. As Figure 12.4 shows,
by a huge margin, the largest piece of the health care "pie"
is the cost of hospitalization.

The modern hospital has a complex, hierarchical administrative structure. At the top is usually a board of trustees,
consisting of community and business leaders charged with
overall policymaking, long-range planning, and fund-raising.
Directly below the trustees are the hospital administrators
and medical staff, and each of those groups has its own line
of authority. The administrative staff deals with the everyday matters of keeping the hospital running smoothly—
monitoring patient accounts, ordering supplies, purchasing
equipment, and maintenance, for example. The medical staff,
which includes the physicians and the nurses, is responsible
for medical treatment. In most American hospitals, physicians are not employees of the hospital. Rather, they are employed in private practice or affiliated with a managed care plan and provide
services at the hospital for their patients through these sources. Most receive
salaries from the managed care plan or bill patients individually.

The Nursing Staff

Nurses are the backbone of the health care system, and the demand for their
services continues to outstrip their supply. Of primary interest are the registered
nurses (R.N.s), who are either nurse practitioners or clinical nurse specialists.
Nurse practitioners have completed bachelor's and master's programs in nursing
as well as training in primary care. They often work with physicians in private
practice, seeing their own patients and providing all routine medical care, including prescribing treatments for various illnesses and conditions. *Clinical
nurse specialists* specialize as health care providers in an area of practice such as
cardiac or cancer care, pediatrics, gerontology, or mental health.

Nurses are in a unique position among a hospital's medical staff. Although
employed by the hospital, they are also assisting the physicians. These multiple
roles sometimes create conflicting demands, such as when a doctor orders an
expensive diagnostic test for a patient, but the hospital administration wants to
discourage use of the test as a cost-containment strategy.

Nursing is a stressful occupation for several reasons. First, nurses experience
tension stemming from conflict between their own professional goals and those
of physicians and hospital administrators. Although both nurses and physicians work from a *cure orientation* in which they seek to restore patients to good
health, nurses also work from a patient *care orientation*. That is, while their primary goal is to heal patients, an equally important goal is to make the healing process as humane as possible. Although they do care about the patients,
hospital administrators have an *institutional orientation,* in which they are concerned primarily with ensuring the smooth flow of services, keeping the physical facilities of the hospital well maintained, and so forth. Caught in the

middle, nurses are especially prone to conflict, dissatisfaction, and a high rate of turnover.

Second, nurses may suffer stress from the conflict between their high level of medical training and low involvement in decision making. For example, unless they are *nurse practitioners,* they are not allowed to prescribe medication, although their experience often makes it obvious when it is needed. Third, nurses often struggle with monumental issues, such as balancing their medical oath to "do no harm" with requests from dying patients to assist them in committing suicide. One *New England Journal of Medicine* study showed that 19 percent of nurses who care for the dying had engaged in *euthanasia* or assisted suicide (Scanlon, 1996). Seven percent had done so on their own, without a physician's request. These conflicts, along with the numerous other stresses of working with sick people, place nurses at high risk of *burnout*—an occupational hazard characterized by emotional and physical exhaustion, a loss of meaningfulness in one's work, and an increasingly depersonalized and cynical attitude toward patients. One explanation suggests that the hurried, fast-lane pace of the modern hospital, coupled with the pain of watching patients suffer, forces burned-out nurses to distance themselves psychologically from their clients and from their career (Parker & Kulik, 1995).

Physician Assistants

Another increasingly important health care provider is the *physician assistant (PA).* As members of one of the ten fastest growing professions in the United States (CNNMoney.com), PAs provide health care services typically performed by a physician, under the supervision of a physician. They take medical histories, examine and treat patients, order and interpret laboratory tests and x-rays, make diagnoses, prescribe medication, and operate more independently of physicians than nurses do. PAs are the principal providers in many rural areas and inner city clinics, where a physician is present for only 1 or 2 days each week. PAs must graduate from an accredited, two-year educational program (most of which are at the graduate level) and pass a national exam to obtain a license (Bureau of Labor Statistics, 2006).

The Changing Health Care System

As medical costs have skyrocketed, the American health care system has undergone many changes. Walk-in clinics, *extended care facilities,* and home help services, for example, handle an increasing proportion of smaller emergencies and long-term care for those who are not seriously ill. Extended care facilities include convalescent homes, nursing homes, and other facilities for patients with chronic illnesses or disabilities that prevent them from living on their own. In addition, *rehabilitation centers* treat those who are recovering from specific conditions, such as stroke, spinal cord injuries, head injuries, and degenerative diseases, while *psychiatric hospitals* offer care for people diagnosed with psychological disorders such as schizophrenia. Finally, *hospices* provide both institutional and home health care for those who are terminally ill.

Managed Care

The most dramatic cost-containment strategy is the increasing prominence of *health maintenance organizations (HMOs)* and other forms of managed care—health care that seeks to control costs by eliminating waste and unnecessary procedures and by providing economically sound treatment guidelines to hospitals and doctors. Under a managed care system, each patient is assigned a *primary care physician,* who manages his or her treatment by acting as a gatekeeper to determine when referrals to specialists within the system are warranted. About one in five insured Americans now belongs to a managed care program. Another type of managed care plan, the *preferred provider organization,* or *PPO,* groups together a network of hospitals and physicians who agree to negotiated rates for members.

One concern about managed care is that medical decision making is being taken out of the hands of doctors and patients and shifted to insurance companies and other third-party providers. Although this keeps costs down, critics complain that it also eliminates the patient's right to choose his or her own doctor or hospital—for example, to stay with the doctor who has been treating the family for years.

Another concern is that the medical care provided by HMOs may not be of the same quality as that provided by private physicians. One study found that, compared to fee-for-service patients, HMO patients tended to have less expensive tests prescribed for them, were less likely to be admitted to a hospital, and, when admitted, were discharged sooner (Miller & Luft, 1994). We have to be careful in generalizing from such results, however. Managed care programs vary greatly in their policies and quality of care, so it's a good idea to shop around and ask careful questions of providers before selecting a plan.

Clearly, the health care system is in flux. Politicians, economists, and medical professionals are all looking for solutions to the health care problem. At the core of the problem is the high cost of medical care. This is why HMOs have become so popular. The goal of managed care has been to allow more companies to afford to provide benefits to employees and to contain runaway health care costs. However, health insurance costs in the U.S. are still prohibitively high, especially for small companies and for individuals seeking insurance outside of a group plan.

The High Cost of Health Care

Why does health care cost so much? One reason is that under the old "fee-for-service model," doctors and hospitals had a financial incentive to throw every treatment option available at every illness or health problem. The more procedures they carried out, the greater their income. And patients, too, had few reasons to worry about the costs of their treatment since third-party payment insurance programs allowed them to pass their bills straight to their insurers almost without regard to costs. When Medicare was enacted into law in 1965, the government seemed to be institutionalizing this "blank check" mentality in which most or all health care costs were covered by private insurers and federal programs. The result was escalating inflation of health care costs that made the

American system the most expensive in the world. In 1980, for instance, Americans spent $247 billion on health care, or 8.9 percent of the gross domestic product (GDP). By 2004, that figure had risen to $1.9 *trillion,* or 16 percent of the GDP (Smith and others, 2006).

Another reason health care costs have skyrocketed is that many doctors say that fear of *malpractice suits* has forced them to practice *defensive medicine,* ordering possibly unnecessary diagnostic tests and procedures that serve primarily to protect them from legal action. Many health experts believe that the economics of health care make it inevitable that the American health care system will ultimately shift to some form of national health insurance program. Most European countries, as well as Japan and Canada, have national health insurance programs that ensure high-quality care for every citizen. In Canada, hospitals are funded almost entirely by the government, while physicians are paid on the basis of the specific services they provide. England has a national health insurance system in which hospitals are financed and run by the government, and physicians are either salaried or paid a flat fee based on the number of patients they treat.

In contrast, the health care system in the United States traditionally has been a unique mixture of public, private nonprofit, and private for-profit hospitals, in which most physicians were compensated on a fee-for-service basis. Their compensation has come from a variety of sources—sometimes from insurance companies, sometimes directly from patients, and sometimes from government programs such as Medicare, Medicaid, or the Veterans Administration.

Still, national health care has its critics. Although the quality of care is generally excellent, critics point to some significant drawbacks, such as the potentially long wait for certain operations and other procedures. In England, when patients began to complain of inadequate access to doctors, more and more wealthy citizens began taking out private health insurance. And Canadian citizens sometimes choose to cross the border into the United States in order to obtain certain health care services that are low priority in nationalized Canadian hospitals. Regardless of who provides health care—nurse or physician or physician's assistant—and whether that care is covered under a fee-for-service or managed care or national health insurance system, the patient–provider relationship is a crucial factor in how effective and satisfying the care is.

Getty Images /DAJ

Japanese Care Japan enjoys high-quality health care, such as the rehabilitation services shown here, for much less than the Unites States spends. In 2004, Japan spent just 7.6 percent of its gross domestic product on health care, compared with 16 percent in the United States. Japan has mandatory health insurance coverage for all its citizens. By contrast, recent estimates suggest that over 40 million Americans are completely uninsured.

Hospitalization

Although the word *hospital* comes from the same root as the word *hospitality,* many patients don't find hospitals to be very hospitable places. Recent studies indicate that more than one-fifth of hospitalized patients experience hospital system problems such as staff providing them with

In 2003, the average hospital stay was 4.8 days, down from 7.3 days in 1980. An increase in same-day surgery, new drug therapies, and cost-management controls account for the shorter average stay. The rate of hospitalization has also declined. In 1980, 168 of 1,000 Americans were hospitalized. That rate dropped nearly 30 percent to 122 per 1,000 population in 1990 and to 120 per 1,000 in 2003.

—National Center for Health Statistics, 2005

conflicting information, and tests and procedures not being done on time (Cleary, 2003). Furthermore, hospitalization is not as safe as it should be. In the United States alone, as many as 98,000 people die in hospitals each year as a result of preventable medical errors (IOM, 2001).

Historically, the psychological well-being of the patient has not been a primary goal of health care (Friedman, 1992). Rather, its goals were to bring together all the necessary medical staff and equipment to cure people who are seriously ill and, in the process, to maximize efficiency. In fact, surveys from around the world consistently reveal that the single greatest stressor for health care providers is to be behind schedule (Zuger, 1998). This need for efficiency has prompted a somewhat one-dimensional, depersonalized view of hospitalized patients.

Loss of Control and Depersonalization

Upon entering the hospital, patients may feel they are being absorbed by what Erving Goffman (1961) described as a *total institution* that takes control of virtually every aspect of life. Hospitalized patients are expected to conform to the rules of the hospital, including its schedule for eating, sleeping, and receiving visitors, and to make their bodies available for examination and treatment. Throughout their hospitalization, patients are expected to remain cooperative, which often leads to passivity and feeling the loss of control.

Patients also often suffer from being treated as a nonperson—a body to be medicated, watched, and managed. Being referred to as "the appendectomy in Room 617" calls attention to the fact that nearly every aspect of a patient's identity—other than his or her reason for being in the hospital—disappears. Sometimes this *depersonalization* is so complete that hospital staff converse among themselves in the patient's presence, using medical jargon that excludes the patient. Although medical terminology was designed to allow physicians and nurses to telegraph their conversations in order to convey a great deal of information quickly, when health providers use it without translation, most patients are left feeling both helpless and anxious (Disbrow and others, 1993).

A need for efficiency is only partly to blame for this depersonalized care. There is also a need to reduce the daily stress of the hospital environment. Hospital staff may attempt to distance themselves emotionally as a way to cope with the pressures of making life-or-death decisions, working in an environment with hazardous chemicals, being exposed to contagious illnesses, and treating patients who may not respond to care or who may die.

Factors Affecting Adjustment to Hospitalization

A patient's adjustment to the hospital experience depends on a variety of factors, including the nature of the health problem, the patient's age, the presence of emotional support, and the individual's explanatory style and coping strategies. For example, older adults generally find it easier to cope with chronic illnesses than do adolescents and younger adults, for whom "out of season" illnesses are unexpected and may seem particularly cruel (Holahan & Moos, 1982).

Explanatory Style

Hospitalized patients may display a variety of adverse psychological symptoms, particularly if they engage in a self-defeating attempt to assign *blame* for their plight. Some people are more likely to feel responsible for what happens to them. Others are more likely to assign responsibility externally—to other people, to bad luck, or simply to fate. Still others do not assign any kind of responsibility. What impact does our explanatory style have on how we adjust to hospitalization? Do people who blame themselves for a serious illness, for example, wallow in guilt or self-hatred that delays their recovery and emotional adjustment? Do people who assign blame externally become bitter and angry, and thereby worsen their own prognosis?

Health psychologists have consistently found that the more patients dwell on assigning blame for their illnesses and other traumatic events—whether to themselves or to others—the more their emotional adjustment suffers (Downey and others, 1990). There is some evidence that seeking to blame others is the greater of the two "emotional evils," perhaps because it is harder to "forgive" others (as when injured, for example, by a drunk driver) than to forgive ourselves (as when smoking or practicing unsafe sex leads to a serious health condition) (Kiecolt-Glaser & Williams, 1987; Taylor and others, 1984).

How Children Cope with Medical Procedures and Minor Injuries

Children cope somewhat differently with the stress of hospitalization and medical procedures. Richard Lazarus' *three-stage model of coping* can be applied to how children cope with acute events such as injury or an anticipated painful diagnostic test or medical treatment (Lazarus & Launier, 1978). The first stage of this model involves *appraisal* of the stressor; the second stage involves *encounter* with the stressor, and the third stage involves *recovery* from the stressor.

Most studies of how children cope with acute pain have focused on the encounter stage, because children rarely appraise potentially harmful situations beforehand—or they would avoid them! In one study, 8-year-old boys and girls were asked to role-play four situations, each designed to assess what the children themselves would do and what they would suggest a friend should do when encountering acute pain (Peterson and others, 1999). The situations involved hypothetical medical procedures (an injection or a blood test) and minor injuries (a bruise on the leg or a cut from a piece of glass).

Children and Medical Procedures In order to get children to undergo difficult or "scary" medical procedures, parents, nurses, and doctors should understand how the child appraises such situations. The parent and nurse here are working together to keep the child calm and focused.

© William Campbell/Corbis Sygma

Table 12.1

Frequency of Children's Coping Responses

Situation	Response[a]		
	Proactive	Neutral	Reactive
Self	62	51	79
Other	105	30	15

[a]Each child can contribute to the analysis more than once.

Source: Peterson, L., Crowson, J., Saldana, L., & Holdridge, S. (1999). Of needles and skinned knees: Children's coping with medical procedures and minor injuries for self and other. *Health Psychology, 18*(2), 197–200.

The children's coping responses were coded into three categories: *proactive coping* (imagine you are someplace else doing something fun, take deep breaths, try to relax your muscles); *neutral coping* (sit still, be quiet, do what the nurse says); and *reactive coping* (yell, cry, hit the doctor). As Table 12.1 reveals, children were more likely to suggest reactive coping strategies for themselves and more proactive responses for friends. These results suggest that children are likely to use less effective coping strategies for themselves than they would recommend to a friend confronting similar stressors. In this regard, they are like adults, who recognize adaptive coping techniques such as relaxation and exercise and recommend them to friends, yet often engage in maladaptive coping behaviors such as smoking and alcohol abuse.

Preparing for Hospitalization

Facing surgery, chemotherapy, and many other invasive procedures is especially daunting, because it means confronting our vulnerability and mortality. Surgeons and anesthesiologists have an old saying: "The way a patient enters anesthesia is the way he or she will come out of it." In other words, patients who approach treatment with an optimistic demeanor, confidence, and a sense of being in control often do better after treatment than do highly anxious people who feel helpless and overwhelmed by the situation. For this reason, psychological interventions are increasingly used to prepare patients for stressful medical procedures.

The most effective interventions are those that increase patients' sense of *control* over their treatment and recovery. Although interventions often overlap in the types of control they emphasize, most can be categorized as primarily promoting increased informational, cognitive, or behavioral control.

Increasing Informational Control

Informational control interventions focus on the particular procedures and physical sensations that accompany a medical treatment. One of the first psychologists to study the role of informational control in hospitalized patients was Irving Janis, who in 1958 studied fear levels in patients before and after surgery. Following a presurgery intervention, which involved analysis of patients' feelings, Janis categorized the patients according to the amount of fear, anxiety, and feelings of vulnerability they reported. After the surgery, Janis reinterviewed the patients to learn how well they had understood and followed the presurgery coping information they had received and to assess their postoperative emotional mood. The results showed that patients who displayed moderate levels of fear had the fewest postoperative emotional problems. Janis attributed these results to the realistic manner in which moderately fearful patients approached their operation. Their concern was appropriate to allow

■ **informational control** refers to patients' knowledge regarding the particular procedures and physical sensations that accompany a medical treatment.

them to gather information about the procedure and to develop optimal defenses and coping strategies. Patients who were extremely fearful or nonfearful did not ask questions or gather information to prepare for the procedure, and they were thus poorly equipped to cope with the pain or discomfort that followed the procedure. High-fear patients were too focused on their own emotions to process the preparatory information, while patients who initially reported low fears tended to become upset or angry after their surgery.

In a follow-up study, Janis examined the impact of a simple presurgery intervention on the recovery progress of patients. Patients in the intervention group were given information about possible unpleasant symptoms they might experience following surgery. Compared with a control group of patients who were given little information, the patients in the prepared group requested less pain medication, made fewer demands on the hospital staff, recovered faster, and reported greater satisfaction with their surgeon and the hospital staff than those who were not given the additional information (Janis, 1958).

Since Janis' pioneering studies, many others have conducted research to determine the type of information that is most helpful to patients. Imagine that you are in the hospital for a minor operation that, although not dangerous, is likely to be followed by a painful recovery. What type of information would you want? Would you want a detailed description of the *medical steps* to be followed before, during, and after the surgery (procedural information)? Or would you like to know how you can expect to *feel* before, during, and after surgery (sensory information)? Sensory information allows you to make an accurate attribution for sensations that you actually do experience. If you are told, for example, that it is customary to feel nauseated for a few days following a particular medical procedure, you will not be surprised when you actually do feel sick to your stomach. More important, armed with accurate information beforehand you will not worry when the symptom appears. Unprepared, however, you might fear that your nausea is a sign that something has gone wrong and that you are not recovering properly. Procedural information, on the other hand, may reduce stress by giving patients an increased sense of control over what their bodies are experiencing. When procedures are expected and predictable, many patients develop greater confidence and become more relaxed.

The results of studies comparing the advantages of procedural and sensory information have been mixed. One reason for the inconsistency in findings is that researchers may define improvement differently. For example, some may use as their criterion the length of the hospital stay while others may use requests for pain medication or improvements in mobility, muscular strength, and other physical measures related to recovery. In a large-scale meta-analysis, researchers reported that although procedural information and sensory information are both beneficial to patients preparing for stressful medical procedures, procedural information appears to help the greatest number of patients. In many instances, of course, providing both types of information produces the maximum benefits (Johnson & Vogele, 1993).

■ **cognitive control** refers to interventions that direct the patient's attention to the positive aspects of a procedure (such as improved health) rather than on feelings of discomfort.

Interestingly, researchers have found that a patient's reaction to procedural or sensory information regarding a stressful medical procedure depends, in part, on his or her style of coping (Shipley and others, 1979). As you might expect, sensitizers tend to deal with stressful medical procedures with constant vigilance and anxious monitoring of the cues of discomfort, while repressors deny stress, actively suppress stressful thoughts, and do not appear to be anxious.

Researchers have also discovered that sensitizers welcome as much detailed information as they can get while they are awaiting stressful medical procedures, while repressors prefer to know as little as possible. In one study, women who were about to undergo diagnostic screening for cervical cancer were first classified as sensitizers or repressors on the basis of their self-reported desire for medical information (Miller & Mangan, 1983). Next, half the patients of each type were given extensive preparatory information about the procedures; the others were given minimal information. The patients who experienced the least physical discomfort during the exam (as measured by average heart rate before and after receiving the information and following the exam) were those who received the appropriate amount of information based on their preferences.

Increasing Cognitive Control

Cognitive control interventions direct the patient's attention to the positive aspects of a procedure (such as improved health) rather than on feelings of discomfort. *Modeling*—learning by watching others—is a widely used intervention for increasing cognitive control. In one study, researchers showed dental patients a videotape of a nervous dental patient who reduced his nervousness by learning to relax and communicate more effectively with the dentist (Law and others, 1994). Patients with a self-reported need for control, who generally felt helpless during dental treatment, had the most beneficial response to the modeling intervention. Compared with control subjects and those with a lower need for control, these patients reported significantly lower levels of pain, anxiety, and stress.

Another example of a cognitive control intervention involves helping patients prepare for a medical procedure by controlling the focus of their attention. In one study, a group of surgical patients was taught to direct their attention away from worries about the discomfort of their upcoming surgery, focusing instead on its potentially positive outcomes (Langer and others, 1975). Other surgical patients were randomly assigned to a comparison group that spent the same amount of time with a psychologist before their operation but focused only on general issues related to hospitalization. Those in the intervention group reported less anxiety and required fewer postoperative pain medications. They were also rated by hospital staff as dealing significantly better with their surgery than control patients.

A number of controversial cognitive control interventions incorporate *guided imagery,* in which patients rehearse instructions for mentally influencing the perception of pain as well as their blood flow, immune functioning, and other "involuntary" processes that may influence their recovery. Although traditional Western medicine has considered these processes to be outside voluntary control, the growing body of psychoneuroimmunology research suggests that people can learn to alter them somewhat and thus improve their chances for a speedy recovery (Pert and others, 1998).

Cognitive control interventions encourage patients to redefine their role—from that of an immobile body being worked on to that of an active participant. Doing so may reap huge health benefits. Consider the effects of a cognitive control intervention on blood loss. Doctors have long been puzzled by the reality that two patients who undergo similar surgical procedures often lose very different (and unpredictable) amounts of blood. In a remarkable study, Henry Bennett (1986) and his colleagues randomly divided patients about to undergo spinal surgery into three groups for a 15-minute presurgery intervention. One group was told only about how the neural functioning of their spinal cords would be monitored during the operations. Another group was also taught how to relax their muscles as they entered anesthesia and again as they were waking up. Those in a third, *blood-shunting,* group were told, in addition to everything the other groups were told, the importance of conserving blood by trying to control their blood flow during surgery. To increase their confidence, they were reminded of how blushing, which reddens the face by increasing blood flow, can be triggered just by being embarrassed. Then they were told that their blood would "shunt" away from the site of surgery during the procedure. Remarkably, patients in the blood-shunting group lost an average of 500 cc less blood than those in either the control group or the relaxation group, where the average amount lost was nearly 1 full liter (900 cc).

Increasing Behavioral Control

Behavioral control interventions teach techniques for controlling pain and speeding recovery during and after a medical procedure. These might include relaxation instructions, breathing exercises, and other techniques to reduce discomfort or speed recovery during or after a stressful medical procedure. Such interventions may provide patients with an even greater sense of control because they focus on actual tools to influence how they are feeling (Manyande and others, 1995).

In a classic study, anesthesiologist Larry Egbert and his colleagues (1964) told 46 patients awaiting abdominal surgery that they could relieve their postsurgical pain by relaxing the muscles surrounding the site of their incision. They also were given breathing exercises to reduce pain. Remarkably, during the days after their surgery these patients requested lower doses of morphine for pain relief and were discharged earlier than a control group of patients who did not participate in a behavioral control intervention.

Lamaze training, which is designed to prepare prospective parents for natural childbirth, is perhaps the most widely used behavioral control intervention. At the heart of the Lamaze technique is relaxation training that enhances the prospective mother's behavioral control over breathing and the muscles of the uterus, which push the baby out. Delivering mothers who are afraid tend

■ **behavioral control** interventions that teach techniques for controlling pain and speeding recovery during and after a medical procedure.

■ **Lamaze training** natural childbirth preparation designed to prepare prospective parents by enhancing their informational, cognitive, and behavioral control over the procedure.

to counteract the natural rhythmic contractions of childbirth by tightening their muscles, which lengthens labor and makes it more painful. Cross-cultural research reveals that women in cultures in which childbirth is anticipated with less fear and apprehension generally report shorter, less painful deliveries, indicating that inadequate psychological preparation may play a role in the difficulty that some mothers experience during labor.

Interventions aimed at increasing behavioral control are most beneficial for medical procedures in which the patient's participation can assist progress. In delivering a baby, for example, the mother-to-be clearly *can* do something to make things run more smoothly. Conversely, behavioral control interventions may be useless when medical procedures require that the patient remain still and passive. For example, cardiac catheterization and dental surgery both require that patients be inactive. There is little that the patient can do to make the procedures more pleasant or to assist the health care providers.

Summing Up

Recognizing and Interpreting Symptoms

1. Detecting physical symptoms and interpreting their medical significance are strongly influenced by psychological processes, including the individual's past experience, personality, culture, gender, and psychological health, as well as by the individual's focus of attention and tendency to either monitor or repress health threats.

2. Sensitizers have a strong internal focus; they detect and report symptoms more quickly than repressors, who are more externally focused. Consequently, repressors are more likely to cope with distressing medical symptoms by distancing themselves from unpleasant information.

3. Illness representations regarding the type of disease, its causes, time frame, consequences, and controllability also influence how people react to and interpret physical symptoms.

Seeking Treatment

4. Social and demographic variables, such as cultural norms, age, gender, and socioeconomic status, influence whether a person seeks treatment.

5. Health services may be underused or overused. Delay behavior may result from a failure to notice symptoms (appraisal delay), refusal to believe one is actually sick (illness delay) or needs professional help (behavioral delay), procrastination in making an appointment (scheduling delay), or belief that the benefits of seeking treatment are not worth the costs (treatment delay).

6. Some people may use health services when there is no real need because they are feigning illness (malingering) or falsely believe they have a disease when they do not (hypochondriasis). In others, bodily symptoms are an expression of emotional stress.

Patient Adherence

7. Adherence means closely following the advice of a health care provider, which less than half of patients do. Patient adherence improves with perceived control (for those who prefer control), optimism, a good mood, trust in the care provider, a strong patient–provider relationship, a simple and clearly explained treatment regimen, and social support.

The Patient–Provider Relationship

8. The central elements of the essential relationship between health care provider and patient are continuity of care, communication, and the overall quality of consultations. Poor communication between health care providers and patients is common, given the time pressures of health care and the fact that providers may lack communication skills. Other factors in miscommunication include the attitudes and beliefs patients and providers have regarding their roles, as well as gender, cultural, and educational differences between providers and patients.

9. The traditional model of the patient–provider relationship has been a paternalistic one in which providers are active and patients remain essentially passive. The con-

sumer movement of the 1960s and 1970s promoted a more active role for patients and mutual participation between provider and patients. Patients who are satisfied with their provider's communication style and with the overall quality of their relationship are more likely to adhere to treatment instructions.

10. Communication skills training is now a fundamental component of medical and nursing education. The quality of the patient–provider relationship may be challenged by enhanced electronic communication and greater access to Internet health and medical information. The burgeoning field of telemedicine has, however, greatly improved health care in remote locations.

The Health Care System

11. There are many types of hospitals, each catering to particular health needs. Among these are extended care facilities, rehabilitation centers, psychiatric hospitals, and hospices. Nurses at all levels as well as physicians' assistants are playing an increasingly important role, along with doctors, technicians, and other health care providers.

12. As medical costs have risen, the health care system has instituted many cost-saving measures. Among these are the advent of walk-in clinics and home help services as well as health maintenance organizations, preferred provider organizations, and other forms of managed care. One concern about managed care is that medical decision making is being taken out of the hands of physicians and shifted to insurance companies. Another concern is that managed care may not be of the same quality as that provided by private physicians.

Hospitalization

13. One of the most persistent problems of hospitals is the depersonalization of patients as a result of a need for efficiency and the need of hospital staff to distance themselves emotionally from their stressful daily experiences.

14. A patient's adjustment to hospitalization depends on a variety of factors, including the nature of the health problem being treated, the patient's age, the presence of emotional support, and the individual's explanatory style.

15. Children, like adults, often use less effective coping strategies for themselves than they would recommend to a friend when confronting similar stressors.

16. Psychological interventions designed to restore or enhance control often improve adjustment to hospitalization and to stressful medical procedures. The benefits of preparatory information, relaxation training, modeling, and guided imagery training have all been documented.

Key Terms and Concepts

collaborative care, p. 360
attentional focus, p. 361
sensitizers, p. 361
repressors, p. 361
illness representation, p. 362
comorbidity, p. 364

lay referral system, p. 369
delay behavior, p. 370
hypochondriasis, p. 371
malingering, p. 371
secondary gains, p. 371
chronic fatigue syndrome (CFS), p. 372

adherence, p. 374
managed care, p. 377
informational control, p. 390
cognitive control, p. 392
behavioral control, p. 393
Lamaze training, p. 393

Managing Pain

*D*uring the 1932 Los Angeles Olympic Games, the Japanese gymnastics team finished dead last—a humiliating defeat that triggered a national mission to become an international gymnastic power. When the games resumed following World War II, the mission was finally fulfilled as the Japanese team won the gold medal in four consecutive Olympics: Rome, Tokyo, Mexico City, and Munich. In their attempt at a fifth straight title at the 1976 Montreal games, however, Shun Fujimoto, their star competitor, broke his kneecap while performing the floor exercise. Remarkably, he didn't disclose the injury to his coaches or teammates. "I did not want to worry my teammates," he recalled. "The competition was so close I didn't want them to lose their concentration with worry about me."

Blessed with incredible strength and a nearly perfect gymnastic physique, Fujimoto was a fierce competitor and team leader whose buoyant spirit and national pride had rallied his teammates many times in previous competitions. But how could he continue? Although Olympic rules prohibited him from taking a painkiller, Fujimoto decided to stay in the competition and endure the excruciating pain. Fortunately, the next apparatus was the pommel horse—an event in which the knees are mostly locked in place. Unless he fell, the pain might be tolerable. Fujimoto completed a nearly flawless performance, receiving a score of 9.5 out of a possible 10.

The final event, however, would be much more demanding. The high rings test arm strength, but vital points can also be lost during the dismount, when the gymnast descends from a great height after a swinging routine that propels him onto the mat at high velocity. "I knew when I descended from the rings, it would be the most painful moment," Fujimoto remembered. "I also knew that if my posture was not good when I landed, I would not receive a good score. I must try to forget the pain."

After another nearly perfect routine, Fujimoto landed, smiled for the judges, held his position for the required few seconds, and then fell to the mat as his injured leg buckled beneath him. Incredibly, his near-perfect score of 9.7 was enough to propel his team to gold medal victory!

Biological, psychological, and social factors contributed to Fujimoto's development as a gymnast, and those same factors played a role in his triumphant Olympic victory. The story also makes clear one of health psychology's most fundamental themes: that the mind and body are inextricably intertwined. Fujimoto's determination not to let his teammates down allowed him to overcome a painful injury that in other circumstances would most certainly have been crippling.

The struggle to understand pain—what causes it and how to control it—is a central topic in health psychology. Until recently, however, researchers knew next to nothing about this common, yet extraordinarily complex, phenomenon. Moreover, medical schools did not spend much time covering the topic of pain. Over the past 3 decades, health psychologists have made considerable progress in filling in the gaps. In this chapter, we discuss the components of pain—the ways in which it is experienced, how it is measured, and the biological, psychological, and social factors that influence the experience of pain. And we will take a look at how pain is treated within medicine and in the latest multidimensional interventions introduced by health psychology.

What Is Pain?

What types of pain have you experienced? Few topics in health psychology are as elusive as pain. Pain is obviously a physical sensation—when we fall and scrape a knee, we feel a stinging sensation that has real, physical substance. Yet the pain of losing a loved one or ending a long-term relationship, which is more psychological than physical in nature, is often just as real. And pain is highly subjective and sometimes not altogether unpleasant. After a hard workout on the track, for example, I often feel a deep muscular fatigue that is definitely uncomfortable, yet somehow warm and almost pleasant, too.

This chapter focuses on **clinical pain,** which is pain that requires some form of medical treatment. Let's begin by considering how many of us suffer pain and how often.

Epidemiology and Components of Pain

Pain is a major public health problem, affecting more than 50 million Americans and costing more than $70 billion each year in health care costs and lost productivity (Gatchel & Mayer, 2000). Moreover, pain is the most common

■ **clinical pain** pain that requires some form of medical treatment.

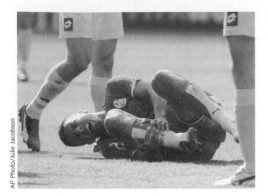

Components of Pain Pain obviously has a strong physical component, as the face of Tunisia's Hamed Namouchi clearly reveals. It also has emotional and psychological components; because the shot that landed him on his ankle won the game for his team, Naumouchi's pain is probably somewhat more bearable, as the joy of winning overshadows the pain.

reason that people seek medical treatment and is so pervasive that it is now being considered a fifth vital sign, along with blood pressure, pulse, temperature, and respiration (Gatchel & Maddrey, 2004). No other class of health problems even approaches this level of impact.

Perhaps more so than any other everyday experience, pain clearly illustrates the biopsychosocial model. This model distinguishes among the biological mechanisms by which painful stimuli are processed by the body; the subjective, emotional experience of pain; and the social and behavioral factors that help shape our response to pain (Turk & Okifuji, 2002).

Let's consider a specific example—striking your thumb with a hammer—to illustrate how these components come together to create the experience of pain. First, you have the physical sensation of pain—an immediate, sharp stab of pain as you strike your thumb. Next, depending upon who is observing and whether your culture dictates stoicism, you either express or inhibit your feelings of pain, which affects your actual pain experience. If the injury is serious and the pain persists, you may avoid using your aching hand, which then becomes weak from inactivity, and you may begin to depend on others for assistance.

Thus, our *pain* experience is shaped by biological, psychological, and sociobehavioral forces which in turn reflect our genetic legacy, previous experiences, personality, and coping resources (Gatchel & Maddrey, 2004).

Significance and Types of Pain

Painful Struggle Ashlyn Blocker's mother, shown here with Ashlyn (right) and her sister, struggles daily with Ashlyn's inability to sense pain, hot, and cold. "Pain's there for a reason. It lets your body know something's wrong and it needs to be fixed. I'd give anything for her to feel pain" (quoted in Bynum, 2004).

Despite the discomfort and stress it can cause, pain is essential to our survival. Stick your toe into hot bath water, and the stinging sensation causes you to jerk your foot out of the water immediately. A nagging pain that radiates down your arm prompts a visit to your doctor to rule out possible cardiovascular disease. Thus, although pain can be bothersome, it is just that bothersome nature that makes it highly adaptive. Pain sounds a warning that something is wrong and alerts you to try to prevent further physical damage.

In fact, not feeling pain is hazardous to your health. Ashlyn Blocker's mother knows. Ashlyn has a rare genetic disorder that prevents her from feeling either pain or extreme hot and cold. Her parents, teachers, playground monitors, and others must therefore check her regularly for accidentally self-inflicted injuries, summertime over-heating, and winter frostbite—none of which she can detect herself.

Types of Pain

In general, researchers divide pain into three broad categories: acute, recurrent, and chronic, depending on its time course. **Acute pain** is sharp, stinging pain that is usually localized in an injured area of the body. Although acute pain can last from a few seconds to several months, it generally subsides as normal healing occurs. Examples include a burn, a fracture, an overused muscle, or pain after surgery. **Recurrent pain** involves episodes of discomfort interspersed with periods in which the individual is relatively pain free that recur for more than 3 months (Gatchel & Maddrey, 2004). Periodic migraine headaches are of this type.

Chronic pain, which is traditionally defined as pain that lasts 6 months or longer—long past the normal healing period-—may be continuous or intermittent, moderate or severe in intensity, and felt in just about any of the body's tissues (Turk & Okifuji, 2002). Chronic pain lowers the person's overall quality of life and increases his or her vulnerability to infection and thus to a host of diseases. Chronic pain can also take a devastating psychological toll, triggering lowered self-esteem, insomnia, anger, hopelessness, and many other signs of distress. Compared with acute pain patients, those with chronic lower back pain tend also to have higher rates of depression and personality disorders, and they are more likely to abuse alcohol and other drugs (Brewer & Karoly, 1992; Kinney and others, 1993).

Hyperalgesia

Another challenge faced by those with chronic pain is that they may become even more sensitive to pain, a condition known as **hyperalgesia.** Hyperalgesia also happens when people are sick or injured, and it may facilitate recovery by stimulating recuperative behaviors such as getting extra rest and following a healthy diet. For example, when you have the flu, you feel weak and achy, which drives you back to bed, which is exactly where you need to be to recover.

Hundreds of experiments over more than 100 years have confirmed that hyperalgesia often occurs as a normal adaptation during sickness. Most kinds of internal pain, from mild indigestion to the agony of certain kidney disorders, are accompanied by increased sensitivity in nearby tissues. In the 1890s, physiologists Henry Head and Mames MacKensie observed this phenomenon and proposed that signals from diseased parts of the body set up an "irritable focus" in the central nervous system that creates areas of enhanced pain sensitivity in nearby body parts. The fact that the increased sensitivity to pain occurs in otherwise healthy tissues strongly suggests that the signals originate in the central nervous system (Cervero, 2000).

acute pain sharp, stinging pain that is short lived and usually related to tissue damage.

recurrent pain involves episodes of discomfort interspersed with periods in which the individual is relatively pain free, that recur for more than 3 months.

chronic pain dull, burning pain that is long lasting.

hyperalgesia a condition in which a chronic pain sufferer becomes more sensitive to pain over time.

Measuring Pain

Because of its multidimensional and subjective nature, pain is not easily measured. Nevertheless, clinicians and researchers have developed a number of ways to assess pain: *physical measures, behavioral measures,* and *self-report measures.*

Physical Measures

There are no objective measures of pain, only subjective ones (Gatchel, 2001). It's not that clinicians and researchers haven't tried to find them. In fact, the problem of measuring pain set the stage for the very earliest *psychophysical studies* in the new field of psychology. These studies highlight the familiar *mind–body* (*psyche,* meaning mind; *physike,* meaning body) *problem:* How does conscious awareness derive from, and affect, the physical sensations of the body?

One way to assess pain is to measure the specific physiological changes that accompany pain. For example, *electromyography (EMG)* assesses the amount of muscle tension experienced by patients suffering from headaches or lower back pain. Researchers have also carefully recorded changes in heart rate, breathing rate, blood pressure, skin temperature, and skin conductance—all indicators of the *autonomic arousal* that may accompany pain. Unfortunately, physical measures have generally not provided any consistent differences between those with and those without a specific type of pain, such as a headache (Andrasik and others, 1982). This failure may well be because pain is only one of many factors that contribute to autonomic changes; others include diet, attention, activity level, stress, and the presence of illness.

Behavioral Measures

Another assessment technique measures signs of pain in a patient's behavior. This can be done by relatives and friends of the patient or by health care professionals in structured clinical sessions.

Wilbert Fordyce (1976), a pioneer in pain research, developed a pain behavior-training program in which an observer, such as the pain sufferer's roommate, is asked to monitor five to ten behaviors that frequently signal the onset of a pain episode. For example, the observer might tally the amount of time the person spends in bed, the number of verbal complaints, and the number of requests for painkillers.

In clinical settings, nurses and other health professionals are trained to systematically observe patients' pain behaviors during routine care procedures. One frequently used pain inventory is the *Pain Behavior Scale,* which consists of a series of target behaviors, including verbal complaints, facial grimaces, awkward postures, and mobility (Feuerstein & Beattie, 1995). The patient is asked to perform various activities, such as walking across the room, touching the toes, and picking up an object from the floor while the observer rates the occurrence of each target behavior on a three-point scale: "frequent," "occasional," and "none" (Ohlund and others, 1994).

Self-Report Measures

The simplest way to measure pain is to have patients fill out a questionnaire, assigning a numerical value to their discomfort in a given situation. *Pain rating scales* may also be based on verbal report, in which the person chooses from a list the word that most accurately describes the pain. Rating scales are so easy to use that they are the preferred means of assessing pain in young children. The numerical scales are also used in verbal reports.

Many clinicians find it useful to have patients keep a *pain diary* in which they rate pain episodes over a period of time, along with daily events, medications, and other details. Pain diaries paint a more accurate picture of an individual's pain than an isolated measurement because they reveal how constant the pain is, whether it follows a pattern, and how it is affected by various activities (Jensen & McFarland, 1993). However, pain diaries may not be appropriate for some patients because they may focus even more attention on the pain and thus interfere with treatment and recovery.

Some years ago, pain research pioneer Ronald Melzack developed a system for categorizing pain along three dimensions (Melzack & Torgerson, 1971). The first dimension, *sensory quality*, highlighted the tremendous variations that occur in the sensation of pain—it can be stabbing, burning, throbbing, or dull, to list only a few possibilities. The second dimension, *affective quality*, focuses on the many different emotional reactions that pain can trigger, such as irritation, fear, or anger. The final dimension is *evaluative quality*, which refers to the sufferer's judgment of the severity of the pain as well as its meaning or significance. From this multidimensional model of pain, Melzack derived the McGill Pain Questionnaire (MPQ), which has become the most widely used pain inventory today (Bradley, 1993) (Figure 13.1).

The MPQ reliably differentiates a number of pain syndromes. People suffering from headaches, for example, tend to choose the same pattern of words to describe their pain, while those suffering from lower back pain choose a different pattern (Melzack & Wall, 1988). However, the MPQ has been criticized for requiring subjects to make fine distinctions among very similar words. What, for example, is the difference between "beating" and "pounding" pain? The MPQ is also of limited usefulness for people for whom English is not the primary language, as well as for children under 12 years of age (Karoly, 1988).

The Physiology of Pain

As you slip on the icy sidewalk, you fall hard on your elbow. In the instant before you feel the pain, a cascade of biochemical and electrical reactions occurs. The processing of all sensory information, including pain, begins when *sensory receptors* on or near the surface of the body convert a physical stimulus—such as the pressure of striking the ground—into neural impulses. The pressure of striking the ground activates the receptors in the skin covering your elbow, which stimulates neurons in the peripheral nervous system that relay the message to your brain. Only when the brain registers and interprets this neural input is pain experienced. What happens in between the stimulation of sensory receptors and the brain's interpretation has been the subject of a great deal of exciting research.

Figure 13.1

The McGill Pain Questionnaire

Part 1. Where Is Your Pain?

Please mark on the drawing below the areas where you feel pain. Put E if external or I if internal near the areas which you mark. Put EI if both external and internal.

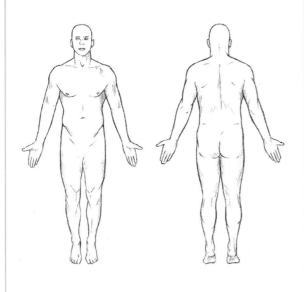

Part 2. What Does Your Pain Feel Like?

Some of the words below describe your <u>present</u> pain. Circle <u>ONLY</u> those words that best describe it. Leave out any category that is not suitable. Use only a single word in each appropriate category—the one that applies best.

1	2	3	4
Flickering	Jumping	Pricking	Sharp
Quivering	Flashing	Boring	Cutting
Pulsing	Shooting	Drilling	Lacerating
Throbbing		Stabbing	
Beating		Lancinating	
Pounding			

5	6	7	8
Pinching	Tugging	Hot	Tingling
Pressing	Pulling	Burning	Itchy
Gnawing	Wrenching	Scalding	Smarting
Cramping		Searing	Stinging
Crushing			

9	10	11	12
Dull	Tender	Tiring	Sickening
Sore	Taut	Exhausting	Suffocating
Hurting	Rasping		
Aching	Splitting		
Heavy			

13	14	15	16
Fearful	Punishing	Wretched	Annoying
Frightful	Grueling	Blinding	Troublesome
Terrifying	Cruel		Miserable
	Vicious		Intense
	Killing		Unbearable

17	18	19	20
Spreading	Tight	Cool	Nagging
Radiating	Numb	Cold	Nauseating
Penetrating	Drawing	Freezing	Agonizing
Piercing	Squeezing		Dreadful
	Tearing		Torturing

Part 3. How Does Your Pain Change With Time?

1. Which word or words would you use to describe the <u>pattern</u> of your pain?

1	2	3
Continuous	Rhythmic	Brief
Steady	Periodic	Momentary
Constant	Intermittent	Transient

2. What kind of things <u>relieve</u> your pain?

3. What kind of things <u>increase</u> your pain?

Part 4. How Strong Is Your Pain?

People agree that the following 5 words represent pain of increasing intensity. They are:

1	2	3	4	5
Mild	Discomforting	Distressing	Horrible	Excruciating

To answer each question below, write the number of the most appropriate word in the space beside the question.

1. Which word describes your pain right now? _____
2. Which word describes it at its worst? _____
3. Which word describes it when it is least? _____
4. Which word describes the worst toothache you ever had? _____
5. Which word describes the worst headache you ever had? _____
6. Which word describes the worst stomach-ache you ever had? _____

Pain Pathways

Unlike vision and hearing, pain is not triggered by only one type of stimulus—nor does it have a single type of receptor. Tissue injury isn't the only thing that will produce pain. The corneas of your eyes, for instance, are exquisitely sensitive. Almost any stimulus, from a speck of dust in the eye to the application of a bit too much pressure when inserting a contact lens, will be experienced as pain, even though the cornea suffers no damage. All of these stimuli trigger the pain response in the brain through different receptors.

Pain Receptors

For more than a century, researchers have been on a quest to find the definitive sensory receptors for pain. Among the candidates are **free nerve endings,** which are found throughout the body: in the skin, muscles (contributing to muscle cramps), internal organs of the visccra (stomachaches), membranes that surround joints and bones (arthritic pain), and even the pulp of teeth (toothaches).

Although free nerve endings are the simplest sensory receptors, they are also the most poorly understood. What we do know is that they respond primarily to temperature change and pressure. They also respond to certain chemicals secreted in damaged body tissues. However they are aroused into action, it appears that free nerve endings begin a process that ends when the brain registers and interprets the sensation as pain. For this reason, researchers refer to free nerve endings that are activated by *noxious* (painful) stimuli as **nociceptors.**

It is important to note, however, that free nerve endings *contribute to* rather than *create* the pain experience. Psychological factors, such as whether we are paying attention to pain, our emotional state, and how we interpret a situation, also contribute to whether pain is experienced. For example, during the excitement of the Olympics, Shun Fujimoto, whose knee injury we described at the beginning of the chapter, experienced much less pain than he reported feeling after the competition, when his attention was not distracted. Patients suffering from a variety of injuries and illnesses often report that their pain is strongest when they are feeling depressed and hopeless (Turk & Nash, 1996). When their emotions rebound, their pain is reduced.

Fast and Slow Fibers

The pain process begins when neural signals from free nerve endings are routed to the central nervous system via **fast nerve fibers** and **slow nerve fibers.** *Fast nerve fibers* are relatively large, myelinated neurons that conduct neural impulses at about 15 to 30 meters per second (myelin is the fatty coating on the axons of some neurons that increases the speed of neural transmission). *Slow nerve fibers* are smaller, unmyelinated fibers that conduct electrical impulses at about 0.5 to 2 meters per second.

The fast and slow fibers are the messengers for two pain systems in the brain: The *fast pain system* (involving the fast nerve fibers) appears to serve only the skin and mucous membranes; the *slow pain system* (involving the slow nerve fibers) serves all body tissues except the brain itself, which does not experience

■ **free nerve endings** sensory receptors found throughout the body that respond to temperature, pressure, and painful stimuli.

■ **nociceptor** (no-chi-SEP-tur) a specialized neuron that responds to painful stimuli.

■ **fast nerve fibers** large, myelinated nerve fibers that transmit sharp, stinging pain.

■ **slow nerve fibers** small, unmyelinated nerve fibers that carry dull, aching pain.

■ **substantia gelatinosa** the dorsal region of the spinal cord where both fast and slow pain fibers synapse with sensory nerves on their way to the brain.

pain (Thompson, 2000). The fast pain system carries pain that is perceived as stinging and localized in one area, whereas slow nerve fibers signal dull, aching pain that may be generalized throughout the body.

Strong mechanical pressure or extreme temperatures normally stimulate fast nerve fibers, whereas slow nerve fibers are typically activated by chemical changes that occur in damaged body tissues. These chemical changes lower the thresholds of both types of nerves, making them more responsive to further stimulation. This is why even the lightest touch on an injured area of skin can be extremely painful.

To get a feeling for the practical differences in the speed of the two pain systems, consider that slow fibers relaying a painful message from your foot could take as long as 2 seconds to reach the brain. In contrast, the faster fibers relay their messages in a fraction of a second. This explains a familiar experience. Sticking your toe in unbearably hot bath water will stimulate the fast pain fibers, producing an immediate sharp pain. The message is carried from the skin to the spinal cord, where it is passed via a single interneuron to motor neurons that cause you to jerk your toe out of the water. But this highly adaptive *spinal reflex* is completed well before you experience the deeper, dull pain that really hurts. The uncomfortable moment you spend waiting for the pain to hit once you're out of the bath occurs because the slow pain system lags behind in getting its message to your brain.

After leaving the skin, the sensory fibers of the fast and slow pain systems group together as nerves to form *sensory tracts* that funnel information up the spinal cord to the brain. Both types of pain fibers enter through the back of the spinal cord, where they synapse with neurons in the **substantia gelatinosa** (Figure 13.2). In the spinal cord, the pain fibers link up with sensory nerves that carry touch, pressure, and limb movement sensations to the thalamus, the brain's sensory switchboard.

On its way to the thalamus, the fast pain pathway triggers neural activity in the reticular formation, which is the brain's mechanism for arousing the cortex in response to important messages and for reducing our awareness of unimportant stimuli. Once in the thalamus, incoming messages are routed to the *somatosensory area* of the cerebral cortex, the area that receives input from all the skin senses.

The amount of somatosensory cortex allotted to various regions of the body determines our sensitivity in that region. For example, even though your back has a much larger surface area than your face, there are many more sensory receptors in the

Figure 13.2

Pain Pathways The thinner line illustrates the pathway for fast, acute pain, which originates with fast nerve fibers in the spinal cord and projects to the somatosensory cortex. The thicker line illustrates the pathway for slow, chronic pain, which begins with slow nerve fibers in the spinal cord.

skin of your face, and therefore more somatosensory cortex dedicated to the face. This means that your face is capable of sensing weaker touch stimuli than is your back. The internal organs of the body are not mapped in the cortex in the same way as the skin. For this reason, although we can sense pain from the body's interior, it is much harder to pinpoint. In fact, visceral (internal) pain often becomes **referred pain,** in that it feels as though it originates on the surface of the body rather than in the body part in which the cause that produced the pain is situated. So reliable is this phenomenon that referred pain is often used to diagnose serious medical conditions. A patient complaining of pain in the shoulder, for example, is often scheduled for an EKG stress test because that type of pain often accompanies advanced heart disease. As another example, we feel pain in the blood vessels of our head as a headache.

The slow pain system follows roughly the same pathway as the fast system up the spinal cord to the brainstem (see Figure 13.2). In the brainstem, slow pain messages are reprocessed; from there, they travel to the hypothalamus, the rear portion of the thalamus, and then to the amygdala of the limbic system. Although many details of these higher regions of the slow pain system have yet to be worked out, a widely held view is that they mediate our subjective experience of pain, including the means by which our emotions and motivational state modulate pain (Willis, 1995).

The Biochemistry of Pain

Like all neurons, those that carry pain messages depend on several types of chemical neurotransmitters to relay information across synapses. One neurotransmitter, called **substance P,** with another neurotransmitter called *glutamate,* continuously stimulates nerve endings at the site of an injury and within your spinal cord, increasing pain messages.

A third group of neurotransmitters called **enkephalins** (the smallest member of the brain's natural opiates, the endorphins) bind to receptors in the brain to deaden pain sensations. Through their synapses with slow fibers, enkephalin-containing neurons are believed to regulate how much substance P is released and, therefore, how much of the slow pain system's message is passed through to the brain. If substance P is not released, or if it is released in small quantities, an incoming pain message may be reduced or completely blocked.

What activates enkephalin neurons? The search for an answer to this question has led researchers to the **periaqueductal gray (PAG)** area of the midbrain. When this area is stimulated, pain is reduced almost immediately, with the *analgesia* (pain relief) continuing even after stimulation is discontinued (Kolb & Wishaw, 2001). So powerful is the analgesia that researchers have actually performed surgery on laboratory animals using no other anesthesia than electrical stimulation of the PAG (Reynolds, 1969). The PAG is also believed to be the primary site at which drugs such as morphine exert their analgesic effects. Even a miniscule amount of morphine will produce substantial pain relief if it is injected directly into cells of the PAG (Basbaum & Fields, 1984).

■ **referred pain** pain manifested in an area of the body that is sensitive to pain, but caused by disease or injury in an area of the body that has few pain receptors.

■ **substance P** a neurotransmitter secreted by pain fibers in the spinal cord that stimulates the transmission cells to send pain signals to the brain.

■ **enkephalins** endogenous (naturally occurring) opioids found in nerve endings of cells in the brain and spinal cord that bind to opioid receptors.

■ **periacqueductal gray (PAG)** a region of the midbrain that plays an important role in the perception of pain; electrical stimulation in this region activates a descending neural pathway that produces analgesia by "closing the pain gate."

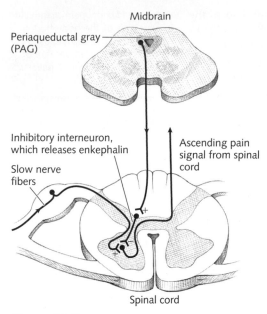

Midbrain

Periaqueductal gray
(PAG)

Inhibitory interneuron,
which releases enkephalin

Slow nerve
fibers

Ascending pain
signal from spinal
cord

Spinal cord

Figure 13.3

The Pain-Inhibiting System
Neural activity resulting from
stimulation of the midbrain's
periaqueductal gray (PAG) activates inhibitory neurons in the
spinal cord. These, in turn, act
directly on incoming slow nerve
fibers to block pain signals from
being relayed to the brain. The
slow nerve fibers contain substance P and glutamate. When
the nerve fibers' release of substance P is inhibited, as it is
here, the ascending pain signal
is aborted (that is, prevented
from traveling to the brain).

■ **stress-induced analgesia
(SIA)** a stress-related increase in
tolerance to pain, presumably
mediated by the body's endorphin system.

■ **naloxone** an opioid antagonist that binds to opioid
receptors in the body to block
the effects of natural opiates
and painkillers.

Thus, it appears that the brain is capable of "turning off"
pain through a *descending neural pathway*—the PAG down to
neurons in the substantia gelatinosa of the spinal cord. This
descending pain control pathway uses the neurotransmitter
serotonin to activate enkephalin-containing spinal neurons,
which, in turn, inhibit pain information coming from substance P fibers (Figure 13.3).

But what turns on the pain-inhibiting cells in the PAG?
The answer to this question was discovered by one of the pioneers of the field of psychoneuroimmunology. While still a
graduate student, Candace Pert discovered that neural chemicals called *peptides* function as "information messengers"
that affect the mind, emotions, the immune system, and
other body systems simultaneously (Pert and others, 1998).
One of the peptides she identified was *endorphin* (meaning,
the morphine within). Endorphins are natural opioids powerful enough to produce pain relief comparable to that of
morphine and other opiates (Julien, 2001).

It turns out that the PAG has numerous opiate/endorphin
receptors. Endorphins produced in the brain and spinal cord
act as neurotransmitters and inhibit pain by binding to receptors in the PAG
and by acting on cells in the spinal cord and brainstem. The presence of endorphin in the PAG initiates the pain-relieving activity of the descending pathway.

The circumstances that trigger the production of endorphins are the subject
of ongoing research. A variety of events have been demonstrated to increase the
level of endorphins. One is stress. **Stress-induced analgesia (SIA)** refers to the
pain relief that results from the body's production of endorphins in response
to stress. A number of animal studies have confirmed that endorphins mediate
stress-induced analgesia. In one study, rats exposed to extremely loud noises
(the stressor) became relatively insensitive to pain for a minute or two after-
ward, as indicated by their unresponsiveness to a normally painful stimulus
(Helmstetter & Bellgowan, 1994). However, rats injected with an endorphin-
blocking drug called **naloxone** before the noise did not show the stress-induced
analgesia, showing clearly that the pain-relieving effect depends on endorphins. Classified as an *opioid antagonist,* naloxone binds to opioid receptors in
the body, blocking the effects of both naturally occurring (endogenous) opiates and artificial (exogenous) painkillers such as morphine. So powerful is
naloxone in counteracting the effects of opiates that the drug is used as the primary treatment for narcotic overdoses. The effects of naloxone, however, are
quite brief, lasting for only 15 to 30 minutes.

Similar neurochemical effects may account for the *placebo effect* in pain relief. Many research studies have demonstrated that one-quarter to one-third of
people suffering pain receive significant relief simply by taking a placebo. A
classic field study of dental pain (Levine and others, 1978) was the first to suggest that endorphins might mediate SIA and thus produce the placebo effect.
Three hours after having a major tooth pulled (ouch!), one-half of a group of

dental patients were given a placebo, which they referred to as a "painkiller." The remaining subjects received an injection of naloxone. One hour later, subjects who had received the placebo were injected with naloxone, and those who had received naloxone were injected with the placebo. After each injection, the participants were asked to indicate on a standard pain-rating scale the degree of pain they were experiencing.

What do you suppose happened? Under the "influence" of the placebo painkiller, patients reported some relief from their dental pain, which provides additional support for the validity of the placebo effect. But what do you suppose happened when the patients were under the influence of naloxone? Since naloxone blocks the effects of opiates, including the body's own endorphins, administering this drug provides a good test of the hypothesis that the placebo effect is mediated by endorphins. Indeed, under the influence of naloxone, patients reported feeling *increased* pain compared to that reported in the placebo condition, indicating that the placebo effect is at least partly the result of the body mustering its own mechanisms of pain relief. More recent research shows that injections of a drug that blocks cholecystokin, a hormone that inhibits the action of endorphins, enhances the placebo effect in pain relief (Sullivan and others, 2004). As we'll see later in the chapter, some other nonmedical techniques for producing analgesia may also work because they trigger the release of endorphins.

Gate Control Theory

In the past, several theories have been proposed to explain pain perception. Most, however, fell short in accounting for all aspects of pain—biological, psychological, and social. In 1965, Ronald Melzack and Peter Wall outlined a **gate control theory** (GCT) that overcame some of the shortcomings of earlier theories. Although the theory has received its share of criticism, it was the impetus for the biopsychosocial model of pain, which is the dominant theory of pain today (Turk & Okifuji, 2002).

The GCT first introduced the idea that the pain experience is not the result of a straight-through sensory channel that begins with the stimulation of a skin receptor and ends with the brain's perception of pain. Rather, as we have seen, incoming sensations that *potentially* signal pain are modulated in the spinal cord as they are conducted to the brain. They are also subject to modification under the influence of descending pathways from the brain.

The theory proposed the existence of neural structures in the spinal cord and brainstem that function like a gate (see Figure 13.4, p. 408), swinging open to increase the flow of transmission from nerve fibers or swinging shut to decrease the flow (Melzack & Wall, 1965). With the gate open, signals arriving in the spinal cord stimulate sensory neurons called *transmission cells,* which, in turn, relay the signals upward to reach the brain and trigger pain. With the gate closed, signals are blocked from reaching the brain, and no pain is felt.

What causes the spinal gate to close? Melzack and Wall (1988) suggested that the mechanism is found in the substantia gelatinosa of the spinal cord. As we saw earlier, both the small and large pain fibers have synapses in the substantia

■ **gate control theory** the idea that there is a neural "gate" in the spinal cord that regulates the experience of pain.

Figure 13.4

The Gate Control Theory of Pain In Melzack and Wall's gate control theory, excitatory signals (pluses) tend to open the gate; inhibitory signals (minuses) tend to close the gate. The drawing on the far left—with a net of +9 excitatory signals—illustrates the conditions that might exist when the pain gate remains open and strong pain is felt. The drawing to the right—with a net of only +1—illustrates the conditions that might exist when the pain gate is closed as a result of strong inhibitory stimulation from the brain and peripheral nerve fibers. In both situations, messages from fast pain fibers tend to close the gate, and messages from slow pain fibers tend to open it.

Source: Melzack, R., & Wall, P. D. (1988). *The challenge of pain.* New York: Basic Books.

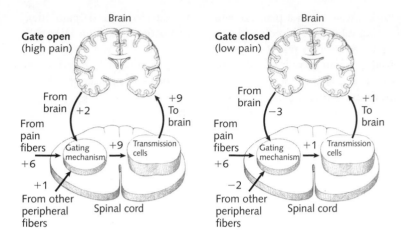

gelatinosa (see Figure 13.2, page 000). Depending on which fibers are activated, the substantia gelatinosa—the "gatekeeper"—will open or close the gates. Activity in the fast pain fiber system tends to close the gate, whereas activity in the slow pain fiber system tends to force the gate open.

To account for the influence of thoughts and feelings on the perception of pain, Melzack and Wall also described a *central control mechanism* by which signals from the brain can also shut the gate. Through this mechanism, anxiety or fear may amplify the experience of pain, whereas the distraction of other activities, such as athletic competitions, can dampen the experience of pain.

Let's see how well the GCT explains several familiar aspects of pain. While running outdoors last winter, I slipped on an icy patch and twisted my ankle. Fortunately, I was close to home and managed to limp to safety, all the while feeling stinging pain. According to the gate theory, the twisting of my ankle activated countless slow pain fibers, forcing the gate open and sending a painful message to my brain.

When I arrived home, I immediately took off my running shoe and began rubbing my swelling ankle. The temporary relief that I felt was the result of stimulating one area to reduce pain in another. Although well known to every school child (and aging, clumsy runners!) who instinctively rub a sore spot, exactly why this method worked was unknown before the GCT provided the answer. According to the GCT, I felt relief because deep massage activated fast pain fibers, which in turn triggered activity in the substantia gelatinosa, which in turn closed the gate in my spinal cord and at least temporaily prevented the twisted ankle pain messages carried by the smaller pain fibers from reaching the brain.

Melzack (1993) now proposes that messages reaching the brain are further processed by a widely distributed network of brain neurons, which ultimately determine a person's perceptual experience. This network of cells also seems to operate even in the absence of sensory input, placing even greater emphasis on the role of the brain in our experience of pain (as in the phantom limb sensation described in the Diversity and Healthy Living Box on page 409) as well as in reducing pain.

■ **phantom limb pain** following amputation of a limb, false pain sensations that appear to originate in the missing limb.

Diversity and Healthy Living

Phantom Limb Pain

Sometimes people experience pain that has no apparent physical cause. One example is **phantom limb pain,** which is the experience of pain in an amputated arm or leg. Although most people with amputated limbs experience phantom sensations of touch, pressure, warmth, cold, position, and movement, between 65 and 85 percent report phantom pain sufficiently severe to disrupt social and work activities for substantial periods of time (Williams, 1996). The pain may be occasional or continuous and is usually described as "cramping," "shooting," "burning," or "crushing."

Phantom pain develops most often in patients who experienced pain in the limb for some time prior to amputation. It is much less common in those who lose a limb suddenly. In addition, phantom pain often resembles, in quality, the type of pain that was present before the amputation. Ronald Melzack (1993) describes a patient who had a painful wood sliver jammed under his fingernail at the time that he lost the same hand in an industrial accident. For years, the patient reported a painful splinter sensation under the fingernail of his phantom hand. Phantom limb sensations are incredibly "real" in their vivid sensory qualities and precise location in space—so real that an amputee may try to step off the bed onto the phantom foot or pick up a telephone with a phantom hand. Even minor sensations of the missing limb are felt, such as a wedding ring on a phantom finger or a painful corn on a phantom foot. Those who suffer from Parkinson's disease may continue to perceive "tremors" like those that occurred in the missing limb before its amputation.

The Search for a Cause The underlying mechanisms of phantom limb pain remain a mystery. Historically, the search for the cause focused on single factors, such as damage to peripheral nerves, or the patient being neurotic and imagining his or her pain. More recent studies have shed light on another possible mechanism in phantom limb pain—evidence that neurons in the brain rewire themselves to seek input from other sources after a limb is amputated. A team of researchers led by Michael Merzenich amputated the middle fingers from a group of adult owl monkeys. After the monkeys recovered, the researchers electrically stimulated the remaining fingers on each monkey's paw while recording electrical activity from the somatosensory area of the monkey's brains. Remarkably, Merzenich found that cortical neurons that originally fired in response to stimulation of the amputated finger responded every time he touched the remaining fingers of the monkeys' paws. The neurons had not responded to stimulation of these fingers before the amputation (cited in Ranadive, 1997).

Vilayanur Ramachandran conducted experiments on people who had lost a finger or a hand (Ramachandran & Rogers-Ramachandran, 2000). Blindfolding his patients, Ramachandran applied pressure to different parts of their bodies and discovered that several subjects reported phantom hand sensations as areas of their face were touched. Ramachandran suggested that his findings made sense because the cortical areas that once served the missing finger or hand are adjacent to those that serve the face. Perhaps neurons in these adjacent areas invade those areas left fallow because sensations are no longer received from the missing limb.

Treatment Phantom limb pain is a condition that is often extremely resistant to conventional pain therapies. One long-term study of over 2,000 people who were treated for phantom limb pain found that only about 1 percent experienced any lasting benefits, despite the use of a variety of techniques (Sherman and others, 1984). Among the treatments that have been tried, with varying degrees of success, are the fitting of prosthetic limbs, ultrasound, transcutaneous electrical nerve stimulation (TENS) (see page 418), anti-inflammatory and anticonvulsant drugs, and nerve blocks such as injections of local anesthetics into trigger points (Williams, 1996).

More recently, researchers have found that blocking glutamate receptors may prevent abandoned cortical neurons, which are no longer communicating with a missing limb, from forming new synapses with neurons linked to other parts of the body. When the blockage to the spinal cord subsides, the original cortical connections and functions remain intact. Research testing whether blocking glutamate receptors will also prevent neural reorganization in those with amputated limbs (thereby reducing phantom limb pain) is presently underway.

In the meantime, Ramachandran has devised a simpler therapy—a mirror box, which allows a person to "see" the phantom limb. For example, when James Peacock, a security guard whose right arm was amputated, slips his intact left arm into the box, mirrors make it appear as if his missing right arm is there as well. The box has provided the only relief Peacock knows from wrenching spasms in his phantom hand. "When I move my left hand," he says, "I can feel it moving my phantom hand" (quoted in Brownlee, 1995, p. 76).

Besides presenting a coherent theory that organizes the many diverse aspects of pain, the GCT has led to several clinical techniques for controlling pain, including one that involves the artificial stimulation of the large pain fiber system. We look at this and other pain management techniques later in the chapter. First, however, let's take a closer look at some of the psychological and social factors that influence our perception of pain.

Psychosocial Factors in the Experience of Pain

The experience of pain is a complex, multidimensional phenomenon involving not only physical events but also psychological factors and social learning from family and the surrounding culture. All pain patients are unique individuals who are acting (and reacting) members of social groups. In this section, we take a look at how such factors influence the experience of pain.

Age and Gender

Across a wide variety of measures, research studies reveal consistent age and gender differences in pain behavior.

Age

Certain pains tend to increase in frequency with age, especially headaches, facial pain, and abdominal pain. In a survey of adults aged 25 to 74, those over 56 were twice as likely as the 25- to 45-year-olds to have experienced two or more pain episodes during the previous month and three times as likely to have had five or more episodes (Mechanic & Angel, 1987). But before we conclude that aging is inevitably accompanied by a world of pain, we do well to ask ourselves whether other factors, such as overall health, differences in socialization, and coping resources might account for age-related differences in pain experiences. As we have seen, it is very easy for researchers examining differences between groups of people (such as age cohorts) to overlook such factors. If we look at the study by David Mechanic and Ronald Angel more closely, we find that adults over age 65 who reported a greater sense of overall well-being complained less about pain than those in other age groups. When questioned, those in the oldest age group were more likely to attribute physical symptoms to normal age-related changes. This finding supports the idea that pain perceptions are influenced by social comparisons with people in other reference groups. For example, adults who reported that their parents had experienced frequent severe pain were themselves more likely to report substantial back, muscle, and joint pain. Older people are also generally more vigilant than young people in monitoring their health status, and they see themselves as more vulnerable

(Skevington, 1995). This may help explain why there is a progressive increase in reports of pain and a decrease in tolerance to experimentally induced pain as individuals grow older (Clark & Mehl, 1971).

Gender

Gender differences in health behavior are already apparent in adolescence, with boys being less likely than girls to seek medical care. Girls feel more vulnerable to illness, place a higher value on health, and accept more responsibility for their own health than do boys (Skevington, 1995). As adults, women are more likely to report medical symptoms to a doctor, to experience more frequent episodes of pain, and to report lower pain thresholds and less tolerance to painful stimuli than are men (Gatchel & Maddrey, 2004; Muellersdorf & Soeder-back, 2000).

Gender differences extend to the types of pain most commonly reported by women and men (LeResche, 2000). Women seem to suffer more than men from migraines and tension headaches, as well as from pelvic pain, facial pain, and lower back pain (Breslau & Rasmussen, 2001). Gender differences are also apparent in how the medical community responds to certain pain syndromes. In a study of medical consultations for a variety of complaints, Lois Verbrugge and Richard Steiner (1981) reported that women and men received similar treatment for chest and back pain. Overall, however, women consistently received 5 to 10 percent more prescription drugs for common complaints than did men. A more recent study asked primary care physicians to treat three hypothetical pain patients (with kidney stones, back pain, and sinusitis). For back pain, male physicians prescribed higher doses of painkillers to males than to females, while female physicians prescribed higher doses to females (Weisse and others, 2001).

A number of researchers believe that the emphasis on differences between women and men is unwarranted and reflects stereotyped medical views about treating men and women rather than responses to specific symptoms (Skevington, 1995). The essential *similarity* of women and men is made clear in studies of gender differences in the experience of pain. Although some researchers have reported that females have a lower pain tolerance than males (Woodrow and others, 1972), others have found only trivial differences (Elton and others, 1983). Moreover, the equivocal conclusions of many early studies of gender differences in pain may be the result of intervening social factors in how the experiments were conducted. This line of reasoning was explored in a study in which college students were exposed to a *cold pressor test* (Levine & DeSimone, 1991). This standard laboratory procedure involves immersing a subject's hand and forearm in a bath of icy water (2 degrees C) for several minutes. The male and female students were randomly and equally assigned to male and female experimenters. The results showed that women reported more pain than men did. More interesting was the fact that men reported significantly lower pain ratings to a female experimenter than to a male experimenter. However, there was no difference in the female students' self-reports of pain to experimenters of either sex. These and other researchers have suggested that gender differences reflect traditional sex roles, with men responding to female experimenters with a more stoic "macho" image (Fillingim, 2000).

Is There a Pain-Prone Personality?

A widely held but inaccurate stereotype of migraine sufferers suggests that they are ambitious, orderly, a bit obsessive, and rigid in their thinking. This example begs the question of whether there is a *pain-prone personality*. To find out, researchers have used a variety of personality tests, especially the Minnesota Multiphasic Personality Inventory (MMPI). The MMPI contains 10 clinical scales, including scales that measure concern with body symptoms, depression, paranoia, social introversion, and other personality traits.

Both acute and chronic pain patients often show elevated scores on two MMPI scales: hysteria (the tendency to exaggerate symptoms and use emotional behavior to solve problems) and hypochondriasis (the tendency to be overly concerned about health and to overreport body symptoms). Chronic pain sufferers also tend to score high in depression (Low & Peck, 1987). In fact, depression is about three to four times more prevalent among lower back pain patients than it is among people in the general population (Sullivan and others, 1992). However, these results could simply be reflecting the challenges of dealing with pain, which can affect psychological functioning.

Some researchers believe that individual differences in how patients *cope* with serious health problems, including chronic pain, are more telling than personality types. Pain researchers Dennis Turk and James Nash (1996) have identified three subtypes of pain patients:

- *Dysfunctional patients* report high levels of pain and psychological distress, feel they have little control over their lives, and are extremely inactive. As one example, increases in recurrent pain associated with sickle cell disease have been linked to increases in self-reported stress and negative mood (Gil and others, 2004).

- *Interpersonally distressed patients* feel they have little social support and that other people in their lives don't take their pain seriously.

- *Adaptive copers* report significantly lower levels of pain and psychological or social distress than those in the other two groups and continue to function at a high level.

Turk believes that tailoring treatments to match a patient's coping style will achieve better, longer-lasting results. In one study, Turk provided a comprehensive stress-management treatment to a group of patients with chronic jaw pain (Turk and others, 1993). The program included an educational component, relaxation training, and a "bite plate" to help the patients learn to monitor muscle tension in their jaws. Although all the subjects reported lower levels of pain and psychological distress following the treatment program, most of those classified as dysfunctional patients relapsed within 6 months. In contrast, adaptive copers continued to report lower levels of pain that remained stable well past the 6-month follow-up. In a subsequent study, Turk and his colleagues added a cognitive therapy component to the standard stress-management program and tested its effectiveness on a second group of dysfunctional jaw pain sufferers. This time, almost none of the subjects relapsed, and the pain improvements lasted well past the 6-month follow-up.

Sociocultural Factors

Cultural and ethnic groups differ greatly in their response to pain, suggesting that different groups establish their own norms for both the degree to which suffering should be openly expressed and the form that pain behaviors should take (Baum and others, 1997). Research studies demonstrate that the sociocultural context also influences how pain is conceptualized, which in turn affects the relationship between pain patients and their health care providers. In one study, for instance, European Americans, Latinos, Puerto Ricans, and Polish Americans in New England and Puerto Rico participated in formal and informal interviews regarding their symptoms and treatment. In Puerto Rico, both providers and patients generally viewed chronic pain as a biopsychosocial experience, and patient–provider relationships were strong. In New England, however, where the traditional biomedical view of mind–body dualism prevailed among virtually all health care providers, patients reported higher levels of stress and alienation in their relationships with their providers (Bates and others, 1997).

Sociocultural variations in the experience of pain are brought into sharp focus in the various religious rituals and rites of passage of many cultures. In Africa, for example, members of certain cultural groups pierce their flesh with spikes with no visible evidence of pain. Stoicism brings high status, while expressions of pain bring shame because they are viewed as signs of cowardice. In contrast, the open expression of pain is encouraged and approved among some Mediterranean peoples (Burrows and others, 1979).

It is important to note that cultural differences in pain reactions are probably related to differences in *pain tolerance,* not to differences in *pain threshold.* Pain threshold, defined as the minimum intensity of a noxious stimulus that is perceived as pain, tends to be more strongly affected by physiological factors, whereas pain tolerance is more strongly influenced by psychological factors, such as expectations about an upcoming experience or the meaning attached to a certain type of pain.

Childbirth provides another vivid example of cultural variation in the experience of pain. Among Yap women in the South Pacific, childbirth seems to be treated as a run-of-the-mill activity that brings little pain. Expectant mothers continue their daily activities almost to the point at which labor pains begin, when they walk to a childbirth hut to deliver their child with the help of a midwife. After a very brief recovery period, the new mother resumes her normal schedule of activities. In sharp contrast to this matter-of-fact approach to having

© Reuters/Peter Morgan/Archive Photos

Psychosocial Influences on Pain The experience of pain is shaped by the meanings we attach to events. In some cultures and religions, seemingly excruciating body piercing is perceived as benign and brings great honor. In many Western cultures today, body piercing and "branding" are not only acceptable behaviors but also are desirable in certain age and social groups. In New York's East Village, the brander heats thin bits of steel and presses them into the customer's flesh.

a baby is the experience of many Latina women (Scrimshaw and others, 1983). In traditional Hispanic cultures, childbirth is viewed as a cause for much greater worry. Even the Spanish word for labor, *dolor,* means sorrow or pain. As expected, researchers have found a significantly higher incidence of painful labor and delivery complications among Latina women than among Yap women (Scrimshaw and others, 1983).

Surveys of American adults suffering chronic lower back pain, postoperative dental pain, and other pain syndromes have shown significant differences in the level of pain reported by Americans of African, Hispanic, Asian, and European descent (Faucett and others, 1994). In addition, surveys of lower back pain sufferers in various countries reveal greater impairment among Americans, followed by Italians and New Zealanders, Japanese, Colombians, and Mexicans (Sanders and others, 1992).

However, as with age and gender differences, we should be cautious in interpreting cultural variation in reported pain. One reason is that cross-cultural studies often are criticized for lacking linguistic and semantic equivalence. For example, while English has at least four basic words to describe pain—ache, sore, hurt, and pain—the Japanese have three words for pain, and the Thais have only two (Fabrega & Tyma, 1976), making it difficult to equate subjective pain reports across groups.

Moreover, as psychologists have long noted, studies of *within-group variation* have been far less popular than studies of *between-group variation.* That is, researchers—like people in general—are frequently victims of faulty reasoning that leads them to focus on the relatively few ways in which certain groups differ rather than on the greater number of ways in which they are the same. In a striking example of this, James Lipton and Joseph Marbach (1984) interviewed facial pain patients, comparing the self-reported pain experiences of African-Americans, Irish-Americans, Italian-Americans, Jewish Americans, and Latin-Americans. Only 34 percent of the participants' responses showed significant intergroup differences, while the remaining 66 percent exhibited similar responses from group to group. In fact, the researchers found much stronger evidence of *intraethnic variation* (individual variation within each group) than they did *interethnic variation.*

A final reason for being cautious in interpreting the results of cultural pain studies is that cross-cultural studies are correlational in design, making it difficult to rule out socioeconomic pressures, social support, coping resources, and other underlying factors that may also be contributing to the differences.

Social Learning

In the early 1980s, an alarming number of Australian keyboard operators and computer programmers began to find themselves in pain—typically, an ache, cramp, or sensation of pinpricks in their forearms or wrists. Soon, a name describing this vague set of symptoms appeared in the medical literature: *repetitive strain injury,* or RSI. The "injury" part of the name was important because RSI came to be seen as an occupational disorder. RSI steadily made its way into public consciousness as newspapers began to report it, government investigations began, lawsuits were filed, doctors began to treat it, and unions began to protest the conditions that seemed to cause it. By the mid-1980s, nearly everyone in Australia had an opinion about RSI. Some felt that it was a genuine occupational injury caused by overuse, and others felt that it was a fake disorder manufactured by malingering workers seeking compensation. Whatever the truth (and many since have suffered from authentic repetitive stress injuries), the skyrocketing early incidence of RSI shows how a change in social context can influence people's experience of pain and actually lead to the *social construction* of an illness (Lucire, 2002).

It seems that social and cultural factors do affect the experience of pain, but how do they exert their influence? Many health psychologists believe that social learning and social comparison play a critical role in determining an individual's future processing of the pain experience. An individual's earliest models for pain behavior are the family and surrounding culture. Observing family members and other people in the reference group helps a person determine what pain behaviors are appropriate in a given situation. How will others react if I cry, for example, or ask for a medication to relieve my suffering?

The social environment also shapes an individual's pain experience by way of operant conditioning. In some social and cultural groups, a person who grimaces or moans in response to pain is reinforced for that response by receiving attention from others, which may lead to more open expressions of pain in the future. In other groups, open expressions of pain are either ignored (leading over time to their extinction) or received with hostility (leading over time to their suppression).

As with many behaviors, how we learn to respond to pain begins in childhood. Children whose parents disregard their pain behavior may grow up more stoic in their approach to pain than children whose parents pay undue attention to every minor ache and pain (Pennebaker, 1982). This process of socialization may explain the finding that firstborn children and only children tend to have a lower tolerance to experimentally-induced pain (Sternbach, 1986). Compared with later-born children, these children's pain may get more attention from their parents because first-time parents are inexperienced and more likely to overreact to illness and injury. Later, when they've learned what to expect, they typically give less reinforcement to pain behavior. On the other hand, children who have many siblings tend to complain *more* about pain, perhaps to compete with their brothers and sisters for parental attention.

Treating Pain

The treatment of pain is big business. It is estimated that Americans consume between 10,000 to 20,000 *tons* of aspirin alone each year (Frank and others, 2000). There are two broad categories of pain treatment: medical interventions and nonmedical interventions, which include cognitive-behavioral treatments such as hypnosis and biofeedback (Milling and others,

2003). Although health care professionals once scoffed at most nonmedical treatments, the proven effectiveness of using psychological techniques with pain patients, as well as evidence that some, such as the placebo effect, work partly by mobilizing the body's physical system of analgesia, have increasingly led to the realization that there is no sharp dividing line between physical and nonphysical pain treatments.

In this section, we'll look first at the more well-known pharmacological, surgical, and electrical stimulation treatments, then at the cognitive-behavioral treatments now widely used in pain control.

Pharmacological Treatments

For most patients, analgesic drugs are a mainstay in pain control. Analgesics fall into two general classes. The first includes *opioid (central acting)* drugs such as morphine. The second category consists of *nonopioid (peripherally acting)* chemicals that produce their pain-relieving and anti-inflammatory effects at the actual site of injured tissue.

Opioid Analgesics

Formerly called *narcotics* (from the Greek word *narke,* which means numbness), the opioids are *agonists* (excitatory chemicals) that act on specific receptors in the spinal cord and brain to reduce either the intensity of pain messages or the brain's response to pain messages.

The most powerful and most widely used opioid for treating severe pain is morphine, which is administered orally, rectally, or intravenously. After binding to receptors in the PAG, the thalamus, and cells at the back of the spinal cord, morphine produces intense analgesia and indifference to pain, a state of relaxed euphoria, reduced apprehension, and a sense of tranquility. Because of morphine's powerful effects, regular users predictably develop tolerance so quickly that doctor-prescribed doses of morphine sometimes have to be increased to retain their effectiveness—from clinical doses of 50 to 60 milligrams per day to as high as 500 milligrams per day over as short a period as 10 days (Julien, 2001).

There is one drawback to the powerful effects of morphine, however: Its effectiveness makes it highly addictive. Therefore, many physicians are reluctant to prescribe opioid analgesics and often *undermedicate* pain patients by prescribing doses that are too weak to produce meaningful relief (Hill, 1995). One solution to the problem of undermedication has been *patient-controlled analgesia*—giving responsibility for administering the pain-killing drugs to the patients. Today, some patients with severe, chronic pain have small morphine pumps implanted near sites of localized pain. Patients can activate the pump and deliver a small pain-relieving dose whenever they need it. Many postsurgical burn and cancer patients are fitted with morphine pumps connected to intravenous lines that allow them to do the same (Morey, 1998).

A 2001 survey of Australian registered nurses found that there was "a clear knowledge deficit" in the management of pain in the elderly. For example, only 4 out of 10 nurses knew that it is unnecessary to avoid giving potent painkillers to frail elderly patients. Nurses who specialized in palliative care showed the greatest knowledge of treating older patients' pain.

—Sloman, Ahern, Wright, & Brown, 2001

A recent alternative to the use of prescription opioids stems from the finding that many chronic pain patients have lower-than-normal levels of endorphins in their spinal fluid. Clinicians are experimenting with synthetic endorphins to boost their stores. Patients have, for example, reported excellent, long-lasting pain relief after receiving injections of a synthetic form of endorphin called *beta-endorphin* (Farrington, 1999).

Nonopioid Analgesics

The nonopioid analgesics include aspirin, acetaminophen, and ibuprofen. Also called **nonsteroidal anti-inflammatory drugs (NSAIDs),** these drugs produce several effects, including:

- Pain reduction without sedation
- Reduction of inflammation
- Reduction of body temperature when fever is present

Although aspirin is a highly effective analgesic for low-grade pain, many people cannot tolerate its side effects, which include heartburn and stomachache, ringing in the ears, thirst, and hyperventilation. As an alternative, they may take acetaminophen (Tylenol) or ibuprofen (Motrin), which are easier to tolerate.

NSAIDs relieve pain by blocking a chemical chain reaction that is triggered when tissue is injured. Consider sunburn pain. One of the chemicals produced at the site of the burn is called *arachidonic acid,* which the body converts into **prostaglandin,** the substance responsible for sunburn pain and inflammation. Prostaglandin also causes free nerve endings to become more and more sensitized as time passes. This is why the tissue injury that accompanies sunburn usually goes unnoticed while you are at the beach. Later that night, however, your skin may be so sensitive that even a cool shore breeze feels painful. NSAIDs work their magic by blocking production of the enzyme needed to convert arachidonic acid into prostaglandin.

Surgery, Electrical Stimulation, and Physical Therapy

For centuries, healers have used surgery in their attempts to relieve severe pain. Their reasoning made sense: If pain is a simple *stimulus–response* connection between peripheral pain receptors and the brain, why not simply cut, or lesion, pain fibers so that the messages don't get through? In their search, surgeons have tested the analgesic effects of lesions that disrupt incoming messages before they reach the spinal cord, as well as lesions placed higher in the "pain highway," such as in the brainstem.

Sometimes surgery is helpful. For example, destroying thalamic cells of the slow pain system has been demonstrated to alleviate some deep, burning pain, such as that experienced by some cancer patients, without altering the sense of touch or the more acute, stinging pain of the fast-pain system. More often, however, surgery has unpredictable results, and its effects are short lived, perhaps because of the nervous system's remarkable regenerative ability that enables pain

■ **nonsteroidal anti-inflammatory drugs (NSAIDs)** aspirin, ibuprofen, acetaminophen, and other analgesic drugs that relieve pain and reduce inflammation at the site of injured tissue.

■ **prostaglandin** the chemical substance responsible for localized pain and inflammation; prostaglandin also causes free nerve endings to become more and more sensitized as time passes.

TENS Back pain can be relieved with transcutaneous electrical nerve stimulation (TENS). Portable TENS machines help relieve the pain of thousands of sufferers. After the person logistically places the pads shown here on either side of the painful area, he or she can hook the small electrical conduit to a belt and continue with daily activities while pulses are delivered to the body.

■ **counterirritation** analgesia in which one pain (for example, a pulled muscle) is relieved by creating another, counteracting stimulus (such as rubbing near the site of the injury).

■ **transcutaneous electrical nerve stimulation (TENS)** a counterirritation form of analgesia involving electrically stimulating spinal nerves near a painful area.

impulses to reach the brain via several alternative paths (Zimmerman, 1979). As a result, some pain patients have endured numerous "hit-or-miss" surgeries that provide only short-term relief and generate substantial risk to their health, staggering medical bills, and untold suffering. And in some cases, patients actually experience *worse* pain due to the cumulative damage of repeated surgeries on the nervous system. For these reasons, surgery is rarely used to control pain today, and only as a last-ditch effort.

More effective than surgery is **counterirritation,** which involves stimulating one area of the body to reduce pain in another part of the body. For example, with **transcutaneous electrical nerve stimulation (TENS),** brief pulses of electricity are applied to nerve endings under the skin near the painful area. Alternatively, stimulating electrodes may be placed or implanted where nerve fibers from the painful area enter the back of the spinal cord. By adjusting the frequency and voltage of the stimulation, patients are able to self-administer treatment. If successful, TENS produces a feeling of numbness that overcomes the sensation of pain.

TENS yields excellent *local pain relief* for some chronic pain patients, particularly when stimulation is applied to regions of the body where touch and pressure sensitivity remains intact. A recent longitudinal study reported that a single trial of TENS produced significant pain relief in 64 percent of patients displaying a variety of pain syndromes, including those caused by nerve injuries or damage to the spinal cord and those with no demonstrable cause (Kim & Dellon, 2001). Four years after the study, of those who had elected to have a permanent stimulator implanted, 21 percent rated their pain relief as excellent, 50 percent as good, and 29 percent as fair.

For more widespread and severe pain (such as that associated with some advanced cancers), another electrical form of analgesia, called *stimulation-produced analgesia (SPA),* involves delivering mild electrical pulses through electrodes that are surgically implanted in the brain. Once again, patients self-administer treatment, determining when and how much stimulation is needed. SPA appears to work by stimulating endorphin neurons, which activate the body's natural system of analgesia. Accordingly, SPA electrodes are implanted in brain sites known to be rich in opioid receptors. Although SPA is expensive and entails the risks associated with brain surgery, many pain patients report that in response their pain seems to melt away. As an added benefit, SPA does not seem to disrupt the other senses, and there is no mental confusion, which often occurs with opioid analgesia (Farrington, 1999).

People who are in pain, as well as those who are suffering disability as a result of disease, injury, or surgery, may also be referred to a physical therapist for assistance. *Physical therapists* are rehabilitation professionals who promote optimal health and functional independence through their efforts to identify, correct, or prevent movement dysfunction, physical disability, and pain.

Physical therapists typically create an individualized program of targeted exercises to improve the patient's muscular strength, flexibility, and coordination. Depending on the individual's needs, they may also concentrate on improving the patient's daily living skills, such as bathing, dressing, and cooking. Physical therapy often begins in the hospital and continues as long as needed.

Cognitive-Behavioral Therapy

Because no single pain control technique has proved to be the most effective in relieving chronic pain, many health care providers today use an *eclectic,* or "cafeteria" approach to helping their patients manage pain. This means that treatment is tailored to each individual case and that the patient is taught several pain-management strategies from which he or she may choose as needed.

One example of such a program is **cognitive-behavioral therapy (CBT),** an umbrella term for a variety of multidisciplinary interventions aimed at changing a person's experience of pain by changing his or her thought processes and behaviors (Grant & Haverkamp, 1995). CBT involves such strategies as distraction, imagery, relaxation training, exercising, and deep breathing.

CBT has become the dominant model for treating chronic pain (Turk & Okifuji, 2002). Although the specific components of CBT vary from one intervention to another, most programs

- include an education and goal-setting component that focuses on the factors that influence pain and clarifies the client's expectations for treatment.
- include cognitive interventions to enhance patients' self-efficacy and sense of control over pain.
- teach new skills for responding to pain triggers.
- promote increased exercise and activity levels.

Education and Goal Setting

CBT counselors often begin by giving patients a brief course that explains the differences between acute and chronic pain; the mechanisms of gate control theory; and the contributions of depression, anxiety, lack of activity, and other controllable factors to pain. Patients are drawn into the educational phase by being encouraged to generate examples from their own pain experiences, perhaps by keeping a daily diary that records pain frequency, duration, and intensity; medication use; and hour-by-hour mood and activity levels. In addition to allowing both patient and counselor to review pain patterns without having to rely on the patient's memory, the diary almost always gives clients new insights into some of the factors that affect their pain experience. These insights are invaluable in promoting an increased sense of control over pain.

This phase is most useful for establishing specific goals for the intervention. As with any behavior management program, goals need to be specific and measurable to prevent miscommunication and the development of unrealistic expectations. Goals should also be phrased in a way that downplays the

■ **cognitive-behavioral therapy (CBT)** a multidisciplinary pain-management program that combines cognitive, physical, and emotional interventions.

common tendency to dwell on pain. For example, rather than "I would like to be able to resume my normal activities without feeling pain," a better goal is "I would like to take a brisk, 30-minute walk, four times a week."

Cognitive Interventions

Our attitudes and beliefs are powerful influences on our health. Faulty reasoning often contributes to poor health outcomes and interferes with treatment. As part of a pain-management program, *cognitive restructuring* challenges maladaptive thought processes and helps pain sufferers to redefine pain as an experience that is more manageable than they once believed (Philips, 1988). It is also directed at correcting the patient's irrational beliefs, which contribute to anxiety and amplify pain.

Health psychologists recognize a general pattern of cognitive errors in the thinking of chronic pain patients, including:

- *Catastrophizing.* Many pain sufferers overestimate the distress and discomfort caused by an unfortunate experience, such as being injured. They also tend to ruminate about painful stimuli, focus excessively on the negative aspects of pain (Michael & Burns, 2004), and use more pain medication than those who think less catastrophically (Severeijns and others, 2004).

- *Overgeneralizing.* Some pain victims believe that their pain will never end and that it will completely ruin their lives. As we have seen elsewhere, such *global* and *stable attributions* of a negative event often lead to depression and poorer health outcomes.

- *Victimization.* Some chronic pain patients feel that they have experienced an injustice that consumes them. Many are unable to get beyond the "Why me?" stage in dealing with their pain.

- *Self-blame.* In contrast, some chronic pain patients come to feel a sense of worthlessness because of their pain, and they may blame themselves for not being able to carry on their normal family and work responsibilities.

- *Dwelling on the pain.* Some pain sufferers simply can't stop thinking about their pain problem. They may repeatedly "relive" painful episodes and replay negative thoughts over and over in their minds.

Because negative beliefs and thoughts are obviously counterproductive to a successful treatment intervention, CBT therapists often use *rational-emotive therapy* (see Chapter 4) to challenge illogical beliefs. Another helpful technique has patients practice developing an *internal dialogue,* in which maladaptive pain thoughts are replaced with more positive and optimistic thoughts. Moreover, because many chronic pain patients have misconceptions or exaggerated fears about their pain and its treatment, simply providing accurate, realistic information often helps them to restructure their thinking.

Cognitive Distraction Earlier, we described several situations in which painful events were either ignored (the injured athlete involved in an intense competition) or perceived as benign (the person undergoing a religious ritual or rite of passage). Other examples come easily to mind: the soldier who is unaware of being wounded until after helping a friend reach safety, or the seriously injured firefighter who ignores his or her own pain while rescuing an unconscious victim from a burning building.

Does this type of *cognitive distraction* have any *practical* usefulness in pain control? Many CBT therapists think so. Think back to your last dental procedure. If your dentist's office is like mine, the treatment room is filled with numerous attention-getting stimuli. Music is piped in, colorful mobiles spin from the ceiling, and dreamy landscapes hang on soothing wallpaper. There's even a pile of stuffed animals sitting in the corner, in the direct line of vision of the unfortunate person sitting in the dental chair.

Do such things work? One study exposed dental patients to one of three conditions. One group listened to music during their dental procedure; another group listened to the music *after* receiving a verbal suggestion that the music might help relieve their pain and stress; a third group served as control subjects and received neither the suggestion nor the music. Compared with control subjects, patients in both of the music conditions reported experiencing significantly less discomfort during their treatment (Anderson and others, 1991). Music is also frequently used to help burn victims distract their attention from painful treatments, such as having wound dressings changed.

Imagery A closely related pain-control technique that is often used with cognitive distraction is *imagery.* Designed to promote changes in a person's perceptions, imagery has two components: a mental process (as in imagining) and a procedure (as in *guided imagery*). Although imagery is often used synonymously with *visualization,* this is misleading: the latter refers only to seeing something in the mind's eye, while good imagery involves using all the senses.

Imagery is actually a form of self-hypnosis because it involves focused concentration and attention. It is incorporated into relaxation techniques that involve suggestions (for example, "Your hands are heavy") and into *mental rehearsal,* which helps prepare patients to undergo an uncomfortable medical treatment. By mentally rehearsing (imagining) surgery or a difficult medical treatment, patients can rid themselves of unrealistic fantasies and thus relieve the anxiety, pain, and side effects that are exacerbated by heightened emotional reactions.

In a typical intervention, the patient first learns a relaxation strategy. Then, while the patient is relaxing, the practitioner describes the treatment and recovery period in sensory terms, taking the patient on a guided imagery "trip." Practitioners are careful to be factual without using emotion-laden or fear-provoking words and to describe, where possible, the medical procedure in a positive way. The patient is also taught coping techniques such as distraction, mental dissociation, muscle relaxation, and abdominal breathing.

Like cognitive distraction procedures, imagery techniques are based on the concept that our attention and awareness have a limited capacity. Therefore, pain is a stimulus that competes for attention with other stimuli in a person's internal and external environments (Morley, 1997). The purpose of the intervention is to teach patients to switch their attention from pain to other stimuli or to restructure their current focus of awareness. For example, a pain patient may be taught to construct a vivid, multisensory image, such as strolling through a lush meadow on a beautiful spring day, focusing intently on the sights, sounds, textures, and smells of the meadow. The elaborated features of the image presumably compete with the painful stimulus and lower its impact.

How effective is imagery in controlling pain? As is true with hypnosis and relaxation training, imagery is most often used to supplement other techniques, so its effectiveness as a stand-alone treatment is based primarily on anecdotal evidence (Eccleston, 1995). The few published results that exist are almost uniformly positive. Thus far, it seems that imagery works best with low to medium levels of pain intensity (Jensen & Karoly, 1991), especially those that are slow to develop and can be anticipated. Compared with untrained control subjects, patients who have been trained in the use of positive imagery may experience a number of benefits, including reduced anxiety and pain during dental procedures, use of fewer pain medications and reduced treatment side effects, and increased pain tolerance to experimentally induced pain (Hardin, 2004).

Imagery is also a fundamental component of *Lamaze training,* the most widely used method of prepared childbirth in the United States (Katz, 2006).

Alamy.

The Culture of Childbirth Pain Childbirth is not feared as a painful event in all cultures. Prepared childbirth that takes place in a calm and comfortable environment, such as in this home birth, in which the new mother is surrounded by loved ones, can greatly reduce both anxiety and the pain it often exacerbates.

The Lamaze method has been mistakenly described as "natural childbirth," but it is really a method for "prepared childbirth" that provides an analgesic effect through cognitive and behavioral rather than chemical means. When my wife and I participated in Lamaze childbirth classes, we received extensive instruction in developing a *focal point—* an actual or imagined image (such as a photograph that holds great personal meaning) that she was to focus on in order to distract her attention away from labor pains. To be effective, the image has to be practiced, controllable, and easy to call up.

Many imagery studies have used only a handful of people and have not been replicated, leaving the effectiveness of imagery open to question. Still, there is enough evidence of a relationship between imagery and pain control that the Office of Alternative Medicine, part of the National Institutes of Health, has called for further and more precise investigation into imagery.

Reshaping Pain Behavior Consider the case of Mrs. Y, a 37-year-old office administrator who entered the University of Washington's pain-management program. For the past 18 years, Mrs. Y has experienced constant lower back pain that allows her to get out of bed less than 2 hours a day. The rest of the time she spends reclining—either reading, watching TV, or sleeping. Although over the years Mrs. Y has had four major surgical procedures (including removal of a herniated disc and a spine fusion), her ability to function continues to deteriorate. At the time of admission to the hospital, she was taking several hundred milligrams of highly addictive opiate painkillers per day, despite the fact that x-rays and a complete physical examination revealed no evidence of any actual organic problem.

Although pain may initially be caused by an injury or underlying organic pathology, over time its expression is often maintained by social and environmental reinforcement. Like Mrs. Y, some chronic pain sufferers may not progress in their treatment because adhering to the role of a pain patient brings them a number of benefits, including plenty of solicitous attention from others, lots of rest, and freedom from daily hassles (such as work). One goal of many comprehensive treatment programs, therefore, is to modify pain behaviors, such as excessive sleeping, complaining about discomfort, and requests for pain medication (Morley, 1997). Stemming from a conditioning model, the intervention begins by identifying the events (stimuli) that precede targeted pain behaviors (responses) as well as the consequences that follow (reinforcers). Treatment then involves changing the *contingencies* between responses and reinforcers to increase the frequency of more adaptive ways of coping with discomfort.

In the case of Mrs. Y, reinforcing consequences (hospital staff attention, rest, and so on) were made contingent on desirable behaviors (such as walking or some other mild form of exercise) rather than on maladaptive pain behaviors such as complaining, dependence, and excessive requests for painkillers. To make the program work, family members—who tend to be overly attentive to signs of pain in their loved ones and thereby reinforce excessive rest and nonparticipation in normal family activities (Morley, 1997)—were also brought into the treatment program. They were taught to change their behavior toward their loved one in order to reduce pain behaviors and increase more positive ways of coping. As a result of the combined efforts of both hospital staff and family members, Mrs. Y's pain behaviors were quickly *extinguished.*

Evaluating the Effectiveness of Pain Treatments

Which approach to pain control works best? The answer seems to be, "It depends." Research studies comparing cognitive-behavioral treatments with traditional physical therapy for chronic pain generally have found that *physical* functioning improves the most in patients who receive physical therapy, while *psychosocial* gains are greatest in patients who receive cognitive-behavioral therapy (Turk & Okifuji, 2002). The most effective pain-management programs are multidisciplinary programs that combine the cognitive, physical, and emotional interventions of CBT therapy with judicious use of analgesic drugs (Peat and others, 2001).

In studies with tension headache sufferers, for instance, biofeedback has proved to be about twice as effective as a placebo in reducing pain and slightly

Recall from Chapter 5 that biofeedback is a technique that provides visual or auditory feedback about certain supposedly involuntary physiological responses so the person can learn to control those responses.

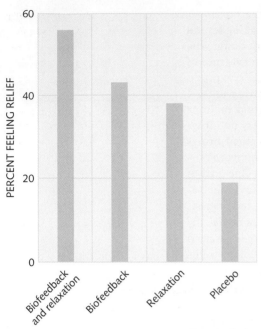

Figure 13.5

Headache Relief Following Biofeedback and Relaxation Training Both biofeedback and relaxation training are more effective than a placebo in relieving the pain of tension headaches. Across many studies, however, the greatest relief occurred when biofeedback and relaxation training were combined.

Source: Holroyd, D. A., & Penzien, D. B. (1990). Pharmacological versus non-pharmacological prophylaxis of recurrent migraine headache: A meta-analytic review of clinical trials. *Pain*, 42, 1–13.

In Chapter 14, we will consider several alternative treatments for pain, including acupuncture, hypnosis, relaxation, meditation, and chiropractic.

more beneficial than relaxation training. As Figure 13.5 shows, however, the greatest relief was experienced by headache sufferers who received biofeedback *and* relaxation training in a combined treatment (Holroyd & Penzien, 1986). Until recently, it was generally believed that migraine headaches were caused by abnormally dilated blood vessels, so most were treated with drugs that constrict blood vessels. However, new research using neuroimaging devices that allow researchers to watch patients' brains during migraine attacks shows that people who are prone to migraines have abnormally excitable neurons in their brainstems (Bahra and others, 2001). This may explain why, for migraine headaches, biofeedback combined with relaxation training appears to be nearly as effective as conventional pharmacological treatments (Holroyd and others, 1995).

Most important, effective programs encourage patients to develop (and rehearse) a specific, individualized *pain-management program* for coping when the first signs of pain appear and as pain intensifies. In doing so, patients learn to redefine their role in managing pain, from being passive victims to being active and resourceful managers who can *control* their experiences. The increased feelings of self-efficacy that follow from these steps are an important element in determining the patient's degree of pain and overall well-being (Keefe and others, 1992).

Unrelieved pain has enormous effects on people, including slowing recovery in patients, creating burdens for caregivers and family members, and increasing costs to the health care system. Recently, a national organization that sets standards for health care programs underscored the psychological effects of pain by establishing new guidelines for the assessment and management of pain (Rabasca, 1999). Under the new guidelines, health care facilities (including nursing homes) are expected to

- recognize that patients have a right to appropriate assessment and management of pain.
- assess the existence, nature, and intensity of pain in all patients.
- facilitate regular reassessment and follow-up.
- educate staff about pain management and assessment.
- establish procedures that allow staff to appropriately prescribe effective pain medications.
- educate patients and their families about effective pain management. (Relaxation training, imagery distraction, calming self-statements, massage, and exercise are recognized as effective nonmedical methods of managing pain.)

The goals of pain management programs extend beyond the control of pain to restoring the patient's overall quality of life by decreasing the reliance on medication, restoring activity levels, and enhancing psychological and social well-being.

Summing Up

What Is Pain?

1. Pain involves our total experience in reacting to a damaging event, including the physical mechanism by which the body reacts; our subjective, emotional response (suffering); and our observable actions (pain behavior).

2. Pain is categorized in terms of its duration as acute, recurrent, or chronic.

Measuring Pain

3. Researchers have tried unsuccessfully to develop objective, physical measures of pain. Because of pain's subjective nature, however, they have had to rely on behavioral measures, rating scales, and pain inventories such as the McGill Pain Questionnaire.

The Physiology of Pain

4. Pain typically begins when free nerve endings in the skin called nociceptors are stimulated. The nociceptors relay this input to fast nerve fibers that signal sharp, acute pain, or slow nerve fibers that signal slow, burning pain. Pain signals travel from these peripheral nerve fibers to the spinal cord, and from there to the thalamus, a message-sorting station that relays the pain message to your cerebral cortex, the reasoning part of your brain. The cortex assesses the location and severity of damage.

5. Endorphins and enkephalins produced in the brain act as neurotransmitters and inhibit pain by acting on cells in the substantia gelatinosa of the spinal cord and the periacqueductal gray region of the brain.

6. The gate control theory suggests that a pain gate exists in the spinal cord. The pain gate may be closed by stimulation of the fast pain fiber system, whereas activity in the slow-pain system tends to open the gate. The gate may also be closed by influences on the brain's descending pathway.

Psychosocial Factors in the Experience of Pain

7. The experience of pain is subject to a variety of psychosocial factors. Although older people and women are more likely to report higher levels of pain than younger people and men, the relationships among pain, gender, and aging are complex. They also may reflect faulty reasoning that tends to exaggerate the relatively few ways in which age groups, women, and men differ, while ignoring the greater number of ways in which they are similar.

8. There seems not to be a "pain-prone personality," though certain traits do affect our ability to cope effectively with pain.

9. Cultural differences in pain reactions are probably related to differences in pain tolerance, rather than differences in pain threshold. Although some researchers have reported ethnic differences in pain, others have found much greater variation among individual members within an ethnic group than variation between ethnic groups.

Treating Pain

10. The most common biomedical method of treating pain is the use of analgesic drugs, including opioids such as morphine. These centrally acting drugs stimulate endorphin receptors in the brain and spinal cord. A less-addictive class of analgesics, the nonsteroidal anti-inflammatory drugs (NSAIDs), produce their pain-relieving effects by blocking the formation of prostaglandins at the site of injured tissue. Electrical stimulation techniques, such as TENS, deliver mild electrical impulses to tissues near the pain-producing area in order to close the pain gate in the spinal cord.

11. The most successful pain treatment programs are multidisciplinary and combine the use of analgesic drugs with eclectic cognitive-behavioral programs. These programs use a mix of techniques to develop individualized pain-management programs, including cognitive restructuring of pain beliefs, distraction, imagery, and relaxation training.

12. Behavioral interventions rely on operant procedures to extinguish undesirable pain behaviors while reinforcing more adaptive responses to chronic pain.

Key Terms and Concepts

clinical pain, p. 397
acute pain, p. 399
recurrent pain, p. 399
chronic pain, p. 399
hyperalgesia, p. 399
free nerve endings, p. 403
nociceptor, p. 403
fast nerve fibers, p. 403
slow nerve fibers, p. 403

substantia gelatinosa, p. 404
referred pain, p. 405
substance P, p. 405
enkephalins, p. 405
periacqueductal gray (PAG), p. 405
stress-induced analgesia (SIA), p. 406
naloxone, p. 406
gate control theory, p. 407
phantom limb pain, p. 408

nonsteroidal anti-inflammatory drugs
   (NSAIDs), p. 417
prostaglandin, p. 417
counterirritation, p. 418
transcutaneous electrical nerve
   stimulation (TENS), p. 418
cognitive-behavioral therapy (CBT),
   p. 419

Complementary and Alternative Medicine

*I*n August 2003, a 53-year-old woman—call her Cynthia—visited an Oregon clinic to undergo chelation therapy. Although she was in good health, against the advice of her doctor Cynthia opted for the unconventional treatment because of its reputed health and antiaging effects. Proponents claim that chelation, which involves intravenous infusions of the drug EDTA, removes heavy metals and other environmental toxins from the body. Although there were no apparent adverse effects from the earlier treatments, about 15 minutes into her fourth infusion Cynthia lost consciousness. She was rushed to the emergency department of a local hospital, where unsuccessful cardiopulmonary resuscitation was initiated. The medical examiner determined the cause of death to be cardiac arrhythmia resulting from abnormally low levels of calcium in Cynthia's body (Quackwatch, 2006).

In contrast to Cynthia's tragic story, consider this testimony to the benefits of unconventional treatment that Andrew Weil, M.D. received in a letter from one of his patients. "Six years ago (I'm now 27) the doctors threw the ugly 'C-word' at me and made it sound like a death sentence. (It was bone cancer.) They decided that they were the authorities and I was the victim and the only way was their way. I walked out of their offices never to return. I took up biking (about five hundred miles a week) and running (about sixty miles a week), and ate fresh fruit, juices, and whole grains. . .nothing else. Too bad more people out there won't acknowledge what a little self-determination and using one's subconscious can do to return a person to wholeness" (Weil, 1998, p. 10).

The National Institutes of Health estimate that less than one-third of the world's health care is delivered by allopathic, or biomedically trained, doctors and nurses (NIH, 2006). The remainder comes from self-care and nontraditional treatments. This may mean a trip to the acupuncturist, massage therapist, or

■ **evidence-based medicine** an approach to health care that promotes the collection, interpretation, and integration of the best research-based evidence in making decisions about the care of individual patients.

■ **holistic medicine** an approach to medicine that considers not only physical health but also the emotional, spiritual, social, and psychological well-being of the person.

chiropractor; on-line purchases of aromatherapy ingredients, herbal medicines, or megavitamins; or a daily hour of meditation.

A visit to any large bookstore reveals an abundance of books about nontraditional health care. Andrew Weil's books on alternative medicine continue to attract a huge audience. Sometimes called "America's doctor" and a "pioneer in the medicine of the future," Weil has published ten books on the body's natural powers of healing, five of which were *New York Times* bestsellers (Nutrition Action HealthLetter, 2006).

Celebrity accounts and personal testimonials on behalf of unconventional treatments contribute to the growing interest in such therapies. Perhaps best known was author and critic Norman Cousins' powerful description of his battle with an incurable illness. Cousins attributed his successful recovery to his unconventional approach to healing: a program of massive doses of vitamin C and comedy movies. The success of his treatment led him to become a crusader for the view that "the hospital is no place for a person who is seriously ill" (Cousins, 1976). This grim warning took on new meaning in November 1999, when a scathing report by the National Academy of Sciences' Institute of Medicine indicated that medical errors kill 44,000 to 98,000 patients in United States hospitals each year, making these errors the eighth leading cause of death—ahead of car accidents and AIDS.

But do these methods work? Unconventional treatments must be subjected to the same rules of **evidence-based medicine** (Spencer, 1999) that traditional biomedical interventions undergo, including rigorous testing and careful evaluation of alleged health benefits. In this chapter, we will consider several alternative treatments, which have varied widely in their tested effectiveness, as we will see.

What Is Complementary and Alternative Medicine?

The term *alternative medicine* has been used to identify a broad range of therapeutic approaches and philosophies that are generally defined as health care practices that are not taught widely in medical schools, not generally used in hospitals, and not usually reimbursed by insurance companies (http://nccam.nih.gov/). A number of these approaches are considered a part of a **holistic medicine** approach, in which the practitioner addresses the physical, mental, emotional, and spiritual needs of the whole client.

In earlier chapters, we discussed several nontraditional techniques, including guided imagery, stress management, and cognitive reappraisal. In this chapter, we focus on larger scale nontraditional therapies that encompass some of these techniques: *acupuncture, mind–body therapies, chiropractic,* and *naturopathy.*

Establishing a Category for Nontraditional Medicine

Some "alternative" methods have been around far longer than antibiotic medicines, angioplasty, and other more recent biomedical therapies. For this reason, the term *alternative* hardly seems appropriate. A more appropriate term, recently coined by health care experts, is *complementary medicine,* which emphasizes that many "alternative medicines" are best used in conjunction with—rather than instead of—regular (or *allopathic*) medicine. For example, hypertension might be treated with a blood-pressure-lowering drug *and* relaxation training: the combined effect of the two interventions exceeds that of either the drug or relaxation by themselves, and relaxation may reduce the doses of the drug needed, thus minimizing any adverse side effects.

In this chapter, we will use the term **complementary and alternative medicine (CAM)** to refer to the range of health-promoting interventions and diagnostic therapies that may not be part of any current Western health care system, culture, or society (Spencer, 1999). Although these therapies all belong to the same category, they are not necessarily based on a common philosophy. In fact, they may have contradictory beliefs about the best way to heal. The Office of Alternative Medicine (OAM) at the National Institutes of Health has recently developed the classification scheme depicted in Table 14.1, which separates CAM practices into five major domains.

■ **complementary and alternative medicine (CAM)** the use and practice of therapies or diagnostic techniques that fall outside of conventional biomedicine.

Table 14.1

Domains of Complementary and Alternative Medicine

Alternative medical systems	Complete health care systems that evolved independently of conventional biomedicine. Examples include traditional Oriental medicine, ayurveda, homeopathy, and medical systems developed by Native American, Aboriginal, African, Middle Eastern, and South American cultures.
Mind–body interventions	Techniques designed to affect the mind's capacity to influence bodily functions and symptoms. Examples include meditation, hypnosis, prayer, music and art therapy, and mental healing.
Biologically-based therapies	Natural and biologically-based interventions and products, often overlapping with conventional medicine's use of dietary supplements. Include herbal and orthomolecular approaches, as well as special diets (e.g., Atkins, Ornish, Pritikin).
Manipulative and body-based methods	Using touch and manipulation with the hands as diagnostic and therapeutic tools. Include chiropractic, osteopathy, and massage therapy.
Energy therapies	Focus either on energy fields originating within the body (biofields) or those from other sources (electromagnetic fields). Examples include Qi Gong, therapeutic touch, Reiki, and the use of magnets.

Source: National Center for Complementary and Alternative Medicine (http://nccam.nih.gov).

Three Ideals of Complementary and Alternative Medicine

Despite the endless variety of alternative therapies, most forms of alternative medicine *do* share several features, which distinguish these interventions from traditional medicine. Most work from three fundamental ideals: to provide health treatment that is natural, that is holistic, and that promotes wellness.

Navajo Healing Complementary and alternative medicine (CAM) includes a wide variety of practices, some more or less accepted in Western civilization. Here, a Navajo medicine person treats a patient with rocks and minerals, creating a sacred sand painting.

Natural Medicine

For many people, the modern world has become too synthetic, too artificial, and too toxic. One person yearns for a closer connection to nature, another chooses to wear only "natural" cotton fibers, and a third grows her own herbs. This "back-to-nature" backlash is a fairly recent phenomenon. During most of the twentieth century, the public seemed to have an undying faith in modern technology, science, and biomedicine.

Then, in the second half of the twentieth century evidence increasingly indicated that advances in health-related technology were not always healthy—and things began to change. Biologist Rachel Carson's 1962 book *Silent Spring* made the public aware of the potential harm of DDT, a chemical developed during World War II and introduced in the 1940s as a miraculous insecticide. After years of widespread aerial spraying of what was believed to be a harmless insecticide, Carson showed, and others confirmed, that the chemical was harming fish and birds by traveling up through the food chain. Ten years after Carson voiced her concerns, the U.S. government banned DDT, and a growing public distrust of science was triggered.

Fueled by evidence of the hazards of DDT and other pesticides, artificial colors and sweeteners, the volatile chemicals given off by disposable diapers, and the environmental toxin du jour, the public's distrust of science has begun to extend to medicine. The growing popularity of CAM seems to indicate a growing desire for more "natural" treatments. Immunization is a powerful example. Although vaccinations are an essential component of pediatric well-child care and are required for entering school, the possibility of adverse side effects and the use of multiple-antigen vaccines are subjects of some controversy (Ellenberg & Chen, 1997; Robbins, 1993). One British survey reported that 21 percent of parents believed the risk of disease to be less than the risk of vaccination and would seek more natural treatments if any illness developed in their children (Simpson and others, 1995).

Although the philosophy of a "natural" medicine inspires many CAM practitioners, it is a mistake to assume that all CAM therapists agree. Herbal therapy and massage certainly are natural, but some other popular alternative treatments are not. Consider the chelation therapy Cynthia tried in our chapter opener. This controversial intervention involves ingesting or injecting into the bloodstream the synthetic chemical EDTA as a treatment for angina and atherosclerosis.

Holistic Medicine

CAM also aims to avoid the narrow specialization of conventional biomedicine. As physician Patch Adams, a pioneer of holistic medicine, noted, "Treat a disease and you win or lose, treat the person and you win every time" (Adams & Mylander, 1998; p. 22). Many patients seek out alternative care because they prefer to work with practitioners who will see (and treat) them as a whole person. Steven Bratman describes one extreme case of a man whose various symptoms eventually led to treatment by six medical specialists: a neurologist (for cognitive symptoms stemming from a stroke), an orthopedist (for bone degeneration), an ophthalmologist (for eye pain), a dermatologist (for skin lesions), a urologist (for bladder problems), and a cardiologist (for heart valve leakage). Until an elderly neighbor (who happened to be a retired general practitioner) realized that the seemingly independent symptoms were similar to the syphilis cases he had often seen 40 years earlier, no one suspected that a simple program of penicillin shots was all the man needed.

Specialization and fragmentation are predictable consequences of the analytical nature of biomedicine, which encourages doctors to focus on the fine details of the symptoms that each patient presents. As a backlash against the overspecialization of conventional medicine, many alternative practitioners broaden their analysis of each patient's complaints to examine diet, emotions, and lifestyle as well the specific symptoms of the disease or condition. This is especially true of traditional Chinese medicine, ayurveda, and homeopathy (a largely unproven system of so-called energy medicine developed in the nineteenth century by Samuel Hahnemann, which advocates such ideas as the "law of similars"—the most effective remedy for a particular disease is a minute quantity of the very substance that would trigger the disease's symptoms in a healthy person).

Promoting Wellness

Given Western biomedicine's historical focus on battling disease, it is understandable that the concept of wellness is too vague for medical science to rally around. Instead, biomedicine orbits around disease, while the primary focus of many alternative treatments is to strengthen the individual, even if the person currently has no serious symptoms.

Alternative practitioners believe that medication, surgery, and other mainstream interventions can fight illness but generally cannot produce an optimal state of healthy vitality. Indeed, although most medical interventions eliminate major symptoms, they often leave behind one or more adverse side effects, such as upset stomach or headache.

Many alternative treatments *do* make the person "feel like a million bucks," even if only temporarily. Acupuncture, aromatherapy, and massage therapy may produce feelings of relaxation—even symptom relief among cancer patients

Ayurvedic Heat Treatments In ayurveda, the practitioner emphasizes treatment of the whole person, including diet, emotions, and lifestyle as well as the specific symptoms of the disease or disorder. The patient in this photo is receiving ayurvedic oils and massage to improve blood circulation at a clinic in New Delhi, India.

▨ **integrative medicine** a multidisciplinary approach to medicine that involves traditional biomedical interventions as well as complementary and alternative medical practices that have been proven both safe and effective.

▨ **vitalism** the concept of a general life force, popular in some varieties of complementary and alternative medicine.

▨ **traditional Oriental medicine** an ancient, integrated herb- and acupuncture-based system of healing founded on the principle that internal harmony is essential for good health.

(Fellowes and others, 2004); chiropractic generates a feeling of being energized. Whether these effects are due to positive suggestion, a placebo effect, or the patient's expectations doesn't matter—the patient still benefits. Furthermore, note CAM advocates the same can be said of medication. Patients so strongly expect that certain treatments such as chemotherapy will make them feel ill that placebos trigger the same symptoms. While medication triggers expectations of illness, many alternative treatments connote a more pleasant, desirable state.

Complementary and alternative medicine is not so rigid that practitioners believe theirs is the only right way; many admit that both disease-focused and wellness-focused approaches are needed, depending on the circumstances. Health care providers who practice **integrative medicine** combine traditional biomedical interventions with CAM therapies for which there is evidence of both effectiveness and safety (NCCAM, 2004). For many varieties of CAM, the concept of wellness is closely connected with belief in the existence of a "life energy" or "vital force," known as **vitalism.** In **traditional Oriental medicine,** as you'll recall from Chapter 1, the life force of *qi* (pronounced *chee* in Chinese and *kee* in Japanese) is believed to flow through every cell of the body. Acupuncture, herbal therapy, and other interventions supposedly restore vitality by correcting blockages, deficiencies, and isolated excesses of qi.

How Widespread Is Complementary and Alternative Medicine?

In the United States, an estimated 36 percent of adults regularly use some form of CAM. When megavitamin therapy and prayer for health reasons are included, the percentage increases to 62% (Table 14.2.) (NCCAM, 2004). Americans visited alternative therapy practitioners some 629 million times in 1997, a 47 percent increase over 1990, and spent approximately $27 billion out-of-pocket dollars on alternative therapies—just about as much as they spent on all physician services the same year (Hwang & Molter, 1998). Even holistic veterinarians for pets are cropping up! When prayer is included in the definition of CAM, mind-body medicine is the most frequently used domain (53 percent). Apart from prayer, biologically based therapies (22 percent) are the most popular forms of CAM (17 percent).

Some people are more likely to use CAM than others. Overall, CAM is used more by women than men, by people with higher education levels, and by people who have been hospitalized during the past year primarily for back problems, anxiety or depression, sleeping problems, and headaches (NCCAM, 2004). Asked why they chose an alternative treatment, respondents to one major survey said they believed that they could achieve faster results if they combined alternative and traditional medicine (72 percent did not tell their biomedical physician). Others said they simply wanted to try every available option to boost their health. Many reported that alternative practitioners were better listeners, and the respondents appreciated the extra time these practitioners were likely to give to them (Eisenberg and others, 1998).

Table 14.2

**Percentage of Physicians (*n* = 176) Using Alternative Medicine and
Classifying Various Treatments as Legitimate or Alternative**

Treatment	Legitimate Medical Practice	Have Used in Practice	Alternative Medicine
Counseling/psychotherapy	97.2	30.8	12.4
Biofeedback	92.5	53.8	18.4
Diet and exercise	92.1	96.6	12.1
Behavioral medicine	91.5	58.9	16.8
Hypnosis	73.7	30.8	30.6
Massage therapy	57.5	35.1	42.0
Acupuncture	55.9	13.5	48.9
Chiropractic	48.9	27.2	45.7
Vegetarianism	45.9	22.2	53.3
Art therapy	39.1	12.9	42.4
Acupressure	38.4	12.9	52.6
Prayer	32.8	30.8	53.4
Homeopathic medicine	26.9	5.3	62.2
Herbs	22.6	6.9	67.7
Megavitamins	21.1	13.5	60.8
Oriental medicine	18.3	1.8	56.1
Electromagnetic applications	17.5	7.1	52.0
Native American medicine	16.9	3.5	60.1

Source: Adapted from Berman, B. M., Singh, B. K., Lao, L., Singh, B., Ferentz, K. S., & Hartnoll, S. M.
(1995). Physicians' attitudes toward complementary or alternative medicine: A regional survey. *The Journal
of the American Board of Family Practice, 8,* 361–368.

The use of unconventional medical therapies is increasing throughout the
world. Even more important, the perceived effectiveness of CAM therapies
seems to be increasing among both the general public and traditional allopathic physicians. A meta-analysis of 12 separate surveys of physicians' perceptions of the effectiveness of CAM therapies conducted throughout Europe and
the Middle East indicated that CAM therapies were considered to be at least
moderately effective (Ernst and others, 1995).

Medicine or Quackery?

Many of the same trends that led to the emergence of health psychology have also fueled increasing interest in alternative forms of medicine. These trends include increasing public concern about

- the costly and impersonal nature of modern medical care.
- the adverse effects of treatment.

■ the seemingly profit-driven nature of health care and medical research that ignores unpatentable (and unprofitable) treatment options, such as herbal medicines.

Ironically, the surge in popularity of CAM is also due, at least in part, to the success of Western biomedicine. Although people living in developed countries are less likely to die from infectious diseases such as smallpox, as average life expectancy has increased, so too have the rates of chronic diseases for which biomedicine has, as of yet, no cure. CAM therapies give people something else to try as they battle such diseases and strive to increase their *average health expectancy.*

Finally, the "doctor knows best" attitude, which has dominated patient–provider relations, seems to be giving way to a more activist, consumer-oriented view of the patient's role. This, coupled with the growing public distrust of the scientific outlook and a reawakening of interest in mysticism and spiritualism, has given strong impetus to the CAM movement.

What Constitutes Evidence?

CAM advocates and conventional physicians and scientists differ most in their views of what constitutes an acceptable research design and which kinds of evidence are needed to demonstrate effectiveness. Biomedical researchers demand evidence from controlled clinical trials, in which hypothesis testing and scientific reasoning are used to tease apart the individual pathogens that cause disease and isolate the treatments that are clinically effective in eradicating or controlling the pathogens. CAM practitioners, whose therapies are based on a more holistic philosophy, claim that treatment variables cannot always be studied independently. A case in point is the testing of herbal remedies. Under the direction and regulation of the FDA, biomedical researchers developing new medications must isolate the active agent in a drug before it can be approved for human trials. But many practitioners of herbal medicine claim that certain tonics and combinations of plant medicines are effective precisely *because* of the interactions among the various substances. According to this view, any attempt to isolate one ingredient from another would render the treatment useless.

As a result of such differences in perspective, many alternative practitioners are willing to endorse interventions even when the evidence backing their claims is far from convincing based on conventional standards of scientific reasoning. Health food stores, for example, have shelf after shelf of impressive-sounding literature that is largely unsupported. As always, one should keep this in mind when evaluating statements made by alternative practitioners.

Finally, the two groups differ in their focus. Rather than just seeking to remove a pathogen or to "cure" a physical condition, as biomedical practitioners do, CAM therapists emphasize the overall quality of a patient's life, broadening their focus to include important psychological, social, emotional, and spiritual aspects. Consequently, many CAM studies appear unfocused, do not use hy-

"I've been told to see a chiropractor, to have my liver flushed out, and to drink hydrogen peroxide! My doctor muttered a nasty word when I said I planned to try alternative medicine. She told me it was all garbage. I'd believe her, except for one thing: I'm in pain, and her treatments are not helping me."

—A lower back pain patient

pothesis testing or large samples, and tend to rely more on verbal reports from patients as evidence of effectiveness. It is not surprising that the quality of CAM studies, as judged by Western scientists, is considered poor (NIH, 1998).

Participant Selection and Outcome Measures

As noted in Chapter 2, scientists have established specific criteria for the proper design of a clinical trial. Besides the obvious need to use the scientific method, researchers must begin by selecting large, representative samples of research participants, grouped by gender, age, socioeconomic status, and similarity of medical condition. These people are then randomly assigned to groups so that each has an equal chance of either receiving or not receiving the treatment of interest.

For both practical and ethical reasons, however, randomized clinical trials sometimes present problems for medical researchers, especially for CAM researchers. Many CAM trials include too few people in a group to allow researchers to determine whether results are statistically significant or due to chance alone. Furthermore, CAM practitioners often find it difficult (or morally unacceptable) to persuade volunteers to participate in a study in which they may be "randomized" into a no-treatment control group. For this reason, CAM evidence is often based on informal case studies. This type of *anecdotal evidence,* based as it is on subjective opinions regarding diagnosis and treatment outcomes, does little to advance the credibility of unconventional treatments.

Another weakness in CAM research is the use of incomplete, biased, or invalidated treatment outcome measures (Spencer, 1999). Many CAM studies rely on self-report. Although within certain guidelines, self-report can yield useful information, skeptics are naturally concerned about the truthfulness of self-report data. Answers can be influenced by the research participants' desire to please the researchers, to appear "normal," and even to persuade themselves that they are experiencing symptom relief. This criticism is made all the more important by the fact that CAM studies too often rely on single-outcome measures rather than on several different measures that might or might not provide converging lines of evidence. The NIH panel evaluating research on acupuncture, for example, concluded that there were few acceptable studies comparing the effectiveness of acupuncture with either placebo or sham controls and so encouraged future researchers to provide accurate descriptions of protocols for the types and number of treatments, subject enrollment procedures, and methods of diagnosing outcomes (NIH, 1998).

Participant Expectancy and the Placebo Effect

Medical students are often taught the story of "Mr. Wright," a California cancer patient who, in 1957, was given only a few days to live. After hearing that scientists had discovered that a horse serum, called *Krebiozen,* might be effective against cancer, he begged his doctor to administer it. Reluctantly, the patient's physician gave Mr. Wright an injection. Three days later, the disbelieving doctor found that the patient's golf-ball-sized tumors "had melted like snowballs on a hot stove." Two months later, after reading a medical report that the serum was, in fact, a quack remedy, Mr. Wright suffered an immediate relapse and died.

Although many doctors dismiss this story as an anecdote, researchers have long recognized that part of medicine's power to heal is derived from the expectations both patients and practitioners bring to therapy. Whenever patients are treated for an illness or health condition, any improvement may be due to one of four explanations:

- The treatment may actually be effective.
- The illness simply improved on its own over time. This is true of most illnesses, including pain, which tend to be cyclical, *self-limiting conditions.* Because most people seek help when they are symptomatic, any intervention that occurs—whether inert or otherwise—is likely to be followed by improvement, often creating a powerful illusory correlation that it is the intervention, rather than the passage of time and the body's self-healing, *autonomous responses,* that was responsible for improvement (Moerman, 2002).
- The patient was misdiagnosed and in fact did not have an illness.
- Patients improve on their own because of some nonspecific effect, such as their belief that the treatment will be beneficial (*placebo effect*).

A placebo is a physiologically inert substance that may nevertheless bring about healing due to the patients' expectations of healing. Placebos have been shown to successfully treat a variety of conditions, including headache, anxiety, hypertension, cancer, and depression. By one estimate, placebos are about 55 to 60 percent as effective for controlling pain as active drugs such as aspirin and codeine (Talbot, 2000). One review of placebo-controlled studies of antidepressant drugs reported that placebos and genuine drugs were equally effective (Blakeslee, 1998). Placebos can work for years, reducing symptoms as long as the patient believes they will do so.

Why do placebos work? According to one explanation, the medical treatments we receive over the course of our lives are like conditioning trials. The physician's white coat, the disinfectant smell of a waiting room, the prick of a needle, and the taste and texture of each pill that is swallowed function as *conditioned stimuli* (see Chapter 1). Over the years, as each stimulus is paired with the biological impact of active drug ingredients (and other therapeutic outcomes), expectations of improvement become stronger and stronger. Later, when given a pill without active ingredients, or some other sham treatment, we may still experience a therapeutic benefit as a *conditioned response* to the same medical stimuli (Vincent & Furnham, 1997). Herbert Benson (1996) has suggested that "remembered wellness" is another conditioned factor in placebo responding. After any therapeutic intervention, he suggests, we have a memory of past events, which helps to trigger a beneficial physical response.

A closely related explanation is that placebos tap into the body's natural "inner pharmacy" of self-healing substances (Brody, 2000). For instance, placebos may reduce levels of cortisol, norepinephrine, and other stress hormones.

Researchers also strongly suspect that at least part of placebo-based pain relief occurs because placebos stimulate the release of endorphins, morphine-like neurotransmitters produced by the brain. In one remarkable study, Fabrizio Benedetti (1996) asked 340 healthy people to repeatedly squeeze hand exercisers while tourniquets on their arms limited blood flow, causing pain that increased over time (Figure 14.1). Throughout the ordeal, the participants periodically rated their pain on a 10-point scale that ranged from 1 (no pain) to 10 (unbearable). When participants reached 7 on the scale, one of several drugs, or saline solution, was administered through an intravenous line, either fully within their view, or surreptitiously.

Benedetti's results were important for several reasons. First, because only a *visible* placebo reduced pain, it was clearly not the placebo itself that reduced the pain but rather the *knowledge* of the placebo that did the trick. Second, placebo-induced analgesia (pain relief) was clearly mediated by the body's autonomous production of endorphins in response to the expectation that a treatment (a visible injection) would be beneficial: Pharmacological interventions that blocked endorphin production (naloxone) disrupted placebo-induced analgesia, while those that enhanced the activity of endorphins (proglumide) strengthened placebo-induced analgesia.

Although any medical procedure—from drugs to surgery—can have a placebo effect, critics contend that CAM is entirely placebo-based. When conventional therapies fail to help, the acupuncturist, chiropractor, or herbalist presents a powerful belief system designed to give the suffering patient hope that help is

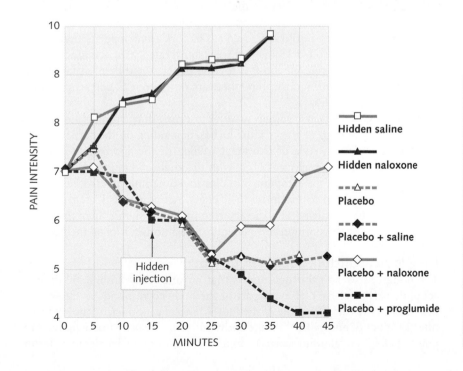

Figure 14.1

Placebo Analgesia Visible injections of placebos were significantly more effective in reducing pain than hidden injections, suggesting that it was not the placebo itself but rather *knowledge* of the placebo that produced analgesia. In addition, injections that blocked endorphin production (naloxone) disrupted placebo-induced analgesia, whereas those that enhanced the activity of endorphins (proglumide) strengthened placebo-induced analgesia.

Source: Benedetti, F. (1996). The opposite effects of the opiate antagonist naloxone and the cholecystokinin antagonist proglumide on placebo analgesia. *Pain, 64(3)*, 540.

■ **acupuncture** a component of traditional Oriental medicine in which fine needles are inserted into the skin in order to relieve pain, treat addiction and illness, and promote health.

available. It is ironic that biomedicine's insistence on rigorous standards of scientific "proof" of the efficacy of a new drug or alternative therapy may have actually provided the strongest testimony for the prevalence of the placebo effect. "Scientific proof" requires the use of a double-blind, randomized controlled trial (see Chapter 2). The method is based on the premise that if either the patient or the researcher knows which treatment is "supposed to work," it would indeed work. Thus, the working assumption is that the placebo effect occurs routinely (Goldstein, 1999).

Does CAM Work?

How good is complementary and alternative medicine? What works and what doesn't? In this section, we will try to answer these questions for several of the most widely used alternative treatments: acupuncture, mind–body therapies, chiropractic, and naturopathic medicine.

Acupuncture

Acupuncture was first practiced during the Bronze Age in ancient China as part of an integrated system of healing that was founded on the principle that internal harmony is essential for good health. In the West, it was recognized only 100 years ago (Lytle, 1993). Although Asian-Americans have a long history with acupuncture, general interest in acupuncture in the United States did not increase noticeably until 1972, when a *New York Times* reporter underwent an emergency operation in China and was later treated with acupuncture for complications and wrote all about it for the paper. Since then, acupuncture schools have begun springing up, and there are now about 12,000 acupuncturists in the United States.

An acupuncture session typically involves inserting thin acupuncture needles superficially or as deep as one or more inches, depending on the particular site and the practitioner's style of treatment. Which of the approximately 2,000 acupuncture points are selected, along with the angle and depth of the needle insertion, varies with the symptom. Needles are sometimes twirled, heated, or electrically stimulated to maximize their effect. Acupuncturists often also incorporate herbal medicine and dietary recommendations in their treatment regimen—two other common components of traditional Oriental medicine.

How Is Acupuncture Supposed to Work?

The honest answer to this question is that no one really knows. Traditional acupuncturists believe that every part of the body corresponds to the whole, whether it's the ear or the sole of the foot. Classical acupuncture theory identifies 14 "lines of energy (qi)" on the body, called *meridians*. Most acupuncture points, believed to allow for corrections of blockages or deficiencies in qi, lie on

Acupuncture Acupuncture, originally practiced in China only, has become increasingly popular throughout Western industrialized nations. It has proved most successful in treating pain, although practitioners contend that it rejuvenates the body.

© J. P. Laffont/Corbis Sygma

these meridians. Treatment typically involves inserting one or more needles at a point at one end of a meridian to produce effects at the other end. Early researchers tried unsuccessfully to match the meridian lines with physical structures in the body.

But many conventional doctors, including those who practice acupuncture, find it hard to accept the concept of an invisible energy path, or qi, preferring instead to explain any treatment success as an example of the placebo effect. Others maintain that the pain of inserting acupuncture needles simply distracts the patient from his or her original pain, or that acupuncture triggers the release of the body's own natural painkillers (endorphins) and anti-inflammatory agents. None of these explanations, however, is widely accepted.

Today, using tools such as functional magnetic resonance imaging (fMRI), researchers are probing the brain in search of specific acupuncture sites and effects. Comparing brain images of 12 chronic pain sufferers before and after acupuncture treatment (Hui and others, 2000), they have found that acupuncture needle manipulation at a point on the hand between the thumb and forefinger produced prominent decreases of neural activity in the nucleus accumbens, amygdala, hippocampus, and hypothalamus. These results suggest that acupuncture-induced analgesia may result from activation of descending pain pathways and other brain structures that modulate the perception of pain (see Chapters 3 and 13). Recent evidence that the analgesic effects of acupuncture are reversed by naloxone, which blocks neural receptor sites for endorphins and other opiates, supports the hypothesis that acupuncture triggers the release of opioid peptides (natural painkillers) (Gardea and others, 2004). In addition, there is some evidence that acupuncture activates the hypothalamic–pituitary–adrenal (HPA) axis (see Chapter 3) and influences the functioning of the immune system (NIH Consensus Conference, 1998).

How Well Does Acupuncture Work?

Although acupuncture is often used for a wide range of medical conditions in China, in the United States its acceptance by allopathic physicians—if at all—is nearly always for the treatment of pain or addiction. Indeed, many chronic pain patients find some relief from acupuncture, escaping the adverse side effects that many prescription and nonprescription painkillers can cause, including gastrointestinal bleeding and liver or kidney problems. Similarly, many substance abusers find relief from painful withdrawal symptoms through acupuncture.

Acupuncture is among the most heavily researched of the CAM therapies. Thousands of studies have been conducted, but many of them have been uncontrolled, have used sample sizes that were too small, or have been otherwise methodologically unsound.

The only scientific way to determine the effectiveness of interventions such as acupuncture is through controlled studies. But such studies are difficult to perform for several reasons: First, the highly individualized nature of acupuncture does not lend itself well to standardized tests. Acupuncturists themselves disagree about the appropriate acupuncture needle sites for a given medical condition. If you ask 10 acupuncturists to identify the appropriate needle sites for sinusitis, you are likely to get 10 different responses. Because some studies allow acupuncturists to choose their own points of stimulation, to control the number of sessions, and to use electrical stimulation if desired, it is very difficult for researchers to isolate independent variables or to compare study results.

Double-blind controls, the mainstay of clinical trials, are even more problematic. Needles can be inserted at points that are inappropriate to a patient's health problem, making the patient blind to treatment, but the acupuncturist has to know whether the points are sham or real, so the study can't be double-blind. In one clever study, one acupuncturist diagnosed the patient's condition and another acupuncturist, who was unaware of the diagnosis, inserted the needles *where the first acupuncturist instructed.* In some patients, the needles were inserted into appropriate points that matched the diagnosis; in others, the needles were inserted into sham sites (Warwick-Evans and others, 1991).

Research trials that use sham acupuncture often show that it has some effect—in some cases, an effect as strong as genuine acupuncture (Fugh-Berman, 1997). Needless to say, the idea that stabbing patients at random points may be nearly as effective as using real acupuncture points is quite disturbing to acupuncturists who spend years memorizing locations.

Yet another difficulty is that operational definitions of successful acupuncture treatments have been inconsistent at best, woefully vague at worst. In the case of addiction research, success has variously been defined as complete abstinence, decreased use, decreased cravings, diminished withdrawal symptoms, improved outlook, and increased productivity (Culliton and others, 1999). Thus, one may report an intervention as successful because substance use decreased overall even though more than half the participants relapsed, while another may report similar findings as indicating a failed intervention. Such variations make it impossible to compare one study to another.

Acupuncture and Pain

More than 100 randomized, clinical trials testing acupuncture's effectiveness on 10 painful conditions have been conducted. These studies provide evidence, although not statistically conclusive, that acupuncture provides *some* patients with *some* relief from painful conditions such as osteoarthritis, fibromyalgia, neck and back pain, migraine headaches, tennis elbow, and postoperative dental pain (see Birch and others, 2004 for a review).

One relatively new form of acupuncture that shows promise—*percutaneous electrical nerve stimulation (PENS)*—uses acupuncture-like needles to stimulate peripheral sensory nerves to assist in the management of cancer bone pain (Gardea, Gatchel, & Robinson, 2004). In one study, 60 patients with chronic low back pain (LBP) were treated on separate occasions with PENS, sham-PENS in which the needles were placed in the same pattern as PENS but no stimulation was applied, transcutaneous electrical nerve stimulation (TENS, see Chapter 13), and a program of spine exercises (Ghoname and others, 1998). Each treatment was administered for a 30-minute period, three times per week, for a total of 3 weeks. The results demonstrated that PENS was significantly more effective in reducing the patients' self-reported pain after each session than any of the other therapies, and in lessening the need for daily analgesic medication. Other researchers have also found that PENS is more effective than TENS for chronic LBP, but this effect gradually fades after the treatment is terminated (Yokoyama and others, 2004). PENS therapy has also been found to be effective in the management of migraine headache pain (Ahmed and others, 2000), and leg and foot pain from diabetes (Hamza and others, 2000).

Acupuncture and Substance Abuse

Excluding 12-step programs, acupuncture is the most widely used CAM method for the treatment of substance abuse, especially of nicotine, alcohol, heroin, and cocaine (Jain, 2003; Margolin, 2003). Some drug courts even mandate its use for the treatment of offenders (Culliton and others, 1999). The goals of acupuncture treatment include reducing the symptoms of withdrawal, including drug craving, keeping abusers in treatment programs, and continued abstinence from drug use.

Patients typically receive treatment in a group setting, seated in large chairs with arms and high backs to provide support. Soothing lighting, soft music, and herbal teas often accompany the session. Both ears are swabbed with alcohol, after which 5-inch sterilized disposable needles are placed into specific sites along the outer ear (auricular acupuncture). At the end of the 40-minute session, the needles are removed.

As with other conditions, evidence regarding the effectiveness of acupuncture in treating substance abusers is mixed at best (Margolin, 2003). For example, two *controlled* studies on the treatment of alcohol relapse—one with 80 patients and another with 54 patients—found that acupuncture treatment was more effective than sham treatment in reducing cravings for alcohol, drinking episodes, and treatment readmissions for detoxification (Bullock and others, 1987; Bullock and others, 1989). In the second study, these effects were maintained over a 6-month follow-up: The placebo group had more than twice the number of drinking episodes and readmissions to detoxification centers.

An 8-week Yale medical school study reported that acupuncture is an effective treatment for cocaine and heroin addiction (Avants and others, 2000). The participants received individual and group counseling and were divided into three groups: an intervention group that received auricular acupuncture; a control group that received acupuncture in other points along the outer ear believed to have no treatment effect; and a second control group that viewed videotapes depicting relaxing images, such as nature scenes. Of those who received auricular acupuncture treatments along with counseling, 53.8 percent tested free of cocaine during the last week of the treatment and had longer periods of sustained abstinence, compared with 23.5 percent and 9.1 percent in the two control groups.

On the other hand, two other studies of acupuncture treatment for cocaine addiction reported negative results (Bullock and others, 1999). The first study randomly assigned 236 residential abusers to true, sham, or conventional treatment. The second applied true acupuncture to 202 randomly selected clients at three dose levels (8, 16, or 28 treatments). Overall, the true, sham, and conventional groups did not differ significantly on any outcomes, including abstinence, retention, and mood.

Despite the inconsistency of research evidence for acupuncture's effectiveness, acupuncture's success rate is among the highest of all alternative medical interventions, and for some individuals it compares favorably with conventional treatments.

Acupuncture Safety Issues

Acupuncture is generally considered quite safe because serious adverse effects are rare. Because disposable needles are used, there is little risk of infection, HIV transmission, or hepatitis. Occasionally, small bruises or bleeding may occur when a careless acupuncturist pierces a blood vessel.

As with all forms of CAM, one danger is that acupuncture patients may abandon conventional therapy and, in so doing, not receive a needed biomedical diagnosis or intervention. Although some alternative practitioners have been accused of discouraging their patients from using conventional treatment, this rarely seems to be the case with acupuncturists, who are generally quite respectful of conventional medicine (Brody, 1998).

Currently, 35 states and the District of Columbia have established clinical practice standards for acupuncturists. These are official statements from professional societies and government agencies that either describe how to care for patients with specific health conditions or illustrate specific techniques. Practitioners who have met these standards are "licensed" or "certified" by the *National Certification Commission for Acupuncture and Oriental Medicine*.

In 1996, the FDA classified acupuncture needles as a type of medical device, boosting the credibility of acupuncturists and increasing the likelihood that an insurance provider will pay for acupuncture treatments. Although the American Medical Association does not officially sanction acupuncture, more than 2,000 of the 12,000 acupuncturists in the United States are MDs. As another sign of growing recognition, the World Health Organization has identified some 50 diseases for which it considers acupuncture an appropriate treatment.

Mind–Body Therapies

The basic premise of mind–body therapies is that cognitive, emotional, and spiritual factors can have profound effects on one's health (NCCAM, 2004). In this section, we'll examine three of the most popular mind–body therapies: hypnosis, relaxation and meditation, and spiritual healing.

Hypnosis

Hypnosis is a psychological state that results from a social interaction in which one person (the hypnotist) suggests to another (the hypnotized person) that certain thoughts, feelings, perceptions, or behaviors will occur.

hypnosis a social interaction in which one person (the hypnotist) suggests to another that certain thoughts, feelings, perceptions, or behaviors will occur.

Hypnosis is most often used to treat pain. Depending on the hypnotherapist, a variety of cognitive processes may come into play during a session of hypnosis, including focused attention, relaxation, imagery, expectation, and role-playing. The most salient feature of hypnosis is the *hypnotic trance,* which is a waking state of attentive and focused concentration in which the subject becomes detached from his or her surroundings and becomes absorbed by the hypnotist's suggestions.

Hypnosis has been used since antiquity, but its history in clinical medicine can be traced to James Braid, who in 1843 discovered that a person could be induced to fall into a state of "nervous sleep." After realizing that subjects in this state were unusually responsive to verbal suggestions, Braid named the phenomenon *hypnosis* after *Hypnos,* the Greek god of sleep. During the last part of the nineteenth century, several prominent physicians, including Jean-Martin Charcot, James Esdaile, and Hippolyte-Marie Bernheim, began using hypnosis in their medical practices. Esdaile reportedly performed numerous painless surgeries, including amputations, using hypnosis as the sole means of anesthesia! With the discovery of ether and other anesthetic drugs in the late nineteenth century, however, hypnosis fell into decline and has only recently experienced something of a revival in clinical medicine (Druckman & Bjork, 1994).

Hypnosis and Pain A typical hypnosis intervention for pain involves several overlapping stages.

- A prehypnotic stage in which the therapist builds rapport with the subject.

- The use of suggestions and imagery to induce relaxation and the focused attention of the hypnotic trance.

- The treatment stage, which may involve various kinds of suggestions and imagery to reduce the experience of pain.

- A "consolidation phase" that may incorporate *posthypnotic suggestions* to be carried out after the hypnosis session has ended.

- A posthypnotic stage, in which the patient is awakened, given additional instructions, and released. The hypnotherapist may also train patients in self-hypnosis so they can practice the therapy at home.

Does Hypnosis Work? Hypnosis does not endow suggestible subjects with special powers. Physiologically, hypnosis resembles other forms of imagery and deep relaxation because it is accompanied by a generalized decrease in sympathetic nervous system activity, a decrease in oxygen consumption and carbon dioxide elimination, a lowering of blood pressure and heart rate, and an increase in certain kinds of brain-wave activity. This suggests to health psychologists that hypnotic phenomena reflect the workings of normal consciousness (Spanos & Coe, 1992). We all probably flow naturally in and out of hynoticlike states all the time—for example, while watching a mind-numbing television program (Gardea, Gatchel, & Robinson, 2004). Many researchers believe that people often move into trancelike states of focused concentration when they are under

"In childhood, fantasizers had had at least one, but usually many, imaginary companions often drawn from storybook characters, real-life playmates who had moved away, and pets and toys whom they believed could talk. One of my subjects had seen the movie *Camelot* as a child and, for two years, imagined being the son of Arthur and Guinevere, commanding the King's court."

—Deirdre Barrett, hypnotherapist (2001)

stress, such as when they are about to experience an uncomfortable treatment. During such moments, when a person in a position of authority issues an instruction, it may have as strong an effect as a posthypnotic suggestion. For example, when a physician distracts a child who is about to receive an injection or makes a statement such as, "This will feel like a little mosquito bite," the power of suggestion at this moment of focused concentration may very well help the child get through the difficult experience. Those who are most likely to report pain relief from hypnosis also tend to be highly suggestible, fantasy-prone people and to be very responsive to authority figures. Evidence from electroencephalograph (EEG) recordings suggests that there are indeed differences between high and low hypnotizable individuals in frontal lobe and temporal lobe activity.

For highly hypnotizable people, hypnosis does appear to be more powerful than a placebo for coping with pain (Jacobs and others, 1995). For people who are low in hypnotizability, hypnotic suggestions of analgesia are no more effective than drug placebos (Miller and others, 1991). For people who are easily hypnotized, however, hypnosis can be an effective intervention for migraine and tension headaches (ter-Kuile and others, 1994), and for the pain of childbirth (Mairs, 1995).

Relaxation and Meditation

As noted in other chapters, relaxation and meditation are related therapies that have proved successful in helping some patients cope with, and recover from, a number of medical conditions. In *progressive muscle relaxation,* which is the most common variety, subjects learn to divide their muscles into seven groups and then to tense and relax each group in turn. As their muscle control improves, subjects learn to control several groups simultaneously and, finally, to monitor, tense, and relax all of their muscles at once.

Meditation is a process in which one tries to achieve greater "awareness without thought" (Fugh-Berman, 1997). Those who practice *mindfulness meditation* learn to pay nonjudgmental, in-the-moment attention to changing perceptions and thoughts. Conversely, in *transcendental meditation,* the person focuses awareness on a single object or on a word or short phrase, called a *mantra.*

In his classic experiment on relaxation, Herbert Benson (1993) fitted experienced practitioners of transcendental meditation with measurement devices to record changes in a number of physiological functions, including oxygen consumption—a reliable indicator of the body's overall metabolic state. After recording the participants' physiological state for a 20-minute baseline period during which they simply sat in a quiet resting position, Benson instructed the participants to begin meditating. The participants were not permitted to change their posture or activity; they simply changed their thoughts to maintain a meditative focus. Following the meditation period, which also lasted 20 minutes, the participants were instructed to return to their normal state of thinking. Compared with the premeditation period, the participants consumed significantly less oxygen while meditating (Figure 14.2). Other changes also oc-

Before　　　During　　　After

Figure 14.2

Oxygen Consumption during Transcendental Meditation The body's metabolic rate, reflected in the amount of oxygen consumed, decreased significantly in experienced meditators when they switched from simply resting (before) to meditating (during); it rose when they stopped meditating (after).

Source: Benson, H. (1993). The relaxation response. In D. Goleman & J. Gurin (Eds.), *Mind–Body Medicine* (pp. 233–257). New York: Consumer Reports Books.

curred during meditation: Breathing slowed from a rate of 14 or 15 breaths per minute to approximately 10 or 11 breaths, and brain-wave patterns included more low-frequency alpha, theta, and delta waves—waves associated with rest and relaxation—and significantly fewer high-frequency beta waves associated with higher states of alertness. In addition, during meditation, the level of lactate (a chemical that has been linked to anxiety) in the participants' bloodstream decreased dramatically.

Relaxation, meditation, and other *physiological self-regulation* techniques are effective in helping to manage a variety of disorders (Gatchel, 2001). In one early study by Jon Kabat-Zinn (1982), 65 percent of the chronic-pain patients who spent 10 weeks in a mindfulness meditation program reported fewer overall symptoms, a significant improvement in mood, and a one-third or more reduction in their pain. Indeed, for patients with chronic lower back pain, relaxation training seems to be more effective than placebo medications or biofeedback (Stuckey and others, 1986). In another study, compared with a control group, patients who received a single hour of relaxation instruction the night before undergoing spinal surgery later required less pain medication, complained less to nurses, and had shorter hospital stays (Lawlis and others, 1985).

A smaller group of researchers have suggested that relaxation and meditation are no more effective than placebos in modulating physiological responses. Daniel Eisenberg and his colleagues (1993), for instance, performed a meta-analysis of research on the effects of relaxation, meditation, and biofeedback on blood pressure levels in patients with hypertension. As shown in Figure 14.3 (p. 446), compared with patients who received no treatment or a wait-list control group, patients receiving the CAM therapies showed a statistically (and

Figure 14.3

Relaxation Therapy and Hypertension A meta-analysis of 26 control trials involving 1,264 hypertensive patients showed that CAM interventions based on relaxation training, meditation, and biofeedback were significantly more effective than no treatment in reducing systolic and diastolic blood pressure. Compared with credible placebo treatment, however, CAM interventions were much less effective; the difference between the treatments was statistically and clinically insignificant.

Source: Adapted from Eisenberg, D. M., Delbanco, T. L., Berkey, C. S., Kaptchuk, T. J., Kupelnick, B., Kuhl, J., & Chalmers, T. C. (1993). Cognitive behavioral techniques for hypertension: Are they effective? *Annals of Internal Medicine, 118,* 964–972.

clinically) significant reduction in both systolic and diastolic blood pressure. However, as compared with a credible placebo intervention (pseudo-meditation or sham biofeedback), the CAM therapies showed a smaller and neither statistically nor clinically significant blood pressure effect. The analysis also showed that no single CAM technique was more effective than any other in reducing blood pressure.

How Might Relaxation and Meditation Promote Health? Just how relaxation or meditation might promote health is the subject of ongoing debate. One suggestion is that the relaxation at the center of these therapies relieves stress, muscle tension, anxiety, and negative emotionality, all of which might exacerbate physical symptoms and increase a person's vulnerability to ill health. Indeed, one study of 25 healthy women found that regular practitioners of yoga had fewer complaints of bodily pain, lower excitability, reduced aggressiveness and emotionality, and greater life satisfaction than a matched group who were not yoga devotees (Schell and others, 1994).

Researchers have also suggested that relaxation and meditation may alter a person's emotional response to symptoms such as pain. "I'm still in constant pain," notes one woman, who joined the pain reduction program at the University of Massachusetts after a bad fall left her with neck and back injuries and the chronic, painful condition called *fibromyalgia.* "Meditation makes the pain more bearable. I have less pain, muscles are more relaxed, and I have much better mobility" (Eisenberg and others, 1998). This makes sense, according to mind–body therapy advocates, because these techniques alter the way pain sufferers respond to painful sensations and the way they feel about them. Relaxation interventions often teach pain sufferers to reinterpret painful sensations, regarding them as "warm, even pleasant" rather than "burning and unpleasant" (Eisenberg and others, 1998).

Relaxation and meditation may also promote health by bolstering the immune system. In one study of 45 elderly people in independent living facilities, one group received relaxation training three times each week, another received social contact three times a week, and the third received no training or social contact. After 1 month, the relaxation group showed a significant increase in immune functioning, and the subjects reported feeling more relaxed. There were no significant changes in the groups that received social contact or no contact (Kiecolt-Glaser and others, 1985).

Transcendental meditators have also been found to have higher daytime levels of serotonin compared with controls, and these levels increase with meditation. Serotonin is a precursor of melatonin, a naturally occurring biochemical that promotes analgesia, lowers blood pressure and heart rate, and has an anti-stress, anti-insomnia effect. Health benefits such as these may help explain the findings of one remarkable study of elderly residents of nursing homes. The study randomly assigned the residents either to daily meditation or to no intervention. After 3 years, 25 percent of the nonmeditators had died, while *all* of those in the meditation group were still alive (Alexander and others, 1989).

Spirituality and Prayer

As noted in Chapter 1, throughout history, religion and medicine have been closely connected as healing traditions. Indeed, spiritual and physical healing were frequently conducted by the same person. As Western biomedicine matured, however, the two traditions diverged. Rather than consulting a spiritual healer to cure infection and prevent disease, people began turning to vaccines, antibiotics, and the growing number of wondrous new weapons in the modern medical arsenal.

There are signs, however, that the wall between medicine and spiritual healing—which never was nearly as high in some countries as in the United States—is beginning to topple. Medical conferences and centers for research on spirituality and healing are cropping up at Harvard, Duke, and other top universities, and more than 70 of 126 U.S. medical schools offered spirituality and health courses in 1999, up from only 3 schools just 10 years earlier (Musick and others, 2003). Moreover, one survey reported that 99 percent of family physicians agreed that "personal prayer, meditation, or other spiritual and religious practices" could increase the effectiveness of medical treatment (Yankelovich Partners, 1998).

The increasing popularity of fundamentalist Christianity, New Age beliefs, and CAM has led to a renewed interest in possible links between spirituality and the healing process. Prayer is being used with increasing frequency in the treatment of many chronic diseases, including cancer (Primack & Spencer, 1996). And many are convinced of the efficacy of spiritual interventions. Anecdotal cases of tumor regression in response to prayer have been reported, as has the effect of prayer in reducing anxiety (Dossey, 1993).

But is there scientific evidence to support this growing movement? Does spirituality promote health, as four of every five Americans believe (Matthews, 1997)? As is often the case with nontraditional interventions, the evidence is mixed. To be sure, there is evidence that faith and spirituality are *correlated* with health. A number of studies have reported that devotees of various religions—Catholic priests and nuns, Trappist monks, and Mormon priests—have lower illness and mortality rates than the general population. One study of mortality rates among nearly 4,000 Israelis reported that those living in orthodox religious communities were about half as likely as those living in nonreligious kibbutz settlements to have died over the 16-year course of the study (Kark and others, 1996).

A review of 27 studies found that in 22 of them, frequency of attendance at religious services was associated with better health (Levin & Vanderpool, 1987). However, most of those studies were uncontrolled, making them vulnerable to mistaken interpretation and unable to pinpoint causation. For example, ill health may prevent many individuals from attending services in the first place. As another example, if religious people shared other health-promoting traits—say, they exercised as much as they worshipped or avoided smoking or excessive alcohol use—religion might have nothing to do with their improved health. Finally, it has been argued that women, who tend to be more religiously active than men, may in large measure account for the spirituality-longevity effect because women in general tend to outlive the less religious members of the other gender (Sloan and others, 1999). Several recent studies have attempted to rule out gender and other uncontrolled variables in the faith–health connection. One study of Californians reported that even after ruling out differences due to gender, ethnicity, age, and education, those who were religiously active were 36 percent less likely to die in any given year than their less religious counterparts (McCullough and others, 2000). In another study, which controlled for the age, race, and gender of the participants, researchers reported that those who rarely attended religious services were 1.87 times more likely to die during the 8-year study than were those who attended frequently (Hummer and others, 1999) (Figure 14.4).

What accounts for the correlation between strong religious practices and longevity? At least three intervening factors remain strong candidates: *lifestyle, social support,* and *positive emotions.* First, compared with those in the general population, those who are religiously active tend to smoke less, consume alcohol more moderately, eat less fat, be more active, and be less likely to engage in high-risk sexual behaviors (Sloan and others, 1999). Second, because religion tends to be a communal experience, those who are religiously active may benefit from more social ties than those in the general population. Throughout this book, we have seen the beneficial effects of social support on each domain of health. Third, religious activity may promote health by fostering more positive emotions, including an optimistic and hopeful worldview, a feeling of accept-

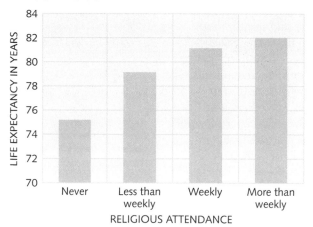

Figure 14.4

Religious Attendance and Life Expectancy The results of this large national health survey conducted by the Centers for Disease Control and Prevention showed that religiously active people had longer life expectancies, even when the respondents' ages, races, and genders were controlled for.

Source: Hummer, R. A., Rogers, R. G., Nam, C. B., & Ellison, C. G. (1999). Religious involvement and U.S. adult mortality. *Demography, 36,* 273–285.

ance and personal control, and a sense that life itself is meaningful (Koenig & Larson, 1998).

Despite the mounting correlational evidence that people who are religiously active are healthier, scientific evidence for the power of prayer in promoting health is virtually nonexistent (Fugh-Berman, 1997). No research to date supports the claim that any form of distant healing (intercessory prayer, mental healing, therapeutic touch, or spiritual healing) works. A meta-analysis of 23 clinical trials of distant healing that included random assignment of participants and placebo-based control groups reported that 13 of the studies (57 percent) yielded statistically significant effects, 9 showed no effect over control interventions, and 1 showed a negative effect. However, the methodological limitations of many of the studies made it impossible to draw definitive conclusions about the efficacy of distant healing (Astin and others, 2000).

So what is the role of faith in the healing process? Richard Sloan and his Columbia University colleagues (1999) believe that doctors should remain cautious in "prescribing" faith. "Linking religious activities and better health can be harmful to patients," they explain, "who already must confront age-old folk wisdom that illness is due to their own moral failure" (p. 665). However, they acknowledge that faith can help patients cope with illness. Although the scientific jury is still out on the connection between faith and healing, "respectful attention must be paid to the impact of religion on the patient's decisions about health care," they conclude (p. 665).

Chiropractic

Therapeutic manipulation of the body dates from the beginning of recorded time: Hippocrates (fifth century B.C.) and Galen (second century A.D.), for example, used some form of it, and *bodywork* was common among physicians until the eighteenth century (Moore, 1993). The two most common forms of therapeutic manipulation today—*chiropractic* and *osteopathy*—are the only major forms of CAM originally developed in the United States.

The word *chiropractic* is derived from the Greek roots *cheir* (hand) and *praktikos* (done by). Its actual practice can be traced back to September 1895, when Daniel David Palmer, a magnetic healer in Iowa, supposedly cured a patient's deafness by realigning the man's spine. Two years later, Palmer founded the first school of chiropractic, based on his belief that the human body has an innate self-healing power and seeks a state of *homeostasis,* or balance. Imbalance is believed to be caused by misalignments of bones within joints or abnormal movements that interfere with the flow of nervous impulses. By manipulating the bones, muscles, and joints, particularly in the spine, chiropractors work to improve the function of the neuromusculoskeletal system and restore homeostasis.

Although Palmer was enough of an ideologue to date things *BC* (Before Chiropractic) and *AC* (After Chiropractic), osteopathy is actually older. Andrew Taylor Sill, the allopathic physician who founded osteopathy, began teaching its principles in 1892, 3 years before Palmer's first chiropractic adjustment (Fugh-Berman, 1997). Although osteopathy is a more complete system of medicine (osteopaths can prescribe drugs, perform surgery, and do just about anything else MDs can do), chiropractic has always been more pervasive. Today, chiropractors provide over 90 percent of the manipulative therapy in the United States (Shekelle and others, 1992; Shekelle & Brook, 1991). Each year, between 3 and 10 percent of the U.S. population consult chiropractors (Eisenberg et al., 1993). In this section, we will focus on chiropractic because it is more commonly practiced in this country.

Today, chiropractors are divided into two major groups, each of which has its own governing body. *Straight chiropractors* are traditionalists who continue to believe that misalignments cause pain and that manipulation is the best form of treatment. *Mixers* combine traditional manipulation along with a broad range of other CAM therapies, including massage, physical therapy, and nutritional therapy. Straight chiropractors maintain that chiropractic treatment can be beneficial for a wide range of ailments—from asthma to lower back pain to impotence. Mixers, on the other hand, tend to recognize its effectiveness for a more limited range of conditions, especially acute lower back pain, headaches, and neck pain.

What to Expect During a Chiropractic Examination

Before performing any type of adjustment, the chiropractor will *palpate,* or feel, your vertebrae to detect misalignment of bones or muscular weaknesses. He or she may also test your reflexes to check neural functioning. X-rays may be taken to reveal any underlying joint problems that might interfere with treatment or be worsened by a chiropractic adjustment.

During a treatment, the chiropractor will adjust your joints one at a time, using a slight thrusting movement that moves a restricted joint just beyond its limited range of motion. You may be asked to lie on a padded table for a spinal adjustment or to sit or stand for an adjustment of the neck and other joints. Although the treatments are usually painless, it is not uncommon to hear joints crack during an adjustment.

Does Chiropractic Work?

The medical profession has been relentlessly hostile to chiropractors. As far back as 1910, Abraham Flexner's government report on medical education in the United States dismissed chiropractic without even the briefest consideration.

Critics charge that chiropractic treatments are at best useless because misaligned vertebra are common and harmless, and they usually clear up on their own. At worst, chiropractic manipulation can cause severe damage to the body if there are fractures or tumors present. Others question the premise that a sound nervous system is the foundation of overall health, pointing to quadriplegics, who often have healthy internal organs despite extensive nerve damage. Some critics accept chiropractic treatment as effective for back pain but argue that it should be restricted to this disorder because there is insufficient evidence to support its efficacy in treating other conditions. Some people use chiropractors as their primary care gatekeepers, which is a cause for concern because chiropractors are not all trained to diagnose all medical conditions.

Despite such criticism, chiropractic remains very popular with the general public, forcing Congress, in 1974, to pass legislation requiring Medicare to pay for chiropractic services. Although still considered a form of alternative medicine by many conventional doctors, chiropractic has achieved mainstream acceptance and is licensed in all 50 states (Gardea and others, 2004). As another testimonial to the growing acceptability of chiropractic, the services of chiropractors generally are covered not only by Medicare and Medicaid, but also by about 85 percent of the major insurance plans.

Evidence for chiropractic's effectiveness in treating back pain has been accumulating since 1952, when a Harvard study reported that this was the most common reason for visiting a chiropractor and that one-fifth of back pain sufferers have used chiropractic successfully (Eisenberg and others, 1993). A 1974 retrospective study of back pain sufferers who had received workers' compensation found that those who received chiropractic treatment were as satisfied as and improved as much as their counterparts who opted for conventional medical treatment (Kane and others, 1974). A 1995 prospective study of acute back pain patients found that chiropractic patients were more satisfied with their treatment than the patients of primary care physicians and orthopedic surgeons (Carey and others, 1995).

Research studies also show that chiropractic treatment may decrease the frequency and intensity of tension and migraine headaches and be beneficial in the treatment of otitis media (Froehle, 1996); hypertension (Crawford and others, 1986); carpal tunnel syndrome (Feuerstein and others, 1999); some sports injuries (Jacchia and others, 1994); and arthritis of the hip, wrist, and hand (Gottlieb, 1997).

Naturopathic Medicine

Naturopathic medicine aims to provide holistic, or whole body, health care by returning humans to their "natural state." This "back to nature" movement has been traced to German doctors such as Vincent Preissnitz (1799–1851), who balked at the harsh treatment used by medical doctors. While medical doctors were "treating" their patients with mercury, bloodletting, and other "modern cures," Preissnitz and other German "nature doctors" were taking patients for walks in the woods and recommending fasting to "detoxify the body," followed by a simple diet and the healing powers of fresh air, sunlight, and bathing in natural hot springs.

At about the same time, the *hygienic movement* was becoming popular in the United States. This movement, founded by Sylvester Graham (originator of the graham cracker), advocated a strict vegetarian diet, herbal treatments, and, naturally, an abundance of whole grains. Another dietary mogul who regarded conventional medicine as a fundamentally wrongheaded attempt to improve on nature through artificial means was John Harvey Kellogg, best known as the founder of Kellogg's cereal.

■ **naturopathic medicine** the system that aims to provide holistic health care by drawing from several traditional healing systems, including homeopathy, herbal remedies, and traditional Oriental medicine.

Benedict Lust (1869–1945), another advocate of natural treatments, coined the word *naturopath*. A German immigrant, Lust also opened the world's first health food store in New York City around 1920. From then until the start of World War II, naturopathic medicine was a popular alternative to conventional medicine. By the 1950s, however, naturopathy was forced out of popularity by the increasingly powerful American Medical Association and by the discovery of penicillin and other potent antibiotics that were effective against many life-threatening diseases.

With the more recent "return to nature" movements, naturopathy has regained some of its earlier popularity. Naturopaths follow seven basic principles, which are in keeping with the major ideals of CAM: *help nature heal, do no harm, find the underlying cause, treat the whole person, encourage prevention, recognize wellness,* and *act as a teacher*. Naturopathic medicine integrates herbal medicine, clinical nutrition, homeopathy, and sometimes other CAM therapies with modern medical methods of diagnosis and treatment.

There are only three accredited naturaopathic medical schools in the United States. Elements of naturopathic medicine therefore seem destined either to be absorbed into conventional medicine or to become a separate branch of it. Although naturopathic physicians are licensed to practice in only 11 states, the majority of other states allow them to practice in limited ways. Naturopathic practice is regulated by state law, and only a few insurance providers cover naturopathic health care.

Herbal Medicine

People have used plants to treat physical, mental, and behavioral conditions since the dawn of time, and all known cultures have ancient histories of folk medicine that include the use of herbs. This knowledge was often grouped into a collection called a *pharmacopoeia*. The ancient Greek and Roman cultures developed extensive pharmacopoeias. Until the thirteenth century, *herbology* was traditionally a woman's art in Europe. When the practice of healing was taken over by male-dominated medical schools as early as the thirteenth century, herbology lost favor, and many women herbalists were prosecuted as witches.

In the United States, physicians relied on medicinal plants as primary medicines through the 1930s. In fact, botany was once an important part of the medical school curriculum. But during the second half of the twentieth century, the use of medicinal plants declined due to developments in the ability to produce pharmaceuticals synthetically.

Today, most herbs are marketed as food supplements because it is illegal for doctors to recommend an herb as a treatment for anything. Doing so is considered the same as prescribing an illegal drug. In practice, of course, herbs are widely used as treatments for numerous health conditions, with annual sales reaching the billions of dollars.

Types of Herbs Derived from the leaves, stems, roots, bark, flowers, fruits, seeds, and sap of plants, herbs can be prepared or marketed in different forms—as supplements, medicines, or as teas—depending on their intended use. Herbs

Herbal Medicines Medicine sellers set up stalls in the open market to display the many herbs used to treat anything from a toothache to lower back pain to cancer. This seller is in Menghan, Yunnan Province, China.

© Mike Yamashita/Woodfin Camp & Associate

can be used as tonics and remedies for virtually every known ailment and condition. Herbal teas can be steeped to varying strengths. Roots, bark, and other plant parts can be simmered into potent solutions called *decoctions*. Today, many herbs (in the form of tablets and capsules) are also available in health food stores, pharmacies, and even groceries. Highly concentrated alcohol-based herb extracts called *tinctures* are also popular.

Herbs play a central role in Chinese medicine, ayurvedic medicine, and Western herbal medicine. Western herbs are categorized in several ways. They may be grouped according to their potency. *Tonics,* or normalizers, have a gentle healing effect on the body, whereas *effectors* have potent actions and are used to treat illness. Herbs are also often grouped according to their effects on the body. These categories include anti-inflammatories, diuretics, and laxatives as well as other, lesser-known classes such as diaphoretics that promote perspiration and nervousness, which allegedly strengthen the nervous system. Herbs are also often grouped according to which of the body's systems they affect. The cardiovascular system, for example, is said to respond to ginkgo, buckwheat, linden, and other herbs claimed to strengthen blood vessels.

Do Herbs Work? Although roughly 25 percent of our pharmaceutical drugs are derived from herbs, physicians often believe that herbs in general are ineffective and potentially dangerous (McCarthy, 2001). Still, there is at least some evidence that plant-based medicines are effective in treating certain conditions. For example, ginger's proven anti-inflammatory and antirheumatic properties, coming from both human and animal trials, suggest that it may be effective in treating arthritis (Srivastava & Mustafa, 1992). As another example, *capsaicin,* an extract from the cayenne pepper, is effective in relieving the pain of osteoarthritis (Zhang & Po, 1994).

On the other hand, the evidence for the effectiveness of some popular herbs is mixed, at best. For example, a meta-analysis of 26 controlled clinical trials (18 randomized, 8 double-blind) examined the effectiveness of the herb *echinacea*. Although the researchers found positive results for 30 of 34 treatment groups, once again most of the trials were of poor methodological quality and therefore questionable (Melchart and others, 1995).

Results such as these make it impossible to offer a definitive, across-the-board answer to the question "Do herbs work?" At present, the safest conclusion seems to be that certain herbs may be beneficial for certain conditions. In general, however, there simply is not enough good evidence that herbs work as well as many would like to believe (Gardea and others, 2004). Furthermore, compared with the often-dramatic power of pharmaceutical drugs, herbs usually have fairly subtle effects. *Standardized extracts,* which have long been available in Europe and increasingly so in the United States, do seem to be more effective, perhaps because the dosages used are generally higher than those found in dried herbs.

Many advocates of herbal medicine claim that the presence of many different active and inactive ingredients in synthetic drugs—known and unknown—makes botanical products safer and more effective. This is mostly speculation because there have been few clinical trials directly comparing herbs and pharmaceuticals in their effectiveness in treating specific diseases and conditions (Relman, 1998). Furthermore, advocates of herbal medicine typically neglect to mention the possible adverse side effects created by the lack of purity and standardization of some herbal products.

Food Supplement Therapy

The use of vitamins and food supplements is a second major emphasis of naturopathy and is perhaps the best known of all CAM treatments. Look through nearly any popular magazine, and you are sure to find at least one recommended supplement, such as vitamin E to deter atherosclerosis and prevent premature aging of the skin, or folic acid to support the immune system. Although most medical experts have yet to fully endorse nutritional supplementation, an estimated 70 percent of adults in the United States take vitamin supplements, 100 million using them regularly (Gardea and others, 2004).

There is no longer any doubt that food supplements can have important health benefits. There is a large body of convincing research evidence that materials derived from foods can be effective in treating a number of diseases. For example, niacin is effective in lowering cholesterol levels, and glucosamine sulfate is effective in reducing the pain of arthritis. Moreover, food supplements often trigger fewer adverse side effects than do drugs of comparable effectiveness.

Food supplements are generally used in two ways: to correct dietary deficiencies (*nutritional medicine*) or in immense doses to trigger a specific therapeutic effect (*megadose therapy*). As nutritional medicine, they are useful in correcting fairly common deficiencies in many essential nutrients, including deficiencies in calcium, folic acid, iron, magnesium, zinc, and vitamins A, B6, C, and E. Although conventional biomedicine supports eating a balanced diet or, short of that, using nutritional medicine to correct deficiencies in vitamins and minerals, the use of megadose therapy is more controversial. Linus Pauling's famous recommendation to take 4,000 to 10,000 mg per day of vitamin C is a prime example. According to naturopaths, this huge dose—equivalent to eating 40 to 100 oranges per day, or 10 to 15 times the official recommended daily allowance (RDA)—is needed because the stresses of modern life and the effects of environmental toxins cause nutritional needs to increase beyond what a normal diet can provide. This claim remains controversial among nutritionists.

Dietary Medicine

Naturopaths have always believed that fruits, vegetables, nuts, and whole grains are "natural foods" and that any refinement of these foods reduces their natural vitality and health-promoting properties. In contrast, until quite recently, conventional biomedicine has paid little attention to diet. Only in the past 2 decades have medical researchers begun to take seriously the idea that what people eat has a major impact on their health. As discussed in Chapter 7, the overwhelming evidence from large-scale epidemiological research has shown that diet plays a central role in preventing most of the major chronic diseases, including heart disease, strokes, and cancer of the breast, colon, and prostate.

Despite this agreement, naturopaths typically go well beyond conventional medicine's recommendations regarding diet. In addition to dramatically reducing consumption of meat and saturated fat, they decry the use of food preservatives, artificial fertilizers, pesticides, and the hormones used in modern farming. Instead, they recommend eating organic foods that are produced without these adulterations.

Another popular dietary concept in naturopathic medicine has to do with the idea of *food allergy* or, more accurately, *food sensitivity*. Diets based on avoiding "trigger" foods such as sugar, wheat, or dairy products are prescribed for many conditions, from arthritis to chronic fatigue (Wheelwright, 2001). When a food sensitivity is suspected, naturopaths typically place the patient on a highly restricted elimination diet of a small number of foods known to seldom cause allergic reactions. Rice, sweet potatoes, turkey, and applesauce are popular choices. If symptoms begin to clear up after several weeks on the restricted diet, foods are gradually added back into the diet, one at a time, while the patient keeps a journal of symptoms such as sneezing and headaches.

But even naturopaths disagree about the elements of a healthy diet. Proponents of *raw food theory*, a naturopathic concept dating back more than 100 years, believe that cooking foods destroys the "vital life force" (along with the vitamins, enzymes, and micronutrients) found in food. In contrast, the popular theory of *macrobiotics* condemns raw foods as unhealthy, considering them a cause of multiple sclerosis, rheumatoid arthritis, and other diseases. Macrobiotic nutritionists insist that all foods, including vegetables, should be cooked.

Do Dietary Modifications and Food Supplements Work? Epidemiological and experimental studies in animals and humans have provided substantial evidence that diet (in the form of foods or as supplements) can have a major effect on risk factors for certain diseases and the progression of disease. For example, over the past 10 years plant-based diets, dietary fiber supplementation, and antioxidant supplementation have become increasingly accepted treatments for managing cardiovascular disease. In fact, along with low-fat diets, aerobic exercise, and stress reduction, these treatments, which were at one time considered alternative therapies, are now considered either complementary or a part of standard medical practice for reducing risk of cardiovascular disease (Haskell and others, 1999).

Similarly, low-fat, high-fiber, basically vegetarian diets such as the *Pritikin diet* and the *Ornish diet* have been demonstrated to be effective in lowering blood glucose levels in people with diabetes. In one study, 60 percent of people with Type 2 diabetes on the Ornish diet no longer required insulin (McGrady & Horner, 1999). A number of epidemiological studies have also suggested a possible decrease in the prevalence of cancer in people who consume higher amounts of fruits and vegetables, perhaps due to their antioxidant effects (Primack & Spencer, 1999).

Elimination diets, megavitamin supplementation, and diets that focus on replacing trace elements are popular forms of CAM therapy that have been used to treat *attention-deficit hyperactivity disorder (ADHD)*. The *Feingold diet,* for example, eliminates food colors, artificial flavors, and highly processed foods from the ADHD child's diet, with mixed results in improving symptoms (Kien, 1990). One controlled study of fifty 7- to 12-year-old ADHD children, whose diagnosis was based on DSM-IV criteria, found a magnesium deficiency in blood and hair samples. The treatment group, who received a 200-mg daily supplement of magnesium for 6 months, showed an increase in the magnesium contents of their hair, which correlated positively with a significant decrease of hyperactivity (Starobrat-Hermelin & Kozielec, 1997).

The value of food supplements, on the other hand, is not so clear. Certain supplements have been proved to be reasonably effective in treating certain conditions—for example, glucosamine sulfate for osteoarthritis, vitamin C for cold symptoms, and zinc for prostate enlargement. Despite these successes, however, megadose supplements rarely are as powerful as synthetic drugs, and supplement therapy alone usually is not adequate in managing serious health conditions. For instance, one double-blind, cross-over clinical trial found that megavitamins were ineffective in managing ADHD and had the added danger of potential toxicity to the liver (Haslam and others, 1984).

Safety Concerns As with herbal medicines, the FDA cautions consumers that some unregulated dietary supplements may contain hazardous substances. For example, in January 1999, the FDA asked dietary supplement manufacturers to recall supplements that contained *gamma butyrolactone (GBL),* which were sold via the Internet and in health food stores and health clubs. Marketed under such brand names as Blue Nitro, GH Revitalizer, and Revivarant, the popular supplement was supposed to build muscles, lower weight, and improve athletic and sexual performance. In fact, GBL contains a chemical also found in commercial floor strippers that affects the central nervous system; slows breathing and heart rate; and can lead to seizures, unconsciousness, and coma. GBL has been linked to at least six deaths and adverse health effects in hundreds of other people (National Drug Intelligence Center, 2001).

As another example, contaminants in the once-popular supplement L-tryptophan—touted as a pain reliever, a remedy for insomnia, and an antidepressant—caused a serious illness, *eosinophilia myalgia syndrome.* Thirty people died in 1989 as a result of using this over-the-counter substance (Berge, 1998).

The FDA also warns against the use of certain herbs and food supplements by those who are also taking prescription medications. For instance, in a February 2000 public health advisory, the FDA cautioned that St. John's Wort had been found to reduce the effectiveness of the AIDS drug Indinavir by 57 percent (Piscitelli and others, 2000). The FDA also cited a Zurich, Switzerland, study reporting that this popular herbal remedy for depression reduced levels of a transplant rejection drug (cyclosporin), increasing the odds that a heart transplant patient might reject a donated heart (Fugh-Berman, 2000).

What to Expect from a Visit to a Naturopath

The herbal medicines, food supplements, and dietary medicines we've discussed in this section are provided by naturopaths, who function as primary, preventive care doctors. A visit to a naturopath generally begins with a standard physical exam, possibly one that includes conventional blood and urine tests, and even radiology. Naturopaths will also spend considerable time recording the patient's medical history, focusing on the patient's lifestyle, including diet, exercise level, stress, and even emotional and spiritual issues.

After this initial examination, patient and naturopath work together to establish a treatment program. Usually, the program emphasizes noninvasive therapies and lifestyle changes such as eliminating unhealthy behaviors. The naturopath may then prescribe dietary changes, food supplements, and/or herbal medicine for any specific complaints. Depending on where the naturopath practices, conventional drugs, vaccinations, or even surgery may be recommended.

Does Naturopathy Work?

Diseases that are strongly affected by lifestyle and environment are among those for which naturopathic treatment is most often reported to be effective. For example, it has been used effectively to treat allergies, chronic infections, fatigue, arthritis, asthma, headache, hypertension, and depression, to name only a few conditions. In a typical case of hypertension, for example, a naturopathic doctor might prescribe a multifaceted treatment that includes dietary changes, vitamin and mineral supplements, herbal medicine, and lifestyle changes designed to reduce stress. For an arthritis sufferer, the regimen might include dietary modifications, herbal medicine, and massage.

Critics of naturopathic medicine raise several concerns. Chief among these is that unsuspecting consumers are flooded with inaccurate or deceptive information carrying extreme claims about the effectiveness of herbs. Herbal therapy is also criticized for being untested according to pharmaceutical standards. Herbalists reply that because herbs are natural products (and therefore cannot be patented), the extremely expensive testing required of pharmaceutical drugs is unlikely to happen. Proponents point out that the modern pharmaceutical industry grew out of herbal medicine, and that many drugs—from the digitalis used to treat heart disease (derived from the foxglove plant) to morphine (from the opium poppy)—are still made from plant extracts. Another concern is safety. For this reason, most herbalists recommend purchasing herbs rather than harvesting them in the wild. Plants have natural variations that can be misleading, and this has caused more than one death from a person's ingesting a toxic plant he or she believed to be a beneficial herb.

CAM and the Elderly

Two chronic conditions striking many elderly people are Alzheimer's disease (AD) and osteoarthritis. AD is a degenerative disorder that alters memory, cognition, and behavior. In the United States, 10 percent of those aged 65 and older have AD; up to 50 percent of those 85 and older have some form of the disease (Alzheimer's Association, 2000). In 2006, roughly 4.5 million individuals in the United States had AD, with the number estimated to triple by 2050 (Luskin and others, 2000; National Institute on Aging, 2006).

In a survey of 101 physicians treating AD patients, 55 percent administered at least one CAM therapy to improve their patients' memory; 20 percent gave three or more treatments. These included vitamins (84%), health foods (27%), herbal medicines (11%), and home remedies (7%) (Coleman and others, 1995).

Gingko biloba extract (GBE) is a prevalent, legal, over-the-counter medicine in Europe. Although the FDA has not yet approved the extract, in the United States it can be purchased as a dietary supplement at health food and grocery stores. GBE has been tested in many randomized, placebo-controlled studies, with patients showing moderate AD symptoms. One study reported that after 1 month of GBE or placebo treatment, attention, memory, and psychomotor ability all improved in the GBE group (Hofferberth, 1994). In another prospective, randomized, double-blind study, researchers reported that the GBE-based improvement in AD symptoms continued over a period of 24 weeks (Kanowski and others, 1996). A third study found that gingko increased the percentage of alpha brain waves, suggesting its role as a cognitive activator (Itil & Martorano, 1995). Finally, a meta-analysis of 25 randomized, placebo-controlled, double-blind studies confirmed that GBE was an effective form of treatment for early-stage AD (Letzel and others, 1996).

Osteoarthritis (OA) is the most common form of arthritis, involving a degenerative joint disease accompanied by inflammation, breakdown, and deterioration of cartilage in weight-bearing joints. Cartilage is the protein cushioning between the bones of joints; when damaged, it can cause severe joint pain, stiffness, and physical disability, making walking and other tasks of everyday living difficult. OA affects an estimated 16 million persons in the United States, mostly elderly women, and is the second leading cause of disability in adults 65 and over (West & Rink, 1997).

Although there is no known cure for OA, conventional treatment is aimed at pain relief and minimizing the disability caused by loss of joint mobility (Luskin and others, 2000). Common treatments include weight-loss programs, moderate aerobic exercise (for example, swimming or walking), physical therapy, use of mechanical support devices (for instance, canes, splints, or walkers), pain relievers (such as aspirin), and surgery (for example, arthroscopy or knee or hip replacement).

CAM therapies are also widely used by OA patients. One survey of 100 OA sufferers found that 64 percent had used some form of "self-therapy" (including heat treatments and folk remedies) and that one-fourth had employed the services of CAM providers—primarily acupuncturists and chiropractors (Gray, 1985). Another survey found that of 384 OA patients surveyed, one-third used nontraditional treatments. A third survey found that CAM use was as high as 94 percent (Hawley, 1984).

Although there have been a number of clinical trials testing CAM's effectiveness as a treatment for OA, much of the research is inconclusive and of poor scientific quality. Acupuncture, which is the most widely used CAM treatment for OA, seems to decrease pain levels in OA sufferers compared with no treatment at all, but the pain relief is often only temporary and no greater than placebo treatment (Berman, and others, 1999).

Looking Ahead: Complementary and Alternative Medicine in Our Future

Growing interest in CAM is viewed by some as one of several indications of a major paradigm shift in medicine and health care in the United States (NCCAM, 2004). One of the changes is a shift from the traditional view of the provider–patient relationship in which patients are willing, passive, and dependent to one in which patients are activist health consumers. New patients are more likely to demand and seek out accurate and timely health information on their own. As a result, new patients no longer accept their doctors' recommendations blindly and are more likely to be critical of traditional medicine and to consider (and use) alternative forms of treatment.

Armed with unprecedented access to health information from the Internet, self-help books, and other media, today's patients are becoming more empowered to manage their own health. Turning to CAM practitioners is a predictable manifestation of this sense of empowerment—choosing your own treatment approach despite what your physician might suggest.

This assessment of changed patient behavior is supported by the results of a 2004 report on the use of CAM published by the *National Center for Complementary and Alternative Medicine (NCCAM)*. The report indicated that most who chose to use CAM did so because they believed CAM would improve their health when used in combination with conventional medical treatments (55 percent). Relatively few respondents reported using CAM because they believed that conventional treatments would not help (28 percent) or were too expensive (13 percent). For this reason, it may be more accurate to predict that alternative medicine will become more *complementary*—that is, a supplement, to allopathic medicine, rather than an alternative or replacement.

Even the government is jumping on the CAM bandwagon. For example, the NIH's Office of Alternative Medicine (OAM) has funded numerous research centers to explore CAM and aging, arthritis, cancer, and cardiovascular disease; chiropractic; botanical supplements and women's health; and acupuncture, to name only a few (NCCAM, 2004). The increase in the number of CAM providers is projected to be 88 percent between 1994 and 2010, whereas the increase in the number of physicians is projected to be only about 16 percent (Cooper & Stoflet, 1996).

The Best of Both Worlds

In the end, no single approach to health care has all the answers; the search for the best solution to a medical condition often requires a willingness to look beyond one remedy or system of treatment. Already, many insurance companies cover certain alternative methods, including acupuncture. And conventional doctors are incorporating alternative therapies into their treatment regimens. For instance, *integrative cancer therapy,* which combines conventional medicine with the use of CAM modalities such as acupuncture, massage, and herbal medicine, is the subject of several ongoing clinical trials (Block, 2004). The NIH estimates that more than half of all conventional physicians use some form of CAM themselves or refer their patients to such forms of treatment (NCCAM, 2004). As a result, there is a growing movement to provide CAM instruction as a regular part of medical school curriculum. A survey of American physicians' knowledge and use of, training in, and acceptance of CAM as legitimate yielded the range of attitudes summarized in Table 14.2. Diet and exercise, biofeedback, and counseling or psychotherapy were most often used.

Thus, health care in the United States is moving toward a more open-minded view of unconventional medicine. Even the American Medical Association (AMA) has shifted its views toward greater tolerance. As late as the mid-1970s, the AMA's official position was that "the fakes, the frauds, and the quackeries need to be identified, exposed, and, if possible, eradicated" (AMA, 1973). By 1995, however, the AMA had substituted "alternative medicine" for "quackery" and passed a resolution encouraging its members to "become better informed regarding the practices and techniques of alternative or complementary medicine" (AMA, 1995). In November 1998, the prestigious *Journal of the American Medical Association* devoted its entire issue to the subject of alternative medicine. And where there once were none, there are now five peer-reviewed journals devoted to alternative medicine.

Still, "let the buyer beware" is sound advice for consumers considering CAM therapies. Statutory requirements for the practice of CAM differ from state to state. Provider-practice acts for massage exist in 22 states. Licensure is now required in 25 states and the District of Columbia. Naturopathy-practice acts exist in 12 states, although each state defines the scope of such practice differently (AANP, 2006).

The Politics of Medicine

The growing acceptability of CAM should not, however, be construed as an indication of its complete acceptance by the biomedical community. Both alternative and conventional medicine are guilty of discounting one another's approach to health care, and both conventional medicine and alternative medicine are mixtures of good and bad health practices. The best course is to be an informed consumer and to be skeptical about unsupported claims.

Clearly, the best result would be for patients to have access to the "best of both worlds." Following a conventional medical evaluation and discussion of conventional allopathic options, patients may choose a CAM consultation. But before doing so, the physician (according to Daniel Eisenberg, 1997), should

- ensure that the patient recognizes and understands his or her symptoms.
- maintain a record of all symptoms, including the patient's own opinions.
- review any potential for harmful interactions.
- plan for a follow-up visit to review CAM effectiveness.

This approach is designed to help keep communication channels open between patient and provider so that the patient receives the most effective and safest treatment.

Summing Up

What Is Complementary and Alternative Medicine?

1. *Complementary and alternative medicine* (CAM) refers to the range of health-promoting interventions that fall outside of conventional, Western biomedicine. Most CAM practitioners work from three fundamental ideals: to provide health treatment that is natural, is holistic, and promotes wellness. Various forms of what we now call CAM have been around for thousands of years, but they were eclipsed during most of the twentieth century by the success of biomedicine.

Medicine or Quackery?

2. Skeptics of CAM raise several concerns about unconventional treatments. Foremost among these concerns is that many CAM therapies have never been subjected to rigorous empirical scrutiny regarding their effectiveness or safety. When CAM studies are conducted, critics contend, the methods are often poor and conclusions questionable. Another concern is that people who rely on CAM therapies instead of conventional medicine may delay or lose the opportunity to benefit from scientifically based treatment.

3. Alternative practitioners counter that it is often impossible to conduct the kinds of formal experiments that mainstream medical researchers are most comfortable with. For example, because many CAM therapies are based on a more holistic philosophy, its advocates claim that treatment variables cannot always be studied independently.

4. CAM skeptics also contend that when conventional therapies fail to help, the acupuncturist, chiropractor, or naturopath presents a powerful belief system, and the CAM techniques then seem to work due to the placebo effect.

Does Complementary and Alternative Medicine Work?

5. Acupuncture was originally practiced as part of an integrated system of healing. Today, its use is sanctioned in the United States primarily for the treatment of pain and addiction.

6. The basic premise of mind–body therapies is that cognitive, emotional, and spiritual factors can have profound effects on one's health. Among the mind–body therapies are hypnosis, relaxation training and meditation, and spiritual healing.

7. Although hypnosis does not involve a unique state of consciousness, it may be effective in relieving pain in some patients. Those who are most likely to report pain relief from hypnosis also tend to be highly suggestible people and to be very responsive to authority figures.

8. Relaxation and meditation may also promote health by bolstering the immune system, reducing pain, and lowering stress hormones. Several studies have found that people who are religiously active are healthier and live longer than their less religious counterparts, perhaps due to differences in lifestyle, social support, and positive emotions.

9. Research studies show that chiropractic treatment may decrease the frequency and intensity of tension and migraine headaches and be beneficial in the treatment of otitis media, hypertension, carpal tunnel syndrome, some sports injuries, and arthritis of the hip, wrist, or hand.

10. Naturopathic medicine aims to provide holistic, or whole body, health care by returning us to our "natural state." Modern naturopathy draws from several CAM traditions, especially herbal medicine, food supplement therapy, and dietary modification.

11. Roughly 25 percent of our modern-day pharmaceutical drugs are derived from herbs. Certain herbs may be beneficial for certain conditions, but caution must be exercised because many herbs remain untested and may have harmful effects.

12. There is substantial evidence from epidemiological and experimental studies on animals and humans that diet (in the form of foods or as supplements) can have a major effect on risk factors for certain diseases and the progression of disease.

Looking Ahead: Complementary and Alternative Medicine in Our Future

13. Growing interest in CAM is viewed by some as one of several indications of a major paradigm shift in medicine and health care in the United States.

Key Terms and Concepts

evidence-based medicine, p. 428
holistic medicine, p. 428
complementary and alternative medicine
  (CAM), p. 429

integrative medicine, p. 432
vitalism, p. 432
traditional Oriental medicine, p. 432
acupuncture, p. 438

hypnosis, p. 442
naturopathic medicine, p. 451

Health Psychology Today and Tomorrow

I wasn't always interested in health. Like many students, when I enrolled at Columbia University in the fall of 1979 I was blessed with a sound mind and body that I took for granted. I rarely exercised, ate too much fast food, slept too little, and even began smoking cigarettes—to "cope" with the stress of grad school, I rationalized. Nor was I interested in what psychology might contribute to our understanding of health. My schedule of classes and research focused on learning theory, neurobiology, and cognition.

Things began to change, however, when I decided to branch out and study applied social psychology with Professor Stanley Schachter. His distinctive approach to research was breaking new ground in the study of emotions, obesity, and addiction. Unlike most of his peers, Schachter always focused on the broader context in which social behaviors were embedded. Nowhere is this more evident than in his effort to understand the biological processes involved in seemingly social phenomena, such as increased cigarette smoking at parties or in response to stress. Much of the emerging field of health psychology was rooted in Schachter's work. I began to see a clearer path toward the contributions to humanity that I was hoping to make. Psychology for me became a tool to promote health.

As my professional interests shifted, my personal interests followed. I recall one seminar when Stan, who was struggling to quit smoking himself, asked me when I was going to take up the battle against nicotine addiction. "Why don't you apply what you've learned here to your own life?" he asked. So I began to do so, and I've tried to be faithful to Schachter's challenge ever since. It was tough, but I did quit smoking many years ago. I also began to exercise, eat a more nutritious diet, and follow a healthier sleep schedule. As new research findings have come along, I've tried to incorporate them into how I cope *with stress; the efforts I make to keep strong, positive, social connections with others; and in how I appraise the events around me.*

My hope is that this book has sparked your interest in the field of health psychology—for some of you as a profession, and for all of you as a tool in promoting your own better health!

Health psychology has traveled a long way since the American Psychological Association first recognized it in 1978. My goal in this closing chapter is to look back—to review what has been accomplished along the way—and to look ahead to the most pressing challenges of the future. Although we will focus on health psychologists' contributions to various health-related goals, it is important to remember that they are not working alone. The medical profession and others in the health care industries all work together to achieve these ends.

Health Psychology's Most Important Lessons

The science of health psychology is still in its infancy, and its contributions are still unfolding. Thus, much work remains to be done. Yet virtually all health psychologists agree that there have been lessons learned during the past 3 decades of research that all of us should heed.

Lesson 1: Psychological and Social Factors Interact With Biology in Health

Good Health is More Than Good Genes Josephine Tesauro and her sister share identical genes, but not identical health. At 92, Josephine is still healthy and active in the community—working part-time in a gift shop and living very independently. Her sister, who has not shared Josephine's physically active lifestyle, suffers dementia and incontinence, has had a hip replaced, and has lost most of her vision. Health psychologists are fascinated to study the lifestyle differences that might affect such dramatic disparity between identical twins.

As we have seen, for many diseases, heredity plays a small role. And not every person with the same genetic vulnerability eventually develops the disease. Bacteria, viruses, and other microorganisms cause some diseases, but being exposed doesn't guarantee that a person will become ill. Stress, negative emotions, coping resources, healthy behaviors, and a number of other factors affect our susceptibility to disease, the progression of disease, and how quickly (if at all) we recover.

Behavior, mental processes, social influences, and health are intimately connected. This is the fundamental message of the *biopsychosocial model* of health. Even those among us with "hardy" genes and healthy immune systems can become ill if we engage in risky health behaviors, live in unhealthy social and physical environments, and develop a negative emotional style and poor stress management techniques.

Unhealthy Behaviors and Social Alienation

The evidence is clear: Unhealthy behaviors such as smoking, alcohol use, poor nutrition, and inactivity lead to or at least accelerate the occurrence of illness and disease. For example, extensive research has eliminated any doubt that smoking is causally related to lung cancer and that alcohol use is related both to diseases of the liver and to traffic fatalities. Similarly, a low-fiber, high-fat diet increases a person's risk of developing cardiovascular disease and some forms of cancer. And, of course, a sedentary life increases the risk of cardiovascular disease and certain kinds of cancer and results in poorer immune functioning.

Numerous studies suggest that psychosocial factors can also affect the development and progression of diseases ranging from a simple cold to chronic conditions such as cardiovascular disease, cancer, and AIDS. Among the psychosocial factors that affect cardiovascular health are socioeconomic status, gender, race, employment, acute and chronic stress, social support versus isolation, anger, and depression (Kuper and others, 2006). The impact of these factors often equals or exceeds that of more traditional risk factors such as hypertension, diabetes, and even smoking (Stansfeld and others, 2004; O'Keefe and others, 2004).

Psychosocial factors are also linked to life expectancy. As a specific example, prospective studies demonstrate that social support reduces the risk of mortality, independent of other factors, such as gender and ethnicity. Lisa Berkman and her colleagues (2004) investigated a sample of 16,699 French workers, obtaining a social integration score for each participant based on marital status, contacts with friends and relatives, church membership, and other group memberships. Over a 7-year follow-up, and after adjustment for age, smoking, alcohol consumption, body mass index, and depressive symptoms, men with low social integration scores had a 2.7 time greater risk of dying than did men with high scores; for women the rate was 3.64. This finding has been replicated in several other major studies (Berkman & Syme, 1994; Wills, 1997).

Researchers cannot yet unequivocally state exactly why social integration is protective against chronic disease. So far, the most valid hypotheses proposed include the following: Social support may buffer the effects of stress on the body; social support may positively influence health behaviors associated with disease (such as diet and exercise); and social support may directly affect underlying physical mechanisms associated with disease (Cohen and others, 1994). In support of the physical mechanisms hypothesis, researchers have found that social integration is negatively correlated with several inflammatory markers of cardiovascular disease (Loucks and others, 2006; Ford and others, 2006). Interestingly, people also *expect* to live longer when they perceive strong social and emotional support in their lives (Ross & Mirowsky, 2002).

Stress

Since the pioneering stress research of Hans Selye (see Chapter 4), there has been mounting evidence that poor stress management can take a negative toll on health, both directly and indirectly—increasing the risk of many chronic diseases, altering the progression of those diseases, and undermining

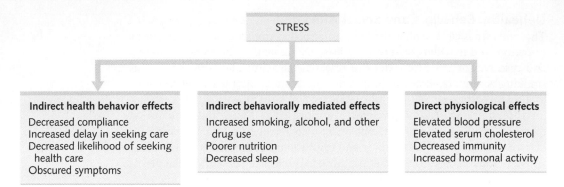

Figure 15.1

Direct and Indirect Effects of Stress on the Disease Process Stress affects health directly by elevating blood pressure and serum cholesterol levels and by decreasing immunity. The indirect effects of stress include reducing compliance with treatment instructions and increasing smoking and a variety of other unhealthy behaviors.

Source: Baum, A. (1994). *Behavioral, biological, and environmental interactions in disease processes.* Washington, DC: NIH Publications.

the effectiveness of treatment (Stansfeld and others, 2004; Booth and others, 2001) (Figure 15.1). Over the past 30 years, health psychologists have delineated the various possible consequences of how a person responds to daily hassles, occupational demands, environmental stressors, and other challenging events and situations. We now understand many of the physiological mechanisms by which stress adversely affects health and increases the likelihood of illness. For example, poorly managed stress can result in elevated blood pressure and serum cholesterol levels (Rau, 2006; Baum & Posluzny, 1999).

Some of health psychology's most dramatic findings have focused on immune function (Miller & Cohen, 2001). For example, temporary psychological stress, including exam taking or daily hassles, can decrease immune function (Robles and others, 2005), especially in people who have poor coping skills and in those who magnify the impact of potential stressors and appraise them as uncontrollable. In addition, chronic stress, such as that arising from natural disasters or caring for a spouse with Alzheimer's disease, can reduce immunocompetence (Kiecolt-Glaser & Glaser, 1995). These findings are part of the burgeoning field of *psychoneuroimmunology.* When we have a calm sense of being in control, we tend to have a comparable emotional and physiological reaction. When we become angry or fearful or feel hopeless because we believe a situation is out of our control, we tend to become emotionally aroused, and consequently our physiological response is more dramatic. Because we know that reactions such as these, if repeated and chronic, can promote illness, it is important for us to learn to manage our thoughts and emotional reactions.

Lesson 2: It Is Our Own Responsibility to Promote and Maintain Our Health

Our society has become increasingly health conscious. As a result, more of us realize that the responsibility for our health does not rest solely in the hands of health care professionals but that we ourselves have a major role to play in determining our overall well-being.

As a nation, for example, Americans have become well informed about the hazards of smoking, substance abuse, poor dietary practices, and sedentary living. We know, too, that stress, our emotional temperament, the quality of interpersonal relationships, and coping resources are important factors in health. We have learned about the importance of having regular check-ups, adhering to our prescribed treatment, and seeking early detection screening for various chronic illnesses, especially if our age, gender, race, or ethnicity places us in the "high-risk" group for these conditions.

This awareness does not guarantee that people will follow through on what they know to be the healthiest course of action. Between 2002 and 2004, a series of midcourse reviews of progress toward the 467 objectives of *Healthy People 2010* demonstrated mixed progress for Americans. The findings included the following:

- Worsening trends in the percentage of overweight and obese individuals, and little or no change in the status of most objectives for physical activity and fitness. In 2002, 38 percent of adults engaged in *no* leisure-time physical activity, compared with 40 percent in 1997.

- Continued decline in the three leading causes of death (heart disease, cancer, and stroke). This may be partly due to decreased tobacco use and the shift of dietary patterns toward more fruits and vegetables, less saturated fats, and no trans-fatty acids.

- A leveling off in the number of new cases and death rate from AIDS.

- Increasing use of preventive and early-detection health services, including PAP smears, mammograms, and childhood immunization.

- Continued increase in life expectancy.

- Continued decline in the infant mortality rate.

Americans have clearly made some gains in improving their health habits. Yet the report also notes that nearly 1 million deaths in this country each year are preventable:

- Control of underage and excess use of alcohol could prevent 100,000 deaths from automobile accidents and other alcohol-related injuries.

- Eliminating public possession of firearms could prevent 35,000 deaths.

- Eliminating all forms of tobacco use could prevent 400,000 deaths from cancer, stroke, and heart disease.

- Better nutrition and exercise programs could prevent 300,000 deaths from heart disease, diabetes, cancer, and stroke.

- Reducing risky sexual behaviors could prevent 30,000 deaths from sexually transmitted infections.

- Providing full access to immunizations for infectious diseases could prevent 100,000 deaths.

It has become quite clear that unhealthy lifestyles are much harder to change than to prevent in the first place. Although lifestyle interventions often meet with initial success, too many people "fall off the wagon." Ex-smokers, former

"I used to tell all the campaign staff: 'If you will just let me get sleep and exercise, I can keep going, but if I start cheating on either one of those, then it will have its consequences.'"

—Senator Bill Nelson (D), Florida (Krupin, 2001)

heavy drinkers, weight-loss program participants, and those who are new to exercise programs too often fall back into their old bad habits, a problem that must continue to be a focus for future health psychologists.

Lesson 3: Unhealthy Lifestyles Are Harder to Change Than to Prevent

Good nutrition, fitness, responsible drinking, and healthy management of body weight, stress, and social relationships are lifelong challenges that are best begun at a young age. Most smokers, for example, take up the habit during adolescence, usually before they graduate from high school. But as we have seen, preventing smoking, like preventing certain risky sexual activities, is a daunting challenge. Many people, especially young people, are more heavily influenced by the immediate "rewards" of smoking—the stimulating "kick" from nicotine, the self-image of doing something that seems mature or perhaps rebellious—than by worries about long-term health consequences.

Preventing poor health habits from developing in the first place will continue to be a high priority for health psychology. New research will investigate the most effective and efficient interventions for reaching the largest number of people in the workplace, schools and universities, and the community. The use of *behavioral immunization programs,* such as those targeting adolescents most likely to engage in risky sex, smoking, drug abuse, and under- or overeating, will also continue to grow. For some health behaviors, interventions will probably need to target even younger "at-risk" individuals. Among these are pediatric "well-parent/well-child" programs designed to teach new parents how to minimize the risks of accidents in the home and car and how to start their youngsters off on a lifetime of healthy eating and cardiopulmonary fitness.

Lesson 4: Positive Stress Appraisal and Management Are Essential to Good Health

One of health psychology's most important contributions in the area of stress and health has been the resolution of the controversy regarding whether stress is external or internal. Research has clearly revealed that it is both: Stress is a *transaction* in which each of us must continually adjust to daily challenges. As we learned in Chapters 4 and 5, each of life's stressful events can be appraised as either a motivating challenge or a threatening obstacle. Viewing life's stressors as challenges that we can handle helps us maintain a sense of control and minimizes the impact on our health. Learning to manage the stress we encounter is crucial to our physical, psychological, and emotional well-being. Research has revealed the benefits of several stress management strategies: keeping stress at manageable levels; preserving our physical resources by following a balanced diet, exercising, and drinking responsibly; establishing a stress-busting social network; increasing our psychological hardiness; disclosing our feelings when something is bothering us; cultivating a sense of humor; reducing hostile behaviors and negative emotions; and learning to relax.

Health Psychology's Future Challenges

Most of health psychology's challenges stem from two major research agendas. The first is the U.S. Department of Health and Human Services report *Healthy People 2010*, which, as we have seen, outlined the nation's highest priorities for promoting health and preventing disease among all Americans. The report was based on the best judgments of a large group of health experts from the scientific community, professional health organizations, and the corporate world. The report's 467 health objectives were organized under two overarching goals: *helping people of all ages increase life expectancy and improve their quality of life, and eliminating health disparities among various socioeconomic and ethnic groups.*

The second research agenda, produced by the American Psychological Association in collaboration with the National Institutes of Health and 21 other professional societies, focuses more specifically on health psychology's role in health care reform. Published in 1995, *Doing the Right Thing: A Research Plan for Healthy Living* identified four research tasks, out of which emerge the five challenges we will discuss in this section.

Challenge 1: To Increase the Span of Healthy Life for All People

The rapid aging of the population draws our attention to a crucial challenge: developing effective interventions that will enable older adults to maintain the highest possible level of functioning, or to improve it, for the greatest number of years.

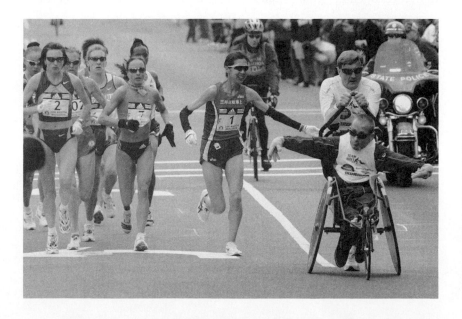

Inspirational Father-Son Team Dick Hoyt was inspired by his then-teenage son Rick, who has congenital physical disabilities, to train for and compete together in a running race for charity. Rick loved the experience and told his dad that for the first time he didn't feel disabled—while flying along in his specially-designed wheelchair. The pair has gone on to compete in hundreds of athletic competitions—including marathons and ironman triathlons—over the past 25 years.

Healthy life is a combination of average life expectancy and quality of life. The challenge for health psychology is to increase the *healthy life expectancy,* or average number of years that a person can expect to live in full health—an index of a person's biological age rather than his or her chronological age—along with a *compression of morbidity*—which refers to a shortening of the amount of time people spend disabled, ill, or in pain.

We have achieved some success, but there is room for much additional improvement. Overall, global healthy life expectancy at birth for women and men combined currently is only 57.7 years, 7.5 years lower than total life expectancy at birth (Nolte and others , 2004). This discrepancy between life expectancy and well years is even larger when we compare various socioeconomic groups and other countries of the world. Lower socioeconomic status is associated with shorter average life expectancy *and* fewer well years. Around the world, the percentage of life expectancy lost to disability ranges from less than 9 percent in the healthiest regions to more than 14 percent in the least healthy.

Challenge 2: To Reduce Health Discrepancies and Increase Our Understanding of the Effects of Gender, Culture, and Socioeconomic Status on Health

Historically, several measures of health have shown substantial differences among various ethnic and sociodemographic groups, as well as between the genders. For example, in 2002, average life expectancy was 75.1 years for white males but only 68.8 years for African-American males, and 80.3 years for white females but only 75.6 years for African-American females (National Center for Health Statistics, 2003). Asking people about their health reveals even greater differences by ethnic group, as shown in Figure 15.2. The reasons for these dis-

Figure 15.2

Quality of Health by Ethnic Group and Gender When asked to describe their health, a surprisingly high percentage of all ethnic groups used "fair" or "poor." Except among Native Americans, women are more likely than men to describe their health in negative terms. Even more telling are the differences between ethnic groups, with whites having the most positive view of their health and Native Americans being least positive.

Source: National Center for Health Statistics. (1999). *Healthy people 2000 review.* Hyattsville, MD: Public Health Service.

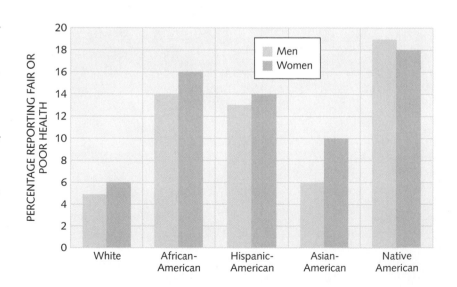

crepancies are undoubtedly complex but may include unequal access to health care, genetic susceptibility to specific diseases, and lifestyle differences.

The negative effects of ethnicity and poverty on health may be the result of factors such as poor nutrition, crowded and unsanitary environments, inadequate medical care, stressful life events, and subjective perceptions that environmental stressors are beyond one's ability to cope. Another factor is less effective use of health screening among certain groups. For example, African-American women delay longer than white women in seeking care for breast symptoms, and older women, who frequently are at increased risk of breast cancer, are less likely to seek preventive care.

However, ethnic group disparities in health are not completely attributable to the social conditions in which people live. For example, Hispanic-Americans generally fare as well as or better than European-Americans on most measures of health, actually having a lower death rate than European-Americans from heart disease, lung cancer, and stroke. This is paradoxical, given the high rates of hypertension, obesity, and tobacco use among Hispanic-Americans. Some researchers believe that this puzzling fact reflects a lag in acculturation because the same trend can be found in all immigrant groups: as immigrants adopt an American lifestyle, they eventually develop the same patterns of illness and mortality (Marwick, 1991).

Another factor that may be important is education. Regardless of ethnicity, people who have achieved higher levels of education live longer and have better overall health than those with less education, most likely because people with fewer years of education generally are more likely to engage in unhealthy behaviors such as smoking and eating a high-fat diet than those with more years of education (Macera and others, 2001).

Health psychologists have not been able to pinpoint the reasons for the discrepancies because until recently, what they knew about health and disease derived from research disproportionately concentrated on young, relatively healthy, white male subjects. Health psychologists have begun to widen the scope of their research to include a more diverse pool of research participants, and in some cases to focus specifically on understudied groups. For example, they have found that women and men have very different psychological, social, and biological characteristics and vulnerabilities and that they therefore differ in their susceptibility to various diseases and in their coping reactions to stress. The same seems to be true of many different ethnic and racial groups.

Clearly, much more research is needed before health psychologists can confidently explain why there are health discrepancies among traditionally understudied groups. One attempt to fill the void is being provided by the *Women's Health Initiative (WHI)*, a long-term national health study focusing on the prevention of heart disease, breast and colorectal cancer, and osteoporosis in postmenopausal women. WHI (2006), which focuses on the effects of the social environment and individual characteristics on health (Figure 15.3, p. 476), includes three components: a randomized, controlled clinical trial of 64,500 women testing the impact of a low-fat diet, hormone replacement therapy, and

Figure 15.3

Sociodemographic Characteristics and Health-Related Quality of Life in Women One goal of the Women's Health Initiative (WHI) is to understand the factors that contribute to the health of postmenopausal women and to evaluate the efficacy of practical interventions in preventing the major causes of morbidity and mortality in older women. They hope to accomplish this in part by testing the model depicted here, which suggests that the effects of the social environment and individual dispositions influence a woman's health through her health-related behaviors and intermediate biological outcomes.

Source: Matthews, K. A., Shumaker, S. A., Bowen, D. J., Langer, R. D., Hunt, J. R., Kaplan, R. M., and others. (1997). Women's Health Initiative: Why now? What is it? What's new?" *American Psychologist, 52,* 101–116.

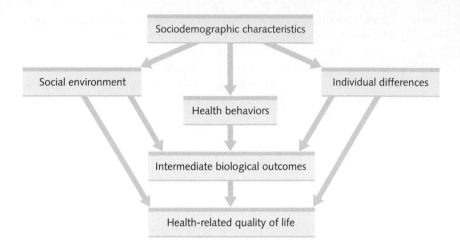

calcium-vitamin D supplementation; an observational study of another 100,000 women, examining the biological and psychological determinants of these chronic diseases in women; and a massive study evaluating eight different model education/prevention programs in communities throughout the United States.

Challenge 3: To Achieve Equal Access to Preventive Health Care Services for All People

As we have seen throughout this book, many minorities and impoverished Americans of every ethnicity and race have limited access to preventive health care. And there is a disproportionate concentration of certain minority groups in unhealthy neighborhoods (Whitfield and others, 2002). These are some of the reasons why minorities and the poor tend to suffer more health problems and have a higher mortality rate. In 2005, 46.6 million working Americans (15.9% of the population) had no health insurance (United States Census Bureau, 2006), making every day, in effect, a roll of the dice with respect to their health. Health psychology faces the continuing challenge of understanding and removing barriers that limit access to health care.

The United States does a poorer job than any other industrialized nation in making health care available to all its citizens. Although we have the most costly health care system in the world, it is not the best (Figure 15.4). For example, we rank only twenty-first in the world in infant mortality, sixteenth in life expectancy for women, and seventeenth in life expectancy for men. In terms of overall performance on eight measures of health, the U.S. health care system ranks thirty-seventh out of the member states of the World Health Organization (WHO, 2000). As we have seen, one reason for these low rankings is the tremendous disparity in the environmental conditions in which Americans live (Taylor and others, 1997).

Underscoring the impact of this disparity in environmental conditions, *Save the Children's YouthNoise,* recently issued its report *Ten Critical Threats to Amer-*

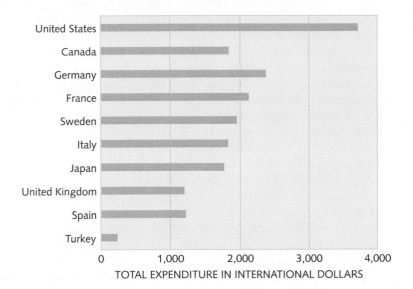

Figure 15.4

Health Care Costs Around the World The United States has the most costly, but not the best, health care system in the world. The United Kingdom and Canada—both of which have socialized medicine—rank above the United States in the overall quality of their health care system but spend less money annually. Thus, improving health care while cutting costs is one of our most pressing challenges as a nation.

Source: Data from *Health Systems: Improving Performance,* by World Health Report, 2000, June 2000 (Annex Table 1, pp. 152–155). Geneva, Switzerland: World Health Organization.

ica's Children (2006). The report outlined the following threats: poverty, lack of health care, substance abuse, crime and dangers in the environment, abuse and neglect at home, inadequate child care, poor schools, teen pregnancy, and absent parents. It is obvious that each of these threats, either directly or indirectly, can have a powerful impact on children's health.

As long as some people have access to quality health care while others have none, we will have a two-tiered health care system in this country: state-of-the-art, high-tech care for those who have managed to get health insurance, and substandard care (or no care) for everyone else. Health care reform remains a continuing challenge—for health psychology as well as for the national political agenda.

Challenge 4: To Adjust the Focus of Research and Intervention to Maximize Health Promotion With Evidence-Based Approaches

In the past, health psychology followed biomedicine's lead in focusing on mortality rather than morbidity. Even when prevention was stressed, health psychologists tended to focus on those chronic diseases that were the leading causes of death. Although reducing mortality will continue to be a priority, health psychology also must devote greater attention toward conditions such as arthritis, which have a minimal impact on mortality rates but a dramatic impact on wellness among the elderly.

A related challenge is to place more emphasis on health-enhancing behaviors and factors that may delay mortality and reduce morbidity. In the past, health psychologists devoted more of their research to studying risk factors for chronic disease and less of their research to learning about health-promoting behaviors that help prevent people from developing illness. The positive psychology movement is beginning to address this imbalance, as researchers pay greater attention to promoting healthy individuals, healthy families and communities, and healthy workplaces.

A continuing challenge for health psychology is to employ *evidence-based approaches* through documentation of the effectiveness of various interventions. This issue comes into sharp focus as the debate continues over the extent to which psychological interventions should be covered by managed health insurance. Even the most exciting new intervention—if backed only by weak or poorly conducted research studies—is likely to meet with the same skeptical reaction from health care professionals that many complementary and alternative therapies have faced (see Chapter 14). Complicating the research picture, true primary prevention studies often take decades to complete, and they require expensive, long-term funding. Fortunately, the U.S. Centers for Disease Control and Prevention has shown considerable interest in continuing behavioral intervention research.

Despite health psychology's successes, much remains to be done before the goals of *Healthy People 2010* are fully met. Although health psychologists continue to focus on eliminating health disparities among various sociocultural groups, emphasis has been shifted away from targeting special groups in favor of improved health for all Americans.

Challenge 5: To Assist in Health Care Reform

As noted in Chapter 12, health care in the United States faces three fundamental problems: It is far too expensive; not all citizens have equal access to high-quality health care; and its services are often used inappropriately. For many years, researchers have therefore been predicting a major revolution in the U.S. health care system. Among the issues needing to be addressed are universal access to health care, comprehensive mandated health benefits, cost containment, quality, accountability, and a shift in emphasis from secondary prevention to primary prevention (Belar & Deardorff, 1996; Kaplan, 2004). Unfortunately, health care in this country continues to focus much more on expensive inpatient care (and other efforts at secondary prevention) than on cost-effective primary prevention and health promotion (Kaplan, 2000).

To improve health care while cutting costs is among the most pressing of needs. One of health psychology's most fundamental messages is that prevention and health promotion or maintenance must be made as important in the health care system as disease treatment is now. Health care must be defined more broadly so that it doesn't focus solely on the services provided by doctors, nurses, clinicians, and hospitals. Many health psychologists emphasize the importance of patients taking responsibility for their own well-being while also recognizing the important roles played by the individual's family, friends, and community. More effective health care will recognize that schools, places of worship, and workplaces are important sites for promoting health and should become part of the network of interconnected services in the nation's health care system.

The important role of psychologists in improving physical health through enhancing treatment outcomes has now been firmly established. This has led to a significant increase in the number of psychologists working in general health care settings. Unfortunately, however, recent efforts to reduce health care costs may threaten this trend. Among hospital administrators and legislators, primary prevention and psychological services are still too often viewed as optional or even a frill. Current health policy places the greatest emphasis on preventing *further* episodes of disease in those who are already sick (secondary prevention) than on preventing the onset of disease in the first place (primary prevention) (Kaplan, 2004; 2000). Secondary prevention is based on the traditional biomedical (disease) model and usually involves medical diagnosis, medication, surgery, and other procedures that are covered by health insurance. In contrast, primary prevention is based on a behavioral rather than a disease model and typically does not involve diagnosis because there is no disease to diagnose.

This is not only unfortunate but also counterproductive because secondary prevention programs are often expensive and may produce few, if any, measurable benefits (Kaplan, 2000). One way to estimate the benefits of preventive actions is with combined measures of life expectancy and quality of life (QALYs). QALYs can be used to calculate the cost effectiveness of various primary and secondary prevention efforts. For example, a pharmaceutical treatment, medical screening procedure, or behavior intervention that improves the quality of life by half (0.5) for two people will result in the equivalent of 1 QALY over a period of 1 year. Researchers estimated that the small benefit of regular mammography among women 40 to 49 years of age (increasing life expectancy by only 2.5 days at a cost of $676 per woman) amounts to a cost of $100,000 for 1 full QALY (Salzmann and others, 1997). As a comparison, researchers have found that regular exercise produces 1 QALY for $11,313—a much more modest expenditure relative to many biomedical secondary prevention interventions (Hatziandreu and others, 1988).

Psychosocial Interventions

Health psychologists perform a wide range of activities, including training future doctors and nurses on the importance of psychosocial factors in patient compliance and recovery and directly intervening to assist patients who are facing difficult procedures and adjusting to chronic illness (Table 15.1, p. 476). Treatment interventions cover every domain of health. In the biological domain, treatment is designed to directly change specific physiological responses involved in the illness. Examples include relaxation to reduce hypertension, hypnosis to alleviate pain, and systematic desensitization to reduce the nausea that often occurs in anticipation of chemotherapy. In the psychological domain, health psychologists have applied both cognitive and behavioral interventions. Cognitive interventions include stress inoculation to decrease anxiety about an

Table 15.1

Examples of Health Psychology's Treatment Interventions

1. Desensitization of fears of medical and dental treatments, including needles, anesthesia, childbirth, or magnetic resonance imaging (MRI) procedures.
2. Treatment to enhance coping with or control over pain, including chronic back pain, headache, or severe burns.
3. Interventions to control symptoms such as vomiting with chemotherapy, scratching with neurodermatitis, or diarrhea with irritable bowel syndrome.
4. Support groups for chronic illness, cardiac rehabilitation, HIV-positive patients, or families of the terminally ill.
5. Training to overcome physical handicaps after trauma, cognitive retraining after stroke, or training to use prosthetic devices effectively.
6. Consultations and program development regarding patient compliance (for example, special aids for the elderly or inpatient units for insulin-dependent diabetic children).

Source: Adapted from Belar, C. E. & Deardorff, W. W. (1996). *Clinical health psychology in medical settings: A practitioner's guidebook.* Washington, DC: American Psychological Association.

upcoming medical procedure, cognitive-behavioral treatment for depression, and anger management for hostile cardiovascular disease patients. Behavioral interventions include teaching skills to improve patient–provider communication, to develop a behavior-change program to modify unhealthy habits, and to help train patients in self-management skills such as daily injections of insulin. Social interventions include establishing support groups for those suffering from chronic illness, providing counseling for families of the terminally ill, and conducting role-playing exercises with young children to socially "inoculate" them against being pressured by peers into risky behaviors.

Such psychosocial interventions can actually yield significant cost savings, particularly when used to prepare patients for surgery and other anxiety-producing medical procedures (Groth-Marnat & Schumaker, 1995). Patients who are overly anxious when facing hospitalization and invasive procedures such as surgery often experience a disintegration of normal coping skills (Horne and others, 1994; Strain & Horne, 2001). Relaxation training, postsurgical exercises, distraction techniques, and control-enhancing techniques can reduce the length of hospitalization and the need for pain-relieving medication and help prevent disruptive patient behavior (Blankfield, 1991; Disbrow and others, 1993). Psychosocial interventions are also perceived as effective and desirable by both patients and their families (Arving and others, 2006; Martire, 2005).

The challenge of cost containment is likely to continue because cardiovascular disease and cancer—chronic, age-related diseases that are extraordinarily costly to treat—will probably remain the leading causes of death for some time to come. Health psychology's emphasis on *prevention,* if widely employed, would help contain overall expenses, despite the initial cost of additional health personnel. One of the best ways to contain these costs is to help people improve their health behaviors to avoid getting sick, and to help those who become sick to recover as quickly as possible.

Blended (Collaborative) Care

As further testimony to health psychology's future role in helping the health care system's efforts to contain costs, the *Human Capital Initiative* has called for greater use of *blended care* (also called collaborative care; see Chapter 12). This interdisciplinary model, in which treatment teams approach diseases from biological, psychological, and sociocultural perspectives, shows great promise in improving treatment while simultaneously cutting costs (Table 15.2).

The success of blended care reflects health psychology's growing acceptance by traditional biomedicine over the past 25 years—a trend that is likely to continue into the future (Daw, 2001). One sign of this acceptance is the dramatic increase in the number of psychologists working in medical schools and academic health centers— the single largest area of placement of psychologists in recent years (APA, 2006). Between 1960 and 2006, psychology has grown from averaging about two psychologists per medical school to nearly 30 psychologists per medical school (APAHC, 2006). Psychologists have become key members of multidisciplinary clinical and research teams in many medical specialties, including family practice, pediatrics, rehabilitation, cardiology, oncology, and anesthesiology. Another sign is the growing role of nurses in delivering psychological services. An increasing number of nurses are obtaining advanced degrees in psychology, and nursing has established the *National Institute for Nursing Research (NINR)*, which focuses on controlled studies of psychological variables in nursing.

Paradoxically, as medical care has grown more specialized and more complex, it has also begun to broaden its scope, incorporating more complementary and alternative aspects of healing. Relaxation training, imagery, and some of the spiritual aspects of non-Western healing traditions are beginning to be accepted by some managed-care programs because these methods are typically inexpensive and yet often effective in helping patients cope with a variety of stress-related symptoms. With ever-rising medical costs, the *cost-effectiveness ratio* of such interventions can't be ignored.

Table 15.2

Reduction in Treatment Frequency with Blended Care

Total ambulatory care visits	−17%
Visits for minor illnesses	−35%
Pediatric acute illness visits	−25%
Office visits for acute asthma	−49%
Office visits by arthritis patients	−40%
Average length of stay in hospital for surgical patients	−1.5 days
Cesarean sections	−56%
Epidural anesthesia during labor and delivery	−85%

Source: *Doing the right thing: The human capital initiative strategy* (report). Washington, D.C.: American Psychological Association, 1994,16.

International Reform

As we have seen, there is great variability in the prevalence of specific diseases throughout the world. Poverty, lack of health care, and ignorance generally contribute to a higher incidence of infectious diseases in developing countries than in developed countries. For example, as smoking continues to decline in this country, its prevalence is increasing in developing parts of the world.

Health psychology can take the lead in carrying the messages of the thousands of research studies from developed nations to other parts of the world in which similar health problems are just beginning to emerge. But the transmission of information can flow in both directions. Health psychologists can help reform the U.S. health care system by helping policymakers understand those things that other countries do *better* than we do. For example, all Canadian citizens are covered through one government-subsidized health insurance provider. Although physicians work as independent service providers in private offices and clinics, much like those in the United States, their fees are fixed through regular negotiations with the government of the province in which they practice. Thus, physicians cannot charge more for their services than the agreed-upon price.

As another example, consider one aspect of the Australian system: well-woman/well-man clinics. The aim of these clinics is to promote the health of the total woman and man, focusing on wellness rather than only on disease. These free clinics, staffed by nurse practitioners, are found throughout the country and focus on education, assessment, and nonmedicinal management of personal and family stress problems.

Conclusion

Health psychology's outlook as a profession is bright. The field has made impressive advances in its brief history, though there is much more to learn. Future health psychologists will face many challenges as they work to improve individual and community health and to help reform the health care system. I hope that your increasing understanding of health psychology will be as motivating to you—both personally and professionally—as it has been to me.

Summing Up

Health Psychology's Most Important Lessons

Lesson 1: Psychological and Social Factors Interact With Biology in Health

Lesson 2: It Is Our Own Responsibility to Promote and Maintain Our Health

Lesson 3: Unhealthy Lifestyles Are Harder to Change Than to Prevent

Lesson 4: Positive Stress Appraisal and Management Are Essential to Good Health

Health Psychology's Future Challenges

Challenge 1: To Increase the Span of Healthy Life for All People

Challenge 2: To Reduce Health Discrepancies and Increase Our Understanding of the Effects of Gender, Culture, and Socioeconomic Status on Health

Challenge 3: To Achieve Equal Access to Preventive Health Care Services for All People

Challenge 4: To Adjust the Focus of Research and Intervention to Maximize Health Promotion With Evidence-Based Approaches

Challenge 5: To Assist in Health Care Reform

Glossary

acculturation the process by which a member of one ethnic or racial group adopts the values, customs, and behaviors of another.

acupuncture a component of traditional Oriental medicine in which fine needles are inserted into the skin in order to relieve pain, treat addiction and illness, and promote health.

acute pain sharp, stinging pain that is short lived and usually related to tissue damage.

adherence a patient both agreeing to and then closely following a treatment regimen as advised by his or her health care provider.

adipocytes collapsible body cells that store fat.

adrenal glands lying above the kidneys, the pair of endocrine glands that secrete epinephrine, norepinephrine, and cortisol, hormones that arouse the body during moments of stress.

agonist a drug that attaches to a receptor and produces neural actions that mimic or enhance those of a naturally occurring neurotransmitter.

AIDS (acquired immune deficiency syndrome) a life-threatening disease caused by the human immunodeficiency virus in which the body's CD4 lymphocytes are destroyed, leaving the victim vulnerable to opportunistic diseases.

AIDS dementia complex an AIDS-related syndrome involving memory loss, confusion, and personality changes.

alcohol abuse a maladaptive drinking pattern in which drinking interferes with role obligations.

alcohol dependence a state in which the use of alcohol is required for a person to function normally.

alcohol expectancies individuals' beliefs about the effects of alcohol consumption on behavior—their own as well as that of other people.

amygdala two clusters of neurons in the limbic system that are linked to emotion, especially aggression.

anatomical theory the theory that the origins of specific diseases are found in the internal organs, musculature, and skeletal system of the human body.

anecdotal evidence research evidence based on informal case histories, in which there is little or no objective documentation regarding a patient's diagnosis or the effectiveness of a treatment.

angina pectoris a condition of extreme chest pain caused by a restriction of the blood supply to the heart.

anorexia nervosa an eating disorder characterized by self-starvation, a distorted body image, and, in females, amenorrhea.

antagonist a drug that blocks the action of a naturally occurring neurotransmitter or agonist.

antigen a foreign substance that stimulates an immune response.

arteries blood vessels that carry blood away from the heart to other organs and tissues. A small artery is called an arteriole.

arteriosclerosis also called "hardening of the arteries," a disease in which blood vessels lose their elasticity.

association cortex areas of the cerebral cortex not directly involved in sensory or motor functions; rather, they integrate multisensory information and higher mental functions such as thinking and speaking.

atherosclerosis a chronic disease in which cholesterol and other fats are deposited on the inner walls of the coronary arteries, reducing circulation to heart tissue.

attentional focus a person's characteristic style of monitoring bodily symptoms, emotions, and overall well-being.

aversion therapy a behavioral therapy that pairs an unpleasant stimulus (such as a nauseating drug) with an undesirable behavior (such as drinking or smoking), causing the patient to avoid the behavior.

basal metabolic rate (BMR) the minimum number of calories the body needs to maintain bodily functions while at rest.

behavioral control interventions that teach techniques for controlling pain and speeding recovery during and after a medical procedure.

behavioral disinhibition the false sense of confidence and freedom from social restraints that results from alcohol consumption.

behavioral intention in theories of health behavior, the rational decision to engage in a health-related behavior or to refrain from engaging in the behavior.

behavioral medicine an interdisciplinary field that integrates behavioral and biomedical science in promoting health and treating disease.

behavioral undercontrol a general personality syndrome linked to alcohol dependence and characterized by aggressiveness, unconventionality, and impulsiveness; also called deviance proneness.

behavioral willingness in theories of health behavior, the reactive, unplanned motivation involved in the decision to engage in risky behavior.

belief bias a form of faulty reasoning in which our expectations prevent us from seeing alternative explanations for our observations.

biofeedback a system that provides audible or visible feedback information regarding involuntary physiological states.

biomedical model the dominant view of twentieth-century medicine that maintains that illness always has a physical cause.

biopsychosocial (mind–body) perspective the viewpoint that health and other behaviors are determined by the interaction of biological mechanisms, psychological processes, and social influences.

birth cohort a group of people who, because they were born at about the same time, experience similar historical and social conditions.

blood alcohol level (BAL) the amount of alcohol in the blood, measured in grams per 100 milliliters.

blood–brain barrier the network of tightly packed capillary cells that separates the blood and the brain.

body mass index (BMI) a measure of obesity calculated by dividing body weight by the square of a person's height.

brainstem the oldest and most central region of the brain; includes the medulla, pons, and reticular formation.

bronchi the pair of respiratory tubes that branch into progressively smaller passageways, the bronchioles, culminating in the air sacs within the right and left lungs (alveoli).

buffering hypothesis theory that social support produces its stress-busting effects indirectly, by helping the individual cope more effectively.

bulimia nervosa an eating disorder characterized by alternating cycles of binge eating and purging through such techniques as vomiting or laxative abuse.

burnout a job-related state of physical and psychological exhaustion.

calorie a measure of food energy equivalent to the amount of energy needed to raise the temperature of 1 gram of water 1 degree Celsius.

cancer a set of diseases in which abnormal body cells multiply and spread in uncontrolled fashion forming a tissue mass called a tumor.

carcinogen a cancer-causing agent such as tobacco, ultraviolet radiation, or an environmental toxin.

carcinoma cancer of the epithelial cells that line the outer and inner surfaces of the body; includes breast, prostate, lung, and skin cancer.

cardiovascular disease (CVD) disorders of the heart and blood vessel system, including stroke and coronary heart disease (CHD).

cardiovascular reactivity an individual's characteristic reaction to stress, including changes in heart rate, blood pressure, and hormones.

carotenoids light-absorbing pigments that give carrots, tomatoes, and other foods their color and are rich sources of antioxidant vitamins.

case study a descriptive study in which one person is studied in depth in the hope of revealing general principles.

cellular theory formulated in the nineteenth century, the theory that disease is the result of abnormalities in body cells.

central nervous system the brain and spinal cord.

cerebellum located at the rear of the brain, this brain structure coordinates voluntary movement and balance.

cerebral cortex the thin layer of cells that covers the cerebrum; the seat of conscious sensation and information processing.

chronic fatigue syndrome (CFS) a puzzling disorder of uncertain causes in which a person experiences headaches, infections of unknown origins, extreme tiredness, and difficulties with concentration and memory.

chronic pain dull, burning pain that is long lasting.

cilia the tiny hairs that line the air passageways in the nose, mouth, and trachea; moving in wavelike fashion, the cilia trap germs and force them out of the respiratory system.

clinical pain pain that requires some form of medical treatment.

cognitive control refers to interventions that direct the patient's attention to the positive aspects of a procedure (such as improved health) rather than on feelings of discomfort.

cognitive reappraisal the process by which potentially stressful events are constantly reevaluated.

cognitive therapy the category of treatments that teach people healthier ways of thinking.

cognitive-behavioral therapy (CBT) a multidisciplinary pain-management program that combines cognitive, physical, and emotional interventions.

collaborative care a cooperative form of health care in which physicians, psychologists, and other health care providers join forces to improve patient care.

comorbidity the simultaneous occurrence of two or more physical and/or psychological disorders or symptoms.

complementary and alternative medicine (CAM) the use and practice of therapies or diagnostic techniques that fall outside of conventional biomedicine.

concordance rate the rate of agreement between a pair of twins for a given trait; a pair of twins is concordant for the trait if both of them have it or if neither has it.

coping the cognitive, behavioral, and emotional ways in which we manage stressful situations.

coronary angiography a diagnostic test for coronary heart disease in which dye is injected so that x-rays can reveal any obstructions in the coronary arteries.

coronary angioplasty cardiac surgery in which an inflatable catheter is used to open a blocked coronary artery.

coronary artery bypass graft cardiac surgery in which a small piece of a healthy vein from elsewhere in the body is grafted around a blocked coronary artery, allowing blood to flow more freely to a portion of the heart.

coronary heart disease (CHD) a chronic disease in which the arteries that supply the heart become narrowed or clogged; results from either atherosclerosis or arteriosclerosis.

correlation coefficient a statistical measure of the strength and direction of the relationship between two variables, and thus of how well one predicts the other.

corticosteroids hormones produced by the adrenal cortex that fight inflammation, promote healing, and trigger the release of stored energy.

counterirritation analgesia in which one pain (for example, a pulled muscle) is relieved by creating another, counteracting stimulus (such as rubbing near the site of the injury).

cross-sectional study a study comparing representative groups of people of various ages on a particular dependent variable.

cytokines protein molecules produced by immune cells that act on other cells to regulate immunity (include the interferons, interleukins, and tumor necrosis factors).

delay behavior the tendency to avoid seeking medical care because symptoms go unnoticed *(appraisal delay)*, sickness seems unlikely *(illness delay)*, professional help is deemed unnecessary *(behavioral delay)*, the individual procrastinates in making an appointment *(scheduling delay)*, or the perceived benefits of treatment do not outweigh the perceived costs *(treatment delay)*.

delirium tremens (DTs) a neurological state induced by excessive and prolonged use of alcohol and characterized by sweating, trembling, anxiety, and hallucinations; a symptom of alcohol withdrawal.

dependence a state in which the use of a drug is required for a person to function normally.

dependent variable the behavior or mental process in an experiment that may change in response to manipulations of the independent variable; the variable that is being measured.

descriptive study research method in which researchers observe and record participants' behaviors, often forming hypotheses that are later tested more systematically; includes case studies, interviews and surveys, and observational studies.

diabetes mellitus a disorder of the endocrine system in which the body is unable to produce insulin (Type 1) or is unable to properly utilize this pancreatic hormone (Type 2).

diathesis-stress model the model that proposes that two interacting factors determine an individual's susceptibility to stress and illness: predisposing factors in the person (such as genetic vulnerability) and precipitating factors from the environment (such as traumatic experiences).

direct effect hypothesis theory that social support produces its beneficial effects during both stressful and non-stressful times by enhancing the body's physical responses to challenging situations.

disinhibition overeating triggered by an event, emotion, or behavior that causes a restrained eater to abandon his or her restraint.

double-blind study a technique designed to prevent observer- and participant-expectancy effects in which neither the researcher nor the subjects know the true purpose of the study or which subject is in each condition.

drug abuse the use of a drug to the extent that it impairs the user's biological, psychological, or social well-being.

drug addiction a pattern of behavior characterized by physical as well as possible psychological dependence on a drug as well as the development of tolerance.

drug potentiation the effect of one drug to increase the effects of another.

drug use the ingestion of a drug, regardless of the amount or effect of ingestion.

electrocardiogram (ECG or EKG) a measure of the electrical discharges that emanate from the heart.

emotion-focused coping coping strategy in which we try to control our emotional response to a stressor.

enkephalins endogenous (naturally occurring) opioids found in nerve endings of cells in the brain and spinal cord that bind to opioid receptors.

epidemic literally, *among the people;* an epidemic disease is one that spreads rapidly among many individuals in a community at the same time. A *pandemic* disease affects people over a large geographical area.

epidemiology the scientific study of the frequency, distribution, and causes of a particular disease or other health outcome in a population.

etiology the scientific study of the causes or origins of specific diseases.

etiology the scientific study of the causes or origins of specific diseases.

evidence-based medicine an approach to health care that promotes the collection, interpretation, and integration of the best research-based evidence in making decisions about the care of individual patients.

expectancy effects a form of bias in which the outcome of a study is influenced either by the researcher's expectations or by the study participants' expectations.

explanatory style our general propensity to attribute outcomes always to positive causes or always to negative causes, such as personality, luck, or another person's actions.

exposure-response prevention a behavioral treatment of bulimia nervosa that attempts to prevent purging (and therefore, reinforcement) following binge eating.

fast nerve fibers large, myelinated nerve fibers that transmit sharp, stinging pain.

female pattern obesity the "pear-shaped" body of women who carry excess weight on their thighs and hips.

fetal alcohol syndrome (FAS) a cluster of birth defects that include facial abnormalities, low intelligence, and retarded body growth caused by the mother's use of alcohol during pregnancy.

free nerve endings sensory receptors found throughout the body that respond to temperature, pressure, and painful stimuli.

gain-framed message a health message that focuses on attaining positive outcomes, or avoiding undesirable ones, by adopting a health-promoting behavior.

gastrointestinal system the body's system for digesting food; includes the digestive tract, salivary glands, pancreas, liver, and gallbladder.

gate control theory the idea that there is a neural "gate" in the spinal cord that regulates the experience of pain.

gateway drug a drug that serves as a stepping-stone to the use of other, usually more dangerous, drugs.

gender perspective theoretical perspective that focuses on gender-specific health problems and gender barriers to health care.

general adaptation syndrome (GAS) Selye's term for the body's reaction to stress, which consists of three stages: alarm, resistance, and exhaustion.

genome all of the DNA information for an organism; the human genome consists of approximately 3 billion DNA sequences.

genotype the sum total of all the genes present in an individual.

germ theory the theory that disease is caused by viruses, bacteria, and other microorganisms that invade body cells.

guided imagery the use of one or more external devices to assist in relaxation and the formation of clear, strong, positive images.

hardiness a cluster of stress-buffering traits consisting of commitment, challenges, and control.

health a state of complete physical, mental, and social well-being.

health behavior a health-enhancing behavior or habit; also called *behavioral immunogen.*

health belief model (HBM) non-stage theory that identifies three beliefs that influence decision making regarding health behavior: perceived susceptibility to a health threat, perceived severity of the disease or condition, and perceived benefits of and barriers to the behavior.

health education any planned intervention involving communication that promotes the learning of healthier behavior.

health psychology the application of psychological principles and research to the enhancement of health, and the prevention and treatment of illness.

hemophilia a genetic disease in which the blood fails to clot quickly enough, causing uncontrollable bleeding from even the smallest cut.

heritability the amount of variation in a trait among individuals that can be attributed to genes.

hippocampus a structure in the brain's limbic system linked to memory.

HIV (human immunodeficiency virus) the retrovirus that causes AIDS; it injects its genome into lymphocytes so that it reproduces when the cells are activated.

holistic medicine an approach to medicine that considers not only physical health but also the emotional, spiritual, social, and psychological well-being of the person.

homeostasis the tendency to maintain a balanced or constant internal state; the regulation of any aspect of body chemistry, such as the level of glucose in the blood, around a particular set point.

hormones chemical messengers, released into the bloodstream by endocrine glands, that have an effect on distant organs.

humoral theory a concept of health proposed by Hippocrates that considered wellness a state of perfect equilibrium among four basic body fluids, called humors. Sickness was believed to be the result of disturbances in the balance of humors.

hydrostatic weighing a method of determining the percentage of body fat by comparing a person's weight underwater with his or her dry weight.

hyperalgesia a condition in which a chronic pain sufferer becomes more sensitive to pain over time.

hypertension a sustained elevation of diastolic and systolic blood pressure (exceeding 140/90).

hypnosis a social interaction in which one person (the hypnotist) suggests to another that certain thoughts, feelings, perceptions, or behaviors will occur.

hypochondriasis the condition of experiencing abnormal anxiety over one's health, often including imaginary symptoms.

hypothalamic-pituitary-adrenocortical (HPA) system the body's delayed response to stress, involving the secretion of corticosteroid hormones from the adrenal cortex.

hypothalamus lying just below the thalamus, the region of the brain that influences hunger, thirst, body temperature, and sexual behavior; helps govern the endocrine system via the pituitary gland.

illness intrusiveness the extent to which a chronic illness disrupts an individual's life by interfering with valued activities and interests and reducing perceptions of personal control, self-efficacy, and self-esteem.

illness representation how a person views a particular illness, including its label and symptoms, perceived causes, timeline, consequences, and controllability.

immune surveillance theory the theory that cells of the immune system play a monitoring function in searching for and destroying abnormal cells such as those that form tumors.

immunocompetence the overall ability of the immune system, at any given time, to defend the body against the harmful effects of foreign agents.

immunotherapy chemotherapy in which medications are used to support or enhance the immune system's ability to selectively target cancer cells.

incidence the number of new cases of a disease or condition that occur in a specific population within a defined time interval.

independent variable the factor in an experiment that an experimenter manipulates; the variable whose effect is being studied.

informational control refers to patients' knowledge regarding the particular procedures and physical sensations that accompany a medical treatment.

Kaposi's sarcoma a rare cancer of blood vessels serving the skin, mucous membranes, and other glands in the body.

kilocalorie a measure of food energy equal to 1,000 calories.

Korsakoff's syndrome an alcohol-induced neurological disorder characterized by the inability to store new memories.

Lamaze training natural childbirth preparation designed to prepare prospective parents by enhancing their informational, cognitive, and behavioral control over the procedure.

lay referral system an informal network of family members, friends, and other nonprofessionals who offer their own impressions, experiences, and recommendations regarding a set of bodily symptoms.

leptin the weight-signaling hormone monitored by the hypothalamus as an index of body fat.

leukemia cancer of the blood and blood-producing system.

life-course perspective theoretical perspective that focuses on age-related aspects of health and illness.

limbic system a network of neurons surrounding the central core of the brain; associated with emotions such as fear and aggression; includes the hypothalamus, amygdala, and hippocampus.

longitudinal study a study in which a single group of people is observed over a long span of time.

loss-framed message a health message that focuses on a negative outcome from failing to perform a health-promoting behavior.

lymphocytes antigen-fighting white blood cells produced in the bone marrow.

lymphoma cancer of the body's lymph system; includes Hodgkin's disease and non-Hodgkin's lymphoma.

male pattern obesity the "apple-shaped" body of men who carry excess weight around their upper body and abdomen.

malingering making believe one is ill in order to benefit from sick role behavior.

managed care health care that seeks to control costs by eliminating waste and unnecessary procedures and by providing economically sound treatment guidelines to hospitals and physicians.

medulla the brainstem region that controls heartbeat and breathing.

melanoma a potentially deadly form of cancer that strikes the melatonin-containing cells of the skin.

meta-analysis a quantitative technique that combines the results of many studies examining the same effect or phenomenon.

metabolic syndrome a cluster of conditions that occur together—including elevated blood pressure and insulin levels, excess body fat, and unhealthy cholesterol ratios—that increase a person's risk for heart disease, stroke, and diabetes.

metastasis the process by which malignant body cells proliferate in number and spread to surrounding body tissues.

mind–body dualism the philosophical viewpoint that mind and body are separate entities that do not interact.

morbidity as a measure of health, the number of cases of a specific illness, injury, or disability in a given group of people at a given time.

mortality as a measure of health, the number of deaths due to a specific cause in a given group of people at a given time.

motor cortex lying at the rear of the frontal lobes, the region of the cerebral cortex that controls voluntary movements.

myocardial infarction (MI) a heart attack; the permanent death of heart tissue in response to an interruption of blood supply to the myocardium.

naloxone an opioid antagonist that binds to opioid receptors in the body to block the effects of natural opiates and painkillers.

naturopathic medicine the system that aims to provide holistic health care by drawing from several traditional healing systems, including homeopathy, herbal remedies, and traditional Oriental medicine.

negative emotionality a state of alcohol abuse characterized by depression and anxiety.

nicotine-titration model the theory that smokers who are physically dependent on nicotine regulate their smoking to maintain a steady level of the drug in their bodies.

nociceptor (no-chi-SEP-tur) a specialized neuron that responds to painful stimuli.

nonsteroidal anti-inflammatory drugs (NSAIDs) aspirin, ibuprofen, acetaminophen, and other analgesic drugs that relieve pain and reduce inflammation at the site of injured tissue.

obesity excessive accumulation of body fat.

observational study a nonexperimental research method in which a researcher observes and records the behavior of a research participant.

overweight body weight that exceeds the desirable weight for a person of a given height, age, and body shape.

palliative care health care that focuses on easing pain and providing comfort, especially at the end of life.

pandemic a worldwide epidemic such as AIDS.

pathogen a virus, bacterium, or some other microorganism that causes a particular disease.

periacqueductal gray (PAG) a region of the midbrain that plays an important role in the perception of pain; electrical stimulation in this region activates a descending neural pathway that produces analgesia by "closing the pain gate."

peripheral nervous system all the neurons outside the central nervous system; consists of both the somatic nervous system and the autonomic nervous system, which includes the sympathetic and parasympathetic nervous systems.

personal control the belief that we make our own decisions and determine what we do and what others do to us.

phantom limb pain following amputation of a limb, false pain sensations that appear to originate in the missing limb.

phenotype a person's observable characteristics; determined by the interaction of the individual's genotype with the environment.

pituitary gland the master endocrine gland controlled by the hypothalamus; releases a variety of hormones that act on other glands throughout the body.

population density a measure of crowding based on the total number of people living in an area of limited size.

positive psychology the study of optimal human functioning and the healthy interplay between people and their environments.

post-traumatic stress disorder (PTSD) a psychological disorder triggered by exposure to an extreme traumatic stressor, such as combat or a natural disaster. Symptoms of PTSD include haunting memories and nightmares of the traumatic event, extreme mental distress, and unwanted flashbacks.

prevalence the total number of diagnosed cases of a disease or condition that exist at a given time.

primary appraisal a person's initial determination of an event's meaning, whether irrelevant, benign-positive, or threatening.

primary prevention health-enhancing efforts to prevent disease or injury from occurring.

problem-focused coping coping strategy for dealing directly with a stressor, in which we either reduce the stressor's demands or increase our resources for meeting its demands.

progressive muscle relaxation a form of relaxation training that reduces muscle tension through a series of tensing and relaxing exercises involving the body's major muscle groups.

prospective study a forward-looking longitudinal study that begins with a healthy group of subjects and follows the development of a particular disease in that sample.

prostaglandin the chemical substance responsible for localized pain and inflammation; prostaglandin also causes free nerve endings to become more and more sensitized as time passes.

psychoactive drugs drugs that affect mood, behavior, and thought processes by altering the functioning of neurons in the brain; they include stimulants, depressants, and hallucinogens.

psychoneuroimmunology (PNI) the field of research that emphasizes the interaction of psychological, neural, and immunological processes in stress and illness.

psychosomatic medicine an outdated branch of medicine that focused on the diagnosis and treatment of physical diseases caused by faulty psychological processes.

quasi-experiment a study comparing two groups that differ naturally on a specific variable of interest.

random assignment assigning research participants to groups by chance, thus minimizing preexisting differences among the groups.

randomized clinical trial a true experiment that tests the effects of one independent variable on individuals (single-subject design) or on groups of individuals (community field trials).

rational-emotive therapy (RET) a confrontational form of cognitive therapy, developed by Albert Ellis, that challenges people's irrational ideas and attitudes.

reactivity our physiological reaction to stress, which varies by individual and affects our vulnerability to illness.

recurrent pain involves episodes of discomfort interspersed with periods in which the individual is relatively pain free, that recur for more than 3 months.

referred pain pain manifested in an area of the body that is sensitive to pain but caused by disease or injury in an area of the body that has few pain receptors.

regulatory control the various ways in which we modulate our thinking, emotions, and behavior over time and across changing circumstances.

relative risk a statistical indicator of the likelihood of a causal relationship between a particular health risk factor and a health outcome; computed as the ratio of the incidence (or prevalence) of a health condition—in a group exposed to the risk factor—to its incidence (or prevalence) in a group not exposed to the risk factor.

relaxation response a meditative state of relaxation in which metabolism slows and blood pressure lowers.

repressive coping an emotion-focused coping style in which we attempt to inhibit our emotional responses, especially in social situations, so we can view ourselves as imperturbable.

repressors people who cope with health problems and other aversive events by ignoring or distancing themselves from stressful information.

resilience the quality of some children to bounce back from environmental stressors that might otherwise disrupt their development.

restraint theory the theory that heightened sensitivity to norms for body weight triggers a pattern of eating that vacillates between strict dieting and binge eating.

reticular formation a network of neurons running through the brainstem involved with alertness and arousal.

retrospective study a backward-looking study in which a group of people who have a certain disease or condition are compared with a group of people who are free of the disease or condition, for the purpose of identifying background risk factors that may have contributed to the disease or condition.

retrovirus a virus that copies its genetic information onto the DNA of a host cell.

rumination repetitive focusing on the causes, meanings, and consequences of stressful experiences.

sarcoma cancer that strikes muscles, bones, and cartilage.

satiation a form of aversion therapy in which a smoker is forced to increase his or her smoking until an unpleasant state of "fullness" is reached.

scatterplot a graphed cluster of data points, each of which represents the values of two variables in a descriptive study.

secondary appraisal a person's determination of whether his or her own resources and abilities are sufficient to meet the demands of an event that is appraised as potentially threatening or challenging.

secondary gains the "rewards" associated with sick role behavior, including increased attention, the ability to rest, freedom from responsibility, and so forth.

secondary prevention actions taken to identify and treat an illness or disability early in its course.

sensitizers people who cope with health problems and other aversive events by closely scanning their bodies and environments for information.

sensory cortex lying at the front of the parietal lobes, the region of the cerebral cortex that processes body sensations such as touch.

set-point hypothesis the idea that each person's body weight is genetically set within a given range, or set point, that the body works hard to maintain.

slow nerve fibers small, unmyelinated nerve fibers that carry dull, aching pain.

social support companionship from others that conveys emotional concern, material assistance, or honest feedback about a situation.

sociocultural perspective theoretical perspective that focuses on how social and cultural factors contribute to health and disease.

stress management the various psychological methods designed to reduce the impact of potentially stressful experiences.

stress the process by which we perceive and respond to events, called stressors, that are perceived as harmful, threatening, or challenging.

stress-induced analgesia (SIA) a stress-related increase in tolerance to pain, presumably mediated by the body's endorphin system.

stressor any event or situation that triggers coping adjustments.

stroke a cerebrovascular accident that results in damage to the brain due to lack of oxygen; usually caused by atherosclerosis or arteriosclerosis.

subjective norm an individual's interpretation of the views of other people regarding a particular health-related behavior.

substance P a neurotransmitter secreted by pain fibers in the spinal cord that stimulates the transmission cells to send pain signals to the brain.

substantia gelatinosa the dorsal region of the spinal cord where both fast and slow pain fibers synapse with sensory nerves on their way to the brain.

survey a questionnaire used to ascertain the self-reported attitudes or behaviors of a group of people.

sympatho-adreno-medullary (SAM) system the body's initial, rapid-acting response to stress, involving the release of epinephrine and norepinephrine from the adrenal medulla under the direction of the sympathetic nervous system.

systematic desensitization a form of behavior therapy, commonly used for overcoming phobias, in which the person is exposed to a series of increasingly fearful situations while remaining deeply relaxed.

systems theory the viewpoint that nature is best understood as a hierarchy of systems, in which each system is simultaneously composed of smaller subsystems and larger, interrelated systems.

tension-reduction hypothesis an explanation of drinking behavior that proposes that alcohol is reinforcing because it reduces stress and tension.

teratogens drugs, chemicals, and environmental agents that can damage the developing person during fetal development.

tertiary prevention actions taken to contain damage once a disease or disability has progressed beyond its early stages.

thalamus the brain's sensory switchboard. Located on top of the brainstem, it routes messages to the cerebral cortex.

theory of planned behavior (TPB) a theory that predicts health behavior on the basis of three factors: personal attitude toward the behavior, the subjective norm regarding the behavior, and perceived degree of control over the behavior.

traditional Oriental medicine an ancient, integrated herb- and acupuncture-based system of healing founded on the principle that internal harmony is essential for good health.

transactional model Lazarus's theory that the experience of stress depends as much on the individual's cognitive appraisal of a potential stressor's impact as it does on the event or situation itself.

transcutaneous electrical nerve stimulation (TENS) a counterirritation form of analgesia involving electrically stimulating spinal nerves near a painful area.

transtheoretical model a widely used stage theory that contends that people pass through five stages in altering health-related behavior: precontemplation, contemplation, preparation, action, and maintenance.

Type A Friedman and Rosenman's term for competitive, hurried, hostile people who may be at increased risk for developing cardiovascular disease.

Type B Friedman and Rosenman's term for more relaxed people who are not pressured by time considerations and thus tend to be coronary-disease resistant.

Type C (cancer-prone) personality a passive, uncomplaining person who tends to repress emotions and may be prone to developing cancer.

veins blood vessels that carry blood back to the heart from the capillaries.

vitalism the concept of a general life force, popular in some varieties of complementary and alternative medicine.

weight cycling repeated weight gains and losses through repeated dieting.

withdrawal the unpleasant physical and psychological symptoms that occur when a person abruptly ceases using certain drugs.

X chromosome the sex chromosome found in males and females. Females have two X chromosomes; males have one.

Y chromosome the sex chromosome found only in males; contains a gene that triggers the testes to begin producing testosterone.

zidovudine (AZT) the first anti-AIDS drug; a reverse transcriptase inhibitor.

zygote a fertilized egg cell.

References

Abbey, A., Zawacki, T., & McAuslan, P. (2000). Alcohol's effects on sexual perception. Journal of Studies on Alcohol, 61, 688–697.

Ablashi, D. V., Eastman, H. B., Owen, C. B., Roman, M. M., Friedman, J., Zabriskie, J. B., Peterson, D. L., Pearson, G. R., & Whitman, J. E. (2000). Frequent HHV-6 reactivation in multiple sclerosis (MS) and chronic fatigue syndrome (CFS) patients. Journal of Clinical Virology, 16, 179–191.

Abood, D. A., & Chandler, S. B. (1997). Race and the role of weight, weight change, and body dissatisfaction in eating disorders. American Journal of Health Behavior, 21, 21–25.

Abraham, C., Sheeran, P., Spears, R., & Abrams, D. (1992). Health beliefs and promotion of HIV-preventive intentions among teenagers: A Scottish perspective. Health Psychology, 11, 363–370.

Abraido-Lanza, A. F. (2004). Social support and psychological adjustment among Latinas with arthritis: A test of a theoretical model. Annals of Behavioral Medicine, 27(3), 162–171.

Abrams, D. B., & Wilson, G. T. (1983). Alcohol, sexual arousal, and self-control. Journal of Personality and Social Psychology, 45, 188–198.

Accreditation Council for Graduate Medical Education. (2001). Outcome Project: Enhancing Residency Education through Outcomes Assessment. Author. www.acgme.org

Accreditation Council for Graduate Medical Education. (2004). Outcome Project. Author. http://www.acgme.org/Outcome/

Ackerman, B. P., Kogos, J., Youngstrom, E., Schoff, K., & Izard, C. (1999). Family instability and the problem behaviors of children from economically disadvantaged families. Developmental Psychology, 35, 258–268.

Adams, P., & Mylander, M. (1998). Gesundheit! Bringing good health to you, the medical system, and society through physician service, contemporary therapies, humor, and joy. Rochester, NY: Inner Traditions International.

Ader, R., & Cohen, N. (1985). CNS-immune system interactions: Conditioning phenomena. Behavioral and Brain Sciences, 8, 379–394.

Adler, N., & Matthews, K. (1994). Health psychology: Why do some people get sick and some stay well? Annual Review of Psychology, 45, 229–259.

Agid, Y., Arnulf, I., Bejjani, P., Block, F., Bonnet, A. M., Damier, P., Dubois, B., et al. (2003). Parkinson's disease is a neuropsychiatric disorder. Advances in Neurology, 91, 365–370.

Agras, W. S. (1993). Short-term psychological treatments for binge eating. In C. G. Fairburn & G. T. Wilson (Eds.), Binge eating: Nature, assessment, and treatment (pp. 270–286). New York: Guilford.

Ahmed, H. E., White, P. F., Craig, W. F., Hamza, M. A., et al. (2000). Use of percutaneous electrical nerve stimulation (PENS) in the short-term management of headache. Headache, 40(4), 311–315.

Ajzen I. (1985). From intentions to actions: A theory of planned behavior. In J. Kuhl & J. Beckman (Eds.), Action-control: From cognition to behavior (pp. 11–39). Heidelberg: Springer.

Al'Absi, M., Hatsukama, D., Davis, G. L., & Wittmers, L. E. (2004). Prospective examination of effects of smoking abstinence on cortisol and withdrawal symptoms as predictors of early smoking relapse. Drug and Alcohol Dependence, 73(3), 267–278.

Alba, R. D., Logan, J. R., & Stults, B. J. (2000). How segregated are middle-class African Americans? Social Problems, 47(4), 543–558.

Albarracin, D., McNatt, P. S., Williams, W. R., Howworth, T., Zenilman, J., Ho, R. M., et al. (2000). Structure of outcome beliefs in condom use. Health Psychology, 19, 458–468.

Aldercreutz, H. (2002). Phyto-oestrogens and cancer. Lancet, 3(6), 364–373.

Alexander, C. N., Langer, E. J., Newman, R. I., Chandler, H. M., & Davies, J. L. (1989). Transcendental meditation, mindfulness, and longevity: An experimental study with the elderly. Journal of Personality and Social Psychology, 57, 950–964.

Alexander, E. (1950). Psychosomatic medicine. New York: Norton.

Allen, J. R., & Setlow, V. P. (1991). Heterosexual transmission of HIV: A view of the future. Journal of the American Medical Association, 266, 1695–1696.

Allen, K., Shykoff, B. E., & Izzo, J. L. (2001). Pet ownership, but not ACE inhibitor therapy, blunts home blood pressure responses to mental stress. Hypertension, 38(4), 815–820.

Altman, D. G. (1995). Sustaining interventions in community systems: On the relationship between researchers and communities. Health Psychology, 14, 526–536.

Alzheimer's Association. (2000). Alzheimer's disease fact sheet. http://alzheimersdc-md.org/alzfacts.html

American Association of Naturopathic Physicians. (2006). Naturopathic medicine: How it works. The American Association of Naturopathic Physicians. http://naturopathic.lv0.net/DesktopDefault.aspx

American Cancer Society. (2006). Cancer facts and figures 2006. Atlanta: Author.

American Diabetes Association. (1997). National standards for diabetes self-management education programs and American Diabetes Association review criteria. Diabetes Care, 20, S67–S70.

American Hospital Association. (2006). Health and Hospital Trends. Author. http://www.aha.org/aha/about/index.html

American Medical Association. (1973). Proceedings of the house of delegates. New York: Author.

American Medical Association. (1995). Proceedings of the house of delegates. Chicago: Author.

American Psychiatric Association. (1997). Diagnostic and statistical manual of mental disorders (4th ed.). Washington, DC: Author.

American Psychological Association. (2006). Psychology's prescribing pioneers. Monitor on psychology, 37(7), 30.

Amigo, I., Buceta, J. M., Becona, E., & Bueno, A. M. (1991). Cognitive behavioral treatment for essential hypertension: A controlled study. *Stress Medicine, 7,* 103–108.

Amundsen, D. W. (1996). *Medicine, society, and faith in the ancient and medieval worlds.* Baltimore: Johns Hopkins University Press.

Anda, R., Williamson, D., Jones, D., Macera, C., Eaker, E., Glassman, A., et al. (1993). Depressed affect, hopelessness, and the risk of ischemic heart disease in a cohort of U.S. adults. *Epidemiology, 4,* 285–294.

Andersen, B., Ho, J., Brackett, J., Finkelstein, D., & Laffel, L. (1997). Parental involvement in diabetes management tasks: Relationships to blood glucose monitoring adherence and metabolic control in young adolescents with insulin-dependent diabetes mellitus. *Journal of Pediatrics, 130,* 257–265.

Anderson, E. A., Balon, T. W., Hoffman, R. P., Sinkey, C. A., & Mark, A. L. (1992). Insulin increases sympathetic activity but not blood pressure in borderline hypertensive humans. *Hypertension, 6,* 621–627.

Anderson, G. L., Manson, J., Wallace, R., Lund, B., Hall, D., Davis, S., Shumaker, S., Wang, C., Stein, E. & Prentice, R. (2003). Implementation of the women's health initiative study design. *Annals of Epidemiology, 13*(9), S5.

Anderson, L. P. (1999). Parentification in the context of the African American family. In N. D. Chase (Ed.), *Burdened children: Theory, research and treatment of parentification* (pp. 154–170). Thousand Oaks, CA: Sage Publications.

Anderson, R. A., Baron, R. S., & Logan, H. (1991). Distraction, control, and dental stress. *Journal of Applied Social Psychology, 21,* 156–171.

Andrasik, F., Blanchard, E. B., Arena, J. G., Teders, S. J., Teevan, R. C., & Rodichok, L. D. (1982). Psychological functioning in headache sufferers. *Psychosomatic Medicine, 44,* 171–182.

Andrews, J. A., Tildesley, E., Hops, H., & Li, F. (2002). The influence of peers on young adult substance use. *Health Psychology, 21*(4), 349–356.

Anton, R. F., & Kranzler, H. R. (1994). *The pharmacology of alcohol abuse.* New York: Springer-Verlag.

Antoni, M. H., Cruess, D. G., Cruess, S., Lutgendorf, S., Kumar, M., Ironson, G., et al. (2000). Cognitive-behavioral stress management intervention effects on anxiety, 24-hour urinary norepinephrine output, and T-cytotoxic/suppressor cells over time among symptomatic HIV-infected gay men. *Journal of Consulting & Clinical Psychology, 68,* 31–45.

Antoni, M. H., Lehman, J. M., Kilbourn, K. M., et al. (2001). Cognitive-behavioral stress management intervention decreases the prevalence of depression and enhances benefit finding among women under treatment for early-stage breast cancer. *Health Psychology, 20*(1), 20–32.

Antoni, M. H., & Schneiderman, N. (2001). HIV and AIDS. In D. W. Johnston & M. Johnston (Eds.), *Health psychology: Comprehensive clinical psychology* (Vol. 8, pp. 237–275). Amsterdam: Elsevier.

Antonovsky, A. (1990). Personality and health: Testing the sense of coherence model. In H. S. Friedman (Ed.), *Personality and disease* (pp. 155–177). New York: Wiley.

Ardell, D. B. (1985). *The history and future of wellness.* Dubuque, IA: Kendall/Hunt.

Arias, E. (2003). United States Life Tables. *National Vital Statistics Reports, 54*(14), 1–40.

Arnetz, B. B., Brenner, S. O., Levi, L., Hjelm, R., Petterson, I. L., Wasserman, J., Petrini, B., Eneroth, P., Kallner, A., & Kvetnansky, R. (1991). Neuroendocrine and immunologic effects of unemployment and job insecurity. *Psychotherapy and Psychosomatics, 55*(2–4), 76–80.

Aron, A., Norman, C. C., Aron, E. N., McKenna, C., & Heyman, R. E. (2000). Couples' shared participation in novel and arousing activities and experienced relationship quality. *Journal of Personality and Social Psychology, 78,* 273–284.

Aronoff, J., Stollak, G. E., & Woike, B. A. (1994). Affect regulation and the breadth of interpersonal engagement. *Journal of Personality and Social Psychology, 67,* 105–114.

Arora, N. K. Patient preferences for medical decision making: Who really wants to participate? *Medical Care, 38*(3), 335–341.

Arthur, C. M., Katkin, E. S., & Mezzacappa, E. S. (2004). Cardiovascular reactivity to mental arithmetic and cold pressor in African Americans, Caribbean Americans, and white Americans. *Annals of Behavioral Medicine, 27*(1), 31–37.

Arving, C., Per-Olow, B., Jonas, L., Annika T., et al. (2006). Satisfaction, utilization and perceived benefit of individual psychosocial support for breast cancer patients: A randomised study of nurse versus psychologist interventions, *Patient education and counseling, 62*(2), 243.

Aspinwall, L. G., Kemeny, M. E., Taylor, S. E., Schneider, S. G., & Dudley, J. P. (1991). Psychosocial predictors of gay men's AIDS risk-reduction behavior. *Health Psychology, 10,* 432–444.

Astin, J. A., Harkness, E., & Ernst, E. (2000). The efficacy of "distant healing": A systematic review of randomized trials. *Annals of Internal Medicine, 132,* 903–910.

Association of Psychologist in Academic Health Centers. (2006). Author. http://www.apa.org/divisions/div12/sections/section8/

Avants, S. K., Margolin, A., Holford, T. R., & Kosten, T. R. (2000). A randomized controlled trial of auricular acupuncture for cocaine dependence. *Archives of Internal Medicine, 160,* 2305–2312.

Ayanian, J. Z., & Epstein, A. M. (1991). Differences in the use of procedures between women and men hospitalized for coronary heart disease. *The New England Journal of Medicine, 325,* 221–225.

Ayanian, J. Z., & Epstein, A. M. (1997). Attitudes about treatment of coronary heart disease among women and men presenting for exercise testing. *Journal of General Internal Medicine, 12,* 311–314.

Azar, B. (1999). Antismoking ads that curb teen smoking. *American Psychological Association Monitor, 30,* 14.

Azar, B. (2001). A new take on psychoneuroimmunology. *Monitor on Psychology, 32*(11), 34–36.

Baer, J. S., Kivlahan, D. R., Fromme, K., & Marlatt, G. A. (1994). Secondary prevention of alcohol abuse with college populations: A skills-training approach. In G. S. Howard & P. E. Nathan (Eds.), *Alcohol use and misuse by young adults* (pp. 83–108). Notre Dame, IN: University of Notre Dame Press.

Bagley, S. P., Angel, R., Dilworth-Anderson, P., Liu, W., & Schinke, S. (1995). Adaptive health behaviors among ethnic minorities. *Health Psychology, 14*(7), 632–640.

Bagozzi, R. P. (1981). Attitudes, intentions, and behavior: A test of some key hypotheses. *Journal of Personality and Social Psychology, 41*, 607–627.

Bahra, A., Matharu, M. S., Buchel, C., Frackowiak, R. S. J., & Goadsby, P. J. (2001). Brainstem activation specific to migraine headache. *The Lancet, 357*, 1016–1017.

Baker, C. (2003). Predicting adolescent eating and activity behaviors: The role of social norms and personal agency. *Health Psychology, 22*(2), 189–198.

Baker, R., & Kirschenbaum, D. S. (1998). Weight control during the holidays: Highly consistent self-monitoring as a potentially useful coping mechanism. *Health Psychology, 17,* 367–370.

Balfour, L., White, R., Schiffrin, A., Dougherty, G., & Dufresne, J. (1993). Dietary disinhibition, perceived stress, and glucose control in young, type 1 diabetic women. *Health Psychology, 12,* 33–38.

Balter, M. (1996). New hope in HIV disease. *Science, 274,* 1988–1989.

Bandura, A. (1977). Self-efficacy: Toward a unifying theory of behavioral change. *Psychological Review, 84,* 191–215.

Bandura, A. (1992). Self-efficacy mechanism in psychobiologic functioning. In R. Schwarzer (Ed.), *Self-efficacy: Thought control of action* (pp. 255–394). Washington, DC: Hemisphere Publishing Group.

Bandura, A. (1997). *Self-efficacy: The exercise of control.* New York: Freeman.

Bandura, A., Cioffi, D., Taylor, C., Brouillard, M. E. (1988). Perceived self-efficacy in coping with cognitive stressors and opioid activation. *Journal of Personality and Social Psychology, 55*(3), 479–488.

Bandura, A., Taylor, C. B., Williams, S. L., Mefford, I. N., & Barchas, J. D. (1985). Catecholamine secretion as a function of perceived coping self-efficacy. *Journal of Consulting and Clinical Psychology, 53*(3), 406–414.

Banks, M. R., & Banks, W. A. (2002). The effects of animal-assisted therapy on loneliness in an elderly population in long-term care facilities. *Journal of Gerontology, 57*(7), M428.

Barefoot, J. C., Larsen, S., von der Lieth, L., & Schroll, M. (1995). Hostility, incidence of acute myocardial infarction, and mortality in a sample of older Danish men and women. *American Journal of Epidemiology, 142,* 477–484.

Bartlett, J. G., & Moore, R. D. (1998). Improving HIV therapy. *Scientific American, 279*(1), 84–87.

Bartholow, B. D., Sher, K. J., & Krull, J. L. (2003). Changes in heavy drinking over the third decade of life as a function of collegiate fraternity and sorority involvement: A prospective, multilevel analysis. *Health Psychology, 22*(6), 616–625.

Baruch, G. K., & Barnett, R. C. (1986). Consequences of fathers' participation in family work: Parents' role strain and well-being. *Journal of Personality and Social Psychology, 51,* 983–992.

Basbaum, A. I., & Fields, H. L. (1984). Endogenous pain control systems: Brainstem spinal pathways and endorphin circuitry. *Annual Review of Neuroscience, 7,* 309–338.

Bates, M. E., & Labouvie, E. W. (1995). Personality-environment constellations and alcohol use: A process-oriented study of intraindividual change during adolescence.

Bates, M. S., Rankin-Hill, L., & Sanchez-Ayendez, M. (1997). The effects of the cultural context of health care on treatment of and response to chronic pain and illness. *Social Science and Medicine, 45,* 1433–1477.

Baum, A. (1999). Health psychology: Mapping biobehavioral contributions to health and illness. *Annual Review of Psychology, 50,* 137–163.

Baum, A., Cohen, L., & Hall, M. (1993). Control and intrusive memories as possible determinants of chronic stress. *Psychosomatic Medicine, 55*(3), 274–286.

Baum, A., Davidson, L. M., Singer, J. E., & Street, S. W. (1987). Stress as a psychophysiological process. In A. Baum & J. E. Singer (Eds.), *Handbook of psychology and health, Vol. 5. Stress* (pp. 1–24). Hillsdale, NJ: Erlbaum.

Baum, A., & Fleming, I. (1993). Implications of psychological research on stress and technological accidents. *American Psychologist, 48,* 665–672.

Baum, A., Garofalo, J. P., & Yali, A. M. (2000). Socioeconomic status and chronic stress: Does stress account for SES effects on health. *Annals of the New York Academy of Sciences, 896,* 131–144.

Baum, A., Gatchel, R. J., & Krantz. (1997). *An introduction to health psychology* (3rd ed.). New York: McGraw-Hill.

Baum, A., & Grunberg, N. E. (1991). Gender, stress, and health. *Health Psychology, 10,* 80–85.

Baum, A., & Posluzny, D. M. (1999). Health psychology: Mapping biobehavioral contributions to health and illness. *Annual Review of Psychology, 50,* 137–163.

Baumann, L. J., Cameron, L.D., Zimmerman, R. S., & Leventhal, H. (1989). Illness representations and matching labels with symptoms. *Health Psychology, 8,* 449–469.

Baumeister, R. F. (1997). Esteem threat, self-regulatory breakdown, and emotional stress as factors in self-defeating behavior. *Review of General Psychology, 1,* 147–174.

Beaglehole, R., Bonita, R., & Kjellstrom, T. (1993) *Basic epidemiology.* Geneva: World Health Organization.

Bechara, A., Dolan, S., Denburg, N., Hindes, A., Anderson, S. W., & Nathan, P. E. (2001). Decision-making deficits, linked to a dysfunctional ventromedial prefrontal cortex, revealed in alcohol and stimulant abusers. *Neuropsychologia, 39,* 376–389.

Beck, K. H., & Frankel, A. (1981). A conceptualization of threat communications and protective health behavior. *Social Psychology Quarterly, 44,* 204–217.

Beckman, H. B., & Frankel, R. M. (1984). The effect of physician behavior on the collection of data. *Annals of Internal Medicine, 101,* 692–696.

Behrman, J. R. & Rosenzweig, M. R. (2004). Returns to birthweight. *The Review of Economics and Statistics, 86(2),* 586-601.

Belar, C. D., & Deardorff, W. W. (1996). *Clinical health psychology in medical settings: A practitioner's guidebook.* Washington, DC: American Psychological Association.

Bell, D. (1987). Gender difference in the social moderators of stress. In R. C. Barnett, L. Biener, & G. K. Baruch (Eds.), *Gender and stress* (pp. 257–277). New York: Free Press.

Bellack, J. P., Graber, D. R., O'Neil, E. H., Musham, C., & Lancaster, C. (1999). Curriculum trends in nurse practitioner programs: Current and ideal. *Journal of Professional Nursing, 15,* 15–27.

Ben-Hur, H. & Zeidner, M. (1996). Gender differences in coping reactions under community crisis and daily routine conditions. *Journal of Personality and Individual Differences, 20*(3), 331–340.

Benishek, L. A. (1996). Evaluation of the factor structure underlying two measures of hardiness. *Assessment, 3,* 423–435.

Bennett, H. L., Benson, D. R., & Kuiken, D. A. (1986). Preoperative instructions for decreased bleeding during spine surgery. *Anesthesiology, 65,* A245.

Bennett, M. P., Zeller, J. M., Rosenberg, L., & McCann, J. (2003). The effect of mirthful laughter on stress and natural killer cell activity. *Alternative Therapies in Health and Medicine, 9*(2), 38–47.

Bennett, P., & Carroll, D. (1997). Coronary heart disease: Impact. In A. Baum, S. Newman, J. Weinman, R. West, & C. McManus (Eds.), *Cambridge handbook of psychology, health and medicine* (pp. 419–421). Cambridge: Cambridge University Press.

Benson, H. (1993). The relaxation response. In D. Goleman & J. Gurin (Eds.), *Mind-body medicine: How to use your mind for better health* (pp. 233–257). New York: Consumer Reports Books.

Benson, H. (1996). *Timeless healing: The power and biology of belief.* New York: Scribner.

Benyamini, Y., Leventhal, E. A., & Leventhal, H. (1997). Attributions and health. In A. Baum, S. Newman, J. Weinman, R. West, & C. McManus (Eds.), *Cambridge handbook of psychology, health and medicine* (pp. 72–77). Cambridge: Cambridge University Press.

Berge, K. G. (1998). Herbal remedies: There's no magic. *Mayo Clinic Health Oasis.* http://www.mayohealth.org/mayo/9703/htm/herbs.htm

Berkman, L. F. (2000). From social integration to health: Durkheim in the new millennium. *Social Science and Medicine, 51*(6), 843–857.

Berkman, L. F., Melchior, M., Chastang, J., Niedhammer, I., et al. (2004). Social integration and mortality: A prospective study of french employees of electricity of France-Gas of France. *American Journal of Epidemiology, 159*(2), 167–174.

Berkman, L. F., & Syme, L. S. (1994). Social networks, host resistance, and mortality: A nine year follow-up study of Alameda County residents. In A. Steptoe & J. Wardle (Eds.), *Psychosocial processes and health: A reader* (pp. 43–67). Cambridge: Cambridge University Press.

Berman, B. M., Singh, B. B., Lao, L., Langenberg, P., et al. (1999). A randomized trial of acupuncture as an adjunctive therapy in osteoarthritis of the knee. *Rheumatology, 38*(4), 346–354.

Berry, J. W. (1997). Immigration, acculturation, and adaptation. *Applied Psychology: An International Review, 46,* 5–34.

Berry, J. W. & Worthington, E. L. (2001). Forgiveness, relationship quality, stress while imagining relationship events, and physical and mental health. *Journal of Counseling Psychology, 48*(4), 447–455.

Biener, L., & Heaton, A. (1995). Women dieters of normal weight: Their motives, goals, and risks. *American Journal of Public Health, 85,* 714–717.

Billings, A. G., & Moos, R. H. (1981). The role of coping responses and social resources in attenuating the stress of life events. *Journal of Behavioral Medicine, 4,* 139–157.

Birch, S., Hesselink, J. K., Jonkman, F. A., Hekker, T. A., & Bos, A. (2004). Clinical research on acupuncture: Part 1. What have reviews of the efficacy and safety of acupuncture told us so far? *The Journal of Alternative and Complementary Medicine, 10*(3), 468–480.

Black, J. S., Sefcik, T., & Kapoor, W. (1990). Health promotion and disease prevention in the elderly: Comparison of house staff and attending physician attitudes and practices. *Archives of Internal Medicine, 150,* 389–393.

Blackburn, G. L., & Bevis, L. C. (2002). The obesity epidemic: Prevention and treatment of the metabolic syndrome. http://www.medscape.com

Blair, S. N., Kohl, H. W., Paffenbarger, R. S., Clark, D. C., Cooper, K. H., & Gibbons, L. W. (1989). Physical fitness and all-cause mortality: A prospective study of healthy men and women. *Journal of the American Medical Association, 262,* 2395–2401.

Blakeslee, S. (1998, October 13). Placebos prove so powerful even experts are surprised. *The New York Times,* pp. D1, D4.

Blalock, S. J., DeVellis, R. F., Giorgino, K. B., DeVellis, B. M., Gold, D. T., Dooley, M. A., et al. (1996). Osteoporosis prevention in premenopausal women: Using a stage model approach to examine the predictors of behavior. *Health Psychology, 15,* 84–93.

Blanchard, E. B., & Hickling, E. J. (1997). *After the crash: Assessment and treatment of motor vehicle accident survivors.* Washington, DC: American Psychological Association.

Blankfield, R. P. (1991). Suggestion, relaxation, and hypnosis as adjuncts in the care of surgery patients: A review of the literature. *American Journal of Clinical Hypnosis, 33,* 172–186.

Block, K. L. (2004). Optimal healing environments and integrative cancer therapy. *Integrative Cancer Therapies, 3*(2), 95–97.

Bloor, L. E., Uchino, B. N., Hicks, A., & Smith, T. W. (2004). Social relationships and physiological function: The effects of recalling social relationships on cardiovascular reactivity. *Annals of Behavioral Medicine, 28*(1), 29–38.

Bolt, M. (2004). *Pursuing human strengths: A positive psychology guide.* New York: W. H. Freeman.

Bondi, N. (1997, March 19). Stressed out? Holding it in may be deadly. *The Detroit News,* p. A1.

Bonebright, C. A., Clay, D. L., & Ankenmann, R. D. (2000). The relationship of workaholism with work-life conflict, life satisfaction, and purpose in life. *Journal of Counseling Psychology, 47,* 469–477.

Bonham, V. L., Sellers, S. L., & Neighbors, H. W. (2004). John Henryism and self-reported physical health among high-socioeconomic status African-American men. *American Journal of Public Health, 94*(5), 737–738.

Booth, R. J., Cohen, S., Cunningham, A., Dossey, L., Dreher, H., Kiecolt-Glaser, J. K., et al. (2001). The state of the science:

The best evidence for the involvement of thoughts and feelings in physical health. *Advances in Mind-Body Medicine, 17,* 2–59.

Bor, R. (1997). AIDS. In A. Baum, S. Newman, J. Weinman, R. West, & C. McManus (Eds.), *Cambridge handbook of psychology, health and medicine* (pp. 343–347). Cambridge: Cambridge University Press.

Bor, R., & Elford, J. (1994). *The family and HIV.* London: Cassell.

Borland, R., Owen, N., & Hocking, B. (1991). Changes in smoking behaviour after a total workplace smoking ban. *Australian Journal of Public Health, 15,* 130–134.

Bosma, H., Stansfeld, S. A., & Marmot, M. G. (1998). Job control, personal characteristics, and heart disease. *Journal of Occupational Health Psychology, 3,* 402–409.

Boutelle, K. N. & Kirschenbaum, D. S. (1998). Further support for consistent self-monitoring as a vital component of successful weight control. *Obesity Research, 6*(3), 219–224.

Bowen, A. M., & Trotter, R. (1995). HIV risk in intravenous drug users and crack cocaine smokers: Predicting stage of change for condom use. *Journal of Consulting and Clinical Psychology, 63,* 238–248.

Bower, J. E., Kemeny, M. E., Taylor, S. E., & Fahey, J. L. (1998). Cognitive processing, discovery of meaning, CD4 decline, and AIDS-related mortality among bereaved HIV-seropositive men. *Journal of Consulting and Clinical Psychology, 66,* 979–986.

Bower, J. E., Kemeny, M. E., Taylor, S. E., & Fahey, J. L. (2003). Finding positive meaning and its association with natural killer cell cytotoxicity among participants in a bereavement-related disclosure intervention. *Annals of Behavioral Medicine, 25*(2), 146–155.

Boyles, S., Ness, R. B., Grisson, J. A., Markovic, N., Bromberger, J., & Cifelli, D. (2000). Life event stress and the association with spontaneous abortion in gravid women at an urban emergency department. *Health Psychology, 19,* 510–514.

Bradley, C. (1997). Diabetes mellitus. In A. Baum, S. Newman, J. Weinman, R. West, & C. McManus (Eds.), *Cambridge handbook of psychology, health and medicine* (pp. 432–436). Cambridge: Cambridge University Press.

Bradley, L. A. (1993). Pain measurement in arthritis. *Arthritis Care and Research, 6,* 178–186.

Brady, S. S., & Matthews, K. A. (2006). Chronic stress influences ambulatory blood pressure in adolescents. *Annals of Behavioral Medicine, 31*(1), 80–88.

Bray, G. A. (1969). Effect of caloric restriction on energy expenditure in obese patients. *The Lancet, 2,* 397–398.

Brems, C., & Johnson, M. E. (1989). Problem-solving appraisal and coping style: The influence of sex-role orientation and gender. *Journal of Psychology, 123,* 187–194.

Brennan, A. F., Walfish, S., & AuBuchon, P. (1986). Alcohol use and abuse in college students: A review of individual and personality correlates. *International Journal of the Addictions, 21,* 449–474.

Breslau, N., & Rasmussen, B. K. (2001). The impact of migraine: Epidemiology, risk factors, and co-morbidities. *Neurology* (Special Issue: Headache-related disability in the management of migraine), *56,* S4–S12.

Brewer, B. W., & Karoly, P. (1992). Recurrent pain in college students. *Journal of American College Health, 41,* 67–69.

Brink, S. (1998). The hospitalist. *U.S. News & World Report, 125*(4), 48–54.

Broadbent, E., Petrie, K. J., Alley, P. G., & Booth, R. J. (2003). Psychological stress impairs early wound repair following surgery. *Psychosomatic Medicine, 65*(5), 865–869.

Brody, H. (2000a, July/August). Mind over medicine. *Psychology Today,* 60–67.

Brody, H. (2000b) *The placebo response.* New York: HarperCollins.

Brody, J. (1996a, February 28). Good habits outweigh genes as key to a healthy old age. *The New York Times,* p. B11.

Brody, J. (1998c, November 30). Diet is not a panacea, but it cuts risk of cancer. *New York Times.* http://www.nytimes.com

Brondolo, E., Rieppi, R., Kelly, K. P., & Gerin, W. (2003). Perceived racism and blood pressure: A review of the literature and conceptual and methodological critique. *Annals of Behavioral Medicine, 25*(1), 55–65.

Bronzaft, A. L., & McCarthy, D. P. (1975). The effect of elevated train noise on reading ability. *Environment and Behavior, 7,* 517–527.

Brook, J., Cohen, P., Whiteman, M., & Gordon, A. S. (1992). Psychosocial risk factors in the transition from moderate to heavy use or abuse of drugs. In M. D. Glantz & R. W. Pickens (Eds.), *Vulnerability to drug abuse* (pp. 359–388). Washington, DC: American Psychological Association.

Brook, J. S., Brook, D. W., Arencibia-Mireles, O. Richter, L., & Whiteman, M. (2001). Risk factors for adolescent marijuana use across cultures and across time. *Journal of Genetic Psychology, 162*(3), 357.

Brown, J. D. (1991). Staying fit and staying well: Physical fitness as a moderator of life stress. *Journal of Personality and Social Psychology, 60,* 555–561.

Brown, J. D., & Siegel, J. M. (1988). Exercise as a buffer of life stress: A prospective study of adolescent health. *Health Psychology, 7,* 341–353.

Brownell, K. D. (2003). *Food fight: The inside story of the food industry, America's obesity crisis and what we can do about it.* New York: McGraw-Hill.

Brownell, K. D., & Wadden, T. A. (1991). The heterogeneity of obesity: Fitting treatments to individuals. *Behavior Therapy, 22,* 153–177.

Brownlee, C. (2006). Eat smart. Foods may affect the brain as well as the body. *Science News, 169,* 136–137.

Brownlee, S. (1995, October 2). The route of phantom pain. *U.S. News & World Report, 119,* 76.

Brubaker, R. G., & Wickersham, D. (1990). Encouraging the practice of testicular self-examination: A field application of the theory of reasoned action. *Health Psychology, 9,* 154–163.

Bruch, H. (1982). Anorexia nervosa: Therapy and theory. *American Journal of Psychiatry, 139,* 1531–1538.

Bullock, M. L., Culliton, P. D., & Olander, R. T. (1989). Controlled trial of acupuncture for severe recidivist alcoholism. *The Lancet, 1989,* 1435–1438.

Bullock, M. L., Kiresuk, T. J., & Pheley, A. M. (1999). Auricular acupuncture in the treatment of cocaine abuse. A study of efficacy and dosing. *Journal of Substance Abuse Treatment, 16,* 31–38.

Bullock, M. L., Umen, A. J., Culliton, P. D., & Olander, R. T. (1987). Acupuncture treatment of alcoholic recidivism: A pilot study. *Alcoholism: Clinical and Experimental Research, 11,* 292–295.

Burack, J. H., Barrett, D. C., Stall, R. D., Chesney, M. A., Ekstrand, M. L., & Coates, T. J. (1993). Depressive symptoms and CD4 lymphocyte decline among HIV-infected men. *Journal of the American Medical Association, 270,* 2568–2573.

Burbach, D. J., & Peterson, L. (1986). Children's concepts of physical illness: A review and critique of the cognitive-developmental literature. *Health Psychology, 5,* 307–325.

Bureau of Labor Statistics. (2006). Physician Assistants. http://www.bls.gov/soc/soc_j1h1.htm

Bureau of Labor Statistics. (2006). Regional variations in workplace homicide rates. U.S. Department of Labor. http://www.bls.gov/opub/cwc/sh20031119ar01p1.htm

Burd, S. (1994). NIH issues rules requiring women and minorities in clinical trials. *The Chronicle of Higher Education, 40,* A50.

Burks, N., & Martin, B. (1985). Everyday problems and life change events: Ongoing versus acute sources of stress. *Journal of Human Stress, 1985, 11,* 27–35.

Burnam, M. A., Timbers, D. M., & Hough, R. L. (1984). Two measures of psychological distress among Mexican Americans, Mexicans, and Anglos. *Journal of Health and Social Behavior, 25,* 24–33.

Burrows, G. D., Elton, D., & Stanley, G. V. (1979). The relationship between psychophysical and perceptual variables and chronic pain. *British Journal of Social and Clinical Psychology, 18,* 425–430.

Burstein, A. (1985). Posttraumatic stress disorder. *Journal of Clinical Psychiatry, 46*(7), 300–301.

Bush, C., Ditto, B., & Feuerstein, M. (1985). A controlled evaluation of paraspinal EMG biofeedback in the treatment of chronic low back pain. *Health Psychology 4,* 307–321.

Butler, E. A., Egloff, B., Wilhelm, F. H., Smith, N. C., Erickson, E. A., & Gross, J. J. (2003). The social consequences of expressive suppression. *Emotion, 3*(1), 48–67.

Bynum, R. (2004, Nov. 1). *Associated Press.*

Byrnes, D. M., Antoni, M. H., Goodkin, K., Efantis-Potter, J., et al. (1998). Stressful events, pessimism, natural killer cell cytotoxicity, and cytotoxic/suppressor T cells in HIV+ Black women at risk for cervical cancer. *Psychosocmatic Medicine, 60*(6), 714–722.

Caetano, R. (1987). Acculturation and drinking patterns among US Hispanics. *British Journal of Addictions, 82,* 789–799.

Calam, R., Waller, G., Slade, P. D., & Newton, T. (1990). Eating disorders and perceived relationships with parents. *International Journal of Eating Disorders, 9,* 479–485.

Calandra, C., Musso, F., & Musso, R. (2003). The role of leptin in the etiopathogenesis of anorexia nevosa and bulimia. *Eating and Weight Disorders, 8*(2), 130–137.

Calhoun, J. B. (1970). Space and the strategy of life. *Ekistics, 29,* 425–437.

Calle, E. E., Miracle-McMahill, H. L., Thun, M. J., & Heath, C.W. (1994). Cigarette smoking and risk of fatal breast cancer. *American Journal of Epidemiology, 139*(10), 1001–1007.

Calle, E. E., Thun, M. J., Petrelli, J. M., Rodriguez, C., & Heath, C. W. (1999). Body-mass index and mortality in a prospective cohort of U.S. adults. *New England Journal of Medicine, 341*(15), 1097–1105.

Cameron, L., Leventhal, E. A., & Leventhal, H. (1993). Symptom representations and affect as determinants of care seeking in a community-dwelling, adult sample population. *Health Psychology, 12,* 171–179.

Cameron, L., Leventhal, E. A., & Leventhal, H. (1995). Seeking medical care in response to symptoms and life stress. *Psychosomatic Medicine, 57,* 37–47.

Camp, D. E., Klesges, R. C., & Relyea, G. (1993). The relationship between body weight concerns and adolescent smoking. *Health Psychology, 12,* 24–32.

Campaign for Tobacco-Free Kids. (2006). Federal tax burdens on U.S. households caused by tobacco use. http://www.tobaccofreekids.org

Cannon, W. (1932). *The wisdom of the body.* New York: Norton.

Canoy, D., Luben, R., Welch, A., Bingham, S., et al. (2004). Abdominal obesity and respiratory function in men and women in the EPIC-Norfolk Study, United Kingdom. *American Journal of Epidemiology, 159*(12), 1140–1149.

Cantor, D. W., Boyce, T. E., & Repetti, R. L. (2004). Ensuring healthy working lives. In R. H. Rozensky, N. G. Johnson, C. D. Goodheart, & W. R. Hammond (Eds.), *Psychology builds a healthy world.* Washington, D.C.: American Psychological Association.

Caplan, R. D., & Jones, K. W. (1975). Effects of work load, role ambiguity, and Type A personality on anxiety, depression, and heart rate. *Journal of Applied Psychology, 60,* 713–719.

Carels, R. A., Darby, L., Cacciapaglia, H., Douglass, O. M., et al. (2005). Applying a stepped-care approach to the treatment of obesity. *Journal of Psychosomatic Research, 59*(6), 375–383.

Carnethon, M. R., Gidding, S. S., Nehgme, R., Sidney, S., et al. (2003). Cardiorespiratory fitness in young adulthood and the development of cardiovascular disease risk factors. *Journal of the American Medical Association, 290*(23), 3092–3100.

Carpenter, K. M., Hasin, D. S., Allison, D. B., & Faith, M. S. (2000). Relationships between obesity and DSM-IV major depressive disorder, suicide ideation, and suicide attempts: Results from a general population study. *American Journal of Public Health, 90,* 251–257.

Carpenter, S. (2001, June). Cognition is central to drug addiction. *Monitor on Psychology* (special issue on substance abuse) *32,* 34–35.

Carter, J. C., & Fairburn, C. G. (1998). Cognitive-behavioral self-help for binge eating disorder: A controlled effectiveness study. *Journal of Consulting and Clinical Psychology, 66,* 616–623.

Cartwright, F. F. (1972). *Disease and history.* New York: Crowell.

Cartwright, M., Wardle, J., Steggles, N., Simon, A. E., Croker, H., & Jarvis, M. J. (2003). Stress and dietary practices in adolescents. *Health Psychology, 22*(4), 362–369.

Carvajal, S. C., Garner, R. L., & Evans, R. I. (1998). Dispositional optimism as a protective factor in resisting HIV exposure in sexually active inner-city minority adolescents. *Journal of Applied Social Psychology, 28,* 2196–2211.

Carver, C. S., & Glass, D. C. (1978). Coronary-prone behavior pattern and interpersonal aggression. *Journal of Personality & Social Psychology, 36,* 361–366.

Carver, C. S., Pozo, C., Harris, S. D., Noriega, V., & Scheier, M. F. (1993). How coping mediates the effect of optimism on distress: A study of women with early stage breast cancer. *Journal of Personality and Social Psychology, 65,* 375–390.

Carver, C. S. & Scheier, M. F. (2002). Optimism. In Snyder, C. R. & S. J. Lopez (Eds.), *Handbook of positive psychology* (pp. 231–243). New York: Oxford University Press.

Carver, C. S., Scheier, M. F., & Weintraub, J. K. (1989). Assessing coping strategies: A theoretically based approach. *Journal of Personality and Social Psychology, 56,* 267–283.

Carver, C. S., Smith, R. G., Antoni, M. H., Petronis, V. M., et al. (2005). Optimistic personality and psychosocial well-being during treatment predict psychosocial well-being among long-term survivors of breast cancer. *Health Psychology, 24*(5), 508–515.

Cash, T. F., & Henry, P. E. (1995). Women's body images: The results of a national survey in the U.S.A. *Sex Roles, 33,* 19–28.

Caspersen, C. J., Bloemberg, B. P., Saris, W. H., Merritt, R. K., & Kromhout, D. (1991). The prevalence of selected physical activities and their relation with coronary heart disease risk factors in elderly men: The Zutphen Study, 1985. *American Journal of Epidemiology, 133,* 1078–1092.

Catalano, R. A., Rook, K., & Dooley, D. (1986). Labor markets and help-seeking: A test of the employment security hypothesis. *Journal of Health and Social Behavior, 27,* 277–287.

Catania, J. A., Binson, D., Dolcini, M. M., Moskowitz, J. T., & van der Straten, A. (2001). Frontiers in the behavioral epidemiology of HIV/STDs. In A. Baum, T. A. Revenson, & J. E. Singer (Eds.), *Handbook of health psychology* (pp. 777–799). Mahwah, NJ: Erlbaum.

CEBM. (2004). Introduction to evidence-based medicine. Oxford Center for Evidence-Based Medicine. www.cebm.net

Celle, D., Hughs, C., Peterman, A., Chang, C., et al. (2002). A brief assessment of concerns associated with genetic testing for cancer: The multidimensional impact of cancer risk assessment (MICRA) questionnaire. *Health Psychology, 21*(6), 564–572.

Centers for Disease Control and Prevention. (2003). *AIDS public information data in the United States for the years 1981–2002.* http://wonder.cdc.gov/wonder/help/aids.html

Centers for Disease Control and Prevention. (2005). *Health, United States, 2005.* National Center for Health Statistics. Hyattsville, MD.

Centers for Disease Control and Prevention. (2005). *National diabetes fact sheet, United States, 2005.* Atlanta, GA: U.S. Department of Health and Human Services.

Centers for Disease Control and Prevention. (2006). *Update: Trends in AIDS Incidence-United States.* Centers for Disease Control and Prevention, *MMWR, 46*(37), 861–867.

Centers for Disease Control and Prevention. (2005, April 1). *Tobacco Use, Access, and Exposure to Tobacco in Media Among Middle and High School Students—United States, 2004. MMWR, 54*(12), 297–301. http://www.cdc.gov/mmwr

Cervero, F. (2000). Visceral hyperalgesia revisited. *The Lancet, 9236,* 1127–1135.

Chamberlin, J. (2001, June). NIAAA to release findings of student drinking study. *Monitor on Psychology* (special issue on substance abuse), *32,* 13.

Champion, V. L. (1994). Strategies to increase mammography utilization. *Medical Care, 32,* 118–129.

Changing America: Indicators of social and economic well-being by race and Hispanic origin. (1998). Washington, DC: The President's Council of Economic Advisers.

Chaplin, W., Gerin, W., Holland, J., Alter, R., Wheeler, R., Duong, D., & Pickering, T. G. (2003). Effects of 9/11/2001 terrorist attacks on blood pressure in four regions of the US. *American Journal of Hypertension, 16*(5), A45.

Chartrand, L. J., & Seidman, E. G. (1996). Celiac disease is a life-long disorder. *Clinical and Investigative Medicine, 19,* 357–361.

Chassin, L., Presson, C. C., Sherman, S. J., et al. (2003). Historical changes in cigarette smoking and smoking-related beliefs after 2 decades in a midwestern community. *Health Psychology, 22*(4), 347–353.

Chassin, L., Presson, C. C., Todd, M., Rose, J. S., & Sherman, S. J. (1998). Maternal socialization of adolescent smoking: The intergenerational transmission of parenting and smoking. *Developmental Psychology, 34,* 1189–1201.

Chermack, S. T., & Giancola, P. R. (1997). The relation between alcohol and aggression: An integrated biopsychosocial conceptualization. *Clinical Psychology Review, 17,* 621–649.

Chiaramonte, G. R., & Friend, R. (2006). Medical students' and residents' gender bias in the diagnosis, treatment, and interpretation of coronary heart disease symptoms. *Health Psychology, 25*(3), 255–266.

Chobanian, A. V., Bakris, A. V., Black, H. R., Cushman, W. C., Green, L. A., et al. (2003). The seventh report of the Joint National Committee on prevention, detection, evaluation, and treatment of high blood pressure. *Journal of the American Medical Association, 289*(19), 2560–2572.

Choi, W. S., Harris, K. J., Okuyemi, K., & Ahluwalia, J. S. (2003). Predictors of smoking initiation among college-bound high school students. *Annals of Behavioral Medicine, 26*(1), 69–74.

Christeff, N., Lortholary, O., Casassus, P., Thobie, N., Veyssier, P., Torri, O., et al. (1996). Relationship between sex steroid hormone levels and CD4 lymphocytes in HIV infected men. *Experimental and Clinical Endocrinology and Diabetes, 104,* 130–136.

Christensen, A. J., Moran, P. J., Wiebe, J. S., Ehlers, S. L., & Lawton, W. J. (2002). Effect of a behavioral self-regulation intervention on patient adherence in hemodialysis. *Health Psychology, 21*(4), 393–397.

Christensen, A. J., Smith, T. W., Turner, C. W., Holman, J. M., & Gregory, M. C. (1990). Type of hemodialysis and preference for behavioral involvement: Interactive effects on adherence in end-stage renal disease. *Health Psychology, 9*(2), 225–236.

Christoffel, K. K., & Ariza, A. (1998). The epidemiology of overweight in children: Relevance for clinical care. *Pediatrics, 101,* 103–105.

Ciechanowski, P. S., Katon, W. J., Russon, J. E., & Walker, E. A. (2001). The patient–provider relationship: Attachment theory and adherence to treatment in diabetes. *American Journal of Psychiatry, 158,* 29–35.

Cinciripini, P. M., Cinciripini, L. G., Wallfisch, A., Hague, W., & Van Vunakis, H. (1996). Behavior therapy and the transdermal nicotine patch: Effects on cessation outcome, affect, and coping. *Journal of Consulting and Clinical Psychology, 64,* 314–323.

Clayton, R. R., & Ritter, C. (1985). The epidemiology of alcohol and drug abuse among adolescents. *Advances in Alcohol and Substance Abuse, 4,* 69–97.

Clement, K., Boutin, P., & Froguel, P. (2002). Genetics of obesity. *American Journal of Pharmacogenomics, 2*(3), 177–187.

Clark, A., Seidler, A., & Miller, M. (2001). Inverse association between sense of humor and coronary heart disease. *International Journal of Cardiology, 80*(1), 87–88.

Clark, K. (1999). Why it pays to quit. *U.S. News & World Report,* November 1, 74.

Clark, W. C., & Mehl, L. (1971). Thermal pain: A sensory decision theory analysis of the effect of age and sex on d', various response criteria, and 50% pain threshold. *Journal of Abnormal Psychology, 78,* 202–212.

Cleary, P. D. (2003). A hospitalization from hell: A patient's perspective on quality. *Annals of Internal Medicine, 138*(1), 33–39.

Cloninger, C. R. (1987). Neurogenetic adaptive mechanisms in alcoholism. *Science, 236,* 410–416.

Cloninger, C. R., Bohman, M., Sigvardsson, S., & von Knorring, A. L. (1985). Psychopathology in adopted-out children of alcoholics. The Stockholm Adoption Study. *Recent Developments in Alcoholism, 3,* 37–51.

CNNMoney.Com (2006). 50 Best Jobs in America. http://money. cnn.com/magazines/moneymag/moneymag_archive/2006/05/ 01/8375749/index.htm

Coates, T. J., Stall, R. D., & Hoff, C. C. (1990). Changes in sexual behavior among gay and bisexual men since the beginning of the AIDS epidemic. In L. Temoshok & A. Baum (Eds.), *Psychosocial perspectives on AIDS: Etiology, prevention, and treatment* (pp. 103–137). Hillsdale, NJ: Erlbaum.

Cochran, S. D., & Mays, V. M. (1990). Sex, lies, and HIV. *New England Journal of Medicine, 322,* 774–775.

Cohen, J. (2006, July 28). The overlooked epidemic. *Science, 313,* 468–469.

Cohen, S., & Herbert, T. B. (1996). Health psychology: Psychological factors and physical disease from the perspective of human psychoneuroimmunology. *Annual Review of Psychology, 47,* 113–132.

Cohen, S., Kaplan, J. R., & Mauck, S. B. (1994). Social support and coronary heart disease: Underlying psychological and biological mechanisms. In S. A. Shumaker, & S. M. Czajkowski (Eds.), *Social support and cardiovascular disease.* New York: Plenum Press.

Cohen, S., & McKay, G. (1984). Social support, stress and the buffering hypothesis: A theoretical analysis. In A. Baum, S. E. Taylor, & J. E. Singer (Eds.), *Handbook of psychology and health* (pp. 253–268). Hillsdale, NJ: Erlbaum.

Cohen, S., & Wills, T. A. (1985). Stress, social support, and the buffering hypothesis. *Psychological Bulletin, 93,* 310–357.

Cohen, S., Doyle, W. T., & Turner, R.B. (2004). Childhood socioeconomic status and host resistance to infectious illness in adulthood. *Psychosomatic Medicine, 66*(4), 553-558.

Cohen, S., Frank, E., Doyle, W. J., Skoner, D. P., Rabin, B. S. & Gwaltney, J. M. (1998). Types of stressors that increase susceptibility to the common cold in healthy adults. *Health Psychology, 17,* 214–223.

Cohen, S., Glass, D. C., & Singer, J. E. (1973). Apartment noise, auditory discrimination, and reading ability in children. *Journal of Experimental Social Psychology, 9,* 407–422.

Cohen, S., Miller, G. E., & Rabin, B. S. (2001). Psychological stress and antibody response to immunization: A critical review of the human literature. *Psychosomatic Medicine, 63*(1), 7–18.

Cohen, S., Sherrod, D. R., & Clark, M. S. (1986). Social skills and the stress-protective role of social support. *Journal of Personality and Social Psychology, 50,* 963–973.

Colditz, G. A., Willett, W. C., Hunter, D. J., Stampfer, M. J., Manson, J. E., Hennekens, C. H., et al. (1993). Family history, age, and risk of breast cancer. Prospective data from the Nurses' Health Study. *Journal of the American Medical Association, 270,* 338–343.

Cole, S. W., Kemeny, M. E., Taylor, S. E., Visscher, B. R., & Fahey, J. L. (1996). Accelerated course of human immunodeficiency virus infection in gay men who conceal their homosexual identity. *Psychosomatic Medicine, 58,* 219–231.

Coleman, L. M., Fowler, L. L., & Williams, M. E. (1995). Use of unproven therapies by people with Alzheimer's disease. *Journal of the American Geriatrics Society, 43,* 747–750.

Colligan, R. C., & Offord, K. P. (1988). The risky use of the MMPI hostility scale in assessing risk for coronary heart disease. *Psychosomatics, 29,* 188–196.

Collins, N. L., Dunkel-Schetter, C., Lobel, M., & Scrimshaw, S. C. (1993). Social support in pregnancy: Psychosocial correlates of birth outcomes and postpartum depression. *Journal of Personality and Social Psychology, 65,* 1243–1258.

Compas, B. E., Haaga, D. A., Keefe, F. J., Leitenberg, H., & Williams, D. A. (1998). Sampling of empirically supported psychological treatments from health psychology: Smoking, chronic pain, cancer, and bulimia nervosa. *Journal of Consulting and Clinical Psychology, 66,* 89–112.

Conner, M., Norman, P., & Bell, R. (2002). The theory of planned behavior and healthy eating. *Health Psychology, 21*(2), 194–201.

Conner, M., & Sparks, P. (1996). The theory of planned behaviour and health behaviours. In M. Conner & P. Normal (Eds.), *Predicting health behavior: Research and practice with social cognition models* (pp. 121–162). Buckingham, UK: Open University Press, 121–162.

Conrad, C. D., Magarinos, A. M., LeDoux, J. E., & McEwen, B. S. (1999). Repeated restrain stress facilitates fear conditioning independently of causing hippocampal CA3 dendritic atrophy. *Behavioral Neuroscience, 13,* 902–913.

Contrada, R. J., Goyal, T. M., Cather, C., Rafalson, L., et al. (2004). Psychosocial factors in outcomes of heart surgery: The impact of religious involvement and depressive symptoms. *Health Psychology, 23*(3), 227–238.

Cook, E. H., Stein, M. A., Krasowski, M. D., Cox, N. J., Olkon, D. M., Kieffer, J. E., & Levanthal, B. L. (1995). Association of attention-deficit disorder and the dopamine transporter gene. *American Journal of Human Genetics, 56*, 993–998.

Cook, S., Weitzman, M., Auinger, P., Nguyen, M., & Dietz, W. H. (2003). Prevalence of a metabolic syndrome phenotype in adolescents: Findings from the third National Health and Nutrition Examination Survey. *Archives of Pediatrics & Adolescent Medicine, 157*(8), 821–827.

Cooper, M. L., Pierce, R. S., & Tidwell, M. O. (1995). Parental drinking problems and adolescent offspring substance use: Moderating effects of demographic and familial factors. *Psychology of Addictive Behaviors, 9*, 36–52.

Cooper, R. A., & Stoflet, S. J. (1996). Trends in the education and practice of alternative medicine clinicians. *Health Affairs, 15*, 226–238.

Cooper, R. S., Rotimi, C. N., & Ward, R. (1999). The puzzle of hypertension in African-Americans. *Scientific American, 280*(2), 56–63.

Corelli, R. L., & Hudmon, K. S., (2002). Medications for smoking cessation. *The Western Journal of Medicine, 176*(2), 131–135.

Cornelis, M. C., El-Sohemy, A., Kabagambe, E. K., & Campos, H. (2006). Coffee, CYP1A2 genotype, and risk of myocardial infarction. *Journal of the American Medical Association, 295*(1), 1135–1141.

Costa, P. T., & McCrae, R. R. (1985). Hypochondriasis, neuroticism, and aging. When are somatic complaints unfounded? *American Psychologist, 40*, 19–28.

Cousins, N. (1976). Anatomy of an illness: As perceived by the patient. *New England Journal of Medicine, 295*, 1458–1463.

Cousins, N. (1979). *Anatomy of an illness as perceived by the patient: Reflections on healing and regeneration* (p. 695). New York: Norton.

Cox, D. J., Gonder-Frederick, L., Julian, D. M., & Clarke, W. (1994). Long-term follow-up evaluation of blood glucose awareness training. *Diabetes Care, 17*, 1–5.

Crawford, A. M. (2002). Familial predictors of treatment outcome in childhood anxiety disorders. *Journal of the American Academy of Child & Adolescent Psychiatry, 40*(1), 1182–1189.

Crawford, J. P., Hickson, G. S., & Wiles, M. R. (1986). The management of hypertensive disease: A review of spinal manipulation and the efficacy of conservative therapeusis. *Journal of Manipulative and Physiological Therapeutics, 9*, 27–32.

Crowell, N. A., & Burgess, A. W. (1996). *Understanding violence against women.* Washington, DC: National Academy Press.

Croyle, R. T., & Uretsky, M. B. (1987). Effects of mood on self-appraisal of health status. *Health Psychology, 6*, 239–253.

Cruess, D. G., Antoni, M. H., McGregor, B. A., Kilbourn, K. M., et al. (2000). Cognitive-behavioral stress management reduces serum cortisol by enhancing benefit finding among women being treated for early stage breast cancer. *Psychosomatic Medicine, 62*(3), 304–308.

Cruikshank, M. (2003). *Learning to Be Old: Gender, Culture, and Aging.* New York: Roman & Littlefield.

CTUMS (Canadian Tobacco Use Monitoring Survey). (2004). *Health Canada.* http://www.hc-sc.gc.ca/hl-vs/tobac-tabac/research-recherche/stat/ctums-esutc/2004/index_e.html

Culliton, P. D., Boucher, T. A., & Bullock, M. L. (1999). Complementary/alternative therapies in the treatment of alcohol and other addictions. In J. W. Spencer & J. J. Jacobs (Eds.), *Complementary/alternative medicine: An evidence-based approach.* St Louis: Mosby.

Cummings, D. E., Foster-Schubert, K. E. & Overduin, J. (2005). Ghrelin and energy balance: Focus on current controversies. *Current Drug Targets, 6*(2), 153–169.

Cunningham, A. J., Edmonds, C. V., Jenkins, G. P., Pollack, H., Lockwood, G. A., & Warr, D. (1998). A randomized controlled trial of the effects of group psychological therapy on survival in women with metastatic breast cancer. *Psycho-oncology, 7*(6), 508–517.

Cvengros, J. A., Christensen, A. J., & Lawton, W. J. (2004). The role of perceived control and preference for control in adherence to a chronic medical regimen. *Annals of Behavioral Medicine, 27*(3), 155–161.

Daffner, K. R., Scinto, L. F., Weintraub, S., Guinessey, J., & Mesulam, M. M. (1994). The impact of aging on curiosity as measured by exploratory eye movements. *Archives of Neurology, 51*, 368–376.

Daley, S. (1998). Dead zones: The burden of shame. *New York Times.* http://www.nytimes.com

Dallongeville, J. Y., Ducimetiere, P., Arveiler, D. Ferrieres, J., et al. (2003). Fish consumption is associated with lower heart rates. *Circulation, 108*(7), 820–825.

D'Amico, E. J., & Fromme, K. (1997). Health risk behaviors of adolescent and young adult siblings. *Health Psychology, 16*(5), 426–432.

Daniels, K. (2006). Rethinking job characteristics in work stress research. *Human Relations, 59*(3), 267–290.

Dattore, P. J., Shontz, F. C., & Coyne, L. (1980). Premorbid personality differentiation of cancer and non-cancer groups: A list of the hypotheses of cancer proneness. *Journal of Consulting and Clinical Psychology, 48*, 388–394.

Davies, G. M., Willner, P., James, D. L., & Morgan, M. J. (2004). Influence of nicotine gum on acute cravings for cigarettes. *Journal of Psychopharmacology, 18*(1), 83–87.

Daw, J. (2001a, April). New rule will change the psychologist/physician relationship. *Monitor on Psychology.* http://www.apa.org/monitor/apr01

Daw, J. (2001b, May). Academic medicine welcomes psychology. *Monitor on Psychology.* www.apa.org/monitor/may.oq

DeAngelis, T. (1995). Primary care collaborations growing. *American Psychological Association Monitor, 26*, 22.

DeAngelis, T. (2004, January). What's to blame for the surge in super-size Americans? *Monitor on Psychology, 35*(1), 46–62.

Deeks, S. G., Smith, M., Holodniy, M., & Kahn, J. O. (1997). HIV-1 protease inhibitors. *Journal of the American Medical Association, 277*, 145–153.

Deffenbacher, J. L., & Stark, R. S. (1992). Relaxation and cognitive-relaxation treatments of general anger. *Journal of Counseling Psychology, 39*, 158–167.

Dekaris, D., Sabioncello, A., Mazuran, R., Rabatic, S., Svoboda-Beusan, I., Racunica, N. L., & Tomasic, J. (1993). Multiple changes of immunologic parameters in prisoners of war. *Journal of the American Medical Association, 270*(5), 595–599.

De La Cancela, V., Alpert, J., Wolf, T., & Dachs, S. L. (2004). Psychological approaches to community health: Community health psychology. In R. H. Rozensky, N. G. Johnson, C. D. Goodheart, & W. R. Hammond (Eds.), *Psychology builds a healthy world.* Washington, D.C.: American Psychological Association.

DeMichele, M., Panico, S., Iannuzzi, A., Celentano, E., et al. (2002). Association of obesity and central fat distribution with carotid artery wall thickening in middle-aged women. *Stroke, 33*(12), 2923–2928.

Dempsey, M. (2002). Negative coping as mediator in the relation between violence and outcomes: Inner-city African American youth. *American Journal of Orthopsychiatry, 72*(1), 102–109.

Denissenko, M. F., Pao, A., Tang, M., & Pfeifer, G. P. (1996). Preferential formation of benzoapyrene adducts at lung cancer mutational hotspots in P53. *Science, 274*, 430–432.

Dentino, A. N., Pieper, C. F., Rao, C. K., Currie, M. S., Harris, T., Blazer, D. G., & Cohen, H. J. (1999). Association of interleukin-6 and other biologic variables with depression in older people living in the community. *Journal of the American Geriatrics Society, 47*(1), 6–11.

DeRosa, C. J., & Marks, G. (1998). Preventive counseling of HIV-positive men and self-disclosure of serostatus to sex partners: New opportunities for prevention. *Health Psychology, 17*, 224–231.

Desvarieux, M., Demmer, R. T., Rundex, T., Boden-Albala, B., Jacobs, D. R., Papapanou, D. N., et al. (2003). Relationship between periodontal disease, tooth loss, and carotid artery plaque: The Oral Infections and Vascular Disease Epidemiology Study (INVEST). *Stroke, 34*(9), 2120–2125.

Devins, G. M., Hunsley, J., Mandin, H., Taub, K. J., & Paul, L. C. (1997). The marital context of end-stage renal disease: Illness intrusiveness and perceived changes in family environment. *Annals of Behavioral Medicine, 19*, 325–332.

Devor, E. J. (1994). A developmental-genetic model of alcoholism: Implications for genetic research. *Journal of Consulting and Clinical Psychology, 62*, 1108–1115.

Dey, A. N., Schiller, J. S., & Tai, D. A. (2004). Summary health statistics for U.S. children: National health interview survey. *Vital and Health Statistics, Series 10, Data from the National Health Survey, 221*, 1–78.

Dhabhar, F. S., McEwen, B. S., & Spencer, R. L. (1993). Stress response, adrenal steroid receptor levels and corticosteroid-binding globulin levels: A comparison between Sprague-Dawley, Fischer 344 and Lewis rats. *Brain Research, 616*(1–2), 89–98.

Diano, S., Farr, S. A., Benoit, S. C., McNay, E. C., et al. (2006). Ghrelin controls hippocampal spine synapse density and memory performance. *Nature Neuroscience, 9*(3), 381–388.

DiClemente, R. J. (1991). Predictors of HIV-preventive sexual behavior in a high-risk adolescent population: The influence of perceived peer norms and sexual communication on incarcerated adolescents' consistent use of condoms. *Journal of Adolescent Health, 12*, 385–390.

Diehr, P., Bild, D. E., Harris, T. B., Duxbury, A., Siscovick, D., & Rossi, M. (1998). Body mass index and mortality in nonsmoking older adults: The Cardiovascular Health Study. *American Journal of Public Health, 88*, 623–629.

Diez-Ruiz, A., Tilz, G. P., Gutierrez-Gea, F., Gil-Extremerak, B., Murr, C., Wachter, H., & Fuchs, D. (1995). Neopterin and soluble tumor necrosis factor receptor type 1 in alcohol-induced cirrhosis. *Heptalogy, 21*, 976–978.

Diez Roux, A. V. (2001). Investigating neighborhood and area effects on health. *American Journal of Public Health, 91*(11), 1783–1789.

DiMatteo, M. R. (1993). Expectations in the physician-patient relationship: Implications for patient adherence to medical treatment recommendations. In P. D. Blanck (Ed.), *Interpersonal expectations: Theory, research, and applications* (pp. 296–315). New York: Cambridge University Press.

DiMatteo, M. R. (1994). Enhancing patient adherence to medical recommendations. *Journal of the American Medical Association, 271*, 79–83.

Dimsdale, J. E., Alper, B. S., & Schneiderman, N. (1986). Exercise as a modulator of cardiovascular reactivity. In K. A. Matthews, S. M. Weiss, T. Detre, T. M. Dembroski, B.

Disbrow, E. A., Owings, J. T., & Bennett, H. L. (1993). Respond. *The Western Journal of Medicine, 159*(5), 735.

Disis, M. L. (2005). *Immunotherapy of cancer.* New York: Humana Press.

Dittman, M. (2002). On the disease trail. *Monitor on Psychology, 33*(8). Washington, DC: American Psychological Association Online. http://www.apa.org/monitor/sep02/disease.html

Dohrenwend, B. P., & Shrout, P. E. (1985). "Hassles" in the conceptualization and measurement of life stress variables. *American Psychologist, 40*, 780–785.

Dolan, B., & Ford, K. (1991). Binge eating and dietary restraint: A cross-cultural analysis. *International Journal of Eating Disorders, 10*, 345–353.

Domino, E. F. (1996). Estimating exposure to environmental tobacco smoke. *Journal of the American Medical Association, 276*, 603.

Doro, P., Benko, R., Matuz, M., & Soos, G. (2006). Seasonality in the incidence of type 2 diabetes: A population-based study. *Diabetes Care, 29*(1), 173–184.

Dossey, L. (1993). *Healing words: The power of prayer and the practice of medicine.* San Francisco: HarperCollins.

Doublas, K. A., Collins, J. L., Warren, C., Kann, L., et al. (1997). Results from the 1995 national college risk behavior survey. *Journal of American College Health, 46*(2), 55–66.

Dougall, A. L., & Baum, A. (2001). Stress, health, and illness. In A. Baum, T. A. Revenson, & J. E. Singer (Eds.), *Handbook of health psychology* (pp. 321–337). Mahwah, NJ: Erlbaum.

Downey, G., Silver, R. C., & Wortman, C. B. (1990). Reconsidering the attribution-adjustment relation following a major negative event: Coping with the loss of a child. *Journal of Personality and Social Psychology, 59*, 925–940.

Dreer, L. E., Ronan, G. F., Ronan, D. W., Dush, D. M., & Elliott, T. R. (2004). Binge drinking and college students: An investigation of social problem-solving abilities. *Journal of College Student Development, 45*(3), 303–315.

Droomers, M., Schrijvers, C. T., & Mackenbach, J. P. (2002). Why do lower educated people continue smoking? Explanations from the longitudinal GLOBE study. *Health Psychology, 21*(3), 263–272.

Drory, Y., Kravetz, S., Florian, V., & Weingartnen, M. (1991). Coronary care—sexual activity after first acute myocardial infarction in middle-aged men: Demographic, psychological, and medical predictors. *Cardiology, 90*(3), 207–211.

Druckman, D. E., & Bjork, R. A. (1994). *Learning, remembering, believing: Enhancing human performance.* Washington, DC: USA National Academy Press.

Dunbar-Jacob, J. & Schlenk, E.A. (2001). Treatment adherence in chronic disease. *Journal of Clinical Epidemiology, 54,* S57–S60.

Duncan, G. E. (2001). Can sedentary adults accurately recall the intensity of their physical activity? *Preventive Medicine, 33*(1), 18–26.

Dunn, A. L., Reigle, T. G., Youngstedt, S. D., Armstrong, R. B., & Dishman, J. (1996). Brain norepinephrine and metabolites after treadmill training and wheel running in rats. *Medicine and Science in Sports and Exercise, 28,* 204–209.

Durazo-Arvizu, R. A., McGee, D. L., Cooper, R. S., Liao, Y., & Luke, A. (1998). Mortality and optimal body mass index in a sample of the U.S. population. *American Journal of Epidemiology, 147,* 739–749.

DSM-IV-TR (2000). *Diagnostic and Statistical Manual of Mental Disorders.* American Psychiatric Association.

Eccleston, C. (1995). The attentional control of pain: Methodological and theoretical concerns. *Pain, 63,* 3–10.

Eckenrode, J. (1984). Impact of chronic and acute stressors on daily reports of mood. *Journal of Personality and Social Psychology, 46,* 907–918.

Edelman, S., Lemon, J., Bell, D. R., & Kidman, A. D. (1999). Effects of group CBT on the survival time of patients with metastatic breast cancer. *Psycho-oncology, 8*(6), 474–481.

Edgar, L., Rossberger, Z., & Nowlis, D. (1992). Coping with cancer during the first year after diagnosis: Assessment and intervention. *Cancer, Diagnosis, Treatment, Research, 69,* 817–828.

Egbert, L. D., Battit, C. E.,Welch, C. E., & Bartlett, M. K. (1964). Reduction of postoperative pain by encouragement and instruction of patients. A study of doctor-patient rapport. *New England Journal of Medicine, 75,* 1008–1023.

Eisenberg, D. M. (1997). Advising patients who use alternative medical therapies. *Annals of Internal Medicine, 127,* 61–69.

Eisenberg, D. M., Davis, R. B., Ettner, S. L., Appel, S., Wilkey, S., Van Rompay, M., & Kessler, R. C. (1998). Trends in alternative medicine use in the United States, 1990–1997: Results of a follow-up national survey. *Journal of the American Medical Association, 280,* 1569–1575.

Eisenberg, D. M., Delbanco, T. L., Berkey, C. S., Kaptchuk, T. J., et al. (1993). Cognitive behavioral techniques for hypertension: Are they effective? *Annals of Internal Medicine, 118*(12), 964–972.

Eitel, P., Hatchett, L., Friend, R., & Griffin, K.W. (1995). Burden of self-care in seriously ill patients: Impact on adjustment. *Health Psychology, 14,* 457–463.

Ellenberg, S. S., & Chen, R. T. (1997). The complicated task of monitoring vaccine safety. *Public Health Reports, 112,* 10–20.

Ellenhorst-Ryan, J. M. (1997). The nature of cancer. In C. Varricchio, M. Pierce, C. Walker, & T. B. Ads (Eds.), *A cancer source book for nurses* (7th ed., pp. 27–34). Atlanta: American Cancer Society.

Ellis, A. (1962). *Reason and emotion in psychotherapy.* Secaucus, NY: Citadel Press.

Elton, D., Stanley, G. V., & Burrows, G. D. (1983). *Psychological control of pain.* Sydney, Australia: Grune & Stratton.

Emmons, C. A., Joseph, J. G., Kessler, R. C., Wortman, C. B., Montgomery, S. B., & Ostrow, D. G. (1986). Psychosocial predictors of reported behavior change in homosexual men at risk for AIDS. *Health Education Quarterly, 13,* 331–345.

Emmons, R. A., & McCullough, M. E. (2003). Personality processes and individual differences—counting blessings versus burdens: An experimental investigation of gratitude and subjective well-being in daily life. *Journal of Personality & Social Psychology, 84*(2), 377–389.

Endler, V. S. & Parker, J. D. A. (1990). State and trait anxiety, depression and coping styles. *Australian journal of psychology, 42*(2), 207–221.

Eng, P. M., Fitzmaurice, G., Kubzansky, L. D., Rimm, E. B., & Kawachi, I. (2003). Anger expression and risk of stroke and coronary heart disease among male health professionals. *Psychosomatic Medicine, 65*(1), 100–110.

Epping-Jordan, J. E., Compas, B. E., & Howell, D. C. (1994). Predictors of cancer progression in young adult men and women: Avoidance, intrusive thoughts, and psychological symptoms. *Health Psychology, 13,* 539–547.

Epping-Jordan, J. E., Compas, B. E., Osowiecki, D. M., Oppedisano, G., Gerhardt, C., Primo, K., et al. (1999). Psychological adjustment in breast cancer: Processes of emotional distress. *Health Psychology, 18,* 315–326.

Eriksen, W. (2004). Do people who were passive smokers during childhood have increased risk of long-term work disability? A 15-month prospective study of nurses' aides. *European Journal of Public Health, 14*(3), 296–300.

Ernst, E., Resch, K. L., & White, A. R. (1995). Complementary medicine: What physicians think of it. *Archives of Internal Medicine, 155,* 2405–2408.

Esplen, M. J., Toner, B., Hunter, J., Glendon, G., Butler, K., & Field, B. (1998). A group therapy approach to facilitate integration of risk information for women at risk for breast cancer. *Canadian Journal of Psychiatry, 43,* 375–380.

Esposito-Del Puente, A., Lillioja, S., Bogardus, C., McCubbin, J. A., Feinglos, M. N., Kuhn, C. M., et al. (1994). Glycemic response to stress is altered in euglycemic Pima Indians. *International Journal of Obesity and Related Metabolic Disorders, 18,* 766–770.

Esterling, B. A., Kiecolt-Glaser, J. K., Bodnar, J. C., & Glaser, R. (1994). Chronic stress, social support, and persistent alterations in the natural killer cell response to cytokines in older adults. *Health Psychology, 13,* 291–298.

Evans, G. W., Hygge, S., & Bullinger, M. (1995). Chronic noise and psychological stress. *Psychological Science, 6,* 333–338.

Evans, R. I. (2003). Some theoretical models and constructs generic to substance abuse prevention programs for adolescents: Possible relevance and limitations for problem gambling. *Journal of Gambling Studies, 19*(3), 287–302.

Everall, I. P., Luthert, P. J., & Lantos, P. L. (1991). Neuronal loss in the frontal cortex in HIV infection. *The Lancet, 337,* 1119–1121.

Everson, S. A., Goldberg, D. E., Kaplan, G. A., & Cohen, R. D. (1996). Hopelessness and risk of mortality and incidence of myocardial infarction and cancer. *Psychosomatic Medicine, 58,* 113–121.

Eysenck, H. J., Grossarth-Maticek, R., & Everitt, B. (1991). Personality, stress, smoking, and genetic predisposition as synergistic risk factors for cancer and coronary heart disease. *The Pavlovian Journal of Biological Science, 26,* 309–322.

Fabes, R. A., & Eisenberg, N. (1997). Regulatory control and adults' stress-related responses to daily life events. *Journal of Personality and Social Psychology, 73*(5), 1107–1117.

Fabes, R. A., Eisenberg, N., Karbon, M., Troyer, D. & Switzer, J. (1994). The relations of children's emotion regulation to their vicarious emotional responses and comforting behaviors. *Child Development, 65,* 1678–1693.

Fabrega, H., & Tyma, S. (1976). Culture, language and the shaping of illness: An illustration based on pain. *Journal of Psychosomatic Research, 20,* 323–337.

Farrington, J. (1999, January). What it means when you hurt. *Current Health, 5,* 166–168.

Fairburn, C. G., & Wilson, G. T. (1993). Binge eating: Definition and classification. In C. G. Fairburn & G. T. Wilson (Eds.), *Binge eating: Nature, assessment, and treatment* (pp. 3–14). New York: Guilford.

Falkner, S. B. Mauck, & R. B. Williams (Eds.), *Handbook of stress, reactivity, and cardiovascular disease.* New York: Wiley.

Farrell, P. A., Gates, W. K., Maksud, M. G., & Morgan, W. P. (1982). Increases in plasma beta-endorphin/beta-lipotropin immunoreactivity after treadmill running in humans. *Journal of Applied Physiology, 52,* 1245–1249.

Farzadegan, H., Hoover, D. R., Astemborski, J., Lyles, C. M., Margolick, J. B., Markham, R. B., et al. (1998). Sex differences in HIV-1 viral load and progression to AIDS. *The Lancet, 352,* 1510–1514.

Faucett, J., Gordon, N., & Levine, J. (1994). Differences in postoperative pain severity among four ethnic groups. *Journal of Pain and Symptom Management, 9,* 383–389.

Fauci, A. S. (2006, July 28). Twenty-five years of HIV/AIDS. *Science, 313,* 409.

Fava, M., Copeland, P. M., Schweiger, U., & Herzog, D. B. (1989). Neurochemical abnormalities of anorexia nervosa and bulimia nervosa. *American Journal of Psychiatry, 146,* 963–971.

Fawzy, F. I., Fawzy, N. W., Hyun, C. S., Elashoff, R., Guthrie, D., Fahley, J. L., & Morton, D. L. (1993). Malignant melanoma: Effects of an early structures psychiatric intervention, coping, and affective state on recurrence and survival 6 years later. *Archives of General Psychiatry, 50,* 681–689.

Feifer, C., & Tansman, M. (1999). Promoting psychology in diabetes primary care. *Professional Psychology: Research and Practice, 30,* 14–21.

Feingold, A., & Mazzella, R. (1996). Gender differences in body image are increasing. *Psychological Science, 9,* 190–195.

Feldman, P. J. & Steptoe, A. (2004). How neighborhoods and physical functioning are related: The roles of neighborhood socioeconomic status, perceived neighborhood strain, and individual health risk factors. *Annals of Behavioral Medicine, 27*(2), 91–99.

Fellowes, D., Barnes, K., & Wilkinson, S. (2004). Aromatherapy and massage for symptom relief in patients with cancer. *Cochrane Database of Systematic Reviews (Online), 2004*(2): CD002287.

Ferroli, C. (1996, January). Anger could be a fatal fault. *The Saturday Evening Post, 268,* 18.

Feuerstein, M., & Beattie, P. (1995). Biobehavioral factors affecting pain and disability in low back pain: Mechanisms and assessment. *Physical Therapy, 75,* 267–280.

Feuerstein, M., Burrell, L. M., Miller, V. I., Lincoln, A., Huang, G. D., & Berger, R. (1999). Clinical management of carpal tunnel syndrome: A 12-year review of outcomes. *American Journal of Industrial Medicine, 35,* 232–245.

Fiatarone, M. A., O'Neill, E. F., Doyle, N., Clements, K. M., Roberts, S. B., Kehayias, J. J., Lipsitz, L. A., & Evans, W. J. (1993). The Boston FICSIT study: The effects of resistance training and nutritional supplementation on physical frailty in the oldest old. *Journal of the American Geriatrics Society, 41,* 333–337.

Fillingim, R. B. (2000). Sex, gender, and pain: Women and men really are different. *Current Review of Pain, 4,* 24–30.

Fiore, M. C. (2000). A clinical practice guideline for treating tobacco use and dependence. *Journal of the American Medical Association, 283*(24), 3244–3254.

Fiore, M. C., Smith, S. S., Jorenby, D. E., & Baker, T. B. (1994). The effectiveness of the nicotine patch for smoking cessation: A meta-analysis. *Journal of the American Medical Association, 271,* 1940–1947.

Fischman, J. (2000, March 13). The "man's illness" can be deadlier to women who don't spot cardiac trouble. *U.S. News & World Report, 128,* 67–68.

Fishbein, H. D. (1982). The identified patient and stage of family development. *Journal of Marital and Family Therapy, 8,* 57–61.

Flack, J. M., Amaro, H., Jenkins, W., Kunitz, S., Levy, J., Mixon, M., & Yu, E. (1995). Epidemiology of minority health. *Health Psychology, 14*(7), 592–600.

Flay, B. R. (1985). Psychosocial approaches to smoking prevention: A review of findings. *Health Psychology, 4,* 448–488.

Fleishman, J. A., & Fogel, B. (1994). Coping and depressive symptoms among people with AIDS. *Health Psychology, 13,* 156–169.

Fleshner, F. (2005). Physical activity and stress resistance: Sympathetic nervous system adaptations prevent stress-induced immunosuppression. *Exercise and Sport Sciences Reviews, 33*(3), 120–126.

Flett, G. L., Hewitt, P. L., Blankstein, K. R., & Mosher, S. W. (1995). Perfectionism, life events, and depressive symptoms: A test of a diathesis-stress model. *Current Psychology: Developmental, Learning, Personality, Social, 14,* 112–137.

Flor, H., & Birbaumer, N. (1993). Comparison of the efficacy of electromyographic biofeedback, cognitive-behavioral therapy, and conservative medical interventions in the treatment of chronic musculoskeletal pain. *Journal of Consulting and Clinical Psychology, 61,* 653–658.

Florian, V., Mikulincer, M., & Taubman, O. (1995). Does hardiness contribute to mental health during a stressful real-life situation? The roles of appraisal and coping. *Journal of Personality and Social Psychology, 68,* 687–695.

Foa, E. B., Riggs, D. S., & Gershuny, B. S. (1995). Arousal, numbing, and intrusion: Symptom structure of PTSD following assault. *American Journal of Psychiatry, 152,* 116–120.

Fogel, J., Albert, S. M., Schnabel, F., Ditkoff, B. A., & Neugut, A. I. (2002). Internet use and social support in women with breast cancer. *Health Psychology, 21*(4), 398–404.

Folsom, V., Krahn, D. D., Naim, K., & Gold, L. (1993). The impact of sexual and physical abuse on eating disordered and psychiatric symptoms: A comparison of eating disordered and psychiatric inpatients. *International Journal of Eating Disorders, 13,* 249–257.

Fondacaro, M. R., & Heller, K. (1983). Social support factors and drinking among college student males. *Journal of Youth and Adolescence, 12,* 285–299.

Ford, E. S., Loucks, E. B., Berkman, L. F. (2006). Social integration and concentrations of C-reactive protein among US adults. *Annals of epidemiology, 16*(2), 78–84.

Fordyce, W. E. (1976). *Behavioral methods in chronic pain and illness.* St. Louis: Mosby.

Forman, T. A. (2002). The social psychological costs of racial segmentation in the workplace: A study of African Americans' well-being. *Journal of Health and Social Behavior, 44*(3), 332–352.

Fowles, D. C. (1992). Schizophrenia: Diathesis-stress revisited. *Annual Review of Psychology, 43,* 303–336.

Foxhall, K. (2001, June). Preventing relapse. *Monitor on Psychology* (special issue on substance abuse), *32,* 46–47.

Frank, E., Sperling, L., & Wu, K. (2000). Aspirin use among women physicians in the United States. *The American Journal of Cardiology, 86,* 465–466.

Frankenhaeuser, M. (1975). Sympathetic-adreno-medullary activity behavior and the psychosocial environment. In P. H. Venables & M. J. Christie (Eds.), *Research in psychophysiology* (pp. 71–94). New York: Wiley.

Frankenhaeuser, M. (1991). The psychophysiology of workload, stress, and health: Comparison between the sexes. *Annals of Behavioral Medicine, 13,* 197–204.

Frankenhaeuser, M., & Gardell, B. (1976). Underload and overload in working life: Outline of a multidisciplinary approach. *Journal of Human Stress, 2,* 35-46.

Fraser, G. E. (1991). Epidemiologic studies of Adventists. *Scope, 27,* 50–55.

Frasure-Smith, N., & Prince, R. (1989). Long-term follow-up of the Ischemic Heart Disease Life Stress Monitoring Program. *Psychosomatic Medicine, 51,* 485–513.

Frasure-Smith, N., Lesperance, F., Juneau, M., Talajic, M., & Bourassa, M. G. (1999). Gender, depression, and one-year prognosis after myocardial infarction. *Psychosomatic Medicine, 61,* 26–37.

Frasure-Smith, N., Lesperance, F., & Talajic, M. (1995). The impact of negative emotions on prognosis following myocardial infarction: Is it more than depression? *Health Psychology, 14,* 388–398.

Frederickson, B. L. (2001). The role of positive emotions in positive psychology: The broaden-and-build theory of positive emotions. *American Psychologist, 56,* 218–226.

Freedman, J. L. (1975). *Crowding and behavior.* New York: Freeman.

Freking, K. (2006, August 30). Rise in obesity weighs on health care experts. *Detroit News.* http://www.detroitnews.com

French, S. A., Story, M., Downes, B., Resnick, M. D., & Blum, R. W. (1995). Frequent dieting among adolescents: Psychosocial and health behavior correlates. *American Journal of Public Health, 85,* 695–701.

Frenn, M., & Malin, S. (2003). Obesity risk factor: Access to low-fat foods increases health eating among adolescents. *Drug Week, October 24,* 273.

Frerichs, R. R. (2000). *John Snow: A portrait.* UCLA Department of Epidemiology. http://www.ph.ucla.edu/epi/snow.html

Friedman, E. (1992). Fact, fallacy and fairness: The ethics of health care reform. *California Hospitals, 6,* 19–20.

Friedman, M., & Rosenman, R. H. (1959). Association of specific overt pattern with blood and cardiovascular findings. *Journal of the American Medical Association, 169,* 1286–1296.

Friedman, M. A., & Brownell, K. D. (1995). Psychological correlates of obesity: Moving to the next research generation. *Psychological Bulletin, 117,* 3–20.

Fries, J. F. (1999). *Living well: Taking care of your health in the middle and later years.* Cambridge: Perseus Publishing.

Froehle, R. M. (1996). Ear infection: A retrospective study examining improvement from chiropractic care and analyzing for influencing factors. *Journal of Manipulative and Physiological Therapeutics, 19,* 169–177.

Fry, W. F. (1977). The respiratory components of mirthful laughter. Journal of Biological Psychology, 19*(2),* 39–50.

Fugh-Berman, A. (1997). *Alternative medicine: What works.* Baltimore: Lippincott Williams & Wilkins.

Fugh-Berman, A. (2000). Herb-drug interactions. *The Lancet, 355,* 134–138.

Fuller, T. D., Edwards, J. N., Sermsri, S., & Vorakitphokatorn, S. (1993). Gender and health: Some Asian evidence. *Journal of Health and Social Behavior, 34,* 252–271.

Furukawa, T. (1994). Weight changes and eating attitudes of Japanese adolescents under acculturative stresses: A prospective study. *International Journal of Eating Disorders, 15,* 71–79.

Gailani, M. R., Leffell, D. J., Ziegler, A., Gross, E. G., Brash, D. E., & Bale, A. E. (1996). *Relationship between sunlight exposure and a key genetic alteration in basal cell carcinoma.* Journal of the National Cancer Institute, *88,* 349–354.

Gainetdinov, R. R., & Caron, M. G. (1999). Genetic models in pharmacology: Present status and future. *Pharmacological Research, 39,* 403–404.

Gallo, L. C., Bogart, L. M., Vranceanu, A. M., & Walt, L. C. (2004). Job characteristics, occupational status, and ambulatory cardiovascular activity in women. *Annals of Behavioral Medicine, 28*(1), 62–73.

Gallucci, W. T., Baum, A., & Laue, L. (1993). *Sex differences in sensitivity of the hypothalamic-pituitary-adrenal axis.* Health Psychology, *12,* 420–425.

Garbarino, J. (1991). The context of child abuse and neglect assessment. In J. C. Westman (Ed.), *Who speaks for the children? The handbook of individual and class child advocacy* (pp. 183–203). Sarasota, FL: Professional Resource Exchange.

Gardea, M. A., Gatchel, R. J., & Robinson, R. C. (2004). Complementary health care. In T. J. Boll, R. G. Frank, A. Baum, & J. L. Wallander (Eds.). *Handbook of clinical health psychology, volume 3: Models and perspectives in health psychology* (pp. 341–375). Washington, DC: American Psychological Association.

Garfinkel, P. E., & Garner, D. M. (1984). Bulimia in anorexia nervosa. In R. C. Hawkins, II, W. J. Remouw, & P. F. Clement (Eds.), *The binge-purge syndrome: Diagnosis, treatment and research* (pp. 442–446). New York: Springer.

Garmezy, N. (1993). Children in poverty: Resilience despite risk. *Interpersonal and Biological Processes* (Special Issue: *Children and Violence*), 56, 127–136.

Gatchel, R. J. (1997). Biofeedback. In A. Baum, S. Newman, J. Weinman, R. West, & C. McManus (Eds.), *Cambridge handbook of psychology, health and medicine* (pp. 197–199). Cambridge: Cambridge University Press.

Gatchel, R. J. (2001). Biofeedback and self-regulation of physiological activity: A major adjunctive treatment modality in health psychology. In A. Baum, T. A. Revenson, & J. E. Singer (Eds.), *Handbook of health psychology* (pp. 95–103). Mahwah, NJ: Erlbaum.

Gatchel, R. J. & Maddrey, A. M. (2004). The biopsychosocial perspective of pain. In J. M. Raczynski & L. C. Leviton. *Handbook of Clinical Health Psychology, Volume 2. Disorders of Behavior and Health* (pp. 357–378). Washington, DC: American Psychological Association.

Gatchel, R. J., & Mayer, T. G. (2000). Occupational musculoskeletal disorders: Introduction and overview of the problem. In T. G. Mayer, R. J. Gatchel, & P. B. Polatin (Eds.), *Occupational musculoskeletal disorders: Function, outcomes, and evidence* (pp. 3–8). Philadelphia: Lippincott, Williams, & Wilkins.

Gavard, J. A., Lustman, P. J., & Clouse, R. E. (1993). Prevalence of depression in adults with diabetes: An epidemiological evaluation. *Diabetes Care, 16*, 1167–1178.

Genest, J. (2004). Watching or doing sports: Children's investment in cardiovascular health. *Canadian Journal of Cardiology, 20*(3), 303–304.

Gerrard, M., Gibbons, F. X., Benthin, A. C., & Hessling, R. M. (1996). A longitudinal study of the reciprocal nature of risk behaviors and cognitions in adolescents: What you do shapes what you think, and vice versa. *Health Psychology, 15*, 344–354.

Gerrard, M. F., Dougherty, D.M. Barratt, E.S., Oderinde, V., et al. (2002). Increased impulsivity in cocaine dependent subjects independent of antisocial personality disorder and aggression. *Drug and Alcohol Dependence, 68(1)*, 105-112.

Gerstein, D. R., & Green, L. W. (Eds.) (1993). *Preventing drug abuse: What do we know?* Washington, DC: National Academy Press.

Gessner, P. K., & Gessner, T. (1992). *Disulfiram and its metabolite, dithiocarb: Pharmacology and status in the treatment of alcoholism, human immunodeficiency virus infections and heavy metal intoxication.* New York: Chapman & Hall.

Ghoname, E. S., Craig, W. F., White, P. F., Ahmed, H. E., et al. (1998). The effect of stimulus frequency on the analgesic response to percutaneous electrical nerve stimulation in patients with chronic low back pain. *Anesthesia and Analgesia, 88*(4), 841–846.

Giannini, A. J., & Miller, N. S. (1989). Drug abuse: A biopsychiatric model. *American Family Physician, 40*, 173–182.

Gibbons, F. X., Gerrard, M., Blanton, H., & Russell, D. W. (1998). Reasoned action and social reaction: Willingness and intention as independent predictors of health risk. *Journal of Personality and Social Psychology, 74*, 1164–1180.

Gibbs, W. W. (1996). Gaining on fat. *Scientific American, 275*, 88–95.

Giedzinska, A. S., Meyerowitz, B. E., Ganz, P. A., & Rowland, J. H. (2004). Health-related quality of life in a multiethnic sample of breast cancer survivors. Annals of Behavioral Medicine, 28(1), 39–51.

Gil, K. M., Carson, J. W., Porter, L. S., Scipio, C., et al. (2004). Daily mood and stress predict pain, health care use, and work activity in African American adults with Sickle-Cell disease. *Health Psychology, 23*(3), 267–274.

Gilada, I. S. (1991). AIDS in Asia. *AIDS Care, 3*, 391–394.

Gillum, R. F., Mussolino, M. E., & Madans, J. H. (1998). Body fat distribution and hypertension incidence in women and men. The NHANES I epidemiologic follow-up study. *International Journal of Obesity and Related Metabolic Disorders, 22*, 127–134.

Gladwell, M. (2006). Homelessness and the power-law paradox. *The New Yorker, February 13*, 96–105.

Glanz, K., Patterson, R. E., Kristal, A. R., & DiClemente, C. C. (1994). Stages of change in adopting healthy diets: Fat, fiber, and correlates of nutrient intake. *Health Education Quarterly, 21*, 499–519.

Glanz, K., Geller, A. C., Shigaki, D., et al. (2002). A randomized trial of skin cancer prevention in aquatic settings: The Pool-Cool program. *Health Psychology, 21*(6), 579–587.

Glaser, R., Kiecolt-Glaser, J. K., Bonneau, R. H., Malarkey, W., Kennedy, S., & Hughes, J. (1992). Stress-induced modulation of the immune response to recombinant Hepatitis B vaccine. *Psychosomatic Medicine, 54*(1), 22–29.

Glaser, R., Kiecolt-Glaser, J. K., Stout, J. C., Tarr, K. L., Speicher, C. E., & Holliday, J. E. (1985). Stress-related impairments in cellular immunity. *Psychiatry Research, 16*, 233–239.

Glass, D. C., & Singer, J. E. (1972). *Urban stress: Experiments on noise and social stressors.* New York: Academic Press.

Glauert, H. P., Beaty, M. M., Clark, T. D., Greenwell, W. S., & Chow, C. K. (1990). The effect of dietary selenium on the induction of altered hepatic foci and hepatic tumors by the perosisome proliferator ciprofibrate. *Nutrition and Cancer, 14*, 261–272.

Global Tobacco Control. (2006). http://www.globalink.org/

Godin, G., Valois, P., & Lepage, L. (1993). The pattern of influence of perceived behavioral control upon exercising behavior: An application of Ajzen's theory of planned behavior. *Journal of Behavioral Medicine, 16*, 81–102.

Goebel, M., Viol, G. W., & Orebaugh, C. (1993). An incremental model to isolate specific effects of behavioral treatments in essential hypertension. *Biofeedback and self-regulation, 18*(4), 255–280.

Goffman, E. (1961). *Asylums.* Garden City, NY: Doubleday.

Gold, P. W., Goodwin, F. K., & Chrousous, G. P. (1988). Clinical and biochemical manifestations of depression: Relation to the neurobiology of stress. *New England Journal of Medicine, 319*, 413–420.

Goldberg, J., Halpern-Felsher, B. L., & Milstein, S. G. (2002). Beyond invulnerability: The importance of benefits in adolescents' decision to drink alcohol. *Health Psychology, 21*(5), 477–484.

Goldfield, G. S., & Epstein, L. H. (2002). Can fruits and vegetables and activities substitute for snack foods? *Health Psychology, 21*(3), 299–303.

Goldring, A. B., Taylor, S. E., Kemeny, M. E. et al. (2002). Impact of health beliefs, quality of life, and the physician-patient relationship on the treatment intentions of inflammatory bowel disease patients. *Health Psychology, 21*(3), 219–228.

Goldstein, M. S. (1999). *Alternative health care: Medicine, miracle, or mirage?* Philadelphia: Temple University Press.

Gonder-Frederick, L. A., Cox, D. J., Bobbitt, S. A., & Pennebaker, J. W. (1989). Mood changes associated with blood glucose fluctuations in insulin-dependent diabetes mellitus. *Health Psychology, 8*, 45–59.

Goodall, T. A., & Halford, W. K. (1991). Self-management of diabetes mellitus: A critical review. *Health Psychology, 10*, 1–8.

Gortmaker, S. L., Must, A., Perrin, J. M., & Sobol, A. M. (1993). Social and economic consequences of overweight in adolescence and young adulthood. *New England Journal of Medicine, 329*, 1008–1012.

Gottlieb, A. M., Killen, J. D., Marlatt, G. A., & Taylor, C. B. (1987). Psychological and pharmacological influences in cigarette smoking withdrawal: Effects of nicotine gum and expectancy on smoking withdrawal symptoms and relapse. *Journal of Consulting and Clinical Psychology, 55*, 606–608.

Gottlieb, B. H. (1996). Theories and practices of mobilizing support in stressful circumstances. In C. L. Cooper (Ed.), *Handbook of stress, medicine, and health* (pp. 339–356). Boca Raton, FL: CRC Press.

Gottlieb, M. S. (1997). Conservative management of spinal osteoarthritis with glucosamine sulfate and chiropractic treatment. *Journal of Manipulative and Physiological Therapeutics, 20*, 400–414.

Graber, J. A., Brooks-Gunn, J., Paikoff, R. L., & Warren, M. P. (1994). Prediction of eating problems: An 8-year study of adolescent girls. *Developmental Psychology, 30*, 823–834.

Grant, L. D., & Haverkamp, B. E. (1995). A cognitive-behavioral approach to chronic pain management. *Journal of Counseling & Development, 74*, 25–32.

Grant, S., Contoreggi, C., & London, E. D. (2000). Drug abusers show impaired performance in a laboratory test of decision-making. *Neuropsychologia, 38*, 1180–1187.

Gray, D. (1985). The treatment strategies of arthritis sufferers. *Social Science and Medicine, 21*, 507–515.

Gray, J. J., Ford, K., & Kelly, L. M. (1987). The prevalence of bulimia in a black college population. *International Journal of Eating Disorders, 6*, 733–740.

Green, B. L., Krupnick, J. L., Rowland, J. H., Eptstein, S. A., et al. (2000). Trauma history as a predictor of psychologic symptoms in women with breast cancer. Journal of Clinical Oncology, 18(5), 1084–1093.

Green, C. A., Perrin, N. A., & Polen, M. R. (2004). Gender differences in the relationships between multiple measures of alcohol consumption and physical and mental health. *Alcoholism, Clinical and Experimental Research, 28*(5), 754–764.

Green, L. W., & Kreuter, M. W. (1990). Health promotion as a public health strategy for the 1990s. *Annual Review of Public Health, 11*, 319–334.

Green, L. W., & McAlister, A. L. (1984). Macro-intervention to support health behavior: Some theoretical perspectives and practical reflections. *Health Education Quarterly, 11*, 323–339.

Greendale, G. A., Barrett-Connor, E., Edelstein, S., Ingles, S., & Halle, R. (1995). Lifetime leisure exercise and osteoporosis: The Rancho Bernardo study. *American Journal of Epidemiology, 141*, 951–959.

Greenfield, S., & Kaplan, S. (1985). Expanding patient involvement in care: Effects on patient outcomes. *Annals of Internal Medicine, 102*, 520–528.

Greenfield, S., Kaplan, S. H., Ware, J. E., Yano, E. M., & Frank, H. J. (1988). Patients' participation in medical care: Effects on blood sugar control and quality of life in diabetes. *Journal of General Internal Medicine, 3*, 448–457.

Greenglass, E. R., & Noguchi, K. (1996). *Longevity, gender and health: A psychocultural perspective.* Paper presented at the meeting of the International Society of Health Psychology, Montreal, CA.

Greenwald, B. S., Mathe, A. A., Mohs, R. C., Levy, M. I., Johns, C. A., & Davis, K. L. (1986). Cortisol and Alzheimer's disease: Dexamethasone suppression, dementia severity, and affective symptoms. *The American Journal of Psychiatry, 143*(4), 442–446.

Greenwood, D., Szapocnik, J., McIntosh, S., & Antoni, M. (1996). African American women, their families, and HIV/AIDS. In R. J. Resnick & R. H. Rozensky (Eds.), *Health psychology through the life span: Practice and research opportunities* (pp. 349–359). Washington, DC: American Psychological Association.

Greer, S. (1991). Psychological response to cancer and survival. *Psychological Medicine, 21*, 43–49.

Greiger-Zanlungo, P. (2001). HIV and women: An update. *Female Patient, 26*, 12–16.

Griffith, J. (1983). Relationship between acculturation and psychological impairment in adult Mexican Americans. *Hispanic Journal of Behavioral Sciences, 5*, 431–459.

Gross, J. J. (1998). The emerging field of emotion regulation: An integrative review. *Review of General Psychology, 2*, 271–299.

Grossarth-Maticek, R., Eysenck, H. J., Pfeifer, A., Schmidt, P., & Koppel, G. (1997). The specific action of different personality risk factors on cancer of the breast, cervix, corpus uteri and other types of cancer: A prospective investigation. *Personality and Individual Differences, 23*, 949–960.

Groth-Marnat, G., & Schumaker, J. (1995). Psychologists in disease prevention and health promotion: A review of the cost effectiveness literature. *Psychology, 32*, 1–9.

Grunberg, N. E. (1986). Nicotine as a psychoactive drug: Appetite regulation. *Psychopharmacology Bulletin, 22*, 875–881.

Grunberg, N. E., & Straub, R. O. (1992). The role of gender and taste class in the effects of stress on eating. *Health Psychology, 11*, 97–100.

Grunberg, N. E., Brown, K. J., & Klein, L. C. (1997). Tobacco smoking. In A. Baum, S. Newman, J. Weinman, R. West, & C.

McManus (Eds.), *Cambridge handbook of psychology, health and medicine* (pp. 606–611). Cambridge: Cambridge University Press.

Grunberg, N. E., Faraday, M. M., & Rahman, M. A. (2001). The psychobiology of nicotine self-administration. In A. Baum, T. A. Revenson, & J. E. Singer (Eds.), *Handbook of health psychology* (pp. 249–261). Mahwah, NJ: Erlbaum.

Gump, B. B., & Matthews, K. A. (2000). Are vacations good for your health? The 9-year mortality experience after the multiple risk factor intervention trial. *Psychosomatic Medicine, 62,* 608–612.

Gus, I., Harzheim, E., Zaslavsky, C., Medina, C., & Gus, M. (2004). Prevalence, awareness, and control of systemic arterial hypertension in the state of Rio Grande do Sul. *Arquivos Brasilieros de Cardiologia, 83*(5), 429–433.

Hackman, R. M. (1998, September). Flavonoids and the French Paradox: Unhealthy-living French have low rate of heart attacks. *USA Today, 127,* 58.

Halaas, J. L., Gajiwala, K. S., Maffei, M., Cohen, S. L., Chait, B. T., Rabinowitz, D., Lallone, R. L., Burley, S. K., & Friedman, J. M. (1995). Weight-reducing effects of the plasma protein encoded by the obese gene. *Science, 269,* 543–545.

Hall, J. A., Irish, J. T., Roter, D. L., Ehrlich, C. M., & Miller, L. H. (1994). Gender in medical encounters: An analysis of physician and patient communication in a primary care setting. *Health Psychology, 13,* 384–392.

Hall, S. M., Herning, R. I., Jones, R. T., Benowitz, N. L., & Jacob, P. (1984). Blood cotinine levels as indicators of smoking treatment outcome. *Clinical Pharmacology and Therapeutics, 35,* 810–814.

Hammarstrom, A. (1994). Health consequences of youth unemployment—review from a gender perspective. *Social Science and Medicine, 38,* 699–709.

Hammer, G. P. (1997). *Hepatitis B vaccine acceptance among nursing home workers.* Unpublished doctoral dissertation, Department of Health Policy and Management, Johns Hopkins University, Baltimore.

Hammond, D., McDonald, P. W., Fong, G. T., Brown, K. S., & Cameron, R. (2004). The impact of cigarette warning labels and smoke-free bylaws on smoking cessation: Evidence from former smokers. *Canadian Journal of Public Health, 95*(3), 201–204.

Hamza, M. A., White, P. F., Craig, W. F., Ghoname E. S., et al. (2000). Percutaneous Electrical Nerve Stimulation: A novel analgesic for diabetic neuropathic pain. *Diabetes Care, 23*(3), 365–370.

Hanna, E., Defour, M. C., Elliott, S., Stinson, F., & Harford, T. C. (1992). Dying to be equal: Women, alcohol, and cardiovascular disease. *British Journal of Addiction, 87,* 1593–1597.

Harburg, E., Erfurt, J. C., Havenstein, L. S., Chape, C., Schull, W. J., & Schork, M. A. (1973). Socioecological stress, suppressed hostility, skin color, and black-white male blood pressure: Detroit. *Psychosomatic Medicine, 35,* 276–-296.

Hardin, K. N. (2004). Chronic pain management. In P. M. Camic & S. J. Knight (Eds.) *Clinical Handbook of Health Psychology: A Practical Guide to Effective Interventions* (pp. 75–99). Ashland, OH: Hogrefe and Huber Publishers.

Hardy, J. D., & Smith, T. W. (1988). Cynical hostility and vulnerability to disease: Social support, life stress, and physiological response to conflict. *Health Psychology, 7,* 447–459.

Harris, D. J., & Kuba, S. A. (1997). Ethnocultural identity and eating disorders in women of color. *Professional Psychology: Research and Practice, 28,* 341–347.

Harris, K. F., Matthews, K. A., Sutton-Tyrrell, K., & Kuller, L. H. (2003). Associations between psychological traits and endothelial function in postmenopausal women. *Psychosomatic Medicine, 65*(3), 402–409.

Harris, M. B., Walters, L. C., & Waschull, S. (1991). Gender and ethnic differences in obesity-related behaviors and attitudes in a college sample. *Journal of Applied Social Psychology, 21,* 1545–1566.

Harrison, M. O., Koenig, H. G., Hays, J. C., Eme-Akwari, A. G., & Pargament, K. I. (2001). The epidemiology of religious coping: A review of recent literature. *International Review of Psychiatry, 13*(2), 86–93.

Hart, S. (1997). Old age and health behaviour. In A. Baum, S. Newman, J. Weinman, R. West, & C. McManus (Eds.), *Cambridge handbook of psychology, health and medicine* (pp. 143–146). Cambridge: Cambridge University Press.

Hartung, B. D. (1987). Acculturation and family variables in substance abuse: An investigation with Mexican American high school males. *Dissertation Abstracts International, 48,* 264.

Haskell, W. L., Luskin, F. M., & Marvasti, F. F. (1999). Complementary/alternative therapies in general medicine: Cardiovascular disease. In J. W. Spencer & J. J. Jacobs (Eds.), *Complementary/alternative medicine: An evidence–based approach* (pp. 90–106). St. Louis: Mosby.

Haslam, R. H., Dalby, J. T., & Rademaker, A. W. (1984). Effects of megavitamin therapy on children with attention deficit disorders. *Pediatrics, 74,* 103–111.

Hassed, C. (2001). How humour keeps you well. *Australian Family Physician, 30*(1), 25–28.

Hassed, C. (2001). Humour in medicine: How humour keeps you well. *Australian Family Physician, 30*(1), 25–28.

Hatziandreu, E. I., Koplan, J. P., Weinstein, M. C., Caspersen, C. J., & Warner, K. E. (1988). A cost-effectiveness analysis of exercise as a health promotion activity. *American Journal of Public Health, 78,* 1417–1421.

Haug, M. R. (1994). Elderly patients, caregivers, and physicians: Theory and research on health care trends. *Journal of Health and Social Behavior, 35,* 1–12.

Haug, M. R., & Ory, M. G. (1987). Issues in elderly patient-provider interactions. *Research on Aging, 9,* 3–44.

Hawkins, J. D., Catalano, R. F., & Miller, J. Y. (1992). Risk and protective factors for alcohol and other drug problems in adolescence and early adulthood: Implications for substance abuse prevention. *Psychological Bulletin, 112,* 64–105.

Hawley, D. J. (1984). Nontraditional treatment of arthritis. *Clinical Nursing in North America, 19,* 663–667.

Hayashi, T., Iwanaga, S., Kawai, K., Ishii, H., Shoji, S., & Murakami, K. (2003). Laughter lowered the increase in postprandial blood glucose. *Diabetes Care, 26*(5), 1651–1652.

Hazuda, H. P., Mitchell, B. D., Haffner, S. M., & Stern, M. P. (1991). Obesity in Mexican-American subgroups: Findings from the

San Antonio Heart Study. *The American Journal of Clinical Nutrition, 53,* 1529S–1534S.

Heim, C., Ehlert, U., Hellhammer, D. H. (2000). The potential role of hypocortisolism in the pathophysiology of stress-related bodily disorders. *Psychoneuroendocrinology, 25*(1), 1–24.

Heath, A. C., & Madden, P. A. (1995). Genetic influences on smoking behavior. In J. R. Turner & L. R. Cardon (Eds.), *Behavior genetic approaches in behavioral medicine* (pp. 45–66). New York: Plenum Press.

Heatherton, T. F., Mahamedi, F., Striepe, M., & Field, A. E. (1997). A 10-year longitudinal study of body weight, dieting, and eating disorder symptoms. *Journal of Abnormal Psychology, 106,* 117–125.

Heatherton, T. F., Nichols, P., Mahamedi, F., & Keel, P. (1995). Body weight, dieting, and eating disorder symptoms among college students, 1982 to 1992. *American Journal of Psychiatry, 152,* 1623–1629.

Heckman, T. G., Barcikowski, R., Ogles, B., Suhr, J., Carlson, B., et al. (2006). A telephone-delivered coping improvement group intervention for middle-aged and older adults living with HIV/AIDS. *Annals of Behavioral Medicine, 32*(1), 27–38.

Heckman, T. G., Miller, J., Kochman, A., Kalichman, S. C., et al. (2002). Thoughts of suicide among HIV-infected rural persons enrolled in a telephone-delivered mental health intervention. *Annals of Behavioral Medicine, 24*(2), 141–148.

Helgeson, V. S., Snyder, P., & Seltman, H. (2004). Psychological and physical adjustment to breast cancer over 4 years: Identifying distinct trajectories of change. *Health Psychology, 23*(1), 3–15.

Heller, K., King, C. M., Arroyo, A. M., & Polk, D. E. (1997). Community-based interventions. In A. Baum, S. Newman, J. Weinman, R. West, & C. McManus (Eds.), *Cambridge handbook of psychology, health, and medicine* (pp. 203–206). Cambridge: Cambridge University Press.

Helmrich, S. P., Ragland, D. R., Leung, R. W., & Paffenbarger, R. S. (1991). Physical activity and reduced occurrence of non-insulin-dependent diabetes mellitus. *New England Journal of Medicine, 325,* 147–152.

Helms, J. E. (1995). An update of Helms' white and people of color racial identity models. In J. G. Ponterotto, & M. J. Casas (Eds.), *Handbook of multicultural counseling* (pp. 181–198). Thousand Oaks, CA: Sage.

Helmstetter, F. J., & Bellgowan, P. S. (1994). Hypoalgesia in response to sensitization during acute noise stress. *Behavioral Neuroscience, 108,* 177–185.

Helzer, J. E., Robins, L. N., & McEvoy, L. (1987). Post-traumatic stress disorder in the general population: Findings of the Epidemiologic Catchment Area survey. *New England Journal of Medicine, 317,* 1630–1634.

Henningfield, J. E., Cohen, C., & Pickworth, W. B. (1993). Psychopharmacology of nicotine. In C. T. Orleans & J. D. Slade (Eds.), *Nicotine addiction: Principles and management* (pp. 24–45). New York: Oxford University Press.

Henry J. Kaiser Foundation. (2000). *Uninsured in America: A chart book.* http://www.kff.org/content/archive/1407/

Henry J. Kaiser Foundation (2004). *The uninsured: A primer.* http://www.kff.org/uninsured/7451.cfm

Herek, G. M., Copitanio, J. P., & WIdaman, K. F. (2003). Stigma, social risk, and health policy: Public attitudes toward HIV surveillance policies and the social construction of illness. *Health Psychology, 22*(5), 533–539.

Herman, C. P., & Polivy, J. (1975). Anxiety, restraint, and eating behavior. *Journal of Abnormal Psychology, 84,* 666–672.

Herman, C. P., & Polivy, J. (1980). Restrained eating. In A. J. Stunkard (Ed.), *Obesity* (pp. 593–607). Philadelphia: Saunders.

Hewison, J. & Dowswell, T. (1994). *Child health care and the working mother.* London: Chapman & Hall.

Higgs, S. (2002). Memory for recent eating and its influence on subsequent food intake. *Appetite, 39*(2), 139–166.

Hilbert, G. A. (1994). Cardiac patients and spouses: Family functioning and emotions. *Clinical Nursing Research, 3,* 243–252.

Hill, C. S. (1995). When will adequate pain treatment be the norm? *Journal of the American Medical Association, 274,* 1881–1882.

Hinds, G. M. F., & McCluskey, D. R. (1993). A retrospective study of the chronic fatigue syndrome. *Proceedings of the Royal College of Physicians, 23,* 10–12.

Hochschild, A. R. (1997). *The time bind: When work becomes home, and home becomes work.* New York: Metropolitan Books.

Hoebel, B. G., & Teitelbaum, P. (1966). Effects of forcefeeding and starvation on food intake and body weight in a rat with ventromedial hypothalamic lesions. *Journal of Comparative and Physiological Psychology, 61,* 189–193.

Hofferberth, B. (1994). The effect of Egb 761 in patients with senile dementia of the Alzheimer's type: A double–blind placebo–controlled study on different levels of investigation. *Psychopharmacologia, 9,* 215.

Hogan, B. E., & Linden, W. (2004). Anger response styles and blood pressure: At least don't ruminate about it! *Annals of Behavioral Medicine, 27*(1), 38–49.

Holahan, C. J., & Moos, R. H. (1982). Social support and adjustment: Predictive benefits of social climate indices. *American Journal of Community Psychology, 10,* 403–415.

Holahan, C. J., Holahan, C. K., Moos, R. H., & Brennan, P. L. (1997). Psychosocial adjustment in patients reporting cardiac illness. *Psychology and Health, 12,* 345–359.

Holden, C. (1996). Bright spots in a bleak Russian landscape. *Science, 283,* 1621.

Holland, J. C., & Lewis, S. (1996). Emotions and cancer: What do we really know? In D. Goleman & J. Gurin (Eds.), *Mind-body medicine: How to use your mind for better health* (pp. 85–109). Yonkers, NY: Consumer Reports Books.

Holroyd, K. A., & Penzien, D. B. (1986). Client variables and the behavioral treatment of recurrent tension headache: A meta-analytic review. *Journal of Behavioral Medicine, 9,* 515–536.

Holroyd, K. A., France, J. L., Cordingley, G. E., Rokicki, L. A., Kvaal, S. A., Lipchik, G. L., & McCool, H. R. (1995). Enhancing the effectiveness of relaxation-thermal biofeedback training with propranolol hydrochloride. *Journal of Consulting and Clinical Psychology, 63,* 327–330.

Holt-Lunstad, J., Uchino, B. N., Smith, T. W., Olson-Cerny, C., & Nealey-Moore, J. B. (2003). Social relationships and ambulatory blood pressure: Structural and qualitative predictors of cardiovascular function during everyday social interactions. *Health Psychology, 22*(4), 388–397.

Horne, D. J., Vatmanidis, P., & Careri, A. (1994). Preparing patients for invasive medical and surgical procedures. 1: Adding behavioral and cognitive interventions. *Behavioral Medicine, 20,* 5–13.

House, J. S., Lepkowski, K. D., Williams, R., Mero, R. P., Lantz, P. M., Robert, S. A., & Chen, J. (2000). Excess mortality among urban residents: How much, for whom, and why? *American Journal of Public Health* (http://www.apha.org/journal/).

Hoyt, M. A., Nemeroff, C. J., & Huebner, D. M. (2006). The effects of HIV-related thought suppression on risk behavior: Cognitive escape in men who have sex with men. *Health Psychology, 25*(4), 455–461.

HRSA Care Action. (2005). Health Resources and Services Administration. U.S. Department of Health and Human Services. http://www.hrsa.gov/

Hsu, L. K. G. (1990). *Eating disorders.* New York: Guilford.

Hughes, T. A., Ross, H. F., Musa, S., Bhattacherjee, S., Nathan, R. N., Mindham, R. H. S., & Spokes, E. G. S. (2000). A 10-year study of the incidence of and factors predicting dementia in Parkinson's disease. *Neurology, 54*(8), 1596–1602.

Hui, K. S., Liu, J., Makris, N., Gollub, R. L., Chen, A. J. W., Moore, C. I., et al. (2000). Acupuncture modulates the limbic system and subcortical gray structures of the human brain: Evidence from fMRI studies in normal subjects. *Human Brain Mapping, 9,* 13–25.

Hull, J. G. (1987). Self-awareness model. In H. T. Blane & K. E. Leonard (Eds.), *Psychological theories of drinking and alcoholism* (pp. 272–304). New York: Guilford.

Hummer, R. A., Rogers, R. G., Nam, C. B., & Ellison, C. G. (1999). Religious involvement and U. S. adult mortality. *Demography, 36,* 273–285.

Humphrey, L. (1987). Comparison of bulimic-anorexic and nondistressed families using structural analysis of social behavior. *Journal of the American Academy of Child and Adolescent Psychiatry, 26,* 248–255.

Hunt, M. E. (1997). A comparison of family of origin factors between children of alcoholics and children of non-alcoholics in a longitudinal panel. *American Journal of Drug and Alcohol Abuse, 23,* 597–613.

Huston, P. (1997). Cardiovascular disease burden shifts. *The Lancet, 350,* 121.

Hutchison, K. E., McGeary, J., Smolen, A., Bryan, A., & Swift, R. (2002). The DRD4 VNTR Polymorphism moderates craving after alcohol consumption. *Health Psychology, 21*(2), 139–146.

Hwang, M. Y., & Molter, R. M. (1998). Alternative choices: What it means to use nonconventional medical therapy. *Journal of the American Medical Association, 280,* 1640.

Hygge, S. (1997). Noise: Effects on health. In A. Baum, S. Newman, J. Weinman, R. West, & C. McManus (Eds.), *Cambridge handbook of psychology, health and medicine* (pp. 139–143). Cambridge: Cambridge University Press.

Hyman, R. B., Baker, S., Ephraim, R., Moadel, A., & Philip, J. (1994). Health belief model variables as predictors of screening mammography utilization. *Journal of Behavior Medicine, 17,* 391–406.

Ickovics, J. R., Grigorenko, E., Beren, S. E., Druley, J. A., Morrill, A. C., & Rodin, J. (1998). Long-term effects of HIV counseling and testing for women: Behavioral and psychological consequences are limited at 18 months posttest. *Health Psychology, 17,* 395–402.

Ickovics, J. R., Thayaparan, B., & Ethier, K. A. (2001). Women and AIDS: A contextual analysis. In A. Baum, T. A. Revenson, & J. E. Singer (Eds.), *Handbook of health psychology* (pp. 817–839). Mahwah, NJ: Erlbaum.

Ingham, R., Woodcock, A., & Stenner, S. (1991). Getting to know you: Young people's knowledge of their partners at first intercourse. *Journal of Community and Applied Social Psychology* (special issue: Social dimensions of AIDS), *1,* 117–132.

Ingledew, D. K., Hardy, L., & Cooper, C. L. (1997). Do resources bolster coping and does coping buffer stress? An organizational study with longitudinal aspect and control for negative affectivity. *Journal of Occupational Health Psychology, 2,* 118–133.

IOM. (2006). Preventing Medication Errors: Quality Chasm Series. *Institute of Medicine.* http://www.iom.edu/CMS/3809/22526/35939.aspx

IOM. (2004). First Annual Crossing the Quality Chasm Summit. *Institute of Medicine,* http://www.iom.edu/CMS/3809/9868/22344.aspx

IOM. (2001). Crossing the Quality Chasm: A New Health System for the 21st Century. *Institute of Medicine.* http://www.iom.edu/CMS/8089/5432.aspx

Ironson, G., Field, T., Scafidi, F., et al. (1996). Massage therapy is associated with enhancement of the immune system's cytotoxic capacity. *International Journal of Neuroscience, 84*(1–4), 205–217.

Ironson, G., Schneiderman, H., Kumar, M., & Antoni, M. H. (1994). Psychosocial stress, endocrine and immune response in HIV-1 disease. *Homeostasis in Health & Disease, 35,* 137–148.

Ishikawa-Takata, K., Ohta, T., & Tanaka, H. (2003). How much exercise is required to reduce blood pressure in essential hypertensives: A dose-response study. *American Journal of Hypertension, 16*(8), 629–633.

Itil, T., & Martorano, D. (1995). Natural substances in psychiatry (ginkgo biloba in dementia). *Psychopharmacology Bulletin, 31,* 147–158.

Iyengar, S. S., & Lepper, M. R. (2000). Personality processes and individual differences—When choice is demotivating: Can one desire too much of a good thing? *Journal of Personality & Social Psychology, 79*(6), 995–1005.

Jablon, S., Hrubec, Z., & Boice, J. D. (1991). Cancer in populations living near nuclear facilities. A survey of mortality nationwide and incidence in two states. *Journal of the American Medical Association, 265,* 1403–1408.

Jacchia, G. E., Butler, U. P., Innocenti, M., & Capone, A. (1994). Low-back pain in athletes: Pathogenetic mechanisms and therapy. *La Chirurgia degli organi di movimento, 79,* 47–53.

Jackson, J. S. (1996). A life-course perspective on physical and psychological health. In R. J. Resnick & R. H. Rozensky (Eds.), *Health psychology through the lifespan* (pp. 39–57). Washington, DC: American Psychological Association.

Jacobs, A. L., Kurtz, R. M., & Strube, M. J. (1995). Hypnotic analgesia, expectancy effects, and choice of design: A reexamination. *International Journal of Clinical and Experimental Hypnosis, 43,* 55–69.

Jacobs, B. L. (1994). Serotonin, motor activity, and depression-related disorders. *American Scientist, 82,* 456–463.

Jacobson, A. M. (1996). The psychological care of patients with insulin-dependent diabetes mellitus. *New England Journal of Medicine, 334,* 1249–1253.

Jacobson, E. (1938). *Progressive relaxation.* Chicago: University of Chicago Press.

Jain, A. (2003). Treating nicotine addiction. *British Medical Journal, 327*(7428), 1394–1395.

James, S. A., Hartnett, S. A., & Kalsbeek, W. D. (1983). John Henryism and blood pressure differences among black men. *Journal of Behavioral Medicine, 6*(3), 259–278.

Janis, I. L. (1958). *Psychological stress.* New York: Wiley.

Janis, I. L., & Feshbach, S. (1953). Effects of fear-arousing communications. *Journal of Abnormal and Social Psychology, 48,* 78–92.

Janz, N. K., Schottenfeld, D., Doerr, K. M., Selig, S. M., et al. (1997). A two-step intervention to increase mammography among women aged 65 and older. *American Journal of Public Health, 87*(10), 1683–1686.

Jargowsky, P. A. (1997). Metropolitan restructuring and urban policy. *Stanford Law and Policy Review, 8,* 47–56.

Jarvis, S. (1994). *Drug prevention with youth.* Tulsa, OK: National Resource Center for Youth Services.

Jeffery, R. W., Forster, S. A., French, S. H., Kelder, H. A., Lando, H. A., McGovern, D. R., Jacobs, D. R., & Baxter, J. E. (1993). The healthy worker project: A worksite intervention for weight control and smoking cessation. *American Journal of Public Health, 83,* 395–401.

Jeffery, R. W., Kelly, K. M., Rothman, A. J., Sherwood, N. E., & Boutelle, K. N. (2004). The weight loss experience: A descriptive analysis. *Annals of Behavioral Medicine, 27*(2), 100–106.

Jemmott, J. B., Croyle, R. T., & Ditto, P. H. (1988). Commonsense epidemiology: Self-based judgments from laypersons and physicians. *Health Psychology, 7,* 55–73.

Jemmott, J. B., Jemmott, L. S., & Fong, G. T. (1992). Reductions in HIV risk-associated sexual behaviors among black male adolescents: Effects of an AIDS prevention intervention. *American Journal of Public Health, 82,* 372–377.

Jenkins, C. D., Jono, R. T., & Stanton, B. A. (1996). Predicting completeness of symptom relief after major heart surgery. *Behavioral Medicine, 22*(2), 45–57.

Jenkins, E. L. (1996). Workplace homicide: Industries and occupations at high risk. *Occupational Medicine, 11*(2), 219–226.

Jensen, M. P., & Karoly, P. (1991). Coping beliefs, coping efforts, and adjustment to chronic pain. *Journal of Consulting and Clinical Psychology, 59,* 431–438.

Jensen, M. P., & McFarland, C. A. (1993). Increasing the reliability and validity of pain intensity measurement in chronic pain patients. *Pain, 55,* 195–203.

Jessor, R. (1987). Problem-behavior theory, psychosocial development, and adolescent problem drinking. *British Journal of Addiction,* Special Issue: Psychology and addiction, *82,* 331–342.

Johnsen, L., Spring, B., Pingitore, R., Sommerfeld, B. K., & MacKirnan, D. (2002). Smoking as subculture? Influence on

Hispanic and non-Hispanic White women's attitudes toward smoking and obesity. *Health Psychology, 21*(3), 279–287.

Johnson, K. W., Anderson, N. B., Bastida, E., Kramer, B. J., Williams, D., & Wong, M. (1995). Panel III: Macrosocial and environmental influences on minority health. *Health Psychology, 14,* 601–612.

Johnson, M., & Vogele, C. (1993). Benefits of psychological preparation for surgery: A meta-analysis. *Annals of Behavioral Medicine, 15,* 245–256.

Johnson, N. G. (2004). Future directions for psychology and health. In R. H. Rozensky, N. G. Johnson, C. D. Goodheart, & W. R. Hammond (Eds.), *Psychology builds a healthy world.* Washington, D.C.: American Psychological Association.

Johnson, R. A., & Meadows, R. L. (2002). Older Latinos, pets, and health. *Western Journal of Nursing Research, 24*(6), 609–620.

Johnson, V. C., Walker, L. G., Heys, S. D., et al. (1996). Can relaxation training and hypnotherapy modify the immune response to stress, and is hypnotizability relevant? *Contemporary Hypnosis, 13*(2), 100–108.

Johnston, D. W., Johnston, M., Pollard, B., Kinmouth, A. L., & Mant, D. (2004). Motivation is not enough: Prediction of risk behavior following diagnosis of coronary heart disease from the theory of planned behavior. *Health Psychology, 23*(5), 533–538.

Jonas, J. M., & Gold, M. S. (1988). The use of opiate antagonists in treating bulimia: A study of low-dose versus high-dose naltrexone. *Psychiatry Research, 24,* 195–199.

Jones, R. T. (1992). What have we learned from nicotine, cocaine, and marijuana about addiction? In C. P. O'Brien & J. H. Jaffe (Eds.), *Addictive states* (pp. 109–122). New York: Raven Press.

Jordan, N. N., Hoge, C. W., Tobler, S. K., Wells, J., Dydek, G. J., Egerton, W. E. (2004). Mental health impact of 9/11 Pentagon attack: Validation of a rapid assessment tool. *American Journal of Preventive Medicine, 26*(4), 284–293.

Jorgensen, R. S., Johnson, B. T., Kolodziej, M. E., & Schreer, G. E. (1996). Elevated blood pressure and personality: A meta-analytic review. *Psychological Bulletin, 120,* 293–320.

Julien, R. M. (2001). *A primer of drug action* (9th ed.). New York: Worth.

Kabakian-Khasholian, T., Campbell, O., Shediac-Rizkaliah, M., & Ghorayeb, F. (2000). Women's experiences of maternity care: Satisfaction or passivity? *Social Science and Medicine, 51,* 103–113.

Kabat-Zinn, J. (1982). An outpatient program in behavioral medicine for chronic pain patients based on the practice of mindfulness meditation: Theoretical considerations and preliminary results. *General Hospital Psychiatry, 4,* 33–47.

Kalichman, S. C., & Hospers, H. J. (1997). Efficacy of behavioral-skills enhancement HIV risk-reduction interventions in community settings. *AIDS, 11* (supplement A), S191–S199.

Kalichman, S. C., Carey, M. P., & Johnson, B. T. (1996). Prevention of sexually transmitted HIV infection: A meta-analytic review of the behavioral outcome literature. *Annals of Behavioral Medicine, 18,* 6–15.

Kalichman, S. C., Heckman, T. G., Kochman, A. R., Sikkema, K. J., et al. (2000). Suicidal ideation among midlife and older adults living with HIV/AIDS. *Psychiatric Services, 51,* 903–907.

Kalichman, S. C., Kelly, J. A., Hunter, T. L., Murphy, D. A., & Tyler, R. (1993). Culturally tailored HIV-AIDS risk-reduction messages targeted to African-American urban women: Impact on risk sensitization and risk reduction. *Journal of Consulting and Clinical Psychology, 61,* 291–295.

Kalichman, S. C., Nachimson, D., Cherry, C., & Williams, E. (1998). AIDS treatment advances and behavioral prevention setbacks: Preliminary assessment of reduced perceived threat of HIV-AIDS. *Health Psychology, 17,* 546–550.

Kalichman, S. C., Weinhardt, L., DiFonzo, K., Austin, J., & Luke, W. (2002). Sensation seeking and alcohol use as markers of sexual transmission risk behavior in HIV-positive men. *Annals of Behavioral Medicine, 24*(3), 229–235.

Kamarck, T. W., & Lichtenstein, E. (1985). Current trends in clinic-based smoking control. *Annals of Behavioral Medicine, 7,* 19–23.

Kamarck, T. W., & Lichtenstein, E. (1998). Program adherence and coping strategies as predictors of success in a smoking treatment program. *Health Psychology, 7,* 557–574.

Kaminski, P. L., & McNamara, K. (1996). A treatment for college women at risk for bulimia: A controlled evaluation. *Journal of Counseling and Development, 74,* 288–374.

Kane, R. L., Olsen, D., & Leymaster, C. (1974). Manipulating the patient: A comparison of the effectiveness of physician and chiropractor care. *The Lancet,* 1333–1336.

Kanner, A. D., Coyne, J. C., Schaefer, C., & Lazarus, R. S. (1981). Comparison of two modes of stress measurement: Daily hassles and uplifts versus major life events. *Journal of Behavioral Medicine, 4,* 1–39.

Kanowski, S., Herrmann, W. M., Stephan, K., Wierich, W., & Horr, R. (1996). Proof of efficacy of the ginko biloba special extract EGb 761 in outpatients suffering from mild to moderate primary degenerative dementia of the Alzheimer type or multi-infarct dementia. *Pharmacopsychiatry, 29*(2), 47–56.

Kaplan, G. (2003). What is the role of the social environment in understanding inequities in health? *Annals of the New York Academy of Sciences, 896,* 116–119.

Kaplan, G. A., & Keil, J. E. (1993). Socioeconomic factors and cardiovascular disease: A review of the literature. *Circulation, 88,* 1973–1998.

Kaplan, G. A., & Reynolds, P. (1988). Depression and cancer mortality and morbidity: Prospective evidence from the Alameda County study. *Journal of Behavioral Medicine, 11,* 1–13.

Kaplan, H. B., & Johnson, R. J. (1992). Relationships between circumstances surrounding initial illicit drug use and escalation of drug use: Moderating effects of gender and early adolescent experiences. In M. D. Glantz & R. W. Pickens (Eds.), *Vulnerability to drug abuse* (pp. 299–358). Washington, DC: American Psychological Association.

Kaplan, M. J. (2004). Consumers as directors. A revised, more active role for healthcare recipients may mean changes for the industry. *Healthcare informatics, 21*(4), 27–29.

Kaplan, R. M. (2000). Two pathways to prevention. *American Psychologist, 55*(4), 382–396.

Kandel, D. B., & Davies, M. (1996). High school students who use crack and other drugs. *Archives of General Psychiatry, 53,* 71–80.

Karasek, R. A., Russell, R. S., & Theorell, T. (1982). Physiology of stress and regeneration in job related cardiovascular illness. *Journal of Human Stress, 8*(1), 29–42.

Kark, J. D., Shemi, G., Friedlander, Y., Martin, O., Manor, O., & Blondheim, S. H. (1996). Does religious observance promote health? Mortality in secular vs. religious kibbutzim in Israel. *American Journal of Public Health, 86,* 341–346.

Karlin, W. A., Brondolo, E., & Schwartz, J. (2003). Workplace social support and ambulatory cardiovascular activity in New York City traffic agents. *Psychosomatic Medicine, 65,* 167–176.

Karoly, P. (1988). Pain assessment in children I: Concepts and measurement strategies. In P. Karoly (Ed.), *Handbook of child health assessment: Biopsychosocial perspectives* (pp. 357–386). New York: Wiley.

Kasl, S. V. (1997). Unemployment and health. In A. Baum, S. Newman, J. Weinman, R. West, & C. McManus (Eds.), *Cambridge handbook of psychology, health and medicine* (pp. 186–189). Cambridge, UK: Cambridge University Press.

Kassirer, J. P. (2000, November/December). Patients, physicians, and the Internet. *Health Affairs, 19,* 115–123.

Katon, W., & Sullivan, M. D. (1990). Depression and chronic medical illness. *Journal of Clinical Psychiatry, 51,* 12–14.

Katz, B. R. (2006). Birthing fathers: The transformation of men in American rites of birth. *Gender & Society, 20*(1), 142–144.

Katz, E. C., Fromme, K., & D'Amico, E. J. (2000). Effects of outcome expectancies and personality on young adults' illicit drug use, heavy drinking, and risky sexual behavior. *Cognitive Therapy and Research, 24*(1), 1–22.

Katzmarzyk, P. T., Mahaney, M. C., Blangero, J., Quek, J. J., & Malina, R. M. (1999). Potential effects of ethnicity in genetic and environmental sources of variability in the stature, mass, and body index of children. *Human Biology, 71,* 977–987.

Kawachi, I., Colditz, G. A., Stampfer, M. J., Willett, W. C., Manson, J. E., Rosner, B., et al. (1994). Smoking cessation and time course of decreased risks of coronary heart disease in middle-aged women. *Archives of Internal Medicine, 154,* 169–175.

Keane, T. M., & Wolfe, J. (1990). Comorbidity in post-traumatic stress disorder: An analysis of community and clinical studies. *Journal of Applied Social Psychology, 20,* 1776–1788.

Keefe, F. J., Dunsmore, J., & Burnett, R. (1992). Behavioral and cognitive-behavioral approaches to chronic pain: Recent advances and future directions. *Journal of Consulting and Clinical Psychology, 60,* 528–536.

Keenan, N. L., Strogatz, D. S., James, S. A., Ammerman, A. S., & Rice, B. L. (1992). Distribution and correlates of waist-to-hip ratio in black adults: The Pitt county study. *American Journal of Epidemiology, 135*(6), 678–684.

Keesey, R. E., & Corbett, S. W. (1983). Metabolic defense of the body weight set-point. In A. J. Stunkard & E. Stellar (Eds.), *Eating and its disorders* (pp. 327–331). New York: Raven Press.

Keesling, B., & Friedman, H. S. (1987). Psychosocial factors in sunbathing and sunscreen use. *Health Psychology, 6,* 477–493.

Kelly, E. L., & Conley, J. J. (1987). Personality and compatibility: A prospective analysis of marital stability and marital satisfaction. *Journal of Personality and Social Psychology, 52,* 27–40.

Kelley, J. A., & Kalichman, S. C. (1998). Reinforcement value of unsafe sex as a predictor of condom use and continued

HIV/AIDS risk behavior among gay and bisexual men. *Health Psychology, 17,* 328–325.

Keltner, D., Ellsworth, P. C., & Edwards, K. (1993). Beyond simple pessimism: Effects of sadness and anger on social perception. *Journal of Personality and Social Psychology, 64,* 740–752.

Kemeny, M., Weiner, H., Taylor, S. E., & Schneider, S. (1994). Repeated bereavement, depressed mood, and immune parameters in HIV seropositive and seronegative gay men. *Health Psychology, 13,* 14–24.

Kempen, G. I., Jelicic, M., & Ormel, J. (1997). Personality, chronic medical morbidity, and health-related quality of life among older persons. *Health Psychology, 16,* 539–546.

Kendler, K. S., Preschott, C. A., Neale, M. C., & Pedersen, N. L. (1997). Temperance Board registration for alcohol abuse in a national sample of Swedish male twins, born 1902 to 1949. *Archives of General Psychiatry, 54,* 178–184.

Kessler, R. C., Foster, C., Joseph, J., Ostrow, D., Wortman, C., Phair, J., et al. (1991). Stressful life events and symptom onset in HIV infection. *American Journal of Psychiatry, 148,* 733–738.

Kessler, R. C., Sonnega, A., Bromet, E., Hughes, M., Nelson, C. B., Breslau, N. (1999). Epidemiological risk factors for trauma and PTSD. In R. Yehuda (Ed.) *Risk factors for posttraumatic stress disorder.* Washington, DC: American Psychiatric Association, 23–59.

Keys, A., Brozek, J., Henschel, A., Mickelsen, O., & Taylor, H. L. (1950). *The biology of human starvation.* Minneapolis: University of Minnesota Press.

Kiecolt-Glaser, J. K. (1985). Psychosocial enhancement of immunocompetence in a geriatric population. *Health Psychology, 4*(1), 25–41.

Kiecolt-Glaser, J. K., Cacioppo, J. T., Malarkey, W. B., & Glaser, R. (199). Acute psychological stressors and short-term changes: What, why, for whom, and to what extent. *Psychosomatic Medicine, 54*(6), 680–685.

Kiecolt-Glaser, J. K., Fisher, L., Ogrocki, P., Stout, J. C., Speicher, C. E., & Glasser, R. (1987). Marital quality, marital disruption, and immune function. *Psychosomatic Medicine, 49,* 13–34.

Kiecolt-Glaser, J. K., Garner, W., Speicher, C. E., Penn, G. M., Holliday, J. E., & Glaser, R. (1984). Psychosocial modifiers of immunocompetence in medical students. *Psychosomatic Medicine, 46,* 7–14.

Kiecolt-Glaser, J. K. & Glaser, R. (1988). Psychological influences on immunity. *Psychosomatics: Journal of Consultation Liaison Psychiatry, 27*(9), 621–624.

Kiecolt-Glaser, J. K., & Glaser, R. (1995). Psychoneuroimmunology and health consequences: Data and shared mechanisms. *Psychosomatic Medicine, 57,* 269–274.

Kiecolt-Glaser, J. K., Glaser, R., & Williger, D. (1985). Psychosocial enhancement of immunocompetence in a geriatric population. *Health Psychology, 4,* 25–41.

Kiecolt-Glaser, J. K., Glaser, R., Gravenstein, S., Malarkey, W. B., & Sheridan, J. (1996). Chronic stress alters the immune response to influenza virus vaccine in older adults. *Proceedings of the National Academy of Science, 93,* 3043–3047.

Kiecolt-Glaser, J. K., Malarkey, W. B., Cacioppo, J. T., & Glaser, R. (1994). Stressful personal relationships: Immune and endocrine function. In R. Glaser & J. K. Kiecolt-Glaser (Eds.),

Handbook of human stress and immunity (pp. 321–339). San Diego, CA: Academic Press.

Kiecolt-Glaser, J. K., McGuire, L., Robles, T. F., & Glaser, R. (2002). Psychoneuroimmunology: Psychological influences on immune function and health. *Journal of Consulting and Clinical Psychology, 70*(3), 537–547.

Kiecolt-Glaser, J. K., Newton, T., Cacioppo, J. T., MacCallum, R. C., Glaser, R., & Malarkey, W. B. (1997). Marital conflict and endocrine function: Are men really more physiologically affected than women? *Journal of Consulting and Clinical Psychology, 64,* 324–332.

Kiecolt-Glaser, J. K., Page, G. G., Marucha, P. T., MacCallum, R. C., & Glaser, R. (1998). Psychological influences on surgical recovery: Perspectives from psychoneuroimmunology. *American Psychologist, 53,* 1209–1218.

Kiecolt-Glaser, J. K., Preacher, K. J., MacCallum, R. C., Atkinson, C., Malarkey, W. B., & Glaser, R. (2003). Chronic stress and age-related increases in the proinflammatory cytokine IL-6. *Proceedings of the National Academy of Sciences of the United States of America, 100*(15), 9090–9095.

Kiecolt-Glaser, J. K., & Williams, D. A. (1987). Self-blame, compliance, and distress among burn patients. *Journal of Personality and Social Psychology, 53,* 187–193.

Kien, C. L. (1990). Current controversies in nutrition. *Current Problems in Pediatrics, 20,* 349–408.

Kilbourne, J. (1994). Still killing us softly: Advertising and the obsession with thinness. In P. Fallon, M. A. Katzman, & S. C. Wolley (Eds.), *Feminist perspectives on eating disorders* (pp. 395–418). New York: Guilford.

Killen, J. D., Fortmann, S. P., Kraemer, H. C., & Varady, A. (1992). Who will relapse? Symptoms of nicotine dependence predict long-term relapse after smoking cessation. *Journal of Consulting and Clinical Psychology, 60,* 797–801.

Kim, D. K., Lim, S. W., & Kim, H. (2003). Serotonin transporter gene polymorphisms in depression. *European Neuropsychopharmacology, 13*(4), S239.

Kim, E. L., Larimer, M. E., Walker, D. D., & Marlatt, G. A. (1997). Relationship of alcohol use to other health behaviors among college students. *Psychology of Addictive Behaviors, 11,* 166–173.

Kim, J., & Dellon, A. L. (2001). Pain at the site of tarsal tunnel incision due to neuroma of the posterior branch of the saphenous nerve. *Journal of the American Podiatric Medical Association, 91,* 109–114.

King, D. A., Peragallo-Dittko, V., Polonsky, W. H., Prochaska, J. O., & Vinicor, F. (1998). Strategies for improving self-care. *Patient Care, 32,* 91–111.

King, K. R. (2005). Why is discrimination stressful? The mediating role of cognitive appraisal. *Cultural Diversity & Ethnic Minority Psychology, 11*(3), 202–212.

Kinloch-de Loes, S., Hirschel, B. J., Hoen, B., Cooper, D. A., Tindal, B., Carr, A., et al. (1995). A controlled trial of zidovudine in primary human immunodeficiency virus infection. *New England Journal of Medicine, 333,* 408–413.

Kinney, R. K., Gatchel, R. J., Polatin, P. B., Fogarty, W. , & Mayer, T. (1993). Prevalence of psychopathology in acute and chronic low back pain patients. *Journal of Occupational Rehabilitation, 3,* 95–103.

Kirschbaum, C., Wolf, O., & Hellhammer, D. (1998). Adrenocortical responsiveness to psychosocial stress in humans: Sources of interindividual differences. In D. S. Krantz & A. S. Baum (Eds.), *Technology and methods in behavioral medicine* (pp. 29–45). Mahwah, NJ: Lawrence Erlbaum.

Klag, M. J., Ford, D. E., Mead, L. A., He, J., Whelton, P. K., Liang, K. Y., & Levine, D. M. (1993). Serum cholesterol in young men and subsequent cardiovascular disease. *New England Journal of Medicine, 328,* 313–318.

Klag, S. & Bradley, G. (2004). The role of hardiness in stress and illness: An exploration of the effect of negative affectivity and gender. *British Journal of Health Psychology, 9*(2), 137–161.

Kobasa, S. C., Maddi, S. R., & Kahn, S. (1982). Hardiness and health: A prospective study. *Journal of Personality and Social Psychology, 42*(1), 168–277.

Kobasa, S. C., Maddi, S. R., Puccetti, M. C., & Zola, M. A. (1985). Effectiveness of hardiness, exercise and social support as resources against illness. *Journal of Psychosomatic Research, 29,* 525–533.

Koenig, H. G., & Larson, D. B. (1998). Use of hospital services, religious attendance, and religious affiliation. *Southern Medical Journal, 91,* 925–932.

Kolb, B., & Wishaw, I. Q. (2001). *Introduction to brain and behavior.* New York: Worth.

Komaroff, A. L., & Buchwald, D. (1991). Symptoms and signs of chronic fatigue syndrome. *Reviews of Infectious Diseases, 13*(supplement 1), S8–11.

Kop, W. J., Gottdiener, J. S., & Krantz, D. S. (2001). Stress and silent ischemia. In A. Baum, T. A. Revenson, & J. E. Singer (Eds.), *Handbook of health psychology* (pp. 669–682). Mahwah, NJ: Erlbaum.

Kop, W. J., & Krantz, D. S. (1997). Type A behaviour, hostility and coronary artery disease. In A. Baum, S. Newman, J. Weinman, R. West, & C. McManus (Eds.), *Cambridge handbook of psychology, health and medicine* (pp. 183–186). Cambridge, UK: Cambridge University Press.

Kozlowski, L. T., Appel, C. P., Fredcker, R. C., & Khouw, W. (1982). Nicotine, a prescribable drug available without prescription. *The Lancet, 6,* 334.

Krantz, D. S. & Baum, A. S. (1998). *Technology and methods in behavioral medicine.* Mahwah, NJ: Lawrence Erlbaum.

Krantz, D. S., Glass, D. G., & Snyder, M. L. (1974). Helplessness, stress level, and the coronary-prone behavior pattern. *Journal of Experimental Social Psychology, 10,* 284–300.

Kraus, W. E., Houmard, J. A., Duscha, B. D., Knetzger, K. J., Wharton, M. B., McCartney, J. S., et al. (2002) Effects of the amount and intensity of exercise on plasma lipoproteins. *New England Journal of Medicine, 347,* 1483–1492.

Kreps, G. L. (2002). Advancing communication as science: The centrality of communication in health promotion. *Journal of Applied Communication Research, 30*(4), 369–381.

Krieger, N., Sidney, S., & Coakley, E. (1998). Racial discrimination and skin color in the CARDIA study: Implications for public health research. *American Journal of Public Health, 88,* 1308–1313.

Kronenberg, F., Pereira, M. A., Schmitz, M. K., Arnett, D. K., Evenson, K. R., Crapo, R. O., et al. (2000). Influence of leisure time physical activity and television watching on atherosclerosis risk factors in the NHLBI Family Heart Study. *Atherosclerosis, 153,* 433–443.

Kronmal, R. A., Cain, K. C., Ye, Z., & Omenn, G. (1993). Total serum cholesterol levels and mortality risk as a function of age: A report based on the Framingham data. *Archives of Internal Medicine, 153,* 1065–1073.

Kulik, J. A., & Mahler, H. I. M. (1993). Emotional support as a moderator of adjustment and compliance after coronary artery bypass surgery: A longitudinal study. *Journal of Behavioral Medicine, 26,* 48–63.

Kumanyika, S. (2002). The minority factor in the obesity epidemic. *Ethnicity & Disease, 12*(3), 316–319.

Kuper, H., Adami, H., Theorell, T., Weiderpass, E. (2006). Psychosocial determinants of coronary heart disease in middle-aged women: A prospective study in Sweden. *American Journal of Epidemiology 164*(4), 349–357.

Kushner, R. F., & Foster, G. D. (2000). Obesity and quality of life. *Nutrition, 16*(10), 947–952.

Kusseling, F. S., Shapiro, M. F., Greenberg, J. M., & Wenger, N. S. (1996). Understanding why heterosexual adults do not practice safer sex: A comparison of two samples. *AIDS Education and Prevention, 8*(3), 247–257.

Lachman, M. E., & Weaver, S. L. (1998). The sense of control as a moderator of social class differences in health and well-being. *Journal of Personality and Social Psychology, 74,* 763–773.

Lachman, M. E., Ziff, M. A., & Spiro, A. (1994). Maintaining a sense of control in later life. In R. P. Abeles & H. C. Gift (Eds.), *Aging and quality of life.* New York: Springer.

LaCroix, A. Z., & Haynes, S. (1987). Gender differences in the health effects of workplace roles. In R. C. Barnett & L. Biener (Eds.), *Gender and stress* (pp. 96–121). New York: Free Press.

Lakka, T. A., & Salonen, J. T. (1992). Physical activity and serum lipids: A cross-sectional population study in Eastern Finnish men. *American Journal of Epidemiology, 136,* 806–818.

Lammers, C., Ireland, M., Resnick, M., & Blum, R. (2000). Influences on adolescents' decision to postpone onset of sexual intercourse: A survival analysis of virginity among youths aged 13 to 18 years. *Journal of Adolescent Health, 26,* 42–48.

Landis, B., Jovanovic, L., Landis, E., Peterson, C. M., Groshen, S., Johnson, K., et al. (1985). Effects of stress on reduction of daily glucose range in previously stabilized insulin-dependent diabetic patients. *Diabetes Care, 8,* 624–626.

Lando, H. A. (1986). Long-term modification of chronic smoking behavior: A paradigmatic approach. *Bulletin of the Society of Psychologists in Addictive Behaviors, 5,* 5–17.

Landrine, H., & Klonoff, E. A. (1994). Cultural diversity in causal attributions for illness: The role of the supernatural. *Journal of Behavioral Medicine, 17,* 181–193.

Landro, L. (2001, February 2). Health groups push 'information therapy' to help treat patients. *The Wall Street Journal,* BI.

Langer, E. J., & Rodin, J. (1976). The effects of choice and enhanced personal responsibility for the aged: A field experiment in an institutional setting. *Journal of Personality and Social Psychology, 34,* 191–198.

Langer, E. J., Janis, I. L., & Wolfer, J. A. (1975). Reduction of psychological stress in surgical patients. *Journal of Experimental Social Psychology, 11,* 155–165.

Langner, T., & Michael, S. (1960). *Life stress and mental health.* New York: Free Press.

LaPerriere, A. R., Antoni, M. H., Schneiderman, N., Ironson, G., Klimas, N., Caralis, P., & Fletcher, M. A. (1990). Exercise intervention attenuates emotional distress and natural killer cell decrements following notification of positive serologic status for HIV-1. *Biofeedback and Self Regulation, 15,* 229–242.

Larsen, R. J. (1992). Neuroticism and selective encoding and recall of symptoms: Evidence from a combined concurrent-retrospective study. *Journal of Personality and Social Psychology, 62,* 480–488.

Latner, J. D., & Stunkard, A. J. (2003). Getting worse: The stigmatization of obese children. *Obesity Research, 11*(3), 452–456.

Lau, M. A. & Segal, Z. V. (2003). Depression in context: Strategies for guided action. *Journal of Cognitive Psychotherapy, 17*(1), 94–97.

Launer, L. J., & Kalmijn, S. (1998). Anti-oxidants and cognitive function: A review of clinical and epidemiologic studies. *Journal of Neural Transmission, 53,* 1–8.

Laux, L., & Spielberger, C. D. (1983). Stress, trait-state anxiety, and learning: Two competing models. *Series in Clinical and Community Psychology, 2,* 145–154.

Lauver, D. R., Henriques, J. B., Settersten, L., et al. (2003). Psychosocial variables, external barriers, and stage of mammography adoption. *Health Psychology, 22*(6), 649–653.

Law, A., Logan, H., & Baron, R. S. (1994). Desire for control, felt control, and stress inoculation training through dental treatment. *Journal of Personality and Social Psychology, 67,* 926–936.

Lawler, K. A., Younger, J. W., Piferi, R. L., Billington, E., Jobe, R., Edmondson, K., et al. (2003). A change of heart: Cardiovascular correlates of forgiveness in response to interpersonal threat. *Journal of Behavioral Medicine, 26*(5), 373–393.

Lawlis, G. F., Selby, D., Hinnant, D., & McCoy, C. E. (1985). Reduction of postoperative pain parameters by presurgical relaxation instructions for spinal pain patients. *Spine, 10,* 649–651.

Lazarus, R. S. (1984). On the primacy of cognition. *American Psychologist, 39,* 124–129.

Lazarus, R. S. (1993). From psychological stress to the emotions: A history of changing outlooks. *Annual Review of Psychology, 44,* 1–21.

Lazarus, R. S., & Launier, R. (1978). Stress-related transactions between person and environment. In L.A. Pervin & M. Lewis (Eds.), *Internal and external determinants of behavior* (pp. 287–327). New York: Plenum.

Leary, M. R., & Kowalski, R. M. (1990). Impression management: A literature review and two-component model. *Psychological Bulletin, 107*(1), 34.

Leclere, F. B., Rogers, R. G., & Peters, K. (1998). Neighborhood social context and racial differences in women's heart disease mortality. *Journal of Health and Social Behavior, 39,* 91–107.

Lee, C. (1993). Attitudes, knowledge, and stages of change: A survey of exercise patterns in older Australian women. *Health Psychology, 12,* 476–480.

Lee, C. D., Folsom, A. R., & Blair, S. N. (2003). Physical activity and stroke risk: A meta-analysis. *Stroke, 34*(1), 2475–2481.

Lee, I. M., Manson, J. E., Hennekens, C. H., & Paffenbarger, R. S. (1993). Body weight and mortality. A 27-year follow-up of middle-aged men. *Journal of the American Medical Association, 270*(23), 2823–2828.

Leedham, B., Meyerowitz, B. E., Muirhead, J., & Frist, W. H. (1995). Positive expectations predict health after heart transplantation. *Health psychology, 14,* 74–79.

Lefcourt, H. M. (2002). Humor. In Snyder, C. R. & Lopez, S. J. (Eds.) *Handbook of positive psychology.* New York: Oxford University Press, 619–631.

Leffell, D. J., & Brash, D. E. (1996). Sunlight and skin cancer. *Scientific American, 275,* 38–43.

Lehrer, P. M., Carr, R., Sargunaraj, D., & Woolfolk, R. L. (1994). Stress management techniques: Are they all equivalent, or do they have specific effects? *Biofeedback and Self Regulation, 19,* 353–401.

Lehrer, P., Feldman, J., Giardino, N., Song, H., & Schmaling, K. (2002). Psychological aspects of asthma. *Journal of Consulting and Clinical Psychology, 70*(3), 691–711.

Leibel, R. L., Rosenbaum, M., & Hirsch, J. (1995). Changes in energy expenditure resulting from altered body weight. *New England Journal of Medicine, 332,* 621–629.

Leigh, B. C. (1989). In search of the seven dwarves: Issues of measurement and meaning in alcohol expectancy research. *Psychological Bulletin, 105,* 361-373.

Lemos, K., Suls, J., Jenson, M., Lounsbury, P., & Gordon, E. E. (2003). How do female and male cardiac patients and their spouses share responsibilities after discharge from the hospital? *Annals of Behavioral Medicine, 25*(1), 8–15.

Lepore, S. J., Revenson, T. A., Weinberger, S. L., Weston, P., Frisina, P. G., Robertson, R., et al. (2006). Effects of social stressors on cardiovascular reactivity in Black and White women. *Annals of Behavioral Medicine, 31*(2), 120–127.

Leproult, R., Copinschi, G., Buxton, O., & Van Cauter, E. (1997). Sleep loss results in an elevation of cortisol levels the next evening. *Sleep, 20,* 865–870.

Lester, T., & Petrie, T. A. (1998). Physical, psychological, and societal correlates of bulimic symptomatology among African American college women. *Journal of Counseling Psychology, 3,* 315–321.

LeResche, L. (2000). Epidemiologic perspectives on sex differences in pain. In R. B. Fillingim (Ed.), *Sex, gender, and pain* (pp. 233–249). Seattle, WA: IASP Press.

Lerman, C., Caporaso, N. E., Audrain, J., Main, D., Bowman, E. D., Lockshin, B., Boyd, N. R., & Shields, P. G. (1999). Evidence suggesting the role of specific genetic factors in cigarette smoking. *Health Psychology, 18*(1), 14–20.

Lerman, C., Hughes, C., Benkendorf, J. L., Biesecker, B., Kerner, J., Willison, J.,and others. (1999). Racial differences in testing motivation and psychological distress following pretest education for BRCA1 gene testing. *Cancer Epidemiology, Biomarkers and Prevention, 8,* 361–368.

Lerman, C., Schwartz, M. D., Miller, S. M., Daly, M., Sands, C., & Rimer, B. K. (1996). A randomized trial of breast cancer risk counseling: Interacting effects of counseling, educational level, and coping style. *Health Psychology, 15,* 75–83.

Leserman, J., Petitto, J. M., Golden, R. N., Gaynes, B. N., Gu, H., Perkins, D. O., et al. (2000). Impact of stressful life events, depression, social support, coping, and cortisol on progression to AIDS. *American Journal of Psychiatry, 157,* 1221–1228.

Leshner, A. I. (2001). What does it mean that addiction is a brain disease? *Monitor on Psychology* (special issue on substance abuse) *32,* 19.

Letzel, H., Haan, J., & Feil, W. B. (1996). Nootropics: Efficacy and tolerability of products from three active substance classes. *Journal of Drug Development and Clinical Practice, 8,* 77–83.

Leutwyler, K. (1995, April). The price of prevention. *Scientific American, 272,* 124–129.

Leventhal, E. A., & Prohaska, T. R. (1986). Age, symptom interpretation, and health behavior. *Journal of the American Geriatrics Society, 34,* 185–191.

Leventhal, E. A., Hansell, S., Diefenbach, M., Leventhal, H., & Glass, D. C. (1996). Negative affect and self-report of physical symptoms: Two longitudinal studies of older adults. *Health Psychology, 15,* 193–199.

Leventhal, H., & Diefenbach, M. (1991). The active side of illness cognition. In J. A. Skelton & R. T. Croyle (Eds.). *Mental representation in health and illness* (pp. 247–272). New York: Springer–Verlag.

Leventhal, H., Benyamini, Y., Brownlee, S., Diefenbach, M., Leventhal, E. A., Patrick-Miller, L., & Robitaille, C. (1997). Illness representations: Theoretical foundations. In K. J. Petrie & J. A. Weinman (Eds.), *Perceptions of health and illness: Current research and applications* (pp. 19–45). Singapore: Harwood Academic Publishers.

Levesque, D. A., Prochaska, J. M., & Prochaska, J. O. (1999). Stages of change and integrated service delivery. *Consulting Psychology Journal: Practice and Research, 51,* 226–241.

Levi, L. (1974). Psychosocial stress and disease: A conceptual model. In E. K. E. Gunderson & R. H. Rahe (Eds.), *Life stress and illness* (pp. 8–33). Springfield, IL: Thomas.

Levin, J. S., & Vanderpool, H. Y. (1987). Is frequent religious attendance really conducive to better health? *Social Science and Medicine, 24,* 589–600.

Levine, F. M., & DeSimone, L. L. (1991). The effect of experimenter gender on pain report in male and female subjects. *Pain, 44,* 69–72.

Levine, J. D., Gordon, N. C., & Fields, H. L. (1978). The mechanism of placebo analgesia. *The Lancet, 8091,* 654–657.

Ley, P. (1988). *Communicating with patients.* London: Chapman and Hall.

Lichtenstein, A.H., Kennedy, E., Barrier, P., Danforth, D., et al. (1998). Dietary fat consumption and health. *Nutrition Reviews, 56*(5), S19–S28.

Lichtenstein, E., & Glasgow, R. E. (1997). A pragmatic framework for smoking cessation: Implications for clinical and public health programs. *Psychology of Addictive Behaviors, 11,* 142–151.

Lichtman, S. W., Pisarska, K., Berman, E. R., & Prestone, M. (1992). Discrepancy between self-reported and actual caloric intake and exercise in obese subjects. *New England Journal of Medicine, 327,* 1893–1898.

Lieberman, M. A. (1982). The effects of social supports on responses to stress. In L. Goldberger & L. Breznitz (Eds.), *Handbook of stress.* New York: Free Press.

Lierman, L. M., Kasprzyk, D., & Benoliel, J. Q. (1991). Understanding adherence to breast self-examination in older women. *Western Journal of Nursing Research, 13,* 46–66.

Lijing, Y. L., Liu, K., Matthews, K. A., Daviglus, M. L., et al. (2003). Psychosocial factors and risk of hypertension: The Coronary Artery Risk Development in Young Adults (CARDIA) Study. *Journal of the American Medical Association, 290*(16), 2138–2148.

Lin, E. H., & Peterson, C. (1990). Pessimistic explanatory style and response to illness. *Behaviour Research and Therapy, 28,* 243–248.

Lindsted, K. D., & Singh, P. N. (1997). Body mass and 26-year risk of mortality among women who never smoked: Findings from the Adventist Mortality Study. *American Journal of Epidemiology, 146,* 1–11.

Linkins, R. W., & Comstock, G. W. (1988). Depressed mood and development of cancer. *American Journal of Epidemiology, 128* (Abstract), 894.

Lipton, J. A., & Marbach, J. J. (1984). Ethnicity and the pain experience. *Social Science and Medicine, 19,* 1279–1298.

Littlefield, C. H., Craven, J. L., Rodin, G. M., Daneman, D., Murray, M. A., & Rydall, A. C. (1992). Relationship of self-efficacy and binging to adherence to diabetes regimen among adolescents. *Diabetes Care, 15,* 90–94.

Long, B. C., & van Stavel, R. (1995). Effects of exercise training on anxiety: A meta-analysis. *Journal of Applied Sport Psychology, 7,* 167–189.

Loucks, E. B., Berkman, L. F., Gruenewald, T.L., Seeman, T. E. (2006). Relation of social integration to inflammatory marker concentrations in men and women 70 to 79 years. *The American Journal of Cardiology, 97*(7), 1010–1017.

Lovallo, W. R., & Pishkin, V. (1980). A psychophysiological comparison of type A and B men exposed to failure and uncontrollable noise. *Psychophysiology, 17,* 29–36.

Low, A. W., & Peck, C. L. (1987). The MMPI and psychological factors in chronic low back pain: A review. *Pain, 28,* 1–12.

Lox, C. L., McAuley, E., & Tucker, R. S. (1996). Physical training effects on acute exercise-induced feeling states in HIV-1 positive individuals. *Journal of Health Psychology, 1,* 235–240.

Luecken, L. J., & Compas, B. E. (2002). Stress, coping, and immune function in breast cancer. *Annals of Behavioral Medicine, 24,* 336–344.

Lundberg, U., & Frankenhaeuser, M. (1999). Stress and workload of men and women in high-ranking positions. *Journal of Occupational Health Psychology, 4,* 142–151.

Lundberg, U., Mardberg, B., & Frankenhaeuser, M. (1994). The total workload of male and female white collar workers as related to age, occupational level, and number of children. *Scandinavian Journal of Psychology, 35,* 315–327.

Lupien, S. J., de Leon, M., De Santi, S., Convit, A., Tarshish, C., Nair, N. P. V., and others. (1998). Cortisol levels during human aging predict hippocampal atrophy and memory deficits. *Nature Neuroscience, 1,* 69–73.

Luskin, F. M., Newell, K. A., Griffith, M., Holmes, M., Telles, S., Dinucci, E., et al. (2000). A review of mind/body therapies in the treatment of musculoskeletal disorders with implications for the elderly. *Alternative Therapies, 6,* 46–56.

Lynch, B. S., Bonnie, R. J., & Nelson, D. E. (1995). Growing up tobacco free. *Journal of Public Health Policy, 16,* 492–493.

Lyness, S. A. (1993). Predictors of differences between type A and B individuals in heart rate and blood pressure reactivity. *Psychological Bulletin, 114,* 266–295.

Lytle, C. D. (1993). *An overview of acupuncture.* Rockville, MD: United States Public Health Service, Center for Devices and Radiological Health, Food and Drug Administration.

Lyubomirsky, S., Caldwell, N. D., & Nolen-Hoeksema, S. (1998). Effects of ruminative and distracting responses to depressed mood on retrieval of autobiographical memories. *Journal of Personality and Social Psychology, 75,* 166–177.

Lyvers, M. (1998). Drug addiction as a physical disease: The role of physical dependence and other chronic drug-induced neurophysiological changes in compulsive drug self-administration. *Experimental and Clinical Psychopharmacology, 6,* 107–125.

MacDonald, T., Zanna, M. P., & Fong, G. T. (1996). Why common sense goes out the window: Effects of alcohol on intentions to use condoms. *Personality and Social Psychology Bulletin, 22,* 763–775.

Macera, C. A., Armstead, C. A., & Anderson, N. B. (2001). Sociocultural influences on health. In A. Baum, T. A. Revenson, & J. E. Singer (Eds.) *Handbook of health psychology* (pp. 427–440). Mahwah, NJ: Erlbaum.

Maes, H. M., Neale, M. C., & Eaves, L. J. (1997). Genetic and environmental factors in relative body weight and human adiposity. *Behavioral Genetics* (special issue: The genetics of obesity), *27,* 325–351.

Maddi, S. R., & Kobasa, S. C. (1991). The development of hardiness. In A. Monat & R. Lazarus (Eds.), *Stress and coping: An anthology* (pp. 245–257). New York: Columbia University Press.

Maddux, J. E. (2002). Self-efficacy: The power of believing you can. In Snyder, C. R. & S. J. Lopez (Eds.), *Handbook of positive psychology* (pp. 227–287). New York: Oxford University Press.

Magni, G., Silvestro, A., Tamiello, M., Zanesco, L., & Carl, B. (1988). An integrated approach to the assessment of family adjustment to acute lymphocytic leukemia in children. *Acta Psychiatrica Scandinavica, 78,* 639–642.

Maier, K. J., Waldstein, S. R., & Synowski, S. J. (2003). Relation of cognitive appraisal to cardiovascular reactivity, affect, and task engagement. *Annals of Behavioral Medicine, 26*(1), 32–41.

Maier, S. F. (2003). Bi-directional immune-brain communication: Implications for understanding stress, pain, and cognition. *Brain, Behavior, and Immunity, 17*(2), 69–85.

Mairs, D. A. (1995). Hypnosis and pain in childbirth. *Contemporary Hypnosis, 12,* 111–118.

Manger, T. A. & Motta, R. W. (2005). The impact of an exercise program on posttraumatic stress disorder, anxiety, and depression. *International Journal of Emergency Mental Health, 7*(1), 49–57.

Manjer, J., Berglund, G., Bondesson, L., Garne, J. P., Janzon, L., Lindgren, A., and others. (2000). Intra-urban differences in breast cancer mortality: A study from the city of Malmö in Sweden. *Journal of Epidemiology and Community Health, 54*(4), 279–285.

Mann, T., Nolen-Hoeksema, S., Huang, K., & Burgard, D. (1997). Are two interventions worse than none? Joint primary and secondary prevention of eating disorders in college females. *Health Psychology, 16,* 215–225.

Mann, T., Sherman, D., & Updegraff, J. (2004). Dispositional motivations and message framing: A test of the congruency hypothesis in college students. *Health Psychology, 23*(3), 330–334.

Manne, S., Markowitz, A., Winawer, S., Meropol, N. J., et al. (2002). Correlates of colorectal cancer screening compliance and stage of adoption among siblings of individuals with early onset colorectal cancer. *Health Psychology, 21*(1), 3–15.

Mansergh, G., Marks, G., & Simoni, J. M. (1995). Self-disclosure of HIV infection among men who vary in time since seropositive diagnosis and symptomatic status. *AIDS, 9,* 639–644.

Manyande, A., Berg, S., Gettins, D., Stanford, S. C., Mazhero, S., Marks, D. F., & Salmon, P. (1995). Preoperative rehearsal of active coping imagery influences subjective and hormonal responses to abdominal surgery. *Psychosomatic Medicine, 57,* 177–182.

Markovitz, J. H., Matthews, K. A., Kannel, W. B., Cobb, J. L., & D'Agostino, R. B. (1993). Psychological predictors of hypertension in the Framingham Study. Is there tension in hypertension? *Journal of the American Medical Association, 270,* 2439–2443.

Markovitz, J. H., Matthews, K. A., Whooley, M., Lewis, C. E., & Greenlund, K. J. (2004). Increases in job strain are associated with incident hypertension in the CARDIA Study. *Annals of Behavioral Medicine, 28*(1), 4–9.

Marlatt, G. A., & Gordon, A. (1985). Abstinence and controlled drinking: Alternative treatment goals for alcoholism and problem drinking? *Bulletin of the Society of Psychologists in Addictive Behaviors, 4,* 123–150.

Martin, R. A. (1988). Humor and mastery of living: Using humor to cope with the daily stresses of growing up. *Journal of Children in Contemporary Society, 20*(1–2), 135–154.

Martin, L. L., & Tesser, A. (1989). Toward a motivational and structural theory of ruminative thought. In J. S. Uleman & J. A. Bargh (Eds.), *Unintended thought* (pp. 306–326). New York: Guilford.

Maru, S., van der Schouw, Y. T., Gimbrere, C. H., Grobbeee, D. E., & Peeters, P. H. (2004). Body mass index and short-term weight change in relation to mortality in Dutch women after age 50. *The American Journal of Clinical Nutrition, 80*(1), 231–236.

Marucah, P. T., Kiecolt-Glaser, J. K., & Favagehi, M. (1998). Mucosal wound healing is impaired by examination stress. *Psychosomatic Medicine, 60,* 362–365.

Maruta, T., Colligan, R. C., Malinchoc, M., & Offord, K. P. (2000). Optimists vs. pessimists: Survival rate among medical patients over a 30-year period. *Mayo Clinic Proceedings, 75,* 140–143.

Marvan, M. L., & Cortes-Iniestra, C. (2001). Women's beliefs about the prevalence of premenstrual syndrome and biases in recall of premenstrual changes. *Health Psychology, 20,* 276–280.

Marwick, C. (1991). Hispanic HANES takes a long look at Latino health. *Journal of the American Medical Association, 265,* 177, 181.

Marx, J. (2003). Cellular warriors at the battle of the bulge. *Science, 299*(5608), 846–849.

Mason, J. W. (1975). A historical view of the stress field. *Journal of Human Stress, 1,* 22–36.

Massey, C. V., Hupp, C. H., Kreisberg, M., Alpert, M. A., & Hoff, C. (2000). Estrogen replacement therapy is underutilized among postmenopausal women at high risk for coronary heart disease. *American Journal of the Medical Sciences, 320,* 124–127.

Masten, A. S. (2001). Ordinary magic: Resilience processes in development. *American Psychologist, 56,* 218–226.

Martire, L. M. (2005). Clinical research—The "relative" efficacy of involving family in psychosocial interventions for chronic illness: Are there added benefits to patients and family members? *Families Systems & Health, 23*(3), 312–327.

Matthews, D. A. (1997). Religion and spirituality in primary care. *Mind/Body Medicine, 2,* 9–19.

Matthews, K. A., Owens, J. F., Allen, M. T., & Stoney, C. M. (1992). Do cardiovascular responses to laboratory stress relate to ambulatory blood pressure levels? Yes, in some of the people, some of the time. *Psychosomatic Medicine, 54,* 686–697.

Matthews, K. A., Raikkonen, K., Sutton-Tyrrell, K., & Kuller, L. H. (2004). Optimistic attitudes protect against progression of carotid atherosclerosis in healthy middle-aged women. *Psychosomatic Medicine, 66*(5), 640–644.

Matthews, K. A., Siegel, J. M., Kuller, L. H., Thompson, M., & Varat, M. (1983). Determinants of decisions to seek medical treatment by patients with acute myocardial infarction symptoms. *Journal of Personality and Social Psychology, 44,* 1144–1156.

Maunsell, E., Brisson, J., Mondor, M., Verreault, R., & Deschenes, L. (2001). Stressful life events and survival after breast cancer. *Psychosomatic Medicine, 63*(2), 306–315.

Mayer, J. D., Salovey, P., Caruson, D. R., & Sitarenios, G. (2001). Emotional intelligence as a standard intelligence. *Emotion, 1*(3), 232–242.

Mays, V. M., So, B. T., Cochran, S. D., Detels, R., Benjamin, R., Allen, E., et al. (2001). HIV disease in ethnic minorities: Implications of racial/ethnic differences in disease susceptibility and drug dosage response for HIV infection and treatment. In A. Baum, T. A. Revenson, & J. E. Singer (Eds.), *Handbook of health psychology* (pp. 801–816). Mahwah, NJ: Erlbaum.

Mazas, C. A., Cofta-Woerpel, L., Daza, P., Fouladi, R. T., et al. (2006). At-risk drinking in employed men and women. *Annals of Behavioral Medicine, 31*(3), 279–287.

Mazer, S. P., & Rabbani, L. E. (2004). Evidence for C-reactive protein's role (CRP) in vascular disease: Atherothrombosis, immuno-regulation, and CRP. *Journal of Thrombosis and Thrombolysis, 17*(2), 95–105.

McCabe, M. P., & Ricciardelli, L. A. (2003). Sociocultural influences on body image and body changes among adolescent boys and girls. *Journal of Social Psychology, 143*(1), 5–26.

McCann, I. L., & Holmes, D. S. (1984). Influence of aerobic exercise on depression. *Journal of Personality and Social Psychology, 46,* 1142–1147.

McCarthy, J. (2001, May). Superfoods or superfrauds? *Shape, 20,* 104–106.

McCullough, M. E., Hoyt, W. T., Larson, D. B., Koenig, H. G., & Thoresen, C. (2000). Religious involvement and mortality: A meta-analytic review. *Health Psychology, 19,* 211–222.

McEwen, B. (1994). Stress and the nervous system. *Seminars in Neuroscience, 6*(4), 195–196.

McEwen, B., & Stellar, E. (1993). Stress and the individual. Mechanisms leading to disease. *Archives of Internal Medicine, 153*(18), 2093–2101.

McEwen, B. S. (1998). Stress, adaptation and disease: Allostasis and allostatic load. *Annals of the New York Academy of Sciences, 840,* 33–44.

McEwen, B. S., & Magarinos, A. M. (1997). Stress effects on morphology and function of the hippocampus. In R. Yehuda & A. C. McFarlane (Eds.), *Psychobiology of posttraumatic stress disorder* (pp. 271–284). New York: New York Academy of Sciences.

McGrady, A. (1994). Effects of group relaxation training and thermal biofeedback on blood pressure and related physiological and psychological variables in essential hypertension. *Biofeedback and Self-Regulation, 19,* 51–66.

McGrady, A. (1997). Outcome of biofeedback-assisted relaxation for neurocardiogenic syncope and headache: A clinical replication series. *Applied Psychophysiology and Biofeedback, 22*(1), 63–72.

McGrady, A., & Horner, J. (1999). Role of mood in outcome of biofeedback assisted relaxation therapy in insulin dependent diabetes mellitus. *Applied Psychophysiology and Biofeedback, 24,* 79–88.

McGrath, J. (2003). Pediatric cardiovascular reactivity: Evidence for stable individual differences and differentiation of higher- and lower-risk children. *Dissertation Abstracts International, 63*(10-B), 4913.

McKegney, F. P., & O'Dowd, M. A. (1992). Suicidality and HIV status. *American Journal of Psychiatry, 149*(3), 396–398.

McKenna, M. C., Zevon, M. A., Corn, B., & Rounds, J. (1999). Psychosocial factors and the development of breast cancer: A meta-analysis. *Health Psychology, 18,* 520–531.

McLaren, L., Hardy, R., & Kuh, D. (2003). Women's body satisfaction at midlife and lifetime body size: A prospective study. *Health Psychology, 22*(4), 370–377.

McMillen, D. L., Smith, S. M., & Wells-Parker, E. (1989). The effects of alcohol, expectancy, and sensation seeking on driving risk taking. *Addictive Behaviors, 14,* 477–483.

McMurran, M. (1994). *The Psychology of Addiction.* Philadelphia: Taylor & Francis.

McMurtrie, B. (1994, July 19). Overweight fatten ranks. *New York Newsday,* p. A26.

McTiernan, A., Kooperberg, C., White, E., Wilcox, S., et al. (2003). Recreational physical activity and the risk of breast cancer in postmenopausal women. *Journal of the American Medical Association, 290*(10), 1331–1336.

Meara, E., Kotagal, U. R., Atherton, H. D., & Lieu, T. A. (2004). Impact of early newborn discharge legislation and early follow-up visits on infant outcomes in a state Medicaid population. *Pediatrics, 113*(6), 1619–1627.

Mechanic, D. (1978). *Medical sociology.* New York: Free Press.

Mechanic, D., & Angel, R. J. (1987). Some factors associated with the report and evaluation of back pain. *Journal of Health and Social Behavior, 28,* 131–139.

Mehilli, J., Kastrati, A., Dirschinger, J., Pache, J., Seyfarth, M., Blasini, R., et al. (2002). Sex-based analysis of outcomes in patients with acute myocardial infarction treated predominantly with percutaneous coronary intervention. *Journal of the American Medical Association, 287*(2), 210–215.

Meichenbaum, D. (1985). *Stress inoculation training.* New York: Pergamon.

Melchart, D., Linde, K., Worku, F., Sarkady, L., Holzmann, M., Jurcic, K., & Wagner, H. (1995). Results of five randomized studies on the immunomodulatory activity of preparations of Echinacea. *Journal of Alternative and Complementary Medicine, 1,* 145–160.

Melzack, R. (1993). Pain: Past, present, and future. *Canadian Journal of Experimental Psychology, 47,* 615–629.

Melzack, R., & Torgerson, W. S. (1971). On the language of pain. *Anesthesiology, 34,* 50–59.

Melzack, R., & Wall, P. D. (1965). Pain mechanisms: A new theory. *Science, 150,* 971–979.

Melzack, R., & Wall, P. D. (1988). *The challenge of pain.* New York: Basic Books.

Mercer, W. B. (2006). Behavioral Health: Addressing hidden health care costs. http://www.mercerhr.com/summary.jhtml?idContent =1089855

Merriman, J. (1999, May 13). These pounds aren't sterling. http://www.abcnews.go.com

Merritt, M. M., Bennett, G. G., Williams, R. B., Edwards, C. L., & Sollers, J. J. (2006). Perceived racism and cardiovascular reactivity and recovery to personally relevant stress. *Health Psychology, 25*(3), 364–369.

Merritt, M. M., Bennett, G. G., Williams, R. A., Sollers, J. J., & Thayer, J. F. (2004). Low educational attainment, John Henryism, and cardiovascular reactivity to and recovery from personally relevant stress. *Psychosomatic Medicine, 66*(1), 49–55.

Metzler, C. W., Noell, J., Biglan, A., & Ary, D. (1994). The social context for risky sexual behavior among adolescents. *Journal of Behavioral Medicine, 17*(4), 419–438.

Meyer, D., Leventhal, H., & Gutmann, M. (1985). Common-sense models of illness: The example of hypertension. *Health Psychology, 4,* 115–135.

Meyer, J. M., & Stunkard, A. J. (1994). Twin studies of human obesity. In C. Bouchard (Ed.), *The genetics of obesity* (pp. 63–78). Boca Raton, FL: CRC Press.

Meyerowitz, B. E., Richardson, J., Hudson, S., & Leedham, B. (1998). Ethnicity and cancer outcomes: Behavioral and psychosocial considerations. *Psychological Bulletin, 123,* 47–70.

Michael, E. S. & Burns, J. W. (2004). Catastrophizing and pain sensitivity among chronic pain patients: Moderating effects of sensory and affect focus. *Annals of Behavioral Medicine, 27*(3), 185–194.

Michie, S., Marteau, T. M., & Kidd, J. (1992). Predicting antenatal class attendance: Attitudes of self and others. *Psychology and Health, 7,* 225–234.

Milberger, S., Biederman, J., Faraone, S. V., Chen, L., & Jones, J. (1996). Is maternal smoking during pregnancy a risk factor for attention deficit hyperactivity disorder in children? *American Journal of Psychiatry, 153,* 1138–1142.

Milby, J. B., Schumacher, J. E., & Tucker, J. A. (2004). Substance use disorders. In T. J. Boll, J. M. Raczynski, & L. C. Leviton (eds.)

Handbook of clinical health psychology, vol. 2 (pp. 43–47). Washington: American Psychological Association.

Milkie, M. A., & Peltola, P. (1999). Playing all the roles: Gender and the work-family balancing act. *Journal of Marriage and the Family, 61,* 476–490.

Millar, M. G., & Millar, K. (1995). Negative affective consequences of thinking about disease detection behaviors. *Health Psychology, 14,* 141–146.

Miller, D. A., McCluskey-Fawcett, K., & Irving, L. M. (1993). The relationship between childhood sexual abuse and subsequent onset of bulimia nervosa. *Child Abuse & Neglect, 17,* 305–314.

Miller, G. A., & Nuessle, W. (1978). Characteristics of the emotional responsiveness of sensitizers and repressors to social stimuli. *Journal of Consulting and Clinical Psychology, 46,* 339–340.

Miller, G. E., & Cohen, S. (2001). Psychological interventions and the immune system: A meta-analytic review and critique. *Health Psychology, 20,* 47–63.

Miller, G. E., Cohen, S., & Ritchey, A. K. (2002). Chronic psychological stress and the regulation of pro-inflammatory cytokines: A glucocorticoid-resistance model. *Health Psychology, 21*(6), 531–541.

Miller, K., & Miller, P. M. (2001). *Journey of hope: The story of Irish immigration to America.* New York: Chronicle Books.

Miller, L. C., Bettencourt, B. A., DeBro, S., & Hoffman, V. (1993). Negotiating safer sex: Interpersonal dynamics. In J. B. Pryor & G. D. Reeder (Eds.), *The social psychology of HIV infection* (pp. 85–123). Hillsdale, NJ: Erlbaum.

Miller, L. J., Holicky, E. L., Ulrich, C. D., & Wieben, E. D. (1995). Abnormal processing of the human cholecystokinin receptor gene in association with gallstones and obesity. *Gastroenterology, 109,* 1375–1380.

Miller, M. F., Barabasz, A. F., & Barabasz, M. (1991). Effects of active alert and relaxation hypnotic inductions on cold pressor pain. *Journal of Abnormal Psychology, 100,* 223–226.

Miller, N. E. (1969). Psychosomatic effects of specific types of training. *Annals of the New York Academy of Sciences, 159*(3), 1025–1040.

Miller, R. H., & Luft, H. S. (1994). Managed care plans: Characteristics, growth, and premium performance. *Annual Review of Public Health, 15,* 437–459.

Miller, S. M., & Mangan, C. E. (1983). Interacting effects of information and coping style in adapting to gynecologic stress: Should the doctor tell all? *Journal of Personality and Social Psychology, 45,* 223–236.

Miller, T. Q., Smith, T. W., Turner, C. W., Guijarro, M. L., & Hallet, A. J. (1996). A meta-analytic review of research on hostility and physical health. *Psychological Bulletin, 119,* 322–348.

Milling, L. S., Levine, M. R., & Meunier, S. A. (2003). Hypnotic enhancement of cognitive-behavioral interventions for pain: An analogue treatment study. *Health Psychology, 22*(4), 406–413.

Mills, P. J., Davidson, K. W., & Farag, N. H. (2004). Work stress and hypertension: A call from research into intervention. *Annals of Behavioral Medicine, 28*(1), 1–3.

Mintz, L. B., & Kashubeck, S. (1999). Body image and disordered eating among Asian American and Caucasian college students:

An examination of race and gender differences. *Psychology of Women Quarterly, 23,* 781–796.

Mintz, L. B., Kashubeck, S., & Tracy, L. S. (1995). Relations among parental alcoholism, eating disorders, and substance abuse in nonclinical college women: Additional evidence against the uniformity myth. *Journal of Counseling Psychology, 42,* 65–70.

Minuchin, S., Rosman, B. L., & Baker, L. (1978). *Psychosomatic families: Anorexia nervosa in context.* Cambridge, MA: Harvard University Press.

Miranda, J. A., Perez-Stable, E. J., Munoz, R., Hargreaves, W., & Henke, C. J. (1991). Somatization, psychiatric disorder, and stress in utilization of ambulatory medical services. *Health Psychology, 10,* 46–51.

Moerman, D. E. (2002). *Meaning, medicine, and the 'placebo effect.'* Cambridge: Cambridge Studies in Medical Anthropology.

Monroe, S. M., & Simons, A. D. (1991). Diathesis-stress theories in the context of life stress research: Implications for the depressive disorders. *Psychological Bulletin, 110,* 406–425.

Montgomery, G. H. (2004). Presurgery distress and specific response expectancies predict postsurgery outcomes in surgery patients confronting breast cancer. *Health Psychology, 23*(4), 381–387.

Monti, P. M., Rohsenow, D. J., Rubonis, A. V., & Niaura, R. S. (1993). Cue exposure with coping skills treatment for male alcoholics: A preliminary investigation. *Journal of Consulting and Clinical Psychology, 61,* 1011–1019.

Moore, J. S. (1993). *Chiropractic in America.* Baltimore: Johns Hopkins University Press.

Moos, R. H. (2002). Life stressors, social resources, and coping skills in youth: Applications to adolescents with chronic disorders. *Journal of Adolescent Health, 30*(4), 22–29.

Morey, S. S. (1998). NIH issues consensus statement on acupuncture. *American Family Physician, 57,* 2545–2546.

Morgan, C. A., Wang, S., Rasmusson, A., Hazlett, G., Anderson, G., Charney, D. S. (2001). Relationship among plasma cortisol, catecholamines, neuropeptide Y, and human performance during exposure to uncontrollable stress. *Psychosomatic Medicine, 63*(3), 412–422.

Morley, S. (1997). Pain management. In A. Baum, S. Newman, J. Weinman, R. West, & C. McManus (Eds.), *Cambridge handbook of psychology, health and medicine* (pp. 234–237). Cambridge: Cambridge University Press.

Morojele, N. K., & Stephenson, G. M. (1994). Addictive behaviours: Predictors of abstinence intentions and expectations in the theory of planned behavior. In D. R. Rutter & L. Quine (Eds.), *Social psychology and health: European perspectives* (pp. 47–70). Aldershot, England: Avebury.

Morrill, A. C., Ickovics, J. R., Golubchikov, V. V., Beren, S. E. & Rodin, J. (1996). Safer sex: Social and psychological predictors of behavioral maintenance and change among heterosexual women. *Journal of Consulting & Clinical Psychology, 64,* 819–828.

Morris, D. L., Kritchevsky, S. B., & Davis, C. E. (1994). Serum carotenoids and coronary heart disease. The Lipid Research Clinics Coronary Primary Prevention Trial and Follow-up Study. *Journal of the American Medical Association, 272,* 1439–1441.

Morrow, G. R., Asbury, R., Hammon, S., & Dobkin, P. (1992). Comparing the effectiveness of behavioral treatment for chemotherapy-induced nausea and vomiting when administered by oncologists, oncology nurses, and clinical psychologists. *Health Psychology, 11,* 250–256.

Moskowitz, J. T., Folkman, S., Collette, L., & Vittinghoff, E. (1996). Coping and mood during AIDS-related caregiving and bereavement. *Annals of Behavioral Medicine, 18,* 49–57.

Moss, A. J., Allen, K. F., Giovino, G. A., & Mills, S. L. (1992). Recent trends in adolescent smoking, smoking-update correlates, and expectations about the future. *Advance Data* No. 221 (Vital and Health Statistics of the Centers for Disease Control and Prevention).

Moss, D. & Gunkelman, J. (2002). Task force report on methodology and empirically supported treatments. *Applied Psychophysiology and Biofeedback, 27*(4), 271–272.

Moss-Morris, R., & Petrie, K. J. (1997). Cognitive distortions of somatic experiences: Revision and validation of a measure. *Journal of Psychosomatic Research, 43,* 293–306.

Moya-Albiol, L., Salvador, A., Costa, R., et al. (2001). Psychophysiological responses to the Stroop task after a maximal cycle ergometry in elite sportsmen and physically active subjects. *International Journal of Psychophysiology, 40*(1), 47–60.

Muellersdorf, M., & Soederback, I. (2000). The actual state of the effects, treatment and incidence of disabling pain in a gender perspective—A Swedish study. *Disability and Rehabilitation, 22,* 840–854.

Muraven, M., Tice, D. M., & Baumeister, R. F. (1998). Self-control as a limited resource: Regulatory depletion patterns. *Journal of Personality and Social Psychology, 74,* 774–789.

Murray, B. (1999, June). Customized appeals may increase cancer screening. *American Psychological Association Monitor, 30,* 35–36.

Murray, M., & Chamberlain, K. (1999). *Qualitative health psychology: Theories and methods.* London: Sage.

Murray, R. P., Connett, J. E., Tyas, S. L., Bond, R., et al. (2002). Alcohol volume, drinking pattern, and cardiovascular disease morbidity and mortality: Is there a U-shaped function? *American Journal of Epidemiology, 155*(3), 242–248.

Musick, D. W., Cheever, T. R., Quinlivan, S., & Nora, L. M. (2003). Spirituality in medicine: A comparison of medical students' attitudes and clinical performance. *Academic Psychiatry, 27,* 67–73.

Myers, H. F. (1982). Coping styles and competence as mediators of self-reported responses to stress. *Psychological Reports, 50*(1), 303–313.

Myers, H. F., Kagawa-Singer, M., Kumanika, S. K., Lex, B. W., & Markides, K. S. (1995). Panel III: Behavioral risk factors related to chronic diseases in ethnic minorities. *Health Psychology, 14,* 613–621.

Myers, L., Coughlin, S. S., Webber, L. S., Srinivasan, S. R., & Berenson, G. S. (1995). Prediction of adult cardiovascular multifactorial risk factors from childhood risk factor levels: The Bogalusa Heart Study. *American Journal of Epidemiology, 142,* 918–924.

Myrin, B. & Lagerstrom, M. (2006). Health behaviour and sense of coherence among pupils aged 14–15. *Scandinavian Journal of Caring Sciences, 20*(3), 339–346.

Naimi, T. S., Brewer, R. D., Mokdad, A., Denny, C., et al. (2003). Binge drinking among U.S. Adults. *Journal of the American Medical Association, 289*(1), 70–75.

Nakamura, M., Tanaka, M., Kinukawa, N., Abe, S., Itoh, K., Imai, K., Masuda, T., & Nakao, H. (2000). Association between basal serum and leptin levels and changes in abdominal fat distribution during weight loss. *Journal of Atherosclerosis and Thrombosis, 6,* 28–32.

Nakao, M., Nomura, S., Shimosawa, T., Yoshiuchi, K., Kumano, H., Kuboki, T., Suematsu, H., & Fujita, T. (1997). Clinical effects of blood pressure biofeedback treatment on hypertension by auto-shaping. *Psychosomatic Medicine, 59,* 331–338.

Naparstek, B. (1994). *Staying well with guided imagery.* New York: Warner Books.

Nasser, M. (1997). *Culture and weight consciousness.* New York: Routledge.

National Center for Health Statistics. (2000). *Health, United States, 2000.* http://www.cdc.gov/nchs

National Institutes of Health. (1998). Technology Assessment Statement: *Acupuncture.* Washington, DC: Author.

National Center for Environmental Health (2006). Asthma. Centers for Disease Control and Prevention. www.cdc.gov/asthma/basics.htm#facts

National Center for Health Statistics. (1999). *Health, United States, 1997.* Washington, DC: U.S. Government Printing Office.

National Center for Health Statistics. (2005). *Health, United States, 2005.* Hyattsville, MD: U.S. Department of Health and Human Services.

National Center for Health Statistics. (2006). United States Life Tables, 2003. *National Vital Statistics Reports, 54*(14). Hyattsville, MD: U.S. Department of Health and Human Services.

National Drug Intelligence Center. (2001). Other dangerous drugs. http://www.usdoj.gov/ndic/pubs07/717/odd.htm

National Institute on Aging. (2006). What is Alzheimer's disease? U.S. National Institutes of Health. http://www.nia.nih.gov/Alzheimers/AlzheimersInformation/GeneralInfo

National Institute on Alcohol Abuse and Alcoholism (NIAAA). (2001, March). *Quick Facts.* Bethesda, MD: National Institutes of Health. http://www.niaaa.nih.gov/databases

National Institutes of Health Consensus Conference. (2003). Acupuncture. *Journal of the American Medical Association, 280*(17), 1518–1524.

National Institutes of Health. (2006). Nontraditional health care. National Institutes of Health. U.S. Department of Health and Human Services. http://health.nih.gov/search_results.asp

National Public Health Institute (2006). North Karelia Project. http://www.ktl.fi/portal/english/

National Vital Statistics Reports (1998). Deaths: Final data for 1996. *47*(9), Hyattsville, MD: National Center for Health Statistics, 26.

National Vital Statistics Reports (2000). Deaths: Final data for 1998. *48*(11), Hyattsville, MD: National Center for Health Statistics, 26.

National Vital Statistics Reports. (2003). Deaths: Preliminary data for 2001. Hyattsville, MD: National Center for Health Statistics.

Nathan, P. E., & O'Brien, J. S. (1971). An experimental analysis of the behavior of alcoholics and nonalcoholics during prolonged experimental drinking: A necessary precursor of behavior therapy? *Behavior Therapy, 2,* 455–476.

NCCAM. (2004). What is complementary and alternative medicine? National Center for Complementary and Alternative Medicine. http://nccam.nih.gov/health/whatiscam/

NCHS. (2004). 2004 asthma data. National Center for Health Statistics. www.cdc.gov/asthma/nhis/default.htm

NCHS. (2005). *Health, United States.* National Center for Health Statistics. Hyattsville, MD: U.S. Public Health Service.

NCHS. (2005). *Health, United States.* 2005. Hyattsville, MD: U.S. Department of Health and Human Services, Table 73, 292.

NCEP. (2006). National cholesterol education program. Washington: Department of Health and Human Services. http://www.nhlbi.nih.gov/about/ncep/index.htm

NCHS. (2006). *Healthy People 2000 Review: National Health Promotion and Disease Prevention Objectives.* National Center for Health Statistics. Hyattsville, MD: Department of Health and Human Services.

Neergaard, L. (1999, June 18). Six deadliest diseases are cheap to prevent. *The Tribune,* p. A3.

Nelson, M. E., Fiatarone, M. A., Morganti, C. M., Trice, I., Greenberg, R. A., & Evans, W. J. (1994). Effects of high-intensity strength training on multiple risk factors for osteoporotic fractures. A randomized controlled trial. *Journal of the American Medical Association, 272,* 1909–1914.

Nesse, R. M., & Williams, G. C. (1998). Evolution and the origins of disease. *Scientific American.* http://www.sciam.com

Nevid, J. S. (1996). Smoking cessation with ethnic minorities: Themes and approaches. *Journal of Social Distress and the Homeless, 5,* 39–54.

Nevid, J. S., Rathus, S. A., & Rubenstein, H. R. (1998). *Health in the new millennium.* New York: Worth.

Newman, M. M., & Halmi, K. A. (1988). The endocrinology of anorexia nervosa and bulimia nervosa. *Neurologic Clinics, 6*(1), 195–212.

Newton, T. L., & Contrada, R. J. (1992). Repressive coping and verbal autonomic response dissociation: The influence of social context. *Journal of Personality and Social Psychology, 62,* 159–167.

NHANES III (2002). *Third national health and nutrition examination survey.* U.S. Department of Health and Human Services. http://www.cdc.gov/nchs/products/elec_prods/subject/nhanes3.htm

NIAAA (2006). College students and drinking. National Institute on Alcohol Abuse and Alcoholism. http://pubs.niaaa.nih.gov/publications/aa29.htm

Niederhoffer, K. G., & Pennebaker, J. W. (2002). Sharing one's story: On the benefits of writing or talking about emotional expression. In Snyder, C. R. & S. J. Lopez (Eds.), *Handbook of positive psychology* (pp. 573–583). New York: Oxford University Press.

Nivision, M. E., & Endresen, I. M. (1993). An analysis of relationships among environmental noise, annoyance and sensitivity to noise, and the consequences for health and sleep. *Journal of Behavior Medicine, 16,* 257–276.

Nolen-Hoeksema, S., Parker, L. E., & Larson, J. (1994). Ruminative coping with depressed mood following loss. *Journal of Personality and Social Psychology, 67,* 92–104.

Nolte, E., McKee, M., & Scholz, R. (2004). Progress in health care, progress in health? *Demographic Research, 2,* 1–26.

Nordstrom, C. K., Dwyer, K. M., Merz, C. N., & Dwyer, S. A. (2003). Leisure time physical activity and early atherosclerosis:

The Los Angeles Atherosclerosis Study. *American Journal of Medicine, 115*(1), 19–25.

Norris, J., Nurius, P. S., & Dimeff, L. A. (1996). Through her eyes: Factors affecting women's perception of and resistance to acquaintance sexual aggression threat. *Psychology of Women Quarterly, 20,* 123–145.

Norvell, N., & Belles, D. (1993). Psychological and physical benefits of circuit weight training in law enforcement personnel. *Journal of Consulting and Clinical Psychology, 61,* 520–527.

Nowak, R. (1994). Nicotine research. Key study unveiled—11 years late. *Science, 264,* 196–197.

Nuclear Energy Agency (1995). Chernobyl ten years on: Radiological and health impact. www.nea.fr/html/rp/chernobyl

Nutrition Action Health Letter (2006, January/February). Supplementing their income: How celebrities turn trust into cash. http://www.cspinet.org/nah/01_06/sup.pdf#search=%22 andrew%20weil%22

Nutrition Action Newsletter, 2001. *The best and worst breakfasts.* http://www.cspinet.org/nah/index.htm

Nyamathi, A., Stein, J. A., & Brecht, M. (1995). Psychosocial predictors of AIDS risk behavior and drug use behavior in homeless and drug addicted women of color. *Health Psychology, 14,* 265–273.

O'Brien, S. J., & Vertinsky, P. A. (1991). Unfit survivors: Exercise as a resource for aging women. *The Gerontologist, 31,* 347–357.

Odendaal, J. S. (2000). Animal-assisted therapy—magic or medicine? *Journal of Psychosomatic Research, 49*(4), 275–280.

Ohlund, C., Lindstrom, I., Areskoug, B., Eek, C., Peterson, L. E., & Nachemson, A. (1994). Pain behavior in industrial subacute low back pain. *Pain, 58,* 201–209.

Oldridge, N. B., (1988). Cardiac rehabilitation exercise programme. Compliance and compliance-enhancing strategies. *Sports Medicine, 6,* 42–55.

Olds, J., & Milner, P. (1954). Positive reinforcement produced by electrical stimulation of the septal area and other regions of rat brain. *Journal of Comparative and Physiological Psychology, 47,* 419–427.

O'Leary, V. E., & Ickovics, J. R. (1995). Resilience and thriving in response to challenge: An opportunity for a paradigm shift in women's health. *Women's Health, 1*(2), 121–142.

O'Keefe, J., Poston, W., Haddock, C., Moe, R. & Harris, W. Psychosocial stress and cardiovascular disease: How to heal a broken heart. *Comprehensive Therapy, 30*(1), 37–43.

Onishi, N. (2001, February 21). In Africa, Rubensesque rules: Women use animal feed, steroids for beauty ideal. *Anchorage Daily News,* A-1, A-5.

Ory, M. G., & Cox, D. M. (1994). Forging ahead: Linking health and behavior to improve quality of life in older people. *Social Indicators Research, 33,* 89–120.

Oster, G., Thompson, D., Edelsberg, J., Bird, A. P., & Colditz, G. A. (1999). Lifetime health and economic benefits of weight loss among obese persons. *American Journal of Public Health, 89,* 1536–1542.

Ostir, G. V., Markides, K. S., Black, S. A., & Goodwin, J. S. (2000). Emotional well-being predicts subsequent functional independence and survival. *Journal of the American Geriatrics Society, 48,* 473–478.

Outlaw, F. H. (1993). Stress and coping: The influence of racism on the cognitive appraisal processing of African Americans. *Issues in Mental Health Nursing, 14*(4), 399–409.

Owen, N., & Vita, P. (1997). Physical activity and health. In A. Baum, S. Newman, J. Weinman, R. West, & C. McManus (Eds.), *Cambridge handbook of psychology, health and medicine* (pp. 154–157). Cambridge: Cambridge University Press.

Pagoto, S., McChargue, D., & Fuqua, R. W. (2003). Effects of a multi-component intervention on motivation and sun protection behaviors among Midwestern beachgoers. *Health Psychology, 22*(4), 429–433.

Pall, M. L. (2000). Elevated, sustained peroxynitrite levels as the cause of chronic fatigue syndrome. *Medical Hypotheses, 54,* 115–125.

Papas, C. A. (1999, June 15). Unlike women, many men avoid doctor even when feeling pain. *USA Today,* p. 11D.

Paran, E., Amir, M., & Yaniv, N. (1996). Evaluating the response of mild hypertensives to biofeedback-assisted relaxation using a mental stress test. *Journal of Behavior Therapy and Experimental Psychiatry, 27,* 157–167.

Parker, R. (2000). Health literacy: A challenge for American patients and their health care providers. *Health Promotion International, 15,* 277–283.

Parker, P. A., & Kulik, J. A. (1995). Burnout, self- and supervisor-rated job performance, and absenteeism among nurses. *Journal of Behavioral Medicine, 18,* 581–599.

Parrott, A. C. (1999). Does cigarette smoking cause stress? *American Psychologist, 54,* 817–820.

Parsons, J. T., Huszti, H. C., Crudder, S. O., et al. (2000). Maintenance of safer sexual behaviours: Evaluation of a theory-based intervention for HIV seropositive men with haemophilia and their female partners. *Haemophilia, 6*(3), 181–190.

Pate, J. E., Pumariega, A. J., Hester, C., & Garner, D. M. (1992). Cross-cultural patterns in eating disorders: A review. *Journal of the American Academy of Child and Adolescent Psychiatry, 31,* 802–809.

Patel, M. (1987). Problems in the evaluation of alternative medicine. *Social Science and Medicine, 25,* 669–675.

Patenaude, A. F., Hirsch, D., Breyer, J., & Astbury, J. (1990). Psychosocial effects of transfusion-related HIV infection in pediatric cancer patients. *Journal of Psychosocial Oncology, 8,* 41–58.

Patterson, T. L., Shaw, W. S., & Semple, S. J. (2003). Reducing the sexual risk behaviors of HIV+ individuals: Outcome of a randomized controlled trial. *Annals of Behavioral Medicine, 25*(2), 137–145.

Patterson, T. L., Shaw, W. S., Semple, S. J., & Cherner, M. (1996). Relationship of psychosocial factors to HIV disease progression. *Annals of Behavioral Medicine, 18,* 30–39.

Pearsall, Paul (2004). *The Beethoven factor: The new psychology of hardiness, happiness, healing, and hope.* New York: Hampton Roads Publishing.

Peat, G. M., Moores, L., Goldingay, S., & Hunter, M. (2001). Pain management program follow-ups. A national survey of current practice in the United Kingdom. *Journal of Pain and Symptom Management, 21,* 218–226.

Pechmann, C., & Shih, C. F. (1999). Smoking scenes in movies and antismoking advertisements before movies: Effects on youth. *Journal of Marketing, 63,* 1–13.

Pender, N. J., Walker, S. N., Sechrist, K. R., & Frank-Stromborg, M. (1990). Predicting health-promoting lifestyles in the workplace. *Nursing Research, 39,* 326–332.

Penedo, F. J., Gonzalez, J. S., Davis, C., Dahn, J. et al. (2003). Coping and psychological distress among symptomatic HIV+ men who have sex with men. *Annals of Behavioral Medicine, 25*(3), 203–213.

Penley, J. A., Tomaka, J., & Wiebe, J. S. (2002). The association of coping to physical and psychological health outcomes: A meta-analytic review. *Journal of Behavioral Medicine, 25*(6), 551–603.

Penedo, F. J., Dahn, J. R., Molton, I., et al. (2004). Cognitive-behavioral stress management improves stress-management skills and quality of life in men recovering from treatment of prostate carcinoma. *Cancer, 100*(1), 192–200.

Pennebaker, J. W. (1980). Perceptual and environmental determinants of coughing. *Basic and Applied Social Psychology, 1,* 83–91.

Pennebaker, J. W. (1982). *The psychology of physical symptoms.* New York: Springer-Verlag.

Pennebaker, J. W. (1992). Inhibition as the linchpin of health. In H. S. Friedman (Ed.), *Hostility, coping, & health* (pp. 127–139). Washington, DC: American Psychological Association.

Pennebaker, J. W. (1995). Emotion, disclosure, and health: An overview. In J. W. Pennebaker (Ed.). *Emotion, disclosure, and health* (pp. 3–10). Washington, DC: American Psychological Association.

Pennebaker, J. W., & Epstein, D. (1983). Implicit psychophysiology: Effects of common beliefs and idiosyncratic physiological responses on symptom reporting. *Journal of Personality, 51,* 468–496.

Pennebaker, J. W., & Francis, M. E. (1996). Cognitive, emotional, and language processes in disclosure. *Cognition & Emotion, 10,* 601–626.

Pennebaker, J. W., Burnam, M. A., Schaeffer, M. A., & Harper, D. C. (1977). Lack of control as a determinant of perceived physical symptoms. *Journal of Personality and Social Psychology, 35,* 167–174.

Penninx, B. W., van Tilburg, T., Boeke, A. J., Deeg, D. J., Kriegsman, D. M., & van Eijk, J. T. (1998). Effects of social support and personal coping resources on depressive symptoms: Different for various chronic diseases? *Health Psychology, 17,* 551–558.

Perez, D. D., Strobel, P., Foncea, R., Diez, M. S., et al. (2002). Effects of alcohol/wine on cartdioprotection and atherosclerosis—Wine, diet, antioxidant defenses, and oxidative damage. *Annals of the New York Academy of Sciences, 957,* 136–145.

Perkins, K. A., Dubbert, P. M., Martin, J. E., Faulstich, M. E., & Harris, J. K. (1986). Cardiovascular reactivity to psychological stress in aerobically trained versus untrained mild hypertensives and normotensives. *Health Psychology, 5,* 407–421.

Perlick, D., & Silverstein, B. (1994). Faces of female discontent: Depression, disordered eating, and changing gender roles. In P. Fallon & M. A. Katzman (Eds.), *Feminist perspectives on eating disorders* (pp. 77–93). New York: Guilford.

Perls, T. T., & Fretts, R. C. (1998). Why women live longer than men. *Scientific American, 2,* 100–103.

Perna, F. M., Antoni, M. H., Baum, A., et al. (2003). Cognitive behavioral stress management effects on injury and illness among competitive athletes: A randomized clinical trial. *Annals of Behavioral Medicine, 25*(1), 66–73.

Perri, M. G. (1998). The maintenance of treatment effects in the long-term management of obesity. *Clinical Psychology: Science and Practice, 5,* 526–543.

Perry-Jenkins, M., Repetti, R. L., & Crouter, A. C. (2000). Relationship Processes: Work and family in the 1990s. *Journal of Marriage and the Family, 62*(4), 981–997.

Persky, V. W., Kempthrone-Rawson, J., & Shekelle, R. B. (1987) Personality and risk of cancer: 20-year follow-up of the Western Electric Study. *Psychosomatic Medicine, 49,* 435–439.

Pert, C. B. (2003). *Molecules of emotion: The science behind mind-body medicine.* New York: Simon & Schuster.

Pert, C. B., Dreher, H. E., & Ruff, M. R. (1998). The psychosomatic network: Foundations of mind–body medicine. *Alternative Therapies in Health and Medicine, 4,* 30–41.

Perz, C. A., DiClemente, C. C., & Carbonari, J. P. (1996). Doing the right thing at the right time? The interaction of stages and processes of change in successful smoking cessation. *Health Psychology, 15,* 462–468.

Peterson, A. V., Kealey, K. A., Mann, S. L., Marek, P. M., & Sarason, I. G. (2000). Hutchinson Smoking Prevention Project: Long-term randomized trial in school-based tobacco use prevention—results on smoking. *Journal of the National Cancer Institute, 92,* 1979–1991.

Peterson, C., & Bossio, L. M. (1991). *Health and optimism.* New York: Free Press.

Peterson, C. & Steen, T. A. (2002). Optimistic explanatory style. In Snyder, C. R. & S. J. Lopez (Eds.), *Handbook of positive psychology* (pp. 244–256). New York: Oxford University Press.

Peterson, C., & Stunkard, A. J. (1989). Personal control and health promotion. *Social Science and Medicine, 28,* 819–828.

Peterson, C., Seligman, M. E. P., Yurko, K. H., Martin, L. R., & Friedman, H. S. (1998). Catastrophizing and untimely death. *Psychological Science, 9,* 127–130.

Peterson, K. (1997). Success in the face of adversity: Six stories of minority career achievement. In H. S. Farmer (Ed.), *Diversity and women's career development: From adolescence to adulthood* (pp. 172–186). Thousand Oaks, CA: Sage Publications.

Peterson, L., Crowson, J., Saldana, L., & Holdridge, S. (1999). Of needles and skinned knees: Children's coping with medical procedures and minor injuries for self and other. *Health Psychology, 18,* 197–200.

Peto, R., Lopez, A. D., Boreham, J., Thun, M., Heath, C., & Doll, R. (1996). Mortality from smoking worldwide. *British Medical Bulletin, 52,* 12–21.

Petrie, K. J., Booth, R. J., & Davison, K. P. (1995). Repression, disclosure, and immune function: Recent findings and methodological issues. In J. W. Pennebaker (Ed.), *Emotion, disclosure, and health* (pp. 223–237). Washington, DC: American Psychological Association.

Pets and Aging (2001). Science supports the human-animal bond. Atlanta: PAWSitive Interaction. www.pawsitiveinteraction.org

Philips, H. C. (1988). Changing chronic pain experience. *Pain, 32,* 165–172.

Phillips, W. T., Kiernan, M., & King, A. C. (2001). The effects of physical activity on physical and psychological health. In A. Baum, T. A. Revenson, & J. E. Singer (Eds.), *Handbook of health psychology* (pp. 627–657). Mahwah, NJ: Erlbaum.

Pierce, J. P., & Gilpin, E. A. (2004). How did the master settlement agreement change tobacco industry expenditures for cigarette advertising and promotions? *Health Promotion Practice, 5*(3), 84–90.

Pike, K. M., & Rodin, J. (1991). Mothers, daughters, and disordered eating. *Journal of Abnormal Psychology, 100,* 1–7.

Pilisuk, M., Boylan, R., & Acredolo, C. (1987). Social support, life stress, and subsequent medical care utilization. *Health Psychology, 6,* 273–288.

Pingitore, R., Dugoni, B. L., Tindale, R. S., & Spring, B. (1994). Bias against overweight job applicants in a simulated employment interview. *Journal of Applied Psychology, 79,* 909–917.

Piscitelli, S. C., Burstein, A. H., Chaitt, D., Alfaro, R. M., & Falloon, J. (2000). Indinavir concentrations and St. John's wort. *The Lancet, 355,* 547–548.

Pistrang, N., & Barker, C. (1995). The partner relationship in psychological response to breast cancer. *Social Science and Medicine, 40,* 689–697.

Pi-Sunyer, X. (2003). A clinical view of the obesity problem. *Science, 299*(5608), 859–860.

Plomin, R., DeFries, J. C., McClearn, G. E., & McGuffin, P. (2001). *Behavioral genetics* (4th ed.). New York: Worth.

Plomin, R., Fries, J. C., McClearn, G. E., Rutter, M., & Rose, S. (1997). Behavioral genetics. *Nature, 388*(6638), 138–139.

Plomin, R., McClearn, G. E., McGuffin, P., & DeFries, J. C. (2000). *Behavioral genetics* (4th ed.). New York: Worth.

Pluhar, E. I., Frongillo, E. A., Stycos, J. M., & Dempster-McClain, D. (2003). Changes over time in college students' family planning knowledge, preference, and behavior and implications for contraceptive education and prevention of sexually transmitted infections. *College Students Journal, 37*(3), 420–434.

Pollay, R. W. (2000). Targeting youth and concerned smokers: Evidence from Canadian tobacco industry documents. *Tobacco Control, 9*(2), 136–147.

Pollock, S. E. (1986). Human responses to chronic illness: Physiologic and psychosocial adaptation. *Nursing Research, 35,* 90–95.

Potter, J. D. (1997). Hazards and benefits of alcohol. *New England Journal of Medicine, 337,* 1763–1764.

Prescott, E., Osler, M., Hein, H. O., Borch-Johnsen, K., Schnohr, P., & Vestbo, J. (1998). Life expectancy in Danish women and men related to smoking habits: Smoking may affect women more. *Journal of Epidemiology and Community Health, 52*(2), 131–132.

Primack, A., & Spencer, J. (1996). *The collection and evaluation of clinical research data relevant to alternative medicine and cancer.* Bethesda, MD: Office of Alternative Medicine, National Institutes of Health.

Prochaska, J. L., DiClemente, C. C., & Norcross, J. C. (1992). In search of how people change: Applications to addictive behaviors. *The American Psychologist, 47*(9), 1102–1114.

Prochaska, J. O. (1996). A stage paradigm for integrating clinical and public health approaches to smoking cessation. *Addictive Behaviors, 21,* 721–732.

Prochaska, J. O., Redding, C. A., Harlow, L. L., Rossi, J. S., & Velicer, W. F. (1994). The transtheoretical model of change and HIV prevention: A review. *Health Education Quarterly, 21,* 471–486.

Prochaska, J. O., Velicer, W. F., Fava, J., & Laforge, R. (1995). Toward disease-state management for smoking: Stage-matched expert systems for a total managed care population of smokers. (Manuscript submitted for publication.)

Pruessner, J. C., Hellhammer, D. H., & Kirschbaum, C. (1999). Burnout, perceived stress, and cortisol responses to awakening. *Psychosomatic Medicine, 61*(2), 197–204.

Ptacek, J. T., & Eberhardt, T. L. (1996). Breaking bad news. A review of the literature. *Journal of the American Medical Association, 276,* 496–502.

Ptacek, J. T., Smith, R. E., & Zanas, J. (1992). Gender, appraisal, and coping: A longitudinal analysis. *Journal of Personality, 60,* 747–770.

Puhl, R., & Brownell, K. D. (2001). Bias, discrimination, and obesity. *Obesity Research, 9*(12), 788–805.

Pumariega, A. J. (1986). Acculturation and eating attitudes in adolescent girls: A comparative and correlational study. *Journal of the American Academy of Child Psychiatry, 25,* 276–279.

Puska, P. (1999). The North Karelia project: From community intervention to national activity in lowering cholesterol levels and CHD risk. *European Heart Journal Supplements, 1,* S1–S4.

Quackwatch. (2006). Implausibility of EDTA chelation therapy. http://www.quackwatch.org/

Quick, J. C., & Quick, J. D. (1984). *Organizational stress and preventive management.* New York: McGraw-Hill.

Quick, J. D. & Quick, J. C. (2004). Happy, healthy, productive work: A leadership challenge. *Organizational Dynamics, 33*(4), 329–337.

Quigley, K. S., Barrett, L. F., & Weinstein, S. (2002). Cardiovascular patterns associated with threat and challenge appraisals: A within-subjects analysis. *Psychophysiology, 39*(3), 292–302.

Quigley, L. A., & Marlatt, G. A. (1996). Drinking among young adults: Prevalence, patterns and consequences. *Alcohol Health and Research World, 20,* 185–191.

Rabasca, L. (1999, November). Imagery, massage and relaxation recognized as ways to manage pain. *American Psychological Association Monitor, 30,* 9.

Rabin, B. S. (1999). *Stress, immune function, and health: The connection.* New York: John Wiley.

Rahe, R. H., Mahan, J. L., & Arthur, R. J. (1970). Prediction of near-future health changes from subjects' preceding life changes. *Journal of Psychosomatic Research, 14,* 401–406.

Raikkonen, K., Matthews, K. A., & Salomon, K. (2003). Hostility predicts metabolic syndrome risk factors in children and adolescents. *Health Psychology, 22*(3), 279–286.

Raloff, J. (1996). Vanishing flesh: Muscle loss in the elderly finally gets some respect. *Science News, 150,* 90–91.

Raloff, J. (2006). Breakfast trends. *Science News, 169*(15), 238.

Ramachandran, V.S., & Rogers-Ramachandran, D. (2000). Phantom limbs and neural plasticity. *Archives of Neurology, 57,* 317–320.

Ramons, K. D., Schafer, S., & Tracz, S. M. (2003). Learning in practice: Validation of the Fresno test of competence in evidence-based medicine. *British Medical Journal, 326,* 319–321.

Ranadive, U. (1997). Phantom limbs and rewired brains. *Technology Review, 100,* 17–18.

Rand, C. S., & Kuldau, J. M. (1990). The epidemiology of obesity and self-defined weight problem in the general population: Gender, race, age, and social class. *International Journal of Eating Disorders, 9,* 329–343.

Rau, R. (2006). The association between blood pressure and work stress: The importance of measuring isolated systolic hypertension. *Work & Stress, 20*(1), 84–97.

Ray, C. (1997). Chronic fatigue syndrome. In A. Baum, S. Newman, J. Weinman, R. West, & C. McManus (Eds.), *Cambridge handbook of psychology, health and medicine* (pp. 408–409). Cambridge: Cambridge University Press.

Redd, W. H., & Jacobsen, P. (2001). Behavioral intervention in comprehensive cancer care. In A. Baum, T. A. Revenson, & J. E. Singer (Eds.), *Handbook of health psychology* (pp. 757–776). Mahwah, NJ: Erlbaum.

Reed, D., McGee, D., Yano, K., & Feinleib, M. (1983). Social networks and coronary heart disease among Japanese men in Hawaii. *American Journal of Epidemiology, 117,* 384–396.

Reed, G. M., Kemeny, M. E., Taylor, S. E., et al. (1999). Negative HIV-expectancies and AIDS-related bereavement as predictors of symptom onset in asymptomatic HIV-positive gay men. *Health Psychology, 18*(4), 354–363.

Reed, G. M., Kemeny, M. E., Taylor, S. E., Wang, H. Y., & Visscher, B. R. (1994). Realistic acceptance as a predictor of decreased survival time in gay men with AIDS. *Health Psychology, 13,* 299–307.

Reiff, M., Zakut, H., & Weingarten, M. A. (1999). Illness and treatment perceptions of Ethiopian immigrants and their doctors in Israel. *American Journal of Public Health, 89,* 1814–1818.

Rejeski, W. J., Focht, B. C., Messier, S. P., Morgan, T., Pahor, M., & Penninx, B. (2002). Obese, older adults with knee osteoarthritis: Weight loss, exercise, and quality of life. *Health Psychology, 21*(5), 419–426.

Relman, A. S. (1998, December 14). A trip to stonesville. *The New Republic Online.* http://www.tnr.com/archive/1298/121498/relman121498.html

Repetti, R. L. (1993). Short-term effects of occupational stressors on daily mood and health complaints. *Health Psychology, 12,* 125–131.

Repetti, R. L., Taylor, S. E., & Seeman, T. E. (2002). Risky families: Family social environments and the mental and physical health of offspring. *Psychological Bulletin, 128*(2), 330–338.

Resnick, H. S., Kilpatrick, D. G., Best, C. L., & Kramer, T. L. (1992). Vulnerability-stress factors in development of posttraumatic stress disorder. *Journal of Nervous and Mental Disease, 180,* 424–430.

Resnick, M. D., Bearman, P. S., Blum, R. W. et al. (1997). Protecting adolescents from harm. Findings from the National Longitudinal Study on Adolescent Health. *Journal of the American Medical Association, 278*(10), 823–832.

Rexrode, K. M., Carey, V. J., Hennekens, C. H., Walters, E. E., Colditz, G. A., Stampfer, M. J., Willett, W. C., & Manson, J. E. (1998). Abdominal adiposity and coronary heart disease in women. *Journal of the American Medical Association, 280,* 1843–1848.

Reynolds, D. V. (1969). Surgery in the rat during electrical analgesia induced by focal brain stimulation. *Science, 164,* 444–445.

Reynolds, P., & Kaplan, G. A. (1990). Social connections and risk for cancer: Prospective evidence from the Alameda County Study. *Behavioral Medicine, 16,* 101–110.

Rich. L. E. (2004, January). Bringing more effective tools to the weight-loss table. *Monitor on Psychology,* 52–55.

Robbins, A. (1993). The children's vaccine initiative. *American Journal of Diseases of Children, 147,* 152–157.

Robert Wood Johnson Foundation. (2001). *Substance Abuse: The Nation's Number One Health Problem.* http://www.rwif.org

Roberts, C. K., Vaziri, N. D., & Barnard, R. J. (2002). Effect of diet and exercise intervention on blood pressure, insulin, oxidative stress, and nitric oxide availability. *Circulation, 106*(20), 2530–2532.

Roberts, S. S. (1998). Working toward a world without type I diabetes. *Diabetes Forecast, 51,* 85–87.

Roberts, T., & Pennebaker, J. W. (1995). Gender differences in perceiving internal state: Toward a his-and-hers model of perceptual cue use. In M. P. Zanna (ed.) *Advances in experimental social psychology, 27,* 143–175.

Robinson, T. E., & Berridge, K. C. (2000). The psychology and neurobiology of addiction: An incentive-sensitization view. *Addiction, 95,* S91–S117.

Robles, T. F., Glaser, R., Kiecolt-Glaser, J. K. (2005). Out of balance: A new look at chronic stress, depression, and immunity. *Current Directions in Psychological Science, 14*(2), 111–115.

Rockhill, B., Willett, W. C., Hunter, D. J., Manson, J. E., Hankinson, S. E., & Colditz, G. A. (1999). A prospective study of recreational physical activity and breast cancer risk. *Archives of Internal Medicine, 159,* 2290–2296.

Rodin, J. (1981). Current status of the internal-external hypothesis for obesity: What went wrong? *American Psychologist, 36,* 361–372.

Rodin, J. (1986). Aging and health: Effects of the sense of control. *Science, 233,* 1271–1276.

Roehling, M. V., & Winters, D. (2000). Job security rights: The effects of specific policies and practices on the evaluation of employers. *Employee Responsibilities and Rights Journal, 12,* 25–38.

Roethlisberger, F. J., & Dickson, W. J. (1939). *Management and the worker.* Cambridge, MA: Harvard University Press.

Rolls, B. J., Morris, E. L., & Roe, L. S. (2002). Portion size of food affects energy intake in normal-weight and overweight men and women. *American Journal of Clinical Nutrition, 76*(6), 1207–1213.

Root, M. P. (1990). Disordered eating in women of color [Special issue: Gender and ethnicity: Perspectives on dual status]. *Sex Roles, 227,* 525–536.

Rosario, M., Shinn, M., Morch, H., & Huckabee, C. (1988). Gender differences in coping and social supports: Testing socialization and role constraint theories. *Journal of Community Psychology* (Special Issue: *Women in the Community*), 16, 55–69.

Rosen, J. C., & Leitenberg, H. (1982). Bulimia nervosa: Treatment with exposure and response prevention. *Behavior Therapy, 13,* 117–124.

Rosenberg, E. L., Ekman, P., & Blumenthal, J. A. (1998). Facial expression and the affective component of cynical hostility in male coronary heart disease patients. *Health Psychology, 17,* 376–380.

Rosenbloom, A. L., Joe, J. R., Young, R. S., & Winter, W. E. (1999). Emerging epidemic of type 2 diabetes in youth. *Diabetes Care, 22,* 345–354.

Rosenfeldt, F., Miller, F., Nagley, P., Hadj, A., et al. (2004). The cardiovascular system: Response of the senescent heart to stress. *Annals of the New York Academy of Sciences, 1019,* 78–84.

Rosengren, A., Wilhelmsen, L., & Orth-Gomer, K. (2004). Coronary disease in relation to social support and social class in Swedish men: A 15-year follow-up in the study of men born in 1933. *European Heart Journal, 25*(1), 56–63.

Rosenthal, E. (1993, October 13). Does fragmented medicine harm the health of women? *The New York Times,* pp. A1, B7.

Ross, C. E. & Mirowsky, J. (2002). Family relationships, social support and subjective life expectancy. *Journal of Health and Social Behavior, 43*(4), 469–489.

Roth, D. L., & Holmes, D. S. (1985). Influence of physical fitness in deterring the impact of stressful events on physical and psychologic health. *Psychosomatic Medicine, 47,* 164–173.

Rothenbacher, D., Hoffmeister, A., Brenner, H., & Koenig, W. (2003). Physical activity, coronary heart disease, and inflammatory response. *Archives of Internal Medicine, 163*(10), 1200–1205.

Rothman, A. J., & Salovey, P. (1997). Shaping perceptions to motivate healthy behavior: The role of message framing. *Psychological Bulletin, 121,* 3–19.

Rotter, J. B. (1966). Generalized expectancies for internal versus external control of reinforcement. *Psychological Monographs, 80*(1), 1–28.

Rozanski, A., Blumenthal, J. A., & Kaplan, J. (1999). Clinical cardiology: New frontiers—impact of psychological factors on the pathogenesis of cardiovascular disease and implications for therapy. *Circulation, 99*(16), 2192–2217.

Rozen, P., Kabnick, K., Pete, E., Fischler, C., & Shields, C. (2003). The ecology of eating: Smaller portion sizes in France than in the United States help explain the French paradox. *Psychological Science, 14*(5), 450–454.

Ruberman, W., Weinblatt, E., Goldberg, J. D., & Chaudhary, B. S. (1984). Psychosocial influences on mortality after myocardial infarction. *New England Journal of Medicine, 311,* 552–559.

Ruble, D. (1972). Premenstrual symptoms: A reinterpretation. *Science, 197,* 291–292.

Russell, M. A. (1971). Cigarette dependence: Nature and classification. *British Medical Journal, 2,* 330–331.

Russell, R. G. (1979). Bulimia nervosa: An ominous variant of anorexia nervosa. *Psychological Medicine, 9,* 429–448.

Rutledge, T., & Hogan, B. E. (2002). A quantitative review of prospective evidence linking psychological factors with hypertension development. *Psychosomatic Medicine, 64*(5), 758–766.

Rutledge, T. & Linden, W. (2003). Defensiveness and 3-year blood pressure levels among young adults: The mediating effect of stress reactivity. *Annals of Behavioral Medicine, 25*(1), 34–40.

Rutter, M. (1979). Protective factors in children's responses to stress and disadvantage. In W. M. Kent & J. E. Rolf (Eds.), *Primary prevention of psychopathology,* vol. 3 (pp. 49–74). Hanover, NH: University Press of New England.

Rutz, D. (1998, September 22). Study tracks causes, treatment of perplexing chronic fatigue syndrome. http://www.cnn.com/health.

Ryff, C. D., Singer, B. H., Wing, E., & Love, G. D. (2001). Elective affinities and uninvited agonies: Mapping emotion with significant others onto health. In C. D. Ryff & B. H. Singer (Eds.), Emotion, social relationships, and health (pp. 133–175). New York: Oxford University Press.

Saab, P. G., McCalla, J. R., Coons, H. L., Christensen, A. J., et al. (2004). The future of health psychology: Technological and medical advances—implications for health psychology. *Health Psychology, 23*(3), 142–146.

Sacks, M. H. (1990). Eating disorders and long-distance running: The ascetic condition. *Integrative Psychiatry, 5,* 205–206.

Saelens, B. E., Sallis, J. F., & Frank, L. D. (2003). Environmental correlates of walking and cycling: Findings from the transportation, urban design, and planning literatures. *Annals of Behavioral Medicine, 25*(2), 80–91.

Saez, E., Tontonoz, P., Nelson, M. C., Alvarez, J. G., Baird, S. M., Thomazy, V. A., & Evans, R. M. (1998). Activators of the nuclear receptor PPARg enhance polyp formation. *Nature Medicine, 4,* 1058–1061.

Safer, M. A., Tharps, Q. J., Jackson, T. C., & Leventhal, H. (1979). Determinants of three stages of delay in seeking care at a medical clinic. *Medical Care, 17,* 11–29.

Salovey, P., O'Leary, A., Stretton, M. S., Fishkin, S. A., & Drake, C. A. (1991). Influence of mood on judgments about health and illness. In J. P. Firgas (Ed.), *Emotion and social judgments* (pp. 241–262). New York: Pergamon.

Salzmann, P., Kerlikowske, K., & Phillips, K. (1997). Cost-effectiveness of extending screening mammography guidelines to include women 40 to 49 years of age. *Annals of Internal Medicine, 127,* 955–965.

SAMSHA. (2006). Alcohol dependence or abuse in substrate areas. U.S Department of Health and Human Services. Substance Abuse and Mental Health Services Administration. http://www.samhsa.gov

Sanders, S. H., Brena, S. F., Spier, C. J., Beltrutti, D., McConnell, H., & Quintero, O. (1992). Chronic low back patients around the world: Cross-cultural similarities and differences. *The Clinical Journal of Pain, 8,* 317–323.

Sapolsky, R. (1992). Do glucocorticoid concentrations rise with age in the rat? *Neurobiology of Aging, 13*(1), 171–174.

Sapolsky, R. (1990). Glucocorticoids, hippocampal damage and the glutamatergic synapse. *Progress in brain research, 86,* 13–20.

Sapolsky, R. M. (1996). Why stress is bad for your brain. *Science, 273,* 749–750.

Sapolsky, R. M. (1998). *The trouble with testosterone and other essays on the biology of the human predicament.* New York: Simon-Schuster.

Sastry, J. & Ross, C. E. (1998). Asian ethnicity and the sense of personal control. *Social Psychological Quarterly, 61*(2), 101–120.

Satterlund, M. J., McCaul, K. D., & Sandgren, A. K. (2003). Information gathering over time by breast cancer patients. *Journal of Medical Internet Research, 5*(3), 15–26.

Savoca, M. R., Evans, C. D., Wilson, M. E., Harshfield, G. A., & Ludwig, D. A. (2004). The association of caffeinated beverages with blood pressure in adolescents. *Archives of Pediatrics & Adolescent Medicine, 158*(5), 473–477.

Save the Children. (2006). 10 critical threats to America's children. *YouthNoise.* http://www.youthnoise.com/page.php?page_id=883.

Sayette, M. A. (1993). An appraisal-disruption model of alcohol's effects on stress responses in social drinkers. *Psychological Bulletin, 114,* 459–476.

Sayette, M. A., & Hufford, M. R. (1997). Effects of smoking urge on generation of smoking-related information. *Journal of Applied Social Psychology, 27,* 1295–1405.

Scanlon, C. (1996). Euthanasia and nursing practice—right question, wrong answer. *New England Journal of Medicine, 334,* 1401–1402.

Schaalma, H. P., Kok, G., & Peters, L. (1993). Reactions among Dutch youth toward people with AIDS. *Journal of School Health, 63,* 182–187.

Schachter, S. (1978). Pharmacological and psychological determinants of smoking. *Annals of Internal Medicine, 88,* 104–114.

Schachter, S. (1971). Some extraordinary facts about obese humans and rats. *American Psychologist, 26,* 129–144.

Schachter, S., Silverstein, B., Kozlowski, L. T., Perlick, D., Herman, C. P., & Liebling, B. (1977). Studies of the interaction of psychological and pharmacological determinants of smoking. *Journal of Experimental Psychology General, 106* 3–12.

Schaubroeck, J., Ganster, D. C., & Kemmerer, B. E. (1994). Job complexity, "type A" behavior, and cardiovascular disorder: A prospective study. *Academy of Management Journal, 37,* 426–438.

Scheier, L. M., & Botvin, G. J. (1997). Expectancies as mediators of the effects of social influences and alcohol knowledge on adolescent alcohol use: A prospective analysis. *Psychology of Addictive Behaviors, 11,* 48–64.

Scheier, M. F., & Bridges, M. W. (1995). Person variables and health: Personality predispositions and acute psychological states as shared determinants for disease. *Psychosomatic Medicine, 57,* 255–268.

Scheier, M. F., & Carver, C. S. (1985). Optimism, coping, and health: Assessment and implications of generalized outcome expectancies. *Health Psychology, 4,* 219–247.

Scheier, M. F., Matthews, K. A., Owens, J. F., & Magovern, G. J. (1989). Dispositional optimism and recovery from coronary artery bypass surgery: The beneficial effects on physical and psychological well-being. *Journal of Personality and Social Psychology, 57,* 1024–1040.

Scheier, M. F., Weintraub, J. K., & Carver, C. S. (1986). Coping with stress: Divergent strategies of optimists and pessimists. *Journal of Personality and Social Psychology, 51,* 1257–1264.

Schell, F. J., Allolio, B., & Schonecke, O. W. (1994). Physiological and psychological effects of Hatha-Yoga exercise in healthy women. *International Journal of Psychosomatics, 41,* 46–52.

Scherwitz, L., Perkins, L., Chesney, M., & Hughes, G. (1991). Cook-Medley Hostility Scale and subsets: Relationship to demographic and psychosocial characteristics in young adults in the CARDIA study. *Psychosomatic Medicine, 53,* 36–49.

Schifter, D. E., & Ajzen, I. (1985). Intention, perceived control, and weight loss: An application of the theory of planned behavior. *Journal of Personality and Social Psychology, 49,* 843–851.

Schleifer, S. J., Keller, S. E., Camerino, M., Thorton, J. C., & Stein, M. (1983). Suppression of lymphocyte stimulation following bereavement. *Journal of the American Medical Association, 250,* 374–377.

Schmidt, J. E., & Andrykowski, M. A. (2004). The role of social and dispositional variables associated with emotional processing in adjustment to breast cancer: An internet-based study. *Health Psychology, 23*(3), 259–266.

Schneiderman, N. E., Gellman, M., Peckerman, A., et al. (2000). Cardiovascular reactivity as an indicator of risk for future hypertension. In McCabe, P. M., N. E. Schneiderman, T. Field, & A. R. Wellens (Eds.), *Stress, coping, and cardiovascular disease* (pp. 181–202). Mahwah, NJ: Lawrence Erlbaum.

Schneiderman, N. E., McCabe, P., & Baum, A. (1992). *Stress and disease processes.* Hillsdale, NJ: Lawrence Erlbaum Associates.

Schnoll, R. A., James, C., Malstrom, M., Rothman, R. L., et al. (2003). Longitudinal predictors of continued tobacco use among patients diagnosed with cancer. *Annals of Behavioral Medicine, 25*(3), 214–221.

Schoenborn, C. A., Adams, P. F., Barnes, P. M., Vickerie, J. L., & Schiller, J. S. (2004). Health behaviors of adults: United States, 1999–2001. *Vital and health statistics. Series 10, Data from the National Health Survey, 219,* 1–79. Hillsdale, NJ: Erlbaum.

Schreiber, G. B., Busch, M. P., Kleinman, S. H., & Korelitz, J. J. (1996). The risk of transfusion-transmitted viral infections. The retrovirus epidemiology donor study. *New England Journal of Medicine, 334,* 1685–1690.

Schuckit, M. A., & Smith, T. L. (1996). An 8-year follow-up of 450 sons of alcoholic and control subjects. *Archives of General Psychiatry, 53*(3), 202–210.

Schulenberg, J., Bachman, J. G., O'Malley, P. M., & Johnston, L. D. (1994). High school educational success and subsequent substance abuse. *Journal of Health and Social Behavior, 35*(1), 45–62.

Schulman, K. A., Berlin, J., Harless, W., Kerner, J. F., Sistrunk, S. H., Garish, B. J., and others. (1999). The effect of race and sex on physicians' recommendations for cardiac catheterization. *New England Journal of Medicine, 340*(8), 618–625.

Schwartz, B. (2004). *The paradox of choice.* New York: Harper Collins Publishers.

Schwartz, J. (1999, January 22). FDA warns against supplement. *Washington Post,* p. A02.

Schwartz, M. B., & Brownell, K. D. (1995). Matching individuals to weight loss treatments: A survey of obesity experts. *Journal of Consulting and Clinical Psychology, 63,* 149–153.

Schwartz, M. B. & Puhl, R. (2003). Childhood obesity: A societal problem to solve. *Obesity Reviews, 4*(1), 57–71.

Schwartz, M. D., Chambliss, H. O., Brownell, K. D., Blair, S. N., & Billington, C. (2003). Weight bias among health professionals specializing in obesity. *Obesity Research, 11*(9), 1033–1039.

Schwartz, M. D., Lerman, C., Miller, S. M., Daly, M., & Masny, A. (1995). Coping disposition, perceived risk, and psychological distress among women at increased risk for ovarian cancer. *Health Psychology, 14,* 232–235.

Scott, L. D. (2001). Living in a complex social world: The influence of cultural value orientation, perceived control, and racism-related stress on coping among African-American adolescents. *Dissertation Abstracts International, 61*(12–A), 4950.

Scott, S. (1999, September 3). Wellness programs benefit bottom line, studies show. *Houston Business Journal.* www.bizjournals.com/houston/

Scrimshaw, S. M., Engle, P. L., & Zambrana, R. E. (1983). *Prenatal anxiety and birth outcome in U. S. Latinas: Implications for psychosocial interventions.* Paper presented at the annual meeting of the American Psychological Association, Anaheim, CA.

Sears, S. F., Urizar, G. G., & Evans, G. D. (2000). Examining a stress-coping model of burnout and depression in extension agents. *Journal of Occupational Health Psychology, 5,* 56–62.

Sedlacek, K., & Taub, E. (1996). Biofeedback treatment of Raynaud's disease. *Professional Psychology: Research and Practice, 27,* 548–553.

Seeman, M., & Lewis, S. (1995). Powerlessness, health and mortality: A longitudinal study of older men and mature women. *Social Science and Medicine, 41,* 517–525.

Segerstrom, S. C., & Miller, G. E. (2004). Psychological stress and the human immune system: A meta-analytic study of 30 years of inquiry. *Psychological Bulletin, 130*(4), 601–629.

Segerstrom, S. C., Taylor, S. E., Kemeny, M. E., & Fahey, J. (1998). Optimism is associated with mood, coping and immune change in response to stress. *Journal of Personality and Social Psychology, 74*(6), 1646–1655.

Segerstrom, S. C., Taylor, S. E., Kemeny, M. E., Reed, G. M., & Visscher, B. R. (1996). Causal attributions predict rate of immune decline in HIV-seropositive gay men. *Health Psychology, 15,* 485–493.

Seid, R. (1994). Too "close to the bone": The historical context for women's obsession with slenderness. In P. Fallon & M. A. Katzman (Eds.), *Feminist perspectives on eating disorders* (pp. 3–16). New York: Guilford.

Self, C. A., & Rogers, R. W. (1990). Coping with threats to health: Effects of persuasive appeals on depressed, normal, and antisocial personalities. *Journal of Behavioral Medicine, 13,* 343–358.

Seligman, M. E. P. (1975). *Helplessness: On depression, development, and death.* New York: W. H. Freeman.

Seligman, M. E. P. (2002). Positive psychology, positive prevention, and positive therapy. In C. R. Snyder & S. J. Lopez (Eds.) *Handbook of positive psychology* (pp. 3–9). New York: Oxford University Press.

Seligman, M. E. P., & Csikszentmihalyi, M. (2000). Positive psychology: An introduction. *American Psychologist, 55,* 5–14.

Seligman, M. E. P., & Maier, S. F. (1967). Failure to escape traumatic shock. *Journal of Experimental Psychology, 74,* 1–9.

Seligman, M. E. P., Reivich, K., Jaycox, L., & Gillham, J. (1995). *The optimistic child.* Boston, MA: Houghton Mifflin.

Selwyn, P. A. (1986). AIDS: What is now known. *Hospital Practice, 21,* 125–130.

Selye, H. (1974). *The stress of life.* New York: McGraw-Hill.

Senchak, M., Leonard, K. E., & Greene, B. W. (1998). Alcohol use among college students as a function of their typical social drinking context. *Psychology of Addictive Behaviors, 12,* 62–70.

Serdula, M. K., Collins, M. E., Williamson, D. F., Anda, R. F., Pamuk, E., & Byers, T. E. (1993). Weight control practices of U.S. adolescents and adults. *Annals of Internal Medicine, 119,* 667–671.

Serdula, M. K., Mokdad, A., Williamson, D. F., Galuska, D. A., Mendlein, J. M., & Heath, G. W. (1999). Prevalence of attempting weight loss and strategies for controlling weight. *Journal of the American Medical Association, 282,* 1353–1358.

Seto, M. C., & Barbaree, H. E. (1995). The role of alcohol in sexual aggression. *Clinical Psychology Review, 15,* 545–566.

Severeijns, R., Vlaejen, J. W. S., Hout, M. M. A., & Picavet, H. J. (2004). Pain catastrophizing is associated with health indices in musculoskeletal pain: A cross-sectional study in the Dutch community. *Health Psychology, 23*(1), 49–56.

Shapiro, D., Tursky, B., Gershon, E., & Stern, M. (1969). Effects of feedback and reinforcement on the control of human systolic blood pressure. *Science, 163,* 588–590.

Sharpe, M., Hawton, K., Simkin, S., Surawy, C., Hackmann, A., Klimes, I., Peto, T., Warrell, D., & Seagroatt, V. (1996). Cognitive behaviour therapy for the chronic fatigue syndrome: A randomized clinical trial. *British Medical Journal, 312,* 22–26.

Shekelle, P. G., Adams, A. H., & Chassin, M. R. (1992). Spinal manipulation for low-back pain. *Annals of Internal Medicine, 117,* 590–595.

Shekelle, P. G., & Brook, R. H. (1991). A community-based study of the use of chiropractic services. *American Journal of Public Health, 81,* 439–442.

Shekelle, R. B., Gale, M., Ostfield, A. M., & Paul, O. (1983). Hostility, risk of coronary heart disease and mortality. *Psychosomatic Medicine, 45,* 109–114.

Sher, K. J., Bartholow, B. D., & Nanda, S. (2001). Short- and long-term effects of fraternity and sorority membership on heavy drinking: A social norms perspective. *Psychology of Addictive Behaviors, 15,* 42–51.

Sherman, R. A., Sherman, C. J., & Parker, L. (1984). Chronic phantom and stump pain among American veterans: Results of a survey. *Pain, 18,* 83–95.

Sherwin, E. D., Elliott, T. R., Rybarczyk, B. D., & Frank, R. G (1992). Negotiating the reality of caregiving: Hope, burnout and nursing. *Journal of Social & Clinical Psychology, 11,* 129–139.

Shiffman, S. (2006). Reflections on smoking relapse research. *Drug and Alcohol Review, 25*(1), 15–20.

Shilts, R. (1987). *And the band played on: Politics, people, and the AIDS epidemic.* New York: St. Martin's.

Shipley, R. H., Butt, J. H., Horwitz, B., & Farbry, J. E. (1979). Preparation for a stressful medical procedure: Effect of amount of stimulus preexposure and coping style. *Journal of Consulting and Clinical Psychology, 46,* 499–507.

Shoff, S. M., Newcomb, P. A., Trentham-Dietz, A., Remington, P. L., Mittendorf, R., Greenberg, E. R., et al. (2000). Early-life physical activity and postmenopausal breast cancer: Effect of body size and weight change. *Cancer Epidemiology 9,* 591–595.

Showalter, E. (1999). *Hystories: Hysterical epidemics and modern culture.* New York: Columbia University Press.

Shumaker, S. A., & Hill, D. R. (1991). Gender differences in social support and physical health. *Health Psychology: Special Issue: Gender and Health, 10,* 102–111.

Siegel, J. M., Angulo, F. J., Detels, R., Wesch, J., & Mullen, A. (1999). AIDS diagnosis and depression in the Multicenter AIDS Cohort Study: The ameliorating impact of pet ownership. *AIDS Care, 11,* 157–170.

Siegel, K., & Krauss, B. J. (1991). Living with HIV infection: Adaptive tasks of seropositive gay men. *Journal of Health and Social Behavior, 32,* 17–32.

Siegel, K., Gluhoski, V. L., & Karus, D. (1997). Coping and mood in HIV-positive women. *Psychological Reports, 81*(2), 435–442.

Siegler, I. C., Costa, P. T., Brummett, B. H., et al. (2003). Patterns of change in hostility from college to midlife in the UNC alumni heart study predict high-risk status. *Psychosomatic Medicine, 65*(5), 738–745.

Siegler, I. C., Peterson, B. L., Barefoot, J. C., & Williams, R. B. (1992). Hostility during late adolescence predicts coronary risk factors at mid-life. *American Journal of Epidemiology, 136,* 146–154.

Sigerist, H. E. (1958). *The great doctors.* New York: Doubleday Anchor Books.

Sihvonen, M., Kayhko, K., & Kekki, P. (1989). Factors influencing the patient-provider relationship. *Vard i Norden, 9,* 4–9.

Silverman, M. M., Eichler, A., & Williams, G. D. (1987). Self-reported stress: Findings from the 1985 National Health Interview Survey. *Public Health Reports, 102,* 47–53.

Silverstein, P. (1992). Smoking and wound healing. *American Journal of Medicine, 93,* 1A–22S.

Simon, G., Gater, R., Kisely, S., & Piccinelli, M. (1996). Somatic symptoms of distress: An international primary care study. *Psychosomatic Medicine, 58,* 481–488.

Simpson, N., Lenton, S., & Randall, R. (1995). Parental refusal to have children immunized: Extent and reasons. *British Medical Journal, 310,* 227–230.

Singer, E. M. (1988). Delay behavior among women with breast symptoms. In T. Field, & P. M. McCabe (Eds.), *Stress and coping across development* (pp. 163–188). Hillsdale, NJ: Erlbaum.

Singer, J. E., Lundberg, U., & Frankenhaeuser, M. (1978). Stress on the train: A study of urban community. In A. Baum, J. E. Singer, & S. Valins (Eds.), *Advances in environmental psychology.* Hillsdale, NJ: Erlbaum.

Sjostrom, L.V. (1992). Morbidity of severely obese subjects. *American Journal of Clinical Nutrition, 55,* 508–515.

Skevington, S. M. (1995). *Psychology of pain.* Chichester, England: Wiley.

Sleet, D. A., Liller, K. D., White, D. D., et al. (2004). Injuries, injury prevention and public health. *American Journal of Health Behavior, 28*(1), S6.

Sloan, R. P., Bagiella, E., & Powell, T. (1999). Religion, spirituality, and medicine. *The Lancet, 353,* 664–667.

Smedley, B. D., Stith, A. Y., & Nelson, A. R. (2003). *Unequal Treatment: Confronting Racial and Ethnic Disparities in Health Care.* Washington, D. C.: National Academy Press.

Smith, C., Cowan, C., Heffler, S., & Catlin, A. (2006). National health spending in 2004: Recent slowdown led by prescription drug spending. *Health Affairs, 25*(1), 186–196.

Smith, D. (2001, June). Treatment of nonviolent drug offenders: A wave of the future? *Monitor on Psychology* (special issue on substance abuse), *32,* 16, 51.

Smith, J. C. (2005). *Relaxation, meditation, and mindfulness: A mental health practitioner's guide to new and traditional approaches.* New York: Springer.

Smith, T. J. (1998). Health service studies in the terminally ill patient. *Cancer Treatment and Research, 97,* 81–97.

Smith, T. W., & Gallo, L. C. (2001). Personality traits as risk factors for physical illness. In A. Baum, T. A. Revenson, & J. E. Singer (Eds.), *Handbook of health psychology* (pp. 139–173). Mahwah, NJ: Erlbaum.

Smyth, J. M., & Pennebaker, J. W. (2001). What are the health effects of disclosure? In A. Baum, T. A. Revenson, & J. E. Singer (Eds.), *Handbook of health psychology* (pp. 339–348). Mahwah, NJ: Erlbaum.

Snodgrass, S. E. (1998). Thriving: Broadening the paradigm beyond illness to health—personal experience with breast cancer. www.looksmart.com

Soldz, S. & Cui, X. (2002). Pathways through adolescent smoking: A 7-year longitudinal grouping analysis. *Health Psychology, 21*(5), 495–594.

Solomon, G. F. (1991). Psychosocial factors, exercise, and immunity: Athletes, elderly persons, and AIDS patients. *International Journal of Sports Medicine, 12*(Suppl. 1), S50–S52.

Solomon, G. F., & Moss, R. H. (1964). Emotions, immunity, and disease: A speculative theoretical integration. *Archives of General Psychiatry, 11,* 657–674.

Solomon, G. F., Segerstrom, S. C., Grohr, P., Kemeny, M., & Fahey, J. (1997). Shaking up immunity: Psychological and immunologic changes after a natural disaster. *Psychosomatic Medicine, 59,* 114–127.

Sorensen, G. (1985). Sex differences in the relationship between work and health: The Minnesota Heart Survey. *Journal of Health & Social Behavior, 26,* 379–394.

Sorkin, D., Rook, K. S., & Lu, J. L. (2002). Loneliness, lack of emotional support, lack of companionship, and the likelihood of having a heart condition in an elderly sample. *Annals of Behavioral Medicine, 24*(4), 290–298.

Spanos, N. P., & Coe, W. C. (1992). A social-psychological approach to hypnosis. In E. Fromm & M. R. Nash (Eds.), *Contemporary hypnosis research.* New York: Guilford.

Spasojevic, J., & Alloy, L. B. (2001). Rumination as a common mechanism relating depressive risk factors to depression. *Emotion, 1,* 25–37.

Spencer, J. W. (1999). Essential issues in complementary/alternative medicine. In J. W. Spencer & J. J. Jacobs (Eds.), *Complementary/alternative medicine: An evidence-based approach* (pp. 1–36). St. Louis: Mosby.

Spiegel, D. (1996). Psychological stress and disease course for women with breast cancer: one answer, many questions. *Journal of the National Cancer Institute, 88*(1), 629–631.

Spiegel, D., Bloom, J. R., Kraemer, H. C., & Gottheil, E. (1989). Effect of psychosocial treatment on survival of patients with metastatic breast cancer. *The Lancet, 2,* 888–891.

Spitzer, R. L., Yanovski, S., Wadden, T., Wing, R., et al. (1993). Binge eating disorder: Its further validation in a multisite study. *The International Journal of Eating Disorders, 13*(2), 137–153.

Srivastava, K. C., & Mustafa, T. (1992). Ginger (*Zingiber officinale*) in rheumatism and musculoskeletal disorders. *Medical Hypotheses, 39,* 342–348.

Stacy, A. W., Bentler, P. M., & Flay, B. R. (1994). Attitudes and health behavior in diverse populations: Drunk driving, alcohol use, binge eating, marijuana use, and cigarette use. *Health Psychology, 13,* 73–85.

Stamler, J., Stamler, R., Neaton, J. D., Wentworth, D., Daviglus, M. L., Garside, D., et al. (1999). Low-risk factor profile and long-term cardiovascular and noncardiovascular mortality and life expectancy: Findings for 5 large cohorts of young adult and middle-aged men and women. *Journal of the American Medical Association, 282,* 2012–2018.

Stampfer, M. J., Rimm, E. B., & Walsh, D. C. (1993). Commentary: Alcohol, the heart, and public policy. *American Journal of Public Health, 83,* 801–804.

Stanovich, K. E., & West, R. F. (1998). Individual differences in rational thought. *Journal of Experimental Psychology: General, 127*(2), 161–188.

Stansfeld, S. A., Marmot, M. G., & Baum, A. S. (2004). Stress and the heart: psychosocial pathways to coronary heart disease. *Contemporary Psychology, 49*(4), 429–431.

Stanton, A. L., Danoff-Burg, S., Cameron, C. L., Bishop, M., et al. (2000). Emotionally expressive coping predicts psychological and physical adjustment to breast cancer. *Journal of Consulting and Clinical Psychology, 68*(5), 875–882.

Stanton, W. R., Mahalski, P. A., McGee, R., & Silva, P. A. (1993). Reasons for smoking or not smoking in early adolescence. *Addictive Behaviors, 18,* 321–329.

Starobrat-Hermelin, B., & Kozielec, T. (1997). The effects of magnesium physiological supplementation on hyperactivity in children with attention deficit hyperactivity disorder (ADHD). Positive response to magnesium oral loading test. *Magnesium Research, 10,* 149–156.

Statistics Canada (1999). *Statistical report on the health of Canadians.* Prepared by the Federal, Provincial and Territorial Advisory Committee on Population Health for the Meeting of Ministers of Health, Charlottetown, PEI, September 16–17.

Stein, J., & Nyamathi, A. (1999). Gender differences in behavioural and psychosocial predictors of HIV testing and return for test results in a high-risk population. *AIDS Care Special Issue: AIDS Impact: 4th International Conference on the Biopsychosocial Aspects of HIV Infection, 12,* 343–356.

Steinmetz, K. A., Kushi, L. H., Bostick, R. M., Folsom, A. R., & Potter, J. D. (1994). Vegetables, fruit, and colon cancer in the Iowa Women's Health Study. *American Journal of Epidemiology, 139,* 1–15.

Steptoe, A. (1997). Stress and disease. In A. Baum, S. Newman, J. Weinman, R. West, & C. McManus (Eds.), *Cambridge handbook of psychology, health and medicine* (pp. 174–177). Cambridge: Cambridge University Press.

Steptoe, A., Fieldman, G., & Evans, O. (1993). An experimental study of the effects of control over work pace on cardiovascular responsivity. *Journal of Psychophysiology, 7,* 290–300.

Steptoe, A., Perkins-Porras, L., McKay, C., Rink, E., Hilton, S., & Cappuccio, F. P. (2003). Psychological factors associated with fruit and vegetable intake and with biomarkers in adults from a low-income neighbourhood. *Health Psychology, 22*(2), 148–155.

Steptoe, A., Wardle, J., Pollard, T. M., & Canaan, L. (1996). Stress, social support and health-related behavior: A study of smoking, alcohol consumption and physical exercise. *Journal of Psychosomatic Research, 41,* 171–180.

Stern, M., Norman, S., & Komm, C. (1993). Medical students' differential use of coping strategies as a function of stressor type, year of training, and gender. *Behavioral Medicine, 18,* 173–180.

Sternbach, R. A. (1986). Pain and "hassles" in the United States: Findings of the Nuprin Pain Report. *Pain, 27,* 69–80.

Sternberg, E. (2000). *The balance within: The science connecting health and emotions.* New York: W. H. Freeman & Company.

Stevens, J., Plankey, M. W., Williamson, D. F., Thun, M. J., et al. (1998). The body mass-index-mortality relationship in white and African American women. *Obesity Research, 6*(4), 268–277.

Stice, E., Mazotti, L., Krebs, M., & Martin, S. (1998). Predictors of adolescent dieting behaviors: A longitudinal study. *Psychology of Addictive Behaviors, 12,* 195–205.

Stice, E., Myers, M. G., & Brown, S. A. (1998). Relations of delinquency to adolescent substance use and problem use: A prospective study. *Psychology of Addictive Behaviors, 12,* 136–146.

Stice, E., Presnell, K., & Spangler, D. (2002). Risk factors for binge eating onset in adolescent girls: A 2-year prospective investigation. *Health Psychology, 21*(2), 131–138.

Stone, A. A., Mezzacappa, E. S., Donatone, B. A., & Gonder, M. (1999). Psychosocial stress and social support are associated with prostate-specific antigen levels in men: Results from a community screening program. *Health Psychology, 18*(5), 482–486.

Stone, G. C., Cohen, F., & Adler, N. (1979). *Health psychology—A handbook.* San Francisco: Jossey-Bass.

Strawbridge, W. J., Wallhagen, M. I., & Shema, S. J. (2000). New NHLBI clinical guidelines for obesity and overweight: Will they promote health? *American Journal of Public Health, 90,* 340–343.

Strecher, V. J., & Rosenstock, I. M. (1997). The health belief model. In A. Baum, S. Newman, J. Weinman, R. West, & C. McManus (Eds.), *Cambridge handbook of psychology, health and medicine* (pp. 113–117). Cambridge: Cambridge University Press.

Striegel-Moore, R. H., Cachelin, F. M., Dohm, F. A., Pike, K. M., et al. (2001). Comparison of binge eating disorder and bulimia nervosa in a community sample, *The International Journal of Eating Disorders, 29*(2), 157–165.

Striegel-Moore, R. H., Silberstein, L. R., & Rodin, J. (1993). The social self in bulimia nervosa: Public self-consciousness, social anxiety, and perceived fraudulence. *Journal of Abnormal Psychology, 102,* 297–303.

Strober, M., Morrell, W., Burroughs, J., Salkin, B., & Jacobs, C. (1985). A controlled family study of anorexia nervosa. *Journal of Psychiatric Research, 19,* 239–246.

Strogatz, D.S., Croft, J.B., James, S.A., Keenan, N.L., Browning, S.R., Garrett, J.M., & Curtis, A.B. (1997). Social support, stress, and blood pressure in black adults. *Epidemiology, 8*(5), 482–487.

Stuart, R. B. (1974). Teaching facts about drugs: Pushing or preventing. *Journal of Educational Psychology, 66,* 189–201.

Stuckey, S. J., Jacobs, A., & Goldfarb, J. (1986). EMG biofeedback training, relaxation training, and placebo for the relief of chronic back pain. *Perceptual and Motor Skills, 63,* 1023–1036.

Stygall, J., Newman, S. P., Fitzgerald, G., Steed, L., et al. (2003). Cognitive change 5 years after coronary artery bypass surgery. *Health Psychology, 22*(6), 579–586.

Suddendorf, R. F. (1989). Research on alcohol metabolism among Asians and its implications for understanding causes of alcoholism. *Public Health Reports, 104,* 615–620.

Sue, S., & Zane, N. (1995). The role of culture and cultural techniques in psychotherapy: A critique and reformulation. In N.R. Goldberger & J. Bennet (Eds.) *The Culture and Psychology Reader* (pp. 767–788). New York: New York University Press.

Sullivan, M., Paice, J. A., & Beneditti, F. (2004). Placebos and treatment of pain. *Pain Medicine, 5*(3), 325–328.

Sullivan, M. J. L., Reesor, K., Mikail, S., & Fisher, R. (1992). The treatment of depression in chronic low back pain: Review and recommendations. *Pain, 50,* 5–13.

Suls, J. & Green, P. (2003). Pluralistic ignorance and college student perceptions of gender-specific alcohol norms. *Health Psychology, 22*(5), 479–485.

Sundstrom, E. (1978). Crowding as a sequential process: Review of research on the effects of population density on humans. In A. Baum & Y. M. Epstein (Eds.), *Human response to crowding* (pp. 31–116). Hillsdale, NJ: Erlbaum.

Surwit, R. S., & Williams, P. G. (1996). Animal models provide insight into psychosomatic factors in diabetes. *Psychosomatic Medicine, 58,* 582–589.

Sussman, S., Simon, T. R., & Stacy, A. W. (1999). The association of group self-identification and adolescent drug use in three samples varying in risk. *Journal of Applied Social Psychology, 29,* 1555–1581.

Sutton, S., McVey, D., & Glanz, A. (1999). A comparative test of the theory of reasoned action and the theory of planned behavior in the prediction of condom use intentions in a national sample of English young people. *Health Psychology, 18*(1), 72–81.

Sutton, S. R. (1996). Can "stages of change" provide guidance in the treatment of addictions? A critical examination of Prochaska and DiClemente's model. In G. Edwards & C. Dare (Eds.), *Psychotherapy, psychological treatments, and the addictions* (pp. 189–205). Cambridge: Cambridge University Press.

Swan, G. E., & Carmelli, D. (1996). Curiosity and mortality in aging adults: A 5-year follow-up of the Western Collaborative Group Study. *Psychology and Aging, 11,* 449–453.

Swarr, A., & Richards, M. (1996). Longitudinal effects of adolescent girls' pubertal development, perceptions of pubertal timing, and parental relations on eating problems. *Developmental Psychology, 32,* 636–646.

Swendeman, D., Rotheram-Borus, M., Comulada, S., Weiss, R., & Ramos, M. E. (2006). Predictors of HIV-related stigma among young people living with HIV. *Health Psychology, 25*(4), 501–509.

Swenson, R. M., & Vogel, W. H. (1983). Plasma catecholamine and corticosterone as well as brain catecholamine changes during coping in rats exposed to stressful footshock. *Pharmacology, Biochemistry and Behavior, 18,* 689–693.

Szasz, T. S., & Hollender, M. H. (1956). A contribution to the philosophy of medicine. *Archives of Internal Medicine, 97,* 585–592.

Talbot, F., Nouwen, A., Gingras, J., Belanger, A., & Audet, J. (1999). Relations of diabetes intrusiveness and personal control to symptoms of depression among adults with diabetes. *Health Psychology, 18,* 537–542.

Talbot, M. (2000, January 9). The placebo prescription. *New York Times Sunday Magazine,* 34–39, 44, 58–60.

Tan, D., Barger, J. S., & Shields, P. G. (2006). Alcohol drinking and breast cancer. *Breast Cancer Online, 9*(4), 1–11.

Taylor, E. (1997). Shiftwork and health: In A. Baum, S. Newman, J. Weinman, R. West, & C. McManus (Eds.), *Cambridge handbook of psychology, health and medicine* (pp. 318–319). Cambridge, UK: Cambridge University Press.

Taylor, R. D., Roberts, D., & Jacobson, L. (1997). Stressful life events, psychological well-being, and parenting in African American mothers. *Journal of Family Psychology, 11,* 436–446.

Taylor, S. E., & Brown, J. D. (1988). Illusion and well-being: A social-psychological perspective on mental health. *Psychological Bulletin, 103*(2), 193–210.

Taylor, S. E., Cousino, L., Lewis, B. P., Grunewald, T. L., Gurung, R. A., & Updegraff, J. A. (2000). Biobehavioral responses to stress in females: Tend-and-befriend, not fight-or-flight. *Psychological Review, 107*(3), 411–429.

Taylor, S. E., Lerner, J. S., Sherman, D. K., Sage, R. M., & McDowell, N. K. (2003). Are self-enhancing cognitions associated with healthy or unhealthy biological profiles. *Journal of Personality and Social Psychology, 85*(4), 605–615.

Taylor, S. E., Lichtman, R. R., & Wood, J. V. (1984). Compliance with chemotherapy among breast cancer patients. *Health Psychology, 3,* 553–562.

Taylor, S. E., Repetti, R. L., & Seeman, T. (1997). Health psychology: What is an unhealthy environment and how does it get under the skin? *Annual Review of Psychology, 48,* 411–447.

Teachman, B. A., Gapinski, K. D., Brownell, K. D., Rawlins, M., & Jeyaram, S. (2003). Demonstrations of implicit anti-fat bias: The impact of providing causal information and evoking empathy. *Health Psychology, 22*(1), 68–78.

ter-Kuile, M. M., Spinhoven, P., Linssen, A., Corry, G., Zitman, F. G., & Rooijmans, H. G. M. (1994). Autogenic training and cognitive self-hypnosis for the treatment of recurrent headaches in three different subject groups. *Pain, 58,* 331–340.

Thackwray, D. E., Smith, M. C., Bodfish, J. W., & Meyers, A. W. (1993). A comparison of behavioral and cognitive-behavioral interventions for bulimia nervosa. *Journal of Consulting and Clinical Psychology, 61,* 639–645.

Thayer, R. E., Newman, J. R., & McClain, T. M. (1994). Self-regulation of mood: Strategies for changing a bad mood, raising energy, and reducing tension. *Journal of Personality and Social Psychology, 67,* 910–925.

Theorell, T., Blomkvist, V., Jonsson, H., Schulman, S., Berntorp, E., & Stigendal, L. (1995). Social support and the development of immune function in human immunodeficiency virus infection. *Psychosomatic Medicine, 57,* 32–36.

Thom, D. H., Hall, M. A., & Pawlson, L. G. (2004). Measuring patients' trust in physicians when assessing quality of care. *Health Affairs, 23*(4), 124–132.

Thomasson, H. R., & Li, T. (1993). How alcohol and aldehyde dehydrogenase genes modify alcohol drinking, alcohol flushing, and the risk for alcoholism. *Alcohol Health and Research World,* Special Issue: Alcohol, Aggression, and Injury, *17,* 167–172.

Thompson, R. (2000). *The brain: A neuroscience primer* (3rd ed.). New York: Worth.

Thompson, S. M., Dahlquist, L. M., Koenning, G. M., & Bartholomew, L. K. (1995). Brief report: Adherence-facilitating behaviors of a multidisciplinary pediatric rheumatology staff. *Journal of Pediatric Psychology, 20,* 291–297.

Tobacco Free Kids. (2006). http://www.tobaccofreekids.org/

Todaro, J. F., Shen, B. J., Niaura, R., Spiro, A., & Ward, K. D. (2003). Effect of negative emotions on frequency of coronary heart disease (The Normative Aging Study). *American Journal of Cardiology, 92*(8), 901–906.

Tomaka, J., Blascovich, J., Kelsey, R. M., & Leitten, C. L. (1993). Subjective, physiological, and behavioral effects of threat and challenge appraisal. *Journal of Personality & Social Psychology, 65*(2), 248–260.

Tomich, P. L. (2004). Is finding something good in the bad always good? Benefit finding among women with breast cancer. *Health Psychology, 23*(1), 16–23.

Tomkins, S. S. (1966). Psychological model for smoking behavior. *American Journal of Public Health and the Nations Health, 56,* 17–20.

Toribara, N. W., & Sleisenger, M. H. (1995). Screening for colorectal cancer. *New England Journal of Medicine, 332,* 861–867.

Torpy, J. M., Cassio, L., & Glass, R. M. (2005). Smoking and pregnancy. *Journal of the American Medical Association, 293*(1), 1286–1287.

Trichopoulous, D., Li, F. P., & Hunter, D. J. (1996). What causes cancer? *Scientific American, 275*(3), 80–87.

Trief, P. M., Ploutz-Snyder, R., Britton, K. D., & Weinstock, R. S. (2004). The relationship between marital quality and adherence to the diabetes care regimen. *Annals of Behavioral Medicine, 27*(3), 148–154.

Trimble, J. E. (1996). Alcohol abuse in urban Indian adolescents and women: A longitudinal study for assessment and risk evaluation. *American Indian and Alaska Native Mental Health Research, 7,* 81–90.

Tsang, Y. C. (1938). Hunger motivation in gastrectomized rats. *Journal of Comparative Psychology, 26,* 1–17.

Tucker, J. S., Orlando, M., Burnam, M. A., Shelbourne, C. D., et al. (2004). Psychosocial mediators of antiretroviral nonadherence in HIV-positive adults with substance use and mental health problems. *Health Psychology, 23*(4), 363–370.

Tucker, M. E. (2002). Lifestyle intervention is clear choice for diabetes prevention. *Internal Medicine News, 35*(15), 4.

Turk, D. C., & Nash, J. M. (1996). Psychologic issues in chronic pain. *Contemporary Neurology Series, 48,* 323.

Turk, D. C. & Okifuji, A. (2002). Chronic pain. In A. J. Christensen & M. H. Antoni (Eds). *Chronic Physical Disorders: Behavioral Medicine's Perspective* (pp. 165–190). Malden, MA: Blackwell Publishing.

Turk, D. C., Litt, M. D., Salovey, P., & Walker, J. (1985). Seeking urgent pediatric treatment: Factors contributing to frequency, delay, and appropriateness. *Health Psychology, 4,* 43–59.

Turk, D. C., Zaki, H. S., & Rudy, T. E. (1993). Effects of intraoral appliance and biofeedback/stress management alone and in combination in treating pain and depression in patients with temporomandibular disorders. *The Journal of Prosthetic Dentistry, 70,* 158–164.

Turner, B. J., Fleishman, J. A., Wenger, N., London, A. S., et al. (2001). Effects of drug abuse and mental disorders on use and type of antiretroviral therapy in HIV-infected persons. *Journal of General Internal Medicine, 16*(9), 625–633.

Turner, H. A., Catania, J. A., & Gagnon, J. (1994). The prevalence of informal caregiving to persons with AIDS in the United States: Caregiver characteristics and their implications. *Social Science and Medicine, 38,* 1543–1552.

Turner, R. J., & Asvison, W. R. (1992). Innovations in the measurement of life stress: Crisis theory and the significance of event resolution. *Journal of Health and Social Behavior, 33,* 36–50.

Tyler, P., & Cushway, D. (1992). Stress, coping and mental well-being in hospital nurses. *Stress Medicine, 8,* 91–98.

U.S. Bureau of the Census. (2000). *Statistical abstract of the United States, 2000.* Washington, DC: U.S. Department of Commerce.

U.S. Bureau of the Census. (2004). *Statistical abstract of the United States, 2004.* Washington, DC: U.S. Department of Commerce.

U.S. Bureau of the Census. (2005). Births: Final data for 2003. National Vital Statistics Reports. Hyattsville, MD: National Center for Health Statistics.

U.S. Bureau of the Census. (2005). Income, poverty, and health insurance coverage in the United States: 2004. United States Department of Commerce.

U.S. Bureau of the Census. (2005). *Statistical abstract of the United States, 2005.* Washington, DC: U.S. Department of Commerce.

U.S. Bureau of the Census. (2006). Health insurance coverage: 2005. http://www.census.gov/hhes/www/hlthins/hlthin05.html

U.S. Department of Health and Human Services (USDHHS). (1998). *Health, United States, 1998.* Washington, DC: U.S. Government Printing Office.

Van der Velde, F. W., & Van der Pligt, J. (1991). AIDS-related health behavior: Coping, protection motivation, and previous behavior. *Journal of Behavioral Medicine, 14,* 429–451.

van Ryn, M., & Fu, S. S. (2003). Paved with good intentions: Do public health and human service providers contribute to racial/ethnic disparities in health? *American Journal of Public Health, 93*(2), 248–255.

Varmus, H. (2006). The new era in cancer research. *Science, 312*(5777), 1162–1165.

Varni, J. W., Setoguchi, Y., Rappaport, L. R., & Talbot, D. (1992). Psychological adjustment and perceived social support in children with congenital/acquired limb deficiencies. *Journal of Behavioral Medicine, 15*(1), 31–44.

Vena, J. E., Graham, S., Zielezny, M., Swanson, M. K., Barnes, R. E., & Nolan, J. (1985). Lifetime occupational exercise and colon cancer. *American Journal of Epidemiology, 122,* 357–365.

Verbrugge, L. M., & Steiner, R. P. (1981). Physician treatment of men and women patients: Sex bias or appropriate care? *Medical Care, 19,* 609–632.

Vickberg, S. M. (2003). The concerns about recurrence scale (CARS): A systematic measure of women's fears about the possibility of breast cancer recurrence. *Annals of Behavioral Medicine, 25*(1), 16–24.

Vincent, C., & Furnham, A. (1997). *Complementary medicine: A research perspective.* Chichester, NY: Wiley.

Vinokur, A. D., Schul, Y., Vuori, J., & Price, R. H. (2000). Two years after a job loss: Long-term impact of the JOBS program on reemployment and mental health. *Journal of Occupational Health Psychology, 5,* 32–47.

Wager, N., Fieldman, G., & Hussey, T. (2003). The effect on ambulatory blood pressure of working under favourably and unfavourably perceived supervisors. *Occupational and Environmental Medicine, 60*(7), 468–474.

Wagner, D. R., & Heyward, V. H. (2000). Measures of body composition in blacks and whites: A comparative review. *American Journal of Clinical Nutrition, 71,* 1392–1402.

Wagner, J., Lacey, K., Abbott, G., de Groot, M., & Chyun, D. (2006). Knowledge of heart disease risk in a multicultural community sample of people with diabetes. *Annals of Behavioral Medicine, 31*(3), 224–230.

Wall, T. L., Garcia-Andrade, C., Thomasson, H. R., Carr, L. G., & Ehlers, C. L. (1997). Alcohol dehydrogenase polymorphisms in Native Americans: Identification of the ADH2*3 allele. *Alcohol and Alcoholism, 32,* 129–132.

Wallace, J. M., Brown, T. N., Bachman, J. G., & LaVeist, T. A. (2003). The influence of race and religion on abstinence from alcohol, cigarettes and marijuana among adolescents. *Journal of Studies on Alcohol, 64*(6), 843–848.

Wallston, K. A., Wallston, B. S., Smith, S., & Dobbins, C. (1997). Perceived control and health. *Current Psychological Research and Reviews* (special issue: Health psychology), *6,* 5–25.

Walters, E .E., & Kendler, K. S. (1995). Anorexia nervosa and anorexic-like syndromes in a population-based female sample. *American Journal of Psychiatry, 152,* 64–71.

Wannamethee, G., Shaper, A. G., & MacFarlane, P. W. (1993). Heart rate, physical activity, and mortality from cancer and other noncardiovascular diseases. *American Journal of Epidemiology, 137,* 735–748.

Wansink, B., & Park, S. B. (2001). At the movies: How external cues and perceived taste impact consumption volume. *Food Quality and Preference, 12*(1), 69–75.

Wardle, J. (1995). Parental influence on children's diets. *Proceedings of the Nutrition Society, 54,* 747–758.

Wardle, J., Pernet, A., Collins, W., & Bourne, T. (1994). False positive results in ovarian cancer screening: One year follow-up of psychological status. *Psychology and Health, 10,* 33–40.

Wardle, J., Robb, K. A., Johnson, F., Griffith, J., et al. (2004). Socioeconomic variation in attitudes to eating and weight in female adolescents. *Health Psychology, 23*(3), 275–282.

Wardle, J. (1997). Dieting. In A. Baum, S. Newman, J. Weinman, R. West, & C. McManus (Eds.), *Cambridge handbook of psychology, health and medicine* (pp. 436–437). Cambridge: Cambridge University Press.

Warwick-Evans, L. A., Masters, I. J., & Redstone, S. B. (1991). A double-blind placebo controlled evaluation of acupressure in the treatment of motion sickness. *Aviation, Space, and Environmental Medicine, 62,* 776–778.

Waterhouse, J. (1993). Circadian rhythms. *British Medical Journal, 306,* 448–451.

Weil, A. (1998). *Eight weeks to optimum health.* New York: Random House.

Weinberg, R. S., & Gould, D. (1995). *Foundations of sport and exercise psychology.* Champaign, IL: Human Kinetics.

Weinberger, D. A., Schwartz, G. E., & Davidson, R. J. (1979). Low-anxious, high-anxious, and repressive coping styles: Psychometric patterns and behavioral and physiological responses to stress. *Journal of Abnormal Psychology, 88,* 369–380.

Weinberger, M., Hiner, S. L., Tierney, W. M. (1987). In support of hassles as a measure of stress in predicting health outcomes. *Journal of Behavioral Medicine, 10*(1), 19–31.

Weinman, J. (2001). Health care. In D. W. Johnston, M. Johnston, A. S. Bellack, & M. Hersen (Eds.). *Health Psychology, Vol. 8, Comprehensive Clinical Psychology* (pp. 79–112). Amsterdam: Elsevier Science.

Weinman, J. (1997). Doctor-patient communication. In A. Baum, S. Newman, J. Weinman, R. West, & C. McManus (Eds.), *Cambridge handbook of psychology, health and medicine* (pp. 284–287). Cambridge: Cambridge University Press.

Weinstein, N. D. (1982) Unrealistic optimism about susceptibility to health problems. *Journal of Behavioral Medicine, 5*(40), 441–460.

Weinstein, N. D., & Sandman, P. M. (1992). A model of the precaution adoption process: Evidence from home radon testing. *Health Psychology, 11,* 170–180.

Weiss, J. M., Glazer, H., Pohorecky, L. A., et al. (1975). Effects of chronic exposure to stressors on avoidance-escape behavior and on brain norepinephrine. *Psychosomatic Medicine, 37*(6), 522–534.

Weisse, C. S., Sorum, P. C., Sanders, K. N., & Syat, B. L. (2001). Do gender and race affect decisions about pain management? *Journal of General Internal Medicine, 16,* 211–217.

Wenzlaff, R. M., Wegner, D. M., & Roper, D. W. (1988). Depression and mental control: The resurgence of unwanted negative thoughts. *Journal of Personality and Social Psychology, 55,* 882–892.

Werner, E. (1997). Endangered childhood in modern times: Protective factors. *Vierteljahresschrift für Heilpädagogik und ihre Nachbargebiete, 66,* 192–203.

Wesley, J. (2003). *Primitive physic: An easy and natural method of curing most diseases.* New York: Wipf & Stock.

West, R., & Rink, L. (1997). Osteoarthritis. In A. Baum, S. Newman, J. Weinman, R. West, & C. McManus (Eds.), *Cambridge handbook of psychology, health, and medicine* (pp. 543–544). Cambridge: Cambridge University Press.

Westmaas, J. L., Wild, T. C., & Ferrence, R. (2002). Effects of gender in social control of smoking cessation. *Health Psychology, 21*(4), 368–396.

Wetter, D. W., Fiore, M. C., Baker, T. B., & Young, T. B. (1995). Tobacco withdrawal and nicotine replacement influence objective measures of sleep. *Journal of Consulting and Clinical Psychology, 63,* 658–667.

Wheelwright, J. (2001, March). Don't eat again until you read this. *Discover, 22,* 36–42.

WHI. (2006). Background and overview of the women's health initiative. Department of Health and Human Services.

National Institutes of Health. http://www.nhlbi.nih.gov/whi/mediakit12-14-05.pdf

Whitaker, L. C. (1989). Myths and heroes: Visions of the future. *Journal of College Student Psychotherapy, 4,* 13–33.

Whitfield, K. E., Weidner, G., Clark, R., & Anderson, N. B. (2002). Sociodemographic diversity and behavioral medicine. *Journal of Consulting and Clinical Psychology, 70*(3), 463–81.

White, E., Jacobs, E. J., & Daling, J. R. (1996). Physical activity in relation to colon cancer in middle-aged men and women. *American Journal of Epidemiology, 144,* 42–50.

White, K. (1999). Nurses' study disproves link of fat to breast cancer. *Journal of Women's Health and Gender Based Medicine, 8,* 437–438.

WHO. (2003). *World Health Report.*

WHO (2000). *Bronchial asthma.* World Health Organization Fact Sheet Number 206. Geneva: World Health Organization.

WHO (2004). *The world health report 2004.* Geneva: World Health Organization.

Wierzbicki, M., & Pekarik, G. (1993). A meta-analysis of psychotherapy dropout. *Professional Psychology: Research and Practice, 24,* 190–195.

Wight, R. G., LeBlanc, A. J., & Aneshensel, C. S. (1998). AIDS caregiving and health among midlife and older women. *Health Psychology, 17,* 130–137.

Wilcox, S., & Storandt, M. (1996). Relations among age, exercise, and psychological variables in a community sample of women. *Health Psychology, 15,* 110–113.

Wilcox, V. L., Kasl, S. V., & Berkman, L. F. (1994). Social support and physical disability in older people after hospitalization: A prospective study. *Health Psychology, 13,* 170–179.

Willett, W. C., Colditz, G. A., & Mueller, N. E. (1996). Strategies for minimizing cancer risk. *Scientific American, 275,* 88–95.

Williams, A. F., & Lund, A. K. (1992). Injury control: What psychologists can contribute. *American Psychologist, 47,* 1036–1039.

Williams, D. A. (1996). Acute pain management. In R. Gatchel & D.C. Turk (Eds.), *Psychological approaches to pain management: A practitioner's handbook* (pp. 55–77). New York: Guilford.

Williams, D. S. (2000). Racism and mental health: The African American experience. *Ethnicity & Health, 5*(3–4), 243–268.

Williams, D. R. (2003). The health of men: Structured inequalities and opportunities. *American Journal of Public Health, 93*(5), 724–731.

Williams, J. E., Paton, C. C., Siegler, I. C., Eigenbrot, M. L., Nieto, F. J., & Tyroler, H. A. (2000). Clinical investigation and reports: Anger proneness predicts coronary heart disease risk: Prospective analysis from the Atherosclerosis Risk in Communities (ARIC) Study. *Circulation, 101,* 2034–2039.

Williams, P. G., Wiebe, D. J., & Smith, T. W. (1992). Coping processes as mediators of the relationship between hardiness and health. *Journal of Behavioral Medicine, 15,* 237–255.

Williams, R. B. (1989). *The trusting heart: Great news about type A behavior.* New York: Times Books.

Williams, R. B. (1996). Hostility and the heart. In D. Goleman & J. Gurin (Eds.), *Mind-body medicine* (pp. 65–83). New York: Consumer Reports Books.

Williams, R. B. (2001). Hostility (and other psychosocial risk factors): Effects on health and the potential for successful

behavioral approaches to prevention and treatment. In A. Baum, T. A. Revenson, & J. E. Singer (Eds.), *Handbook of health psychology* (pp. 661–668). Mahwah, NJ: Erlbaum.

Williamson, D. F., Serdula, M. K., Anda, R. F., Levy, A., & Byers, W. (1992). Weight loss attempts in adults: Goals, duration, and rate of weight loss. *American Journal of Public Health, 82,* 1251–1257.

Willis, W. D. (1995). Neurobiology, cold, pain and the brain. *Nature, 373,* 19–20.

Wills, T. A. (1997). Social support and health. In A Baum, S. Newman, J. Weinman, R. West, & C. McManus (Eds.), *Cambridge handbook of psychology, health, and medicine* (pp. 168–171). Cambridge: Cambridge University Press.

Windle, M., & Windle, R. C. (2001). Depressive symptoms and cigarette smoking among middle adolescents: Prospective associations and intrapersonal and interpersonal influences. *Journal of Consulting and Clinical Psychology, 69,* 215–226.

Wing, R. R. (1993). Behavioural treatment of obesity: Its application to type II diabetes. *Diabetes Care, 16,* 193–199.

Wing, R. R., & Jeffery, R. W. (1999). Benefits of recruiting participants with friends and increasing social support for weight loss and maintenance. *Journal of Consulting and Clinical Psychology, 67*(1), 132–138.

Winkleby, M. A., Kraemer, H. C., Ahn, D. K., & Varady, A. N. (1998). Ethnic and socioeconomic differences in cardiovascular disease risk factors: Findings for women from the third national health and nutrition examination survey, 1988–1994. *Journal of the American Medical Association, 280,* 356–362.

Winslow, R. W., Franzini, L. R., & Hwang, J. (1992). Perceived peer norms, casual sex, and AIDS risk prevention. *Journal of Applied Social Psychology, 22,* 1809–1827.

Wolfgan, L. (1997). Charting recent progress in alcohol research. *Ninth Special Report to the U.S. Congress on Alcohol and Health.* www.niaa.nih.gov

Wolin, S. (1993). *The resilient self: How survivors of troubled families rise above adversity.* New York: Villard Books.

Wonderlich, S., Klein, M. H., & Council, J. R. (1996). Relationship of social perceptions and self-concept in bulimia nervosa. *Journal of Consulting and Clinical Psychology, 64,* 1231–1237.

Wood, M. D., Vinson, D. C., & Sher, K. J. (2001). Alcohol use and misuse. In A. Baum, T. A. Revenson, & J. E. Singer (Eds.), *Handbook of health psychology* (pp. 249–261). Mahwah, NJ: Erlbaum.

Woodrow, K. M., Friedman, G. D., Siegelaub, A. B., & Collen, M. F. (1972). Pain tolerance: Differences according to age, sex and race. *Psychosomatic Medicine, 34,* 548–556.

Worden, J., & Flynn, B. (1999). Multimedia-TV: Shock to stop? *British Medical Journal, 318,* 64.

Workman, E. A., & La Via, M. F. (1987). Immunological effects of psychological stressors: A review of the literature. *International Journal of Psychosomatics, 34,* 35–40.

World Health Organization. (2000). *Health systems: Improving performance.* World Health Report. Geneva: Author.

World Health Organization. (2000). *The world health report, 2000.* Geneva: Author.

World Health Organization (2002). *World health report 2002.* Geneva: Author, Annex Table 4, pp. 198–199.

World Health Organization. (2004). *The world health report: Changing history.* Geneva: Author.

World Health Organization. (2006). *The world health report 2006: Working together for health.* Geneva: Author.

Wulfert, E., & Wan, C. K. (1993). Condom use: A self-efficacy model. *Health Psychology, 12,* 346–353.

Wulfert, E., Wan, C. K., & Backus, C. A. (1996). Gay men's safer sex behavior: An integration of three models. *Journal of Behavioral Medicine, 19,* 345–366.

Wynder, E. L., Fujita, Y., & Harris, R. E. (1991). Comparative epidemiology of cancer between the United States and Japan. *Cancer, 67,* 746–763.

Yankelovich Partners (1998). Are faith and health linked? *Advocate HealthCare.* http://www.advocatehealth.com/system/about/community/faith/ministry/linked.html

Yee, B., W. K., Castro, F. G., Hammond, W. R., John, R., Wyatt, G. E., & Yung, B. R. (1995). Risk-taking and abusive behaviors among ethnic minorities. *Health Psychology, 14*(7), 622–631.

Yehuda, R. (1999.) *Risk factors for posttraumatic stress disorder* (pp. 23–59). Washington, DC: American Psychiatric Association.

Yehuda, R. (2000). Biology of posttraumatic stress disorder. *Journal of Clinical Psychiatry, 61*(7), 14–21.

Yokoyama, M., Sun, X., Oku, S., Taga, N. et al. (2004). Pain Medicine—Comparison of percutaneous electrical nerve stimulation with transcutaneous electrical nerve stimulation for long-term pain relief in patients with chronic low-back pain. *Anesthesia and Analgesia, 98*(6), 1552–1556.

Young, K., & Zane, N. (1995). Ethnocultural influences in evaluation and management. In P. M. Nicassio & T. W. Smith (Eds.), *Managing chronic illness: A biopsychosocial perspective.* Washington, DC: American Psychological Association.

Yudkin, P., Hey, K., Roberts, S., Welch, S., Murphy, M., & Walton, R. Abstinence from smoking eight years after participation in randomized controlled trial of nicotine patch. *British Medical Journal, 327*(7405), 28–29.

Zepf, B. (2005). Lifestyle changes most effective in preventing diabetes. *American Family Physician, 65*(11), 2338–2448.

Zhang, S., Hunter, D. J., Forman, M. R., Rosner, B. A., Speizer, F. E., Colditz, G. A., Manson, J. E., Hankinson, S. E., & Willett, W. C. (1999). Dietary carotenoids and vitamins A, C, and E and risk of breast cancer. *Journal of the National Cancer Institute, 91,* 547–556.

Zhang, W. H., & Po, A. L. (1994). The effectiveness of topically applied capsaicin: A meta-analysis. *European Journal of Clinical Pharmacology, 46,* 517–528.

Zhang, Y., Proenca, R., Maffei, M., & Barone, M. (1994). Positional cloning of the mouse obese gene and its human analogue. *Nature, 372,* 425–432.

Zimmerman, D. C. (1979). Preplanning, surgical, and postoperative considerations in the removal of the difficult impaction. *Dental Clinics of North America, 517,* 451–459.

Zisook, S., Shuchter, S. R., Irwin, M., Darko, D. F., Sledge, P., & Resovsky, K. (1994). Bereavement, depression, and immune function. *Psychiatry Research, 52,* 1–10.

Zonderman, A. B., Costa, P. T., & McCrae, R. R. (1989). Depression as a risk for cancer morbidity and mortality in a nationally representative sample. *Journal of the American Medical Association, 262,* 1191–1195.

Zuckerman, D. M. (1989). Stress, self-esteem, and mental health: How does gender make a difference? *Sex Roles, 20,* 429–444.

Zuger, A. (1998, March 24). At the hospital, a new doctor is in. *The New York Times,* p. B19.

Name Index

Subject Index

Page numbers followed by "f" denote figures; those followed by "t" denote tables; those followed by "b" denote boxes.